Understanding Music with AI: Perspectives on Music Cognition

Understanding Music with AI: Perspectives on Music Cognition

Edited by Mira Balaban, Kemal Ebcioğlu, and Otto Laske

Cambridge • Menlo Park • London
The AAAI Press/The MIT Press

The musical examples in Chapter 12 (no. 73, no. 18, no. 100, no. 22, no. 210, no. 128, and no. 48) have been taken from Charles Sanford Terry's *The Four-Park Chorals of J. S. Bach* (Oxford University Press, 1964). They are reprinted here with permission from the publisher.

The trademarked terms that appear throughout this book are used in an editorial nature only, to the benefit of the trademark owner. No infringement of any trademarked term is intended.

Copublished and distributed by
The MIT Press
Massachusetts Institute of Technology
Cambridge, Massachusetts, and London, England.

ISBN 0-262-52170-9   BALUP

Book Design by John C. Russell

Manufactured in the United States of America

Contents

Foreword: A Conversation with Marvin Minsky

Marvin Minsky & Otto Laske

Introduction

The following interview with Marvin Minsky took place at his home in Brookline, MA., on January 23rd, 1991. The interview is a conversation about music, its peculiar features as a human activity, the special problems it poses for the scientist, and the suitability of AI methods for clarifying and/or solving some of these problems. The conversation is open-ended, and should be read accordingly, as a discourse to be continued at another time.

A Science Fiction Novel

OL: So, you are writing a science fiction novel. Is that a first for you?

MM: Well, yes, it is, and it is something I would not have tried to do alone. It is a spy-adventure techno-thriller that I am writing together with my co-author Harry Harrison. Harry did most of the plotting and invention of characters, while I invented new brain science and AI technology for the next century.

OL: What is the time frame for events in the novel?

MM: It's set in the year 2023.

OL: I may just be alive to experience it, then …

MM: Certainly. And furthermore, if the ideas of the story come true, then anyone who manages to live until then may have the opportunity to live forever more…

OL: How wonderful …

MM: ... because the book is about ways to read out the contents of a person's brain, and then download those contents into more reliable hardware, free from decay and disease. If you have enough money...

OL: That's a very American footnote ...

MM: Well, it's also a very Darwinian concept.

OL: Yes, of course.

MM: There isn't room for every possible being in this finite universe, so, we have to be selective ...

OL: And what is the selective mechanism?

MM: Well, normally one selects by fighting. Perhaps somebody will invent a better way. Otherwise, you have to have a committee ...

OL: That's worse than fighting, I think.

The Notion of "Formalizing" Musical Knowledge

OL: I wish we could read people's brain when they are engaged in music–making. Since that is, alas, beyond the state of the art of AI, we are forced to deal with such epistemological issues as how to represent knowledge on the basis of what people tell us they do, which in most cases isn't very close to what they are actually doing. A further problem is that we can't use what they are telling us in the form it is reported; rather, we have to translate their verbalizations into even more formal code that is still farther removed from actual musical activities than the initial report. So, of course, two questions immediately come to mind, viz., how should one formalize musical knowledge, and, can it be done effectively, i.e., so as to generate some kind of musical action?

MM: And that in turn raises the question of "is formalizing the right idea?" There are many kinds of reasons for writing descriptions, and here we ought to have a softer concept than "formalize." When we write down things we know about other crafts, we don't usually feel any need to imitate mathematicians. Why should we always feel compelled to do that when describing our musical dispositions?

OL: Indeed, this convention is not much questioned. One thinks backwards from one's research goals, and since one knows how to compute, one concludes with little hesitation that one ought to formalize. The term "formalizing" is linked to the notion of computation ...

MM: Quite so—ever since the earliest days of computing. Maybe because most of the first pioneers were concerned with mathematical matters. Consequently, what we call "computer science" quickly became quite technical. In some domains of computer development that was a good thing. But in other areas, particularly in the semantics of programming, it seems to me that the currently popular formalisms are premature and unnecessarily limited in conception, being inadequate for expressing some of the most important aspects of computation. For example, mathematical logic plays a dominant role in contemporary formalizations, and yet is quite inept at expressing the kinds of heuristic knowledge we need for developing Artificial Intelligence.

OL: "Formalization" typically amounts to making a post facto summary of some state of affairs that is based on specific interpretations. One looks at some description and attempts to "straighten out" things that don't fit the chosen formalism, in order to make them look more "logical."

Problems With Formalization

MM: Well, yes, I like how you put that. Indeed we can use logic to make things look more logical but we can also use it to produce illusions. I suppose that the term originally referred to matters involving understanding and knowledge. But in current computer science "logical" now means mainly to try to express everything in terms of two quantifiers, viz., "for all X," and "for some X,"—and two values, viz., "true" and "false." But those menus seem just too small to me! We need much richer ideas than that.

OL: In the past, we've had other logics, such as, for instance, Hegel's dialectical logic where one doesn't work with two quantifiers, but with the notions of thesis, antithesis, and synthesis. (Antithesis dates from Plato's idea of "Other" in the dialog entitled Sophistes.) So, one always knew there is some other way ...

MM: Well, I'm not familiar with any applications of dialectic logic, but I certainly would favor going beyond binary logics. However, the extensions that I've seen in the so-called modal logics seem no improvement to me. Yes, they can express some ideas like "it is possible," or "it is necessary," and so forth, but extensions like those seem inconsequential. We much more urgently need ways to express ideas like "usually" or "it is often useful to," or "for all objects that resemble X in regard to aspect Y."

OL: So you think computer science—or at least AI—needs other, richer kinds of descriptive ideas and terms?

The Need For a Variety of Methods

MM: Yes indeed. I want AI researchers to appreciate that there is no one "best" way to represent knowledge. Each kind of problem requires appropriate types of thinking and reasoning—and appropriate kinds of representation. For example, logical methods are based on using rigid rules of inference to make deductions. This works well inside formal domains—those artificial worlds that we imagine for ourselves. But to cope with the unknowns and uncertainties of reality, we must base our actions on experience—and that requires us to reason by analogy, because no two situations are ever quite the same. In turn, this means that we have to be able to recollect similar experiences and understand which differences are relevant. But in the logical world, ideas like "similar" and "relevant" are alien because logic can only answer questions like "what is this an instance of?" or "what is this a generalization of?" The trouble is that concepts like instance and generalization apply only to ideas—because no actual object or event can be an instance of anything else. However, real things can be seen as related—at least in an observer's mind—by apparent similarities of structures, effects, or useful applications. Certainly this is the case in music.

OL: Yes, I think reasoning in terms of similarity is very pertinent to music, especially since notions like "similarity" and "contrast" are often the only ones that give a musical actor a handle on what he is dealing with (especially in the sonic domain, i.e., in sound synthesis and orchestration). And since much of musical knowledge is really action knowledge (i.e., knowledge derived from, and destined for, pursuing action), that is of great relevance to music-making. Music is something we do, not just something we understand, and much of what we try to understand regarding music is meant to lead to the making of it.

MM: And it is hard to understand all that making and understanding because they involve so many different mechanisms—I like to think of them as like many different animals inside each brain. When you hear a piece of music, different parts of your brain do different things with it, but we know too little about those different processes. One obstacle to understanding such matters is that psychologists still strive for a science that resembles physics, where it is usually better to treat different explanations as competitive, instead of looking for ways to combine them. That strategy indeed works well in physical science—presumably because there actually are only a very few fundamental laws of nature. But our ancestors had to deal with many different kinds of practical problems, and this lead to the evolution of brains that have hundreds of distinct regions with significantly different micro-architectures and different principles of operation.

OL: You were saying that in listening to music, a lot of things are happening simultaneously, and our task seems to be to understand the interrelationship between the different structures and processes involved in musical reaction and understandings.

MM: Yes, and we can still only guess what some of them are. Certainly, our musical apprehensions involve quite a few partially separable processes involved with rhythm, melody, harmony, timbre, texture, and many other local phenomena—and each of these appear to involve multiprocessing aspects of their own, such as timbral and contrapuntal voice separation. Sometimes it seems that one can sense some of the distinctness of those processes, as when it seems that one part of the mind is annoyed at the monotonously repetitive rhythmic structure of a certain composition—while other parts of the mind don't mind this at all—perhaps because they treat those repeating structures as structures not deserving attention themselves but serving as skeletons or scaffoldings, like a branching Christmas tree on which you hang the decorations. In this view, the significant features are the higher level differences between musical portions or segments that are otherwise extremely similar or analogous. It is those higher-level recognitions that let us treat the repetitive aspects of the music not as an irritating monotony but merely as a textural background.

OL: In all media of communication one encounters a lot of redundancy, just to make it possible to get across those few gems ...

MM: Precisely. But still, perhaps among all the arts, music is distinguished by this sublimely vulgar excess of redundancy, and we should try to understand its possible neurological consequences. I think Lukas Foss once remarked that anything repeated often enough can become interesting. Perhaps this phenomenon can be seen not as a paradox but as evidence that supports the idea of multiple processing levels. The function of the repetition is then to anesthetize the lower levels of cognitive machinery. (We know that this is the usual rule in neurology: decay of response to constant or repetitive signals.) But the result of this could be to suddenly and strangely free the higher levels of the brain from their mundane bondage to reality—to then be free to create new things.

"Music" or Musics?

OL: Would you say that holds for all kinds of music? "Music" seems to be a notion like "God" or "love," something everybody can identify with, but which actually covers many different, even opposite, phenomena ...

MM: I think calling so many different things by the same name, "music," certainly makes it hard to think about those subjects. The modern tendency, to be tolerant and say "anything is music," is bad for the mind, both of the listener and of the critic also. (I don't know whether it's bad for the composer, if he can make a living.) A portmanteau word like "music" that is used for so many activities can not be an element of a serious discussion.

OL: So, we would have to speak of "musics," and would have to define what we mean in any particular instance, which would be very cumbersome.

MM: Yes, like having to say we are going to talk about certain German music from the eighteenth century, or Indian music from such a place at a certain time. And then one can ask, to what extent do these engage similar mental activities?

OL: How should we proceed, music being really a universal?

MM: For serious analysis, I think we simply must avoid such universal. When I write about some mechanism of intelligence or learning, I try not to use words like "intelligence" and "learning"—except in the title or summary.

Music as a Label for Societal Acceptance

OL: That is indeed the usual practice in studies in AI and music, where you find, for instance, systems for doing harmonic analysis, or systems that generate compositional material,— these are all specific kinds of things, and the claim is not that we know what music is. It seems to me that, viewed in the light of such studies, the term "music" expresses rather an acceptance on the side of society that something is o.k. The composer, as composer, doesn't care whether something is music. He is driven to generate something, and if an audience finds that what he produced is acceptable, or is "music," he is likely to be happy, and otherwise he is not—but it's essentially not his doing as much as it is society's.

MM: That raises an exciting and interesting question—that many people are reluctant to consider, which is the question: what is, or ought to be, o.k.? One thing I like to do is to consider the major human activities, and try to get people to ask: "is it ok?" All over the world many people listen to music for hours each day; in this country many spend substantial portions of their incomes on recordings, high-fis, personal earphone devices, rock concerts, and tolerate background music in their workplaces, restaurants, airplanes, and what not. Is that all right? Similarly, we ought to wonder whether it is reasonable to engage in sports. I ask people, "isn't there something funny about grown people gathering in a huge stadium to see other grown people kicking a ball from one end to the other?" Each of those persons is using a multitrillion synapse brain. It would be fun to ask the religious ones to consider whether it is not a sin to waste such wondrous hardware on watching adults kicking balls around? My own view is that this is less a sin than a symptom—of infection by a parasitic meme (namely, one that carries the idea that such an activity is o.k.) which has self–propagated through our culture like a software virus, a cancer of the intellect so insidious that virtually no one thinks/dares to question it. Now, in the same way we see grown people playing and working in the context of popular music that often repeats a single sentence or melodic phrase over and over and over again, and instills in the mind some harmonic trick that sets at least part of one's brain in a loop. Is it o.k. that we, with our hard earned brains, should welcome and accept this indignity—or should we resent it as an assault on an evident vulnerability?

Music as a Device for Directing Human Activity

OL: You have suggested somewhere that music is often used for escaping the painfulness of thought.

MM: Certainly that is how music seems to be used at times. It seems very much as though a person can exploit music as an external intervention (in contrast to using an internal, perhaps chemical, regulatory system) to suppress one or another part of the brain—e.g., parts that might otherwise be occupied with sexual or social or other types of thinking which that person may presently not want to entertain. Clearly, people use music for directing their mental activities. After all, that's what it means when we speak of music as stimulating, or as soothing, as like an opiate for relieving pain or anxiety. Or encouraging us to march and fight, or to sorrow at a funeral.

OL: The idea that music can be used to control inner states is, of course, a very old idea. There is after all such a thing as music therapy …

MM: There are also other ways of listening to music that people like you and I use a lot. Sometimes when hearing some music, I react in the ways we just mentioned, but at other times, when my attention is drawn to music. I find myself more concerned with how to make music that sounds that way. What's that sequence? How would you finger it? How did the composer get that idea? What would I have to learn to be able to do that myself? Heavens, how appropriate to double the horn and the oboe here. Did the composer figure that out anew or get the idea from some previous piece? Thus music can be the most stressful of all activities—from the perspective of the potential composer, because each intriguing new idea portends some unmastered aspect of ability, or newly recognized deficiency in one's own musical machinery. From this viewpoint, it can be very stressful to find oneself forced (from somewhere else within oneself) to like a piece of music without understanding the psycho-musical trick that makes it so effective.

OL: So, in that case music is not something that gives pleasure.

MM: Right. And even when it does give pleasure, there is no reason to take that pleasure at "face value." What pleases you can also control you, by causing you to do something other than you would have done otherwise. The way an adolescent can be enslaved by, and infatuated with, a pretty face borne by a person with no other evident merit. I think Paul Goodman once suggested that "Pleasure is not a goal; it is a feeling that accompanies an important seeming activity."

Music as a Tool for Emotional Exploitation

OL: Apparently, then, music can be used in part as an exploitative device?

MM: Yes. To be a popular composer, what is it you must do? Perhaps you must learn enough tricks that cause people to have pleasant sensations without too much stress. What are the tricks for making something that catches on in a listener's mind, and keeps repeating long after the performance? There is a superb novel,"The Demolished Man," by Alfred Bester that depicts how the tunesmiths of the future develop jingle-composing to such a degree that it can be used, in effect, for mental assassination. A victim infested by such a tune is helpless to do any useful work, and must hire a specialized therapist to help remove the tune from memory.

OL: However, wouldn't such a use of music entail knowing the person one is imprisoning very well?

MM: That is a profound question: how universal are our musical techniques? And even if there are powerful universals, there must also be powerful non-universals and, so, perhaps in the future when we have better brain reading instruments, people may commission composers to produce works designed not for audiences, but for particular clients? Surely you can write a much better piece of music for a single listener ("better," of course, in that person's view). And then perhaps it will be considered most masterful to write a piece that only that single client will adore, and everyone else will abhor.

OL: Now, if such a work were possible, wouldn't we have almost no reason at all to understand music as something that has universality, and addresses itself to some characteristic people share?

MM: Good question. One could argue that even if we find compositional techniques that are widely universal, in the sense that they evoke strong and similar reactions in most listeners, those techniques would by that fact be in some sense rather shallow—because, in being so nearly universal, then it must simply be because of filling some niche, or exploiting some mechanism, or taking advantage of some bug that all human brains have. Consider how many people tend to tap the foot to the rhythm of a piece of music without knowing that they're doing it. An alien being might regard that as some sort of mechanical bug, even if humans regard it as natural.

The Present AI and Music Scene

OL: If we look at what people in AI and music do these days, we'll find that problems like those we have discussed are on nobody's agenda. What one tries to do, instead, is to go a single step beyond verbalizing music's effect on people, or verbalizing how one composes music, by "formalizing" verbal information (mostly public, not personal information). For instance, in this book, you'll find a discussion of issues in knowledge representation, and of attempts to rationally reconstruct certain musical activities such as composing, performing, learning, and analyzing music. The presupposition that is made in such studies seems to be that we already know what music is, and that the goal of research is just a matter of spelling out that knowledge more clearly (whereby it is not always evident for whom). I think a very strong and, in my view, pernicious, idea in the field, —if today it can be called a field at all—is that you can take AI as it is, and "apply" it to music, where "music" is a medium we already know well. As a consequence, one is harnessing the means of present-day AI to the task of "explicating" music, rather than to try to re-invent AI on the basis of musical knowledge other than just verbal knowledge.

MM: Yes, well, that's largely true—and perhaps it is also because AI isn't advanced enough yet, even to explain how we use language—for example, to understand stories. That surely would be an obstacle if it turned out that much of musical thinking involves those same mechanisms. This reminds me of how, in my childhood, there were musicians who talked about music theory. But when I asked what music theory was, it turned out that "music theory" was little more than nomenclature—the classification of chords and sequences. A syntax with no semantics whatever—with virtually no ideas how the music conveys its meanings, or whatever it is that makes us react. The situation is a good deal better, in AI-based language theories, because we have the beginnings of theories about the nature of "stories" and how they affect us. For example, Wendy Lehnert developed a nice theory about the most usual sorts of constraints on the structures of acceptable stories. A respectable story must introduce some characters—typically, a protagonist and an antagonist, and some sort of problem or anomaly that must eventually be resolved. Lehnert shows how such plots could be assembled, recursively, from elementary activities that she calls "plot units." These presumably are what help you construct, elaborate, comprehend, and (perhaps most important of all) remember, a story. For example, according to this model, if character A does something bad to character B then, eventually, A must compensate by doing something good for B—or else something bad must also befall A, so that B can "get even." Of course there can be exceptions to this—but not too many, or else the reader will be compelled to ask, "what is the point; this story rambles; it makes no sense; it is not a story at all." To "understand" a story one needs a well-controlled agenda of concerns about conflicts among its elements.

OL: So, you want to look at music as a kind of "pseudo-story?" (I did that myself in a 1986 paper entitled "Toward a Computational Theory of Musical Listening").

MM: Exactly, that's just what I was reaching for. At least in some kinds of "music," as in most kinds of stories, there mustn't be too many loose ends, unresolved problems, irrelevant material, and pointless excursions. However, acceptable compositions differ from acceptable stories in permitting far more repetition. In works of music, there is a lot of redundancy, as shown by the fact that, in much of classical music, measures are of the same length, and there is a binary tree structure: two phrases are repeated to make what music theorists call a period, and two periods repeat to make a musical sentence. In my 1980 paper I suggested the obvious thing: that certain parts of the brain might apply to this a hierarchical analysis that, in effect, parses this input into a binary (or, rarely, ternary) tree-like structure; then the meaning can be extracted from the now easily–recognizable differences between the corresponding parts. Why else would you repeat something so many times except either to learn it by repetition, or to point out to the listener certain small differences between sequences. For instance, we notice in a typical 4-line tune that one of the phrases goes up the first time, near the end, and the second one goes down, that's a sort of pair of parentheses; and we get used to that.

OL: Yes.

MM: In a computation-based treatment of musical expression you would expect to see attempts to describe and explain such sorts of structure. Yet the most "respectable" present-day analyses—e.g., the well-known Lerdahl & Jackendoff work on generative grammars for tonal music—seem to me insufficiently concerned with such relationships. The so-called "generative" approach purports to describe all choices open to a speaker or composer—but it also tries to abstract away the actual procedure, the temporal evolution of the compositional process. Consequently, it cannot even begin to describe the choices composers must actually face—and we can understand that only by making models of the cognitive constraints that motivate an author or composer. I suspect that when we learn how to do that, many regularities that today are regarded as grammatical will be seen as results of how the composer's motivations interact with the knowledge-representation mechanisms shared by the composer and the listener. In any case it seems to me that, both in music and language, one must understand the semantics of tension-producing elements—at least in the forms that resemble narrative. Each initial discord, be it melodic, rhythmic, harmonic, or whatever, can be seen as a problem to be later resolved. A lot of what a composer does is setting up expectations, and then figuring out how to frustrate them. That gives the composer some problems to solve. The problems and their solutions are then like elements of a plot, and composition becomes a kind of story telling.

OL: If we could understand composing as a variety of story-telling, and performed music as a pseudo-story, wouldn't that help us to arrive at a theory of musical discourse?

The Heart of AI

MM: Yes, indeed. And if we hope to apply AI ideas to that, we'll want to exploit the best tools that AI can offer—different sorts of processing, different ways to represent knowledge, and so forth. But the enterprise of making an artificial intelligence involves not only some tools but also a larger-scale outlook. And AI will fail to illuminate music, just as linguistics did (because of trying to isolate meaning apart from syntax) if we use only the parts but reject the heart. For just as linguistics has a heart—to find how we communicate, so AI too does have a heart—to find out how machines can be made to solve significant problems. Now, in past years we have seen a certain amount of applying AI tools to traditional music analysis. But I would like to see more from the heart of AI, the study of problem solving, applied to issues of how you solve musical problems.

Making a Composer

OL: So, then, for you to apply AI to music, if one can say apply…

MM: … would be making composers, or at least listeners…

OL: By "making," do you mean to produce a robot-like creature that does certain things like, observably composing?

MM: Yes, indeed. And in the case of listening it would have to know when to say "oh, this is exciting," or "how very tender," and the like. I haven't seen much of that.

OL: In Japan, one has built a robot that is capable of reading music and then play it on the piano.

MM: Yes, that fellow at Mazda.

OL: Is that something you have in mind here?

MM: Not at all. Because I'm more concerned about what happens at larger scales of phrase and plot. Our listening machine would have to understand the music well enough to recognize from each moment to the next which problems have been solved, and which remain open.

OL: How would such understanding have to become manifest?

MM: Well, for example, an understanding listener can hear a piano concerto and appropriately say things like "that was a good idea here in the cadenza, but he didn't carry it through." I'd want the robot to make similar analyses.

OL: To do that, the robot must be able to recognize solutions, good or bad. How would it communicate such solutions to others?

MM: One way might be to have it write the sorts of sentences that critics write. Or to have them work more in the musical realm by performing as a teacher does, explaining differences by demonstration—"Look how much better it would be to delay a little these notes here, and make those near the end more staccato, like this, and this." And of course if our machine turned out to able to produce interesting enough interpretations, then we might be satisfied by that alone—if many listeners were to agree that "really, that performer has a lot of good ideas about this music, and brings out stuff that I didn't realize was there."

Does Music Need a Body?

OL: For me, this brings to mind the people, especially at MIT, who have begun to build robotic insects. This "nouvelle AI" seems to be an approach that is in some contrast to the top-down symbolic approach AI has used in the past. I don't know whether you see the matter quite my way. Regarding a musical robot, for instance, I would want to know how it is programmed. Is it programmed on the basis of symbolic representations (i.e., high level constructs), or rather on the basis of a multitude of simple circuits, or of neural networks, —or do all of these have a role to play?

MM: Well, surely understanding music requires many levels, and a good deal of cultural knowledge.

OL: Don't you also need a body level to build an artificial composer or a listener, to render actions?

MM: I don't think that this will be important.

OL: So you don't consider this to be a critical problem—that emotion, as distinguished from cognition, in all known cases manifests itself through an organic body?

MM: Not really, because I don't expect that emotional behavior will turn out to be singularly hard to simulate. I'm inclined to agree with Niko Tinbergen that the basic emotions come from the activities of various almost separate processes, brain-systems that each have different, and rather clear-cut goals. For example, in the brain stem at least a dozen such systems have evolved and, to a large extent, they behave like different animals. In *The Society of Mind* I called them "Protospecialists.." When you're low on sugar, the protospecialist for "hunger" gets activated—and causes you to apply your available knowledge to find a way to get food. If you're too cold, then another specialist gets activated, suppressing the others; it uses the available knowledge to get out of the chill and into the sun, or to cover your body with insulators, or to huddle together with your friends. I think most people assume that emotions are very deep and complicated, because they seem so powerful and hard to understand. But my view is just the opposite: it may be largely because they are basically simple—but wired up to be powerful—that they are hard to understand. That is, they seem mysterious simply because they're separate and opaque to your other cognitive processes. However, there is also another thing that makes these emotions hard to understand, at least in their older, more adult forms. It is that although an emotion may be simple by itself—for example, a brain center that is genetically wired to learn actions that keep one warm—the end result of what it may learn can become arbitrarily complicated. The problem is that each infantile emotion, such as hunger, defense, nutrition, or sex, can eventually acquire a huge cognitive system for achieving its own goal, perhaps by exploiting the other emotions. And presumably virtually every adult cognitive activity develops in some complex way from infantile activities. So I see as false the commonsense distinction between "intellect" and "emotion." It would be better to emphasize the development over time from simple to complex. Nevertheless, music appears to depend for some of its effects on being able to arouse emotions; therefore, in order to build a competent composing or listening machine, we might need to understand such activities well enough to simulate them. Some of this could surely be done with the sorts of decentralized agents and agencies being used in those insect-like AI's—but I don't suppose they would work well for this unless we managed to program them with roughly the required emotions and cognitions. I have never heard of any non-artificial insect that could learn to prefer Schubert to Mendelsohn.

OL: Right. These artificial insects would have to climb the tree of knowledge first.

The Need for An Emotional Culture

MM: Yes, indeed. And to use them inside our music machine, they might have to evolve to be quite similar to the ones inside our human brains. Our reactions to the sound of a violin may exploit our reactions to the pitch centers of female voices; the sound of a cello may seem more male. A machine that was really competent to listen to nineteenth century classical chamber music might well need some knowledge-understanding of human social affairs—about aggression and conciliation, sorrow and joy, and family, friendship and strangership. And of course there are other constraints on how we use those instruments. Generally the cello will have to play longer and slower notes that emphasize foundational notes of the chord and there's nothing sexual about that—but nevertheless, our human perceptual experience will tend to associate the higher notes with children's voices, the middle octave with female, and the lower one with male voices. It might even be natural to link yet lower tones with those of large fierce animals.

OL: There is sufficient historical evidence that suggests what you are saying is entirely to the point. The violin was developed in Renaissance Italy, by people who were very eager to simulate the human voice. For them, the human voice was the telos which they strove to re-embody in the instruments of the violin "family."

MM: I have to admit that the first time I encountered a modern synthesizer, the most exciting stop for me was the choral stop, the high female voices. Having been a pianist all my life, it was so astounding to be able to touch a key, and have those soprano voices come out, and basses, tenors, contraltos. Completely entrancing. For an hour or two, like a fairyland. But eventually it seemed wrong that I couldn't make these voices talk, they were always making the same bleating sound. But what a marvelous experience....

Requirements of Being a Music Scientist

OL: We were wondering why none of these ideas about cognition and emotion seem to be of relevance in present-day AI and music research...

MM: I think that's because the AI people have suffered from the same misconception that most cognitive psychologists have suffered from, viz., the idea that "well, we'll do the easy things first, like understanding memory and simple reasoning and so forth; but emotions are surely too difficult, so let's put off researching them for now." I once came across a statement by Freud in which he complains along lines like this: —"people think I work on emotions because those are the profound, important things. Not so, What I'd really like to understand is common sense thinking. And it is only because that's so difficult, so incredibly complicated, that I work on emotions instead—because emotions are so much more simple."

This is why I like Douglas Lenat's project to build a commonsense data base. I'm sure that Freud would have liked it too. This is a big project; the CYC data base will involve millions of different items, fragments of our cognitive machinery. But until our machines have access to commonsense knowledge, they'll never be able to understand stories—or story-like music. One reason that AI has not gone very far in such domains is because researchers have been afraid to say: "I think emotions are simple enough that we can make useful models of them." I'm not saying that emotions are trivial, they merely involve some complicated machinery. But you can't make progress unless you're willing to begin with simple theories, to serve as first approximations to the science we'll eventually need to understand musical activities.

OL: Could you explain that a little further?

MM: Sure. I mean that one should not be daunted by the apparent complexity of emotions, because it may be feasible to get a good start by making what may seem to be oversimplifications. You could begin by saying "maybe there are only three basic emotions"— happy, sad, and, whatever you like. The "sentics" model of Manfred Clynes stipulates seven. It doesn't matter, so long as you start somewhere. I want to avoid the disaster that has befallen syntactic linguistics which, for all its apparent accomplishments, is dead in the water because of failing to include even the simplest caricature of a theory of what words mean. In my view, syntax has led to some useful discoveries, but to fewer than would have come from building more comprehensive models of language production and understanding. So I would like to see some music-theorists start with models based on simulating a few postulated emotions, each linked to a few procedural rules about how various sorts of rhythmic, harmonic, and melodic elements might work to arouse, suppress and otherwise engage a listener's various feelings and attitudes. Unless you start somewhere you'll go nowhere.

OL: Are you saying: the best way to approach music is to go at it from some hypothesized basic emotions, rather than from ideas about problem solving, or the idea that music is a sort of intellectual game like chess, or is something explainable by psychoacoustics?

Music as a Pseudo-Story

MM: Well, emotion might not be the right word, but we must somehow formulate and engage what we believe are the important musical problems. And clearly, an important aspect of "understanding" music experience is the listener's experience of apprehensions, gratifications, suspense, tensions, anxieties, and reliefs—feelings very suggestive of pains and joys, insecurities and reassurances, dreads and reverences, and so forth. So, just as a good story confronts us with conflicts and resolutions, so do good musics, which take over the listener's disposition with feelings like: "I'm worried that something bad will happen unless this conflict is resolved." Problems and solutions. Once I was trying to finish a two-part invention but there was something wrong with it. I asked a musical friend for help and was surprised to hear a simple answer. "Look here, you went up into this octave but then you never made anything of it. You can't do that. When you let a voice get into a new range, like breaking new ground, you must have a good reason for it, and you must also think of a way to get that voice out of there afterwards. But here you just left those notes hanging up there, and I ended up wondering what will happen to them." Now I wonder if this doesn't reflect some sense of territoriality instinct, in which the listener is disturbed by not knowing who controls which area....

OL: Well, it also relates to rules of musical discourse, doesn't it? If you put forth an argument, you have to follow it up ...

MM: Right—and that reminds me again of the constraint-like operations of Lehnert's Plot Units. Those dangling high notes evidently require follow-up, some resolution, and unless the composer brings them down, the listener is left with some unresolved conflict, concern, or problem. As though one of your emotional protospecialists were left in an active state. After all, what are musical problems if not problems having to do with the resolution of conflict?

OL: Any book on counterpoint will instruct you that "having made a particular step, there are only so many things you can do," as well as "not following up this step is a mistake in terms of the rule system we are adhering to." Whereas you were saying, following up some compositional decision is required for being emotionally or story-wise consistent in one's music.

Where All Those Rules Go ...

MM: Yes, and that raises questions about the numbers of and characters of those "rules"—and those two dimensions are far from independent. Indeed, this is what I was thinking about in that analogy with syntax. For if you tried to analyze contrapuntal music, you could write rule after rule to constrain its surface structure, but you'd never get quite enough rules to tell composers what to do. However, I suspect that if we managed to build the right sort of model for musical plots and conflicts, we might end up with a more compact theory that solves many more problems. A theory that takes account of both transmission and reception, of composing and listening.

Chapters 22 and 26 of my book "The Society of Mind" proposes such a theory of how language works. The idea is that when a speaker explains something to a listener, the goal is to produce in the listener a structure that resembles a certain semantic network in the speaker's brain. Many linguistic tricks are used for controlling the growth of that network. My conjecture is that mechanisms of this sort could lead to good descriptions of what utterances are understandable—and could do this, I suspect, with simpler and fewer rules than the usual kinds for describing sentential grammar—because many grammatical rules that seem separate and independent might result from these deeper mechanisms. It is OK to begin by looking at surface regularities.

Musicological Taboos

UL: It's certainly a step forward to have begun to describe musical products in terms of the rules that may underlie their generation (although in most cases, such as Lehrdahl and Jackendoff, such rules are rarely if ever tested empirically, and therefore have little cognitive reality.) Rules codify actions, or elements making up an action. For the longest time, a taboo has existed in music theory and musicology regarding any attempt of understanding music as an activity. Researchers have typically concentrated on music as an object, an artifact, a product, rather than studying the process by which music is generated, both in the composer and the listener. How do you explain this taboo? Are you aware of analogous taboos in other sciences?

MM: I think the taboo made sense in the past simply because before the advent of modern theories of complex information processing, there really was no useful way to think about how minds might do such things. In my view, the theories of philosophers before the era of Freud, Piaget, and Tinbergen were too primitive to provide much insight. Freud recognized that higher forms of human thought involved the pursuit of goals by acquiring and exploiting knowledge. But it was not until the 1960s that workers like Allen Newell and Herbert Simon formulated adequate theories of systems with goals. To be sure, there were earlier attempts to base psychology on simple principles of association—as in the models of Pavlov and Skinner—but it was never clear how these could lead to higher levels of cognition. Nevertheless, crude surface-behavioral descriptions became dominant, at least in American Psychology—and in my view this included both Skinner and Chomsky, despite their famous debate; neither of them seemed comfortable with the idea of making models of the internal processes that underlie behavior. In any case, outside of psychoanalytic circles, making complex theories about mental processes did become taboo.

OL: This taboo might be called "paradigmatic," then; it is built into the paradigm of what good research was supposed to be.

MM: I think so, considering the lack of progress on most other mental activities. But beginning with the 1950s, AI and computer science started to produce an enormous quantity of new concepts. Just look at the lingo—a "stack," a "push down list," "default inheritance." In these fields, there emerged literally a thousand new ideas and terms for describing mental processes, whereas before, maybe there were a few dozen, in language. So, humanity was just not prepared to understand anything as complicated as the process of a thinking machine. Until it had some practice with it, due to the computer.

OL: Do you have the impression, as I do, that the taboo we've talked about is still in force, even in AI and music today?

MM: Yes, especially in music. There, the taboo is often justified by arguing that too much inquiry will spoil it. There's the apprehension that if you understood music, you would lose your interest and destroy the beauty of it.

OL: There is also this Western notion of a "work of art," as something that is just too good to be drawn into the question of how it was made, and the further notion that it would be best to forget that it was made at all (something that my teacher Th. W. Adorno was the first to notice in his sociology of music) …

MM: Right—and we know what Freud would say about any such notion, viz., that, if there is such a fear, it's because you're worried that there's not so much there, and you're repressing your worries. The more angry you get when it's questioned, the more you are giving yourself away.

I once had an extended argument with a chemist friend because I said: "why don't we synthesize good wine? Why be at the mercy of the weather and the vintages?" And he replied: "That simply can't be done; it is impossible; the sense of taste is infinitely complicated." And I replied: "Well, why not analyze some wine; we might find that there only a few important chemicals in each good wine, and then we just figure out the amounts of them." And he said: "No, there must be a million chemicals." I said: "And you can taste them all, and they all matter?" "Yes," he said, "they all stick together to form one indescribable whole." The argument seemed interminable and I wondered, did this outstanding chemist unconsciously fear that chemistry itself was inadequate? Did he fear the thought that he himself might be "merely" chemical? Or did he fear that all his likes and dislikes could be explained—and then there'd be no mystery to life? Is there a danger if we understand music, or art, or liking food, there will be nothing important left to do? I'm not worried, myself, about running out of mysteries.

How Do Works of Music Relate Their Process?

OL: There is another question worth investigating, viz., the relationship between a work and the process that produces it. For me at least, that question is the crux of any inquiry deserving the name "musicological." It is not enough to make explicit the structure of the work (as is done in music analysis and traditional musicology), nor is it sufficient to make explicit the structure of the process that produced the work (as is done in AI and Cognitive Science). The crucial musicological question regards the link between product and process, the issue of whether one can describe the link, and in what way. And this problem, of relating product and process, for me has always been one of the crucial issues in all of the human sciences, not only in musicology.

MM: Very interesting idea. We're used to seeing completed works—but it would be interesting to see the steps in between. Suppose you were to watch an artist making a painting. Of course, that doesn't show you the artist's thoughts, but it shows some of the planning and structure. How would that affect your relation to the painting? Similarly when you hear music, the steps are concealed—but some composers do work at the keyboard, and it would be interesting to have recordings of those activities. Beethoven made many revisions in some of his manuscripts of Opus 111, some bits written over many times, and pages of alternative sketches; but only the final results are performed. We should ask the next Beethoven to provide us with recordings of his improvisatory sketches. But perhaps that won't be necessary if, over another few decades, we find ways to more directly record a composer's actual brain activities.

This touches on the relation between composing and improvising. In composing you can be out of real time, and make revisions, and cover your tracks. Improvisors cannot be quite so devious—and therefore, in some cases, they may communicate more successfully. And this reminds me of a different experience when I was a student; reading books on mathematics always seemed peculiarly difficult and always took a long time. But one day, I ran across a book by John von Neumann on "Mathematical Foundations of Quantum Theory" and it was the clearest, most pleasant mathematics book I'd ever read. I remember understanding his explanation of the Metric Density theorem as like a real time experience, like being inside another person's head. (This is a theorem about probability or, more precisely, about measurable sets. It says, for example, that if a certain subset U of a square S has probability larger than zero—that is, if when you throw a dart at the square there is a non-zero probability of hitting a point in U—then there must exist smaller squares in S in which the U-points have probabilities arbitrarily close to 1.) I mentioned this to my friend Stanislaw Ulam, who had worked with von Neumann, and Ulam thought he recalled that von Neumann had been in a hurry when he wrote the book, it was a first draft and he never revised it. And so, he was writing down how he thought about the problems.

OL: He improvised the book ...

MM: Yes, and I found that once I had read it, I never had to go back. Whereas most other math books have been made terribly tight; all extra or "unnecessary" words removed, and all traces of how the author actually thinks about the problem. My point is that it can take much longer to read a shorter book with the same content. So too, in music, it sometimes might be nice to have the composers' first drafts—that is, from composers we like, and who improvise at the keyboard ...

Knowledge Acquisition in Music

OL: Of course, making music with computers gives you the possibility of doing knowledge acquisition. In the OBSERVER and the PRECOMP projects (see Laske, this volume) I have presented children as well as adults with a compositional problem to be solved by using a particular program for computer-aided composition. During these experiment, I have generated what H. Simon would call a "protocol," i.e., a document capturing the actions the problem solver had used to find a solution to the given problem.

MM: So, these composers have to shape a piece by applying some operators to the material given them ...

OL: Yes, one might call that task-based knowledge acquisition, since knowledge is here being elicited in the framework of a specific task for which an appropriate environment has been built using a computer. The resulting protocol is not a verbalization of expert knowledge, as in today's knowledge acquisition for expert systems; rather, it is a document that simply captures the usage of problem solving operators over the time of the experiment. It is then the task of the knowledge elicitor/analyst ("musicologist") to understand that operator sequence in terms of its control structure, and to relate his procedural insights to what he/she declaratively knows about the structure of the product ("work") composed during the experimental session....

MM: Then you could also ask the composers why they did what they did, I suppose...

OL: You could, perhaps not children, but professional composers, or people who are learning to be composers ...

MM: They might not be able to tell you anything useful, though. One just doesn't know those processes. It's just like asking somebody why they used a certain clause in their sentence, … what could they tell you?

OL: Not much indeed. I don't in any way presume such processes would be conscious knowledge. Exactly for this reason, I decided to avoid asking musicians to verbalize what they do (except in a study on music analysis called KEITH published in 1984). I wanted to catch them in the act music-making.

MM: But you could look over the (action) protocol, and maybe find things that you never otherwise find …

OL: Yes, that's my point. For the first time in music history, we are able to produce empirical traces of a musical process; we can then study such a process in terms of the actions it is composed of. Common sense tells me that a musical form derives from the process that produced it, and I would think, therefore, that the control structure of that process is intimately linked to the musical form emerging from it. (See also Marsella/Schmidt in this volume.)

Music As A Bug Between Brain Areas

MM: Yes—and perhaps in some years from now we'll be able to see those processes even more directly by using high-resolution brain activity imaging instruments. I would certainly like to be able to see what's happening in my brain when I improvise, because I have virtually no direct insight into that; I'm thinking about other things when I do it—sometimes even about some completely different piece of music. I suspect that my music production machinery is mostly in my motor brain regions—that is, in the front half of the brain—more than in than the back or sensory half of the brain. (I really hate to hear so many people repeating superstitions about the left and the right sides of the brain; the brain has hundreds of different parts, so you can divide it in too in many ways.) The result of this is really annoying to me; I have great difficulty writing down music on paper until my hands play it on the keyboard so that I can hear it. Now, I don't actually mean hearing, literally, because I can play it on an imaginary keyboard in the air. But I can't hear the music nearly so well without moving the fingers. This probably means that in order to close the loop, I have to use some bundles of nerve fibers that tunnel under the central sulcus from the motor regions back to the sensory regions of the cortex. It would be nice to understand this—and there's no reason why not, with new instruments.

OL: If you are right with your hunch that to understand how humans make music we need to know how they use their brains, then, of course, we are right at the question of how music developed in the history of the human brain.

MM: Yes, and that should be extremely interesting because music seems to have no evolutionary origin. So I suspect that in each musical person there has been some early incident in which some musical process-knowledge comes to occupy some piece of brain that isn't dedicated to something else, and it probably happens somewhat differently in each person. I don't think anybody has mapped this very much.

OL: You just said something for me quite astonishing, viz., "Music seems to have no evolutionary origin."

MM: Well yes, in the sense that one can't see anything much related to it in animals descended from our ancestors.

OL: There are no traces …

MM: … of musical concerns or abilities in our ancestors or relatives—so far as I know, no sign of musical interest in any other primates. Nor, so far as I know, in any other animals. I know of no animals that even tap their feet to rhythms or any thing like that. I don't consider bird-songs to be songs; yes, they have communicative functions but no reason to relate that to music. Or whale songs. We call them songs but we still have no idea about their functions—and again, I see no reason to call them musical. (I suspect that they contain information about major ocean currents or coastline features or lists of where various individuals have been seen, or other functional things like that. But no one knows.) Of course we all meet romantic people who maintain that their plants enjoy and thrive in musical environments. But the only careful experiment I've seen only demonstrate that vibrations tend to retard plant growth by injuring rootlets. My best guess is that music became possible because of some anatomical innovation that just happens to facilitate interactions between other, older functions—for example between some of the brain that does planning for paths in space and some of the parts involved with language, or story-like memory systems. If that were the case, it might explain why hearing certain kinds of sounds might come to give you the feeling that you understood something, or give you the experience of being in some other place. If so, we could even regard music as being related to some sort of "hardware bug" perhaps involving brain areas concerned with visualization, kinetic imagery, language, or whatever—some combination of structures that could lead to almost autonomous kinds of activity that we label "musical."

OL: Looking back at ancient Greek culture, you'll find that the term *mousike* denotes something very specific, viz., the linkage between poetry and sound. This culture really has no term for instrumental music as we know it. Sound-making that was not linked to the human voice was considered as being a kind of "techne," and thus much more lowly than mousike. It seems, then, that the split between poetry and music, and the coming into being of music as we know it today (i.e., instrumental and electroacoustic musics), is a rather recent event, even in terms of the short history of humanity.

MM: Right.

OL: Of course, one would have to look at other cultures.

MM: Surely. And in any case, however the brain is involved, music clearly interacts with many memory mechanisms. Not only in music but in other realms, it seems much easier to remember things that are grouped in regular temporal structures that resemble rhythm and meter. The other day, I complained to Carl Sagan that we have no good theory of why people are so attracted to regular rhythms. He pointed out that the mother's heartbeat is a prominent context of every baby's development. I'm sure that there is something to that—except that dogs and cats hear heartbeats too, but do not seem to tap their feet or otherwise show much sign of being affected by music.

A Musical Common Sense Data Base

OL: Indeed, music is a human privilege, a reflection of the human condition, and it probably holds the key for much that psychology is attempting to unearth about human nature. Alas, our time is almost up. Therefore, to conclude our conversation, could I ask you what you think has been achieved in the field of AI and music so far, and beyond that, what you think should be worked on, or might be worked on, in the next decade or so? Is that a fair question to put to you?

MM: A vital question. And to guess at an answer, we need to understand our position in history. AI is only 30 or 40 years old, but people are always asking: "What has it done lately?" or: "What are its important achievements?" The trouble is, we can't really say, because what seems important at one moment may not be what turns out to have been important 10 or 20 years later. We can't be certain which are the good ideas yet. Perhaps we need more research on case-based reasoning. Or on structures like Lehnert's plot units, to understand more about the structures of stories—and of musical compositions. (In Roger Schank's recent theories of learning and reasoning, story-structures play critical roles.) Or, perhaps, most important of all, we need to know more about common sense reasoning, and the data structures that underlie it. Because no computer in the world today yet knows the meaning of enough words to understand a story.

OL: And this will remain true for some time to come …

MM: That is the gap that Doug Lenat is trying to fill, viz., by working on a common sense data base. And similarly we need some sort of musical common sense data base.

OL: So it would seem.

MM: In college, I attended one of Walter Piston's courses. He used to complain that no one knew enough about what makes good tunes. He said that there were only rules of thumb, like the rules for good manners or good behavior; a good melody must show some sense of direction and return; it shouldn't be too jerky—and it shouldn't be too smooth—but there were no useful formal theories about such things. And I remember thinking then—before I ever thought about AI—maybe there actually can't be such rules. Because perhaps it works a different way, by analogy. Perhaps I match each tune I hear with a hundred tunes that I learned when I was a baby. A machine to do this might have to know all those nursery rhymes and folk songs and lullabies and Christmas carols. Perhaps the reason why we like certain tunes is largely because of already liking other similar ones?

OL: Most likely.

MM: And if that were so, then the important thing about a tune would be how well it resembles some of those repertoried tunes—and what are their interesting differences. In any case, those music courses didn't seem to know how to tell me how to compose. They were infuriating ...

OL: They still are ...

MM: Now, today, things ought to be better. We have so many new good ideas. Case-based ideas, grammatical ideas, problem-solving ideas. Expert-system ideas. So much has been accomplished that we may be ready for the renaissance of many an old inquiry. Perhaps the research community as a whole already has a critical mass of the needed insights—and is only waiting for someone to see a way to pull them together. Anyway, in my view the most critical thing, in both music research and general AI research, is to learn how to build a common music data base. But nobody in music research works on that yet, do they?

OL: Not that I know of ... There exist, to be sure, small data bases of scores of the so-called Western tradition, but that is not what you have in mind here ...

MM: It's mostly the same in AI. Most hope to understand language by using compact theory-tricks, like formal grammars. But that simply can't do enough by itself. You need some sort of data base, of experience. A few little stories about each word. And the same for music. Surely you can't react "properly" unless you possess some "stories" about each chord sequence, or melodic turn, or rhythmic variation.

OL: So, that's what you call a common sense musical data base: a collection of stories about important compositional or auditory constructs?

MM: Precisely. And consequently, despite all those popular, fancy, formal theories, we're missing all the substance beneath. We need a musical Lenat to start a musical CYC project.

References

Laske, O. 1986. "Toward a Computational Theory of Music Listening." In L.Apostel et al. (eds.), *Reason, Emotion, and Music,* 363–392. Ghent, Belgium: *Communication and Cognition.*

Laske, O. 1984. "KEITH: A Rule-System for Making Music-Analytical Discoveries." M. Baroni et al. (eds), *Musical Grammars and Computer Analysis,* 165–199. Florence, Italy: Leo S. Olschki.

Laske, O. and S. Drummond, 1980. "Toward an Explicit Theory of Musical Listening." *Computer Music Journal,* 4(2): 73–83. Cambridge, MA: The MIT Press.

Lehnert, W. 1982. Plot Units: A Narrative Summarization Strategy. In Lehnert, W. and M. Ringle (Eds.), *Strategies for Natural Language Processing.* Hillsdale, NJ: Lawrence Erlbaum.

Lehnert, W. and C. Loiselle 1985. Plot Unit Recognition for Narratives. In G. Tonfoni (Ed.). *Intelligence and Text-Understand: Plot Units and Summarization of Procedures,* pp 9–47. Parma, Italy: Edizioni Zara.

Alker, H. R., Lehnert, W. G. and D. K. Schneider 1985. Two Reinterpretations of Toynbee's Jesus: Explorations in Computational Hermeneutics. In G. Tonfoni (Ed.). *Intelligence and Text-Understanding: Plot Units and Summarization of Procedures,* pp. 51–94. Parma, Italy: Edizioni Zara.

Tonfoni, G., Ed. 1985. *Intelligence and Text-Understanding: Plot Units and Summarization of Procedures.* (Quaderni di Ricerca Linguistica, 6.) Parma, Italy: Edizioni Zara.

M. Minsky 1989. "Music, Mind, and Meaning." *The Music Machine,* 639–656. Cambridge, MA: The M.I.T. Press.

M. Minsky 1986. *The Society of Mind.* New York, NY: Simon and Schuster.

M. Minsky 1980. "K-Lines: A Theory of Memory." *Cognitive Science* 4: 117–133.

Introduction

The term "artificial intelligence and music," coined by Curtis Roads (Roads 1980), refers to research that focuses on music as a cognitive process, or a set of activities, modeled with the aid of computer programs. Explorations in this discipline, which began in the late 1960s, are driven by questions having to do with the nature of musical knowledge, such as:

1. What is musical knowledge/intelligence?
2. Is musical knowledge an autonomous human competence, or a collection of historically assembled unrelated competences?
3. Is musical competence different from linguistic and other kinds of competence?
4. Is musical competence invariable over historical periods and cultures, yielding musical universals?
5. How does musical knowledge relate to musical action?

Such questions are markedly different from the traditional problems raised in the sciences of music. The disciplines of music theory and musicology primarily deal with music as a cultural product, rather than as a creative activity and a mental process. On the other hand, research in fields like the psychology of music and music education, that by nature concentrates on the mental process of music cognition, tends to be focused on the local phenomena of perception and learning. While such phenomena are indeed essential to the overall music process, they do not account for the control structures of music processes as expertly carried out activities. By contrast, the study of such control structures is among the main goals of the AI and music research field.

We think that Curtis Roads was right when he thought the field of AI and music seemed to imply "a new and possibly deeper way of looking at music" (Roads 1980). Many of the epistemological puzzles, which music poses as a human capability and experience, have been neglected, or treated in cavalier fashion, by the traditional music sciences. We feel that many terms that have been taken for granted by the traditional music disciplines need a deeper study than they have received, including the term "music" itself.

AI and Music: A New Discipline

The ultimate goal of the field of AI and music can be taken to be, as Minsky puts it, "making a composer, or perhaps a listener." We believe that we can get closer to this, probably unreachable, goal by modeling observable human musical activities. We share this conviction with AI researchers who believe that by modeling human behavior, they can succeed in building systems demonstrating human intelligent behavior (where the notion of intelligence is part of a scientific belief system, rather than a thoroughly defined term). Hence, it seems reasonable, at least as a start, to adopt methods developed in AI for the modeling of musical activities.

However, there are also major differences between traditional AI research and research in AI and music. One difference has to do with the inherently obscure nature of the reference domain of musical activities. What, after all, is "music"? Many AI trends, e.g. in natural language processing, have concentrated on modeling real world situations, where the exact utterances used to describe the real world phenomena are of secondary importance. Making music, for Minsky and Laske for example (see their conversation in this volume), is analogous to telling a story of some kind. What is the reference world of such a story? It is a well known peculiarity of music (and other arts, such as poetry) that, in contrast to language, music has no assigned connotation—an insight first made explicit by the philosopher and aesthetician Susanne K. Langer (Langer 1953). It is not even clear whether the reference domain of music is emotional, perceptual, intellectual, physiological, or whether all of these domains interplay. For this reason, most researchers find it difficult to unravel the intensional world of music, let alone directly model its objects (but see the chapters by Smoliar and Riecken in this volume). Therefore, in music, as in poetry, and unlike many domains of AI research, the sonic constructs musicians use to "describe" the unknown reference world of music, and the exact ways in which such constructs are put together by composers, listeners, and other musicians, are objects of primary importance.

Most experiments researching human musical activities model the sonic phenomenon of music, not its denotation. This difference in focus indicates that many of the existing AI methods may not be adequate for the task of musicological research. But, we feel this deficiency could be an incitement for developing new approaches capable of extending the scope of AI research.

Modeling Musical Activities

Modeling a phenomenon involves making an image of that phenomenon from the point of view that particularly interests an observer. In AI, the phenomena of interest are not easy to define, and are only partially, and possibly erroneously, known. Hence, information about phenomena cannot be fully spelled out and condensed into a set of equations, as happens in models of the natural sciences. This insight has led to the development of discrete, explicit, incremental, and modular frameworks of modeling. Examples are logic systems, production systems, inheritance networks, and planning strategies. Beyond that, AI theorists are still investigating the fundamental issues in modeling, and no satisfying answers as to the architecture and nature of AI models have so far been given. The range of approaches (see Kirsh 1991) includes, among others, connectionism (McClelland et al. 1986, Rumelhart et al. 1986), distributed AI (Hewitt 1991, Gasser 1991), logicism (Nilsson 1991, Hobbs and Moore 1985), indexing and case-based reasoning (Schank and Riesbeck 1981, Slade 1991), and knowledge-based systems (Lenat and Feigenbaum 1991).

Researchers in the discipline of AI and music share the dilemma regarding the nature of their systems with other domains of AI. For instance, it is not clear whether the constructs of a system can be given direct semantics (which is the basis for the logic approach), independently of the system's intended usage, history, and the human agent whose beliefs the system is modeling. The simple Tarski-style semantics (which is, so far, the only feasible candidate for specifying direct semantics) ignores the above factors. However, being unable to provide direct semantics for a system means that there is no specification of the system's intended behavior. Without such a specification, AI systems are no more than engineering products; they can be employed for solving or posing problems, their behavior can be statistically inspected, but they cannot be proven to work correctly.

The Knowledge Level Approach

Most present-day research in AI emphasizes the importance of knowledge level representations and conceptualization. Both are, of course, abstracted from natural language. The main idea behind this approach is that usually, there is no single, uniform body of knowledge that describes the modeled phenomena; rather, a phenomenon can be described on various levels of knowledge, each reflecting a different perspective. Knowledge levels may elaborate on each other, or might be unrelated. On each knowledge level, various concepts (abstractions) that characterize the modeled phenomena are singled out, and modeling is developed in their terms. The classification of knowledge into separate levels fits well with the multiple viewpoints employed in describing musical knowledge, and with the variety of known musical activities. Indeed, all chapters in this collection rely on the conceptualization of some aspect(s) of music, and some also include experiments in formalizing interrelationships among different levels of musical knowledge (see, for example, Bel's chapter on sound objects, in this volume).

About the Contributions

The majority of chapters collected in this volume derive from two international workshops on AI and music held in the United States (1988, 7th AAAI Conference, St. Paul, MN; 1989, 11th IJCAI, Detroit, MI) and from a European workshop (St. Augustin, Germany) preceding the 1988 International Computer Music Conference. Most certainly, the chapters pose more questions than they answer, but this is in harmony with the infancy of the field they represent.

None of the questions presented in this preface are directly discussed in these chapters. What these chapters share is the decision to suspend the totality claim of the term "music" in favor of an empirical inquiry into specific musical tasks, and into general musical capabilities underlying the performance of such tasks. This decision is made in the hope that from the empirical clues generated, one might be able, in the future, to compose a view of music that will indirectly answer many of the questions discussed here.

Nature of This Anthology

It has been the goal of the editors to stimulate the growth of research in AI and music, by publishing a volume summarizing the state of the art in the field. After over twenty years of research in AI and music, the time has perhaps come to acknowledge the existence of this new field of endeavor. We would like to contribute to the development of a science of musical activity, by facilitating the collaboration of different research constituencies with the practicing musician of today. Given this goal, this book addresses itself to four different communities:

1. The professional musician (especially the musician working with computers),

2. The professional music technologist and designer of music systems,

3. The professional AI researcher, and

4. The professional cognitive scientist and cognitive psychologist.

It goes without saying that this book also addresses itself to teachers of music. This book could serve as a textbook for a course introducing questions of musical problem solving and performance, as well as the nature of musical knowledge and of theories of music. Last but not least, the book should be of benefit to readers generally interested in the relationship of music and technology. Given this broad scope, we have tried to avoid technical jargon where possible, and reduced the actual programming code to a minimum.

Overview of the Book

Over and above the Foreword and this Introduction, this book comprises the following seven sections:

1. Two Views on Cognitive Musicology (O. Laske, P. Kugel)
2. General Problems in Modeling Musical Activities (S. W. Smoliar, B. Bel, M. Balaban, E. B. Blevis et al.., F. Courtot)
3. Music Composition (C. Ames and M. Domino, R. D. Riecken, S. C. Marsella and C. F. Schmidt, O. Laske)
4. Analysis (K. Ebcioglu, H. J. Maxwell, D. Cope)
5. Performance (B. Bel and J. Kippen, S. Ohteru and S. Hashimoto)
6. Perception (C. Linster, B. O. Miller et al., P. Desain and H. Honing)
7. Learning and Tutoring (M. J. Baker, G. Widmer).

In section 1, O. Laske and P. Kugel discuss different views of the nature of AI and music, understood as Cognitive Musicology. Laske sees Cognitive Musicology as an *action science* meaning that it "creates communities of inquiry in communities of social practice" (C. Argyris et al. 1987), and is thus not a solely theoretical endeavor, but an instrument of social change. P. Kugel emphasizes that a distinction should be made between *ordinary* and *limiting* computations, the latter being computations that, ultimately, could permit researchers to deal with musical creativity, not only musical problem solving.

In section 2, different epistemological positions giving rise to differences in modeling musical activity are at the center of attention. As it is typical for a domain with non-explicit semantics, the nature of the primitives used for representing knowledge is a subject for discussion.

The chapter by S. W. Smoliar argues that the primitives of a system that tries to model the behavior of a listener are the mental states of the listening agent, and that logical propositions are not sufficient for modeling communication and manipulation of these mental states. This approach follows M. Minsky's ideas about modeling human memory, as described in (Minsky 1980, 1986).

The other four chapters in this section take a different stance: Their primitives are musical objects, not hypothesized denotations of such objects. In B. Bel's work, the primitives are *sound-objects*, i.e., the messages that trigger sounds from a digital sound processor. Bel develops a grammar-based representation for structures of sound objects with incomplete temporal and sonic information needed for performance, and suggests an algorithm for determining such properties.

M. Balaban's chapter is based on the assumption that *hierarchy* and *time* are two fundamental aspects of music, and neither can be independently described. The chapter presents a framework for interleaving the two aspects in music representation, regardless of the nature of the primitives.

The chapters by E. B. Blevis, M. A. Jenkins, and J. I. Glasgow and by F. Courtot describe type-based representations of musical notions and operations for assisting in compositional processes. The chapter by Blevis et al. is a design exercise for a typed music language, while Courtot describes a project for construction of a compositional assistant that can represent, abstract, and induce new musical notions.

In section 3, the topic is music composition as an autonomous problem solving process, discussed in light of the purpose of formulating an empirical theory of composition. This purpose entails an implicit critique of the many speculative attempts, of musicologists and music theorists, to define the nature of individual composition processes. A related goal is to rescue composition from its fate in previous music research, of being reduced to a kind of listening process carried out by an idealized listener, who is in most cases difficult to distinguish from the inquiring music analyst or musicologist him or herself.

In this section, the chapter by C. Ames and M. Domino presents a computer program that automatically generates pieces in jazz, rock, and ragtime styles; the authors hope to thereby explicate the knowledge that is both required and sufficient for composing music in those styles.

In the subsequent chapter, D. Riecken proposes a conception of composition that deviates from the familiar notion of this process as a strictly syntax-directed kind of problem solving; by introducing the metaphor of *emoting potential* of musical constructs. Inspired by Minsky's work on memory modeling (Minsky 1980, 1986), Riecken tries to show what a composition process that is controlled by emotional goals might look like. This chapter is followed by the proposal by S. Marsella and F. Schmidt, who construe composition as a process of stepwise problem reduction search, following a familiar AI paradigm. Finally, O. Laske reports on two approaches to knowledge acquisition in music, in which verbalization is bypassed in favor of directly documenting keyboard actions of musicians involved in a composition and design task.

In section 4, we have a selection of chapters related to music analysis. "Elementary" musical tasks, such as harmonic analysis of tonal music, are often regarded as solved problems by music theorists. But early attempts at creating computer models of such tasks have already shown that the knowledge provided by existing treatises is far from being precise for writing algorithms, or for providing an adequate model of a given style of music. A different approach seems to be needed for producing musically plausible results with a computer. The chapter by H. J. Maxwell in this section is an attempt to create an algorithmic model of the harmonic analysis of J. S. Bach's French Suite movements, using a rule-based AI approach. The chapter by K. Ebcioglu reports on a program with 350 rules, attempting to model the four-part chorale harmonization task in the style of J. S. Bach; while the chapter by D. Cope describes an expert system that aims to generate music in different styles, based on samples of works by different composers. These are preliminary but promising efforts toward giving a more precise meaning to a musical style than the traditional analysis approach, and toward understanding the complexities of producing musical results with a computer model.

Section 5 includes two chapters that deal with two different aspects of musical performance. B. Bel and J. Kippen describe a grammar-based tool that was developed for the simulation of improvisation techniques in traditional drum music, and was, later on, extended to support rule-based composition in contemporary music. The chapter by S. Ohteru and S. Hashimoto gives us a glimpse of research work done in Japan toward computer modeling of human activities related to music and dance. The chapter describes a musician robot equipped with a CCD camera, a speech synthesizer and an electronic keyboard, which can perform various musical activities.

Section 6 presents two chapters on the perception of meter, and one chapter on time quantization. C. Linster's chapter describes a neural network designed for generating the hierarchical grouping of a given rhythmical sequence. B. O. Miller, D. L. Scarborough, and J. A. Jones study and compare two contrasting psychological approaches for modeling the development of hierarchical representation of metric structures by listeners: A rule-based approach versus a parallel constraint satisfaction network approach. The chapter by P. Desain and H. Honing describes and compares traditional and AI approaches to the problem of time quantization in music, i.e., the problem of separation between the continuous and discrete time systems in music. The chapter suggests that a connectionist network approach might have more promise.

The last section presents two chapters on learning and tutoring. M. J. Baker's work deals with the architecture of a tutoring system, intended to intelligently guide novice musicians in the study of concepts underlying knowledge of musical structure and interpretation. The chapter by G. Widmer describes an application of the explanation based learning technique used in AI, to the field of species counterpoint. Widmer's system is capable of efficiently creating new rules in its knowledge base, when provided with positive or negative feedback about a fragment of species counterpoint that it generates; the new rule's merits are then evaluated by the user.

In summary, we feel that the collection of chapters in this book is a good sample of current work in AI and music. It is our hope that the publication of this volume will inspire further research in the field.

Acknowledgments

We would like to thank the people who have inspired this book project, and who have made the realization of this project possible, above all William Clancey, David Mike Hamilton, Marvin Minsky, and Curtis Roads. We are indebted to the AAAI Press, Menlo Park, CA, for its support and facilities. We dedicate this book to the authors whose work created this field over the last twenty years, and to the new generation of researchers and musicians now beginning its work.

Mira Balaban, Kemal Ebcioglu, &Otto Laske
June 1992

References

Argyris, C., et al. 1987. *Action Science*. San Francisco: Jossey-Bass.

Gasser, L. 1991. Social Conceptions of Knowledge and Action: DAI Foundations and Open Systems Semantics. *Artificial Intelligence* 47(1–3): 79–106.

Hewitt, C. 1991. Open Information Systems: Semantics for Distributed Artificial Intelligence. *Artificial Intelligence* 47(1–3): 79–106.

Hobbs, J. R., and Moore, R., eds. 1985. *Formal Theories of the Commonsense World*. Norwood, N.J.: Ablex.

Kirsh, D. 1991. Foundations of AI: The Big Issues. *Artificial Intelligence* 47(1–3): 3–30.

Langer, S. K. 1967. *Mind: An Essay on Human Feeling*. Baltimore: Johns Hopkins University Press.

Langer, S. K. 1953. *Feeling and Form*. New York: Charles Scribner and Sons.

Lenat, D. B., and Feigenbaum, E. A. 1991. On the Thresholds of Knowledge. *Artificial Intelligence* 47(1–3): 185–250.

McClelland, J. L.; Rumelhart, D. E.; and the PDP Research Group, eds. 1986. *Parallel Distributed Processing: Explorations in the Microstructure of Cognition, Psychological and Biological Models, volume 2*. Cambridge, Mass.: The MIT Press.

Minsky, M. 1986. *The Society of Mind*. New York: Simon and Schuster.

Minsky, M. 1980. K-Lines: A Theory of Memory. *Cognitive Science* 4(2).

Nilsson, N. J. 1991. Logic and Artificial Intelligence. *Artificial Intelligence* 47(1–3): 31–56.

Roads, C. 1980. *Computer Music Journal* 4(2). Cambridge, Mass.: The MIT Press.

Rumelhart, D. E.; McClelland, J. L.; and the PDP Research Group, eds. 1986. *Parallel Distributed Processing: Explorations in the Microstructure of Cognition, Psychological and Biological Models, volume 1*. Cambridge, Mass.: MIT Press.

Schank, R. C., and Riesbeck. 1981. *Inside Computer Understanding*. Hillsdale, N.J.: Lawrence Erlbaum.

Slade, S. 1991. Case-Based Reasoning: A Research Paradigm. *AI Magazine* 12(1): 42–55.

Two Views on Cognitive Musicology

Abstract

This chapter provides an introduction to the history, scope, and methodology of cognitive musicology as a science regarding the structure and procedures of musical thought. The new science is seen as an action science geared to understanding the intrinsic tacit knowledge of musical agents (theoretical musicology), on the one hand, and to improving the way in which musical agents act and perform (applied musicology), on the other. It is conceived as strongly motivated by anthropological as well as artificial intelligence concerns, and is thought to be based on knowledge acquisition from empirical sources, and on the computer modeling of musical thought.

Chapter 1

Artificial Intelligence and Music: A Cornerstone of Cognitive Musicology

Otto E. Laske

They speak of singing
who have never heard song; of living
whose deaths are legends
for their kind.   *LeRoi Jones, "The end of man is his beauty"*

Cognitive Musicology: A New Science

Musicology Revisited

Advances in the development of computers, the cognitive sciences, artificial intelligence, and musical software engineering have made it imperative to broaden the notion of musicology, a discipline now a hundred years old. While it was once thought that this discipline's scope could be captured by dividing it into systematic and historical musicology, this idea is now in doubt. Given this situation, I claim the entire range of studies that have emerged through work with computers in music as an integral, indeed a fundamental, part of musicology. To support this contention, I discuss the theoretical and methodological underpinnings of the new science of cognitive musicology that was born in the 1970s. As the discipline's name indicates, the topics of primary concern in this new science are those of understanding musical and musicological thought, and its link to musical action.

The thrust of my proposal regarding the new musicology lies in the distinction between two aspects of this science, namely, theoretical and applied musicology. The former is an hypothesis-formulating and problem-posing, discipline. The latter is driven by attempts at building computer systems serving as intelligent assistants to musicians of all kinds, and directly or indirectly disproving hypotheses formulated in theoretical musicology. Moreover, applied musicology gives rise to hypotheses never before envisioned.

History of the Field

In his book *The Mind's New Science: A History of the Cognitive Revolution* (1985), Howard Gardner points out how philosophy, the oldest of the cognitive sciences, has since 1850 given rise to empirical inquiries dealing with human cognition. This development has spawned such present-day sciences as generative linguistics, cognitive psychology, artificial intelligence, and cognitive anthropology. Gardner was unable to include cognitive musicology among these new sciences, since its major writings have never been gathered in a single place.

As Bernard Vecchione rightfully suggests in "La révolution musicologique des années 1970-1980" (Vecchione 1990), as far as the arts are concerned, recent developments in cognitive anthropology (Blacking 1973) seem related to older initiatives, in particular, historical psychology (Meyerson 1948) and historical sociology (Francastel 1970). These initiatives were reinforced, during the seventies and eighties, by developments from within European structuralism, especially semiotics (Nattiez 1975, 1987), and poetics (Passeron 1984). Writings in the French epistemological tradition draw into doubt crucial assumptions of the Chomsky School, such as the historical immutability of cognitive functions (Lerdahl et al. 1983); moreover, these writings make a strict distinction between the creative act itself (*conduite instaurative*) and the finished work (*oeuvre*), suggesting that each should be investigated on its own terms (Kristeva 1969, Vecchione 1990).

The New Science

Cognitive musicology is among the youngest of the cognitive sciences. It is also one of the most promising, since it might be able to elucidate, in an empirical way, the limitations of the contemporary cognitive science paradigm (Anderson 1983,1985; Goldman 1986). This paradigm one-sidedly draws on the logico-mathematical and linguistic intelligence of humans, and on a model of the human information-processor as a serial computer. Both of these assumptions must seem dubious to anybody having done research in musical knowledge.

Cognitive musicology evolved during the 1970s, from such diverse sources as cognitive anthropology, artificial intelligence, cognitive psychology, linguistics, musicology, neuroscience, psychoacoustics, speech recognition, and semiotics. For many of its founders, the computer provided an intriguing model of music cognition, as well as a new source of data, and an aid in formulating and testing hypotheses. Cognitive musicology is a highly interdisciplinary venture; the topic of this science is knowledge-based (designed) musical action, considered as a distinctive human faculty apart from other human competences, but nevertheless closely linked to them. The interdisciplinary viewpoint in musicology has long been its nemesis. This science has remained thoroughly unfocused. What it has been lacking is a core set of methods shared by all its inquiries, as well as adequate tools for testing hypotheses. I submit that the notion of knowledge representation provides such a core set. Although controversial and far from monolithic, this notion is capable of establishing a common base for widely divergent hypotheses regarding musical knowledge.

Cognitive musicology has as its goal the modeling of musical knowledge in its many forms. Since such knowledge is action-based, strongly perception-bound, and at the same time seems to develop independently of the perception of objects in the physical environment, it is highly controversial. What is more, in a culture such as ours dominated by Cartesian principles—where knowledge is investigated independently of the action it serves and guides at the same time—it has always been difficult to secure a fair hearing for a faculty that is so strongly linked to belief systems and emotions, and whose foundations humans share with their ancestors in the organic world.

Somewhat paradoxically, it has been the notion of computation that gave a strong focus to the writings of the first practitioners of cognitive musicology. This is not astonishing. For the first time in the history of musical research, the computer program provided a medium for formulating theories of musical activity, whereas prior to its emergence only theories of musical artifacts had existed. As well, computer programs inevitably drew attention to the structure of musical decision-making in real time, thus to musical processes; they demonstrated the possibility of formulating musical knowledge in a procedural form, thereby highlighting the fact that musical knowledge in humans takes largely that form. However, it took some time to realize that the Cartesian notion of knowledge (viz., the separation of knowledge from action and being-in-the-world) that underlies recent artificial intelligence research (Winograd & Flores 1986) is largely inapplicable to music research.

Although the notion of knowledge is not a synonym for that of intelligence, but rather encompasses the latter, it is important to note a reorientation in recent intelligence studies. In his work *Frames of Mind: The Theory of Multiple Intelligences* (1983), H. Gardner presents empirical evidence that various types of human intelligence including musical intelligence are generically distinct. This stands in contrast to the traditional view of musical intelligence as a derivative of linguistic or logico-mathematical competences. On the basis of research in neuroscience and psychology, Gardner stipulates the following criteria for defining an intelligence as an autonomous organism: (1) Potential isolation by brain damage, (2) the existence of *idiots savants*, prodigies, and other exceptional individuals, (3) an identifiable core operation or set of operations, (4) a distinctive developmental history, along with a definable set of expert end-state performances, (5) an evolutionary history and evolutionary plausability, (6) support from experimental psychological tasks, (7) support from psychometric findings, and (8) susceptibility for encoding in a symbol system.

Gardner finds that in all of these regards, musical intelligence is a highly plausible candidate for study as a cognitive system in its own right, related to, but independent of, research in other intelligences, such as linguistic, logico-mathematical, spatial, bodily-kinesthetic, and personal. In so doing, Gardner implicitly endorses a research agenda for cognitive musicology as a discipline studying musical intelligence. A first agenda for this endeavor was presented in the mid-1970s (Laske 1974, 1977a, 1977b).

Theoretical and Applied Musicology

The distinction between a theoretical and an applied part of musicology is as natural in cognitive musicology as it is in artificial intelligence. Formulating models of musical knowledge and perception is one thing, using such models to build intelligent assistants for musicians, another. Regardless of how the claim that programs can be theories may be decided, if it ever will be, the pragmatics of using computer programs introduces a notion of theory that is beneficially beyond old disputes. In a field such as music, notions of truth that are not linked to a notion of effectiveness are not very relevant, since knowing music and acting musically are so closely linked.

Briefly, programs serve two distinct functions in musicology. First, they serve to substantiate hypotheses regarding musical knowledge, and second, they are the medium for designing structured task environments (such as programs for interactive composition). While it is not a prerequisite for building intelligent music systems, to have a full-fledged theory of the activity one wants to support, it is certainly more effective to design such systems on as much theory as one can harness. What is more, systems, once built, can serve as a focused research environment for a deeper understanding of the activity concerned, a fact largely neglected at present.

In music studies generally, we are trying to understand how musicians form mental models of sonic experiences, syntactic/semantic structures, forms and representations, and how these models are used in performing musical tasks, real or imagined. If understanding music means having a working model of it, and if the human mind itself is a device for constructing working models, then theoretical musicology is about constructing working models of a device for constructing working models (Johnson-Laird 1983). This amounts to saying that theories of knowledge-intensive activity, such as musicological theories, are inextricably linked to a meta-theory of their domain. By contrast, in applied musicology we put formulated theories to test by embodying them in artifacts used by practicing musicians, thus informally testing their effectiveness. These artifacts serve the purpose of creating new, and replicating old, music, and old music only lives through living human beings (in this sense, there is no old music).

Three Dimensions of Music Knowledge

The Scope of Cognitive Musicology

The scope of cognitive musicology is best circumscribed by introducing the three following notions: local knowledge (task environment), competence, and performance. Each of these is best understood as designating a dimension, not a kind, of musical knowledge (Geerts 1983). To accomplish any musical or musicological task whatsoever, one is required to activate all three dimensions: first, knowledge about one's tools, materials, and cultural niche (task environment, or local knowledge), second, knowledge about the domain (competence), and third, knowledge regarding the deployment of knowledge under real-time constraints (performance).

Of these three dimenions, the task environment is often relegated to historical or sociological studies; rarely is it a topic of anthropological inquiry (Blacking 1973). While it is true that history is the musical task environment in the most general sense, the prevalent notion of music history as a storehouse of terminological conventions and notated works is too simplistic a notion for work in cognitive musicology. Music history is the history of a biological organism that climbed the tree of knowledge, step by step developing an intelligence for *objets sonores* as designed artifacts, an organism that, detaching itself from immediate purposes dictated by the physical and social environment, generated a novel kind of intelligence. To reconstruct this evolution scientifically is a tall order, to which the so-called works give only faint support. As artifacts, these works are not generically different from the machines (called computers) that today serve as the basis for modeling human reason, except that they testify to a kind of intelligence different from purely logical intelligence. Possibly, these artifacts—works and computers—could throw light on each other since, anthropologically, as well as in terms of historical psychology, they belong to the same category. To quote Meyerson (1948: 86):

> Man is a maker and an incarnator. All of his efforts lead to artifacts (oeuvres) in the broad sense, that often he wants to outlast him; all of his activities are informed by that purpose and guided by it. But what is more, it is by means of culture that Man's mind manifests itself, viz., by embodying itself in matter and taking on(material) form. This even characterizes the way Man develops (through evolution): by the creation of forms. For, all that "comes to mind" tends to embody (incarnate) itself, and it is by finding a form that psychological states gain precison, and truly become what they are.

Needed today is the integration of work in cognitive musicology with computers. This integration reveals something about the nature of music and musicology that has long been hidden from view: that music as well as musicology are a kind of "knowledge engineering," or rather, knowledge modeling, namely, the attempt of modeling human reason on the basis of artifacts. As Meyerson points out, this attempt is Man's way of developing the human potential.

The emphasis that cognitive musicology is both a theory of activities (*conduites*) and of artifacts (*oeuvres*) has a methodological purpose. It is meant to forestall the "knowledge engineering in reverse" accepted up to now, by which one thought to distill theories of musical activity and thinking by way of analyzing (i.e., modeling) documents of notated music. Results of this endeavor have remained inconclusive. Musicologists never adopted a task-oriented view, and therefore never distinguished what is true of the composer investigated (if that could be known at all), the idealized listener implied by the analysis, and the analyst himself. Artificial intelligence and music is a cornerstone of cognitive musicology precisely because it introduces a task-oriented perspective on music—a perspective that so far has equally been absent from music theory (Lerdahl et al. 1983) and perception studies (Deutsch 1982).

Musical Task Environments

The best intuitive grasp of what it means to deal with musical task environments can be gleaned from ethnomusicology. There, the assumption is that one is investigating a foreign musical culture whose practitioners one does not initially understand, and that, therefore, the linguistic and social environment, the communication network, and the means of production of musicians have to be understood first, before analyzing the knowledge invested specifically in musical artifacts. As a consequence, much of ethnomusicological research is anthropological. Soundscape studies are another example of studying local knowledge (Truax, 1984). Turning to task environments of smaller scope, say, a classical sound synthesis studio, certainly the spatial setup of the studio, the layout of the work space, the manuals for hardware and software, as well as the public-knowledge theories used, would constitute the immediate task environment. As experience shows, any change in the task environment has immediate consequences for the work accomplished within it.

Task environment studies investigate musicians coupled to the universe of tools and conventions which inform their thinking (e.g., Kippen et al. 1989). The link to present-day knowledge elicitation methods in building knowledge-based systems is obvious: in order to conceptualize an expert's knowledge, and to define requirements of a system supporting his work, one first has to understand the corporate, institutional, or other culture within which the expert is working. Only after having a model of his habitat, can one hope to understand his task knowledge (competence) and his performance. For this reason, the study of music history as an archeology of task environments is highly relevant in cognitive musicology. In this context, history is an ordered sequence of task environments.

Musical Competence

A distinction of competence and performance is required because a theory of what an expert knows cannot serve as a prediction of how he may decide to use his knowledge (Chomsky 1957). Competence and performance models must be distinguished; they result from different perspectives on the knowledge being modeled, viz., the What, and the How of its use (Laske 1972, 1973a; chapter 2).

Suppose a musician knows the concept of chord (competence). How does he actually deploy this knowledge when writing a chord progression (performance)? To answer this question, one obviously first needs a theory of harmonic knowledge. How is this theory to be formulated? This goes to show that as soon as one speaks of competence one encounters a problem in knowledge representation.

Let us assume that a speech-knowledge (post facto) view of musical competence can be formulated in terms of some propositional representation encodable in a programming language such as Prolog. Using Prolog assertions, one could then state an assumption of competence. One might, for instance, stipulate the musician understands that three tones together form a motive called motive-x:

```
element (c#, 1, motive-x).
element (d#, 2, motive-x).
element (e, 3, motive-x).
length (motive-x, 3). ,
```

where the last assertion defines the length of motive-x.

Given this small knowledge base of Prolog facts, the musician can ask the following procedural questions given in Figure 1.

In pursuing a task involving motive-x, any of these queries might be appropriate. However, those actually considered in the musician's performance process, would depend on the problem the musician is solving, the musician's plans and goals, and the actual task environment (historical situation) in which the musician is working. All of these queries refer to one and the same knowledge base. One would say in the parlance of cognitive musicology that the knowledge base explicates the musician's competence, and that the way in which the musician deploys the knowledge base in posing and solving problems constitutes the musician's performance (Laske 1971, 1972, 1973a/b).

```
element (X,1,motive-x).      ;which tone is the first element of motive-x
element(d#,X,motive-x).      ;in which position does D# occur in motive-x
element(e,3,X).              ;what motive(s) comprise(s) E as a third tone
element(X,Y,motive-x).       ;what are all the elements and their associated
                             ;positions in motive-x
element(X,_,motive-x).       ;what are all the tones in motive-x irrespective of position
element(_,Y,motive-x).       ;how many position (elements) are in motive-x
element(_,_,motive-x).       ;is there a motive-x
element(X,Y,Z).              ;what are all the motives in the musical
                             ;knowledge base
```

Figure 1. Possible Queries to a Mucical Knowledge Base.

In addition to exemplifying the competence/performance distinction in a nut-shell, the example just given also makes it clear that it would be overtaxing a competence formulation if one were to use it as a performance prediction (viz., of how competence will actually be used). This methodological error has been committed by music theorists since days immemorial. However, the use of available competence depends on many factors changing from situation to situation. There is simply not enough procedural information available in a knowledge base formulation of competence to make that determination.

Musical Performance

The musical notion of performance does not coincide with the Chomskyan notion, or with the notion of performance in cognitive musicology which is derived from that notion. The knowledge a musician brings to bear on the music he performs evidently comprises all three dimensions of knowledge discussed. Performance in the musicological sense is that part of the musician's knowledge which pertains to his use of competence and of local knowledge under real-world conditions. Whereas much competence knowledge is speech knowledge of music, performance is largely action knowledge of music, or to speak with Seeger, music knowledge of music (Seeger 1977).

To state the previous thoughts about musical knowledge more precisely, linking it to the use of memory, let us employ a more performance-oriented artificial intelligence language such as OPS5 (Brownston et al. 1985). OPS5 is a production-system language (Post 1943, Newell 1973) well suited to a post facto analysis of an activity. We make the assumption that one can model the use of competence in a musical task performance in terms of a global data base called a memory. The memory is twofold, consisting of working memory and production memory. Working memory is a repository of current musical situations, or knowledge states. Production memory is a rule memory containing sets of rules that state the conditions under which certain actions (which change knowledge states) are taking place .

The generic form of the rules in production memory is as follows:

IF <conditions X> THEN <actions Y> .

The performance system (production system) modeling the musician comprises an interpreter proceeding in the following way. Whenever the conditions stated on the left-hand side of a rule (LHS) are true descriptions of the present state of working memory (i.e., match one or more conditions held therein), the actions defined on the right-hand side (RHS) of the rule are carried out, and the situation current in working memory changes correspondingly.

To give an example of this concept, we define an initial situation in working memory, and a rule that changes the situation into another, related one. The name of the (performance) rule here used is M1 (see Fig. 2). The assumption is made that the musician is currently pursuing an analytical task based on listening.

In this rule, the fact that there exists a motive called motive-x consisting of tones

```
(Rule M1
   goal understand-piece-X                    ; IF the presently active goal
                                              ; is to understand piece X,

   start-listening                            ; the start flag has been set,
   tones pitch-class [C# D# E]                ; and the tones presently attended to
                                              ; are C#, D#, and E,

succession pitch-class [C# D# E]
                                              ; occurring in linear form,—
|—>|                                          ; THEN
   make motive name motive-x                  ; input to working memory
   make motive pitch-content [C# D# E]
                                              ; a token for motive-x,
write "Tones C#, D#, and E form motive-x."
                                              ; specify its pitch content,
remove statements 2, 3, 4                     ; clean up memory
make subgoal continue-listening
                                              ; and proceed to the next subgoal.
)                                             ; end of rule M1).
```

Figure 2. Production Rule for Recognizing Motive-x.

C#, D#, E, is embedded in considerations pertaining to a specific performance situation (in which the point is to recognize that the three tones form a recurring motive). How is this rule used?

Assume that working memory (cognitively speaking, short-term memory) is initially defined by the following knowledge state:

```
Knowledge_state.1:
((goal understand-piece-X)
(start-listening)
(tones pitch-class (c# d# e))
(succession pitch-class (c# d# e))
)
```

Since this situation (knowledge state) exactly matches the LHS of rule M1 (see Figure 2), the actions listed to the right of the arrow token (RHS) will be executed by the performance system. In cognitive terms, the musician modeled by the system will cease to regard C#, D# and E as independent tones; instead, the musician will identify them as constituting an autonomous unit, motive-x. This analytical insight changes the musician's previous knowledge state into the following one:

```
Knowledge_state.2:
((goal understand-piece-X)
(subgoal continue-listening)
```

(motive name motive-x)
(motive pitch-content (c# d# e))
)

The Representation of Musical Knowledge

The successsive knowledge states of a musician engaged in a task performance, when rendered in some knowledge representation, define a performance "program" that can be run on a computer. This program is a micro-theory of the task performance in question. (A macrotheory would require the comparison of several performances). In the parlance of cognitive musicology one would say that musical performance has been explicated on the representational level (Pylyshyn 1984). What has been formulated is an explicit and formal (post facto) description of music actions irrespective of the details of the perceptual process and its associated acoustic and neurophysiological correlates. On the basis of this representational account one can say that musicians who understand that (in some context) the three tones C#, D#, and E form a motivic unit, share one and the same representational state. This state is defined by symbol structures that can be inferred from empirical data (above all, concurrent reports generated by the musician during his performance of the task). The empirical basis of the knowledge representation is thus secure; we are dealing with an actual, not an idealized, musician.

By contrast, in competence hypotheses one is dealing with stipulations regarding an idealized musician liberated from all constraints of time and space. Therefore, competence hypotheses are in need of falsification, and are valid only for prototypical situations. Music analyses and music theories form a huge storehouse of unverified competence hypotheses. Unfortunately, they are of little use to musicology as a science of musical action, except as hypotheses suggesting directions of empirical research.

Summary of Dimensions of Knowledge

We have discussed three distinct, but inseparable dimensions of musical knowledge one ought to distinguish in cognitive musicology. As the above choice of encoding media indicates, representations should be *cognitively natural*, i.e., expressive of the peculiar features of the knowledge in question. Just as one would misrepresent competence knowledge in a medium emphasizing real-time constraints, so one would distort performance knowledge in a declarative language such as Prolog. As to modeling local knowledge, any object-oriented language or shell that permits implementing a structured task environment can be used.

A possible misconception should be pointed out here. Programming language representations of musical knowledge are post-facto renditions. Even though they may be cognitively natural, they cannot claim psychological reality, in the sense of being simulations of active musical knowledge. They do not model musical knowledge per se, but rather a speech-knowledge understanding of such knowledge. This points to the paradoxical enterprise of musicology, where one attempts to formulate a theory or machine (thus an alloreferential construct) explicating a self-referential activity. For such an activity, there is no speech knowledge analog; the only reason for this engaging in paradox is that we are striving for explanations (an old human aspiration).

The Musicological Level as a Metalevel

Problems with Traditional Musicology

Traditional musicology can be seen as the prolegomenon to a science still to be created. Its peculiar assumptions, most of which derive from nineteenth century scientific conventions, deserve to be treated in a separate volume. One of its most perceptive practitioners and critics, Charles Seeger (Seeger 1977), saw musicology's principal flaw in its heavy and uncritical reliance upon the art of speech, due to which the investigation of processes (music time) is fated to lose out against that of static taxonomies and schemata (music space). In other words, there is a problem of knowledge representation.

Traditional musicology is thoroughly Cartesian (based on the view expressed by Descartes as "Cogito, ergo sum"); it is based on the dichotomy of knowledge and action, subject and object, and therefore cannot discern the peculiarity of musical action. By the same token, musicology has presently no way of doing justice to procedural musical knowledge; nor has it exhibited the slightest interest in doing so. As a consequence, systematic musicology has become a producer of abstract competence models of mainly historical interest, whereas historical musicology is the producer of learned mélanges of task environment and competence studies, in which uncontrolled inferences regarding musical performance (as here understood) are the general rule. After exercising this methodology for a good hundred years, the time has come to cover more of the *terra incognita* of music than has been attempted. This is what cognitive musicology is meant to achieve.

The Need for a Systematic Link

Empirical research in cognitive musicology strives to formulate theories of musical knowledge (competence) and action (performance). In working towards this goal, one can follow two different approaches. One can either model musical activities *directly*, as is done in cognitive science and knowledge acquisition (Laske 1979, and in this book), or one can model them *indirectly*, by analyzing their end result (viz., notated or recorded artifacts), as is done in traditional musicology (e.g., Andrews

1966, Leibowitz 1949). The indirect approach is predominantly geared to competence and task environment models, the direct approach, to performance models.

The crux of the problem, as we see it, lies in the systematic linkage of the two approaches. As is well known, a predominant research topic in the artificial intelligence research of the 1970s has been the duality of declarative versus procedural knowledge representations. It is time for the musicologist to learn from this discussion.

The Musicological Bottleneck

The problems of traditional musicology are all rooted in its knowledge acquisition bottleneck. Since most of the musicians with whom it has been dealing have been long dead, retrospective reports of these experts (answering questions of method and technique, or esthetics) are not available to substantiate competence hypotheses. Equally unavailable are concurrent reports of these experts, in which they would verbalize their problem-solving while being engaged in it. As a consequence, knowledge acquisition has to be done by *knowledge engineering in reverse*, i.e., by inferring, from the analysis of artifacts, the structure of the activity that produced them.

Clearly, this method has stark limitations; it yields only unverified competence hypotheses and (more or less structured) models of the task environments in which competence has been deployed. However, it cannot yield working models of musical activity. While one is thus tempted to say that, from the vantage point of artificial intelligence, the research agenda of musicology has failed overall, there are, to be just, many methods and problem formulations which artificial intelligence research and practice could learn from. I refer especially to hermeneutic methods, originally developed in theology, whose operationalization would be of great relevance for developing argumentation theory in artificial intelligence (Pospelov 1990).

The major reason for the deficiency of traditional musicological research is the fact that its tools, natural language statements, and its data sources, common musical notation, are less than equal to the task of understanding music scientifically. A description of music is only as good as the data sources employed to formulate it. If one has no way of rendering the structure of musical processes, one naturally ends up defining musical knowledge as a disembodied entity impossible to relate to actual uses of musical knowledge.

Natural Language and Music Live in Different Worlds

The ambiguity of natural language has a strong survival function; it permits people to communicate via interpretations, without being bound to replicating insights exactly, or duplicating the so-called real world. (Rather, the world is a body of interpretations.) Ambiguity is the price humans pay for the endless creativity of language use. However, in scientific discourse ambiguity is not always an asset, at least not as long as computers are not intelligent enough to make good use of it.

The ambiguity of natural language descriptions of music is due to the simple but crucial fact that such descriptions rely, for their understanding, on the linguistic as well as the musical competence of their readers or hearers which determine their interpretations. They have communicative and pedagogical purposes over and above strictly theoretical ones. An example from the music literature will make these reflections easier to follow. In their work *Sonic Design* (Cogan & Escott 1976), the authors make the following historical statements:

> Machaut revealed some of the possibilities of combining different speeds of activity, either in succession or superimposition. These exciting and immensely fertile ideas were explored and extended by successive generations of composers. (254).

The descriptive adequacy of this statement is founded on a large number of purely analytical statements about Machaut's work, in particular an analysis of the Amen from the *Credo* of the *Messe de Notre Dame*, such as:

> Although each individual voice attacks and moves differently, the voices join together at certain common attack points. In Example 3.5 (a rhythmic reduction of the Amen O.L.), the line marked "simultaneous attacks" indicates (by means of the numbers 3 or 4) the exact points where three or four voices attack notes simultaneously. The relative weight of several voices attacking notes together creates accents at those points. These accent points are spaced regularly in time (230–232).

It would require another chapter, to model the dialog of the historians with their evidence (Collingwood 1946) through which these statements were generated. No data for developing such a model exist. Another model a cognitive musicologist would like to see is that of the reader's understanding of these statements. Such data could be developed. As a first step, it would be desirable to clarify what has been said. Since no performance modeling is required in this case, one can use Prolog (Ennals 1984, 1985).

The Many Steps Toward the Goal of Explanation

Let us make the following *gedankenexperiment*. Assume that it has been possible to formulate a model of the process of understanding the musicological statements cited above, by using an appropriate programming language. What would one have gained thereby? One would possess an explicit model of musical performance pertaining to the task of understanding discourse about Machaut's music. This would still be a far cry from fully understanding the knowledge base required for following Machaut's music, and from understanding the analyst's competence, not to speak of an understanding of the processes carried out by the composer himself.

What outwardly appears to those innocent of artificial intelligence as a description of an artifact is really a complex appeal to the reader of music descriptions, to activate his/her implicit tacit knowledge about language as well as music (and music history). Naturally, the description leaves unexplicated the processes whereby readers actually understand the statements. Only when forgetting these underlying mental processes can one take a description of musical artifacts at face value. From a cognitive perspective, artifact descriptions always beg the question they are trying to answer, since no matter what artifact (A) a musicologist investigates, he, too, is creating an artifact (A'), and most of the questions regarding artifact A can be answered by understanding the process through which artifact A' is created. Rather than reflecting some outside musical reality, artifact descriptions are self-referential; they refer directly to the analyst's reasoning process, and only secondarily to the artifact. For this reason, cognitive musicology includes investigations into the musicological and music-analytical enterprises, on a par with those of other musical activities.

What Is a Musicological Level?

We can view knowledge-intensive activities as existing on several levels that have a certain relationship. In Figure 3, the *action level*, the level of activity as a whole, is the metalevel of all subordinate levels, namely, the planning, task, domain, and task environment levels. Each level except the action level has a metalevel, and each such metalevel is potentially a musicological level. How do these levels interrelate?

The task environment level supports the domain level, being simultaneously selected by it; the task level applies the contents of the domain level, while the planning level controls the task level. All levels are in the service of the action level where actions are designed on the basis of ideas. Let us consider these relationships in more detail. The (physical and social) task environment level includes physical materials, historical culture, and tools without which the activity is unthinkable. This level supports the deployment of knowledge as much as it is selected on the basis of that knowledge. The meta-level of the task environment level is that of domain knowledge. This is the level of declarative and inferential knowledge an expert musician has. In order to be able to use such knowledge, an expert requires methods and strategies, as held on the task level. Their use is, however, impossible without planning, which conceptually occupies still another level. A musical action is the result of functioning on all of these levels. The orchestration and integration of these levels is the crux of expert activity.

In musicological discourse, any meta-level may be conceived as a set of rules, the execution of which determines how knowledge is used at a subordinate level of the activity. The notion of a meta-level is an operational one: there are as many musicological levels as there are musical object levels (subordinate levels). Together, these rule sets form a knowledge base. To give a historical example, much of the domain knowledge required for creating Gregorian Chant grew out of the organization of the church service, that is, the task environment level of the medieval musician.

Reviewing artificial intelligence renditions of musical activity from this perspective, one notices that most of them select the domain level and, more often than not, the inference level within it, for scrutiny. They then go on to speak of "musical knowledge," and sometimes even, "deep" musical knowledge. That's quite a hyperbole! Considering recent musicological descriptions from this vantage point, one

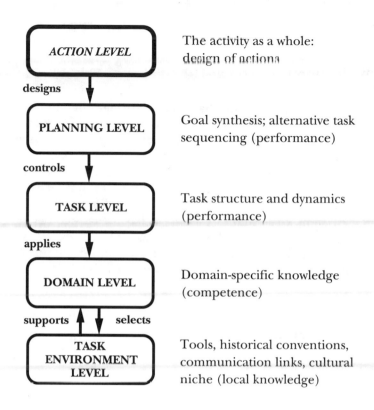

Figure 3. Levels of Musical Activity.

finds that most of them deal with the musical domain level, often for the purpose of formulating competence models of music activity (Lerdahl et al., 1983). In more traditional approaches, competence level formulations (inferred from notation) are kept intertwined with reflections on the musician's task environment (conceptualized as history). Where investigations are more strictly technical, descriptions may deal with a musician's task level, i.e., the structure of his subtasking (often called style). Only in rare cases (e.g., in investigations of Beethoven's sketchbooks) have such descriptions been made of the planning level, and then only based on notation (using knowledge engineering in reverse), as well as without the benefit of knowing the artificial intelligence literature on planning. Consequently, no comprehensive musicological model of music activity exists at present. This state of affairs is about to change as musicologists begin to conceive of themselves as anthropologists, viz., as knowledge elicitors working with (living) musicians—capturing, analyzing, modeling, and eventually, implementing, musical knowledge in the form of knowledge-based systems. In this pursuit, the description of musical artifacts at the domain level has the legitimate function of supporting the codification of the surrounding levels of music activity.

Musicology and Technology

The Emergence of Knowledge-Based Systems

Knowledge-based systems apply inference mechanisms to formal encodings of knowledge elements forming a knowledge base. A knowledge base is a data base whose elements are knowledge elements, or facts characterizing some chosen domain. In contrast to a conventional data base, a knowledge base can be turned into an active medium in which knowledge elements beget other knowledge elements. This is accomplished by an inference engine kept separate from the knowledge base; the engine activates (fires) the rules making up the knowledge base according to a preordained control structure. Convention has it that knowledge-based systems are called \intelligent. Often, such systems are also called expert systems, the assumption being that an expert has perfect speech knowledge of his activity. (This is, of course, untrue; what makes the expert an expert is precisely the forgetting of his knowledge, that is, the compiled nature of it, which enables him to act with great efficiency and seeming effortlessness.) Knowledge-based systems can serve a multiplicity of functions, such as communication between different task domains, reasoning, decision support and accounting, problem solving memory, shielding from interruption, knowledge distribution, knowledge synthesis, or knowledge management, to name a few.

The relevance of knowledge-based systems for cognitive musicology cannot be overstated (Roads 1980, 1983, 1985). Such systems enable musicologists to represent knowledge of and about music formally and explicitly, and to assess the sounding consequences of their beliefs, assumptions, and esthetic evaluations (Clynes1978, 1986, Sundberg 1983). The contemporary musicologist can experiment with different data models, knowledge bases, and process models, and can refine them to any degree of detail desired. He can also distribute musical knowledge in ways never thought possible before, both for pedagogical and scientific purposes.

Among the forms explicit musical knowledge can take, rules stand out as instructions for musical action, and a medium for codifying secure knowledge. As the existence of fields such as music theory, counterpoint, and theory of harmony shows, the awareness that musicians formulate and use rules is an old one. Rules are post-facto formulations of action knowledge for the sake of guiding future action on the basis of experience (Laske 1984; Sundberg 1983), or on the basis of imagining the possible (Koenig 1970a, 1970b).

What has been lacking in musicology is a medium for representing music knowledge in a formal and explicit, and moreover executable, way, as well as a control structure determining how that knowledge is to be used in actual musical tasks. Knowledge-based systems, providing both a medium and a control structure for heuristic theory formation, are likely to revolutionize notions of theory and composition, as well as pedagogy. Such systems enforce what Charles Ames refers to as music-theoretical empiricism, in contrast to speculation. At the very least, they show researchers what, in music, does not yield to rule formulations, requiring perception-based, rather than logic-based, constructs. Knowledge-based systems are thus exploratory devices and tools of criticism, rather than definitive accounts of knowledge. They are artifacts not generically different from artistic works, since they, too, embody human thought in a material form (Meyerson 1948). However, being based entirely on speech knowledge, they are able to mirror only a very narrow spectrum of human long-term memory, all the more so since, so far, they have failed to learn anything.

Computers Help Salvage the Humanistic Tradition

Since the beginning of this century, musicologists have made many strained attempts at establishing the scientific validity of their field. Many ideological linkages have been tried, either with the natural sciences, mathematics, the social (historical) sciences, or semiotics/hermeneutics. All of them have been temporary fashions, and none has added much to the validity of musicology as a science. A simple lesson learned from computer science puts all those fashions in perspective.

Computers are physical systems which are simultaneously symbol manipulators and pattern recognizers. They provide, by their very existence, a demonstration of how it is possible for a physical system, to carry out mental pursuits, whether symbol- or percept-based (symbolic or subsymbolic). With this demonstration, the traditional gulf between the natural sciences and the humanities, at least in the domain of music studies, loses much of its justification. A hybrid of information and knowledge (namely, inference- or knowledge-based information) is about to emerge, which supports musical action in strikingly novel ways. Whether the absorption of artificial intelligence studies into musicology is just another fashion will be determined by the substance of musicological studies as reported in this book.

In short, there now exists the challenge of modeling musical knowledge in terms of objects, methods, rules, blackboards, constraints, neural networks, and related constructs. Rather than only dealing with artifacts of past musical acticity, the contemporary musicologist is starting to work with living musicians whose knowledge and practice he is trying to understand and to improve. As a scientist elucidating musical action, the modern musicologist is a humanist fast becoming a knowledge engineer in the service of anthropology.

A Doorknocker for Traditional Musicology

Both systematic and historical approaches to musicology as we know them are strictly theoretical endeavors. In its traditional form, musicology lacks an applied field that is at the cutting edge of current technology. We call such a field *applied musicology*. (The adjective 'applied' does not signal secondary status here, as in Newtonian science.)

Perusing the *Proceedings* of the International Computer Music Conferences of the 1980s, and those of the most recent musicology workshop (Bel et al. 1990) conveys a good impression of what has happened in music studies. Musicology has renewed itself from without, not for ideological reasons, but out of necessity. What used to be called psychology of music, psychoacoustics, history of music instruments, computational musicology, and AI and music has encroached upon the academic field of musicology, and now forces it to rethink its ways. Similarly, historical psychology and sociology, as well as poetics and semiotics, have redefined the sense of the musicological enterprise (Vecchione 1990). G. Adler's *Hilfswissenschaften* are knocking on the door of the master science. The doorknocker is called symbolic processing (mainly by knowledge-based systems), on the one hand, and connectionism (neural networks), on the other. The domain of the former is speech knowledge, that of the latter, perception.

Building knowledge-based systems for supporting the work of musical experts is an interdisciplinary and thus difficult one. We cannot enter into all the difficulties here. What is difficult, aside from the knowledge elicitation effort involved, is the task of building such systems as practical software. Several reasons stand out (Partridge 1986). First, knowledge engineering is a craft located at the intersection of artificial intelligence, the social sciences, and cognitive science, and therefore does not as yet count many expert practitioners able to deploy a structured methodology. Second, knowledge elicitiation, analysis, and modeling, which are part of theoretical musicology, are complex undertakings that cannot simply be improvised (Cahier 1986), and the tools for operationalizing modeled knowledge (languages, shells, or object-oriented environments) are no child's toys. Third, the kind of musical knowledge that, if implemented, would improve computer music tools is often not public or even shared among experts, but personal, idiosyncratic knowledge. (Building, managing, and utilizing an orchestra library are examples.) By contrast, knowledge-based systems of today at best deal with public (textbook) knowledge, and only in rare cases with knowledge shared among experts. The elicitation of personal knowledge, and of action knowledge, still awaits a methodology, and easy-to-use, interactive support tools (Laske, in this volume).

The majority of existing knowledge-based systems for music are best described as structured task environments (for instance, Zicarelli et al. 1986). These systems do not comprise complete knowledge bases explicating some aspect of musical competence (competence models), nor are they simulations of processes using knowledge in some specific task (performance models). In the majority of cases, the design emphasis in these systems falls on visualizing the materials an expert works with, and on symbolizing the tools for doing so, with little or no attempt at simulating the expert's thinking processes. While this is a departure from the orthodoxy of artificial intelligence research—its claim of reconstructing human intelligence—it is certainly in the mainstream of applied artificial intelligence work in industry. In fact, it very much reflects the nature of musical expertise which is inseparable from action and requires knowledge management.

The structured musical task environments now in existence already form a repertory for musicological research. These systems are the embodiment of musical intelligence in its many forms, and while the knowledge bases they incorporate are in most cases not very novel, the way in which they represent and distribute musical knowledge is revolutionary. For in-depth musicological studies in musical action knowledge, there are no better tools than these structured task environments.

A Truly Contemporary Musicology

It is not difficult to state what a truly contemporary musicology would be like. Its practitioners would be knowledge elicitors and modelers specializing in musical expertise in some chosen anthropological setting; they would be experts in using the tools of applied artificial intelligence. Having absorbed the state of the art in that field, they would set out to develop novel artificial intelligence constructs, and would build systems we have called structured task environments, competence and performance models. Eventually, they might be able to build integrated systems that not only make access to musical knowledge easy, but that automate those parts of musical knowledge that an expert does not care to handle manually and intuitively. By developing its applied branch, musicology could once and for all overcome both its empiristic sterility and its mere retrospectiveness (not to speak of its Cartesian prejudice in favor of knowledge divorced from action). Musicology could become an action science "establishing a community of inquiry within a community of practice" (Argyris 1987), and elaborating theoretical topics, such as knowledge representation, in the framework of contemporary musical practice (Laske 1992a).

Artificial Intelligence and Music

The Challenge of Artificial Intelligence and Music

Musicology, like many of the humanities, has remained a predominantly hermeneutic science, focusing on the meaning of music structures for idealized listeners, and on some vague collective spirit (often tinged with national colors). Its inception falls into the heyday of philosophical inquiry based on the artifact of a subject, used in modeling human creativity and knowledge. A subject was conceived by Kant as a transcendental entity dependent upon empirical input, but structured so as to adhere, in its manipulations of that input, to certain irreducible schemata (such as time and space); these schemata were thought to determine the subject's output, namely, its understanding of reality.

With E. Husserl's method of transcendental phenomenology, the philosophical subject was released from its obligation of constituting reality. Instead, the subject's internal knowledge representations per se, regardless of a referential reality, became the principal topic of philosophical inquiry. Husserl's move toward artificial intelligence was countered by M. Heidegger with the stipulation that being precedes knowing—and not vice versa, as Husserl had assumed. In the end, the notion of mankind as a subject vis-a-vis the world as an object fell into disrepute, and with it all the ethical and esthetic premises that had been attached to the notion of a subject. At about the same time, Schoenberg and his pupils wrote music reflecting the downfall of the subject from its former glory, while other composers, especially Varèse and Stravinsky, took leave of the subject. Until the end of the present century, hermeneutic musicology has acted as if the subject were still in place, and no catastrophe had occured; a revision of its nineteenth century methodology was not on its agenda.

In this context, it comes as a philosophical shock to realize that much of the research program of artificial intelligence is a reformulation of the failed research agenda of subjectivist philosophies from roughly 1450 to 1950 (Nicolaus of Cusa to Theodore Adorno). In this endeavor, most of the Cartesian assumptions (such as the separation of knowledge and action) have remained intact and even unquestioned. In artificial intelligence, as in the subjectivist tradition, reason is ascribed to a subject, whether individual or universal, and the question is asked how that subject, conceived as intelligence, functions. In contrast to subjectivist philosophy, however, human reason is modeled by artificial intelligence on the basis of the artifact of a virtual machine (Turing machine), a human artifact promoting greater precision of speaking about subjective reason. The machine functions, first, as an information-processor and, second, as a manipulator of knowledge representations (where knowledge has the restricted meaning of inference-based information logically derived from facts, i.e., formalized speech knowledge). Unfortunately, the epistemological presuppositions made in designing and using artifacts called intelligent computer programs are rarely considered.

The focus of artificial intelligence inquiry is not human knowledge about the world (as in the philosophical tradition), but human task knowledge relating to a particular segment of the social world that serves as the environment of some task. Changing the basis of modeling from a subject to a machine, while it makes possible a more precise way of speaking, still is burdened by the familiar deficiencies of traditional subjectivist philosophies of reason. This deficiency is only slightly diffused where the subject is turned into a multiplicity of agents whose transcendental nature lies in their parallel connectedness, although this conceptualization cuts a path toward a new theory of human action, if not imagination (Minsky 1986).

The main deficiency of subjectivist approaches to modeling reason as intelligence lies in the fact that human reason is cut off from human action, and is simultaneously viewed as the agency that controls action. (This is the legacy of Descartes and Kant.) Due to this dichotomy, which is paramount in knowledge acquisition, the relationship of knowing and acting remains a mystery, and the symbolic level of action is artificially separated from subsymbolic support systems. As well, the difference between what people say (espoused theory) and what they actually do (theory-in-use) cannot be accounted for (Argyris 1987). Consequently, artificial intelligence becomes the undertaking of formalizing espoused theory (speech knowledge), and misses out on capturing theory-in-use, namely, the cognitive (often subsymbolic) schemata that determine action.

The logic of the artificial intelligence approach, when applied to music, discourages insight into action knowledge, especially if the research task is seen as an application of existing artificial intelligence constructs to music phenomena. In this case, no rethinking of the subjectivist foundations of artificial intelligence takes place, and the link between musical reason and musical action remains hidden from view. No real alternative to traditional musicology is being offered. As is to be expected, a majority of the results of present-day AI research in music tends to consist of formalizations of speech knowledge regarding musical variables and parameters, without any new insights into how these elements are used in actual musical pursuits. Since music is primarily a human activity, and musical knowledge is largely action knowledge, few new, if any, anthropological insights into music emerge from such research. The achievement is rather in the form of a critique, namely, a (valuable) clean-up of speech knowledge illusions about music, and of inconsistencies of music theory. (The nouvelle AI at the Massachusetts Institute of Technology. in the early 1990s, led by Rodney Brooks, would suggest that building musical insects could be a good first step toward building a musical robot. One will have to see whether such insects will be able to climb the tree of knowledge, to become capable of more highly environment-independent action, as exemplified, for instance, by musical performers.

Musicology as an Action Science

What, then, is the real challenge of AI and music, as put forth in this book?

Following (C. Argyris 1987), we see the real challenge of AI and music in establishing cognitive musicology as an action science. In contrast to mainstream (Newtonian) science, on the one hand, and to historic-hermeneutic science, on the other, an action science is geared (1) to understanding the theory-in-use of actors (theoretical musicology), and (2) to improving the way in which the actors act (applied musicology). Accordingly, formalizations and implementations of espoused (i.e., speech) knowledge theories of music action have mainly a critical value, in that they show what is not understood about musical action.

It is in this context that the debate over the relationship of symbolic and subsymbolic representations of musical action assumes relevance. (Subsymbolic processing should not be equated with connectionism; the latter acknowledges no such distinction and, indeed, ought to be entirely free of it.) Since symbolic representations of action are deficient, in that they capture only its speech-knowledge (intelligence, or espoused-theory) aspect, one could hope that an integration, into AI, of subsymbolic approaches to modeling musical action, might take us closer to the actual theory-in-use of musicians. That theory is not a set of propositional statements (as in Newtonian, or even hermeneutic science), but a cognitive and/or biological schema enabling musicians to design musical action. Since from an evolutionary as well as epistemological point of view, being/action precedes knowing/thought, an integration of neuronal and biological modeling into symbolic representations has considerable promise (Radermacher 1990, Todd et al. 1991).

One might hope, for instance, that AI and music, mastering the integration of symbolic and subsymbolic approaches to knowledge representation, could accomplish a rational reconstruction of the way in which musical knowledge evolved from the biological base of human activity; how, being initially restricted to narrow social task environments, musical intelligence emerged as a relatively autonomous agency (without thereby losing its root in the biological foundation of human capabilities). Should the intelligence simulation claim of the field fail (as we think, it will), the knowledge acquisition and modeling claim—and thus, the musicological essence the field—seems secure. Moreover, since the novel knowledge distribution, restructuring, publication, as well as training, possibilities of the field will far outpace the ideological intelligence claim, and will reinforce the pragmatic achievements of computer sound synthesis and manipulation, the effort that began in the seventies will most likely pay off.

The claim of AI and music, to be the new cognitive musicology, rests on rather solid ground. The new field is a science of the artificial (Simon 1969); it focuses, not on intelligence, but on knowledge, which is a much broader notion; more specifically, it focuses on musical knowledge as an agency for designing musical action (theory-in-use), rather than on an agency supposedly understanding some sounding reality 'out there,' and pretty far removed from the shallow speech knowledge intelligence that is thematic in research of the 1970s and 1980s.

On Future Research in Cognitive Musicology

The field of cognitive musicology is coming of age at a time when the limits of strictly logical uses of the computer as a model for intelligent human action have become apparent. The awareness of the limitations of contemporary models of knowledge-intensive activity has grown from within the field of computing itself. Were it not for the state of infancy of cognitive musicology, one could have expected a demonstration of the insufficiencies of this model from cognitive musicology.

The promise of cognitive musicology seems to point in the direction of models of computation that are more strongly inspired by problems in perception and action than by logical inference. From studies in robotics as well as vision (Marr 1982), it has become increasingly evident that transduction and the (early) stages of human perception are fundamentally and massively parallel in nature. This finding, no doubt, also holds for auditory perception and, more generally, musical action generally. Secondly, the classical theory of categorization, which assumes that each concept is defined by a finite set of non-overlapping features, has been drawn into doubt by anthropological studies (Rosch 1978). Certainly, these studies draw into question many of the central assumptions in psychoacoustics, music theory, and music history. The conclusion seems to be that a combination of the cognitive sciences and of artificial intelligence is challenging all tenets of classical theorizing about music, whatever its intellectual origin.

To put it in a nutshell, we expect of cognitive musicology more than that it will absorb the lessons from its natural co-disciplines; we expect it rather to become a force of its own, and to become instrumental in elaborating models of cognition as computation that are closer to human action, common sense, and the imagination, than the narrowly deterministic, prescriptively controlled sequences of assignments counting as computation today. For fashioning new models of computation, research in music, and in the arts generally, could well become a discipline of choice in the future.

References

Anderson, J. R. 1985. *Cognitive Psychology*. New York: Freeman.

Anderson, J. R. 1983. *The Architecture of Cognition*. Cambridge, Massachusetts: The MIT Press.

Andrews, H. K. 1966. *The Technique of Byrd's Vocal Polyphony*. London, England.

Apostel, L. et al. eds. 1986. *Reason, Emotion, and Music*. Ghent, Belgium: Communication and Cognition.

Argyrin, C. 1987. *Action Science*. San Francisco: Jossey-Bass.

Baroni, M. and L. Callegari eds. 1984. *Musical Grammars and Computer Analysis*. Florence, Italy: Leo S. Olschki.

Bel, B., and Vecchione, B. eds. 1990. *Proceedings. Colloque Musique et assistance informatique*. Laboratoire Musique et Informatique Marseille (M.I.M.). Marseille, France.

Blacking, J. 1984. What Languages Do Musical Grammars Describe? In *Musical Grammars and Computer Analysis*, M. Baroni and L Callegari eds., 363–370. Florence, Italy: Leo S. Olschki.

Blacking, J. 1973. *How Musical is Man?* Seattle, WA: University of Washington Press.

Breuker, J. A., and Wielinga, B. J. 1986. Use of Models in the Interpretation of Verbal Data. In *Knowledge Elicitation for Expert Systems*, ed. A. Kidd. New York: Plenum Press.

Broeckx, J. 1981. *Muziek, Ratio, en Affect*. Antwerp: Belgium. Metropolis.

Brownston, L. et al.1985. *Programming Expert Systems in OPS5*. Reading, Massachusetts: Addison-Wesley.

Cahier, J. P. 1986. L'I.A. au tournant de la cognitique. *Le Monde Informatique* (Septembre 1986) également sur série.

Chomsky, N. 1957. *Syntactic Structures*. The Hague: Mouton.

Clynes, M. 1986. Generative Principles of Musical Thought. In *Cognitive Musicology*, ed. O. Laske, 3(3): 185-223. Ghent, Belgium: Communication and Cognition.

Clynes, M. 1978. *Sentics: The Touch of Emotions*. Garden City, N.Y.: Anchor Press/Doubleday.

Cogan, R. 1984. *New Images of Musical Sound*. Cambridge, Massachusetts: Harvard University Press.

Cogan, R. and P. Escott 1976. *Sonic Design*. Englewood-Cliffs, N.J.: Prentice-Hall, Inc.

Collingwood, R. G. 1946. *The Idea of History*. Oxford: Oxford U. Press.

Deutsch, D. ed. 1982. *The Psychology of Music*. New York: Academic Press.

Ennals, R. 1985. *Artificial Intelligence: Applications to Logical Reasoning and Historical Research*. Chichester, England: Ellis Horwood.

Ennals, R. 1984. Computers and History. In *Teaching History*. History Teachers Association of New South Wales.

Fodor, J. A. 1983. *The Modularity of Mind*. Cambridge, MA.: The M.I.T. Press.

Francastel, P. 1970. *Etudes de sociologie de l'art*. Paris: Denoël/Gonthier.

Gardner, H. 1985. *The Mind's New Science: A History of the Cognitive Revolution*. New York: Basic Books.

Gardner, H. 1983. *Frames of Mind: A Theory of Multiple Intelligences*. New York: Basic Books.

Geerts, C. 1983. *Local Knowledge*. New York: Basic Books.

Goldman, A. I. 1986. *Epistemology and Cognition*. Cambridge, Massachusetts: Harvard University Press.

Johnson-Laird, P. N. 1983. *Mental Models*. Cambridge, Massachusetts: Harvard University Press.

Jones, L. 1964. *The End of Man is his Beauty*. New York: Grove Press Inc.

Kippen, J., and Bel, B. 1989. "Can a Computer Help Resolve the Problem of Ethnographic Description?" *Anthropological Quarterly* 62(3): 131–144.

Koenig, G. M. 1970a. *Project One*. Electronic Music Reports No. 1. Utrecht, The Netherlands: Institute of Sonology.

Koenig, G. M. 1970b. *Project Two*. Electronic Music Reports No. 2. Utrecht, The Netherlands: Institute of Sonology.

Kristeva, J. 1969. *Sémiotikè, recherches pour une sémanalyse*. Paris: Seuil.

Kunst, J. 1978. *Making Sense in Music: An Inquiry into the Formal Pragmatics of Art*. Ghent, Belgium: Communication and Cognition.

Laske O., 1992a. An Epistemic Approach to Systematic Musicology. In *Music Processing*, ed. G. Haus. Madison, WI: A-R Editions, Inc.

Laske, O. 1992b. Sciences humaines comme science de l'artificiel. In *Interface* 21(1–2). Amsterdam, The Netherlands: Swets & Zeitlinger.

Laske, O. 1992c. In Search of a Generative Grammar for Music. In *Machine Models of Music*. S. Schwanauer et al., eds. Cambridge, MA: The MIT Press.

Laske, O. 1991. Toward an Epistemology of Composition. In *Interface*, ed. O. Laske, 20(3–4): 235–269. Amsterdam, The Netherlands: Swets & Zeitlinger.

Laske, O. 1990a. The Computer as The Artist's Alter Ego. *Leonardo*, 23(1): 53–66. New York: Pergamon Press.

Laske, O. 1990b. Two Paradigms of Music Research: Composition and Listening. In *Proceedings, Colloque Musique et assistance informatique*, eds. B. Bel and B. Vecchione, 179–185. Marseille, France: Laboratoire Musique et Informatique Marseille.

Laske, O. 1989a. Composition Theory: An Enrichment of Music Theory. *Interface*, 18(1-2): 45–59. Lisse, The Netherlands: Swets & Zeitlinger.

Laske, O. 1989b. Comments on the First Workshop on AI and Music, St. Paul, MN, 1988. In *Perspectives of New Music*, ed. J. Rahn, 27(2): 290–298. Seattle, WA.

Laske, O. 1988a. Can We Formalize and Program Musical Knowledge?: An Inquiry into the Scope of Cognitive Musicology. *Musikometrika*, 1: 257–280. Bochum, F.R.G.: Studienverlag N. Brockmeyer.

Laske, O. 1988b. Introduction to Cognitive Musicology. *Computer Music Journal*, 12(1): 43–57. Cambridge, MA: The M.I.T. Press.

Laske, O. 1986. Toward a Computational Theory of Musical Listening. In *Music, Reason, and Emotion*, L. Apostel et al. eds. Ghent, Belgium: Communication and Cognition.

Laske, O. 1984. KEITH: A Rule-System for Making Music-Analytical Discoveries. In *Musical Grammars and Computer Analysis*, M. Baroni and L. Callegari eds. Florence, Italy: Leo S. Olschki.

Laske, O. 1981. *Music and Mind: An Artificial Intelligence Perspective*. San Francisco, California: Computer Music Association.

Laske, O. 1979. Goal Synthesis and Goal Pursuit in a Musical Transformation Task for Children Between Seven and Twelve Years of Age. In *Interface* 9(2): 207–235. Lisse, The Netherlands: Swets & Zeitlinger.

Laske, O. 1977a. *Music, Memory, and Thought: An Exploration in Cognitive Musicology.* Ann Arbor, Michigan: University Research Press.

Laske, O. 1977b. Verification and Sociological Interpretation in Musicology. In *Intern. Rev. Soc. & Aesthetics of Music,* vol. 8(1): 212–236. Zagreb, Yugoslavia: Academy of Music.

Laske, O. 1974. Toward a Center of Musical Intelligence Studies: Observer. *Numus West,* 5: 44–46. Mercer Island, Washington.

Laske, O. 1973a. *Introduction to a Generative Theory of Music.* Utrecht, The Netherlands: Institute of Sonology.

Laske, O. 1973b. On the Understanding and Design of Aesthetic Artefacts. in *Music und Verstehen,* P. Faltin ed. Cologne, F.R.G.: Arno Volk Verlag.

Laske, O. 1972. *On Problems of a Performance Model for Music.* Utrecht, The Netherlands: Institute of Sonology.

Laske, O. 1971. An Acoulogical Performance Model for Music. In *Electronic Music Reports,* 4: 31–64. Utrecht, The Netherlands: Institute of Sonology.

Leibowitz, R. 1949. *Schoenberg and his School.* New York: Da Capo.

Leman, M. 1990. Some Epistemological Considerations on Symbolic and Subsymbolic Processing. In *Actes, Colloque Musique et assistance informatique,* B. Bel and B. Vecchione eds. Marseille, France: Laboratoire Musique et Informatique Marseille.

Leman, M. 1986a. Using Dialectical Logics for an Account of Default Reasoning in Musical Language. *Report,* Seminar of Musicology, Ghent University, Ghent, Belgium.

Leman, M. 1986b. A Process Model for Musical Listening Based on DH-Networks. In *Cognitive Musicology,* ed. O. Laske, 3(3): 225–240. Ghent, Belgium: Communication and Cognition.

Lerdahl, F., and Jackendoff, R. 1983. *A Generative Theory of Tonal Music.* Cambridge, Massachusetts: The MIT Press.

Lévi-Strauss, C. 1969. *The Raw and the Cooked.* New York: Harper & Row.

Lischka, C. and H.W. Güsgen1986. A Constraint-Based Approach to Musical Knowledge Representation. In *Proceedings of the 1986 ICMC.* The Hague, Holland.

Longuet-Higgins, H.C. 1979. The Perception of Music. In *Proceedings, Royal Society of London, Series B 205.* London, England.

Marr, D. 1982. *Vision: A Computational Investigation Into the Human Representation and Processing of Visual Information.* San Francisco: Freeman.

Meyerson, I. 1948. *Les fonctions psychologiques et les oeuvres.* Paris: Vrin.

Minsky, M. 1986. *The Society of Mind.* New York: Simon & Schuster.

Minsky, M. 1981. Music, Mind, and Meaning. *Computer Music Journal,* 5.28–44.

Nattiez, J.-J. 1987. *Musicologie generale et semiologie.* Paris: Bourgois.

Nattiez, J.-J. 1975. *Fondements d'une sémiologie dela musique.* Paris, France: Union Générale d'Editions.

Newell, A. 1973. Production Systems: Models of Control Structures. In *Visual Information Processing,* ed. W. C. Chase. New York: Academic Press.

Partridge, D. 1986. *Artificial Intelligence: Applications in the Future of Knowledge Engineering.* Chichester, England: Ellis Horwood, Ltd.

Passeron, R. 1989. *Pour une philosophie de la création.* Paris: Klinsieck.

Poitou, J. P. 1990. *Psychisme et Histoire.* Technologies, Idéologies, Pratiques, 8, 1–4, Université de Provence, Aix-en-Provence, France.

Pospelov, D. 1990. Hermeneutics in Expert Systems. In *Knowledge-Based Systems,* 3(1): 25–27. Guilford, U.K.: Butterworths Scientific Ltd.

Post, E.L. 1943. Formal Reductions of the General Combinatorial Decision Problem. *American Journal of Mathematics,* 65.

Pylyshyn, Z. W. 1984. *Computation and Cognition: Toward a Foundation for Cognitive Science.* Cambridge, Massachusetts: The MIT Press.

28   *O. Laske*

Radermacher, F. J. 1990. Modeling and AI In *Applied Artificial Intelligence,* ed. R. Trappl. New York & Washington: Hemisphere Publication Corporation.

Roads, C. 1985. Research in Music and Artificial Intelligence. *ACM Computing Surveys,* 17(2):163–190.

Roads, C., and Laske, O.1983. Musik und Künstliche Intelligenz: Ein Forschungsüberblick. In *Feedback Papers,* no. 30. Cologne: Feedback Studio Verlag (translated from the English, with a commentary, by O. Laske).

Roads, C. 1980 (ed.). Artificial Intelligence and Music. *Computer Music Journal,* 4(2–3).

Rosch, E. and B.B. Lloyd 1978. *Cognition and Categorization.* Hillsdale, N.J: Lawrence Earlbaum.

Seeger, C. 1977. *Studies in Musicology 1935–1975.* Berkeley, California: University of California Press.

Simon, H. A. 1969. *The Sciences of the Artificial.* Cambridge, MA: The M.I.T. Press.

Sloboda, J. A. 1988. *Generative Processes in Music: The Psychology of Performance, Improvisation, and Composition.* New York: Oxford University Press.

Sundberg, J. ed. 1983. *Studies in Music Performance.* Stockholm: Royal Swedish Academy of Music, no. 39.

Sundberg, J., B. Lindblom, 1976. Generative Theories in Language and Music Descriptions. *Cognition,* 4(1):99–122.

Todd, P. M. et al. 1991. *Music and Connectionism.* Cambridge, MA: The MIT Press.

Truax, B. 1984. *Acoustic Communication.* Norwood, N.J.: Ablex Publishing Corporation.

Vecchione, B. 1990. La révolution musicologique des années 1970–1980. In *Proceedings, Colloque Musique et assistance informatique,* B. Bel and B. Vecchione eds. Marseille, France: Laboratoire Musique et Informatique Marseille.

Wielinga, B. J. et al.1989a. Synthesis Report for KADS. *Deliverable Y3, Esprit Project P 1098.* Amsterdam, Holland: Department of Social Science Informatics, University of Amsterdam.

Wielinga, B. J. et al. 1989b. A Knowledge Acquisition Perspective on Knowledge-Level Models. *Report,* University Amsterdam, Department of Social Science Informatics. Amsterdam, Holland.

Winograd, T. and F. Flores 1986. *Understanding Computers and Cognition.* Norwood, N.J.: Ablex Publishing Corporation.

Zicarelli, D. et al. 1986. M: The Interactive Composing and Performing System. Albany, N.Y.: Intelligent Music Systems.

Abstract

This paper differs from the others in this book. Whereas they deal primarily with musical thinking, this paper deals primarily with the way we think about musical thinking. What it says is that the way that most cognitive musicologists do it today—using only ordinary computations—is too weak to deal with all of musical thinking. But the message of this paper is not just about what is wrong. It also suggests what cognitive musicologists might do to set it right. They should also allow themselves to use the limiting computations of Gold 1965 and Putnam 1965. And it suggests some reasons why this might be worth doing.

Chapter 2

Beyond Computational Musicology

Peter Kugel

Computer Science Department, Boston College

From a Theoretical Point of View

Beyond Computation

Today, cognitive musicology (Laske 1988) typically tries to characterize musical thinking in strictly computational terms. And for good reasons. Computations meet three important criteria for scientific descriptions. They (or rather, the programs that define them) are precise. They make precise predictions that can be determined by running the programs and, thus, can be tested against observations. And they can be useful since, if you have a program that characterizes some aspect of musical thinking, that program can be run to produce the results of that thinking.

Thus, if you have a computer program that purports to describe how Mozart wrote piano sonatas, you can read that program (or, better, an English description of that program) and see both how it works and what it does. You can also run the program to see if it produces piano sonatas that really are in the style of Mozart. And you can run your program to automatically compose piano sonatas in Mozart's style...presumably including some sonatas that Mozart never actually wrote.

That's the good news about computations. The bad news, at least potentially, is that computations, alone, might not be powerful enough to describe all of musical thinking. It is at least possible that Mozart used ways of thinking that are more powerful than computations. If that were so, then people who were trying to characterize all musical thinking strictly in computational terms might be forced to leave things out of their accounts of Mozart's musical thinking. What they were doing, in trying to characterize Mozart's musical thinking in strictly computational terms, would be like trying to paint a landscape without using green. You might be able to do that if the landscape you were painting were covered with snow. But you would have a lot more trouble if it was full of grass.

I believe that cognitive musicologists, who limit their conceptual palette to computations alone, are forced to leave important elements of musical intelligence out of their portrayals of it. Musical thinking is a lot like a landscape with some green in it, and trying to characterize it in strictly computational terms is a lot like trying to paint it with strictly non-green paint. In this paper, I want to suggest at least one color that, I believe, cognitive musicologists should add to their palette.

I want to say something about what this color is like. (It is just another kind of paint. Not something wholly different.) I want to suggest what it is about musical intelligence that they might be able to paint more accurately if they added this new color to their palettes. And I want to say a few words about what it tells us about musical intelligence to say that this additional conceptual machinery (or color) is necessary to characterize it fully.

This claim, that computation alone is not enough to characterize all musical thinking, is not new. Almost forty years ago, Myhill 1952 suggested that artistic thinking in general, and musical thinking in particular, might involve more than computations. Some people who make this claim do so because they want to argue that artistic thinking cannot be described precisely, or studied scientifically. That was not what Myhill wanted to say. He seems to have been convinced that artistic thinking could be described precisely and studied scientifically. He seems to have wanted to suggest that to do so would require more powerful conceptual tools that would not, however, take us beyond the range of scientific precision.

In terms of my previous scenery-painting analogy, what he was saying was not that landscapes cannot be painted at all—perhaps because nature is too lovely to be wholly captured on canvas (although that is almost certainly true). What he was saying was simply "If you want to paint nature accurately, you are going to have to put another color on your palette." And he went on to say something about what that other color might be like.

Today, we can express Myhill's suggestion more precisely, using ideas subsequently developed by Gold 1965 and Putnam 1965. What cognitive musicology puts on its palette today are *ordinary* computations. What it needs to add, to do the whole job of "painting an accurate picture of musical intelligence," is what we might call, following Gold, *limiting* computations. Such limiting computations are a lot like ordinary computations, much as green paint is a lot like orange or yellow. Adding them to the cognitive musicologist's palette is thus, a relatively small change. But, I shall argue, a crucial one.

"Uncomputable" Need Not Mean "Unscientific"

One reason some people feel that all account of musical thinking should be computational is that they believe that the alternative is a vague or unscientific account. That is not necessarily so.

What is happening today in cognitive science seems, to me, to be a lot like what happened in the times of Pythagoras. As today, people are trying to account for the mental world in scientific terms, so the Pythagoreans were trying to account for the physical world in such terms. Just as cognitive scientists today are convinced that if the mental world is to be accounted for scientifically, then all mental processes must be capable of being characterized in terms of *computer programs*, so the Pythagoreans were convinced that, if the physical world were to be accounted for scientifically, then all physical magnitudes must be capable of being characterized in terms of *numbers.*

For the Pythagoreans a problem arose because they were convinced that the only kinds of numbers there were were the *rational* ones. Thus, when they discovered that the hypothenuse of the 1x1 right triangle had a length of √2, and that there was no rational number that exactly equalled √2, they grew concerned. They feared the game was up because here was a physical magnitude that could not be characterized numerically.

Today, we laugh at that response because, to us, √2 is a perfectly good number. It just happens not to be a rational one. Well, just as there are numbers that are not rational, there are things that computer programs can be used to do that are not computational. And so, today, we might find it useful to include some of these uncomputational uses of computer programs in our notion of what computer programs can do, in order to be able to come up with precise accounts of parts of the mental world, much as western thought found it useful to add the real numbers to the numbers it would use to account for the physical world.

Myhill suggested that musical thinking might be one kind of thinking for which this might be true. And, if he was right, then that would suggest that just as the Pythagoreans reacted to their crisis (There is something we cannot account for with our current set of conceptual tools.) by adding the irrational numbers to their conceptual toolkit, so we should react to our crisis by adding some kind of uncomputations to our conceptual toolkit.

And now the resemblance gets a bit eerie. Just as you get to the irrational numbers, like √2, by a process known as "passing to the limit," so you get to things that computers cannot do by passing to the limit. These more powerful ways of using computer programs are known, following the terminology of Gold 1965, as *limiting computations.*

Limiting Computations

These limiting computations are like *ordinary computations* in that they can be run on computers (as irrational numbers can be added and subtracted like rational ones). But they are unlike ordinary computations in that they fail to meet what I have called (Kugel 1086) the *announcement condition.*

A procedure is said to meet the announcement condition if it can tell us, once and for all, when it has finished doing its job. Suppose, for example, that we wanted to design a procedure that could determine, for an arbitrary program P with input

I, whether or not P(I) (the program P, run on the input I) would or would not eventually stop. (You can think of such a procedure being used by a computing center to check out runs submitted by users. When a user asks the center to run program P on an input I, the center's computer applies this procedure (Call it *H?* for "Halting?") to P and I. If H? tells it that the job just submitted will halt, then the center runs it. If H? says the job will not halt, the center rejects it on the grounds that it does not want its computer jammed up with a program that runs forever.

The problem of designing such a procedure is called *the halting problem* and it is known to be unsolvable by a computation. (This was proved in Turing 1936. For an accessible account of this proof, see Harel 1987.) To see why a computation can't solve it, let's try to design a program for one that will. Let's have our procedure run a simulation of the program P, running on the input I. When this simulation halts, it prints YES. So far so good. But what if the simulation does not halt? Then our procedure can print NO only if it can somehow determine that the simulation will never halt. That's what it cannot do. Which is why it can compute a YES answer, but not a NO one.

It may seem that there is a rather simple way to handle the NO half of the problem. Let our procedure print NO *before* it starts running the simulation of P, working on I. Then let it start running its simulation as before. If the simulation halts, then let our program erase the NO and replace it with a YES. Count the *last* result this procedure produces as its final result. This procedure's final result is always right, but our new procedure does not solve the halting problem because it is not a computation, even though a computer can run it.

It is not a computation because, when run, it fails to meet the announcement condition. It does not, and cannot be made to, announce when it has produced its final result. A YES result is not the problem. As soon as the simulation halts, and the YES is printed, the procedure can stop and announce that *(Eureka!)* it has found the right answer. But if the correct result is NO, then there is no general way that it can decide when that NO is its final result. It is always possible that running the simulation for one or two more minutes will bring it to a halt and that therefore the NO will turn out to be wrong.

What makes a process, run on a computer, a computation, is not just what the computer does while running it. It is also what we take to be its *result.* When you run a program as a *computation,* you get the computer to go through a series of steps and, when it prints its *first* output, you take that as its result. (If you wish, you can also stop the machine that is running it.) On the other hand, when you run a program in this other way, you get the computer to go through a series of steps and count the *last* output it produces as its result. The difference is between whether you take the first result or the last. And the reason that that makes a difference is that you can always tell when an output is the first, but not when it is the last because the computer, going after that last can always change its mind. Procedures run on computers for their first outputs are the ordinary computations. The ones that are run for their last result are the limiting computations because there is a sense in which they produce their results only in the limit. And when you are running a program as a limiting computation you cannot always stop the computer. You may have to run it, in principle, forever.

It is, I believe, interesting to think about how we might talk about one aspect of this situation in English. We might say that, when you get a result from an ordinary computation, you *know* that that is its result. But if you get a result from a limiting computation you only *think* that that is its result. It may be only a coincidence that English uses the word 'think' both for information processing that is intelligent and to express the fact that a conclusion is only tentative. But, I will suggest later, it also may express an important relationship between intelligence and tentativeness (or open-mindedness).

The difference between ordinary computations and limiting ones is important from a mathematical point of view because you can prove a theorem to the effect that limiting computations can solve problems that regular ones cannot and that, therefore, the difference between them is mathematically significant.

Of course, for our purposes, that is not enough. We also need to demonstrate that the something more that limiting computations can do is needed in some kinds of musical thinking. What this means is shown in Figure 1, below.

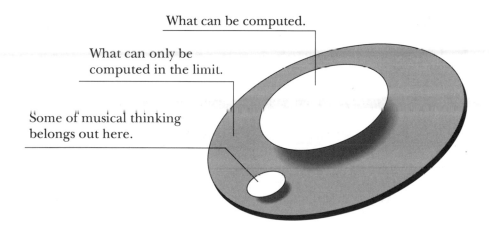

Figure 1. The Basic Thesis of This Paper Visualized.

How to Look for Uncomputability

If you plan to look for something, and we are about to look for examples of musical thinking that require more than ordinary computing, it pays to know something about the kind of thing you are looking for. If you don't, you are likely to head off in the wrong direction or use the wrong instruments. After all, you don't go to Africa to look for polar bears, and you don't use a microscope to look for elephants.

We are looking for a theoretical construct because an uncomputable process is, like an irrational number, a theoretical construct. And you don't go looking for such things in the real physical world just as you don't go looking for an irrational $\sqrt{2}$ in the physical world. The Pythagorean theorem tells us that the hypothenuse of a one foot by one foot right triangle will be $\sqrt{2}$ feet long. But if you draw such a triangle, and measure its length with a ruler, you will find that it is (say) 1.41 feet long. And that is a rational length. To find an hypotenuse that has a length of an irrational $\sqrt{2}$, you have to look at idealized, or abstract, right triangles. And you will have to prove theorems about the lengths of their hypotenuses, not measure them with rulers.

A practical person, say a carpenter, might have trouble understanding why you were doing that sort of thing. The carpenter might tell you that, for any practical purposes, 1.41 is a perfectly good approximation for $\sqrt{2}$. You can't saw boards more accurately than a hundredth of a foot. So who cares that, if you try to write out a decimal number exactly equal to $\sqrt{2}$, you will never be able to get it exactly right?

But the irrationality of $\sqrt{2}$ has nothing to do with the real world. It has to do with the conceptual tools you use to deal with the real world. It has to do with your thinking about that world. And, similarly, our concern with whether or not musical thinking involves uncomputations has to do, not with musical thinking, but with the way we think about such thinking.

Look at it this way. Most cognitive musicologists are trying to build theories, and so that is what most of the other papers in this book are about. If this were a book about houses, those papers would be about building houses. That's important, but that's not what I am talking about here. If this were a book about building houses, this paper would be about the tools we use to build houses—about hammers and nails and saws. And I would be asking the question "Are the tools we are now using to build houses adequate?"

Of course, this book is not about building houses. It is about musical intelligence and one does not find out if the tools one is using to study musical intelligence are adequate by looking in one's toolkit. One does theory. And to do theory one idealizes things. Which is what I am about to do.

So, instead of computers, I will be talking about idealized computers—machines that theoreticians call *Turing machines.* Such machines have unlimited time and space to work with and never make clerical errors. The reason one deals with such idealized machines is to see what computing machines can do in principle (and to see what they cannot do in principle). To find this out, one ignores such matters as how long a process takes, or how much space it requires. What one is doing is very much like what one does in physics when one studies motion. One begins by studying of idealized motion—motion in which friction and gravity are both ignored—although, in the real world, the effects of gravity and friction are impossible to ignore.

From a Musical Point of View

Looking for Partial Computability with a Brahms Machine

Let's see how well such idealized Turing machines might deal with the problem of characterizing certain aspects of musical thinking. Consider the problem (Myhill 1952) of determining whether or not a set of notes is consonant in the usual sense. Properly trained human beings can do this and it is not hard to write a computer program that will, given any set of notes, output YES if that set is consonant and NO if it is not. A problem for which this is possible (which is to say that there exists a single program that gives us both the YES and the NO answers) is called *totally computable.*

Now consider the problem of determining whether or not a given composer will or will not ever use a given chord. To fix ideas, take Brahms. In practice, our problem (for the case of Brahms) can be solved by a computation because Brahms is dead and our program can mechanically check all the pieces he ever wrote for the appearance of the given chord. But that way of going about the job is neither interesting, nor does it tell us much about either Brahms or musical thinking. If we are going to learn anything about such things, we need to construct a theoretical Brahms to pit against our theoretical Turing machines. Turing machines were developed to allow us to ignore practical difficulties so that we could focus on the underlying structures. To say that such an idealized machine can solve a practical problem (like checking all of Brahms' known output for the appearance of a given chord) is, therefore, neither interesting nor does it give us much insight.

To construct a theoretical Brahms to pit against our theoretical Turing machine, we think of Brahms as represented by an abstract machine that, like the Turing machine, also has unlimited time and space to work with and makes no clerical errors. (In a sense, that levels the playing field.) What our Brahms machine does is to grind out compositions in the style of Brahms. But not just the compositions that Brahms actually wrote. That would be trivial for such a machine because it could simply store the entire corpus in its unlimited memory before it got started. To be theoretically interesting, it has to grind out all the compositions Brahms actually wrote and all the ones he might have written. In short, all possible compositions in the style of Brahms.

And now let's ask whether or not this abstract Brahms machine will ever use our chord in any of the infinitely many Brahmsian compositions it can generate. It looks as though there is a simple way for a Turing machine to determine this. Let it simulate our Brahms-composing program, a step at a time. Each time the simulation produces a chord, let it check that chord against the sought-for chord and if new one matches it, let our Turing machine halt the simulation, print a YES, and stop. But now we have the same problem we had earlier when we tried to solve the halting problem. What if the chord does not appear?

Well, then, what we can do will depend a bit on the nature of the chord. If the chord is sufficiently dissonant (Perhaps it is a tone cluster from Schönberg.), then I think we can agree that the answer is NO without checking everything. We don't have to look at everything Brahms might possibly have written to determine that he would never have used that chord because we know he never used real dissonance. But this need not always be possible and if it is not, then we may have no alternative but to go through all of the Brahms machine's compositions. And, if we do that, there will not necessarily come a time at which we can say that we have looked at enough so that we (or rather our program) can conclude, with certainty, that the given chord will never be used.

Such programs—that can compute a YES answer, if there is one, but not a final NO answer—are called *partially computable.* The distinction between the totally computable and the partially computable may seem trivial, but it is not. For one thing, we can prove that it is mathematically significant—that there are problems that can be solved by partial computations that cannot be solved by total ones.

For another thing, the distinction between total and partial computations played a significant role in the invention of the general-purpose digital computer. This is because, if you define the intuitive idea of a computation by the formal idea of a total computation (which seems quite natural) then Turing's (1936) fundamental *universal machine theorem* would be false. There is no single Turing machine (or computing machine) that will compute all and only the totally computable functions, given the right program. On the other hand, there is a single universal Turing machine that will compute all possible partially computable functions, given a suitable program. This universal machine was the prototype of the universal digital computer and the theorem that showed it existed convinced people that such a machine was possible. So one could argue that, if Turing had not expanded his definition of computation to include the partial computations, his theorem would have failed and we would not have the general-purpose computer today.

Expanding your conceptual tools can have such unexpected consequences.

Looking for Limiting Computability in a Beethoven Machine

Now consider the problem of writing music, or composing, by machine. A composing machine generates a sequence of compositions. And we can think of it as generating each composition, chord by chord. At any point, its problem is deciding what chord it is to generate next. Again, to fix ideas, let's pick a composer and a piece. We'll use Beethoven writing his violin concerto.

My choice is not an accident. I chose Beethoven because he was a notorious reviser and I chose his violin sonata because the final score for it was not delivered until the day of its first performance. (One can imagine how delighted the performers must have been.)

Again, let's idealize Beethoven and turn him into an abstract machine that generates all compositions in the style of Beethoven. We will give that machine not only arbitrary amounts of paper to work with, but also arbitrary amounts of time so that it too can produce infinitely many pieces, this time in the style of Beethoven.

Our machine no longer has to deliver its concerto in time for the concert on December 23, 1806. It only has to deliver it in finite time. So it can be really Beethovenesque and change its choice of the next chord as often as it likes. The only restriction that we make is that one of these revisions will be its last. It may, in other words, change its mind only finitely often. And thus we say that the choice of the next chord (in some given place in a composition) for our abstract Beethoven machine is the one it settles on eventually or, as Gold 1965 would put it, *in the limit.*

This Beethoven machine, differs from the other two examples of (computing) machines that we had above in two respects. One is that it does not come out with just YES and NO answers. It comes out with specific chords in place of the YES's. That is not an essential difference from a theoretical point of view. The other difference, however, is essential. The YES output—or, more properly, the last chord—is now not, as it was in the case of those machines, the *first* output the machine generated, but its *last*.

When our first two procedures told us that yes, that chord is consonant and yes, that chord will be used by the idealized Brahms, we *knew* that that answer was right. When this Beethoven procedure tells us that such and such a chord belongs in this spot in this composition, we can only *think* that this is the case. We cannot be sure because the procedure could always change its mind and replace it with another.

Again, this difference is crucial. The conclusions of computations are final and, I believe, the conclusions of intelligent thinking are always tentative. Knowing is, to my mind, one of the greatest impediments to thinking and the apparent pun that underlies this—the two senses of think—seems to me to carry a good deal of truth (I have given my arguments for this elsewhere in Kugel 1986.) For another, it too makes a mathematical difference and we can prove that that switch from counting the first output to counting the last enlarges the set of things that procedures can do. (That means that if we decide that such open-mindedness is crucial to musical intelligence, then at least a part of musical intelligence will fall where Figure 1 shows it to be—outside of the range of computability.)

And this difference makes an important difference from a philosophical point of view too. To put this briefly, consider Popper's view account of science. Popper asked how the sciences differed from the nonsciences, such as astrology. He decided that the difference lay, not in the fact that the sciences came up with better truths, but that the sciences, in contrast to the nonsciences, came up with no final truths at all. A scientific conclusion is always, Popper argued, tentative. It is always subject to revision and many people believe that the notion of limiting computability—counting the last result instead of the first—is a precise version of what Popper had in mind when he suggested this. Accepting Popper's view of science, in place of the more traditional one which sees science as adding to our collection of truths, makes a difference. It says that such scientific facts as that the earth is round, are not facts at all but hypotheses that are always revisable. We don't know

that they are true. We only think so or, to put it in other words, all scientific knowledge is really scientific thinkedge. (It is interesting to note—in the context of this
paper—that Popper [1974] attributes the discovery of this idea largely to his speculations about music.)

Popper's view leads to a much more open-minded view of the nature of scientific
knowledge and of knowledge in general. That it is not trivial is something that you
can probably recognize if you ask yourself whether you really believe that your
belief that the earth is round is only tentative. That is certainly not what most science teachers teach in school.

My claim here is that musical knowledge—I've been using the knowledge
Beethoven must have had to write his violin concerto as an example—is just as tentative as scientific knowledge and that cognitive musicology should treat it as such.

This is not an empirical claim that might be disproved by asking Beethoven (if he
were still alive) or by producing a machine that *computed* the infinite set of compositions that Beethoven might have written. It is not even a mathematical claim that
can be proved or disproved. It is, rather, a suggestion about how musical thinking—
or at least aspects of that thinking—might be thought about. It is, in other words, a
suggestion of a way of looking at things, and such suggestions are neither true nor
false, neither provable nor disprovable.

That is not to say that mathematical theorems, scientific observations and/or computer programs cannot bear on the viability of such suggestions. The theorem that
tells us that limiting computations can do things that partial computations cannot
do, tells us that this claim at least has some mathematical content. The fact that some
composers might think of their pieces as being forever revisable might have some
bearing on it too. And the fact that somebody built (or programmed) a Beethoven
machine that did not use such mind-changing tactics might argue against it.

But basically, this claim is a suggestion that we are adopting a point of view and
such suggestions are not the kinds of things that are true or false. A point of view can
be useful or not, it can be appealing or not, it can be sensible or pointless, but it can
hardly be true or false. I shall give some reasons for thinking that this particular point
of view might be useful later, but first, let me suggest another way of arguing for it.

And Again with a Mozart Machine

The fact that musical thinking may be as tentative, and as open minded, as scientific thinking is only one feature of musical thinking that suggests the adoption of
a limiting-computable model of musical thinking. Another is what we might call
the *creativity* of such thinking.

To sketch the argument from this point of view, I'll use Mozart as an example.
Mozart's compositional thinking has been contrasted with Beethoven's. (See, for
example, Gardner 1982.) Where Beethoven revised, Mozart is reputed to have seen
new compositions in a flash. And having seen one, all that remained was to write it

out. Where Beethoven kept revising, Mozart got the whole thing right (so we are told) the first time through.

Now, I grant you that this contrast between Beethoven's perspiration-based approach to composing, and Mozart's inspiration based approach, may be misleading. It can be argued that what seems, to its users, to be inspiration may be the result of a lot of perspiration expended subconsciously. There may have been lots of hard thinking without the intervention, or awareness, of their conscious minds. But, be that as it may, we can take Mozart as at least a possible example of composition without revision and ask ourselves "Is there anything else that might lead us to a limiting-computable account of such composing?" One possibility is what we can think of as self-awareness.

Several things distinguished Mozart from a less-talented composer, such as (say) Salieri. Mozart seems to have had a better musical sense. Related to this, but slightly different, is the fact that Mozart was able to develop a more personal style. And it is often this ability not just to compose, but also to develop a personal style—something that allows a listener to say "Oh, yes. That sounds like Mozart."—that distinguishes the great composers from the merely good.

What does it mean to develop your own style? It could mean that you just dream something up that nobody had ever dreamt up before—random deviation from what went before. But it seems more plausible that you also have to know what the existing style is and to know how to change it in a significant manner. Let's try to characterize this process of creating your own style in terms of abstract machines.

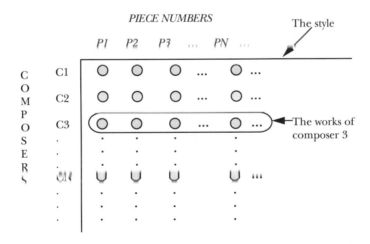

Figure 2. A Style as the Work of the Composers in It.

One way to think of a style—say the *pre-Mozart style*—in such terms, is to think of it as defined by a set, or collection, of abstract machines, with each machine in this set representing one possible composer, working in the pre-Mozart style. (See Figure 2.) Assume that these individual composing machines all have the same machinery, but that they run different programs. Each machine is thus defined by its program (call the programs for composers 1,2,...,n... $C_1, C_2,...,C_n...$) and each such program generates, as our Brahms machine did, an infinite sequence of pieces $(P_1, P_2,...,P_n....)$. Each composition that each such machine generates is in that pre-Mozart style. And now we can use an idea of Cantor 1915 to combine all these machines into a single one that prints out all the pieces generated by all the composers as a single list. (See Figure 3.) This machine, which grinds out all the pieces in it, defines the style in much the same sense that our Beethoven machine defined the style of Beethoven.

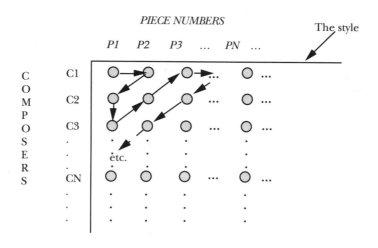

Figure 3. One Way to Combine the Individual Outputs into One.

Cantor used the technique shown in Figure 3 to demonstrate that there were no more rational numbers (which include the fractions) than there were whole numbers. But, in the same paper, he used another technique to show that there were more real numbers (numbers that can be expressed in terms of non-terminating decimals) between 0 and 1 than there were real numbers altogether. This method is known as *Cantor's diagonal method* and it plays an important role in the theory of the uncomputable, or *recursion theory*. (You can think of this paper as suggesting that this theory of the uncomputable, or recursion theory, should play an important role in cognitive musicology.)

Cantor's diagonal method can be used to produce a composer that is not in this list of composers in the pre-Mozartian style. Draw a diagonal line down the array of Figure 3, picking up the first composition of composer one, the second of composer two, and, in general, the n-th piece of composer n. (See Figure 4.)

Now, change these in some uniform way and you have a sequence that could not have been in your original list. Its first piece differs from the first piece of first

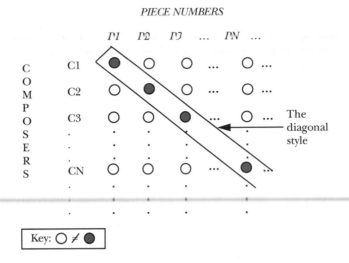

Figure 4. The "Diagonal" Style.

composer's corpus. Its second piece differs from the second piece of the second composer's corpus. And, in general, the nth piece differs from the nth piece of composer number n.

This construction does not quite do the job of producing a new style for us for two reasons. One is that my construction does not yet guarantee that the pieces of this diagonal composer aren't all already somewhere in the original list. There are several ways to avoid this that I will not discuss because I feel that it would take us too far afield. The other is that this construction is wholly mechanical and has no musical point. That, I am afraid, is often the case with a mathematical construction. Finding musically valid reasons for using such constructions is another matter that I will also refrain from discussing here.

It is, after all, not this specific procedure that I claim Mozart used. What I claim is that some musicians have the kinds of cognitive abilities that this kind of construction requires, namely the ability to see what makes for the style of one's day, and the ability to go beyond it. And the reason that this claim is relevant to our concerns here is that, if you give these powers to the right kind of abstract machine that can already carry out ordinary computations, it is thereby turned into a machine that is capable of also carrying out limiting computations.

The Structure of the Arguments

These two arguments—the one based on the Beethoven machine and the other based on the Mozart machine—are based on two different ways that theoreticians go from the ordinary computable to the limiting computable. One way is by passing to the limit, which is due to Putnam 1965 and Gold 1965. The other way is by diagonalizing, which is due to Kleene 1943. Notice that these two arguments do not only use different techniques. They are also based on different features of musical thinking, and they have a slightly different character. The first is more direct than the second. It says that musicians seem to be somewhat tentative, or open to revision, and that characterizing their thinking in terms of computations—with their one-shot conclusions—does not do justice to that aspect of musical thinking. The second argument does not claim that musicians have a certain capability that carries their thinking into the uncomputable. It says that they have a certain capability that leads you into uncomputability, if you want to give a smooth-running account of that capability.

This argument is a lot like the one that Chomsky 1957 used to argue—against the behaviorists—that the mind is not a finite automaton. English, Chomsky noted, allows the embedding of clauses within clauses. Although there is a clear upper bound on how deeply such embedding can be carried out in practice, it makes sense to characterize the machinery (or grammar) that the mind brings to bear on this embedding as though there were no such limit. Why?

For very much the same reasons why we don't say that there is a largest integer. Because it makes for a smoother-running theory and because the resulting theory gives us a better handle on the underlying structure. Chomsky was not trying to capture what English-speakers could do (or their *performance*), but what they knew (or their *competence*). Similarly, we are not trying to characterize what Mozart and Beethoven *could do*. We are trying to characterize what they *knew*.

Think of what Mozart and Beethoven knew as being represented by some kind of program in their heads. In running those programs (or thinking) they were, of course, limited by practical considerations. That violin concerto had to be delivered by December 23rd. Even if they don't have deadlines, composers know that they have finite lifetimes so that revision has eventually to stop. And, if they are willing to leave future revisions to their heirs, they face such ultimate deadlines as the expiration of all mankind or the heat death of the universe. But the programs in their heads—which capture their knowledge of music—do not have these limitations built into them and it is the structure of these programs that we are trying to get at.

Not in detail, of course. We are trying to determine what kinds of machinery are involved. The details can be filled in later.

From a Theoretical Point of View (Variations on the Theme)

So What?

I have given some reasons for believing that musical thinking requires limiting computing. Suppose that we accepted those reasons (or others) and agreed to add limiting computations to the tools we are willing to use to characterize, or think about, musical thinking. What would follow?

Well, in some respects, our thinking about musical thinking, or cognitive musicology, would get worse. Accounts of musical thinking, based on limiting computations, have some serious disadvantages over accounts based on ordinary computations. Both kinds of accounts can be characterized in terms of finite, precise, programs. But it is harder to determine what a limiting computable account predicts, in practice, than what an account in terms of ordinary computations predicts. And limiting computable procedures are not quite as easy to use as totally computable ones. All of which suggests that cognitive musicologists should use ordinary computations wherever they can.

But there is a danger in using concepts that are not powerful enough. If, to paraphrase Maslow, you have only a conceptual hammer, then everything in the world will look like a nail. As a result, there are many things you won't see and, if you restrict your toolkit to hammers, many things you can't build. Which suggests that there will be times when limiting computations should be used.

Now, just as the practicing carpenter might argue that the real value of $\sqrt{2}$ is 1.41 exactly because the length of boards cannot be measured to greater accuracy, so it is tempting to argue that all musical thinking can be characterized by computations in practice because, in practice, the amount of time we can wait for a final result is always finite. (We are reminded, again, that we die, or that the universe eventually comes to an end.) But such arguments are misleading. One could use a similar argument to argue that there really aren't any real numbers and if one did that, one might miss discovering well-tempered tuning, which depends on the irrational number $12\sqrt{2}$. And if we had done that, we would have missed having classical music as we know it.

At the same time, if we adopted limiting computations, as well as ordinary ones, our musical thinking would improve in some respects because the claim that parts of musical thinking involve uncomputations is not wholly negative. I have also said something about what those uncomputations are like and that clarifies the original picture that I gave in Figure 1 (above). We would have more powerful procedures that would let us see more and those procedures, if they were expressed in terms of limiting computations, would still be scientifically precise. And we would now be able to say some things about this territory beyond the edge of ordinary computation. (See Figure 5, below.) The geography of this territory—where the uncomputable procedures live—has been studied by mathematicians for years. They call it *recursion theory* and it provides a fertile source of mathematical ideas for the cognitive musicologists. These ideas could add a certain amount of mathematical depth to what they can say about musical thinking.

And some of these mathematical ideas provide them with new conceptual tools. New conceptual tools give us, not just new things we can do, but also new ways of looking at things. They can provide a new metaphor, if you prefer, a new paradigm (in the sense of Kuhn 1962), for the science of cognitive musicology. The limiting computational metaphor can open up new areas for cognitive musicology to explore.

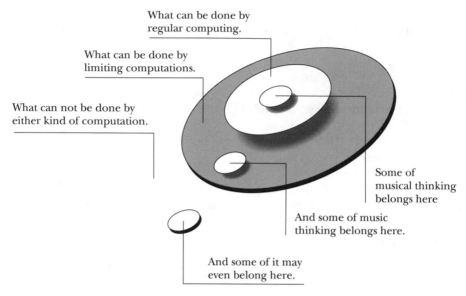

Figure 5. The Basic Thesis of This Paper Refined.

This metaphor has a curious resonance with the history of physics. Recall that the introduction of irrational numbers, and the associated concept of passing to the limit, into the conceptual machinery of the physicists, allowed them to study physical motion. I believe that the introduction of the very-closely-related notion of carrying computations to the limit will allow us to better study motion—which is to say change and development—in musical thinking.

Many people will find this new metaphor as uncomfortable as they find Popper's approach to scientific truths. The feeling of stability that comes from the belief that one knows is, for many, much more appealing than the feeling that comes with the awareness that one can only think. My only suggestion is that not all cognitive musicologists have to use the new conceptual tools. For those who can't stand the heat of open-mindedness in musical thinking, there is plenty of room in the cooler, more computational, parts of the cognitive-musicological kitchen.

Let them work with computations. There are lots of things that can be done with normal computations in cognitive musicology. But there are some things that can't be.

Myhill's Thesis

In an earlier version of this paper (Kugel 1990), I suggested that the claim that *a complete rendition of musical thinking requires more than computing* should be called *Myhill's thesis* because Myhill 1952 seems to have been the first person to propose it in print. In his 1952 paper, Myhill also suggested a nice intuitive way to express this proposal.

He distinguished problems whose solutions can be found by what he called *technique,* from those whose solutions can be found only by *insight.* A problem that can be solved by the thoughtless (or at least relatively thoughtless) application of a recipe (or what we now call an *algorithm)* requires only technique. The solution of a problem requires insight if you have to understand the problem in order to solve it.

Whether or not a problem can be solved by technique or not is relative to what you know. Turning a problem, that used to require insight, into one that does not, can be a major step forward. Thus, for example, it used to require insight (long ago) to divide two numbers. When an algorithm for doing long division was discovered, the problem of dividing 5678 by 12 was reduced to a problem that could be solved by technique. This reduction made it possible for many more people to do division, and for those who could do it to handle much larger numbers and do so more easily.

Giving a computational account of some aspect of musical intelligence—which is what most of the people whose papers appear in this volume are trying to do—is a worthwhile thing to do because it reduces musical problems, that used to be thought to require insight, into ones that now can be solved by applying technique.

True, people who have devoted serious efforts to developing the ability to have such insights, and whose self esteem may rest heavily on their ability to deal with them, may not like that. Those whose ability to do division was trivialized by the discovery of an algorithm for doing it probably didn't like that either. I feel sorry for those whose insights are displaced by techniques, and I sympathize with their desire to claim that the techniques do not fully capture their insight. (And sometimes they have a point.)

But while we argue against those who argue that our techniques are not enough to do what they can do, we need to guard against assuming that therefore techniques can do everything. There are people who believe that all problems can, in principle, be solved by technique. According to them, our failure to find techniques to solve any given problem is, as Myhill 1952 put it, "merely an accidental gap in knowledge which will be closed in the next few thousand years if death and dynamite do not intervene."

Well, they may be wrong too. Myhill suggested that there were some problems whose solutions simply could not be reduced to technique, no matter how hard we try. Some of these are problems, whose solutions cannot be reduced to technique, are, he suggested, problems of artistic (including musical) creation. But there are also such problems in science and mathematics and other disciplines.

If you can do some kinds of musical problem solving by techniques, or ordinary computations, alone, by all means go ahead and do so. But be prepared for some kinds of musical problem solving to require more powerful ideas...to require something like insight—perhaps something like limiting computations.

If green paint is hard to come by, or difficult to handle, or you simply don't like it, then by all means try painting your landscapes without using the damned stuff. But be prepared to run into trouble when you try painting grass, or leaves, or other growing things.

As Einstein once put it, "a scientific theory should be as simple as possible. But not simpler."

Acknowledgments

I want to thank Otto Laske and Charles Ames for helpful comments on an earlier version of this paper (Kugel 1990).

References

Cantor, G. 1915. *Contributions to the Founding of the Theory of Transfinite Numbers.* Tr. P. E. B. Jourdain. Chicago, Ill.: Open Court.

Chomsky, N. 1957. *Syntactic Structures.* The Hague: Mouton & Co.

Gardner, H. 1980. The Compositions of Mozart's Mind. In *Art, Mind and Brain*, H. Gardner, 358-368. New York: Basic Books.

Gold, E. M. 1965. Limiting Recursion. *Journal of Symbolic Logic* 30:28–48.

Harel, D. 1987. *Algorithmics: The Spirit of Computing.* Reading, Mass.: Addison-Wesley.

Kleene, S. C. 1943. Recursive Predicates and Quantifiers. *Transactions of the American Mathematical Society.* 53:41–73.

Kugel, P. 1986. Thinking May Be More Than Computing. *Cognition* 22:137–198.

Kugel, P. 1990. Myhill's Thesis: There's More Than Computing in Musical Thinking. *Computer Music Journal.* 14:3 (in press).

Kuhn, T. S. 1962. *The Structure of Scientific Revolutions.* Chicago, Ill.:The University of Chicago Press.

Laske, O.E. 1988. Introduction to Cognitive Musicology. *Computer Music Journal.* 12:43–57.

Myhill, J. 1952. Some Philosophical Implications of Mathematical Logic: Three Classes of Ideas. *Review of Metaphysics* 6:165–198.

Popper, K. 1959. *The Logic of Scientific Discovery.* New York: Basic Books.

Popper, K. 1974. Intellectual Autobiography. In *The Philosophy of Karl Popper*, ed. P.A. Schilpp. La Salle, Ill.: Open Court.

Putnam, H. 1965. Trial and Error Predicates and the Solution to a Problem of Mostowski. *Journal of Symbolic Logic.* 30:49–57.

Turing, A. M. 1936. On Computable Numbers, With an Application to the Entscheidungsproblem. *Proceedings of the London Mathematical Society, Series 2.* 42:230–265.

Section Two

General Problems in Modeling Musical Activities

Modeling music and musical activities pose hard problems, some of which were discussed in the introductory article to this book. The modeler has to take decisions about the exact nature of the reference domain of his or her system, and about the kind of tools used to specify the formal model. Determining answers for such questions is always hard, and is particularly difficult in an artistic field like music. On one extreme there can be a *mobotics* like approach (Brooks 1991) that denies the validity of any system that is not, directly, grounded in the musical world it manipulates. According to such a view, no abstraction is needed, as the music system uses direct, immediate algorithms to respond to the stimuli it gets from the musical reference domain. Approaches on the other extreme would strive for absolute abstraction and separation between the reference domain and the formal model, with direct semantics for specifying the relationship between them. In between these two extremes there can be a wide range of approaches that support some mixture of abstraction with direct manipulation of the objects of the musical world.

The nature of the primitives or the reference domain was and still is a constant subject for discussion in modeling music. Until about ten years ago, prior to the MIDI based music systems period (Loy 1985), all music modeling was done in terms of symbolic representation of notes, and sometimes even in terms of graphical score notations (Erickson 1975). The MIDI based systems, that communicate with their environment in real time, using musical input-output channels, realize, in a sense, the idea of grounding the modeling system within its reference domain. But most of these systems concentrate on providing user friendly interfaces; their level of abstraction is, usually, very shallow, and restricted to the level of the sound objects. Exceptions are systems like ARCTIC (Dannenberg et al. 1986), FORMES (Rodet & Cointe 1984), FORMULA (Anderson & Kuivila 1989), and (Buxton 1978), that use higher level structuring of the sound objects.

The projects described in this section seem to form a new generation of computer music systems. Their main concern is the nature of the music processing theory they wish to implement, and the kind of formal tools that are most appropriate for that task. Implementation-related decisions, and design of friendly interfaces, belong to a later stage in the development of a music processing system. The following chapters present a diversity of approaches to the modeling of music processing. Smoliar suggests a connectionist approach, that directly manipulates mental states; Bel and Balaban both handle the aspects of *time* and *hierarchy* in the framework of incomplete knowledge, but Bel uses grammar based tools, while Balaban takes a functional approach. Blevis et al. and Courtot are concerned with the kind of operations, transformations and associations that are typical for such musical activities as composition. They both use a type system approach.

In chapter 3, "Representing Listening Behavior: Problems and Prospects," S. W. Smoliar criticizes the unreflected use of logic in studies in AI and music. He sketches a framework for the study of musical behavior, in which the postulated primitives are mental states or dispositions, not musical constructs such as notes or sounds. Smoliar views music as a domain of human *action;* he argues that musical action is mediated by a certain mental disposition, which, in Minsky's definition, gives rise to a "momentary range of possible behaviors". Smoliar goes on to discuss the possible nature of musical memory, and the issues and problems of representing it within a computer. Smoliar's ideas toward modeling musical memory, which do not include, yet, a realization plan, are derived from Minsky's research (Minsky 1980, 1986).

Bernard Bel's chapter "Symbolic and Sonic Representations of Sound-Object Structures," presents a two part framework that consists of: a symbolic, grammar based representation that accounts for the hierarchy and symbolic time aspects in music; and an interpretation algorithm that assigns sonic properties, and physical dates, to the objects of the abstract representation. The symbolic representation consists of strings that can be generated by a grammar, or more generally, by a rule-based system. The terminal symbols of such a grammar stand for sound objects and symbolic dates. The grammar allows for hierarchical groupings of these symbols, and can be combined with a synchronization algorithm that induces a total ordering on the symbolic time primitives. The interpretation algorithm is the bridge between the abstract handling of the music and the real performance. The input to the interpretation algorithm is an abstract structure, comprising various parameters concerning the expected structure of time; the output can be dispatched to a digital sound processor.

The interpretation algorithm provides partial *grounding* to the abstract representation; it defines the intended musical meaning for a grammatically correct string. The grounding is partial as the interpretation algorithm is uni-directional, from symbolic representation to actual performance: Performance results cannot affect the abstract representation. It is possible that studies of musical activities like composition, listening, and learning will yield insight that can contribute to a better grounding of modeling concepts within the intended musical domain.

The chapter "Music Structures: Interleaving the Temporal and Hierarchical Aspects in Music," by M. Balaban, presents a functional framework for interleaving the aspects of *hierarchy* and *time* in music representation, regardless of the nature of the primitives. The framework supports partial or complete, and implicit or explicit, descriptions, and can account for additional aspects of music via an *attributes' mechanism*. The music structures language is suggested as an underlying representation for explorations of music and music activities. It is based on the assumption that hierarchy and time are fundamental, inter-related aspects of music, and that neither can be independently described.

Comparing the chapters of Bel and Balaban seems rather interesting as the two chapters handle, essentially, the same aspects of music: hierarchy and time. Both representations allow for interleaving the two aspects, and support incomplete abstract descriptions. Yet, the resulting languages are considerably different. A thorough comparison that would point to the limitations and advantages of each language, and would explicate how the different formal tools affect the resulting framework, still has to be written.

The chapter "On Designing a Typed Music Language," by E. B. Blevis, M. A. Jenkins and J. I. Glasgow, describes a design exercise for a rich, typed music language targeted to support compositional and analytical processes. The authors conceive of a language that can represent high level structuring of the musical material, and can account for musically natural relationships such as similarities and differences between sequences of musical parameters, associations of such sequences, and generalizations of event sequences. The plan for the language includes polymorphic type constructors, and powerful operations like abstraction, constraints, non-deterministic selection, and equational unification. The chapter does not provide formal, or operational semantics for the language constructs.

Francis Courtot, in his chapter entitled "Logical Representation and Induction for Computer Assisted Composition," describes a compositional apprentice tool, based on a formalism for representing and discovering music structures. The formalism has two major parts: A type-based framework for describing and processing compositional notions; and a learning component that supports inference of new types and methods from given examples.

The typed language underlying this project is particularly designed to support high level compositional notions. The language has three kinds of terms: primitive types, complex types, and associations. Primitive types stand for musical parameters, complex types stand for objects formed by musical combinations (such as horizontal and vertical combinations), associations stand for type combinations (such as assigning a duration to a type, or associating a *description* with a given type). On top of this type base there are *methods* that account for transformations of types, and *concepts* that account for constraints among types. The learning component consists of heuristic rules that propose new types, based on a given set of types, and a sophisticated learning algorithm that discovers new rules, and selects the most general ones.

A comparison between the contributions of Blevis et al. and Courtot would seem fruitful, as their goals and conceptions are closely related. Both works conceive of a high level compositional assistant tool, that can represent and generalize compositional notions. Both contributions rely on a (not explicitly spelled out) belief in the existence of *compositional universals*, that characterize the kind of operations, associations, and abstractions that composers use. This approach can be contrasted with that of older music systems, like (Hiller 1966, 1972), that assume universals on much lower levels, such as musical parameters. The two chapters differ in the kinds of formal tools they develop: Blevis et al. aim at developing a programming language for music composition and analysis, and their approach seems inspired by research in automated deduction, logic, and functional programming. Courtot's system is similar to a logic proof system, and seems more musically motivated. A more formal background for both approaches still has to be developed.

References

Anderson,D. P.; and R Kuivila 1989. "Continuous Abstractions for Discrete Event Languages," *Computer Music Journal,* 13(3): 11-23.

Brooks, R. A. 1991. "Intelligence without Representation," *AI Journal* 47(1-3): 139-159.

Buxton, W.; Reeves, W.; Baecker, R.; and & Mezei, L.1978. "The Use of Hierarchy and Instance in a Data Structure for Computer Music," *Computer Music Journal,* 2(4): 10-20.

Dannenberg, R. B.; McAvinney, P.; and Rubine, D. 1986. "Arctic: A Functional Language for Real Time Systems," *Computer Music Journal,* 10(4): 67-78.

Erickson, R. F. 1975. "The DARMS Project: A Status Report," *Computers and the Humanities,* 9(6): 291-298.

Hiller, L. and Leal, A. 1966. "Revised MUSICOMP Manual," Tech. Rep. no. 13, University of Illinois Experimental Music Studio, May 1966.

Hiller, L. 1972. "Computer Programs Used to Produce the Composition HPSCHD," Tech. Rep. no. 4, SUNY at Buffalo, NY, August 1972.

Loy, G 1985. ''Musicians Make a Standard: The MIDI Phenomenon," Computer Music Journal, 9(4): 8-26.

Minsky, M.1980. "K-Lines: A Theory of Memory," *Cognitive Science Journal,* 4(2) April-June. Ablex Publishing.

Minsky, M. 1986. *The Society of Mind.* New York: Simon and Schuster.

Rodet,X., and P. Cointe 1984. "FORMES: Composition and Scheduling of Processes," *Computer Music Journal,* 8(3): 32-50.

Chapter 3

Representing Listening Behavior: Problems and Prospects

Stephen W. Smoliar

The Divergence of Representation from Music

Any attempt to apply artificial intelligence to the study of music must begin with a process of *abstraction*—a technique which, in his classic monograph on data structuring, Tony Hoare called "the most powerful tool available to the human intellect" (Hoare, 1972). Because there is a strong tendency to invoke abstraction without a clear understanding of what that invocation entails, it is valuable to recall Hoare's analysis of the process and, in particular, the way in which he decomposed it into four stages (Hoare, 1972):

1) Abstraction:[1] the decision to concentrate on properties which are shared by many objects or situations in the real world, and to ignore the differences between them.

2) Representation: the choice of a set of symbols to stand for the abstraction; this may be used as a means of communication.

3) Manipulation: the rules for transformation of the symbolic representations as a means of predicting the effect of similar manipulation of the real world.

4) Axiomatisation: the rigorous statement of those properties which have been abstracted from the real world, and which are shared by manipulations of the real world and of the symbols which represent it. Hoare's monograph was intended to address scientific and engineering applications of the computer. However, since abstraction is equally important to any understanding of music, it is worth while to see where things stand with respect to these four stages.

The most important, of course, is the first stage: the conscious decision to delimit one's universe of objects, selecting which properties will be invoked to describe objects, and which will be rejected as irrelevant. The latter decision, that of rejecting a body of information, lies at the heart of abstraction. In other words, abstraction entails the recognition that one cannot address *all* information associated with an object, and that reasoning cannot begin until that information is cut down to size.

The next most important observation is that the representation stage can only take place *after* one has committed oneself to the results of an abstraction stage. In other words, representation is intended to *reflect* an abstraction, rather than *define* it. Representation involves laying out criteria for what constitutes well-formed expressions of symbols; but unless each such expression *denotes* (Tennent, 1976) some construct which is part of the selected abstraction, the representation will be superfluous, containing symbolic structures which exist for nothing more than their own sake.

The criteria for well-formedness then lead to the next stage—defining the means by which those expressions may be *manipulated* to yield other expressions. Since the results of those manipulations must, themselves, be well-formed expressions, those results will have denotations which reflect back upon the original abstraction. Thus, manipulation is ultimately the instrument of reasoning about that abstraction; it is the means by which one may take given observations and deduce new ones. This increased knowledge about the abstraction may then reflect into increased knowledge of that universe of objects which was abstracted.

The final stage is essentially one of rigorous summary. If one has performed the first three stages properly, then the results of all of them may be embodied in some formal symbolic logic. One may then use that formalism to reason about the abstraction process, itself. This is particularly important if one wishes to establish that one's results are both logically consistent and complete.

How, then, may this characterization of abstraction and its contribution to reasoning be applied to music? The most important lesson is to avoid premature concerns with representation and to begin any application by addressing the nature of the appropriate abstraction. In other words any application must begin by asking *what is the universe of objects, and which properties will be invoked to describe those objects.* There is still a danger of premature consideration of representation, however, because so much of the study of music has a tendency to orient itself around *artifacts of notation.* In this respect David Lewin (Lewin, 1986) has taken a bold step forward in his recent claim that music theory has more to do with *behavior* than with such artifacts.[2] This is a worthy universe which Lewin has proposed for the first stage of Hoare's process, but what are the objects which inhabit it? This must be the first question to address, after which it will be possible to consider those objects associated with current representational systems and see if there is any correspondence.

The Objects of Musical Behavior

In attempting to identify objects of musical behavior, it is helpful to begin by considering the broad scope which Lewin wished the term to encompass (Lewin, 1986):

Actually, I am not very sure what a theory of music might be, or even a theory of modern Western art-music, but so far as I can imagine one (of either) that includes a theory of musical perception, I imagine it including the broader study of what we call people's "musical behavior," a category that includes competent listening to be sure, but also competent production and performance. Here I understand production and performance not only in the sense of high art but also as manifest in everyday acts of musical "noodling," and in a whole spectrum of intermediate activities. Under the rubric of noodling I include rhythmic gestures, conscious or unconscious, like patterns of walking, finger-drumming, or nervous scratching; I also include singing, whistling, or humming bits of familiar or invented tunes, or variations on familiar tunes; I also include timbral productions like twanging metal objects, knocking on wooden ones, making vocal or other bodily sounds without pitched fundamentals or direct phonemic significance, blowing on conch-shells, through hose-pipes, through blades of grass, and so on.

At first blush there would appear to be little that all these examples have in common which might constitute the objects of musical behavior. However, one approach to commonality may be found in Thomas Clifton's observation that musical objects are posited by active-receptive participatory acts (Clifton, 1975). Thus, one view of the objects of musical behavior is that they are simply *actions which are taken*. (Note that Clifton's characterization is consistent with Lewin's examples if one allows for the possibility that the actor and the receiver are the same individual.)

Is there anything which distinguishes musical behavior from any other form of behavior? If one takes the intentional stance of phenomenology (Dennett, 1987), the only distinction lies in the mind that perceives the behavior: the receiver in Clifton's characterization. Thus, if one wishes to focus on musical behavior, one should concern oneself with appropriate ways to *describe actions*, regardless of whether or not those actions are ultimately *perceived* as musical.

How can one go about describing such actions? One viable approach is to assume, as a first step, that natural language provides what is required. Actions are described with *verb phrases*; and a suitably endowed *case grammar* (Fillmore, 1968) will furnish a foundation for the appropriate structuring of a verb phrase based on any given verb (even as awkward a verb as to noodle).

Thus, if one decides to study music in terms of Lewin's proposed universe of musical behavior, the objects which inhabit that universe will be *actions*; and the task of description will be in defining how those actions may be described. A first-order solution to that task is to turn to the verbs and verb phrases of a natural language, such as English. (The full flexibility of English remains beyond the scope of any computer processing capabilities; but that is why this solution is described as first-order. If one is to invoke the use of a computer, one must scale down one's vocabulary, which is nothing more than a further stage of abstraction.) Furthermore, having settled on such verb phrases as a basis for one's abstraction, one may then invoke the representational tools offered by case grammars. Such representations, however, are usually perceived as rather remote from the concerns of music; so the next step should be to review those representational objects which *have* been considered relevant to music.

The Objects of Representational Systems

What, then, are representational systems; and what have they to do with musical behavior? Just as there is broad variety in what may count as musical behavior, there has been equally broad variety in the name of representation. (Consider, for example, the many different approaches taken in the examples collected in John Cage's *Notations* (Cage, 1969).) Where, in the face of such diversity, can one find any hope of commonality?

In the case of musical behavior, one could seek out a lowest common denominator in the form of actions, themselves, which could be described by *verb phrases*. In the case of representations, one may take a semiotic approach (Morris, 1955) and establish a similar lowest common denominator in the symbols which give rise to those representations. For any given representation one may then ask two questions.

The first question is actually a compound: What are the primitive symbols upon which a representation is based, and how may those symbols be combined to form representational structures? This is the question of *syntax*. It embodies two critical assumptions.

The first assumption is that one can identify an appropriate set of *primitive symbols*. The important point here is that, given a representation, one must be able to deal with it as more than simply a monolithic entirety. The primitive symbols may be an arbitrary set defined in advance by the composer. They may even include words in natural language. However, it is important that one be able to identify the *fundamental ingredients*, so to speak, of any given representation.[4]

The second critical assumption about syntax is that symbols are assembled according to some consistent set of *rules*. Thus, when confronted with a representation, one should be able to determine what rules were used to form it from the primitive symbols. This determination is known as *parsing*.[5]

The second question about representations concerns how a given representational structure is *interpreted*. This is essentially the question of semantics. If one assumes that a representational structure is intended to elicit some form of musical behavior, then one must ask if and how actions are related to the primitive symbols and rules for combining those symbols. Such relations, if they can be stated explicitly, are known as a *denotational semantics* (Tennent, 1976). A denotational semantics not only captures the connection between representation and behavior but also captures the expressive scope of the representation, i.e. how much behavior may be realized through the process of interpretation. When this scope includes musical behavior, then one may say that one is *making music* from the representation.

Where does this leave the problem of representing musical behavior? Given the premise that the objects which constitute the universe of musical behavior are actions, the problem reduces to how such actions are elicited by interpreting a given symbolic representation. Any proposed solution to this problem must, in turn, be based on an understanding of the agent that actually performs the interpretation. What, ultimately, gives rise to musical behavior on the part of that agent?

The next section will attempt to explain such interpretation by considering the *mental state* of the agent doing the interpretation and by trying to characterize the relationship between such a mental state and that agent's *ability to perceive*.

Mental State, Perception, and Behavior

In trying to determine what gives rise to musical behavior, one might begin with the broader question of what determines behavior, in general. The simplest mathematical abstraction of behavior is the *state machine* (Minsky, 1967). This is a device which, at discrete units of time, is capable of performing some action from a predetermined repertoire. *Which* action is performed is a function of an *input* which is passed to the device at that unit of time and the current *internal state* of the device. This internal state is essentially an abstraction of the device's *past history* since the state at the next unit of time is determined by both the input and the state at the current unit of time. Given that time can always be traced back to an initial time and an *initial state*, the current state is always a function of those inputs which have been received since the initial time. In other words, in a simple state machine it is the memory of past inputs (i.e. stimuli) which determines what action will be taken in response to a new input.

The state machine abstraction of behavior dates back to the pioneering work of Alan Turing (Turing, 1965), who also recognized that the concept of internal state amounted to the state of mind of a computing agent. Thus, in considering the behavior of an intelligent agent, one might begin by asking how a simple state machine may be generalized to such an agent with the concept of internal state evolving into that of *mental state*. Of course the scope of mental states is much broader than that of the states of any state machine which has been investigated; but one approach to artificial intelligence is to assume that the distinction between machine state and mental state is simply a matter of size, as opposed to any major difference in fundamental nature.

Just as internal state delimits the scope of the behavior of a state machine, so does mental state delimit the behavior of an intelligent agent. (In his pioneering work on memory, Marvin Minsky uses the words 'disposition,' rather than 'delimit.' In (Minsky, 1980) a disposition is "a momentary range of possible behaviors;" and Minsky's society of mind approach to artificial intelligence is founded on the observation that any model of memory must be able to embody such dispositions, rather than the declarative sentences of formal logic.) Thus, it is mental state which gives rise to behavior; and if one is to understand musical behavior, then one must first consider how dispositions to such behavior are associated with mental state.

There is one important element which distinguishes mental states from the internal states of most computing devices. In general the internal state of a mechanical device may be directly set through some engineering technique. Thus, when one turns on the power of a personal computer, there is an automatic process which puts that machine in an initial state from which it is disposed to interact with the user through its set of available commands. Human beings do not work this way. Indeed, Minsky has demonstrated how an ability to directly set a human mental state would ultimately be fatal (Minsky, 1986).

Thus, mental state may only be determined by indirect means. In Minsky's society of mind theory there are two primary factors which influence an agent's mental state: *sensation* and *memory*. Drawing upon an approach which may be traced back to Hume (Hume, 1911), Minsky has developed a model in which immediate sensations are responsible for both the installation and retrieval of memories and in which the memories which are retrieved affect what is actually perceived in the data furnished by the sensors. (This recursive relationship between sensation and memory is called "closing the ring" [Minsky, 1986]) In other words a new mental state is induced by the interaction of the sensations which are received and those memories which are available to a current mental state.

Musical behavior is thus associated with mental states induced, through closing the ring, by both sensations and memories. The sensations may be not only auditory but also tactile and perhaps come from other sources. Similarly, memories may involve recollections of both musical and non-musical experiences. The next section will attempt to focus specifically on the nature of *musical* memories in the context of this model of mind and behavior.

What Constitutes Musical Memory?

What is important about Minsky's approach is that it focuses its attention on the memorable experience, itself, as opposed to some notational representation which attempts to document that experience. Thus, in the case of music, it is the music experience which is memorable and serves as a source of dispositions. Music experiences are not to be confused with representational systems, such as those considered in the previous section, The Objects of Musical Behavior. Rather, representational systems provide means by which musical experiences may be reduced to the *propositional* forms of symbolic logic. Minsky discusses the nature of this distinction as follows (Minsky, 1986):

> When do we actually use logic in real life? We use it to simplify and summarize our thoughts. We use it to explain arguments to other people and to persuade them that those arguments are right. We use it to reformulate our own ideas. But I doubt that we often use logic actually to solve problems or to "get" new ideas. Instead, we formulate our arguments and conclusions in logical terms *after* we have constructed or discovered them in other ways; only then do we use verbal and other kinds of formal reasoning to "clean things up," to separate the essential parts from the spaghetti-like tangles of thoughts and ideas in which they first occurred.

In other words the propositional nature of representational systems of music may serve to *summarize* musical behavior but not to *affect* it. Such influence on behavior can only come from a memory which induces mental states; and such a memory must be able to capture music as it has been (or is) experienced.

Does it make sense to think in terms of a memory based on actual musical behavior? Rather than attempting to address the full scope of such behavior as Lewin has envisaged it, consider the more limited extent of behavior involved in *listening* to music. How might memories of such listening experiences be modeled? Given current sampling technology, there is no reason why a computer could *not* have access to the raw data which may synthesize such experiences. After all, large bodies of those data are already available in machine-readable form on compact discs. Furthermore, it is important to remember that individuals do not tend to recall compositions as entire units. Rather, one recalls fragments which may then be tied together by some rather flexible association structures.[6] Thus, if one is to build a model of memory, one should begin with an abstraction based on such fragments, that is, contiguous temporal intervals of auditory stimuli. One may view these fragments as the fundamental ingredients which must be captured by a representation which must also address means by which connections may be established among them. Such a representation would amount to a database consisting of some library of sounds recorded on compact discs endowed with access mechanisms for retrieving appropriate tracks from appropriate discs. The heart of the representation problem then becomes one of developing a suitable *schema* (Date, 1977) for this data base which provides connections by which one may associate one record of a recalled fragment of sound with another.

When one considers a representation based directly on auditory stimuli, one is inevitably confronted with the question of *segmentation*—the assumption that, given any sort of audio input, one is obliged to parse it into notes before doing anything further with it. However, excessive attention to segmentation may ultimately be a distraction from more fundamental issues of behavior. There is no reason to assume that any fundamental ingredients based on immediate stimuli must be isomorphic to some passage which can be clipped out of a score, so to speak. It is more likely that one is going to remember a particular time interval of *sound* than some stream of notes which happens to be embedded in that interval (Handel, 1989). Such time intervals form the basis for those events which are the fundamental ingredients of Lewin's proposed model of musical perception (Lewin, 1986).

What Do We Do with Our Memories?

How may memories of music experiences be involved in the actual behavior of listening? This is the question of interpretation which shifts concern from the syntactic nature of a representation to semantic matters. At the same time the modeling of any behavior arising from interpretation will require addressing matters of how the representation being interpreted will be manipulated. Three hypotheses of interpretation will now be offered, each of which approaches Minsky's process of closing the ring, as presented in the section Mental State, Perception, and Behavior, from a different point of view.

The first hypothesis is that *listening behavior is simply a matter of structuring what one hears, perhaps just for the sake of building those structures.* This hypothesis appears to form the basis for the approach to listening which has been taken by Fred Lerdahl (Lerdahl, 1988). Previous music experiences are recalled because they facilitate this structuring activity. According to the theory which Lerdahl has developed with Ray Jackendoff, there are actually four types of structures which occupy the mind (Lerdahl, 1988):

> ...*grouping structure,* or the segmentation of the musical flow into units such as motives, phrases, and sections; *metrical structure,* or the pattern of periodically recurring strong and weak beats associated with the surface; *time-span reduction,* or the relative structural importance of events as heard within contextually established rhythmic units; and prolongational reduction, or the perceived pattern of tension and relaxation among events at various levels of structure.

Note that while Lerdahl's analyses have tended to focus on the symbols of music notation, his structures have been characterized with sufficient generality that they may be equally applicable to recalled fragments of music experiences. Thus, manipulation must be able to support operations of *retrieval* of appropriate records from the database proposed in What Constitutes Musical Memory? as well as *constructors* which allow for the synthesis of Lerdahl's structures from those retrieved records.

The second hypothesis is that one does not listen to music as an isolated activity; rather, *one listens in a context based on what one has heard before,* so that what one hears assumes different levels of familiarity. The mind uses the recognition of familiarity as a means to establish points of reference in the course of listening; so without a context which serves to *define* such familiarity, the mind, in a sense, has nothing to listen to. Leonard Meyer (Meyer, 1956) has discussed the importance of *expectation* in listening to music. Recognition of familiarity is a likely source from which such expectations may arise. From this point of view, one may consider the analytical symbology for the representation of functions of implication and realization, developed by Eugene Narmour (Narmour, 1984), as a basis for manipulation. That is, while the first hypothesis requires operations of retrieval and synthesis of Lerdahl's structures, this second hypothesis would engage similar retrieval operations in the construction of implications and evidence of their realization.

The third hypothesis is that *memories of music experiences form associations with non-musical memories, many of which may induce emotional states.* Manipulation must thus be concerned with how those associations are instantiated. A variety of approaches have been taken concerned with how this may take place.

Probably the oldest source of such associations resides in the early connection between music and rhetoric. George Buelow summarizes the nature of this connection in Baroque music as follows (Buelow, 1980):

> During the Baroque period the composer was obliged, like the orator, to arouse in the listener idealized emotional states—sadness, hate, love, joy, anger, doubt and so on—and every aspect of musical composition reflected this affective purpose. While it was easier to appreciate it in music associated with a text, the aim in instrumental music was the same.

Thus, for the Baroque audience, the very nature of the listening experience involved the ability to associate what one heard with the communication of emotional state.

The use of motifs in a rhetorical manner was further extended by Deryck Cooke (Cooke, 1959). Cooke attempted to generalize the emotional content of such gestures to encompass music written both before and after the Baroque period. Unfortunately, as has been reported by (Sloboda, 1985), attempts to validate Cooke's thesis through controlled psychological experiments have not yielded conclusive results.

Another approach is that which Meyer first proposed in his book, *Emotion and Meaning in Music* (Meyer, 1956). For Meyer, non-musical associations, such as those which induce emotions, are not issues of rhetoric. Instead, he based his theory on connections between principles of gestalt psychology and emotional implications.

An important point to consider is that, except in a situation like that of the Baroque use of rhetorical devices in which emotional content was essentially predetermined, any connection between music experiences and resulting emotions may be less principled and more coincidental. If one associates particular sounds with pleasure or pain, then one may be inclined to attach similar associations to fragments of musical memory with similar characteristics, regardless of whether or not those characteristics are in any way universal. Emotional response may simply be a mechanism by which the recollection of a memory may induce a mental state (Minsky, 1986). (Arguments for and against the universality of emotional response have been considered in (Sloboda, 1985); but even if one allows for the possibility of such universality, it may not necessarily be founded on either Cooke's vocabulary of motifs or Meyer's gestalt principles.)

Each of these hypotheses says, in effect, "Memories of music experiences facilitate some other mental activity." However, one may ask why the mind should bother with that other activity. What are the behaviors which emerge from such subsequent mental activity? Each of these hypotheses may, therefore, be so investigated.

The first hypothesis assumes that each music experience is its own event. That is, music inputs are processed strictly for the sake of processing music inputs. This is a very narrow point of view, and it leaves open the critical question of why there should be music experiences at all. Thus, this hypothesis ultimately says very little about the relationships among music, the mind, and behavior.

The second hypothesis relates any mental activity to processing of all past music experiences, but it assumes no connection between music experiences and other experiences. This is still a very narrow point of view. Furthermore, it is probably inadequate since it overlooks such issues as the role of text in music.

The third hypothesis implies that music contributes to a more general view of communication. A major element of getting along in the world is a mind's ability to communicate with other minds. However, there is no reason to assume that communication should be restricted to the exchange of sentences in some verbal language (see, for example, the work of Warren Lamb [1979]), in which case it will be worth investigating the role which music plays as part of the mind's concern with communication.

Conclusion

Mental State, Perception, and Behavior explored the possibility that memories may be based more on dispositions than on *propositions*. Under this premise one is obliged to consider that communication may involve more than an exchange of propositional sentences among communicating agents. What constitutes that more? There may not yet be a good answer to this question, but music *obliges* one to think about it because music experiences cannot be reduced to those propositional sentences. Unfortunately, attempts to apply artificial intelligence to the study of music have allowed themselves to be confined by such propositional limitations, rather than considering the broader issues of what actually constitutes musical behavior. However, a more procedural approach to artificial intelligence, such as that exhibited by Minsky in his work on a society of mind, may provide a foundation upon which such broader issues may ultimately be tackled.

Acknowledgments

The material presented in this paper grew out of a position paper I submitted for a panel discussion on the topic "Music Representation and Notation: Symbolic Approaches," which was held at the Second International Workshop on Artificial Intelligence and Music on August 20, 1989 in Detroit, Michigan. I wish to thank the participants in this workshop for many valuable contributions which emerged in the course of discussion. I also wish to thank John Rahn and Roger Lustig for their subsequent review of this position paper and their suggestions regarding its expansion. This paper has also benefitted from many valuable conversations (both in vivo and through electronic mail) with Otto Laske, David Lewin, Eliot Handelman, Eduard Hovy, Jay Rahn, and Fred Lerdahl.

Notes

1) Note that Hoare is using the noun "abstraction" to refer to both the overall process and the first stage of that process (as well as the *result* of the process). However, it should not be difficult to resolve the appropriate denotation of the term from context.

2) This is not to say that Lewin was the first to make such a claim. In considering the problems of developing a *performance* model for music (Laske, 1972), Otto Laske was concerned with matters of behavior at least a decade before Lewin began to articulate his views.

3) Note that this may be only a *first* step. Musicologists, such as Charles Seeger (Seeger, 1977), have addressed the limits of linguistic communication as a *model* of musical behavior; but that does not prevent the use of natural language as a point of departure for the development of a suitable abstraction.

4) It should be noted that these fundamental ingredients should not be *ad hoc*. John Sloboda (Sloboda, 1985) has discussed the extent to which even music which is *not* based on a notation, but rather on an oral tradition, may still be described in terms of some basis of fundamental ingredients. Thus, the primitive symbols of a representation should, following Hoare's methodology for abstraction, correspond to the fundamental ingredients of the music itself.

5) Note that parsing need not necessarily yield a unique result. A given symbol structure may arise from more than one set of rules. Such a structure would be syntactically valid but is said to be ambiguous (Winograd, 1972).

6) Lewin himself has offered some useful proposals regarding the nature of such structures (Lewin, 1986).

References

Buelow, G. J. Rhetoric and Music, 1980. In Sadie, S. (Ed.), *The New Grove Dictionary of Music and Musicians.* London: Macmillan.

Cage, J. 1969. *Notations.* New York, NY: Something Else Press.

Clifton, T. 1975. Some Comparisons Between Intuitive and Scientific Descriptions of Music. *Journal of Music Theory,* 19(1): 66–110.

Cooke, D. 1959. *The Language of Music.* London: Oxford University Press.

Date, C. J. 1977. *An Introduction to Database Systems..* Second Edition. Reading, MA: Addison-Wesley.

Dennett, D. C., and Haugeland, J. C. 1987. Intentionality. In Gregory, R. L. (Ed.), *The Oxford Companion to the Mind.* New York: Oxford University Press.

Fillmore, C. 1968. The Case for Case. In Bach, E., and Harms, R. eds., *Universals in Linguistic Theory.* New York: Holt, Rinehart and Winston.

Handel, S. 1989. *Listening: An Introduction to the Perception of Auditory Events.* Cambridge, MA: The MIT Press.

Hoare, C. A. R. 1972. Notes on Data Structuring. In Dahl, O.-J., Dijkstra, E. W., and Hoare, C. A. R. eds., *A. P. I. C. Studies in Data Processing. Structured Programming.* New York: Academic Press.

Hume, D. 1911. *A Treatise of Human Nature.* London: Dent.

Lamb, W., and Watson, E. 1979. *Body Code: The Meaning in Movement.* Routledge & Kegan Paul.

Laske, O. E. 1972. *On Problems of a Performance Model for Music.* Utrecht, Netherlands: Institute of Sonology—Utrecht State University,.

Lerdahl, F. 1988. Cognitive Constraints on Compositional Systems. In Sloboda, J. A. ed., *Generative Processes in Music: The Psychology of Performance, Improvisation, and Composition.* New York: Oxford University Press.

Lewin, D. 1986. Music Theory, Phenomenology, and Modes of Perception. *Music Perception,* 3(4), 327–392.

Meyer, L. B. 1956. *Emotion and Meaning in Music.* Chicago: The University of Chicago Press.

Minsky, M. L. 1967. *Comtutation: Finite and Infinite Machines.* Englewood Cliffs, NJ: Prentice-Hall

Minsky, M. 1980. K-Lines: A Theory of Memory. *Cognitive Science,* 4, 117–133.

Minsky, M. 1986. *The Society of Mind.* New York: Simon and Schuster,

Morris, C. 1955. Foundations of the Theory of Signs. In Neurath, O., Carnap, R. and Morris, C. (Eds.), *Foundations of the Unity of Science, Volume I.* Chicago: University of Chicago Press.

Narmour, E. 1984. Toward an Analytical Symbology: The Melodic, Harmonic and Durational Functions of Implication and Realization. In Baroni, M., and Callegari, L. eds., *Quaderni Della Rivista Italiana di Musicologia Vol. 8: Musical Grammars and Computer Analysis.* Florence, Italy: Leo S. Olschki.

Seeger, C. 1977. Speech, Music, and Speech about Music. In *Studies in Musicology: 1935–1975.* Berkeley, CA: University of California Press.

Sloboda, J. A. 1985. *The Musical Mind: The Cognitive Psychology of Music.* Oxford:Clarendon Press.

Tennent, R. D. 1976. The Denotational Semantics of Programming Languages. *Communications of the ACM,* 19(8), 437–453.

Turing, A. M. 1965. On Computable Numbers, With an Application to the Entscheidungs Problem. In Davis, M. ed., *The Undecidable: Basic Paperson Undecidable Propositions, Unsolvable Problems and Computable Functions.* Hewlett, NY: Raven Press.

Winograd, T. 1972. *Understanding Natural Language.* New York: Academic Press.

Abstract

This chapter deals with a representation of music at the symbolic and sonic levels in the context of rule-based musical composition. In this representation, the basic components are not notes but *sound-objects,* here taken to mean sequences of messages dispatched to a real-time digital sound processor.

At the symbolic level, (sequential or concurrent) sound-object structures are represented as strings that may be produced by a rewriting system. Well-formed strings are called *polymetric expressions.* A polymetric expression may not contain all the information needed for synchronizing the sound-object structure it denotes, i.e. determining a mapping of its objects to a set of symbolic dates. In response to this, each sound-object is first assigned a symbolic tempo. Ordering all sound-objects in a sound-object structure is possible once all tempos have been assigned consistently; rules for determining symbolic tempos are therefore proposed. These are imbedded in an algorithm interpreting incomplete polymetric expressions. The relevant features of this interpretation are commented.

An example in conventional music notation is given to illustrate the advantage of using (incomplete) polymetric representations instead of event tables when the complete description of the musical piece and/or its variants calls for complicated computations of durations.

Given the ordering of sound-objects summarized in a phase diagram, the next step is to calculate the dates at which messages will be dispatched. This requires a description of sound-object prototypes along with their sonic (asyntactic) properties, and various parameters related to the musical performance itself (e.g. smooth or striated time, tempo, etc.). Sonic properties are discussed in detail and a polynomial-time constraint-satisfaction algorithm for the time-setting of a sound-object structure is introduced. Musical examples computed by this algorithm are shown and discussed.

Chapter 4

Symbolic and Sonic Representations of Sound-Object Structures

Bernard Bel

Groupe Représentation et Traitement des Connaissances (GRTC)

> [...] not only do individuals and groups give different verbal meanings to music; they also conceive its structures in ways that do not permit us to regard musical parameters as objective acoustical facts. In music, thirds, fourths, fifths, and even octaves, are social facts, whose syntactical behaviour can differ as much as that of *si*, *see*, and *sea*, *beau*, *bow*, and *bo*, or *buy*, *bye*, *by* and *bai*.
>
> *[Blacking 1984:364]*

Pierre Schaeffer, the father of musique concrète [Schaeffer 1966], introduced a taxonomy of musical objects on the basis of their distinctive features. Musical objects may also be called *sonemes*, i.e., equivalence classes on acoustic musical events, each musical event being in turn an acoustic variant of the soneme. The musical object approach certainly contributed to significant developments of electroacoustic music. Nevertheless, composers who had been in search for a higher degree of freedom in sound manipulation felt the need to explore the potential of digital sound synthesis:

> I felt that electronic music yielded dull sounds that could only be made lively through manipulations which, to a large extent, ruined the control the composer could have over them. On the other hand, musique concrète did open an infinite world of sounds to music—but the control and manipulation one could exert upon them was rudimentary with respect to the richness of the sounds, which favored an aesthetics of collage.
>
> *[Risset 1989:67]*

Followers of *musique concrète* have now replaced audio tape with sampling techniques and scissors with various kinds of sequencers, notators or tools for computer-aided composition. As far as digital sound synthesis is concerned, most digital sound processors offer an access to real-time external control through communication devices such as MIDI[1] Therefore, both musical object and sound model designers [Borin et al. 1990] are now operating in environments enabling a control on both sound structures and acoustical parameters. Nevertheless, most of the music software available on the market is specialized either for the manipulation of structures (mainly cut-and-paste operations) or sounds (digital filtering or controlling parameters in a sound processor).

The present study[2] is an attempt to deal with musical objects that may be handled both at the symbolic level and at the level of elementary actions. The nature of these actions is not specified because it depends on the hardware/software configuration of the sound processor and, to a lower extent, on the communication device used for the real-time control of the processor. The motivation of our project, therefore, has been the implementation of efficient procedures handling musical objects as lists of messages (at a macro or micro-level) unrelated to music notation conventions. Some information about the task environment of this work is given in §2.

Representations of time and sound-object structures are discussed in part A. In part B we introduce *polymetric expressions,* string representations of universes of concurrent processes, along with an algorithm that infers the missing time information in incomplete expressions. An application to music in conventional notation is discussed in §9.

In part C we take into account that the terminal symbols of a polymetric expression may be arbitrary labels assigned to sound-objects. A *sound-object* may be viewed as an instance of some predefined sound-object prototype. Each prototype contains (1) a sequence of (time-stamped) messages destined to a sound processor and (2) a list of (inheritable) sonic properties. These properties are defined in the sections on Encoding a Sound-Object Structure and Metrical Properties of Nonempty Sound-Objects..

In §10 a time-setting algorithm is informally introduced. This algorithm calculates the accurate positioning of all sound-objects in a sound-object structure, given the definitions of their prototypes. Its main operation is the resolution of a system of constraints resulting from the sonic properties of sound-objects, the nature of time (smooth or striated) and its structure (e.g. a metronomic or irregular beat). The time-setting algorithm is analyzed in The Time-Setting Algorithm section and examples of its output are commented in §18.

1 Related Work

In the same way computational linguists, e.g. [Jakobson 1963; Chomsky & Halle 1968], have attempted to deal with phonological models of natural language, the work presented here is part of the design of a *sonological* component of musical (formal) grammars:

Supposed sonological segments of music are composed of sound-objects realizing certain syntactical structures.

It is reasonable to assume that no unambiguous one-to-one correlation of such segments with acoustical (i.e. physical) sound properties exists. On the level of the *sonic* representation—mediating between the acoustical and the sonological levels—one therefore expects to find a representation of properties which are acousmatic[3] (independent of sound sources in the physical sense) as well as asyntactic (independent of syntactical classes of musical formatives).

[Laske 1972:30]

The aim of this work is to introduce performance parameters into musical pieces generated by computations on abstract symbols. Our basic assumption is that these parameters should be determined altogether by (1) the musical structure, (2) interpretation rules, and (3) the properties of sound-objects.

The notion of symbolic time introduced in part A is close to Jaffe's [1985] basic time and to virtual time in the *Formula* musical programming environment [Anderson et Kuivila 1989:11–23].

The sonological interpretation [Laske 1972:24] of a musical item may first be handled by a rewriting system whose terminal alphabet is a finite set of sound-object labels.[4] Rules in this system reflect the sonological properties of sound-objects. Part B of this chapter deals with a second step of the sonological interpretation: the inference of missing precedence/simultaneity relations in structures of sound-objects. The intuitive interpretation of superimpositions (see §5.1), leading to the concept of *symbolic tempo* (see §6.1), may be viewed as a kind of semantic interpretation of time structures.

Sonic properties[5] of sound-objects are features unrelated with the syntactic structure of musical pieces in which they appear. The only properties considered in part C of this chapter are the ones controlling the time-scaling of sound-objects (i.e. metrical properties) and acceptable mutual relations of their time-span intervals (i.e. topological properties). Starting from a complete representation of a sound-object structure, these sonic properties are taken into account for determining the accurate timing of sound-objects, as shown in §12, §13, and §16.

Our approach may be viewed as a compromise between top-down (goal-driven) and bottom-up (data-driven) compositional strategies in music. In the former, rules and procedures are used to compute the final sound output on the basis of information entirely imbedded in its symbolic description. In the latter, a structure may emerge from some specific arrangement of elementary acoustic events. The top-down strategy is the main one available in conventional score editors and MIDI composition tools. A bottom-up strategy for the design of discrete structures, which inspired this work, has been proposed by Stroppa (see §10, [Duthen & Stroppa 1990]).

Since the algorithms described here are neither related to a particular musical system nor to sound generation techniques or data-communication standards, they could as well be applied to the time-setting of processes outside the domain of computer music. There is formally no difference between a message destined to a sound processor and one controlling a laser beam, a robot, etc. Nevertheless, for

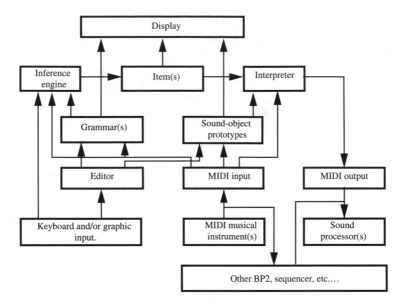

Figure 1. A Block Diagram of BP2*..*

the sake of clarity, the concepts and terminology will be introduced in reference to a particular musical environment.

2 The Task Environment of This Study

The algorithms presented below have been implemented in a computer environment for design-based (stipulatory) or improvisational rule-based composition; [Laske 1989:51,53] called Bol Processor (BP2), in which it is possible to design sets of musical items by way of rewriting rules.[6] Several operational modes are available in BP2, from the one that leaves all decisions to the machine (stochastic improvisation), to the one that prompts the composer to take stepwise decisions. The interaction of modules is summarized in the block diagram of Figure 1.

Three fields are used for storing a grammar, items generated by the grammar (on the basis of decisions taken by the inference engine) and sound-object prototypes loaded from a MIDI musical instrument (and edited manually). The terminal alphabet of the grammar is the set of labels of sound-objects. The interpreter works in three stages:

1) The item generated by the grammar is interpreted as a polymetric expression. The output is a complete expression (i.e., a bidimensional array of terminal symbols) (see §3.2, §7.2).

2) The expression is interpreted as a sound-object structure, using information about the structure of time and object prototype definitions. The main output is an array containing the performance parameters of objects in the structure: their start/clip dates, time-scale ratios, etc. (see §11).

3) MIDI messages are dispatched in real time to control the generation of sound-objects by the sound processor (see the time-setting function, §19.3). The block diagram indicates that an external control can be exerted on the inference engine, grammars, and the interpretation module. Specific MIDI messages may be assigned to changes of rule weights, tempo, and the nature of time (striated/smooth). Other messages may be used for synchronizing events in the performance or assigning computation time limits. These features are used in improvisational rule-based composition.

Several BP2's may be linked together and with other devices such as MIDI sequencers. Messages on the different MIDI channels may be used for making machines communicate or controlling several sound processors. Therefore it must be kept in mind that sound-objects do not necessarily produce sounds. Depending on the implementation they may contain any kind of control/synchronization message as well.

Part A: Definitions

3 The Basic Representation Issues

3.1 Representation of Discrete Sound-Object Structures

Let us assume that a, b, c, e, f, g and "–" are labels of arbitrary sound-objects. Label "–" may be reserved to silences, which are viewed as particular objects. The picture below represents a structure of two sequences which, in first approximation, may be notated $S_1 = a \ b \ c \ a$ and $S_2 = c - f \ g$.

In Figure 2 a set of strictly ordered symbolic dates $D = \{t1, t2, \ldots\}$ is introduced along with θ_i, an injective mapping of each S_i into D. By convention, each θ_i is a monotonous increasing function: sequentiality implies that all objects appearing in a sequence are ordered in increasing symbolic dates. Each mapping θ_i may in turn be viewed as a restriction to S_i of a general mapping θ which we call the *rhythmic structure*[7] of the sound-object structure. The utility of NIL markers will be shown later.

Mappings of sequences to the set of symbolic dates introduce information about the ordering of any pair of events belonging to either sequence. In this way, a structure of sound-objects is described symbolically. Here, for instance, S_1 and S_2 are partly overlapping.

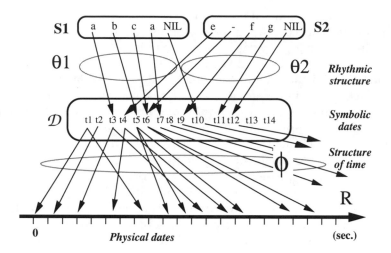

Figure 2. A Representation of Sequences S1 and S2.

The set of symbolic dates D is then mapped to physical time, i.e. the set of real numbers **R**. We call this mapping Φ the structure of time[8.] In the example shown above, Φ is a multivocal mapping, which means, for instance, that each sound-object a and e at symbolic date t_3 would be performed twice. In the rest of this chapter only strictly increasing (univocal) mappings will be considered, i.e.:

$$\forall i,j \in \mathbf{N}, t_i < t_j <=> \Phi(t_i) < \Phi(t_j) \ .$$

In this case, if we consider $\mathrm{Dist}(t_i,t_j) = |\Phi(t_j)—\Phi(t_i)|$ (the absolute value of the difference), Dist is a distance on D. Besides, since

$$\forall i,j,k \in \mathbf{N}, \mathrm{Dist}(t_i,t_j) + \mathrm{Dist}(t_j,t_k) \geq \mathrm{Dist}(t_i,t_k)$$

(D, Dist) is also a *metric* space. (D, Dist) is *Euclidian* (**metronomic time**) if the additional property holds:

$$\forall i,j,k,l \in \mathbf{N}, j—i = l—k => \Phi(t_j)—\Phi(t_i) = \Phi(t_l)—\Phi(t_k)$$

The composition of the two mappings ($\Phi \circ \theta$) is the in-time structure of the musical item, i.e., the mapping that permits its actual performance. Structure of time and in-time structures are two concepts borrowed from Xenakis [1963; 1972:57]. We find these concepts essential as they deal with sets of physical dates not necessarily structured as an Euclidian space.

3.2 Phase Diagram

Both sequences of this example may be represented together in a single array (the phase diagram), the columns of which are labelled and ordered on symbolic dates:

t1	t2	t3	t4	t5	t6	t7	t8	t9	t10	t11	t12	t13	t14
–	–	a	–	b	c	a	–	–	NIL	–	–	–	–
–	–	–	e	–	–	–	–	f	–	g	NIL	–	–

The array contains empty sound-objects "_" which may denote the prolongation of the preceding sound-object. These should not be confused with silences "–."

Using the information displayed in the array, S_1 and S_2 may be properly notated:

$S_1 = a \_ b c a \_ \_$ $S_2 = e \_ - \_ \_ f \_ g$

In general, there are several possible equivalent phase diagrams representing the same sound-object structure. An equivalent diagram would be for instance:

			e		c	a			NIL				
–	–	–	e	–	c	a	–	–	NIL	–	–	–	–
–	–	a	–	b	–	–	–	f	–	g	NIL	–	–

At this stage, we call symbolic duration of a sound-object the relative position of the next non-empty sound-object or NIL marker. A complete definition taking into account the dilation ratio will be proposed in §11. For example, in S_2 the symbolic durations of objects e, "–," f and g are two, three, two and one, respectively. In S_1, there are two consecutive occurrences of *a* with respective durations two and three. If, for example, a, b, etc. would represent notes, assuming that b is a quarter note would imply that *e* is a half-note and "–" a dotted half-note rest.

3.3 Out-Time Objects

Sound-objects have strictly positive symbolic durations. In some cases it is useful to dispose of flat objects with null durations which we call *out-time objects*. These may be defined from sound-objects whose actions are executed simultaneously or in a very short sequence (§19.2). In the BP2 environment, a typical application of out-time objects is the exchange of parameters or synchronization messages.

Given a sound-object labelled *a,* the corresponding out-time object is labelled <<a>>. Using this convention, a string like <<a>> b represents a structure in which out-time object <<a>> starts at the same symbolic date as sound-object b.

4 Smooth Versus Striated Time

Pierre Boulez introduced the notions of *smooth time* (temps lisse) and *striated time* (temps strié) to characterize two typical situations in music performance. Striated time is filled with (regular or irregular) pulse, whereas smooth time does not imply any counting:

> [...] dans le temps lisse, on occupe le temps sans le compter dans le temps strié, on compte le temps pour l'occuper. [...] ce sont les lois fondamentales du temps en musique.
>
> *[Boulez 1963:107]*

A particular case of striated time is the metronomic pulse. Examples of smooth time are common outside Baroque music, e.g., melodic introductions in Indian *raga* music.

In computer-generated music, these notions are bound to the structure of time (the Φ mapping): in striated time, Φ is known in advance, whereas in smooth time it is determined at the time of performance. Therefore, a *striated structure of time* is a set of physical dates defining reference streaks on which sound-objects should be positioned (e.g. see §18.3.2), whereas a *smooth structure of time* is a set of dates determined by the sound-objects themselves (e.g. see §18.3.1).

Part B: Polymetric Structures

5 The Synchronization Problem

We call *synchronization problem* the task of mapping all sound-objects in a structure to a set of symbolic dates. This mapping is the rhythmic structure θ of the musical piece (see §3.1). Imbedding the complete rhythmic structure in the definitions of musical sequences introduces a rigidity that goes against the versatility of rewriting systems, as discussed in §5.1. In response to this, incomplete representations can be envisaged so long as a method is available for inferring the missing time information. A method for synchronizing incomplete descriptions sound-object structures, thereby completing their sonological interpretation, will be proposed in §7–8.

5.1 Rhythmic Structures in a Formal Grammar—Example

Suppose that we wish to superimpose two sequences A and B defined by rules:

A → a b c
A → d e f g
B → h i

in which *a, b, ... i* are labels of sound-objects. Alternate definitions of *A* indicate that it may contain either three or four objects. To start with, we do not know how to interpret the exact superimposition of two sequences: combining *abc* and *hi* may for example yield the following phase diagrams:

```
    a b c          a b c          a _ b _ c _      a _ b c          etc...
    h i _          _ h i          h _ _ i _ _      h i _ _
    (1)            (2)               (3)             (4)
```

Prolongational symbols "_" could also be replaced with silences "–." However, since silences do not explicitly appear in the grammar, we may postulate that creating them is not a valid choice. Further we discard interpretations (1) and (4) in which equal symbolic durations are not maintained within the same string *h i*. Finally, it is reasonable to expect a synchronization of both the start and clip points of the synchronized sequences. Therefore there is no reason to start *a* before *h* as in interpretation (2).

Finally, the most intuitively appealing interpretation of a superimposition (in the absence of any additional information) is the one shown in (3). A notation of superimpositions is now introduced: {A,B} (equivalently, {B,A}) is the superimposition of sequences *A* and *B*. We call {A,B} a polymetric expression whose arguments are *A* and *B*. Nested expressions will be introduced in §5.2.

Using this notation, a grammar yielding all acceptable superimpositions of *A* and *B* would be:

S → {A1,B1}
S → {A2,B2}
A1 → a _ b _ c _   B1 → h _ _ i _ _
A2 → d e f g   B2 → h _ i _

Once a string like {d e f g, h _ i _} has been produced, it is necessary to check that it contains equally many terminal symbols in both arguments, failing to which the phase diagram cannot be constructed.

Evidently it is cumbersome to be forced to give two possible versions of B, the more so because they point to identical ratios of symbolic durations: B2 is similar to B1 in every respect. Ideally, the following grammar should be used:

S → {A,B}
A → a b c
A → d e f g
B → h i

expecting that there will be a method for interpreting a production like {a b c, h i} i.e., an incomplete polymetric expression, as {a _ b _ c _ , h _ _ i _ _ }, i.e., a complete polymetric expression (see formal definition §7.2).

5.2 Event Universe

The concept of an *event universe*, a finite set of objects structured with three time relations, is defined in [Bel 1991:9]. These relations are precedence, simultaneity and sequentiality. The latter relation also implies precedence this implication is part of consistency conditions binding the three relations.

The word event may be used to denote a time point, a time interval, or any other entity on which these relations may be applied meaningfully. In this study, events denote sound-objects ordered by their symbolic dates.[9] In the event universe shown in Figure 9, a, b, etc., are sound-objects arranged in five sequences: ab, cdefghij, etc. The simultaneity relation is notated with thick arrows, e.g., a is simultaneous with e. Each sequence terminates on an end-marker λ1, λ2, etc. (see the NIL markers in string representations §3.1).

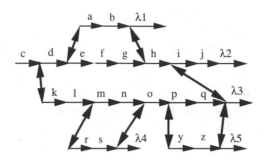

Figure 3. A Polymetric Structure.

This structure of sound-objects may be represented with the polymetric expression: c { d { e f g, a b } h, k l { m n, r s } o { p q, y z } } i j which is an extension of the notation introduced in §5.1. An event universe represented with a polymetric expression is called a *polymetric structure.*

Events λ1, λ2, ... are not indicated in the polymetric expression because the closing bracket is sufficient to mark the end of a sequence. Other equivalent expressions may be written since the order of arguments between brackets is arbitrary. The precedence relation is not shown on Figure 3. It is easy to infer, for instance, that d precedes r, but no such relation can be proved between f and n. Both the graphic representation and the polymetric expression are therefore incomplete.

The polymetric expression representing the event universe of Figure 3 is easy to write because it describes a universe partitioned in sequences. Each sequence is an argument of the expression. Nevertheless, there are (incomplete) event universes that do not lend themselves to a polymetric representation even though they are partitioned in sequences. Figure 4 is an example. The necessary properties enabling a polymetric representation of an incomplete event universe are listed in [Bel 1990b:109].

In spite of this, any complete event universe, i.e., one in which all precedence relations are known, may be represented with a polymetric expression (see §7.1 or [Bel 1990b:110]). Therefore, in this study only (possibly incomplete or inconsistent) polymetric structures will be considered.

6 Inferring the Missing Time Relations in a Polymetric Structure

The problem is to find a general approach to the synchronization problem in an event universe represented with a polymetric expression. In the universe shown in Figure 3, for instance, we hope to know the relative ordering of sound-objects g and n. Evidently, if these objects were (metric) time intervals stringed together in sequences, then computing durations would solve the problem. This is the traditional numerical approach. Allen [1983] has proposed a more flexible representation,

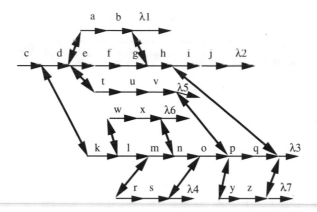

Figure 4. An Arbitrary Event Universe.

starting from the formalization of all possible topological configurations of time-span intervals, from which it is possible to infer the list of plausible temporal relations between any pair of objects.[10] We estimate, though, that reasoning on time-span intervals at such an abstract level of the musical representation is too restrictive. In §16 it will be shown how to deal with time-span intervals in a realistic sense.

6.1 Symbolic Tempo

The concept of tempo is introduced here in response to the bias against time-span intervals. This concept is purely abstract even though, at a lower level, it has implications on the locations of sound-objects on the physical time axis (see §10, §15.2).

Let E be an event universe. We call *symbolic tempo* any mapping V of E to the set of strictly positive rational numbers $\mathbf{Z}^+$ that fulfills the property:

⌐ ▯▯▯▯▯▯▯▯▯ ▯▯▯▯▯▯▯▯

Let "<" denote the precedence relation and "=" the simultaneity relation.
Let there be two sequences
$e_i \dots e_{i+p}$ and $e_j \dots e_{j+p}$
such that $e_i = e_j$ (i.e. starting on simultaneous events)
Then:

$$\sum_{l=i}^{i+p-1} \frac{1}{V(e_l)} = \sum_{l=j}^{i+q-1} \frac{1}{V(e_l)} \Leftrightarrow e_{i+p} = e_{j+q}$$

$$\sum_{l=i}^{i+p-1} \frac{1}{V(e_l)} < \sum_{l=j}^{j+q-1} \frac{1}{V(e_l)} \Leftrightarrow e_{i+p} < e_{j+q}$$

The preceding relations make sense intuitively if one equates $\frac{1}{V(e_i)}$ to the symbolic duration of e_i. It can be proved that if all tempos are known then the synchronization problem can be solved using these relations. [Bel 1990b, theorem VII.2] The problem, therefore, is to define a set of rules for tempo assignment and a procedure for propagating tempos that makes it possible to maintain the consistency of the event universe.

6.2 Tempo Assignment

6.2.1 Explicit Tempo Marker.
We use the syntactic form $/\!n$ to indicate that the next event in a sequence is assigned an integer tempo n. For example, $/\!n$ e_i means that: $V(e_i) = n$. This notation indicates infomally that the symbolic durations of objects following $/n$ are divided by n.

Using empty sound-objects "_" it is possible to apply this notation to non-integer tempos. For example, the tempos of a and b in the sequence $/3$ a _ _ _ $/3$ b _ are ¾ and ⅔ respectively, which means, conversely, that the respective symbolic durations of a and b are ⅘ and ⅔.

6.6.6 Default Assignment.
The default tempo of the first event in a sequence is 1.

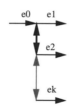

Figure 5. A Divergence in a Polymetric Structure.

6.2.3 Tempo Propagation After a Divergence.
If e_0 e_1 is a sequence and there exist events $e_2, ..., e_k$ such that $e_1 = e_2 = ... = e_k$, then $V(e_1) = V(e_0)$ by default.

This means that when entering the polymetric structure ... e_0 {e_1..., e_2..., ..., e_k...}... the default tempo of the first argument is $V(e_1) = V(e_0)$. This rule will be illustrated in §7.3, in which the consistency condition will be used to determine the tempos of other sequences. Consistency may also impose a tempo $V(e_1) \neq V(e_0)$ whenever one of the arguments of the polymetric expression contains an explicit tempo marker.

6.2.4 Tempo Propagation After a Convergence.
$$V(e_{jn}) = V(e_{j(m-1)})$$
Informally, the tempo after a polymetric expression is the same one as before the expression.

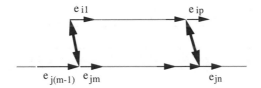

Figure 6. Divergence and Convergence in a Polymetric Structure.

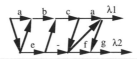

Figure 7. A Complete Event Universe.[11]

6.2.5 Tempo Propagation in a Sequence. If e_i e_j is a sequence and there is no k such that $e_j = e_k$, then $V(e_j) = V(e_i)$

7 Interpreting and Representing Polymetric Expressions

The interpretation algorithm has been introduced in [Bel 1990a] and explained in detail in [Bel 1990b:chapter VIII]. This and the following paragraph summarize its main features.

7.1 Polymetric Representation of a Complete Event Universe

In §5.2 it was stated that in a complete event universe it is possible to assign each event a symbolic date. Therefore it is possible to represent the universe as a phase diagram whose columns are labelled with symbolic dates, as illustrated in §3.2. Conversely, a given phase diagram may lead to a polymetric expression. For example, Figure 7 is an interpretation of the diagram shown in §3.2. Thick one-way arrows indicate the precedence relation.

This universe does not fulfil the conditions yielding a polymetric representation, as indicated in [Bel 1990b:109–110]. Yet it can be replaced with equivalent ones fulfilling these conditions. For example, a silence may be appended to S_1, yielding the new phase diagram

t1	t2	t3	t4	t5	t6	t7	t8	t9	t10	t11	t12	t13	t14
–	–	a	–	b	c	a	–	–	–	–	NIL	–	–
–	–	–	e	–		–	–	f	–	g	NIL	–	–

i.e., the complete polymetric expression: { a _ b c a _ _ _—_ , _ e _—_ _ f _ g }. Another way of representing the universe of Figure 7 as a polymetric expression consists of splitting the sound-object f. For this we use a concatenation symbol notated &, by way of which two segments of the same sound-object may appear in different arguments.[13] Thus we get for example { a _ b c a _ _ , _ e _—_ _ f& } &f g or equivalently: a& { &a b c a _&, e _—_ _ } { &a, f& } &f g etc.   Each expression implies a particular surface structure, here taken to mean segmentation. The latter one is illustrated in Figure 8.

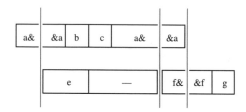

Figure 8. A Segmentation of Sound-Objects Yielding a Polymetric Expression.

Since it is not possible to determine the surface structure of an arbitrary sound-object structure, the input of the polymetric interpretation algorithm is a well-formed polymetric expression, not a phase diagram.[13]

7.2 Complete Polymetric Expressions

Let Vt be a set of labels of sound-objects. A syntactic definition of complete polymetric expressions over Vt is proposed now.

Definition

1) $\forall\, x_i \in$ Vt,
    x_i , x_i&, &x_i and "_" are complete polymetric expressions of identical symbolic durations. (See §11 the definition of the symbolic duration of a single object x_i .)

2) Given a list of complete polymetric expressions $P_1,...,\ P_{imax}$ of symbolic duration *n*,
    $\forall i \in$ [1, imax-1],
    {P_i} and {$P_1,...,\ P_{i+1}$} are complete polymetric expressions of symbolic duration *n*.

3) If P_1 and P_2 are two complete polymetric expressions of respective symbolic durations n_1 and n_2 , then $P_1\ P_2$ is a complete polymetric expression of symbolic duration (n_1+n_2).

4) If P is a complete polymetric expression of symbolic duration *n*,
    $\forall k \in$ **N** with k ≥ 1,
    /k P is a complete polymetric expression of symbolic duration n/k .

7.3 Interpreting a Polymetric Expression

The basic idea of the interpretation algorithm is illustrated here on a simple example.[14] In §5.1 the method for superimposing two sequences of different lengths was informally introduced. Given the incomplete expression{ a b, c d e } the tempo propagation rule in §6.2.5 yields a set of equivalent complete expressions

$$\{a\_\_b\_\_,c\_d\_e\_\}$$
$$\{a\_\_\_\_\_b\_\_\_\_\_,c\_\_\_d\_\_\_e\_\_\_\}$$
$$\{a_____b_____,c\_\_\_\_\_d\_\_\_\_\_e\_\_\_\_\_\}$$

etc.,

with respective durations six, twelve, eighteen, that may be notated

/m {a _ _ b _ _ , c _ d _ e _ },

where m is an arbitrary strictly positive integer denoting the tempo of the polymetric structure. The symbolic duration of the whole structure is $\frac{6}{m}$.

To determine m we use the rule in §6.2.3, i.e., informally, the default tempo of a polymetric structure is the one of its first argument taken separately. The first argument is a b with default tempo one (see rule in §6.2.2), which may be indicated by an explicit tempo marker: {/1 a b, c d e }. According to the definition in §7.2, the symbolic duration of the structure must be two. Therefore m = 3 and the correct interpretation is: /3 {a _ _ b _ _ , c _ d _ e _ }.

The rule in §6.2.3 cannot be used if at least one argument in the expression contains an explicit tempo marker, e.g., in the expression {a b {/3 a b c, d e}, f g h i j k}. Therefore, the interpretation algorithm performs the transformations

$$\{a\,b\,/6\,\{a\_b\_c\_,d\_\_e\_\_\},f\,g\,h\,i\,j\,k\}$$
$$\{/6\,a\_\_\_\_\_b\_\_\_\_\_\{a\_b\_c\_,d\_\_e\_\_\},f\,g\,h\,i\,j\,k\}$$
$$\{/6\,a\_\_\_\_\_b\_\_\_\_\_\{a\_b\_c\_,d\_\_e\_\_\},/6\,f\_\_g\_\_h\_\_i\_\_j\_\_k\_\_\}$$

yielding the complete polymetric expression

/6 { a _ _ _ _ _ b _ _ _ _ _ {a _ b _ c _ , d _ _ e _ _ }, f _ _ g _ _ h _ _ i _ _ j _ _ k _ _ }

and a possible phase diagram:

```
a                     b   ▬  ▬  ▬  ▬  ▬  a     b     c     NIL
_   _   _   _   _   _   _   _   _   _   _   d   _   _   e   _   _   NIL
f   _   _   g   _   _   h   _   _   i   _   _   j   _   _   k   _   _   NIL
```

7.4 Polymetric Representation of a Sequence

Introducing a string of empty objects as the first argument of a polymetric expression is a good method for suppressing explicit tempo markers in a sequence, as will be shown in the example: a b c _ /3 d _ e. This sequence may be notated a b c _ /3 { , d e}, which is equivalent to a b c _ /3 {3, d _ e}, using the convention that any string of n empty objects "_" which does not follow a non-empty object, may be replaced with integer n itself. The following transformation

    a b c _ {3/3, d _ e}
    a b c _ {1, d _ e}
    a b c _ { _ , d _ e}

is valid even though it leads to an incomplete polymetric expression.

An advantage of this notation is visible when the expression is used in a grammar, as for example:

    S   →   /2 A /3 A
    A   →   a b c _ { 1 , d _ e}
             ...   [other rules]

An intuitive meaning of this grammar is that the musical item denoted by variable A should be performed twice. The tempos of the successive occurrences will be two and three.

The unique production of this grammar is

    /2 a b c _ { 1 , d _ e} /3 a b c _ { 1 , d _ e}

which the interpretation algorithm will transform as follows:

                /6 a _ _ b _ _ c _ _ _ _ _ { 3 , d _ e} a _ b _ c _ _ _ { 2 , d _ e}
                /6 a _ _ b _ _ c _ _ _ _ _ { 3 , d _ e} a _ b _ c _ _ _ /6 { 2 , d _ e}
                /6 a _ _ b _ _ c _ _ _ _ _ { 3 , d _ e} a _ b _ c _ _ _ /18 { 6 , d _ _ _ e _ }
                /6 a _ _ b _ _ c _ _ _ _ _ { 3 , d _ e} a _ b _ c _ _ _ /9 { 3 , d _ e}
                /6 a _ _ b _ _ c _ _ _ _ _ d _ e a _ b _ c _ _ _ /9 d _ e

It can be seen that for example the symbolic duration of sound-object d is $\frac{2}{6}$, i.e. $\frac{1}{3}$, in its first occurrence, and $\frac{2}{9}$ in its second occurrence. Thus the tempo has been multiplied, as expected, by $\frac{3}{2}$. The same remark applies to all sound-objects.

7.5 Undetermined Rests

It is possible to insert (one single) undetermined rest, notated "...," in an argument of a polymetric expression. This rest may have different durations depending on other arguments of the expression. For example, {/3 a ... b, /2 c d} should be interpreted {/3 a—b, /2 c d} since the duration of the structure is determined by the second argument of the expression.

In a similar way {a {b c, d e f}, /2 ... g h i j } is interpreted:

    /6 { a _ _ _ _ _ { b _ _ _ _ _ c _ _ _ _ _ , d _ _ _ e _ _ _ f _ _ _ } ,—_ _ _ _ _ g _ _ h _ _ i _ _ j _ _ }

The general idea is that the rest should have a duration corresponding to the most evident solution [Bel 1990b:121; 1991:21]. If no solution is consistent then the algorithm returns an error message: *not enough time for inserting a rest.* An undetermined rest is used in the example of §9.

8 Minimal and Dilated Notations of a Polymetric Structure

The primary motivation of rescaling polymetric expressions is to save memory and yield the simplest phase diagram of a sound-object structure. The *dilation ratio* defined in §8.2 is used to encode sound-objects and calculate their time-scale ratios as shown in §15.

8.1 Simplifying a Sequence

Simplifying a sequence means trying to suppress empty objects in its notation. For example,

/6 a _ _ b _ _ c _ d _   is simplified   /2 a b /3 c d

/5 a _ _ b _ _ c _ _ _ _ d _ _ _   is simplified   /5 a _ _ b _ _ /1 c /5 d _ _ _

8.2 Dilation Ratio

In the second example above it was not possible to suppress all empty objects. However, let us multiply all tempi by the same scale factor s, for instance s = 24. The dilated sequence becomes:

/120 a _ _ b _ _ /24 c /120 d _ _ _   which is simplified   /40 a b /24 c /30 d

It is easy to figure out that the lowest acceptable value of s is twelve, yielding a minimal notation:

/20 a b /12 c /15 d

Let *Prod* be the lowest common multiple (LCM) of all tempi (20, 12, 15), i.e. sixty. The number of empty objects appended to each occurrence of a or b is:

$60/20 - 1 = 2$

The same operation yields four empty objects after c and three after d, hence the *dilated notation* of this sequence: a _ _ b _ _ c _ _ _ _ d _ _ _ This notation is used for setting the columns of the phase diagram. Compared with the original notation, it multiplies all durations by a ratio of five that we call the *dilation ratio*. It is easy to prove that the dilation ratio is:

Ratio = $Prod/s$

8.3 Simplifying a Polymetric Expression

The preceding operations are valid for a polymetric expression provided that the scale factor s is the same in all its arguments. If $s_1,..., s_i,..., s_{imax}$ are the scale factors of minimal notations of arguments $A_1,..., A_i,..., A_{imax}$, then any s which is a common multiple of all s_i's is valid.

Figure 9. A Musical Score.

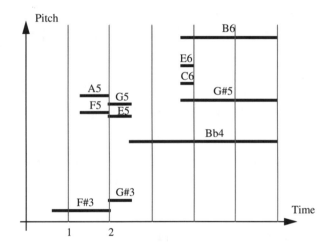

Figure 10. The Pitch/Time Diagram.

Period	Duration	Pitch
0.667	0.667	R [rest]
0.667	1.333	F#3
0.667	0.667	F5, A5
0.5	0.5	G#3, E5, G5
1.25	3.5	Bb4
0	2.25	C6, E6
2.25	0.25	G35, B6

Figure 11. The Event Table.

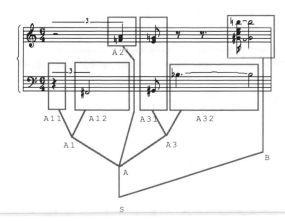

Figure 12. A Possible Hierarchy.

The detailed computation of {i {a b, c d e}, j k} has been given as an illustration of the interpretation algorithm [Bel 1990b:125–128]. The result is {/6 i {/6 a b, /9 c d e}, /4 j k} in which Prod = LCM (6,9,4) = 36 and the dilation ratio:

$$\text{Ratio} = {}^{\text{Prod}}\!/_{s} = {}^{36}\!/_{6} = 6$$

The corresponding dilated expression is

{i _ _ _ _ _ {a _ _ _ _ _ b _ _ _ _ _ _ , c _ _ _ d _ _ _ e _ _ _ }, j _ _ _ _ _ _ _ _ _ k _ _ _ _ _ _ _ _ }

yielding for instance the phase diagram:

i	_	_	_	_	_	a	_	_	_	_	_	b	_	_	_	_	_	NIL
						c				d				e		_	_	NIL
j	_	_	_	_	_	_	_	_	k	_	_	_	_	_	_	_	_	NIL

The interpretation of polymetric structures with out-time objects is explained in [Bel 1990b:128–129; 1991:24].

9 Polymetric Interpretation of a Conventional Musical Score

This example is taken from the *COMPOSE Tutorial and Cookbook* [Ames 1989:2]. See the musical score in Figure 9. This score may be represented with the pitch-versus-time[15] diagram of Figure 10. In COMPOSE the score is stored as an event table similar to Figure 11 [Ames 1989:3]. In Ame's terminology, *period* stands for the time elapsed from the on-setting of an event (note, rest or chord) to the on-setting of the next event. Both periods and durations are measured with a time unit which is the duration of a quarter note.

If the piece, or a variation of it, has been generated by a grammar, its deep structure should be visible at some level of the representation. In Figure 12 we propose one of the many possible structural analyses of Ame's example.

As suggested by this tree, some rests (e.g., A11) may be viewed as part of the structure while others are just functioning as delays.

The tree-structure in Figure 12 could be the parsing tree of a production by the context-free grammar:

S	→ {A , ... B}			
A	→ {2, A1,— A2} {4, A3}			
A1	→ A11 A12	or equivalently	A1 →	{A11 A12}
A3	→ A31 A32	or	A3 →	{A31 A32}
A11	→ —	or	A11 →	{–}
A12	→ {2, F#3}			
A2	→ {F5, A5}			
A31	→ {1/2, G#3, E5, G5}			
A32	→ {3/2, Bb4&} {2, &Bb4}			
B	→ {1/4, G#5&, C6, E6, B6&} {2, &G#5, &B6}			
... etc.	[Other rules]			

Using only the rules listed above yields the unique production

{{2, {- {2, F#3}}, 2 {F5, A5}} {4, {1/2, G#3, E5, G5} {3/2, Bb4&} {2, &Bb4}}, ... {1/4, G#5&, C6, E6, B6&} {2, &G#5, B6}}

displaying the surface structure of this particular production (see §7.1).

In this expression, G#5& and &G#5 denote two segments of the same object G#5 (see §7.1). The expression contains an undetermined rest "..." (see §7.5) produced by the first rule in the grammar.

Time information is redundant in this polymetric expression, yet it is consistent. The interpretation algorithm yields the complete polymetric expression which is displayed

```
{{{-_ _ _ _ _ _ _ {F#3_ _ _ _ _ _ _ _ _ _ _ _ _ _ _ }} , -_ _ _ _ _ _ _ -_ _ _ _ _ _ {F5_ _ _ _ _ _
_ , A5_ _ _ _ _ _ }}{{G#3_ _ _ _ _ , E5_ _ _ _ _ , G5_ _ _ _ _ }{Bb4_ _ _ _ _ _ _ _ _ _ _ _ _
_ _ _ &}{&Bb4_ _ _ _ _ _ _ _ _ _ _ _ _ _ _ _ _ _ _ _ }} , -_ _ _ _ _ _ _ -_ _ _ -_ _ -_ _ -_
_ -_ _ -_ _ -_ _ -_ _ -_ _ _ {G#5_ _ & , C6_ _ , E6_ _ , B6_ _ &}{&G#5_ _ _ _ _ _ _ _
_ _ _ _ _ _ _ _ _ _ _ _ , &B6_ _ _ _ _ _ _ _ _ _ _ _ _ _ _ _ _ _ _ _ _ _ }}
```

while it is stored in minimal notation by BP2:

{{{/18 -, {/9 F#3}}, /18—- {F5, A5}}{{/24 G#3, E5, G5} {/8 Bb4&} {/6 &Bb4}}, 5/16 {/48 G#5&, C6, E6, B6&} {/6 &G#5, B6}}

Let us for instance examine why it is acceptable to write a rule like A12 → 2, F#3} knowing that, although F#3 is a half-note on the score, its actual duration is $\frac{4}{3}$ units (i.e. 1.333 as shown on the second line of the event table, Figure 11). The additional information allowing a correct interpretation is contained in rules:

A	→	{2, A1,— A2} {4, A3}
A1	→	A11 A12

The first rule indicates that the piece is made of two sections, the first one lasting two units of (symbolic) time and the second one 4 units. In the first section, A1 has a two unit duration while A2 has a $\frac{2}{3}$ unit duration like each of the two silences "–". Then we derive:

A1 ⇒ A11 A12 ⇒ A11 {2, F#3} ⇒ — {2, F#3}

In the last expression, "-" and F#3 share ⅓ and ⅔ of the duration of the sequence respectively. Therefore the actual duration of F#3 is: $\frac{2}{3}$ x 2 = $\frac{4}{3}$.

Representing the piece as a tree-structure (an outcome of some musicological analysis) makes it easy to relate it to a set of acceptable variations, i.e. a language generated by a grammar. The initial grammar can be modified to generate this set rather than a unique piece. Let us for example decide that in another variation F#3 should be slightly longer. We may write:

A12 → {3, F#3}

so that A1 is now derived as "– {3, F#3}" in which "–" and F#3 share $\frac{1}{4}$ and $\frac{3}{4}$ of the duration of the structure respectively. Now the duration of F#3 is: $\frac{3}{4}$ x 2 = $\frac{3}{2}$ The polymetric interpretation algorithm automatically readjusted the duration of the rest preceding F#3. To enter the same modification in the event table Figure 11 it would be necessary to recalculate both the duration of the rest (now 0.5) and the period of F#3 (now 0.833). Understandably, the interpretation algorithm takes care of such modifications.

A system manipulating a grammar and interpreting its productions as polymetric expressions is therefore aware of the structure of the piece, by which we mean constraints on synchronization yielding information on durations and start/clip times. Due to the structure of the piece indicated in the grammar, the statement *F#3 should be longer* means that its start time must be earlier while its clip time remains synchronized with the clip time of chord {F5, A5}. Therefore, a limitation of the event list representation is that it makes synchronization explicit only on start-times.

Part C—Time-Setting Sound-Object Structures

10 The Time-Setting Problem—An Informal Introduction

In the rest of this chapter we deal with the problem of instantiating the sound-objects of a complete polymetric structure. Informally, instantiating a sound-object means dispatching to the sound processor all the messages that are defined in its prototype (§19).

A naive interpretation of sequences of sound-objects would be to arrange all corresponding time intervals in a strictly sequential way. Duthen and Stroppa [1990] have suggested a more abstract approach, starting from the assumption that any sound-object may possess one or several time points playing a particular role, e.g. a climax. These points are called *time pivots*. Further they suggest to construct sound structures using a set of synchronization rules. When two objects are synchronized, two pivots—the ones selected in that particular context—are superimposed while other pivots may be used to infer the new pivots of the compound object. Figure 13

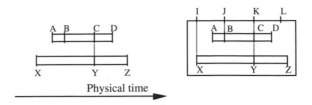

Figure 13. Synchronizing Two Sound-Objects à la *Stroppa.*

represents two sound-objects with respective pivots (A, B, C, D) and (X, Y, Z) being used to build a compound object, assuming that there is a rule saying that C and Y should coincide. Other rules assign pivots (I, J, K, L) to the compound object. Note that some of the new pivots, like L, may not coincide exactly with lower-level pivots.

This approach is attractive but it is hard to implement if the formalism of synchronization rules remains too general. Moreover, in our approach, synchronization is primarily a matter of symbolic time: the partial ordering of objects in a polymetric structure. Therefore we retained a simplified version of Stroppa's idea, assigning each object one single pivot.

Let us for instance consider a polymetric structure {S1,S2,S3} derived as {a _ b c d _ e , a _ f _ g h _ , a i _ a _ i _ } yielding the phase diagram:

a		b	c	d	_	e	NIL
a	_	f	_	g	h	_	NIL
a	i	_	a	_	i	_	NIL

Suppose that all sound-object prototypes labelled a, b, c, …, i are defined—they may have been recorded from a musical instrument as suggested in §2. As will be shown below (§12), the definition of each object contains the relative location of its pivot and metrical properties allowing the calculation of its time-scale ratio—informally, a factor adjusting the duration of the sound-object to the current tempo of performance.

Figure 14 is a graphic representation of a possible instance of this polymetric structure. The structure of time is an irregular pulsation represented with vertical lines (time streaks). The time-span interval of each sound-object is shown as a rectangle with arbitrary vertical width and position. These positions have been chosen to separate objects on the graph: it is clear for example that c, f, g and a have overlapping time-span intervals between the third and fourth streaks. Lengths of rectangles represent the physical durations of sound-objects. Out-time objects are not shown in these examples as they would appear as vertical segments.

Vertical arrows indicate time pivots. As shown with object e, the pivot is not necessarily a time point within the time-span interval of the sound-object.

This graph represents the *default positioning* of objects, with pivots located exactly on time streaks. Although it is reasonable that instances of c, f and a are overlapping between the third and fourth streaks since they belong to distinct sequences

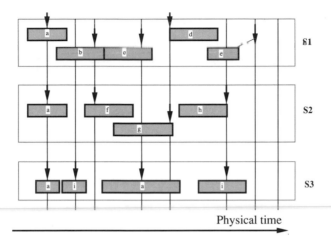

Figure 14. A Structure of Sound-Objects.

which are performed simultaneously, it may not be acceptable that f overlaps g in a single sequence S2; the same with d and e in sequence S1. For similar reasons, it may not be acceptable that the time-span intervals of a and i are disjoint in sequence S3 while no silence is shown in the symbolic representation. The philosophy of our approach is to bind these topological constraints to properties of objects (see §13) instead of imbedding all the information in a symbolic representation. Therefore, the symbolic representation contains no more information than the ordering of pivots.

The topological situations of time-span intervals depend on the structure of time. For example, although the two instances of i in S3 have identical symbolic durations, their physical durations (i.e. their time-scale ratios) are different because the beat offsets (i.e. the duration from one streak to the next) are different.

How could one deal with a constraint such as <<*the end of sound-object e may not overlap another sound-object in the same sequence*>> ? If object g is relocatable then it may be delayed (shifted to the right) until the constraint is satisfied. We call this a *local drift* of the object (see §12.1). Yet the end of g will also overlap the beginning of h. Assume that this too is not acceptable and h is not relocatable. One should therefore look for another solution, for example truncate the beginning of h (see §14). If this and other solutions are not acceptable then one may try to shift f to the left or to truncate its end. In the first case it might be necessary to shift or truncate a as well.

So far we mentioned a kind of constraint propagation within one single sequence. In the time-setting algorithm the three sequences are considered in order S1, S2, S3. Suppose that the default positioning of objects in S1 satisfies all constraints and no solution has been found to avoid the overlapping of f and g in

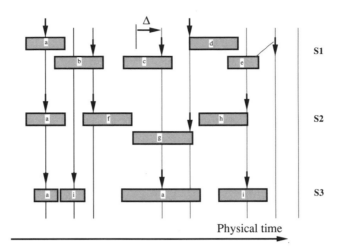

Figure 15. A Structure with "Break of Tempo."

S2. Another option is to envisage a *global drift* to the right of all objects following f in S2. The global drift is notated Δ on Figure 15. All time streaks following the third one are delayed (see dotted vertical lines).

This solution is labelled Break tempo because its effect is similar to the *organum* in conventional music notation. Although the global drift increases the delay between the third and fourth streaks, the physical durations of sound objects are not changed because their time-scale ratios have been calculated beforehand.

Now the positioning of objects in S2 is acceptable, but it might have become inacceptable in S1: there may be a property of b or c saying that their time-span intervals cannot be disjoint, so that c could be shifted to the left, etc. Evidently, whenever a global drift is decided the algorithm must start again from the first sequence.

The process of locating—i.e. instantiating—sound-objects, as illustrated in this example, is the task of the *time-setting algorithm* which will be partly described in §16.

11 Encoding a Sound-Object Structure

The essential data structures used by the time-setting algorithm are introduced here. In §3.1 we indicated that the structure of time Φ is a strictly increasing function mapping the set of symbolic dates $\{t_i\}$ to physical time. Therefore the structure of time is encoded as an increasing list of physical dates $\{T(i): i = 1, ..., imax\}$ such that $T(i) = \Phi(t_i)$.

In striated time all $T(i)$ are given as input data. In smooth time they are calculated only once the sound-objects have been located in the first sequence.

For example, let us consider the structure /3 ab { cde, ab } cd which may be represented in the phase diagram (dilation ratio, see §8.2: Ratio = 6):

```
n _ b _ a _ _ b _ _ c _ d _ NIL
_ _ _ _ c _ d _ e _ NIL
```

Symbols a, b, ..., designate sound-objects E_k, in which k is an arbitrary index ($k \geq -1$). Symbol "_" designates the empty sound-object E_0. NIL is mapped to a virtual object E_{-1} delimitating the end of each sequence.

The strictly positive values of k in this structure may be for instance:

1		2		3			4			5		6	
a	_	b	_	a	_	_	b	_	_	c	_	d	_
				c	_	d	_	e	_				
				7		8		9					

All k's are contained in a bidimensional array called the *phase table* Seq(nseq,i):

Phase table Seq(nseq,i)

i =	1	2	3	4	5	6	7	8	9	10	11	12	13	14	15
nseq =1	1	0	2	0	3	0	0	4	0	0	5	0	6	0	-1
nseq =2	0	0	0	0	7	0	8	0	9	0	-1	0	0	0	0

E_k is the k-th sound-object, with k = Seq(nseq,i). The column index i is the *rank* of object E_k in its sequence. If we call *inext* the rank of the next non-empty sound-object or NIL marker in the sequence, the *symbolic duration* of sound-object E_k is:

$$d(k) = {}^{inext-i}/_{Ratio}$$

in which *Ratio* is the dilation ratio (see §8.2).

T(i) is the date of the *reference streak* of objects with rank i in the structure. If T(i) and the complete polymetric expression are known, it is possible to compute performance parameters, thereby determining the dates of all elementary messages contained in sound-object prototypes (§19). These parameters are listed in an array, the instance table, for example:

Instance table

k	1	2	3	4	5	6	7	8	9
Obj(k)	1	2	1	2	3	4	4	4	4
d(k)	⅓	⅓	½	½	⅓	⅓	⅓	⅓	⅓
t1 (k), t2 (k), α(k), etc...	...	...	...						

In this table, d(k) is the symbolic duration of F_k. Parameters t1(k) and t2(k) are the physical start/clip dates of the k-th sound-object, and α(k) its time-scale ratio (see §12.2). Obj(k) is a pointer allowing object identification in the symbol table:

Symbol table

j =	1	2	3	4	5
symbol	a	b	c	d	e

Each E_k (with $k \geq 0$) may be seen as an instance of an object prototype Ep_j with $j = Obj(k)$. If $k = 0$ the object is empty (labelled "_"), therefore Ep_0 is the empty-object prototype. Object prototypes are formally defined in §19. The encoding of out-time objects is illustrated in [Bel 1990b:136–137 1991:34].

12 Metrical Properties of Non-Empty Sound-Objects

In this and the next three paragraphs, sonic properties and transformations of sound-objects are introduced. These are used by the time-setting algorithm.

A *sonic property* P of a sound-object E_k is a predicate $P(j)$ defined by the corresponding sound-object prototype Ep_j, with $j = Obj(k)$. In this way, all properties of a sound-object are inherited from the (unique) sound-object prototype bearing the same label.

12.1 Time Pivot

Once a sound-object E_k (given $k = Seq(nseq,i)$) has been instantiated by the time-setting algorithm, its time pivot is located at physical date: $T(i) + \Delta(i) + \delta(k)$ in which $\delta(k)$ is the local drift of the object and $\Delta(i)$ the global drift of its reference streak. If $\delta(k) \neq 0$ the object has been relocated. Relocation is only allowed for objects with a property notated Reloc (see §12.3.1).

An object which is assigned a pivot is called a *striated sound-object*. An object which has no definite pivot is a *smooth sound-object*. In reality, a smooth object is assigned a pivot at the beginning of its time-span interval and declared with property Reloc, so that the pivot location is only a default value.

Physical dates $tmin(j)$ and $tmax(j)$ are the respective start/clip dates of the object prototype Ep_j, taking its pivot as the time origin, while $Dur(j) = tmax(j)-tmin(j)$ is its physical duration (§19).

The following is a (non-limitative) list of properties relevant to the positioning of striated objects.

12.1.1 Pivot in the Beginning (PivBeg), In the End (PivEnd).   The pivot coincides with the first (resp. last) message of the sound-object. Therefore,

Case PivBeg: $tmin(j) = 0$, $tmax(j) = Dur(j)$
Case PivEnd: $tmin(j) = -Dur(j)$, $tmax(j) = 0$

12.1.2 Pivot Centered (PivCent).   The pivot is exactly in the middle of the time-span interval of Ep_j, hence:

$tmin(j) = -tmax(j) = {-Dur(j)}/{2}$

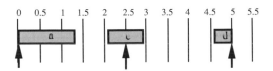

Figure 16. Three Typical Objects and Their Time Pivots.

12.1.3 General Case (PivSpec). The pivot is at some specified date t0 in reference to the first message. Therefore: tmin(j) = - t0 , tmax(j) = Dur(j) - t0

Figure 16 shows a sequence of three objects labelled a, e, d with respective properties PivBeg, PivCent, PivEnd, and physical durations 1.3 s., 0.8 s. and 0.4 s., arranged on a metronomic structure of time with period 0.5 s.

12.2 Scaling Objects in Time

The *physical duration* of a non-empty sound-object is generally not the same as the one of its prototype. The actual physical duration of E_k is $\alpha(k)$ • Dur(j) where $\alpha(k)$ is the time-scale ratio and Dur(j) the duration of sound-object prototype Ep_j, given j = Obj(k). Methods for calculating $\alpha(k)$ are proposed in §15. The way $\alpha(k)$ is taken into account for calculating the dates of elementary messages is explained in §3 of section 19.

Certain ranges of values of $\alpha(k)$ may not be acceptable. For instance, some objects should never be stretched while others should not be contracted. The following properties define acceptable ranges of $\alpha(k)$.

Elasticity (OkRescale, FixScale, OkExpand, OkCompress)

Case OkRescale: any value of $\alpha(k)$ is acceptable.

Case FixScale: $\alpha(k) = 1$.

Case OkExpand: $\alpha(k) \geq 1$ is acceptable.

Case OkCompress: $\alpha(k) \leq 1$ is acceptable.

If the value calculated for $\alpha(k)$ (see §15) is not in an acceptable range, then the value $\alpha(k) = 1$ is imposed.

12.3 Relocating Sound-Objects or Streaks

These properties are relevant to the *local drift* $\delta(k)$ of objects and the *global drift* $\Delta(i)$ of streaks.

12.3.1 Relocatability (Reloc). An object is *relocatable* if its local drift $\delta(k)$ is allowed to take positive or negative values. A classical example of relocatable objects on a metronomic structure of time is the performance of *rubato*.

12.3.2 Break of Tempo (BrkTempo).   There is a break of tempo on sound-object E_k (given $k = \text{Seq}(\text{nseq},i)$ with $k > 0$) if all streaks following the reference streak of the object are delayed, i.e., the global drift $\Delta(\text{ii}) > \Delta(i)$ for all $\text{ii} > i$. An object allowed to break tempo has property BrkTempo.

13 Topological Properties of Non-Empty Sound-Objects

These properties are used to check whether or not topological configurations of time-span intervals are acceptable in a sequence (see informal example in §10).

13.1 Covering the Beginning (OverBeg), the End (OverEnd)

The OverBeg property means that the beginning of the time-span interval of an object may be covered by other objects in the same sequence. OverEnd is defined similarly.

13.2 Continuity in the Beginning (ContBeg), in the End (ContEnd)

A sound-object has property ContBeg if its time-span interval must be connected with (or overlap) the time-span interval of one of the preceding objects in the sequence. ContEnd is defined similarly: the time-span interval must be connected with (or overlap) the one of any object following it in the sequence.

14 Reshaping Sound-Objects

Many transformations of sound-objects could be imagined, e.g., a non-linear distorsion of the local time of an object (see $\text{LocalTime}_k(t)$ in §3 of section 19), or even adding/suppressing messages. The only transformation we consider here is truncating the beginning or the end of a sound-object. Properties allowing this are labelled TruncBeg and TruncEnd respectively.

A variable notated $\text{TrBeg}(k)$ indicates the amount of physical time by which the beginning of sound-object E_k has been truncated. Similarly, $\text{TrEnd}(k)$ is relative to the truncating of its end. Evidently,

$$0 \leq \text{TrBeg}(k),\ 0 \leq \text{TrEnd}(k),\ \text{and}\ \text{TrBeg}(k) + \text{TrEnd}(k) < \text{physical duration of}\ E_k.$$

Truncating a sound-object does not mean that all elementary messages contained in the truncated part have been deleted. Some of them are relocated at the new start/clip dates of the object, as shown in §3 of section 19.

15 Calculating Time-Scale Ratios

The time-scale ratio $\alpha(k)$ of a sound-object E_k depends on its symbolic duration $d(k)$, its nature (smooth or striated) and the structure of time (smooth or striated). This paragraph introduces rules for calculating $\alpha(k)$.

A sound-object prototype Ep_j may be defined in reference to a metronome beat, the period of which is notated $Tref(j)$. If no metronomic reference is used then conventionally $Tref(j) = 0$.

15.1 Calculating Time-Scale Ratios in Smooth Time

In smooth time it is possible to imagine that there is a clock with period Tclock measuring physical durations. This case is called *measured smooth time*. If no such clock is available we always take: $\alpha(k) = d(k)$ where $d(k)$ is the symbolic duration of E_k. The duration of sound-object prototype Ep_j is $Dur(j)$. Empty objects "_" are mapped to prototype Ep_0 such that $Dur(0) = 0$. In measured smooth time, $\alpha(k)$ is calculated as follows:

Object type	Tref(j)	Dur(j)	$\alpha(k)$
striated	> 0	≥ 0	$d(k).^{Tclock}/_{Tref(j)}$
smooth	$= 0$	> 0	$d(k).^{Tclock}/_{Dur(j)}$
smooth	$= 0$	$= 0$	$d(k)$

Using this table, $\alpha(k)$ cannot be calculated in silences, i.e. non-empty sound-objects conventionally notated "-" for which both $Tref(j)$ and $Dur(j)$ are undetermined. A physical duration is therefore assigned to a silence in reference to the local period. Let E_{kprec} be the non-empty sound-object immediately preceding E_k in the sequence. The local period is:

$$P = ^{t2(kprec) - t1(kprec)}/_{d(kprec)}$$

in which $t1(kprec)$ and $t2(kprec)$ are the respective start/clip physical dates of E_{kprec}, and $d(kprec)$ its symbolic duration. The physical duration of silence E_k will therefore be: $P.d(k)$. An error message is generated if a sequence of sound objects starts with a silence in measured smooth time, as *kprec* is not defined in this case.

15.2 Calculating Time-Scale Ratios in Striated Time

15.2.1 Striated Sound-Objects. The value proposed for $\alpha(k)$ is:

If $d(k) > 0$,
$$\alpha(k) = ^{T(inext) - T(i)}/_{Tref(j)}, \text{ with } j=Obj(k) \text{ and } k=Seq(ligne,i)$$

where *inext* is the rank of the next non-empty sound-object or the NIL marker in the sequence, or, if $d(k) = 0$ (case of out-time objects), $\alpha(k) = 0$.

15.2.2 Smooth Sound-Objects. To calculate $\alpha(k)$, Tref(j) is replaced with Dur(j). This yields:

If $d(k) > 0$,
$\alpha(k) = {}^{T(inext) - T(i)}/\text{Dur}(j)$, with j=Obj(k) and k=Seq(ligne,i)

or, if $d(k) = 0$ (case of out-time objects), $\alpha(k) = 0$.

The physical duration (see §12.2) of a smooth object E_k is therefore

$\alpha(k) \cdot \text{Dur}(j) = T(inext) - T(i)$

for a sound-object, and zero for an out-time object.

16 The Time-Setting Algorithm

The main features of the time-setting algorithm informally introduced in §10 will be summarized now. Readers eager to see musical examples may first read §18. More details about the algorithm, proofs of its correctness and complexity calculation have been published in [Bel 1990b:chapter IX] and [Bel 1991:39–53].[16]

Instantiating (i.e., setting in time) a sound-object structure means determining the performance parameters $\alpha(k)$, $\delta(k)$, t1(k), t2(k), TrBeg(k), TrEnd(k) and $\Delta(i)$ for all sound-objects E_k such that k = Seq(nseq,i) with i = 1,…,imax and nseq = 1,…,nmax. Variable *i* is the index of the reference streak of sound-object E_k.

Time-scale ratios $\alpha(k)$ are first calculated and the start/clip dates t1(k) and t2(k) of each object E_k are fixed to their default values, i.e., with its time pivot located exactly on its reference streak. The resulting situation may not be acceptable because of topological constraints on sound-objects. A function called Locate() is therefeore invoked to scan each sequence of the sound-object structure, modifying the start/clip dates of sound-objects until all constraints are satisfied.

16.1 The Locate() Function

Each sequence is scanned from left to right (i.e., increasing dates). The flowchart in Figure 17 shows the detailed operation.

The main test in this function is Situation acceptable? (see §16.2). If the situation of E_k does not fulfill topological constraints, then a first solution set sol_set1 is calculated. This set contains possible corrections of E_k aimed at changing its start date t1(k). Its clip date t2(k) may also incidently be changed in this process. Each time the program jumps at New_choice1, a solution is tried and deleted from the set. This correction is called correction 1. If sol_set1 is empty, the situation of one of the preceding sound-objects must be revised (see Decrementation). Another solution set sol_set2 is calculated, yielding correction 2, i.e., mainly a modification of the clip date t2(k). To facilitate backtracking, both sol_set1 and sol_set2 are stored as arrays indexed on *i*.

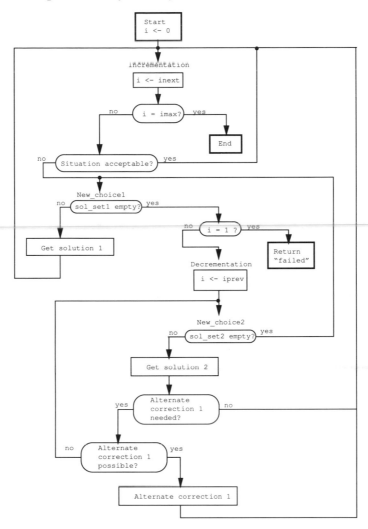

Figure 17. The Locate() Flowchart.

16.2 Formalizing Topological Constraints

While scanning the sequence from left to right, the program stores the clip date of the rightmost sound-object encountered. In Figure 18, E_{kk} is the rightmost object preceding E_k in the sequence. Let $t2(kk)$ be the clip date of E_{kk}. We notate $Ts(i)$ the maximum value of $t2(kk)$ for $ii < i$, with $kk = Seq(nseq,ii)$.

Depending on the value of shift = $Ts(i) - t1(k)$ and on the topological properties of both E_k and E_{kk}, four situations may be envisaged. The only relevant properties of E_{kk}, in this context, are ContEnd and OverEnd. These have been stored as Con-

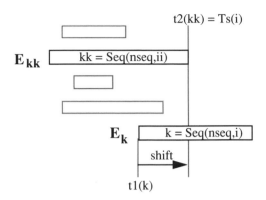

Figure 18. Finding Ts(i) and Shift.

tEndPrev(i) and OverEndPrev(i) respectively. The four situations are listed in Figure 19 along with the conditions that make them acceptable.[2] For instance, in situation 3 the rightmost preceding object E_{kk} overlaps E_k. This is acceptable if both the end of E_{kk} and the beginning of E_k can be covered (see §13.1).

16.3 Corrections 1-2

We call *canonic correction 1* the smallest modification of t1(k) yielding an acceptable solution. It is easy to prove that the canonic correction 1 is:

   t1[k] <— t1[k] + shift

There are three possible transformations yielding this canonic correction:

- Local drift: both the start and clip dates are incremented.
- Global drift (only if shift > 0): same as above, but the reference streak is also relocated.
- Truncating the beginning (only if shift > 0): only the start date is changed.

Correction 2 is similar to correction 1 except that it is aimed at modifying t2(k). It may truncate the end of the sound-object instead of its beginning (see details in [Bel 1991:49–50]).

16.4 Alternate Correction 1

Changing the clip date t2(k) of sound-object E_k modifies the topological constraints on objects following E_k in the sequence. These constraints will be evaluated and taken into account while further scanning the sequence. Once a solution has chosen in sol_set1(i), correction 1 is performed and the following objects in the sequence are examined (see incrementation on the flowchart, Figure 17).

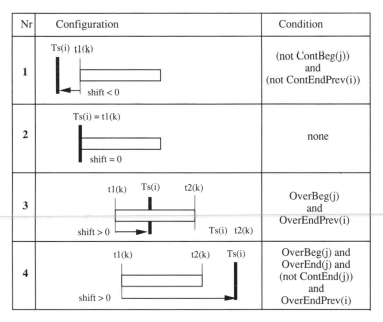

Figure 19. The Four Situations.

On the other hand, whenever correction 2 modifies the start date of E_k it is necessary to check that the constraints on all objects preceding E_k in the sequence are still satisfied. Let E_{kk} and *shift* be defined as in §16.2. The function Alternate_correction1() checks the topological situation between E_k and E_{kk} (as per Figure 19). In situation 3 it attempts to truncate the beginning of E_k. If the correction was successful then '0' is returned and incrementation starts again (see flowchart). Otherwise, another solution is selected for correction 2. If sol_set2(i) is empty, then another solution is tried for correction 1, etc.

It is proved [Bel 1990b:164] that correction 2 always improves the situation and that if there is a solution it will be found in a finite number of steps.

17 Complexity of the Time-Setting Algorithm

The following results have been proved in [Bel 1990b:165–168]:

- The Locate() procedure halts after a finite number of steps.
- If, for some value of *nseq*, Locate() returns a solution with $\Delta(i) \neq 0$ for some value of i (i.e. a global drift), then there is a solution in which $T(i)$ may be replaced with $T(i)+\Delta(i)$.

- In the worst case the time complexity of the Locate() procedure is $O(imax^3)$, where *imax* is the number of objects in the sequence.
- If no global drift is created, the time complexity of the time-setting algorithm is $O(nmax.imax^3)$, where *nmax* is the number of sequences and *imax* the maximum length of a sequence. In the worst case, the time complexity is $O(nmax^2.imax^3)$.

18 Typical Examples

18.1 Non-Empty Sound-Object Prototypes

The table below defines six non-empty striated sound-object prototypes. Objects a and a' are identical as far as messages are concerned, but they differ in their durations and sonic properties.

The first line in the table is the duration of the object prototype in seconds. Reference periods (the metronome value when entering the prototype) are given on the second line.

	a	a'	b	c	d	e
Dur(j)	1.0	1.5	2.0	4.0	1.0	0.5
Tref(j)	1.0	1.5	1.0	2.0	2.0	1.0
Properties	PivBeg	PivBeg	PivBeg	PivBeg	PivBeg	PivCent
	OkRescale	OkRescale	OkRescale	OkRescale	OkRescale	OkRescale
	OverBeg	Reloc	Reloc	OverBeg	OverBeg	OverBeg
	OverEnd	BrkTempo	OverEnd	OverEnd	OverEnd	OverEnd
	TruncEnd	TruncEnd	TruncBeg			

18.2 Calculating Time-Scale Ratios and Time-Setting a Sequence

(This is an application of rules listed in §15) Consider the polymetric expression /2 abc /3 de and its dilated notation /6 a _ _ b _ _ c _ _ d _ e _ with dilation ratio: Ratio = 6 (see §8.2). The sequence contains: imax = 14 symbols.

i	1	2	3	4	5	6	7	8	9	10	11	12	13	14
E_k	a	_	_	b	_	_	c	_	_	d	_	e	_	NIL

18.2.1 Non-Measured Smooth Time. The solution is shown in Figure 20. It is obtained with $\alpha(k) = 0.5$ for a, b and c, and 0.33 for d and e.

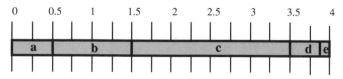

Figure 20. /2 a b c /3 d e (Nonmeasured Smooth Time, Smooth or Striated Sound-Objects).

18.2.2 Striated Sound-Objects in Measured Smooth Time.   Let us take Tclock = 1s. The instance table yields:

	-a	b	c	d	e
d(k)	½	½	½	⅓	⅓
Durj(j)	(1s.)	(2s.)	(4s.)	(1s.)	(0.5s.)
Tref(j)	1	1	2	2	1
$\alpha(k)$	0.5	0.5	0.25	0.166	0.33
physical duration	0.5s.	1s.	1s.	0.16s.	0.16s.

Data between brackets have not been used.

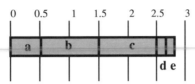

Figure 21. /2 a b c /3 d e (Measured Smooth Time, Striated Sound-Objects).

18.2.3 Sequence of Smooth Sound-Objects in Measured Smooth Time.   Here we suppose for a while that all objects defined in §18.1 are smooth.

	a	b	c	d	e
d(k)	½	½	½	⅓	⅓
Durj(j)	(1s.)	(2s.)	(4s.)	(1s.)	(0.5s.)
$\alpha(k)$	0.5	0.25	0.125	0.33	0.66
physical duration	0.5s.	0.5s.	0.5s.	0.33s.	0.33s.

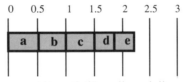

Figure 22 /2 a b c /3 d e (Measured Smooth Time, Smooth Sound Objects).

18.2.4 Striated Sound-Objects in Striated Time.   Let us assume a metronomic structure of time with period 3 seconds. The following is the table of T(i) in seconds and the corresponding objects in the sequence:

i	1	2	3	4	5	6	7	8	9	10	11	12	13	14
T(i)	0	0.5	1	1.5	2	2.5	3	3.5	4	4.5	5	5.5	6	6.5
E_k	a	–	–	b	–	–	c	–	–	d	–	e	–	NIL
k	1	0	0	2	0	0	3	0	0	4	0	5	0	-1

$\Delta(i) = 0$ for every *i*. As to b, for instance, i = 4, inext = 7 and Tref(j) = 1 s. Therefore

$$\alpha(2) = {}^{T(inext)-T(i)}\!/\!_{Tref(j)} = {}^{3-1.5}\!/\!_1 = 1.5$$

The physical duration of this object is: $\alpha(2).Dur(j) = 1.5 \times 2 = 3$ s.

Positioning objects implies taking into account properties PivBeg for a, b and c, PivEnd for d and PivCent for e. The final lay-out is shown in Figure 23.

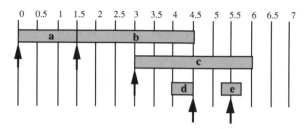

Figure 23. /2 a b c /3 d e, i.e. /6 a _ _ b _ _ c _ _ d _ e _ ,
(Metronomic Striated Time, Period 3s., Striated Sound-Objects).

18.3 Time-Setting Polymetric Structures

Consider /3 ab { cde, ab } cd which is interpreted

   /6 a _ b _ { c_ d _ e _ , a _ _ b _ _ } c _ d _

yielding a possible phase diagram: (Ratio = 6):

a	_	b	_	a	_	_	b	_	_	c	_	d	_	NIL
_	_	_	_	c	_	d	_	e	_	NIL				

18.3.1 Non-Measured Smooth Time, Smooth Sound-Objects.   The first sequence (ababcd) makes no difficulty. Then streaks are created by interpolating the physical durations of non-empty sound-objects in the first sequence. See the dotted lines on Figure 24.

The next step is the time-setting of the second sequence, using the interpolated streaks, as illustrated in Figure 25.

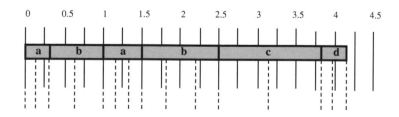

Figure 24. Interpolating Streaks in the First Sequence.

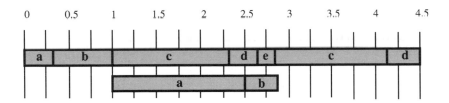

Figure 25. /3 ab { cde , ab } cd, i.e. /6 a _ b _ { c _ d _ e _ , a _ _ b _ _ } c _ d _
(Nonmeasured Smooth Time, Smooth Sound-Objects).

18.3.2 Striated Time.   Consider examples:

        /3 ab { cde , ab} cd
i.e. /6 a _ b _ { c _ d _ e _ , a _ _ b _ _ } c _ d _
        /3 a'b { cde , a'b} cd
i.e. /6 a' _ b _ { c _ d _ e _ , a' _ _ b _ _ } c _ d _

These have similar symbolic representations but different time-settings because of the properties of sound-objects a and a'. With metronomic time, period 3 s., we get the solutions shown in Figures 26–27.

In the latter example, since a' does not have property OkCompress it cannot accept $\alpha(k) = 0.66$, therefore $\alpha(k)$ is forced to 1. Object b should start before a' clips, but b does not have property OverBeg. Therefore the beginning of b is truncated. Since a' does not have OverBeg, its second instance cannot start before b clips. A local drift of a' solves this constraint. Now b may overlap a', which is not acceptable, therefore b is truncated in its beginning.

The last example

           {b - ba, /2 a'c {de, /3 a - c}}
i.e. /6 {b _ _ - _ _ b _ _ a _ _ , a' _ _ c _ _ {d _ _ e _ _ , a_ - _ c _ }}

is shown in two performances (Figure 28–29) with respective metronome periods 3 s. and 2 s. The fact that a' does not have the OverEnd property forces a correction 2 (with negative drift δ) to prevent it from overlapping c.

Part D

19 Formal Definitions of Object Prototypes

The formal definitions of object prototypes are given here as a guide-line for the design of a procedure dispatching elementary messages in real time. The procedure itself is not described as it is highly dependant on the implementation. The

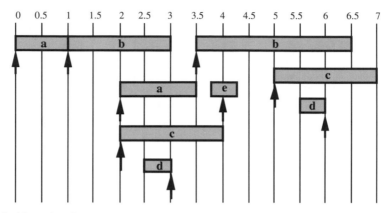

Figure 26. /6 a _ b _ { c _ d _ e _ , a _ _ b _ _ } c _ d _
(Metronomic Time, Period 3 s.)

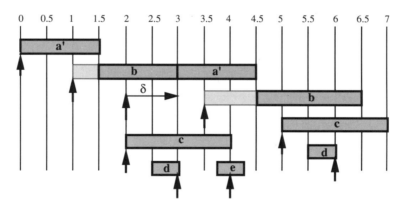

Figure 27. /6 a' _ b _ { a' _ _ b _ _ , c _ d _ e _ } c _ d _
(Metronomic Time, Period 3 s.)

main design requirement, which this formalism helps fulfilling, is a low-level representation of musical items that does not contain all the information stored in sound-object prototypes, so that in the end very large sound-objects can be instantiated and performed in real time.

19.1 Sound-Object Prototypes

Let $\mathbf{A} = \{A_1,\ldots,A_N\}$ be an arbitrary set of elementary actions or messages destined to a sound processor, $P(\mathbf{A})$ the set of all subsets of $\mathbf{A}$, and $\mathbf{R}$ the set of real numbers, representing physical time. In a macro-level description of sound, A_i may be an

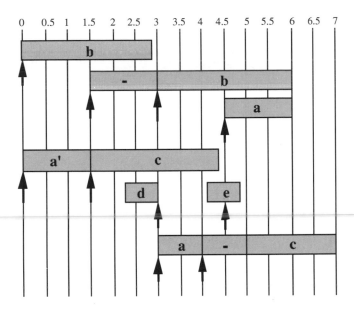

Figure 28. /6 { b _ _ - _ _ b _ _ a _ _ , a' _ _ c _ _ { d _ _ e _ _ , a _ - _ c _ }}
(Metronomic Time, Period 3 s.)

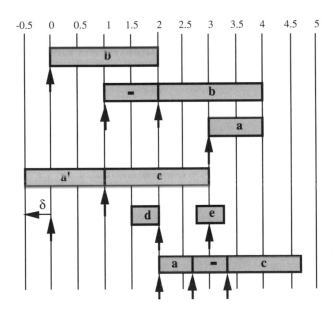

Figure 29. /6 { b _ _ - _ _ b _ _ a _ _ , a' _ _ c _ _ { d _ _ e _ _ , a _ - _ c _ }}
(Metronomic Time, Period 2 s.)

instruction label (e.g. a MIDI code), whereas in a micro-level description it may be a vector of numerical parameters. Both representations may coexist in the same implementation.

Let {Ep_j | j = 0, ... jmax} designate a finite set of sound-object prototypes defined as follows:

Definition

The j-th sound-object prototype is a mapping
$Ep_j: \mathbf{R} \cup \{nil\} \rightarrow P(\mathbf{A})$
such that $Ep_j(nil) = \varnothing$, and $Ep_j(t) \neq \varnothing$ for a finite set of values of $t \in \mathbf{R}$.

Conventionally, the time origin indicates the pivot of the sound-object. The utility of the nil value will be shown below.

It is assumed that sound-object prototypes are predefined. They may be played on an instrument (see §2) and edited as a list of time-stamped MIDI codes. They may also be defined as arbitrary functions mapping time to macro-level or micro-level parameters (see [Truax 1990:101–102]).[18]

By convention, Ep_0 designates the prototype of the empty sound-object labelled "_," with $Ep_0(t) = \varnothing$ for any $t \in \mathbf{R}$. Ep_1 may designate the silence notated "–."

Given an arbitrary time origin, the start/clip dates of the prototype are respectively tmin(j) and tmax(j) such that:

$$Ep(tmin(j)) \neq \varnothing , Ep(tmax(j)) \neq \varnothing , \text{ and } \forall t \notin [tmin(j), tmax(j)], Ep_j(t) = \varnothing .$$

Therefore, $Ep_j(tmin(j))$ contains the very first message of the object and $Ep_j(tmax(j))$ its last message.[19] An illustration of the Ep_j mapping of a sound-object prototype is given in Figure 30.

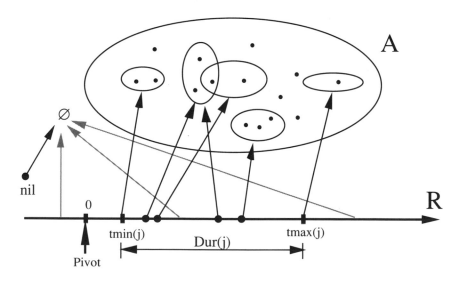

Figure 30. A Sound-Object Prototype and the Ep_j Mapping.

19.2 Out-Time Object Prototypes

Given a sound-object prototype Ep_j, the prototype of the corresponding out-time object $E'p_j$ is:

$E'p_j(0) = \overset{\cup}{_{t \in [tmin,tmax]}} Epj(t)$

$E'p_j(t) = \varnothing \; \forall t \neq 0$

Informally, an out-time object has all its messages at the same date. In an actual implementation, the strict ordering of messages may be maintained while the delay from one message to the next is rendered very small. Figure 31 shows the $E'p_j$ mapping of the out-time object prototype corresponding to the sound-object prototype defined in Figure 30.

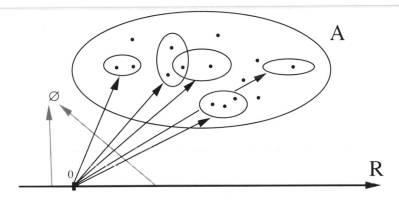

Figure 31. An Out-Time Object Prototype and the E'p_j Mapping.

19.3 The Time-Setting Function f(t)

Let $t1(k)$ and $t2(k)$ be the physical start/clip dates of a (non-empty) sound-object F_1. The object may be truncated, in which case either $TrBeg(k)$ or $TrEnd(k)$ in nnni tive (see §14). Its time pivot is located at physical date $T(i) + \Delta(i) + \delta(k)$, where i is the rank of its reference streak and $k = Seq(nseq,i)$.

Let *imax* and *nmax* be the maximum values of i and *nseq* in a sound-object structure (i.e. the dimensions of the phase diagram). We call time-setting of the sound-object structure the function $f: \mathbf{R} \rightarrow \mathbf{P}(\mathbf{A})$ such that

$\forall t \in \mathbf{R},$

$f(t) = \left(\overset{\cup}{_{nseq=1,nmax}^{i=1,imax}} [Epj(LocalTime_k(t))] \right) \cup \left(\overset{\cup}{_{seq=1,nmax}^{i=1,imax}} [E'p_j(LocalTime'_k(t))] \right)$

with $j = Obj(k)$ and $k = Seq(nseq,i)$

The first member of $f(t)$ is the set of instances of sound-objects (i.e. E_k with $d(k) > 0$), for which local time is defined as follows:

(1) $\forall t \in [t1(k), t2(k)]$,
$$\text{LocalTime}_k(t) = {}^{t\text{-}T(i)\text{-}\Delta(i)\text{-}\delta(k)}\!/\!_{\alpha(k)}$$
with $j = \text{Obj}(k)$ and $k = \text{Seq}(nseq,i)$

(2) $\forall t < t1(k)$,

(2.1) $\text{LocalTime}_k(t) = $ nil if $\text{Ep}_j(\text{LocalTime}_k(t))$ is of type ON

(2.2) $\text{LocalTime}_k(t) = \text{LocalTime}_k(t1(k))$ otherwise

(3) $\forall t > t2(k)$,

(3.1) $\text{LocalTime}_k(t) = $ nil if $\text{Ep}_j(\text{LocalTime}_k(t))$ is of type ON

(3.2) $\text{LocalTime}_k(t) = \text{LocalTime}_k(t2(k))$ otherwise.

Cases (2) and (3) refer to objects truncated in the beginning and the end respectively. The type ON subsets of **A** are the ones that contain a message initiating a process in the sound processor (e.g. a NoteOn message in a MIDI implementation). These are deleted if found in the truncated part of an object (see cases 2.1 and 3.1). Other messages are kept but they are relocated at the start/clip dates of the object (see cases 2.2 and 3.2). Figure 32 shows a truncated sound-object whose prototype could be the one shown in Figure 30.

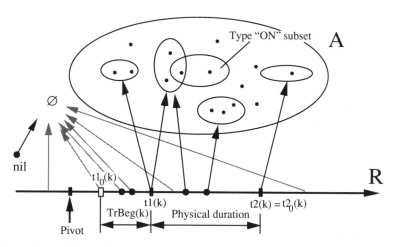

Figure 32. A Sound-Object Truncated in its Beginning.

The second member of $f(t)$ is the set of instances of out-time objects (i.e. E_k with $d(k) = 0$), for which local time is:

$\text{LocalTime'}_k(t) = t - T(i) - \Delta(i) - \delta(k)$.

Given the time-setting function $f(t)$, all messages referenced by $f(t)$ can be dispatched in real time to the sound processor. Instantiating a sound-object is therefore possible as soon as $\alpha(k)$, $t1(k)$, $t2(k)$, $\text{TrBeg}(k)$ and $\text{TrEnd}(k)$ have been calculated. The actual sequence of messages defining the object prototype may be retrieved from some other part of the memory—possibly a hard disk.

Since for every *t*, f(t) is a subset of **A**, messages are not arranged in a strict sequence. In a practical implementation an arbitrary ordering of simultaneous elementary actions may be imposed so that the corresponding messages are dispatched in sequence with a very small delay.

An additional necessary feature is the management of ON/OFF processes: when a sound-object structure containing several sequences is instantiated, the same process may be invoked several times (by several occurrences of the same type ON message) before it is stopped by a type OFF message. This can be avoided, either by ignoring redundant ON messages or by sending an additional OFF message just before triggering again the process.

20 Conclusion

The musical examples in §18 give an indication of the variety of solutions proposed by the time-setting algorithm (on the basis of properties of sound-objects and different structures of time) for the performance of a given musical item. Equally versatile is the interpretation of polymetric expressions generated by formal string-grammars, as shown in part B. Both approaches, therefore, contribute to compensate the rigidity of the timing of computer-generated musical pieces: the synchronization and accurate timings of concurrent musical processes are handled by the computer on the basis of (possibly incomplete) information on structures and sound-objects. This allows a composer to explore sets of musical productions generated by rewriting rules, either in a systematic way—assessing every decision of the machine—or in situations involving one or several computers/sound processors interacting in real-time improvisation.

Acknowledgement

I would like to express thanks to the editor Mira Balaban for her patience in helping me to clarify many ꞁꞁꞁꞁꞁꞁꞁ ꞁꞁ ꞁꞁꞁꞁꞁ ꞁ ꞁꞁ ꞁꞁꞁꞁꞁꞁꞁꞁ ꞁꞁꞁꞁ ꞁꞁꞁꞁ ꞁ

Notes

1) Musical Instrument Digital Interface.

2) The implementation mentioned in this chapter was undertaken by ISTAR France in 1989–90 with a modest financial support of Laboratoire Musique et Informatique de Marseille. Theoretical issues are part of a phD dissertation at Aix-Marseille III University [Bel 1990b].

3) The term *acousmatic* refers to sounds whose physical source is either unknown or is intentionally neglected; the term is taken over from Pierre Schaeffer's *Traité des Objets Musicaux*, [...] 1966:61. [Original footnote]

4) See for instance context-sensitive substitutions: §3 of "Bol Processor grammars" in this volume.

5) The expression sonic properties is borrowed from [Laske 1972:27] but it is used here in a more restrictive sense. In Laske's view [op.cit.:30], a sound-object itself is a set of sonic properties.

6) See "Bol Processor grammars" in this volume.

7) This term is justified in [Bel 1990a:114].

8) This was called *structure temporelle* by Xenakis [1963:190–1,200]

9) In [Bel 1990b] the pair containing a sound-object label and a symbolic date is called a *time-object*.

10) Similar representations of time relations in music have been suggested by Vecchione [1984] and Oppo [1984].

11) Note that this graph contains less information than the phase diagram. It would be unchanged if for instance the column labelled t8 were deleted; additional columns containing only "_" could also be inserted at will.

12) See for instance notes B6 and G#5 in the musical example of §9. The limitation of this notation (ambiguity) is discussed in [Bel 1990c].

13) This was implied by the last sentence of §5.2.

14) The interpretation of a nested polymetric expression is illustrated in [Bel 1990b:125–128].

15) In this paragraph we deal with symbolic, not physical time, although the presumed structure of time is a metronomic pulse.

16) In this paragraph the start/clip dates of a sound-object E_k are notated t1(k) and t2(k), whereas in the actual algorithm (see [Bel 1991]) temporary values are stored in arrays t'1(), t1(), etc., indexed on i. For similar reasons we use shift instead of shift1.

17) Conditions in situations 1-4 are more restrictive than necessary, considering the definition of the continuity property given in §13.2 that cannot be handled by a single array like ContEndPrev().

18) Non-linear mappings generating chaotic objects are being implemented in Bol Processor BP2.

19) In smooth sound-objects (see §12.1) the time origin is such that tmin = 0, i.e. the default position of the pivot is the date of the first message.

References

Allen, J. F. 1983 Maintaining Knowledge about Temporal Intervals. *Communications of the ACM*, 26, 11:832–843.

Ames, C. 1989 *Tutorial and Cookbook for COMPOSE*. Oakland CA: Frog Peak Music.

Anderson, D. P. and Kuivila, R. 1989 Continuous abstractions for discrete event languages. *Computer Music Journal*, 13, 3:11–23.

Bel, B. 1991 *Two algorithms for the instantiation of structures of musical objects*. Internal report, Groupe Représentation et Traitement des Connaissances, CNRS, Marseille (France).

Bel, B. 1990a Time and musical structures. *Interface*, 19, 2-3:107–135.

Bel, B. 1990b *Acquisition et Représentation de Connaissances en Musique*. Thèse de Doctorat, Faculté des Sciences de St-Jérôme, Université Aix-Marseille III.

Bel, B. 1990c *Bol Processor BP2: reference manual*. ISTAR France, Marseille.

Blacking, J. 1984 What languages do musical grammars describe? In *Musical Grammars and Computer Analysis*, eds. M. Baroni and L. Callegari, 363–370. Firenze: Olschki.

Borin, G. De Poli, G. and Sarti, A. 1990 Formalization of the sound generation process—Structures and metaphors. In *Le fait musical—Sciences, Technologies, Pratiques*, eds. B. Vecchione and B. Bel. Forthcoming.

Boulez, P. 1963 *Penser la musique aujourd'hui*. Paris: Gonthier.

Chomsky, N. and Halle, M. 1968 *Principes de phonologie générative*. Paris: Seuil, 1973. Original edition: New York: Harper and Row.

Duthen, J. and Stroppa, M. 1990 Une représentation de structures temporelles par synchronisation de pivots. In *Le fait musical—Sciences, Technologies, Pratiques*, eds. B. Vecchione and B. Bel. Forthcoming.

Jaffe, D. 1985 Ensemble timing in computer music. *Computer Music Journal*, 9, 4:38–48.

Jakobson, R. 1963 *Essais de linguistique générale*. Paris: Éditions de Minuit.

Laske, O. 1989 Composition Theory: An Enrichment of Music Theory. *Interface*, 18:45–59.

Laske, O. 1972 *On problems of a performance model for music*. Utrecht: Institute of Sonology, Utrecht State University.

Oppo, F. 1984 Per una teoria generale del languaggio musicale In *Musical Grammars and Computer Analysis*, eds. M. Baroni and L. Callegari, 115–130. Firenze: Olschki.

Risset, J.C. 1989 Computer music experiments 1964-... In *The Music Machine*, ed. C. Roads, 67–74. Cambridge MA: MIT Press.

Schaeffer, P. 1966 *Traité des objets musicaux*. Paris: Seuil.

Truax, B. 1990 Chaotic Non-Linear Systems and Digital Synthesis: An Explanatory Study. In *Proceedings of the International Computer Music Conference* (ICMC), Glasgow:100–103.

Vecchione, B. 1984 *Pour une science de la réalité musicale*. Thèse de Doctorat, Université de Provence Aix-Marseille I.

Xenakis, I. 1972 Vers une métamusique. In *Architecture et Musique*, 38–70. Paris: Casterman.

Xenakis, I. 1963 *Musiques formelles*. Paris (France): La Revue Musicale. Augmented translation: *Formalized music*, 1971. Bloomington: Indiana University Press.

Abstract

A functional framework for interleaving the aspects of hierarchy and time in music representation, regardless of the nature of the primitives, is presented. The framework supports partial or complete, and implicit or explicit descriptions, and can account for additional aspects of music via an attributes' mechanism. The music structures language is suggested as an underlying representation framework in explorations of music and music activities. It is based on the assumption that hierarchy and time are fundamental, inter-related aspects in music, and neither *can be independently described.*

Chapter 5

Music Structures: Interleaving the Temporal and Hierarchical Aspects in Music

Mira Balaban

The study of music and musical activities such as composition, listening, perfor-mance, perception, analysis, learning and tutoring, involves theorizing about music at various levels of knowledge. Each of these subjects has its own set of concepts and characterizations, imposed on the music domain. Theorists of composition try to conceptualize the compositional process and its relationship to its end product, while theorists of tutoring try to understand the various abstractions used in music teaching. The assumption that understanding such cognitive musical skills relies on modeling the knowledge musicians have about them is common to most theorists.

The subject of this paper is the concept of *Music-piece*. We believe that a proper characterization of this concept is necessary for any study of music, and it might also lay the ground for establishing a standard for music representation. The commercial MIDI standard ([IMA 1983], [Loy 1985], [Droman 1983] [Anderton 1987]) is not a ~~satisfactory candidate, as it provides no characterization of the approved real proper-~~ ties of the notion of "a music piece." It is a way of digitizing simultaneous sound events; no insight about the properties and structure of this notion is involved.

There are two underlying assumptions to our study of the Music-piece concept:

1) The concept Music-piece is common to all domains of musical activities. Hence, this concept cannot include domain specific aspects like rhythmic patterns, composition protocols or learning rules, nor can it include stylistic or periodical aspects like music forms and musical gestures. It even cannot assume a specific set of primitive objects, as the primitives of a theory of lis-tening are different from those of rhythmical analysis, and both are very dif-ferent from the primitives for musical typesetting.

2) There is a single architecture underlying this concept, independent of the musical subject, task or activity.

The first assumption implies that in our study of the Music-piece concept we should concentrate on general aspects that can be found in every form of music and music processing, and ignore the details of how these aspects are realized in every particular task. The second assumption means that we should try to characterize the structure of a domain that consists of these aspects, again, without making any assumption about a particular musical task.

In this study we suggest the aspects of *hierarchy* and *time* as the basic aspects underlying every handling of music pieces. We characterize the world of music pieces as a world of structures in which the hierarchy and time aspects are interleaved together, and provide a representation formalism, entitled "music structures," for this world. We believe that music structures can be the basis for any study of music and musical activities, as well as the basis for music processing systems such as music workstations.

The aspects of hierarchy and time can be found in every viewpoint, activity or direction in music processing. In analysis, various internal relationships within a complete musical piece are singled out. These relationships, usually, rely or imply a hierarchical internal organization of the musical material along a time axis. In listening, the listener usually identifies partially perceived patterns and puts some hierarchical relationships among them, again, along the time axis. In composition, the hierarchy + time aspects appear in two ways: In the end product and in the process of the compositional activity. The hierarchy + time aspects in musical typesetting are, certainly, very different: Hierarchy consists of graphical partition into pages, lines and bars, and the flow of time is identified with the horizontal layout of the graphical symbols.

Both the hierarchy and time aspects in music were much studied. Hierarchy is the basic building block in the generative grammars approach of [Lerdahl & Jackendoff 1983], and of much of the research that followed it. Temporal issues in music were studied by musicians such as Xenakis. Initial experiments at formalizing this aspect are described in Bel's chapter on representations of sound-object structures, in this volume.

The music structures concept tries to capture the inter-relationships between the two aspects, with no commitment to a specific hierarchical form, or to some distinguished temporal system. It reflects the view that the skeleton of the Music-piece concept is a uniform combination of the hierarchy and temporal aspects. On top of this basis, specification of partial or complete musical material, in an explicit or implicit form, can be built. *Note:* The essential status of hierarchy and time applies only to the Music-piece concept. There are, of course, theoretical musical concepts that do not relate to a realized piece, and in which hierarchy and time do not play a major role. Examples are: The set of pitch classes of a chord, and various structures of pitch classes or of loudness primitives.

Historically, music structures emerged from the Twelve Tone Strings defined within a more general research concerning the development of a knowledge base for the common terminology of Western Tonal Music ([Balaban 1986], [Balaban 1988a], [Balaban 1987b]). Later on they were extended within a music workstation project ([Balaban 1988b]), and within AI research concerning a calculus for hierarchical temporal knowledge ([Balaban & Murray 1989], [Balaban & Murray 1990]). The version described here is, actually, a special case of the time structures, developed in the later research.

In this chapter, we try to emphasize the musical motivation for the music structures representation. Hence, we avoid plain definition of its syntax and semantics, and adopt a presentation by examples style. We hope that this way we can highlight the various specification forms in the music structures framework, from a musical viewpoint. A formal definition of the formalism appears in [Balaban & Murray 1990]; the syntax is defined at the end of this chapter.

In the following sections, after describing related work, we describe the musical world of reference for this work: A domain of structures in which the hierarchy and time aspects are interleaved. No assumption is made about the precise nature of individuals from which these structures are built. The section entitled Music Structures describes music structures and their relationship to the described musical phenomenon. Four forms of specifications are distinguished: Explicit, implicit, partial, and complete. The section entitled Extensions to Music Structures shortly covers two additional subjects: User defined functions and attributed music structures. We conclude the chapter with an example of an implicit, complete music structure, encoding music by Bach.

Related Work

In the field of computer music, representational issues play a major role in systems geared towards analytical or cognitive purposes ([Laske 1972], [Laske 1975], [Winograd 1968], [Frankel et al. 1976], [Frankel et al. 1978], [Smoliar 1976], [Smoliar 1980], [Ebcioglu 1986], [Kassler 1977], [Lidov & Gabura 1973], [Leman 1986], [Minsky 1981], [Balaban 1986]). The traditional problem of these systems is their input/output (i/o) bottleneck. Musicians aid tools, like compositional tools, music workstations, tutoring systems, and typesetting programs, have an opposite nature: they usually provide convenient i/o channels, but are based on weak, task specialized, and typically poorly formulated data structures. These systems cannot be combined together to extend their scopes, and if standardization is at all possible, it would be on the stream-like structureless level of MIDI, that is not adequate to support sophisticated analysis of music.

In commercial systems, like those discussed in [Yavelow 1985], [Yavelow 1986]—Personal-composer, Mockingbird ([Maxwell & Ornstein 1983]), Musprint ([Hamel 1984])—to name just a few—the representation of the task environment, i.e., the music, is deeply embedded in the system. In more research oriented systems like the Music Description Languages (MDLs) DARMS ([Erickson 1975], [Erickson 1977]), SMUT ([Byrd 1974], [Byrd 1977]), MIDI, [Gourlay 1986] and projects like PLA ([Schottstaedt 1983]), FORMES ([Rodet & Cointe 1984]), SSSP ([Buxton 1978], [Buxton et al. 1978]), IOS ([Roads 1983]), ARCTIC ([Dannenberg et al. 1986] and

[Hamel et al. 1987]), straightforward, off-the-shelf data structures are used to represent the music. The music material is, typically, viewed as a, possibly multi-dimensional, sequence of notes, augmented with print or performance information about instruments, key signatures, and the like. Explicit structuring of the music and inclusion of abstract musical concepts is not common. Exceptions are [Buxton et al. 1978] that uses hierarchical structures, though they are embedded in the program; FORMES, where the music structure is realized by the structure of the objects generated through a program run; and ARCTIC that uses functional representation.

Music Description Languages can be, roughly, classified as declarative and procedural. The declarative MDLs describe the music, including its time aspect, as a static data structure, usually concentrating on description of printed scores. Representatives of this approach are DARMS ([Erickson 1975], [Erickson 1977]), SMUT ([Byrd 1974], Byrd 1977]), MSS ([Smith 1973], [Droman 1983], [Yavelow 1986]), and [Gourlay 1986]. The objectives of these MDLs are usually restricted to computer typesetting. Consequently, they do not support musical concepts, relationships or activities that do not explicitly appear in a printed score. Except for [Gourlay 1986] and MIDI, they were all designed to solve the input-output problem of music processing systems, in times where graphic or keyboard interfaces were either not available or rare. Their more modern versions are the graphic score editing systems that use internal, hardware dependent structures as MDL ([Yavelow 1985], [Miller 1985], [Hamel 1984], [Maxwell & Ornstein 1983]). MIDI has been widely embraced as a standard for computer-keyboard interface in the computer music industry. Gourlay's language was suggested as a standard for music typesetting.

In the procedural approach, the music is represented by a program, and a program execution corresponds to music performance. The time aspect moves—in part or as a whole—from the explicit data structures to the program's control. Representatives of this approach are [Smoliar 1971], SCORE ([Smith 1976]), PLA ([Schottstaedt 1983]), and FORMES ([Cointe & Rodet 1983]). The objectives of the procedural MDLs are, usually, much broader than those of the declarative ones. They are intended to provide a rich environment for musical activities. Therefore, they would typically try to support processing of musical aspects like hierarchical organization of music, specification of tentatively defined musical symbols (like dynamics symbols), etc. Surveys of MDLs can be found, among many others, in [Roads 1985], [Loy & Abbott 1985], [Pennycock 1985], [Gourlay 1986], and [Balaban 1991]. [Blombach 1976] and [Brook 1970] provide surveys of the early MDLs.

The main deficiency of most MDLs is that their constructs fail to carry direct musical meaning. In the early MDLs—like DARMS, SMUT—this failure appears already in the basic constructs that represent notes and their properties. In DARMS pitches are denoted by staff-lines numbering, and occurrence of notes in the piece is encoded by their relative position on a printed score. SMUT is similarly nonappealing. In more recent MDLs the atomic data structures are indeed pitch, duration, register, dynamics, etc., but higher level, composite constructs enforce rigid, unnatural description, and lack the flexibility needed for being musically appealing. In SCORE the music is necessarily decomposed into *instruments*, which are collections of arrays describing, each, a line of notes and their properties. PLA decomposes the music into *voices*, which are similar to SCORE's instruments, and to *sections*, which are collections of voices. Both languages enforce a rigid polyphonic view of all music, and use *artificial formal constructs*—collections of arrays of musical properties—to describe the music. Gourlay's language is designed for music printing, and therefore all higher level constructs correspond to partitionings of a printed score by measures. The language is not appropriate for standardizing music description since the notion of hierarchy in music does not, necessarily, coincide with the measures partitioning, but rather with musical objects like parts, sections, phrases, motifs, themes, etc. Consequently, the language cannot describe phrases that override the measures partition, or music that overrides the rows structure.

Systems that are more closely related to the Music Structures Language are ARCTIC, [Buxton et al. 1978] and FORMES. ARCTIC shares with our language the functional approach with explicit representation of time; FORMES and Buxton's system share the hierarchical structuring of objects. The Music Structures language combines the two aspects within a single formalism.

Music as a Temporal-Hierarchical Phenomenon

Human beings can communicate even if involved in different musical activities. The composer can transfer the results of his/her work to the publisher, the music theorist can communicate with the editor of his/her work. The music instructor can communicate musical ideas to students, etc. Behind all these communication lines, there is a common music notation, usually augmented with informal conventions about grouping the musical material in various ways. The notion of grouping discussed by music theorists reflects, probably, the realization of theoretical concepts in the music, while the notion of grouping discussed by a typesetter involves paging, bar lines and other print level information. Yet, all those grouping notions share one property: they combine independent subparts along a time scale. We call this property *Temporal Combination*. Figure 1 tries to convey the intuitive idea of temporal combination.

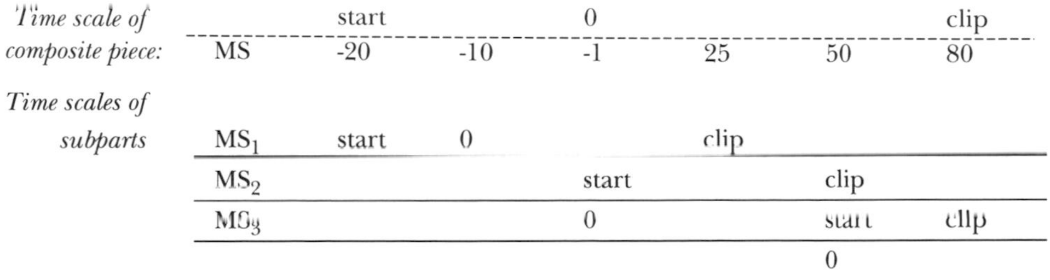

Time scale of composite piece:	start		0			clip
MS	-20	-10	-1	25	50	80

Time scales of subparts						
MS$_1$	start	0		clip		
MS$_2$			start		clip	
MS$_3$			0		start	clip
					0	

Figure 1. Temporal Combination.

Figure 1 depicts a structured view of a piece called MS that consists of three parts: part one, called MS_1, that occurs at time point -10 (an introduction), part two, called MS_2, that occurs at -1, and part three, called M_3, that occurs at 50. As can be seen in the figure, the components of the structure have their own time lines, with their own Zero (beginning), and start and clip points. The temporal combination operation takes several such structured pieces and combines them along the time line of the composite piece.

This uniform notion of interleaving hierarchy with time motivates a unified view of the world of music pieces, as a collection of structured music pieces, each corresponding to a single structured view of a music piece. The simplest, elementary, structured music piece is an occurrence of a sound. A *structured music piece* is a collection of time stamped structured pieces. The collection can be empty—the empty music piece, finite—most music, or infinite, e.g., *glissandi*.

A structured piece has its own time line. An elementary piece has a single occurrence of a sound object along its time line: in its beginning (zero); the duration of the occurrence is that of the sound object. In general, the components of a structured piece, which are, themselves, structured music pieces (elementary or not), have their own time lines. The time stamp of a component denotes the displacement of its beginning from the beginning of the structured piece. Note that a piece does not, necessarily, start in its beginning. There might be an introduction or a delay.

A *time line* is a totally ordered set of objects called *time points*, that corresponds to a subset of the real numbers. One time point is distinguished as the zero (beginning); points preceded by zero are positive and points preceding zero are negative. The time line is closed under the usual arithmetical operations.

The nature of the sound objects from which the structured piece is built depends on the subject of the musical activity. In plain music processing these would be durationless sound objects, i.e., all properties—apart from duration—of the sound objects from which the music piece consists. In analysis, and in studies of musical activities, the sound object can be any subset of sound properties on which the activity focuses. There is no requirement for uniformity: Some structured pieces can be built from loudness primitives, while others can be built from pitchclasses. Note that when the subject of exploration is rhythm, the sound objects are vacuous entities (the subset of sound properties—apart from duration—is empty): The rhythmical content is given by the temporal properties of the structured piece.

In Figures 2 through 5, the structured view of several known musical forms is graphically presented.

The structured view of music does not enforce structuring of music. On one extreme, one is free to assign music a MIDI like description as a stream of time stamped sound objects; on the other extreme one can strive for an account of rhythmic and music patterns and their interrelationships. For the same music piece, many structured views might make sense, depending on one's point of view. All different structured views of a piece share the same denotation: the MIDI-like, flat description.

		start	d			clip
			0			
Components:	MS	start		clip		
	MS		start			clip

Figure 2. A Two-Voice Round.

			Introduction	Part 1	Part 2	
		start		0		clip
		-d				
Components:	Introduction	start		clip		
	Part 1			start	clip	
	Part 2			0	start	clip
					0	

Figure 3. A Two-Part Melody with an Introduction.

			start	clip	
		0	d		
Voices:	Voice 1		start	clip	
			0		
	Voice 2		start	clip	
			0		
	Voice 3		start	clip	
			0		
	Voice 4		start	clip	
			0		

Figure 4. A Four-Part Choir that Starts with a Delay.

	start		clip	
	0			
Elementary piece with duration d_1	start	clip		
	0	d_1		
Elementary piece with duration d_2	start		clip	
	0		d_2	
Elementary piece with duration d_3	start			clip
	0			d_3

Figure 5. A Three-Note Chord: Simultaneous Combination of Elementary Music Pieces.

Summary of the Domain of Structured Music Pieces:

There are three kinds of objects:
- Durationless sound objects.
- Time points (used to specify both durations and time stamps).
- Structured music pieces: elementary or not.

Music Structures

In this section we describe a representation language called Music Structures, developed to account for the structured view of music described in the previous section. Corresponding to the three kinds of objects in the domain of discourse, there will be three types of expressions: Time expressions, sound expressions, and music structures, that can be elementary or not.

The time symbols are the real (or rational) numbers. Any expression that evaluates to a real number can be considered as denoting a time point. Therefore, a time stamp for a component or the duration of an elementary piece can be described by numbers or by expressions like "n+m," or "**duration**(MS)" where *MS* is a given music structure, and **duration** is a function that computes the durations of music structures.

The sound symbols depend on the music domain. In essence they can be any symbolic representation for durationless sound objects. For example, assume that a composer has already synthesized a collection of sounds, and that their duration property can be separated from their other properties (This is the usual case. If not, then the primitives of the music structures language are elementary music structures—see below). Then, the sound symbols might be names for the durationless sound objects, like "Happy-bird," "Wind in-the-bush," etc. In general, the sound symbols can be any combination, possibly empty, of symbols denoting sound properties.

Music structures can be elementary or composite. Elementary music structures form the primitive type of music structures. Composite music structures are formed by applying music structures' operators to music structures. Music structures are further classified as explicit or implicit and as partial or complete. These properties characterize kinds of appropriate musical applications, and direct the selection of processing methods. We now describe, first, elementary music structures, and then various classes of music structures' operators. The section concludes with a discussion of the four, just mentioned, properties.

Elementary Music Structures

An elementary music structure is a pair, [p,d] that associates a term p, denoting a sound object, with a term d, that denotes a non-negative time point. The term d is called the duration of [p,d]. An elementary music structure represents an occurrence of a sound object for a "length of time" denoted by its duration. Some examples of elementary music structures are shown below. The explicit and complete represntation of notes and rests (Figure 6), the implicit sound component (Figure

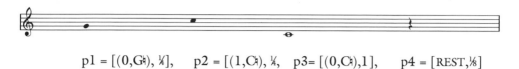

$$p1 = [(0,G\sharp), \tfrac{1}{4}], \quad p2 = [(1,C\sharp), \tfrac{1}{4}, \quad p3= [(0,C\sharp),1], \quad p4 = [REST,\tfrac{1}{8}]$$

Figure 6. An Explicit and Complete Representation of Notes and Rests.

$[(0,G\sharp) \oplus (0,FOURTH,DIM),\tfrac{1}{4}]$ which denotes

Figure 7. Implicit Sound Component.

7), and the implicit duration component (below) are in the Twelve Tones System. The implicit durator component with vacuous sound object is for a rhythm study.

1) Implicit duration component, [(0,Eb), **duration**(MS)], where MS is a music structure: This elementary music structure denotes an occurrence of Eb in the 0 octave that lasts for a period of time equal to the duration of a piece denoted by the music structure MS.

2) Implicit duration component with vacuous sound object: [_ , **duration**(MS)].

Concatenation Operators

The music structures described in this section are constructed by operators that belong to a group of concatenation operators. A *concatenation operator* directly denotes a way of combining structured music pieces into a new structured music piece. The arguments of the concatenation operators are, always, direct components of the new piece. Hence, a music structure, constructed by applying a concatenation operator to explicit music structures, is always explicit.

Musical Concatenation.   Recall that a structured music piece is a collection of structured music pieces, each associated with a time stamp stating the displacement of its beginning from the piece's beginning. This structure can be described using a list like notation as follows: NIL describes the empty music piece; (ms$_1$@t • ms$_2$), for ms$_1$ ≠ NIL, describes the piece denoted by ms$_1$, augmented with the music piece denoted by ms₁, with t as a time stamp. The music structure (ms₁@t • ms₂) is read "ms₁ at t, concatenated to ms₂." The • symbol, called *musical concatenation*, is the basic music structures operator. All other concatenation operators can be defined in terms of the • operator.

Examples.

For simplicity, a music structure like:(ms₁@t₁ • (ms₂@t₂ •...• (msₙ@tₙ • tail)...)) is written (ms₁@t₁ ms₂@t₂...msₙ@tₙ • tail). If tail is NIL it is omitted, and we get a list of time stamped music structures.

1) The structured piece described in Figure 1 can be represented by a music structure, MS, as (MS₁@-10 MS₂@-1 MS₃@50), where MS₁, MS₂, MS₃ represent the three parts of the piece according to this view. Suppose now that MS₁ represents a structured piece consisting of an introduction whose beginning falls at time point -10 of MS₁, and is followed by one part whose beginning coincides with that of MS₁. Then MS₁ is (INTRODUCTION@-10 MS₁₁@0) and the music structure MS is

   ((INTRODUCTION@-10 MS₁₁@0)@-10 MS₂@-1 MS₃@50).

2) A music structure describing a two voice round as in Figure 2, would be (MS@0 MS@d), d > 0.

3) A music structure for a two part melody with an introduction, as in Figure 3, would be (INTRODUCTION@-d PART₁@0 PART₂@**duration**(PART₁)).

4) A music structure for a four part choir that starts with a delay, as in Figure 4, would be ((VOICE₁@0 VOICE₂@0 VOICE₃@0 VOICE₄@0)@d)).

5) A music structure for the three notes chord in Figure 5 would be ([p₁,d₁]@0 [p₂,d₂]@0 [p₃,d₃]@0).

6) The piece described in Figure 8 can be represented by
   MS₁ := ([(0,G♯),¼)]@0 [(0,C♯),1]@¼);
   the piece described in Figure 9 can be represented by
   MS₂ := ([(0,G♯),¼]@0 [REST,⅛]@¼ [(1,C♯),¼]@⅜ [REST,⅛]@⅝);
   the piece described in Figure 10 can be represented by
   MS₃:= (MS₁@0 MS₂@¼).

Figure 8.

Figure 9.

Figure 10.

Due to the context independent nature of music structures, they can be used to describe pieces that can be repeated at different time points in a larger piece. The essence of the musical concatenation constructor is the repeated relativization of different time lines; the ability to describe structured pieces as in the above examples derives from this essence.

Horizontal and Vertical Concatenation. *Horizontal concatenation,* denoted by "—," means "followed immediately by," and *vertical concatenation,* denoted by "|," means "starts simultaneously with." Music structures generated by horizontal/vertical concatenation are called horizontal/vertical, respectively.

Examples.

1) A melody, whose sound objects with their durations are denoted by the elementary music structures $e1,\ldots,en$, can be described by the music structure $e1—e2—\ldots—en$ (or, for short: $\overset{n}{\underset{i=1}{—}} e_i$).

2) A chord consisting of these primitives would be $e1 \mid e2 \mid \ldots \mid en$ (or, for short: $\overset{n}{\underset{i=1}{\mid}} e_i$).

3) A *harmonic sentence,* that is, a sequence of chords, would be $\overset{k}{\underset{j=1}{—}} \overset{n_j}{\underset{i=1}{\mid}} P_{ij}$.

4) A *polyphonic sentence,* that is, a simultaneous combination of melodies, would be $\overset{k}{\underset{j=1}{\mid}} \overset{n_j}{\underset{i=1}{—}} P_{ij}$.

5) The structured piece of Figure 3 can be described by
$$((\text{INTRODUCTION} —\text{PART}_1—\text{PART}_2)@\text{-d}),$$

6) The four part choir of Figure 4 can be
$$((\text{VOICE}_1 \mid \text{VOICE}_2 \mid \text{VOICE}_3 \mid \text{VOICE}_4)@\text{d}).$$

7) The structured pieces of Figure 8 and Figure 9 can also be described by

$$\text{MS}_1 := [(0,\text{G}\sharp), \tfrac{1}{4}] \longrightarrow [(0,\text{C}\sharp),1]$$
$$\text{MS}_2 := [(0,\text{G}\sharp), \tfrac{1}{4}] \longrightarrow [\text{REST}, \tfrac{1}{8}] \longrightarrow [(1,\text{C}\sharp), \tfrac{1}{4}] \longrightarrow [\text{REST}, \tfrac{1}{8}].$$

The horizontal and vertical concatenations can be defined in terms of the temporal concatenation, and the start and clip time operators (see below). The formal definitions are straightforward but tedious; they are left to the end of this chapter. However, these operators are more than just abbreviations. A melodic structure $e1 \longrightarrow e2 \longrightarrow \ldots e_n$ (n>1) states that ei (i>1) plays right after e_{i-1}, and not in a predefined time point, which might be unknown if e_{i-1} is a partial music structure. This information is important, especially, in a dynamic environment, where the duration of components or their stamp points may be changed. In the music workstation, horizontal and vertical concatenations are kept internally, up to the "playback" time, where the real music is needed.

Overlap Horizontal Concatenation.   *Overlap horizontal concatenation* denotes a horizontal combination of structured music pieces, in which the last sound object(s) of the first music piece overlaps (or is unified with) the first sound object(s) of the one that follows. In the Bach example that concludes this chapter we use the overlap horizontal concatenation operator; it is denoted by ~.

Horizontal and Vertical Beginnings' Concatenations.   These operators are analogous to the horizontal and vertical ones, but they relate the beginnings (rather than the start points) of music structures, to follow "right after" or start "simultaneously with." The horizontal beginnings' concatenation describes a situation where the beginning of a music structure immediately follows another music structure. The vertical beginnings' concatenation describes a situation where the beginnings of music structures are simultaneous.

Music Operators

Music operators apply to the sound components in a music structure, not to its structure. For example, in the Twelve Tones system, such operators can be defined on the basis of the additive arithmetic of twelve tones intervals.

Example: Transpose.   This operator transposes a music structure up or down by a given interval. Two versions can be defined: transpose-up and transpose-down. For an elementary music structure [p,d], and an interval i

$$\text{transpose-}^{\text{down}}_{\text{up}}\,([p,k],i) = \begin{cases} [p \pm i, d] & p \text{ denotes a note} \\ [p, d] & p = \text{REST} \end{cases}$$

For a music structure $(\alpha@t \bullet \beta)$,

$$\text{transpose-}^{\text{down}}_{\text{up}}\,((\alpha@t\bullet\beta),\,i) = (\text{transpose-}^{\text{down}}_{\text{up}}(\alpha,\,i)@t \bullet \text{transpose-}^{\text{down}}_{\text{up}}\,(\beta,\,i)).$$

The upward transposition by a minor third (denoted by (0,2,-1), i.e., an interval that includes 0 octaves, distance of 2—when counting intervals from 0, and is smaller by half tone from the major one) of the music structure MS_3 describing Figure 10 can be computed as follows:

transpose-up(MS_3, (0,2,-1)) =
= (transpose-up(MS_1, (0,2,-1))@0 transpose-up(MS_2, (0,2,-1))@ ¼)=
= (([(0,G♯)⊕O(0,2,-1), ¼]@0 [(0,C♯)⊕O(0,2,-1),1]@ ¼)@0
([(0,G♯)⊕O(0,2,-1), ¼]@0 [REST, ⅛]@ ¼ [(1,C♯)⊕O(0,2,-1), ¼]@ ⅜ [REST, ⅛]@ ⅝)@ ¼) =
= (([(0,Bb), ¼]@0 [(0,Eb),1]@ ¼)@0
([(0,Bb), ¼]@0 [REST, ⅛]@ ¼ [(1,Eb), ¼]@ ⅜ [REST, ⅛]@ ⅝)@ ¼)

which denotes the piece (Figure 11).

Figure 11.

The concluding example of this chapter demonstrates the usage of music operators.

A different kind of music operators operate on the duration components within a music structure. For example there might be operators that stretch or squeeze a music structure by a given factor, or an operator that splits all elementary music structures of a given duration d into n, horizontally concatenated, elementary music structures of duration $\frac{d}{n}$, etc.

Transformation Operators

Operators can map certain structurings to other structures. For example, it might be desired to map various structurings of the same flattened version (see below) among themselves, as in **transform** $(\frac{k}{j=1} \frac{n}{i=1} e_{ij})= \frac{n}{j=1} \frac{k}{i=1} e_{ij}.e_{ij}$. This would amount to relating different readings or analyses of the same piece. One special operator of this kind is the **flatten** operator that translates a given music structure into a flat music structure whose components are time stamped elementary music structures. The flat music structure can be considered as the canonical form of the music structure; all structured views of a piece share the same canonical form. It reflects the chronological ordering of the sound objects embedded in the music structure. For example,

flatten (([a,5]@-20 ([b,10]@5 [a,5]@2)@8)) = ([a,5]@-20 [b,10]@13 [a,5]@10).

In playback time, a music structure should first be flattened into its canonical form. The relationship between music structures, canonical forms and music pieces is:

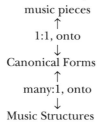

Canonical Forms

many:1, onto

Music Structures

Partial Music Structures

The music structures described so far denote only fully specified music pieces, since only constants of various kinds are used in their construction. Such music structures are called *complete*. The inclusion of variables allows us to describe partially specified music structures and musical patterns. We use lowercase italic letters for variables.

For example, if we know that MS$_3$ that describes Figure 10 is just a part of a larger piece that includes additional, yet unknown, occurrences, the known occurrences can be musically concatenated to a variable denoting the unknown part. The new MS$_3$ would be (MS$_1$@0 MS$_2$@ ¼ • *rest*). We often tend to call the unspecified part of a music structure its "continuation," or "ending," but note that additional constituent music structures could be given any time stamp and thus can describe any part of the larger music structure. Variables also can be used to describe patterns of music structures, i.e., music forms. For example, a music form that consists of two identical music structures, one following the other, can be described by the pattern *ms—ms*. A pattern describing a certain timing of three occurrences would be (ms_1@t ms_2@$\mathbf{f}_1(t)$ ms_3@$\mathbf{f}_2(t)$) where $\mathbf{f}_1$, $\mathbf{f}_2$ are time functions. The pattern of a round can be (ms@t ms@$\mathbf{f}(ms)$), where $0 < \mathbf{f}(ms) <$ **duration** (ms), and the very popular A-B-A pattern can be ms_1—ms_2—ms_1.

Two kinds of partially specified music structures that seem especially valuable for music analysis are durationless music structures and rhythmic patterns. In *durationless music structures* all elementary structures have unspecified (variable) duration; in *rhythmic patterns* all elementary structures have an unspecified sound component. (If the music application domain involves rhythm alone, it is possible that no other sound objects' properties are included, and sound objects are, therefore, vacuous. In that case, rhythmic patterns may be complete: They might fully specify a rhythmic pattern.) Durationless music structures are useful, for example, for analysis that ignores the rhythmic aspect, like in harmonic analysis; rhythmic patterns are useful for the study of the rhythmic aspect in music. Together, they can account for a rich representation of music. The Bach example later in this chapter relies, heavily, on a merge operator that combines structurally compatible durationless structures and rhythmic patterns. Note that the merged music structure may be complete, although not ground.

Time Operators

Time operators compute temporal properties of music structures. The most useful time operators are those computing the start and clip points of a music structure with respect to its own time line and with respect to a context time line. Based on these operators other temporal properties of music structures can be computed, e.g. duration and their time span interval with respect to their own, or to a context, time line. The self-clip time of a music structure ms is written $\mathbf{clip}_{self}(ms)$; intuitively it is the latest point on the time line of ms at which one of its constituents clips. The self-start time of ms, written $\mathbf{start}_{self}(ms)$ is similarly defined; the duration, written $\mathbf{duration}(ms)$, is their difference. For instance, let MS be ([a,5]@-20 ([b,10]@5 [a,5]@2)@8). Then $\mathbf{clip}_{self}(MS) = 23$ and $\mathbf{start}_{self}(MS) = -20$; the duration is 43. For the music structure MS presented in Musical Concatenation for describing Figure 1,

$$\mathbf{start}_{self}(MS) = -20, \ \mathbf{clip}_{self}(MS) = 80, \ \mathbf{duration}(MS) = 100$$

The $\mathbf{start}_{self}$ and $\mathbf{clip}_{self}$ functions provide bottom-up temporal analysis of a music structure. One very intuitive way to view this is to imagine "flattening" a music structure into a set of time stamped elementary music structures. The self-start of a music structure is just the minimum of the time stamps in the flattened version; the self-clip is the maximum sum of the time stamp and duration over all elements of the flattened version. Detailed definitions appear at the end of the chapter.

We may now discuss $\mathbf{clip}(ms_1, ms_2)$ and $\mathbf{start}(ms_1, ms_2)$, the more useful relative clip and start times for a music structure ms_1 that occurs within ms_2. (These are given plain names since they turn out to be more useful; they represent a top-down temporal analysis.) This is not quite as simple as we might expect. As in the example above, a music structure may occur more than once in a larger music structure, and each such occurrence has a clip and start time relative to the overall structure. Therefore, $\mathbf{clip}(ms_1, ms_2))$ and $\mathbf{start}(ms_1, ms_2)$ each yield a list of time points, one for every occurrence of ms_1 in ms_2.

In the previous example, $\mathbf{clip}([a,5], MS) = \{-15 \ 15\}$ and $\mathbf{start}([a,5], MS) = \{-20 \ 10\}$. Of course, the first argument can be composite: For example,

$$\mathbf{start}(([b,10]@5 \ [a,5]@2), TS) = \{10\}.$$

For the music structure MS describing Figure 1,

$\mathbf{start}(MS_1, MS) = \{-20\} \quad \mathbf{clip}(MS_1, MS) = \{25\}$
$\mathbf{start}(MS_2, MS) = \{-1\} \quad \mathbf{clip}(MS_2, MS) = \{50\}$

Intuitively, to compute $\mathbf{start}(ms_1, ms_2)$, we flatten ms_2 "just enough" so that all occurrences of ms_1 appear as list elements of the partially flattened version. The relative start time is then just a set of sums of the time stamps and self-start times of occurrences of ms_1 in the partially flattened version of ms_2. The corresponding definition for relative clip is obvious.

The **interval** function computes a set of pairs of time points that describe intervals during which a given music structure is "playing" within another music structure. For the example above, **interval**([a,5],MS) = {-20 -15} {10 15}. This function is definable from **start** and **clip**. The complete formal definitions for **start, clip, flatten,** and **interval** are straightforward and presented at the end of the chapter.

Properties of Music Structures

We distinguish four properties of music structures, according to the four combinations of explicit/implicit with partial/complete. An *explicit music structure* is one that explicitly specifies the sound properties (i.e., those included in the sound objects) and the temporal combination. (The notion of explicit specification is closely related to Levesque's vivid representation [Levesque 1986]). An *implicit specification* is one where some processing is needed to find out the denoted structured piece. For example, a music piece described as the transposition of another piece, or as the merge of two other pieces, or with a duration component that is implicitly given as the duration of some elementary piece is implicitly specified. A *complete description* is one where the denoted music piece is fully specified by the description. For example, in analysis or in plain music processing, this probably is the typical case. In composition or in studies in music perception, it is important to be able to partially describe a music piece. *Partial descriptions* are also used to specify musical patterns.

The four properties of music structures imply different processing methods. Complete music structures fully specify the denoted structured music piece. Hence, their properties can be computed, and they can be flattened and dispatched for playback. Partial music structures require further inference of the missing information. This can be done either by the user or by the system. Explicit music structures support fast processing, as queries can be directly answered, while implicit structures require preprocessing. Preprocessing of complete implicit structures might yield explicit structures; preprocessing of partial implicit structures is more involved, as not all implicit connections can be computed.

Determining whether a music structure is explicit or implicit is easy: For elementary music structures, each sound object property and the duration component should be specified by an appropriately typed symbol. For composite music structures, it depends on the constructing operators. Operators, whose meaning is directly given in the music structures semantical process (e.g., the concatenation operators), yield explicit music structures. Music structures that are not constructed from such operators are implicit. Determining the complete/partial property is more involved, as it depends on the semantics of the constructing operators. Certainly, a ground music structure is complete, but a nonground music structure can be complete as well (e.g., the merge of two, partial, music structures, denoting a durationless music structure and a rhythmic pattern).

Extensions to Music Structures

User Defined Functions (Lambda-Abstraction and Naming Mechanism)

At this point, our construction lacks a capability that no programmer would give up: the ability to define transformations of music structures. This can be obtained by adding a function definition mechanism (the λ-abstraction and β-reduction of the λ-calculus) or, in a more restricted way, by the addition of a naming mechanism. A round, for example, was described by the pattern $(ms@t\ ms@\mathbf{f}(ms))$. A user might want to define a new function round$(ms,t) = (ms@t\ ms@\mathbf{f}(ms))$. Then its application (β-reduction) to a given music structure MS and a given time term t_0 yields the round $(\text{MS}@t_0\ \text{MS}@\mathbf{f}(\text{MS}))$. The particular language used for function definitions can borrow from the implementation language. User defined functions are a powerful machinery. A naming mechanism (like a restricted assignment) is a "practical" replacement for user defined functions. It can be understood as syntactic sugar or a "macro operation," where a name should always be replaced by the music structure that it stands for. We have already used this option in previous sections.

Attributed Music Structures

The music structures described so far can account for hierarchical organization of the sound objects. But a music piece includes additional information, like, composer name, piece name, key signature, performance instructions, etc. One way to account for this information is to allow the sound object in elementary music structures to denote any musical object, such as "⌢" (fermata), "·" (staccato), "|" (bar line), text, etc. For example, a fermata over a music structure MS would be MS [⌢ , $\mathbf{f}(\mathbf{duration}(\text{MS}))$] where $\mathbf{f}$ is a time function (the duration of the fermata depends on the duration of MS); if MS is to be played with staccato, this can be denoted by MS |[. , $\mathbf{duration}(\text{MS})$]; if the key signature of MS is G# and is not embedded in MS (the G's in MS are written as G ♮ whenever G# is meant), this can be described by MS [(key-sgn G#), $\mathbf{duration}(\text{MS})$]; bar lines can be used with duration 0. Alternatively, the additional information can be considered as attributes. This would yield a new data structure that can be called an *attributed music structure*, which is a pair of a music structures associated with a set of attributes or attribute-value pairs. An attribute is just a name (denoted, below, with an underscore); a value can be anything. For example, a fermata over a music structure MS would yield the attributed music structure < MS, (*fermata*) >; a phrase by the name of "MS," described under the key signature G# and played legato and with crescendo, would yield the attributed music structure < MS, ((*name*, First-motif), (*key-sgn*, G#), *legato*, (*dynamics*, crescendo)) >. Attributed music structures also can include theoretical information such as the scale of a piece, chord analysis, etc.

The two options seem equal as far as expressive power or efficiency is concerned, and the selection between them is more a matter of taste. The first option is in the same line as the Time Structures representation (of which Music Structures form a special case, see [Balaban & Murray 1990]), since in Time Structures the atemporal (durationless) objects can be just anything atemporal. However, the second option seems to yield a more concise description, and to emphasize the distinction between the sound objects themselves from information about them. In the Music Structures–based music workstation, currently under development at Ben-Gurion University, the second option was adopted. The example in the next section also follows the second option.

An Example: Allemande, Partita No. 2, by J. S. Bach

This description by a complete, implicit music structure demonstrates the use of music structures for analytical or plain music processing purposes. We describe the first phrase (roughly, first line) trying to provide a full, somewhat extravagant, account of rhythmic and melodic analyses. The description is complete since the denoted music piece is fully specified; it is implicit since it is given in terms of music operators such as transpose and merge. The sound objects assumed by this description consist of the pitch property alone. Hence, rhythmic patterns are partial music structures (variable sound expressions). The phrase extends from markpoints A to B; its components are marked after their names in the analysis below (Figure 12).

The Overall Context, i.e., the Allemande Has the Following Attributes Information: ((*context* PARTITA2) (*key-sgn* Bb Eb Ab) (meter 4/4)). Being a bottom up description, the music structure ALLEMANDE is yet unknown.

The rhythmic pattern $\sqrt{}$ can be denoted as follows:
THREE_16 ::= $[p_1, \frac{1}{16}]$—$[p_2, \frac{1}{16}]$—$[p_3, \frac{1}{16}]$ with no associated attributes information. Note that p_1, p_2, p_3 are three different variables. The rhythmic pattern $\sqrt{}$ can be denoted by FIVE_16 ::= $[p_1, \frac{1}{16}]$—$[p_2, \frac{1}{16}]$—$[p_3, \frac{1}{16}]$—$[p_4, \frac{1}{16}]$—$[p_5, \frac{1}{16}]$ with no associated attributes information. The two rhythmic patterns can be combined together to form: RHYTHM1 ::= ((THREE_16—FIVE_16)@$(-\frac{3}{16})$) which denotes the pattern $\sqrt{}$ $\sqrt{}$ starting at time point $-\frac{3}{16}$.

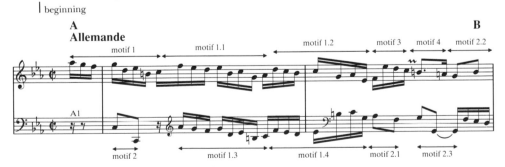

Figure 12. The First Phrase of the Allemande, from Bach's Second Piano Partita.

The melodic line (Figure 13) can be denoted by the durationless music structure 3NOTES1 ::= [1A♮, d_1]—[1G♮, d_2]—[1F♮, d_3] followed by the attributes information ((*context* ALLEMANDE)), which points to ALLEMANDE as including, among other context features, the key signature. Note that all durations are left unspecified.

The melodic line (Figure 14) can be denoted by the durationless music structure: 5NOTES1 ::= [1G♮, d_1]—[1D♮, d_2]—[1E♮, d_3]—[0B♮, d_4]—[1C♮, d_5] followed by the attributes information ((*context* ALLEMANDE) (*override-key-sign* B♮)), which states that ALLEMANDE is the context and the Bb in the inherited key signature is overridden by B♮.

The horizontal combination of the melodic lines 3NOTES1 and 5NOTES1 yields the horizontal durationless music structure NOTES1 ::= ((3NOTES1—5NOTES1) @(-$\frac{3}{16}$)) with no attributes information. It denotes the melodic line shown in Figure 15.

Now NOTES1 and RHYTHM1 can be merged, yielding the motif MOTIF1 ::= **merge**(NOTES1, RHYTHM1) whose denotation is given in Figure 16.

The next motif (Figure 17) can be obtained from MOTIF1 by a diatonic-shift, two steps downward: MOTIF1.1 ::= **diatonic-shift**(MOTIF1, -2) with the attributes information ((*context* ALLEMANDE) (*override-key-sign* B♮)). The third motif (Figure 18) would be MOTIF1.2 ::= **diatonic-shift**(MOTIF1.1, -2) with the same context information as MOTIF1.1.

Figure 13.

Figure 14.

Figure 15.

The first motif, played by the left hand (Figure 19) would be MOTIF1.3 ::= **transpose-down**(MOTIF1,(1, 0,0)). (1,0,0) denotes an octave interval). Similarly, MOTIF1.4 is MOTIF1.4 ::= **transpose-down**(MOTIF1.1, (1,0,0)). The rhythmic pattern ♪♪ is described by TWO_8 ::= $[p_1, ⅛]$—$[p_2, ⅛]$. The motif in Figure 20 would be MOTIF2 ::= **merge**([-1C♮, d_1]—[-2C♮, d_2], TWO_8); MOTIF2.1 (Figure 21) would be MOTIF2.1 ::= **merge**([-1A♮, d_1]—[-1F♮, d_2], TWO_8); MOTIF2.2 (Figure 22)

Figure 16.

Figure 17.

Figure 18.

would be MOTIF2.2 ::= merge([1G♮, d_1]—[1B♮, d_2], TWO_8) with the attributes information ((*context* ALLEMANDE) (*override-key-sgn* B♮)); and MOTIF 2.3 (Figure 23) is MOTIF2.3 ::= **stretch-last**(**transpose-up**(MOTIF2, (0,4,0)), ¹⁄₁₆), where stretch-last is an operator that stretches the last note(s) of a music structure by the duration given as its second argument. The definition of stretch-last might depend directly on the canonical form or a last operator. "(0,4,0)" denotes a perfect fifth interval.

The third and fourth motives can be described similarly:

PHRASE1 ::=   (MOTIF1—MOTIF1.1—MOTIF1.2—MOTIF3—MOTIF4—MOTIF2.2)
                ([REST, ¹⁄₁₆]—[REST, ⅛]—MOTIF2—[REST, ¹⁄₁₆]—
                MOTIF1.3—MOTIF1.4 ~ MOTIF2.1—MOTIF2.3)

followed by the attributes information ((*context* ALLEMANDE)). Note that MOTIF1.4 and MOTIF2.1 are connected by ~, the overlap horizontal concatenation mentioned in Overlap Horizontal Concatenation.

beginning

Figure 19.

Figure 20.

Figure 21.

Figure 22.

Figure 23

Syntax of the Music Structures Language

In correspondence with the three types in the domain of structured music pieces, there are three kinds of terms: *sound terms* that denote sound objects, *time terms* that denote temporal objects, and *music structures* that denote music pieces. All are terms of first order logic. Given: C = a set of constant symbols. S = {s,t,mp}—sort symbols, that correspond to the three types S (Sounds), T (Times), MP (Music Pieces). $0 \in C$—intended to denote the Zero object of T. NIL $\in$ C—intended to denote the empty piece in MP. V = a set of variables. F = a set of function symbols. [ ] $\in$ F— intended to describe elementary music pieces. $\bullet \in$ F—intended to describe composite music pieces. $\bullet$ is called the musical concatenation operator; it is the basic music structures operator. sgn = a mapping as follows: sgn: C $\rightarrow$ S, V $\rightarrow$ S, $F^{(n)} \rightarrow \underset{i=1}{\overset{n+1}{\times}}$ S, sgn(0) = t, sgn(NIL) = mp, sgn([ ]) = (s,t,mp), sgn($\bullet$) = (mp,t,mp,mp).

Terms: Defined as usual, with sort restrictions taken into account as follows: The sort of constants and variables is merely their signature; the sort of $f(t_1, \dots ,t_n)$ is the last element of the signature of f, provided that the ith element of the signature of f agrees with the sort of t_i, 1<i<n. Restriction on $\bullet$ terms: 1-st argument is not NIL. Note also that in the chapter we used $\bullet$ as an infix operator; i.e., we wrote $(ms_1@t \bullet ms_2)$ instead of $\bullet$ (ms_1, t, ms_2).

Definition.   Music Structures are all terms of sort mp.

The following axioms characterize the relationship between $\bullet$ and [ ], the intended meaning of all sort mp terms and the commutativity and idempotence properties of $\bullet$. Axiom ($\bullet$ [ ]) states that an elementary music structure ms and a composite one that includes ms as its single occurrence at time point 0 have the same denotation.

$$\forall\text{—p,d} ([p,d] = \bullet ([p,d], 0, \text{NIL})) \hspace{4cm} (\bullet[])$$

Axiom ($\bullet$mp) states that the denotation of every sort mp term is that of some $\bullet$ term:

$$\forall\text{—ms} ((\text{sgn}(ms)=mp \wedge ms \neq \text{NIL}) \Rightarrow \exists ms_1, ms_2, t (ms = \bullet (ms_1, t, ms_2))) \hspace{1cm} (\bullet\text{mp})$$

Note that this $\bullet$ term is unique up to repetitions and commutativity.
Idempotence:

$$\forall\text{—}ms_1, t_1, ms \bullet (ms_1, t_1, \bullet (ms_1, t_1, ms)) = \bullet (ms_1, {}_1 1, ms) \hspace{2cm} (\bullet\text{idp})$$

Commutativity:

$$\forall\text{—}ms_1, t_1, ms_2, t_2, ms_3 \hspace{7cm} (\bullet\text{cmt})$$
$$\bullet (ms_1, t_1, \bullet (ms_2, t_2, ms_3)) = \bullet (ms_2, t_2, \bullet (ms_1, t_1, ms_3))$$

The semantics of the music structures language directly defines the intended meaning of NIL, [ ], and $\bullet$ terms. The intended meaning of all other mp terms is defined in terms of these "interpreted symbols." For example, we might have () = NIL, introducing additional notation for the empty piece, or HALFNOTE = [note, ½], introducing a "name" for all half notes.

The idempotence property is controversial. It states that repeated occurrences

Figure 24.

(time stamped music structures) can be omitted, i.e., that duplicating an occurrence does not change the denotation. But this assumption seems to ignore a common phenomenon like duplicating notes, as in Figure 24.

We feel that the issue should be determined on philosophical grounds. With the view that music is a temporal phenomenon per se, every occurrence is unique. In the duplicated note case it means that it is not exactly the same note that occurs simultaneously. But, if only the pitch and duration properties of a note are captured, then it is the same note after all! We prefer to leave this issue open for future discussions.

Music Structures Operators

1) **start**$_{self}$, **clip**$_{self}$

    For primitive music structures, the time functions self-clip, duration, and self-start are defined by the equations

    $\mathbf{start}_{self}([p,d]) = 0$

    $\mathbf{clip}_{self}([p,d]) = d = \mathbf{duration}([p,d])$

    $\mathbf{start}_{self}(\text{NIL}) = \infty$

    $\mathbf{clip}_{self}(\text{NIL}) = -\infty$

    For a composite music structure MS = $(\text{ms}_1 @ t_1 \bullet \text{ms}_2)$ we have

    $\mathbf{start}_{self}(\text{MS}) = \min(\mathbf{start}_{self}(\text{ms}_1) + t_1, \mathbf{start}_{self}(\text{ms}_2))$

    $\mathbf{clip}_{self}(\text{MS}) = \max(\mathbf{clip}_{self}(\text{ms}_1) + t_1, \mathbf{clip}_{self}(\text{ms}_2))$

2) duration

    $\mathbf{duration}(\text{MS}) = \mathbf{clip}_{self}(\text{MS}) - \mathbf{start}_{self}(\text{MS})$

3) start, clip

    The relative time functions are the **start** and **clip** functions; each takes two music structures as arguments.

    $\mathbf{start}(\text{MS}, \text{NIL}) = \mathbf{clip}(\text{MS}, \text{NIL}) = \Phi$

    $\mathbf{start}([p_1,d_1], [p_2,d_2]) = \mathbf{clip}([p_1,d_1], [p_2,d_2]) = \Phi$

    $\qquad\qquad\qquad\qquad$ if $[p_1,d_1]$ does not match $[p_2,d_2]$

    $\mathbf{start}((\text{MS}_1 @ t_1 \bullet \text{MS}_2), [p,d]) = \mathbf{clip}((\text{MS}_1 @ t_1 \bullet \text{MS}_2), [p,d]) = \Phi$

    $\mathbf{start}(\text{MS}, \text{MS}) = (\mathbf{start}_{self}(\text{MS}))$ MS ≠ NIL

    $\mathbf{clip}(\text{MS}, \text{MS}) = (\mathbf{clip}_{self}(\text{MS}))$ MS ≠ NIL

Otherwise,

start (MS, ($MS_1@t_1 \bullet MS_2$)) =
$\qquad$ **union** ($\oplus$ (t_1, **start**(MS, MS_1)), **start**(MS, MS_2))

clip (MS, ($MS_1@t_1 \bullet MS_2$)) =
$\qquad$ **union** ($\oplus$ (t_1, **clip**(MS, MS_1)), **clip**(MS, MS_2))

where $\oplus$ produces a set by adding its first argument to each member of its second argument.

4) Interval

The interval function takes the same parameters as start and clip and returns a set of pairs. Each pair corresponds to the start and clip times of an occurrence of the first argument within the second.

interval(MS, NIL) = Φ
interval ($[p_1,d_1]$, $[p_2,d_2]$) = Φ $\qquad$ if $[p_1,d_1]$, does not match $[p_2,d_2]$

interval ($(MS_1@t_1$ o+ $MS_2)$, $[p,d]$) = Φ
interval (MS, MS) = ((**start**$_{self}$(MS) **clip**$_{self}$(MS))) MS $\neq$ NIL

Otherwise,

interval (MS, ($MS_1@t_1 \bullet MS_2$)) =
$\qquad$ **union** ($\oplus$ (t_1, **interval** (MS, MS_1)), **interval** (MS, MS_2))

5) —, |

Horizontal and vertical concatenation can be defined in terms of musical concatenation as follows:

MS_1—MS_2—...—$MS_n \bullet MS_{tail}$ = $(MS_1@0\ MS_2@t_2...MS_n@t_n \bullet MS_{tail})$
$\qquad$ iff **clip**$_{self}$ (MS_i) + t_i = **start**$_{self}$ (MS_{i+1}) + t_{i+1} $1 \le i \le$ n-1

If MS_{tail} is NIL, it is omitted. Note that the commutativity of $\bullet$ does not extend to "—." In general, within a set of equal $\bullet$ expressions, at most one expression satisfies the definition of —.

MS_i | MS_2|...|$MS_n \bullet MS_{tail}$ = ($MS_i@t_1\ MS_2@t_2...MS_n@t_n \bullet MS_{tail}$)
$\qquad$ iff **start**$_{self}$ (MS_i) + t_i = 0 $1 \le i \le$ n

6) Flatten

flatten(MS) = **relative-flatten** (MS,0)
relative-flatten ($[p,d]$,t) = ($[p,d]@t$)
relative-flatten ($(MS_i@t_i \bullet MS_2)$, t) =
$\qquad$ **union**(**relative-flatten** (MS_i,t_i+t), **relative-flatten** (MS_2,t))

Conclusion

In this chapter we have described a representation formalism that concentrates on the hierarchy and time aspects in music. We have shown that the formalism supports partial or complete and implicit or explicit descriptions. An account for additional aspects of music can be built on top of the music structures language via the attributes' mechanism.

We are now in the process of extending the music structures representation into object-oriented music structures (OOMS), which are an elaboration of the attributes' mechanism described here. In OOMS, every music structure is an object, whose description is given by its attributes and methods. The content of an object is given by the music structure it stands for. The hierarchical structure of music structures induces a partial ordering of the objects in OOMS; inheritance of attributes and methods is defined along this ordering.

It seems that the music structures language provides an adequate account for the Music-piece concept, since it supports complex, possibly partial, descriptions of this notion without being overrestrictive. This characteristic results from concentrating on the essential operation of grouping over time (musical concatenation) without making any other assumptions about the "grouped" objects. We believe that this language can be used as an underlying representation framework in explorations of music and music activities and is also appropriate for standardizing music representation. We have started building a music workstation based on the music structures model [Balaban 1988b]. It is now being extended to account for OOMS. The workstation is planned as a kernel system that can, later on, be extended to support research in various directions, such as composition, tutoring, and analysis.

References

[Anderton 1987] C. Anderton, *MIDI for Musicians*, Amsco Publications, 1987.

[Balaban 1983] M. Balaban, "Towards a General Computer Study of Western Tonal Music—I: Level of Representation and Most Basic Concepts," Technical Report 83–11, SUNY Albany, Department of Computer Science, 1983.

[Balaban 1986] M. Balaban, "A Formal Basis for Research in Theories of Western Tonal Music— an Artificial Intelligence Approach," *Communication and Cognition—Artificial Intelligence, Special Issue on Cognitive Musicology*, Laske, O., (ed), vol. 3(3), pp. 211–268, 1986.

[Balaban 1987b] M. Balaban, "CSM: A Computer Basis for a General, Formal Study of Western Tonal Music," *Proceedings, the First Annual Artificial Intelligence & Advanced Computer Technology Conference/EAST*, pp. 197213, Atlantic City, NJ, 1987.

[Balaban 1988b] M. Balaban, "A Music Workstation Based on Multiple Hierarchical Views of Music," *Proceedings, ICMC-88*, pp. 56–65, Cologne, West Germany, 1988.

[Balaban 1988a] M. Balaban, "The TTS Language for Music Description," *International Journal of Man-Machine Studies*, vol. 28, pp. 505–523, 1988.

[Balaban & Murray 1989] M. Balaban and N.V. Murray, "The Logic of Time Structures: Temporal and Nonmonotonic Features," *Proceedings, IJCAI-89*, pp. 1285–1290, Detroit, Michigan, 1989.

[Balaban & Murray 1990] M. Balaban and N.V. Murray, "Time Structures: Hierarchical Representation for Temporal Knowledge," Technical Report FC–TR-027 MCS319, Department of Mathematics and Computer Science, Ben-Gurion University, Israel, 1990.

[Balaban 1991] M. Balaban, *Music Description Languages,* 1991. In *Encyclopedia of Microcomputers,* Marcel Dekker Inc.

[Blombach 1976] A.K. Blombach, "A Conceptual Framework for the Use of the Computer in Music Analysis," Ph.D. Dissertation, The Ohio State University, 1976.

[Brook 1970] B.S. Brook, (ed), *Musicology and t he Computer,* The City University of New York Press, New York, 1970.

[Buxton 1978] W. Buxton, "Design Issues in the Foundation of a Computer-based Tool for Music Composition," Tech. Rep. CSRG-912, Computer Systems Research Group, Univ. of Toronto, Toronto, Ontario, Canada, 1978.

[Buxton et al. 1978] W. Buxton, W. Reeves, R. Baecker, and L. Mezei, "The Use of Hierarchy and Instance in a Data Structure for Computer Music," *Computer Music Journal,* vol. 2(4), pp. 10–20, 1978.

[Byrd 1974] D. Byrd, "A System for Music Printing by Computer," *Computers and the Humanities,* vol. 8, 1974.

[Byrd 1977] D. Byrd, "An Integrated Computer Music Software System," *Computer Music Journal,* vol. 1(2), pp. 55–60, 1977.

[Cointe & Rodet 1983] P. Cointe and X. Rodet, "FORMES: A New Object-Language for Managing of Hierarchy of Events," Internal Report, Institut de Recherche et de Coordination Acoustique Musique, Paris, 1983.

[Dannenberg et al. 1986] R.B. Dannenberg, P. McAvinney, and D. Rubine, "Arctic: A Functional Language for Real Time Systems," *Computer Music Journal,* vol. 10(4), pp. 67–78, 1986.

[Droman 1983] D. Droman, *Exploring MIDI The Musical Instrument Digital Interface,* IMA Publications, North Hollywood, CA, 1983.

[Ebcioglu 1986] K. Ebcioglu, "An Expert System for Chorale Harmonization," *Proceedings, AAAI-86,* pp. 784–788, Philadelphia, PA.

[Erickson 1975] R.F. Erickson, "The DARMS Project: A Status Report," *Computers and the Humanities,* vol. 9(6), pp. 291–298, 1975.

[Erickson 1977] R.F. Erickson, "MUSICOMP 76 and the State of DARMS," *College Music Symposium,* vol. 17(1), pp. 90–101, 1977.

[Frankel et al. 1976] R.E. Frankel, S.J. Rosenschein, and S.W. Smoliar, "A LISP-Based System for the Study of Schenkerian Analysis," *Computers and the Humanities,* vol. 10, pp. 21–32, 1976.

[Frankel et al. 1978] R.E. Frankel, S.J. Rosenschein, and S.W. Smoliar, "Schenker's Theory of Tonal Music—Its Explication Through Computational Processes," *Int. J. Man-Machine Studies,* vol. 10, pp. 121–138, 1978.

[Gourlay 1986] J.S. Gourlay, "A Language for Music Printing," CACM, vol. 29(5), pp. 388–401, 1986.

[Hamel 1984] K. Hamel, *Musprint Manual,* Triangle Resources, Cambridge, MA, 1984.

[Hamel et al. 1987] K. Hamel, B. Pennycook, B. Ripley, and E. Blevis, "A Functional Approach to Composition," Proceedings of the 19 87 *International Computer Music Conference,* pp. 33–39, Urbana, IL, 1987.

[IMA 1983] International MIDI Association, *MIDI Musical Instrument Digital Interface Specification 1.0,* International MIDI Association, North Holywood, 1983.

[Kassler 1977] M. Kassler, "Explication of the Middleground of Schenker's Theory of Tonality," *Miscellanea Musicologica*, vol. 9, pp. 72–81, 1977.

[Laske 1972] O. Laske, "On Problems of Performance Model for Music," Technical Report, Utrecht: Institute of Sonology, 1972.

[Laske 1975] O. Laske, "Introduction to a Generative Theory of Music," *Sonological Reports*, vol. 16, Utrecht: Institute of Sonology, 1975.

[Leman 1986] M. Leman, "A Process Model for Musical Listening Based on DH-Networks," *Communication and Cognition—Artificial Intelligence, Special Issue on Cognitive Musicology*, Laske, O., (ed), vol. 3(3), pp. 225–240, 1986.

[Lerdahl & Jackendoff 1983] F. Lerdahl and R. Jackendoff, *A Generative Theory of Tonal Music*, The MIT Press, Cambridge, Mass, 1983.

[Levesque 1986] H.J. Levesque, "Making Believers Out of Computers," *AI*, vol. 30(1), pp. 81–108, 1986.

[Lidov & Gabura 1973] D. Lidov and J. Gabura, "A Melody Writing Algorithm Using a Formal Language Model," *Computer Studies in the Humanities and Verbal Behavior*, vol. 4(3/4), pp. 138–148, 1973.

[Loy 1985] G. Loy, "Musicians Make a Standard: The MIDI June 6, 1991—49—Phenomenon," *Computer Music Journal*, vol. 9(4), pp. 8–26, 1985.

[Loy & Abbott 1985] G. Loy and C. Abbott, "Programming Languages for Computer Music Synthesis, Performance and Composition," *ACM Computing Surveys*, vol. 17(2), pp. 235–266, 1985.

[Maxwell & Ornstein 1983] J.T. Maxwell and S.M. Ornstein, "Mockingbird: A Composer's Amanuensis," CSL-83-2, Xerox Corporation, Palo Alto, CA, 1983.

[Miller 1985] J. Miller, "Personal Composer," *Computer Music Journal*, vol. 9(4), pp. 27–37, 1985 .

[Minsky 1981] M. Minsky, "Music, Mind and Meaning," *Computer Music Journal*, vol. 5(3), pp. 28–44, 1981.

[Pennycook 1985] R.W. Pennycook, "Computer Music Interfaces: A Survey," *ACM Computing Surveys*, vol. 17(2), pp. 267–289, 1985.

[Roads 1983] C. Roads, "Interactive Orchestration Based on Score Analysis," *Proceedings of t he 1983 International Computer Music Conference*, Venice, Italy, 1983.

[Roads 1985] C. Roads, "Research in Music and Artificial Intelligence," *ACM Computing Surveys*, vol. 17(2), pp. 163–190, 1985.

[Rodet & Cointe 1984] X. Rodet and P. Cointe, "FORMES: Composition and Scheduling of Processes," *Computer Music Journal*, vol. 8(3), pp. 32–50, 1984.

[Roedermacher 1983] M. Rademacher, "Plato: A Composer's Idea of a Language," *Computer Music Journal*, vol. 7(1), pp. 11–20, 1983.

[Smith 1973] L.C. Smith, "Editing and Printing Music by Computing," *Journal of Music Theory*, vol. 17(2), 1973.

[Smith 1976] L.C. Smith, "SCORE—A Musician's Approach to Computer Music," *Journal of the Audio Engineering Society*, vol. 20 (1), pp. 7–14, 1976.

[Smoliar 1971] S.W. Smoliar, "A Parallel Processing Model of June 6, 1991—50—Musical Structures," Rep. AI TR-242, Dept. of Computing and Information Science, MIT, Cambridge, Mass, 1971.

[Smoliar 1976] S.W. Smoliar, "An Approach to Music Theory Through Computational Linguistics," *Journal of Music Theory*, pp. 105–131, Spring 1976.

[Smoliar 1980] S.W. Smoliar, "A Computer Aid for Schenkerian Analysis," *Computer Music Journal*, vol. 4(2), pp. 41–59, 1980.

[Winograd 1968] T. Winograd, "Linguistics and the Computer Analysis of Tonal Harmony," *Journal of Mu sic Theory*, vol. 12 , pp. 2–49, Spring 1968.

[Yavelow 1985] C. Yavelow, "Music Software for the Apple Macintosh," *Computer Music Journal*, vol. 9(3), pp. 52–67, 1985.

[Yavelow 1986] C. Yavelow, "MIDI and Apple Macintosh," *Computer Music Journal*, vol. 10(3), pp. 11–47,

Abstract

CALM is a programming language design exercise. It is specifically targeted for writing programs that analyze or generate musical compositions (in the form of symbolic descriptions of acoustical events, such as a score), and that do so in a manner that allows for the individual methodologies of composers. This chapter establishes the general context of CALM in terms of its motivations, sources, and design criteria. As well, it communicates some of the initial design ideas that we expect to be of general interest. This chapter first appeared as part of a Workshop on AI and Music. Here, the chapter is presented as it appeared in the Workshop proceedings, with some very few corrections and the addition of some comments about the research that succeeds it added at the end. At the present time, CALM is not implemented, but a small prototype of a composition analysis system has been built based on ideas that have evolved from this work. This chapter is, to our knowledge, the first to incorporate notions of types in structured representations of music. As such, it is primarily of historical interest in the development of the literature on AI and Music. More detailed type-based approaches have since appeared. Those in the "to-type" camp of the structured representations of music literature argue that the types provide a natural way to encode music-theoretic notions by providing implicit associations between various musical parameters and various collections of transformations. Our later work has followed larger issues in the interaction between accounts of musical behaviour and their representations on a machine, in the areas of theories of meaning for music logics and case-based composition and analysis systems.

In this chapter, we describe our work on the design of the CALM, the Composition Analysis/Generation Language for Music. CALM is specifically targeted to express the analysis and generation of high level representations of musical compositions in a musically intuitive manner. By *high level representations*, we mean the symbolic encoding of large scale musical objects, such as phrases, motifs, or even complete compositional forms. By *generation*, we mean the process of creating or structuring such representations, and by *analysis*, we mean the process of extracting abstract descriptions or re-structuring the representations.

Chapter 6

Motivations, Sources, and Initial Design Ideas for CALM: A Composition Analysis/ Generation Language for Music

Eli B. Blevis, Michael A Jenkins, and Janice I Glasgow

Sources

This research is not without precedent. Some ten years ago, William Buxton published and spoke about the high level representation of the structure of music on a computer [Buxton, 78]. A number of other researchers have since addressed the high level music representation issue. Gareth Loy and Curtis Roads have surveyed and described the need for such research ([Loy, 87], [Loy and Abbott, 85], and [Roads, 85]). Some of the important contributors to applications of these ideas include Mira Balaban, author of the programming language IIS and a formalism called Music Structures [Balaban, 87A & 87B], David Cope, who has combined Schenkarian analysis with Augmented Transition Network grammars to create the EMI system of composition [Cope, 87], and Keith Hamel, author of the CDS system for musical composition [Hamel, et al., 87]. The present authors contributed to the CDS system, and consequently it has a strong influence on the approach used in the design of CALM.

CALM was developed as a language embedded within the Nial programming language ([Jenkins, 87A & 87B] and [Jenkins, et al., 88]). Additional programming language sources for this research included [DeGroot & Lindstrom, 85], [Glaser, et al., 84], [Cardelli & Wegner, 85], [Cousineau, et al., 85], and [Backus, 78].

Design Criteria and Motivations

The design criteria for CALM are the following:

- CALM is to be a computationally tractable programming language in the sense that it consists of a formally defined syntax and a mathematical semantics, and in the sense that it should be implementable on a machine and it should execute programs efficiently.

- Since composers often utilize analytic processes in the generation of new works, CALM should provide equally for analysis and generation of high level representations of music.

- Common Practice Notation (CPN) is primarily an explicit representation of time and pitch, and secondarily a representation of other interpretive features of a composition. CPN is therefore inappropriate for a variety of musics in which time and pitch may not be the most important aspects of the sound. Many music programming languages and systems have followed this practice. As an alternative to this tradition, CALM should treat all musical data uniformly. For example, durations and pitch should not be higher class objects than dynamics and timbre; one should be able to express computations about the timbral and dynamic objects in a composition, independently of their orientation in the time and pitch domains (For a general discussion of the problems of music notation, see [Cole, 74]).

- The computational paradigm used by CALM should be decided by the domain of music composition. This is a unique and complex domain. It differs from traditional programming language domains in that there are no problems for which correct solutions are sought, but only results that satisfy individual or sociocultural aesthetic criteria.

- In so far as there is no conflict with the previous point, CALM will make use of current ideas and trends in research-level programming languages; functional, declarative, and typed languages in particular.

- CALM should allow composers to model their individual methods and approaches to the composition process, rather than force composers to follow a prescribed method. Thus, the data structures of CALM should not be biased towards a particular representation of music, neither should its control structures be biased towards a particular method of structuring the representation.

- The representation of music and structuring operations used by CALM should be malleable in the sense that they should allow for multiple taxonomies of the same data. This criterion reflects the idea that analyses are probably not unique, and that several different taxonomies of the same musical material may be part of the composition process.

Conceptual Overview of CALM

There are many unresolved problems in the design of CALM. Nevertheless, we can give an informal conceptual framework for the language. We currently conceive of four basic components of CALM that correspond roughly to the components of any functional language.

Musical Parameters (Types) may be pre-defined or constructed by the composer/programmer. *Constructed types* (called Basic Types) are specified by the composer as a combination of a symbolic type and an interval type. *Symbolic Types* are (possibly infinite) collections of similar symbolic objects that correspond in computational terms to primitive data types and in musical terms to musical parameters, such as durations, pitch, attacks, dynamics, timbres, etc. An *Interval Type* is an everywhere defined relation between objects in a symbolic type. In the sections "Abstraction Operations (Generation by Example)" and "Types (Musical Parameters)," we will demonstrate that the interval types provide a musical inference mechanism that will allow us to treat event sequences (below) as examples for generating similar event sequences.

Events (Data Objects) are typed relational tuples that denote musical objects or classes of musical objects. Events may have explicit terms (constants), implicit terms (variables), and partially explicit terms (subtypes). Events can be combined to form lists called *event sequences.*.

Musical Transformations (Operations & Forms) are operations that may be applied to one or more event sequences. These may be primitive (pre-defined) or constructed by the composer/programmer. We currently consider that there are the following classes of primitive operations in CALM: polymorphic constructors that allow event sequences of mixed types to be combined; abstraction operations that allow event sequences to be treated as examples; constraint and non-deterministic selection operations that transform more general event sequences into less general ones; unification operations that define a notion of similarity and difference for event sequences; search operations that transform event sequences to abstractions (expressions involving operations) that describe them; and, input/output operations that make CALM ultimately useful for building music systems.

Meta-control expressions (Control Structures) describe computations involving event sequences and musical transformations. These are not well conceived in our research to date, and are not described further in this chapter. Meta-control expressions should allow for larger scale manipulation of event sequences and musical transformations.

Initial Design Ideas

Event Sequences (Musical Objects)

Musical objects are represented as Event Sequences. Event Sequences are ordered collections of tuples with terms of explicit type and an implicit abstraction mechanism. By explicit type, we mean that a symbol denoting type must be given for each term of a tuple. The motivations here are (1) clarity, (2) stating types explicitly is one method for inferring the kinds of operations that are associated with that type, and (3) instances of symbols for a type need not be unique to that type when the types are stated explicitly. The explicit abstraction mechanism will be described in the section "Abstraction Operations." In the event sequence notation

    <note,dur>:<C,4><E,4><G,4>

the syntax to the left of the ":" describes the type tuple of the event sequence. The components "note" and "dur" of the type tuple are called type identifiers. The syntax to the right of the ":" describes the event tuple sequence of the event sequence. Each object enclosed by angle brackets "<" and ">" is an event tuple, and each item of each tuple is a constant term that has the type of its corresponding type identifier in the type tuple. Thus, the symbols C, E, and G are constant terms of type note, and the symbol 4 is a constant term of type dur. An event sequence can contain other kinds of terms besides constants, but we do not consider these until a later section. Whenever an event sequence has only constant terms in its event tuple sequence, we say that it is a *ground event sequence.*

The following are all examples of event sequences and their notation as CALM expressions:

    <note.:<C#>
    <note,dur>:<C,4><E,4><G,4>
    <dyn,style>:<fff,rude><mf,dolce>
    <note,octave,dur,start,dyn>:<C,1,2,0,pp><Eb↓,1,4,0.25,pp><G,0,4,0.5,mf>

The last example corresponds to Figure 1, a musical example in Common Practice Notation (the "↓" symbol denotes a quarter tone shift down in pitch).The third example shows that it is easy to represent combinations of musical attributes in CALM without attaching them to note, start, or duration attributes; this would be difficult to represent in Common Practice Notation.

Figure 1. A Musical Example in Common Practice Notation.
The "↓" symbol denotes a quarter tone shift down in pitch.

Note that the event tuples are ordered positionally in an event sequence, but they are not ordered in time. Time ordering is accomplished by the presence of a type that denotes it:

    <note,dur,start>:<C,2,1.0><E,4,1.25><G,2,1.0>

The motivation for not ascribing time-dependent meaning to the ordering within an event sequence is that the representation is now sufficiently flexible to allow for the representation of musical parameters without having them be fixed in time. Thus, it is possible in CALM to express a concept of a specific collection of say, timbres. Note also that an event tuple can have only one occurrence of a given type (in order to allow for type inference), and that the ordering of terms within an event tuple is syntactic, not semantic:

<note,note,dur>:<C,C,2> is not an event sequence
<note,dur>:<C,2> is semantically equivalent to <dur,note>:<2,C>

In the case that an event sequence has a type tuple with only one component type identifier, we can omit the angle brackets, using square brackets instead to delimit an event sequence. Then,

[note : C D Eb F G Ab Bb C] is a shorthand notation for
<note>:<C><D><Eb><F><G><Ab><Bb><C>

Identifiers can be associated with event sequences. This is accomplished in a straightforward manner, for example:

let MajorTriad be [note : C E G]
let MinorTriad be [note : A C E]
let Dot be [dur : 4. 8]
let MajorScale be [note : C D E F G A B]

The general form of the definition construct is

let <identifier> be <event sequence>

Polymorphic Constructor Operations (Combining Musical Objects)

Polymorphic (defined for more than one type) constructor operations are used to form new event sequences from lists of event sequences. These operations allow event sequences of disjoint types and lengths to be combined. At the present time, we have defined only two operations of this class, the binary concatenation operator *o*, and its generalization, the combining operator *combine* that applies to lists of event sequences. The intent of the combine operator is to allow for a notion of treating musical fragments as patterns to be combined.

We can see the effect of combining two event sequences of like type tuples:

let MajorTriad be [note : C E G]
let MinorTriad be [note : A C E]
combine MajorTriad MinorTriad = [note : C E G A C E]

Combining two event sequences that are completely disjoint in their type tuples causes the shorter event sequence to be "distributed over" the longer one by filling with terms from the shorter one:

let Dot be [dur : 4. 8]
combine Dot MajorTriad = <dur,note>:<4.,C><8,E><4.,G

Filling with terms from the shorter event sequence makes "combine" a commutative operation (semantically).

combine MajorTriad Dot = <note,dur>:<C,4.><E,8><G,4.>

That is, the order of the arguments doesn't matter:

(combine MajorTriad Dot) = (combine Dot MajorTriad)

Combine associates the binary concatenation operator with items of a list of event sequence in right-to-left order (the decision about right-to-left order is arbitrary, and not necessarily final). When the type tuples of the event sequences to be combined share some type identifiers in common, but are not equivalent, the event sequences are coerced to be homogeneous in type by considering only the disjoint types, and then concatenated:

combine Dot MajorTriad MinorTriad
= Dot o (MajorTriad o MinorTriad)
= Dot o [note : C E G A C E]
= <dur,note>:<4.,C><8,E><4.,G><8,A>,4.,C><8,E>

combine MajorTriad MinorTriad Dot
= MajorTriad o (MinorTriad o Dot)
= MajorTriad o <note,dur>:<A,4.><C,8><E,4.>
= <note,dur>:<C,4.><E,8><G,4.><A,4.><C,8><E,4.>

We should note that there are potentially many other versions of the combine operator that combine musical patterns in different ways.

Abstraction Operations (Generation by Example)

Abstraction operations treat event sequences as examples from which similar event sequences are constructed. The binary apply operator "apply" is such an operation. To understand exactly how an event sequence can be treated as an example requires more details about how types are constructed in CALM. We proceed with some intuitive examples involving "apply," and then fill in some of the details in the next section on types.

In the following example, the "apply" operator is used to build a major triad on the note A:

let MajorTriad be [note : C E G]
MajorTriad apply [note : A] = [note : A C# E]

It can do so, because the type "note" has built into it an implicit abstraction mechanism (not notated, but inferred from the syntax) that musicians know as intervals; in simple terms, the distances between the notes of the event sequence MajorTriad are calculated and then added successively to the argument note,"A."

In the previous example, the event sequence associated with the identifier MajorTriad was applied to an event sequence with only a single event tuple. In the presence of an event sequence with more than one event tuple as right argument, "apply" builds similar sequences for each event tuple and combines them. For example,

MajorTriad apply [note : A B] = [note : A C# E B D# F#]

We can get the same effect from the expression:

combine (MajorTriad apply [note : A]) (MajorTriad apply [note :B])
= [note : A C# E B D# F#]

When the type tuples on either side of the "apply" operator share some types in common (but are not equivalent as sets), the result "applies" only to the types that are in common:

[dur : 4 3*4 3*4] apply <note,dur>:<C,8>
= [dur : 4 12 12] apply <note,dur>:<C,8>
= combine [note : C] [dur : 8 24 24]
= <note,dur>:<C,8><C,24><C,24>

In the preceding example, notice that the type "dur" also has an implicit abstraction mechanism that allows "apply" to infer a similar sequence of durations in the result as in the left argument. Here, the implicit mechanism used to calculate intervals for constant terms of type "dur" is ratio with fractions formed from the reciprocals of the arguments. The constant term "3*4" denotes in musical terms a duration of 1 of 3 in the time of 4, that is, $\frac{1}{12}$ of a beat.

In some cases, we would like "apply" to form its result based on an event tuple other than the first one in its left argument event sequence. We indicate this by placing the symbol "→" in front of the desired event tuple of the sequence:

let ATurn be [note : C# →D E D]
let AnotherTurn be [note : C# D E D]
ATurn apply [note : F] = [note : E → F G F]
AnotherTurn apply [note : F] = [note : F Gb Ab Gb]

The "→" symbol is called the *base indicator* of an event sequence, and the event tuple it modifies is called the *base event tuple* of the event sequence. In the absence of an explicit base indicator, the first event tuple of an event sequence is the base.

Types (Musical Parameters)

The types "note" and "dur" are pre-defined in CALM. Not all types are. We can write an event sequence with any type identifier and constant terms we please. For example,

Let Unusual be [glorp : pluck scrape]

We can use "Unusual" in CALM expressions involving the "combine" operator:

combine Unusual MajorTriad = <glorp,note>:<C,pluck><E,scrape><G,pluck>

However, if we try to use "Unusual" as the left argument of an "apply" expression, a CALM interpreter should return an error message:

[glorp : pluck scrape] apply [glorp : bow]
− ?don't know how to abstract <glorp>

We need to tell an interpreter what the implicit abstraction mechanism for "glorp" is before we can get a meaningful result from the "apply" operator. This is accomplished by writing a type definition expression type glorp is Circle [pluck,scrape,bow]

We now refine our terminology for types. The type "glorp" is called a basic type that consists of an interval type and a symbolic type. The last part of the definition is a list of symbols that are allowed as constant terms of basic type "glorp." The list is the symbolic type of "glorp."

The "Circle" is a pre-defined keyword that denotes a method of abstracting the constant terms; it is the interval type of "glorp." The Circle interval type is defined as circular positional difference for the ordered list of symbols in the symbolic types. It allows "apply" to infer that, for example, "scrape" is to "bow" as "bow" is to "pluck," based on the positions of these symbols in the list of symbolic types. There are other interval types besides "Circle," and we will elaborate on them later in this section. With the type definition for "glorp" in place, the interpreter yields a different evaluation:

[glorp : pluck scrape] apply [glorp : bow] = [glorp : bow pluck]

Types can be used before they are defined using a type definition, since they do more than prescribe how to abstract event sequences for the "apply" operator. The types prescribe how "combine" and operators like it can combine lists of event sequences. As well, their presence allows the CALM interpreter to be efficient, and allows the possibility for a CALM compiler in the future. After a type has been defined, or if it is pre-defined, it can be used by operators like "apply" to infer similar event sequences from example event sequences.

Some further examples illustrate the expressiveness of the type mechanism in CALM:

type start is Difference Reals
type dur is Ratio DurationSymbols
type dyn is Spectrum [ppp,pp,mp,mf,f,ff,fff]
type timbre is Spectrum [sweet,warm,bright]
type attack is Circle [pluck,strike,blow,bow]

The first definition states that basic type "start" has interval type "Difference" and symbolic type "Reals." This means that constant terms of type start are real numbers, and that we can treat the constant terms of type "start" in an event sequence as an example by finding the difference between them as real numbers. The definition of the basic type "dur" has the interval type "Ratio" that is defined as ratio for fractions; the symbolic type "DurationSymbols" are the strings that can be formed from integer symbols and the symbols "*" and ".". The duration symbols are easily interpreted as fractions in their conventional musical sense. The third definition has the interval type "Spectrum" that is defined as positional difference, and the last definition has the interval type "attack" that is defined as circular positional difference. In the latter case, we can infer that "pluck" follows "bow," whereas in the former case we cannot infer that "ppp" follows "fff."

The pre-defined interval type of "note" is rather more involved than the other interval types we have mentioned, but nonetheless, it is uniformly abstract. To include Western Tonal Music convention, we need an abstraction mechanism that will preserve the enharmonic symbols and allow for an arbitrary set of such symbols. The system we prefer is a generalization of one due to [Clements, 86]. Consequently, we have the "Clements" interval type, and its associated symbolic type is a quintuple: the first argument is a list of note name symbols; the second is a list of integer valued divisions of the octave corresponding to each note name; the third argument is an integer denoting the total number of divisions in an octave; the fourth argument is a list of enharmonic symbols; and the last argument is a list of shift values associated with each of the enharmonic symbols. The predefinition of "note" is

```
type <note,octave> is Clements
<{C,D,E,F,G,A,B}, [0,20,40,50,70,90,110], 120,
[bb,↓↓,b,↓,↑,#,↑↑,x] [-20,-15,-10,-5,5,10,15,20]>
```

The type definition that involves a type tuple "<note, octave>," rather than a single type identifier is permitted in CALM, but we will not present the details here. The CALM programmer can redefine the type <note, octave> to include arbitrary divisions of the octave and an arbitrary "grain" for the enharmonic symbols. The actual interval abstraction mechanism is encoded by our generalized version of a system due to Clements that preserves the enharmonic information in the conventional musical way (see [Clements, 86] and [Hamel, et. al., 87]). There is no requirement here to define pitches in this way. The interval type for "note" could just be "Circle" and the interval type for "octave" could just be "Spectrum," if we don't need, as ethnomusicologists say, the feature of preserving enharmonic symbols.

A formal treatment of the role of types in CALM is under preparation. The musical justification for this model of types is that it lets the composer/programmer use symbols freely; it makes the underlying computational mechanism implicit for inferring similarity between event sequences; it allows event sequences to be treated as examples; and it provides a uniform mechanism for inferring common musical effects, such as sequences or other transformations, in a way that is not restricted to pitches and durations.

Generalized Event Sequences (Constraints and Stochastic Selection)

So far in our discussion, we have only used event sequences that contain constant terms. A *generalized event sequence* is one that can as well contain variable terms or subtype terms. A *variable term* is one that denotes an arbitrary element of its symbolic type. We will say that any symbol beginning with the string "var" is a variable. A *subtype term* denotes an element of an explicit subset of its symbolic type. We notate it as a set with elements that are constant terms; for example, "{C, C#}" is a subtype term of the type "note."

The expression let ExtendedNotionOfATurn be [dyn : var1 →var2 var3 var2] defines a generalized event sequence that denotes the set of ground event sequences that have four event tuples, and that have equivalent terms of type "dyn" in the second and fourth event tuples.

The expression [dyn : {pp,mf} var1 fff] denotes another generalized event sequence that describes the set of ground event sequences that have three event tuples, and that have as the first term of type "dyn" either the constant "pp" or the constant "mf," and that have as the third term of type "dyn" the constant "fff."

The scope of an identifier denoting a variable term is the event sequence in which it appears. Then, the identifier "var1" in the event sequence [dur : 4. var1 var1] is distinct from the identifier "var1" in the event sequence [dur : 4. var2 var1].

We can use generalized event sequences everywhere that we used ground event sequences. For example, the "apply" operator can be used to build similar event sequences from generalized event sequences that it treats as examples:

Let ATurn be [note : {C,C#} →D {E,Eb} D]
ATurn apply [note : G#] = [note : {F#,Fx} →G# {A#,A} G#]

The "random" operation can be used to (non-deterministically) select a ground event sequence from the class of event sequences denoted by a generalized event sequence:

Let ATurn be [note : {C,C#} →D {E,Eb} D]
random ATurn = [note : C →D Eb D]

In this context, we say that the generalized event sequence is being used as an *aleatoric selector*. The non-determinism of the "random" operator and its use of generalized event sequences as aleatoric selectors yields a partial model of stochastic processes in CALM.

The binary "constrain" operation constrains the constant and subtype terms of its right argument to include only those constant symbols that appear in its left argument, if it can do so:

let MajorScale be [note : C D E F G A B]
Let ATurn be [note : {C,C#} →D {E,Eb} D]
(MajorScale apply [note : F#]) constrain (ATurn apply [note : G#])
= [note : F# G# A# B C# D# E# F#]
constrain [note : {F#,Fx} →G# {A#,A} G#]
= [note : F# →G# A# G#]

In musical terminology, the expression above is used to denote "create a turn on G# in the key of F# Major."

Unification Operations (Similarity and Difference)

The notion of generalized event sequences permits us to introduce the operations "generalize" and "issimilar" that rely on unification to support notions of similarity and generalization in CALM. Our use of unification is conventional in the sense of first-order unification under a theory of equality (see [Siekmann, 84] for a formal treatment, and [Subrahmanyam & You, 85] or [Kahn, 85] for informal treatments).

In musical terminology, we can think of the "generalize" operation as one that "gathers" musical objects we consider to be similar into generalizations that describe them as a class. In more immediate terminology, the "generalize" operation constructs generalized event sequences from lists of event sequences. At this time, we consider that the event sequences in the list must all be the same length for "generalize" to be defined (we return to this point below). "Generalize" is similar to the "combine" operation for equal-length arguments, except that it forms subtype terms from corresponding pairs of constant terms of the same type, and it may replace variable terms with constant or subtype terms:

    let SomeTurn be [note : C →D Eb D]
    let AnotherTurn be [note : C# →D E D]
    generalize SomeTurn AnotherTurn = [note : {C,C#} →D {Eb,E} D]

The sense of (equational) unification in the result above is that "SomeTurn" is unifiable (equivalent in meaning) with "AnotherTurn" if we are willing to agree that "C" or "C#" will serve equally as well as the constant term of type "note" in the first event tuple of the result, and that, similarly, "E" or "Eb" will serve equally as well as the constant term of type "note" in the third event tuple of the result.

In many cases, it will be desirable to use the "apply" operator to coerce an event sequence to the base event tuple of an event sequence with which it is to be generalized:

    let SomeTurn be [note : C →D Eb D]
    let StillAnotherTurn be [note : F# →G A G]

    generalize SomeTurn StillAnotherTurn
    = [note : {C,F#} →{D,G} {Eb,A} {D,G}]

    generalize SomeTurn (StillAnotherTurn apply [note : D])
    = generalize SomeTurn [note : C# D E D]
    = [note : {C,C#} →D {Eb,E} D]

The binary "issimilar" operation is a predicate that asks if its arguments can be generalized without creating subtype terms in event tuples of the result that do not occur in any of the corresponding event tuples of the arguments:

    let MyPattern be [dyn : {pp,mf} var1 fff var1]

    generalize MyPattern [dyn : pp mf fff var2] = [{pp,mf} mf fff mf]
    MyPattern issimilar [dyn : pp mf fff mf] = [truth-value : Truth]

    generalize MyPattern [dyn : pp mf fff p] = [dyn : { pp, mf} {p, mf} fff {p, mf}]
    MyPattern issimilar [dyn : pp mf fff p] = [truth-value : False]

    generalize MyPattern [dyn : fff mf fff mf] = [dyn : {pp,mf,fff} mf fff mf]
    MyPattern issimilar [dyn : fff mf fff mf] = [truth-value : False]

Notice that if E1 and E2 are any event sequences, then:

    E1 issimilar (generalize E1 E2) = [truth-value : Truth]

From a musical point of view, the idea that the "generalize" and "issimilar" operations are only defined for equal-length arguments is not a reasonable restriction on our notion of similarity and generalization, and merits further research. For example, we cannot yet express the musical notions of prolongation and truncation (patterns that match in non-corresponding subterms). In order to do so, we will have to develop a notion of variables that can be associated with event tuples or subsequences of event sequences.

Summary

In this chapter, we have described sources, motivations and design criteria for a programming language, CALM, that is specifically targeted for writing programs that encode music composition and analysis. We have as well reported on some of our initial design ideas for the language. In the remainder of this section, we summarize some of these ideas and point to areas of future research.

Event sequences, together with the primitive operations "apply," "combine," "random," and "constrain" allow us to write expressions that describe the generation of musical objects. The "generalize" and "issimilar" operations are analytic in nature, but we have not shown how they can be used to actually express analyses, or how the analysis and generation notions might interact. In order to argue that CALM provides equally for analysis and generation, we will have to include a notion of defined operations, search operations that extract defined operations, and control structures that provide the interaction.

Event sequences, together with our notion of types allows us to denote musical objects in a manner that is both extensible, and not dependent on any fixed notion of musical parameters or their interdependence.

Because of the type definition mechanism, event sequences are not biased towards any particular representation of music. We have not yet addressed the more difficult, if not unsolvable, issue of providing control structures that do not force CALM programmers to use a particular method of structuring event sequences.

In this work, we have tried to justify our design ideas in terms of musical practice, rather than conformance to established programming language ideas. The initial design ideas are in fact drawn from both functional and logic programming languages. In order to demonstrate that CALM is useful in musical practice, we will have to provide an implementation that includes sophisticated input/output operations that write and read event sequences to and from synthesizers, that graphically display event sequences and CALM expressions, and that allow CALM expressions to be graphically edited. Moreover, only users of the language can evaluate its success as a tool.

Succeeding Research

It is now two years since this chapter first appeared, and since then there have been many interesting developments in the AI and Music literature as well as in our own work. Other research concerned with adding types to structured representations of music has since appeared, most notably [Courtot, 89]. Also, Otto Laske has described "composition theory" as a research area under which this chapter on CALM falls comfortably [Laske, 89].

Our own research has followed a course that first attempted to establish a foundation for structured representations of music in terms of the meanings and constructions of logical formalisms. Proceeding in this manner caused an evolution in both the understanding and syntax of the data structures in CALM to those described in [Blevis, et. al.,89] as "associations." This work also raised the contentious issue of whether "Music Logics" are required or could be considered to have meanings in terms of Truth at all, given that it is not clear what it means for a passage of music or a compositional act to be "true."

On the more practical side, what CALM lacked was a paradigm for interpretation of the musical acts of composition and analysis. We suggest such a paradigm based upon a case-based reasoning procedure in [Blevis, 90] and [Blevis and Jenkins, 90]. In [Blevis, 90] we provide unification algorithms that are one solution to the "prolongation" and "truncation" problem described in this chapter on CALM in the section on unification.

Acknowledgments

For numerous discussions and advice about these ideas, we are indebted to Bruce W. Pennycook, Keith A. Hamel, Edmund Robinson, Colin Banger, Otto Laske, Mira Balaban, Christoph Lischka, and Marc Leman.

References

John Backus. 1978. Can Programming be Liberated from the von Neumann Style? *ACM Communications* 21(8). pp. 613–41.

Mira Balaban. 1987A. The TTS Language for Musical Description. SUNY at Albany. Technical Report No. 87–18.

Mira Balaban. 1987B. Music Structures: A Temporal Hierarchical Representation for Music. SUNY at Albany. Technical Report No. 8–27, and MusikoMetrika 2 1990, 2–54.

Eli Blevis. 1986. Queen's University M. Sc. Dissertation. Kingston, Canada. M. Sc. Thesis. Queen's University at Kingston.

Eli Blevis, Michael Jenkins, and Edmund Robinson. 1989. On Seeger's Music Logic. *Interface.* 18(1–2). pp. 9–31.

Eli Blevis and Michael Jenkins. 1990. A Computational Paradigm for Exploring Creative Musical Thought. Proceedings of the Second International Conference on Musical Structures and Information Technology. Marseille: Laboratoire Musique et Informatique de Marseille.

Eli Blevis. 1990. An Approach to Interactive Creative Reasoning Systems. Queen's University Ph. D. Dissertation. Kingston, Canada.

William Buxton. 1978. The Use of Hierarchy and Instance in a Data Structure for Computer Music. *CMJ* 2(4). pp. 10–9. And, in [Roads and Strawn, 85]:pp. 443–66. Luca Cardelli and Peter Wegner. 1985. On Understanding Types, Data Abstraction, and Polymorphism. *ACM Surveys* 17(4). pp. 471–522.

Peter Clements. 1986. A System for the Complete Enharmonic Encoding of Musical Pitches and Intervals. Proceedings ICMC-86. pp. 459–461.

H. Cole. 1974. *Sounds and Signs: Aspects of Musical Notation.* Oxford University Press. London.

David Cope. 1987. An Expert System for Computer-assisted Composition. *CMJ* 11(4). pp. 30–46. A shorter version appears in Proceedings ICMC-87. pp. 174–81. Guy Cousineau, Pierre-Louis Curien, and Bernard Robinet (Editors). 1985. *Combinators and Functional Programming Languages.* Anthology. Springer-Verlag L. N. C. S. No. 242.

Francis Curtot. 1989. Representation and Machine Learning for Musical Structures. Proceedings of the Second Workshop on AI and Music. Detroit, Michigan: IJCAI-89. pp. 72–87.

Doug DeGroot and Gary Lindstrom (Editors). 1985. *Logic Programming: Functions, Relations, and Equations. Anthology.* Prentice-Hall. Englewood Cliffs. Hugh Glaser, Chris Hankin, and David Till. 1984. *Principles of Functional Programming.* Prentice-Hall International, Inc. London.

Keith Hamel, Bill Ripley, Bruce Pennycook, and Eli Blevis. 1987. Composition Design System: A Functional Approach to Composition. Proceedings ICMC-87. pp. 33–9.

Michael Jenkins, Janice Glasgow, Eli Blevis, Elizabeth Hache, Raymond Chau, and Denise Lawson. 1988. The Nial AI Toolkit. Avignon, France: Proceedings of the Avignon '88 Eighth International Workshop on Expert Systems and Their Applications.

Michael Jenkins. 1987A. T*he Q'Nial Reference Manual: Release 1 Version 4.* Nial Systems Limited, Kingston.

Michael Jenkins. 1987B. Artificial Intelligence Toolkit for Q'Nial: Release 1 Version 4. Nial Systems Limited, Kingston.

Kenneth M. Kahn. 1985. Uniform: A Language Based upon Unification which Unifies (much of) Lisp, PROLOG, and Act 1. in [DeGroot & Lindstrom, 85]:pp. 411–440.

Otto Laske. 1989. Composition Theory: An Enrichment of Music Theory. *Interface* 18(1–2). pp. 45–60.

Gareth Loy. 1987. Compositional Algorithms and Music Programming Languages. UCSD Center for Music Experiment. Technical Report No. Q-037.

Gareth Loy and Curtis Abbott. 1985. Programming Languages for Computer Music Synthesis, Performance, and Composition. *ACM Surveys* 17(2). pp. 235–266.

Bruce Pennycook. 1985. Computer-Music Interfaces: A Survey. *ACM Surveys* 17(2). pp. 267–289.

Curtis Roads. 1985. Research in Music and Artificial Intelligence. *ACM Surveys* 17(2). pp. 163–90.

Curtis Roads and John Strawn (Editors). 1985. *Foundations of Computer Music. Anthology.* MIT Press. Cambridge, Mass.

John Roeder. 1987. A Declarative Model of Atonal Analysis. UBC School of Music at Vancouver. Unpublished Communication.

J. H. Siekmann. 1984. Universal Unification. in 7th International Conference on Automatic Deduction. Springer-Verlag. L. N. C. S. No. 170.

P. A. Subrahmanyam & Jia-Huai You. 1985. FUNLOG: A Computational Model Integrating Functional and Logic Programming. in [DeGroot & Lindstrom, 85]:pp. 157–200.

Abstract

Our work concerns the issue of representing and discovering musical structures in a computer assisted composition environment. We define a basic level language of typed terms for the representation of musical objects. Within this language, a composer can describe his/her own musical concepts. The system then plays a double role, regarding to assistance in composition. First, once the composer has defined some structures representing the musical objects, the system provides automatically new musical structures, useful for him. Second, once the composer/programmer has defined some methods aimed at the generation and manipulation of previously defined musical structures, the system can learn other methods from examples of their behaviour. Our tool is currently evaluated by composers working at IRCAM.

Chapter 7

Logical Representation and Induction for Computer Assisted Composition

Francis Courtot

Our motivation is to build a Computer Assisted Composition tool that would not be entirely devoted to a single composer's approach. We are only dealing with composers writing down their music with score-like notations. Our goal is different from automatic composition or assisted analysis. In automatic composition, the complete composing act is to be undertaken, from the birth of ideas to a musical score. In assisted analysis, the goal is to research the compositional consistency of a given completed score. Both differ from assisted composition because the formalisms used in automatic composition or assisted analysis may be different from the ones used by the composer. It is a priority in assisted composition to respect the composer's formalism.

The aim of the project, called CARLA (Composition Assistée par Représentation Logique et Apprentissage), is to represent the musical knowledge used by a composer when he is using a computer assisted composition tool. For such a purpose, we must solve at least three problems.

1) Generally, a composer does not completely formalise the language he uses. Some weak definitions of the objects used are sufficient for the composer to compose his piece, but not to build a program. Therefore, the first problem is assistance to the musical formalisation. This problem is undertaken by a type base formalisation of musical objects together with some basic knowledge acquisition techniques aimed at discovering new types, automatically constructed by the system.

2) The second problem refers to the lack of previous training in programming a computer, a common situation for most composers. We must then deal with an assistance to programming. This is solved by the use of a graphical interface, and some Induction tools.

3) Composers are often defining their objects with the aim in mind that they represent some aspects of a more abstract view of their piece. This aspect can be seen as the formal aspect of the piece, describing how musical objects evolve in time, according to their definition. The last problem is to define an abstract representation that can provide a formal account for the musical aspects of the compositional process. This problem is taken into account by a model, that represents the conceptual view of the composer when he deals with musical objects.

In this article, we try to solve these three problems. In the following parts of this article, we first define the representation we choose, and give its formal definition in logic. Then we present the conceptual level of our system, together with the methods that can be applied. Lastly, we present the Induction tool aimed at the automatic construction of some predicates.

Representation of Musical Objects: The Types

In this section, we describe a framework for musical representation, formalised in a subset of second-order logic. We are using logic as a standard way of formalization. We also use logic because of its close relationship with the programming language Prolog. We first emphasize the need for an abstract representation. Then we define primitive and complex types, that formalise the musical syntax. Then a semantic structure, called conceptual graph, is associated to this type base.

Motivations

Composers often deal with the same formal definition of a given musical object, but the actual compositional world (that includes the way the objects are treated) lying behind the straight definition can differ. This explains why composers often use their own specific vocabularies.

Differences among syntactical formats used by composers may be important. For example, M. Stroppa singles out a limited number of features of a chord (what he calls "vertical pitch structures"[1]). Chords are restricted to meet constraints imposed on such features as number of pitches, coefficient of stability, standard deviation in the intervallic content, and so on. The approach of P. Hurel[2] is quite different. He uses chords as banks of pitches that are associated with a completely different object (called pattern[3]) in order to obtain a voice in a polyphony. These chords are often made by some processes derived from synthesis techniques, and use frequencies translated into quarter tones, unlike Stroppa.

Our idea is to enable composers to provide their own musical language, that evolves according to the particular problem the composer solves. Representation of musical objects has been recently studied by several researchers,[4] but none of the suggested frameworks easily allows such an evolution.

We now define this abstract type structure. It includes *primitive types*, such as pitch-name, octave, and alteration and *complex types*, such as pitch, defined from previous ones.

Primitive Types

A primitive type is represented by four features: *domain, cutting, circularity, invertibility*.

The *domain* is the set of possible values for the type; that is, if the type of x is t, and d is the domain of t, then x belongs to d. The domain can be a numeric one (either signed integers or reals), a numeric interval or a symbolic domain.

We represent the signed integers by the distinguished symbol **Z**, and the reals by **R**. We represent an interval by the notation <x,y>, where x and y are respectively the lower and the upper limit, belonging to **Z** or **R**. If the domain of the type of z is <x,y>, then $x \leq z \leq y$. In every interpretation, we identify the number symbols with their numerical value.

We represent a symbolic domain by $\{x_1, x_2, \ldots x_n\}$, where $x_1, x_2, \ldots x_n$ are constants. When the domain is symbolic, it is always considered as finite. For example, for the pitch name type, the domain is: {do, re, mi, fa, sol, la, si}.

The *cutting* of a type is a characterization of the distance separating each pair of elements of the domain.[5] This distance is "conceptual" and may not correspond to an objective, physically observable difference.

It can be linear (constant), exponential, logarithmic, variable or undefined.[6] For example, the cutting of the pitch-name type is variable, since there is a semi-tone between mi and fa and si and do, whereas other pitch names are separated by a tone.

If the cutting is undefined, the domain is considered as not ordered. For the other values of the cutting, the order is the usual order on numbers, or an order given by the user.

The *circularity*[7] is a boolean stating if the last element of the domain is followed by the first or not.

Informally, the *invertibility* states whether the domain is symmetrical or not. For example, the alteration type domain {♭, ♮, ♯} is symetrical around the center ♮. The invertibility is represented by a boolean. When a type is invertible, we must define a neutral element (the center, or *origin* of the type).

Here are some examples of primitive types.

The type corresponding to the octave may be defined as follows:

type: octave;
domain: <-3,+8>,
cutting: linear,
circularity: no,
invertibility: no.

The pitch-name type may be defined as follows:

type: pitch_name;
domain:{do,do#,re,mib,mi,fa,fa#,sol,sol#,la,sib,si},
cutting: linear,
circularity: yes,
invertibility: no.

Note that some attributes may be defined with a different value by other composers/programmers. This choice may be a compositional one or a programmer's implementing choice.

Here is an example of a circular type for pitch variation; in this example, the circularity is a composer's choice:

type: modulation;
domain:{ord,poco_vib,vib,molto_vib,trille,tremolo,glissando, portando}
cutting: linear,
circularity: yes,
invertibility: no.

We now give the formal definition of a primitive type.

Notations

Let **V** be the set of variable symbols: $\mathbf{V} = \{x_i\}$, i∈ **N**.
Let **C** be the set of constants (the 0-arity functional symbols): $\mathbf{C} = \{c_i\}$, i∈ **N**.
Let $\mathbf{F_n}$ be a set of n-ary functional symbols, $\mathbf{F_n} = \{f_i\}$, n, i∈ **N**, n≠0.
Let $\mathbf{Pred_n}$ be the set of n-ary predicate symbols: $Pred_n = \{P_i\}$, i, n∈ **N**.

In order to define a primitive type, we use a distinguished 2-ary predicate symbol, Def-type.

Definitions: A *primitive type definition* **is a** functional term **in the form of**:

type(d, c, l, i), with type $\in \mathbf{F_4}$ and d, c, l, is defined as:
- d is the domain of the type;
d∈ { **Z**, **R** }, or d=<x,y>, where x and y are either signed integers or reals, or d= $\{x_1, x_2, ..., x_n\}$, where x_i (1≤ i ≤n) is a constant.
- c is the cutting of the type;
c∈ {linear, exponential, logarithmic, variable, undefined}.
- l is the circularity of the type; l∈ {yes, no}.
- i is the invertibility of the type; i∈ {yes, no}.
t **is a** *primitive term* **iff** t=f(x), x∈ **C**∪**V**, and Def-type(f(x), p) is true, p being a *primitive type definition*, and f being a 1-ary functional symbol, denoting the *name* of the type.

A primitive term $f(x_i)$ is said to be a *t-variable* iff x_i is a variable. A primitive term $f(c_i)$ is said to be a *t-constant* iff c_i is a constant. For example, the pitch-name type is defined by:

∀**X**, Def-type(pitch_name(**X**),
        type({do,do#,re,mib,mi,fa,fa#,sol,sol#,la,sib,si},
            linear,yes, no)) .

This formula is representing all the pitch-names; in the following parts of this article, the variable **X** will not be explicitly universally quantified.[8]

Complex Types

The primitive types defined above, are not sufficient for representing most objects of musical languages. The next step is, then, to account for complex objects. For that purpose, we need to elaborate some *composition type operators*. So far, we have designed five such operators. These operators are sub-divided into three different categories.

The first category refers to the usual list-constructor, representing an ordered set of terms. We use two list-constructors that take into account the temporal aspect of music, that is horizontality or verticality. The second category corresponds to taxonomic constructors,[9] that is the composition of some types considered as attributes of a more complex type. The last category is simply the type union.

We now define each of the operators:

- ho (horizontal) is a 1-ary functional symbol that corresponds to a composition of types according to a temporal succession. For example, once the pitch type is defined, a composition of this type by ho represents the type of simple-melodies (list of pitches without duration).

- ve (vertical) is a 1-ary functional symbol that corresponds to a composition of types according to a temporal simultaneity. For example, once the pitch type is defined, the chords type is defined by a composition of the pitch type by ve.

- nup is a n-ary functional symbol that corresponds to a composition of types without any constraint (union of defined attributes). For example, once the pitch and duration types are defined, a simple-note type is defined by the composition of these types by nup.

- prod is a n-ary functional symbol that corresponds to a composition of types with some restrictions on the terms resulting from this composition. This occurs when compositional syntactic constraints are used in the definition of some objects. For example, if the pitch-name, alteration, and octave types are composed to define the pitch type, some constraints are needed to state that some pitches are equal, like si#1 and do2.

- union is a 2-ary functional symbol that corresponds to the union of two types.

We can now state the following definitions:

Definitions

A composed type definition **is** a functional term **in the form of** $F(d_1, d_2, \ldots d_n)$, where d_i ($1 \le i \le n$) is a type definition and F is a composition type operator ($F \in \{$ ho, ve, nup, prod, union $\}$).

t **is a** *complex term* **iff** Def-type(t, d) is true, d being a *composed type definition*, t being a 1-ary functional symbol, denoting the *name* of the complex type.

In the case of complex types, Def-type(t, d) is defined by:

For F=ho, or F= ve:
Def-type$(f([t_1, t_2, \ldots t_n]), F(d))$ is true **if** $\forall$ i Def-type(t_i, d).

For F=nup, or F= prod, or F= union:

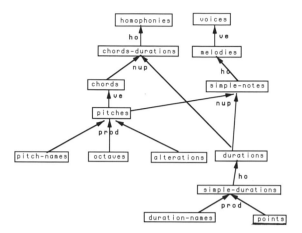

Figure 1. Example of a Signature.

Def-type(f(t$_1$, t$_2$, ... t$_n$), F(d$_1$, d$_2$, ... d$_n$)) is true **if** " i Def-type(t$_i$, d$_i$).

The types appearing in the definition of a composed type definition (defining a type t) are said to be *sub-types* of the type t. Likewise, the terms t$_1$, t$_2$, ... t$_n$ in the term t=f(t$_1$, t$_2$, ... t$_n$) are said to be *sub-terms* of the term t.

The composition type operators can therefore construct a partial order on the set of type names. A type name f1 is said to be lower (according to the set of type names) than a type name f2 **iff** f1 is a sub-type of f2.

For example, the alteration type name is lower than the pitch type name, as the pitch type is a composition of the pitch-name, alteration and octave types. This order is indeed partial, as there are some types that cannot be compared, for example pitch and duration: both of them are lower than simple-note, but not comparable.

We can therefore construct an oriented graph stating the order on type names, that we name a *signature*.[10] In Figure 1, an example of a simple signature is shown.

The terms corresponding to ho and ve composition will be denoted by the use of a functional symbol denoting the type name, and the usual list constructors.[11] Thus a term of type chords, defined as a composition by the operator ve of type pitches, will be denoted by: chords([pitches(X), pitches(Y), ...]). Note that a variable V used in the term chords([pitches(X)|V]) is defined by the type chords.

In order to avoid unboundedness, we define some syntactic restrictions on our typed terms. These restrictions are not musically important, and are conceived in order to allow the system to use the Induction tool described in the section entitled Induction. The length problem is coming from the use of the list-like operators ho and ve. Our solution is then to check the number of elements in terms defined by types using ho or ve. This number of elements is formalized by the notion of n-definition, where n stands for the maximum length of a list.

Definitions

The primitive terms and the complex terms whose type is not defined by one of the composition type operators ho or ve are said 0-defined.

A complex term t whose type τ is defined by one of the composition type operators ho or ve is said n-defined **iff**

1) n is the maximum length of the list forming any complex term of τ, and

2) for every sub-terms t_i of t, there exists m such that t_i is m-defined.

We now define the terms of our logic.

Definitions

A complex term t is *well-formed* **iff** its functional symbols have a signature, and if there exists n such that t is n-defined.

The set of all Well-Formed Terms is denoted WFT.

Example

We shall take as an example the pitch-space. P. Boulez[12] names such a space a parametric space. For some composers dealing with semi-tones, the type representing pitches consists of three types.

The octave type may be defined as follows:[13]

Def-type(octave(O), type(<-3,+9>, linear, no, no)).

The pitch name type is represented as:

Def-type(pitch-name(P),type({do,re,mi,fa,sol,la,si},variable,yes, no))

Finally, the alteration type may be defined by the type:

Def-type(alteration(A),type({♭, ♮, ♯},linear,no,yes))

The pitch space is defined by the following type composition:

Def-type(
    pitch(octave(O),pitch-name(P),alteration(A)),nup(T1,T2,T3)
) is true iff
        Def-type(octave(O), T1) ∧
        Def-type(pitch-name(P), T2) ∧
        Def-type(alteration(A), T3).

The element α in Figure 2 is therefore represented by the term:

pitch(octave(+1) , pitch-name(re), alteration(♯)).

Type Associations

We now introduce a notion of *type association*. The operators presented above define the representation of the syntax of musical objects. The notion of type association accounts for the semantic of the signature. This knowledge will be used later in order to automatically provide the user with some types, possibly useful for him (see Evolution of the Type Base). There are four *type association operators*, described below.

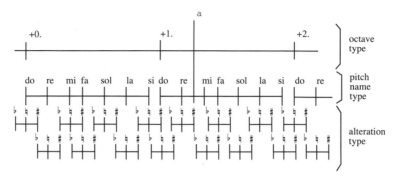

Figure 2. Pitch-space.

The first type association operator allows one type to be associated with another representing its duration. The problem lies in the fact that we must define this representation without any information about the composer's choice of temporal representation. The composition type operator ho is unable to handle such an association, because it only defines the fact that some elements are consecutively ordered in time. It is important to notice that contrary to traditional musical notation, a musical representation must be able to attribute duration to any parameter. In fact, in traditional musical notation, such associations are graphically realised, the best example probably being intensity: in the example in Figure 3 the duration of the intensity **p** is a quarter-note, revealing a desynchronization (admittedly, obvious in this case) between pitch-duration and intensity.

Figure 3. Simple Desynchronization.

The second association type operator is used to handle a somewhat different aspect of representation. To make a comparison, when a physicist is drawing a line associating points representing experimental results, he must accept some deviations around each point; this is what we called a *description* of a point. In music, these descriptions depend of course on a composer's thinking. We can find examples of a conscient use of this syntactic category in Mantra, by K. Stockhausen, and more recently in the works of B. Ferneyhough, for example the Sonatas for string quartet .

Some musical "side-parameters" may also be interpreted as descriptions. For example, a trill, a vibrato, or a tremolo can be regarded as descriptions of the pitch parameter, and crescendo, decrescendo, sforzando as descriptions of the intensity parameter.

The second type association operator explicitly associates the description and the parameter types. This is necessary for two reasons:

1) The parameter and the description have a somewhat different nature: A parameter may exist without any description, unlike a description which always *applies* to a parameter.

2) A description could be used to solve a well-known problem in Machine Learning, namely the presence of noise in the examples: This syntactic category could take *a priori* the responsibility for this noise. Two examples can share parameters but not descriptions. The descriptions also point at the need for the temporal association operator discussed above. Each description could (depending on the composer's whim) receive its own rhythmic structure; B. Ferneyhough often shows this kind of complicated musical writing.

For any composer working with objects in a compositional way, it is useful to calculate intervals lying between the objects. The problem is that there is no assumption on the way these intervals are represented. The solution is to define two types, and associate them. This is the purpose of our third association type operator, called Int.

The last association operator answers a remark often made by composers. It is often said that a musical object can be seen from different points of view, and this is indeed true. In order to take into account this multiple choice, we must be able to deal with an eventual multiple representation of the same musical object, that is, authorize more than one type for an object. To take an example, for composers working with the notion of harmony-timbre,[14] a frequency is often transcribed into a pitch or inversely. This association also formalizes some change of representation used in computer assisted composition systems in order to accelerate the calculations.

In order to obtain a graph where all types used in the signature are present, we introduce a general association operator: *Sub-type*.

We can now define formally an association type operator.

Definitions

An association type operator **is a** predicate symbol whose arguments are type names. The five authorized predicate symbols are:

- Tempo: corresponds to an association between two types, the latter defining the type of the duration of the former.
- Des: corresponds to an association between two types, the latter defining the type of the description of the former.
- Int: corresponds to an association between two types, the latter defining the type of the interval lying between two elements of the former.
- Equal: corresponds to an association between two or more types, representing differently the same objects.
- Sub-type: only syntactic relation between types.

With these five association operators, we obtain a *conceptual graph*.[15] A *conceptual graph* is a bipartite labelled oriented graph. The graph tops are divided in:

- The set of type names
- The set of association type operators.

In **An Example**, we present an example of such a conceptual graph, and in the Evolution of the Type Base section, we show how this conceptual graph is used in the automatic evolution of the type base.

Methods, Concepts

The type base presented previously allows one to formalize the objects used by the composer. However, this cannot, all by itself, deal with a compositional aided-process. First, a musical object is obviously something that can be transformed. We call *methods* the representation of transformations applied to musical objects. Second, a musical object may be more compositionally understood as an instance of a more abstract structure that holds relations between some types. We call this structure a *concept*.

Primitive Methods

In order to provide useful methods for the composer/programmer, the system has built-in *primitive methods*, defined together with the type base. A *primitive method* is a general-purpose predicate, available for most defined types. We briefly present some of these methods below.

For each primitive type, a primitive method called succ (arity 2) is defined. For any term of a primitive type with an ordered domain, this method calculates its successor (e.g. the successor of do is re). For non-ordered types, this method randomly yields an element of the domain.

If a primitive type t1 is associated with a type t2 via the operator Int , then the primitive method difference (arity 3) is defined. This method takes as arguments two elements of t1, x1 and x2, and an element of t2, representing the interval between x1 and x2. This method is based on the four primitive type features previously defined.

For complex types, the methods succ and difference are inherited (calculated) from the primitive methods of the sub-types, according to the composition type operator. The operators ho and ve give rise to common lists' operations. For example, first_element (car), rest_of_list (cdr), member and the like. The prod and nup operators yield a primitive method called extraction, which looks for sub-terms of a given complex term.

The set of primitive methods is later used by the composer to build more complex methods.

Class of Methods

All methods are represented by predicates, since capturing properties via a relation seems attractive for musicians.

The methods used to manipulate objects are sub-divided into four categories.

1) The first category groups methods used for generating instances of musical objects. Such methods are called *theories*.

   The first kind of a theory is a formalization of a class of objects, used as a generator. For example, the Vertical Pitch Structures defined by Marco Stroppa can be regarded as a general theory used to generate chords.

   The second kind of theories are intuitive rules that composers define in order to generate objects (see P. Hurel's example in An Example). The problem lies in the fact that these rules are over-general, and may generate a considerable number of objects.[16] A composer generally loosely defines his theory; he later uses it with some constraints (either intuitive or well defined) that reduce the number of available objects. Our choice is to follow the definition of the composer, and provide him with a set of constraints, used to reduce the amount of search of these particular objects.

2) The second category groups constraints. Indeed, these constraints are those which are important with regard to the formal aspect of the musical piece the composer plans to write.

3) The predicates of the third category hold on transformations of objects. For example, numeric results from some predicates can be transformed into pitches, or into durations. Also, for each pair of types associated by Equal, there is a predicate that translates one type into the other.

4) The last category groups outputs, that can be graphic or not.

Characteristics and Concepts

From a compositional point of view, an object is an instance of a more general structure. This structure corresponds to the use of more complex ideas to compose a piece. It is a vital aspect for an assisted composition tool to deal with such structures. In fact, this conceptual structure refers to what P. Boulez[17] calls the thematic aspect of the composition and M. Stroppa, organisms.[18] We use the term *concept* for referring to this structure. A *concept* is captured by a predicate, stating a relation between types. The arguments of a concept are called *characteristics*.

For example, M. Stroppa's formalization of chords as Vertical Pitch Structures can be seen as a concept (see Motivations). Another example is the formalization of a list of pitches. The arguments of the concept corresponding to this formalization are the pitches themselves, the intervallic content corresponding to the pitches, the shape of the pitches (directions of the intervals between successive pitches in the list), the interval between the first and last pitches, and so on. All these characteristics are constrained during the compositional process to enforce direction at the form of the piece. For example, the beginning of a piece can use the "list-of-pitches" concept, with the shape characteristic constrained such that ascending intervals prevail.[19] During the piece, the constraint on this characteristic will be replaced by a constraint on the intervallic content, and so on.

In CARLA, a concept can be defined in three ways.

1) If the characteristics are formally defined by a composer, this definition is sufficient to be incorporated in the system, as a theory (like Stroppa's example).

2) If the composer is still on progress in the definition of his concept, he must use some methods previously defined. The composer assembles these methods in such a way that the objects he plans to use are all defined (see An Example). The set of methods is structured in the form of a *constraint network*. A *constraint network* is a conjunction of relations (defined by methods) between types. From an implementation point of view, this network can be regarded as a graphic tool used to make programs. We have implemented such an interface,[20] and it is used for searching interesting objects (similarly to Prolog goals), or a help in the programming of predicates. An example of the use of these constraint networks is given in An Example.

3) The last way to define concepts links the previous ones. An abstraction mechanism is defined that allows one to define a predicate from a set of methods. The characteristics must be designated by the composer, and the system automatically constructs the correct predicate.

An Example

In this section, we show how the previous ideas are used by a French composer, P. Hurel. He uses the first version of CARLA, implemented in Prolog.

Figure 4 shows a part of the signature used by P. Hurel. This signature has been defined by P. Hurel, using some graphic tools aimed at the design of types.

A part of the conceptual graph is represented in Figure 5, where only associated

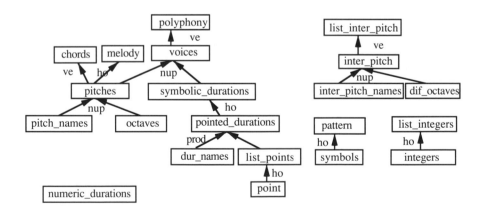

Figure 4. P. Hurel's Signature.

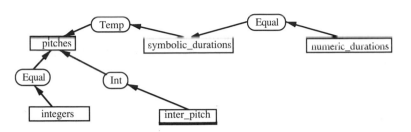

Figure 5. P. Hurel's Conceptual Graph.

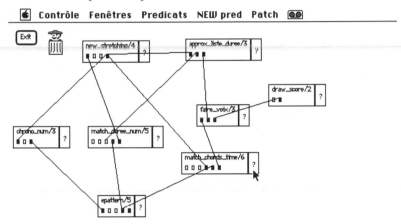

Figure 6. Example of a Constraint Network.

types, apart from the Sub-type associator, are shown.

For him, the theory lies in a recursive structure of symbols called a *pattern*. The eight letters, a b c d e b f d form such a pattern. When repeated five times, the same structure (called the *accent pattern* and represented in upper case) reappears every five symbols:

Abcdebfd abCdebfD abcdEbfd aBcdebFd abcDebfd.

These patterns are represented by a concept in CARLA (see the epattern/5 box in Figure 6).

Once a pattern has been defined, one might like to associate it with pitches, taken from a bank of chords. There is a method aimed at this task, called match_chords_time, that takes as arguments an instance of a pattern, a list of chords, a list of durations for each chord, and the resulting "melody."

In the case of P. Hurel, psycho-acoustical results on the perception of stream formation are used to guide the perception of the listener from a polyphonic texture to the impression of a single timbre. In order to grasp this evolution, some intervallic based constraints are defined, that constrain the shape of the voice in such a way that the psychological impression of a stream is formed. In order to obtain a polyphony, the correct solutions for each voice are stored, and the composer associates every voice by considering vertical constraints.

Figure 6 shows an example of a network, realized by P. Hurel, and corresponding to a single voice for a polyphony.

Each *box* represents a predicate, chosen from a menu, in which predicates are classified according to the above categories. When the user clicks on the "?" part of the box, a window displaying commentaries is shown, stating the semantics of the predicate and its arguments. The little boxes within a predicate box are arguments. Their color, white or black, stands for having a value or not, respectively.

The *connections* represent equality constraints. There is a type verification that prohibits illegal equalities.

In order to assign constant values to arguments, the user graphically selects the argument by double-clicking in it, and the system calls an appropriate *editor*. There are a pitch editor, a chord editor, and a duration editor. Furthermore, some editors specially conceived for P. Hurel are available too, like a pattern editor, numeric editors and the like. When no editor specific to the type of the argument selected is available, then a general, alpha-numeric editor is called.

It is possible to store the Prolog goal corresponding to the network, save the network itself, and run and interrupt the program thus constructed. The order in which the predicates are evaluated is done automatically by the system, according to an order on the predicate categories.

The first graphical result of Figure 6 is shown in Figure 7.

Induction

In previous sections, we sketched a representation model for the notion of a "composer's concept." The representation can evolve in two directions.

Concerning the type base, a composer can define, retract and modify type definitions. In Evolution of the Type Base, we show how this evolution can be aided by the system.

Concerning methods, it is particularly evident that they depend on the composer's whim; hence, there are two solutions: associate a programmer with a composer and expect them to define these particular methods, or design an automatic programming tool. The latter solution is the subject of the last parts of this article.

Evolution of the Type Base

Various types are usually necessary in order to formalize the different objects used by a composer. It is useful to provide the composer with new types, thus relieving him from the need to define these types by himself. We have defined some heuristics aimed at the automatic discovery of new types, from the type base (signature and conceptual graph). The system can therefore propose a new type

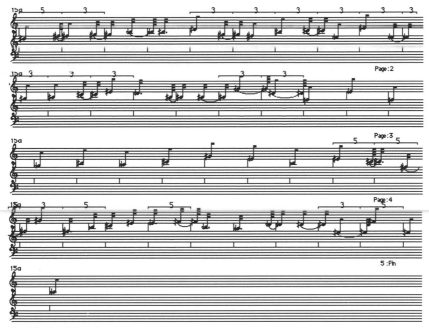

Figure 7. Musical Result of Figure 6.

definition, ask the user if he accepts it or not, and if he does, request a name. We have defined so far three heuristics. They are based on some known techniques in knowledge acquisition, i.e. the use of analogy. The first two heuristics intend to add types to the signature. The third intends to add a relation to the conceptual graph.

We can represent the heuristics in the following way: A graph is used to represent some condition. This graph is either a part of the signature or a part of the conceptual graph. Another graph is used to state the result of the application of the heuristic. In this latter graph, the bold boxes stand for the new things produced by the heuristic. This latter graph may be an addition to the signature (heuristics 1 and 2) or to the conceptual graph (heuristic 3).

Heuristic 1.   This heuristic states that if two known types are associated with the operator Int, then it is generally useful to define the horizontal and vertical composition of the former and the latter. For example, if the types pitches and interval-pitches are defined, it is certainly useful to provide the user with the type aggregate, as a vertical pitch structure, the type melody as a horizontal pitch structure, the types list-interval-pitches and list-interval-pitches' as horizontal and vertical interval-pitches structures, corresponding to the intervallic content. From a more general point of view, this heuristic states that we are rarely working with an object, but more often with a list of objects.

If the relation t1←Int←t2 appears in the conceptual graph, then propose the

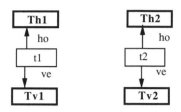

Figure 8.

user the types Th1, Th2, Tv1, Tv2, in order to obtain in the signature the sub-graphof Figure 8, if not previously present.

For stating this heuristic in logic, we must define it as an inference rule.[21]

Heuristic 1

$$\frac{\text{Int}(F1,F2) \wedge \text{Def-type}(V1,T1)) \wedge \text{Def-type}(V2,T2) \wedge P}{\text{Def-type}(Z1, \text{ho}(T1)) \wedge \text{Def-type}(Z2, \text{ho}(T2)) \wedge \text{Def-type}(Z3, \text{ve}(T1))}$$

$\wedge \text{Def-type}(Z4, \text{ve}(T2)) \wedge P$,

where V1 and V2 are t-variables whose functional symbol is respectively F1 and F2, and Zi are t-variables whose functional symbol is the name of the new type (introduction of new functional symbols).

Heuristic 2.   This heuristic may be defined as follows: If the relation t1→Equal→t2 appears in the conceptual graph, and if T ho $\overleftarrow{\text{(resp. ve)}}$ t_1 appears in the signature, then propose a new type T', defined as a ho (resp. ve) composition of the type t2, in order to obtain in the signature the following sub-graph:

T' $\overleftarrow{\text{ho (resp. ve)}}$ t_1'

For example, given t1=pitches and t2=frequency, if the aggregate type is defined as a vertical composition (by ve) of t1, then the second heuristic proposes a spectrum type, defined as the vertical composition of frequency.

Here is the inference rule corresponding to this heuristic, when the ho operator is used:

Heuristic 2

$$\frac{\text{Equal}(t1,t2)\wedge\text{Def-type}(x1,d1)\wedge\text{Def-type}(v1,\text{ho}(d1))\wedge\text{Def-type}(x2,d2)\wedge P}{\text{Def-type}(z1, \text{ho}(d2)) \wedge P}$$,

where x1 is a t-variable whose functional symbol is t1, x2 is a t-variable whose functional symbol is t2 , v1 is a t-variable whose functional symbol is T and z1 is a t-variable whose functional symbol is T'.

Other heuristics may complete the conceptual graph. The third heuristic is an example of this category.

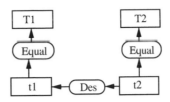

Figure 9.

Heuristic 3.   If the relations shown in Figure 9 appear in the conceptual graph, then propose to the user the relation T1←**Des**←T2 in order to complete the conceptual graph.

Heuristic 3

$$\frac{\text{Equal}(t1, T1) \wedge \text{Equal}(t2,T2) \wedge \text{Des}(t1,t2) \wedge P}{\text{Des}(T1, T2) \wedge P} .$$

These heuristics form a simple set aimed at the evolution of the type base. This automatic discovery is rather elementary, but allows the system to efficiently assist the composer in the task of building the type base.

Learning Predicates

The problem to solve is to automatically learn new predicates from examples of their behaviour given by the composer. The basic groundwork for induction may be found in Shapiro's research.[22] Starting from the study of automatic debugging of logic programs, he proposed algorithms used for building logic programs, using oracles[23] both to reduce the amount of search and assure the validity of inferred rules. In the music, this oracle is the composer, and he cannot judge if a logical formula is correct or not. Hence, we have elaborated some predicate learning operators. We present them in The INTRA Operator and The INTER Operator. We now provide the terminology to be used in the presentation of these operators.

We use classical logic definitions for formulas, clauses, adapted to typed terms. In the rest of this article, all terms belong to WFT.

The classical logical definitions for unification and substitution are easily adapted to our typed terms. As the functional symbols in typed terms denote type names, we must keep them in substitutions. Such substitutions are called here *typed substitutions*, or *t-substitutions*.

For example, the typed terms chords([pitches(X)|Y]) and chords([pitches(1), pitches(5),pitches(8)]) can be unified with the following t-substitutions:

pitches(X)←pitches(1),
chords(Y)←chords([pitches(5),pitches(8)]).

Typically, the methods a composer wishes to write, and in particular the constraint methods, are simple (some constraints in CARLA are written in five lines). Hence, the format of rules[24] to be learned is designed to meet a simplicity and a expressive power constraints. These rules have the following form:

Definition

A *typed linked rule* (TLR) is a (typed) rule in which

1) There is at most 1 t-variable in the head that is not in the tail.

2) Every t-variable in the tail, is present in another literal, in the tail or head of the rule.

For example, the following rule is a TLR:

reverse(melody([pitch(X) | L1]), melody(L2)) ⇐
    reverse(melody(L1), melody(L3))
    simple_append(melody(L3), pitch (X), melody(L2)) .

In this rule, the t-variables melody(L1), melody(L2), pitch(X) are all present both in the tail and the head, and melody(L3) appears twice in the tail, hence the two conditions of a TLR are satisfied.

Similarly, the following rule is a TLR; in this rule, pitch(Y) is the only t-variable present in the head and not in the tail:

member(pitch(X), chord([pitch(Y)|Z])) ⇐
    member(pitch (X), chord(Z)).

On the contrary,

head(figure(X)) ⇐ tail(figure(Y), figure(Z)).

is not a TLR, as both figure(Y) and figure(Z) are not present in any other literal.

We have defined a way to decompose a term. This decomposition is used by the learning operators. The *compatible-terms* of a ground term T is defined as a set of terms S satisfying the following conditions:

1) S = {T} or

2) if the type of T is a complex type constructed by operator nup or prod: S is the union of the compatible terms of the arguments of T.

3) if the type of T is a complex type constructed by operator ho or ve, then T = $F([.t_1, t_2, \ldots t_n])$ and $S = \{t_1\} \cup S'$, where S' is the set of compatible terms of $F([t_2, \ldots t_n])$.

For example, the compatible-terms of lf([f(1),f(2)]) are {lf([f(1),f(2)])}, and{f(1), lf([f(2)])}and{f(1), f(2)}.

We have defined a nondeterministic procedure, called compatible-terms, that computes these terms. The successive solutions for this procedure are ordered by a *descending* order of *complexity*.

The complexity of a term is defined as follows:

• The complexity of t-constants and t-variables is defined as 1.

- The complexity of a term whose type is constructed by operator ho or ve (list typed terms) is the sum of the complexity of its sub-terms (a variable ending a list has a complexity of 0).
- The complexity of a complex term is c+1, c being the sum of the complexities of the arguments of the complex term.

Another notion needed for achieving rules generalization is *inverse t-substitution*. This will give us the basis for the learning of predicates from example. We define the *inverse t-substitution* in such a way that if we apply the inverse t-substitution f(1) →f(X) to the term lf([f(1),f(2)]), the resulting term will be lf([f(X),f(2)]). Likewise, the inverse t-substitution lf([f(2)])→lf(Y) applied to lf([f(1),f(2)]) will give lf([f(1) | Y]).

The compatible-terms procedure is used to define inverse t-substitutions. For example, the inverse t-substitutions for the terms resulting from the compatible-terms procedure used with the example shown previously will respectively give:

lf([f(1),f(2)])→lf(X); (complexity = 1)
f(1)→f(X) , lf([f(2)])→lf(Y), and hence
   lf([f(1),f(2)])→lf([f(X) | Y]); (complexity = 2)
f(1),f(2)→f(X), f(Y), and hence
   lf([f(1),f(2)])→lf([f(X),f(Y)]) (complexity = 3).

The inverse t-substituted terms obtained in the above example are in order of *ascending* complexity. Note that a more complex term is a term containing more type specifications. Hence, a more complex term is less general than a less complex term. Therefore, the most general term among the inverse t-substituted terms is lf(X) and the most specific is lf([f(X),f(Y)]). This is used in order to obtain the most general rules first.

In the next section, we define the learning operators and how these operators are used. Their definitions are strongly influenced by the inversed-resolution principle, as used by Buntine and Muggleton.[25] These operators are the *Intra* operator, specialized at the learning of predicates without any tail, and the *Inter* operator, that learns Typed Linked Rules.

The INTRA Operator

This operator is specially conceived for the learning of rules without tail. It performs an inverse t-substitution close to the "turning constants into variables rule" of Michalski.[26]

Assume the composer needs the predicate member, that assesses whether or not a pitch belongs to a chord.

Let E be an example of the method to be learned:

E = member(pitch(1), chord([pitch(1),pitch(2),pitch(3)])).

The Intra operator first separates the arguments of the example. Then, it looks at the compatible terms within each argument and tries to find at least one in common. The compatible term of the first argument of E is {pitch(1)}. The compatible terms of the second argument are, following the definition of the procedure:

{chord([pitch(1),pitch(2),pitch(3)])}, then
{pitch(1), chord([pitch(2),pitch(3)])}, then
{pitch(1), pitch(2), chord([pitch(3)])}, and finally
{pitch(1), pitch(2), pitch(3)}.

Then the Intra operator chooses pitch(1) $\to$ pitch(X), and chord([pitch(2), pitch(3)])$\to$ chord(Y) as the inverse t-substitutions, because the term pitch(1) is a compatible term of both arguments.

Performed on the example, these inverse t-substitutions give:

Intra(E) = member(pitch(X), chord([pitch(X) |Y])).

The inferred rule is then

    member(pitch(X), chord([pitch(X) |Y])) $\Leftarrow$ true.

Note that there are other possibilities for the inverse substitutions not being taken into account, because we are only looking for the most general rule.

This rule is not sufficient to formulate the complete definition of the predicate member. We see in the next section how the other clause can be learned.

The INTER Operator

As stated above, this operator intend to learn TLR from examples. To make this operator effective, we must assume that the correct rules necessary for the program to be learned exist.

The Inter operator is searching for a TLR in six stages. In some stages, search is reduced due to constraints that are based on the definition of TLRs. These stages are demonstrated in the following example.

Assume that the two following rules are known from the system:

R1: calcul(chord([pitch(X), pitch(Y)]),lint([int(Z)])) $\Leftarrow$
    interval(pitch(X), pitch(Y), int(Z))]) .
R2: interval(pitch(U), pitch(V), int(W)) $\Leftarrow$ difference(U, V, W) .

The user supplies the Inter operator with the heads of rules R1 and R2:

calcul(chord([pitch(X),pitch(Y)]),lint([int(Z)])) and
interval(pitch(U),pitch(V),int(W))

and defines the set of examples as the singleton {E}, where

E=calcul(chord([pitch(1),pitch(2),pitch(4)]),lint([int(1),int(2)]))) .

1) As the Intra operator, the Inter operator looks first for compatible terms of the arguments of the example. The compatible terms of example E are: For the first argument of the example
    C_1= {pitch(1), pitch(2), chord([pitch(4)]) } ;
    for the second argument of the example
    C_2= {int(1), lint([int(2)]) } .
The union of C1 and C2 is called CTE (Compatible Terms of the Example).

2) Then, the Inter operator searches for compatible terms of the arguments of each head. This search is directed by two constraints:

Constraint 1. For each head, there must be at most one compatible term that cannot be unified with one term of CTE.

Constraint 2. In each head, every set of compatible terms of each argument must contain at least one term that can be unified with one term of CTE, except if this set is the argument itself (condition 1 in the definition of compatible terms).

For the first head of our example, the good compatible sets are:

Ct_{11}= {pitch(X), chord([pitch(Y)]) } for the first argument
and Ct_{12}= {lint([int(Z)]) } for the second.

For the second head, the good compatible sets for each argument are respectively:

Ct_{21}= { pitch(U)} ,
Ct_{22}= {pitch(V)} ,
and Ct_{23}= {int(W)} .

3) The operator then performs all the possible unifications between the compatible terms of the heads and the terms of CTE, according to a third constraint:

Constraint 3. For every head, if a term of the decomposition is not instantiated after the unification, then there must be another term in another head that can be unified.

For the given example, this link between the heads is: pitch(V) = pitch(X).

4) At this point, resulting from the previous unifications, all the heads must be bound. We must verify that these unifications are correct, that is the resulting heads are true. We try to do this verification without the use of an oracle.[27] We state that the unifications are correct if the bound heads are either true or are members of the set of examples.

Hence, with our example, the heads are:

calcul(chord([pitch(2),pitch(4)]),lint([int(2)])) and
interval(pitch(1),pitch(2),int(1)).

Both are true, according to rules R1 and R2.

5) Given all compatible terms, the Inter operator performs the inverse t-substitutions on the example and the heads. Therefore, the inverse t-substitutions are, for our example:

pitch(1)→pitch(X), pitch(2)→pitch(Y) ,
chord([pitch(4)])→chord(Z),
int(1)→ int(T), lint([int(2)])→lint(U) .

Hence, the rule that can be learned is:[28]

calcul(chord([pitch(X),pitch(Y)|Z]),lint([int(T)|U])) ⇐
    calcul(chord([pitch(Y)|Z]),lint(U))
    calint(pitch(X),pitch(Y),int(T)) .

6) The operator then retries other substitutions and other compatible terms to find other rules.

With this example and these rules, our implementation[29] of this operator has found the correct rule after 7863 ms[30]. The program has given the explanation:

calcul(chord([pitch(1),pitch(2),pitch(4)]),lint([int(1),int(2)]))
is true because the conjunction of
 calcul(chord([pitch(2),pitch(4)]),lint([int(2)]) and
 calint(pitch(1),pitch(2),int(1)) is true.

And at the end of the search , it has displayed the following messages.

Number of substitutions examined for the example: 9
Number of substitutions examined for the heads: 430
Number of rules examined: 2
Number of correct rules found: 1
Total time for the search: 19425 ms.

Again, an important point is that the search is performed from the more complex terms to the simpler, according to the results of the search for compatible terms. With this strategy, the most general rules are found first.

The order on the compatible terms procedure is also used to reduce the search. When the first rule is found, the complexity of the set of compatible terms of the example (CTE) is calculated. According to the definition of the compatible terms procedure, the complexity of CTE is constant or increasing. If it increases, the resulting rule (if any!) is consequently more specific than the first one. As we are only looking for the most general rules, the program can give up its search.

In the last section, we present how the learning algorithm uses the operators previously discussed.

The Learning Algorithm

Given a set of examples, the algorithm first applies the INTRA operator for each example. Then, it sorts the rules produced by ascending order of complexity (i.e. the most general rules first). The user then chooses the correct rule.

Then, the INTER operator is applied to each example. Once this search is done, we are provided with a set of rules, whose number is less or equal to the number of examples, as there can be some examples from which the program may not infer any rule.

The next step is to find an order in the set. First we try to define some pairs of rules such that the first element of the pair is more general than the other. We say that rule R1 is more general than rule R2 iff R1 covers more examples than R2.

The algorithm proceeds as follows: Each rule is associated with the example that was used for its creation; for each rule R_i and for each example different from the one associated with the rule (that is an E_j, such that $i \neq j$), the algorithm tries to verify if it is covered by the rule. When it is impossible to demonstrate an example (E_k)

from the rule R_i, the rule associated to this example (R_k) is experimented to verify the example of the rule R_i. If it succeeds, then the second rule is more general than the first and the pair (R_k, R_i) is produced; if it fails, then the rules R_k and R_i are non-comparable and no pair is produced.

Once these pairs are determined, we try to find order (or orders) that summarizes all the pairs. In order to keep the most general rules, the maximum rules of each order are produced and later asserted.

Conclusion

In this article, we have outlined an abstract framework for processing compositional objects. The basis of this framework consists of the notion of primitive type, with its four features and the type composition and association operators. We believe that these three components can capture the notion of syntax in a composition.

The higher level of the representation includes *methods* used to transform objects, and *concept definitions*, used to represent formal structures attached to a more abstract view of the composer's musical objects. We have also briefly discussed the automatic discovery of new types, and presented two operators for learning new methods from old methods and examples.

Some problems still occur. The methods the system learns are only general programs, with no possibility of making tests on constants. This could be achieved by a third learning operator that will perform the least general generalization on the set of examples.

Second, the operators perform a selection operation in the set of methods attached to the concepts of created objects. A larger set of methods will reduce the efficiency of the search. A new operator is needed in order to rewrite the tail of a rule with heads of previously defined rules.

Third, the learning operators must know all the rules necessary for the definition of the new rule. This, in general, is not the case. We have now defined other induction operators that can discover missing predicates.

We are now incorporating new inductive operators, using a more oracle based approach, and are experimenting with the use of the learning predicates with composers, some of them using CARLA's tools for methods.

Acknowledgments

I would like to thank Andrew Gerzso, Jacques Nicolas, Gerhard Eckel, Ramon Gonzalez-Arroyo, Jacques Duthen, Marco Stroppa and Philippe Hurel for numerous discussions and commentaries on earlier drafts of this article.

Notes

1) [Stroppa, 1988b]; [Courtot, 1989].
2) Currently working with CARLA, for a commission of the Ensemble Intercontemporain.
3) See example in An Example.
4) Among others, [Balaban, 1988], [Blevis, 1988], [Chemillier, 1987], see also [Loy, 1985].
5) The cutting corresponds to Boulez's notion of "coupure" (Boulez, 1963, p. 95).
6) We represent the possible values of the cutting by these special constant symbols: linear, exponential, logarithmic, variable, undefined.
7) The language structure of the object representation is derived from [Michalski, 1983].
8) We will use upper case letters for variables in the remaining parts of the paper.
9) [Michalski, 1983].
10) The idea of representing ordered typed terms within such a graph is derived from [Ait-Kaci, 1986].
11) We shall use the Prolog Edinburgh notations for the list constructors: [ ] and |.
12) [Boulez, 1963].
13) As we stated earlier, the variables **O**, **P**, and **A** in the type definitions are universally quantified.
14) In particular, G. Grisey, T. Murail.
15) [Sowa, 1984].
16) See, for example, [Chemillier, 1990] for an example of this problem.
17) [Boulez, 1990].
18) [Stroppa, 1988a].
19) Example of this kind of shape's constraints can be seen in B. Ferneyhough's "La chute d'Icare," for clarinet and ensemble.
20) [Courtot, 1990].
21) By notational convention, all the predicates Int(X,Y) must be read $\exists X \ \exists Y$ Int(X,Y) in the inference rules; the same convention applies to Equal, Temp, and Des. Similarly, the predicates Def-type(X,T) must be read $\forall X \ \exists T$ Def-type(X,T).
22) [Shapiro, 1981, 1982].
23) An oracle gives for every logical formula generated by a computer system its truth value in a model.
24) The rules are extensions or variations of g-clauses, often used in Induction research. We authorize a term of the head that does not belong to the tail, and use typed terms.
25) [Muggleton, 1988].
26) [Michalski, 1983].
27) We have later designed other operators making a more intensive use of oracles.
28) This rule could be very useful if the "pitch" type is in fact the *symbolic* pitch type. In this case, the program therefore inferred is the one that calculates the intervallic content of any chord. This was taken as a characteristic by M. Stroppa.
29) So far, this implementation is independent of CARLA itself. We now incorporate in CARLA learning operators.
30) With a Prolog II compiler, running on a Macintosh II.

References

[Aït-Kaci, 1986] Aït-Kaci, H. et Nasr, R. LOGIN: A Logic Program with Built-In Inheritance. *The journal of logic programming* :185–215.

[Balaban, 1988] Balaban, M. The TTS Language for Music Description. *Man-Machine Studies* 28:505–523.

[Boulez, 1989] Boulez, P. *Jalons (pour une Décennie)*. Paris: Christian Bourgois ed.

[Boulez, 1963] Boulez, P. *Penser la musique aujourd'hui*. Paris: Denoël/Gonthier ed.

[Blevis, 1988] Blevis, E. and al. Motivations, Sources, and Initial Design for CALM: a Composition Analysis/Generation Language for Music. In Proceedings of 1st Workshop on AI and Music, 99–112. Minneapolis/St Paul MI (USA).

[Muggleton, 1988] Buntine, W. and Muggleton, W.Towards Constructive Induction in First-Order Predicate Calculus, Research Memoranda, TIRM-88-031, The Turing Institute, Glasgow.

[Courtot, 1989] Courtot, F. Une Experimentation de CAO en Prolog: Analyse et Engendrement "d'Accords." IRCAM Internal document.

[Courtot, 1990] Courtot, F. A Constraint-Based Logic Program for Generating Polyphonies. In Proceedings of ICMC 1990. Glasgow.

[Chemillier, 1987] Chemillier, M. Monoïde Libre et Musique. *Informatique théorique et application*, 20 n° 2, February 1983.

[Chemillier, 1990] Chemillier, M. Langages musicaux et automates. La rationalité du langage sériel. In Proceedings of the Music and Information Technology Conference. October 1990, Marseille, France.

[Hurel, 1989] Hurel, P. "Pour l'image," for 14 instruments. Score Billaudot G42-18-B, CD "Villa medicis 1988," Trajectoire-Salabert AD-184, ADDA.

[Loy, 1985] Loy, G. and Abbott, C. Programming Languages for Computer Music Synthesis, Performance, and Composition. Computer surveys, 17 n° 2, June 1985.

[Michalski, 1983] Michalski, R. A Theory and Methodology of Inductive Learning. *Artificial Intelligence, an International Journal*, 20 n° 2, February 1983.

[Shapiro, 1981] Shapiro, E. An Algorithm that Infers Theory from Facts. In Proceedings of IJCAI 1981: 446–451.

[Shapiro, 1982] Shapiro, E. Algorithmic Program Debugging. MIT Press, Cambridge, Massachusetts.

[Sowa, 1984] Sowa, J. F. Conceptual Structures. The systems programming series, Addison-Wesley.

[Stroppa, 1988a] Stroppa, M. Musical Information Organisms: an Approach to Composition. In *La musique et les sciences cognitives*, ed. S. Mc Adams & I. Deliège, 131–165, Mardaga, Lièges-Bruxelles.

[Stroppa, 1988b] Stroppa, M. Structure, Categorisation, Generation and Selection of Vertical Pitch Structures. IRCAM Internal document.

Section Three

Music Composition

The process of music composition is typically discussed in the context of notions such as genius, master piece, baroque (or other) tradition, and cultural heritage. In contrast to this culturally affirmative perspective, we are here interested in composition as an observable human activity that leaves certain traces in the environment, and that one can therefore investigate empirically. We think it makes sense to suspend the value judgment that we already know what music is, and to investigate quite simply how something that by society is called "music" might come about when an expert called a "composer" decides to select, and work with, sound materials he considers to be of value. We refuse, at this point, to make any distinction between creativity and problem solving, although we have a hunch that the former notion cannot be reduced to the latter one. Indeed, we think that problem solving is but one of the many tools for acting creatively, but regard it as impossible, at this point, to delimit the boundaries between the two concepts.

The term *composition theory* is used here to designate a new discipline of music research oriented toward an empirical theory of compositional processes in music. By *empirical theory* we mean a theory formulated on the basis of empirical data regarding the mental process of composition, such as thinking-aloud protocols, video traces, retrospective reports, documents monitoring action sequences of a musician engaged in computer-aided composition, and other such knowledge acquisition materials.

Composition theory has become a necessity because music analysts and music theorists continue to construe music composition from an ideal listener's point of view, thereby disregarding the control structure of the composition process and reformulating it as an idealized listening process. In contrast to such practice, composition theory intends to capture the compositional process as a process sui generis, different from analysis and listening processes.

Historically, composition theory is the outcome of computer applications in music carried out over the last 35 years. It originated in the 1950s and 1960s, when composers like Hiller (Hiller 1959), Barbaud (Barbaud 1961), Xenakis (Xenakis 1963), and Koenig (Koenig 1970) began to publish their programs for, and comments on, computer-aided composition. (Prior to that, composers like Boulez, Stockhausen, Ligeti, and Babbitt had formalized their compositional thinking; however, they did not work with computer programs, although Babbitt came very close to doing so when working with synthesizers.) To this day, these publications have been interpreted as anecdotal personal statements of composers rather than as writings providing the foundation for a scientific discipline in its own right, viz., composition theory. The insight that a new discipline was in the making gained in acceptance only gradually, when composers began, either to undertake studies in the acquisition of compositional knowledge with the aid of computers (Laske 1974), or to create "intelligent" programs for computer-aided composition, exhibiting some capability for evaluating their results (Ames 1982).

Composition is best investigated empirically by building and utilizing computer music systems. Such systems constitute a unique task environment for empirical research, since they only do what they are told to do, and since they are capable of retaining information about the compositional process of their user that ordinarily gets lost. The present section on composition systems comprises four chapters. In all cases, the theory presented is based on output from a specific program for computer-aided composition; it thus documents tasks thought to be central to composing music.

CYBERNETIC COMPOSER

Principles of music composition have been speculated about on theological, philosophical, pedagogical, and "music-theoretical" grounds since the Middle Ages. In all of these speculations, it was assumed that one already knew what "music" is, and that what was needed was only to abstract out some guiding principles that seemed to be offering themselves to the theorist inspecting notated music, or listening to actual performances of music, or both. It is a different matter to construct a mechanism for putting such speculations to test, by comparing the output of the mechanism with the constraints defining its input, and coming to conclusions about the sufficiency, or lack thereof, of the constraints used.

In their overview of CYBERNETIC COMPOSER, Charles Ames and Michael Domino present an example of music-theoretic empiricism. The CYBERNETIC COMPOSER automatically generates compositions in jazz, rock, and ragtime styles, working from scratch without human intervention. A rhythm-generating stage refines harmonic rhythm into primary notes, ornamental notes, and rests. Then, a pitch-generating stage employs a constrained search with backtracking to seek out pitch sequences that are varied, yet which conform to the rhythmic functions, to the harmonies, and to the thematic context.

Stylistic determinants include thematic templates, chordal progressions, rhythmic grammars, and "ornament generators" that suggest choices for the pitch-selection stage. By attempting to approximate procedures that are both necessary and sufficient to produce identifiable styles, programs such as the cybernetic composer provide a very good means of verifying music-theoretic speculations.

WOLFGANG

The chapter by D. Riecken approaches music composition from the vantage point of emotion. Riecken explores the notion of "emoting potential" as a metaphor for understanding composition. As does Smoliar (in this volume), Riecken uses notions deriving from Marvin Minsky's *Society of Mind*. In his outline of the WOLFGANG system, Riecken describes the architecture and functions of an artificial composer building up his own stylistic repertory over time; this is accomplished in the framework of a simplified version of the 19th century sonata form. What transpires is a software design that seems to have some promise for answering questions about the way in which syntactic-semantic decision-making and culturally determined emotional evaluation interact in music composition. Although this is still a far cry from dealing with composition as creation, rather than problem solving, it is perhaps a fruitful beginning for making such a distinction. (For composition as creation rather than problem solving, also see Kugel, in this volume.)

On the Application of Problem Reduction Search to Automated Composition

In the next following chapter, Marsella and Schmidt present an example of how questions about composition might be posed in a new way, inspired by notions developed in AI research. One of the questions regarding composition that has surfaced in work with computers is whether it might be possible to understand the surface structure of compositions—what one can point to in notated music—on the basis of insight into the control structure of the problem-solving process that generated the music.

Marsella and Schmidt pursue this question in terms of the method of problem reduction, a method by which problems are recursively broken down into simpler subproblems until they can be solved directly. What emerges is an hypothesis due to which "the structure of the composition is viewed as homomorphic to the structure reflected in the history of the decisions (made) in forming the composition." This hypothesis has composition-theoretic as well as analytical consequences, which remain to be explored further.

The Observer Tradition of Knowledge Acquisition

It would seem to be a natural idea to use existing computer programs for composition, especially interactive programs, for finding out in more empirical detail how composers actually think when developing musical ideas. Nevertheless, knowledge-acquisition, i.e., the elicitation, analysis, and modeling of musical knowledge for the double purpose of understanding experts in composition, and of building tools for supporting their work based on such an understanding, is a much neglected topic of music research. It is a difficult topic since much of human knowledge of and about music is not available to musicians in a verbal or verbalizable form; it is, rather, "compiled action knowledge," that one can perhaps capture by bypassing verbalization.

In his contribution to the topic of knowledge acquisition, Otto Laske reviews the—by now twenty years old—tradition deriving from his and Truax's OBSERVER system of the early 1970s (Laske 1974, 1977), as well as from a successor system, PRE-COMP, built during the late 1980s (Laske 1990b, Koenig 1979). In this context, one can speak of task-based knowledge acquisition. The reader will rightfully draw the conclusion that an empirical theory of compositional activity is in its very beginning, and that better knowledge acquisition and modeling tools are required for progress in the field—a finding equally true regarding knowledge acquisition in task domains other than music.

References

Ames, C. 1982."Protocol: Motivation, Design, and Production of a Composition for Solo Piano," *Interface* 11.4:213. Amsterdam, The Netherlands: Swets & Zeitlinger.

Ames, C. 1989 (1991). *User Manual for compose; Tutorial and Cookbook for COMPOSE.* Eggertsville, NY: Self-published.

Barbaud, P. 1961. *Musique—Discipline Scientifique.* Paris: Dunod.

Brun, H. 1970."From Musical Ideas to Computers and Back," in H. Lincoln, ed., *The Computer and Music,* Ithaca, NY: Cornell University Press.

Hiller, L. & Isaacson, L. 1959. *Experimental Music.* New York: McGraw-Hill.

Hiller, L. 1970."Music Composed with Computers: A Historical Survey," In H. Lincoln, ed., *The Computer and Music,* Ithaca, NY: Cornell University Press.

Koenig, G. M. 1979. Protocol. Sonological Reports no. 4. Utrecht, The Netherlands: Institute of Sonology.

Koenig, G. M. 1970. Project One, Electronic Music Reports no. 2. Utrecht, The Netherlands: Institute of Sonology.

Koenig, G. M. 1970. Project Two. Electronic Music Reports no. 3. Utrecht, The Netherlands: Institute of Sonology.

Lachartre, N. 1969."Les musiques artificielles," Diagrammes du Monde, no. 146 (April). Monte Carlo.

Laske, O. 1974. "The Information-Processing Approach to Musical Cognition," *Interface* 3(2):109-136. Amsterdam, The Netherlands: Swets & Zeitlinger.

Laske, O. 1977. Music, Memory, and Thought: Explorations in Cognitive Musicology, Ann Arbor, MI: UMI Research Press [esp. chapter 10].

Laske, O. 1989a. "Composition Theory: An Enrichment of Music Theory," *Interface,* 18(1-2):45-50. Amsterdam, The Netherlands: Swets & Zeitlinger.

Laske, O. 1989b. "Composition Theory in Koenig's Project One and Project Two." In (C. Roads, ed.) *The Music Machine,* 119-130. Cambridge, MA: The MIT Press.

Laske, O. 1990a. "Two Paradigms of Music Research: Composition and Listening." In (B. Bel & B. Vecchione, eds.), *Actes, Colloque Musique et Assistance Informatique,* 179-185. Centre de Recherche en Sciences de la Musique, Aix-en-Provence, France.

Laske, O. 1990b. "The Computer as the Artist's Alter Ego." *Leonardo,* 23(1-2): 53-66. New York: Pergamon Journals.

Laske, O. 1991. "Toward an Epistemology of Composition." In (O. Laske, ed.) *Interface* 20(3-4):109-144. Amsterdam, The Netherlands: Swets & Zeitlinger.

Roads, C. 1985. *Composers and the Computer.* Los Altos, CA: William Kaufman Inc..

Xenakis, I. 1963. *Musiques Formelles,* Paris: Richard Masse.

Abstract

Until now, musical theory has by-and-large been a speculative endeavor. It is often held in contempt by musicians at large (even as logically-minded a musician as Stravinsky, who once rated the *Journal of Music Theory* unfavorably to *MAD Magazine*). With the arrival of digital computers and artificial intelligence, it now becomes possible to subject theoretical speculations about music to rigorous empirical evaluation. The new methodologies offered by computer technology have gained very little acknowledgement so far from professional music theorists. Many such professionals may well grow directly hostile toward AI, since in our estimate some cherished music-theoretic doctrines will likely be revealed under rigorous empirical scrutiny as neither *necessary* nor *sufficient* to explain musical processes. We strongly believe that true empiricism is the only way to restore credibility to the field.

The Cybernetic Composer is an example of music-theoretic empiricism. It was developed by the Kurzweil Foundation Automated Composition Project to show how artificial intelligence can be applied to musical composition. In its current versions, the Cybernetic Composer composes an endless stream of musical compositions in four genres: "standard" jazz, Latin jazz, rock, and ragtime. The results are realistic enough that an unknowing listener cannot discern their artificial origin. The program now exists in two versions, both implemented on the Apple Macintosh. An exhibition version dedicated to the Kurzweil 250 synthesizer has been touring U.S. Science Museums since January 1987 with the exhibition *Robots and Beyond: The Age of Intelligent Machines,* and since June 1987 it has been on permanent display in the *Smart Machines* exhibit at the Boston Computer Museum. A synthesizer-independent version has been distributed as freeware. The Cybernetic Composer's music-composition routines—the subject of this article—were programmed by Charles Ames; its performance routines, graphics, and Macintosh interface were designed and implemented by Michael Domino.

The Cybernetic Composer continues a tradition of music-theoretic empiricism initiated by Hiller and Isaacson's 1957 *Illiac Suite* for string quartet. It is also a direct descendent of Mix and Match, a melody-writing program developed by Hiller and Ames for the 1985 Tsukuba Exposition (Hiller and Ames, 1985; Ames, 1985). Although the Cybernetic Composer employs a wide range of techniques, the primary criteria establishing it as an AI program in our minds are its capabilities to undertake value judgements and to backtrack in response to impasses in the decision-making process. Similar capabilities exist in the programs described by Gill (1963), Ebcioglu (1980), Ames (1982), Ebcioglu (1988; previously described 1984), Thomas (1985), and Ames (1986).

Chapter 8

Cybernetic Composer:
An Overview

Charles Ames and Michael Domino
Kurzweil Foundation Automated Composition Project

The Compositional Process

For each genre in its repertory, the Cybernetic Composer has access to several different *models* describing information pertinent to how pieces can be structured. Each model has a chordal scheme (which also describes the phrase structure) and a thematic scheme.

Cybernetic Composer ensembles have four layers: solo part, background chords, bass line, and drums. The solo and bass parts both are monophonic; the background layer is a homophonic texture in three or four parts; and the drum layer is a polyphonic texture of unpitched drum and cymbal sounds. Except for the information provided by the model, individual layers generally have very little "awareness" of what the other layers are doing. (An exception is the ragtime genre; here the background and bass layers work in close coordination.) Because the instrumental roles in jazz, rock, and ragtime ensembles are well defined, the program often gives the illusion of true interplay when the layers are actually going their separate ways.

Chordal Scheme

The chordal scheme of a model describes a phrase structure and lists alternate chordal progressions appropriate to this structure. To illustrate this, Figure 1 details a four-measure chordal scheme, taken from the Bebop blues model of the Cybernetic Composer's standard jazz genre. The elements in the diagram are

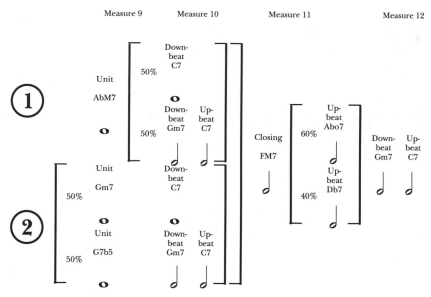

Figure 1. Chordal Scheme for Bebop Blues (measures 9–12).

described by a rhythmic duration, a metric function, a chord root expressed here relative to the key of F, and a chord quality. Chord qualities are designated by the following abbreviations: M7: major 7th chord, m7: minor 7th chord, 7: dominant 7th, 7b5: dominant 7th with lowered 5th, o7: diminished 7th, ø7: half-diminished 7th. Rectangular brackets delimit alternative rhythmic streams; the percentages indicate random weights associated with these streams.

Figure 2 illustrates one of the many alternative progressions described by Figure 1. This progression employs the upper substream of stream 2 in measures 1–2 and the upper stream for beats 3 and 4 of measure 3. Chordal progressions are derived in much the same way for the Latin jazz, rock, and ragtime genres. Ragtime requires additional instructions detailing what kinds of chordal inversions are permissible.

Figure 2. Sample Progression.

Rhythm

The first step taken when the Cybernetic Composer generates a melody is to derive a chordal rhythm such as the sample depicted in Figure 2. The chordal rhythm provides a basic framework to which the program applies refinements characteristic of particular instrumental roles within each genre. These refinements produce a complete rhythmic description of a melody, including when notes start, how long notes last, and *how notes function melodically.*[1] Each note of the chordal rhythm assumes a *primary* melodic function. In solo and background melodies these primary functions include primary chord tones and cadence tones; in bass lines new chords are anchored by statements of the chordal roots. The *refinements* to the chordal rhythm divide primary notes into chunks and establish these chunks as notes or rests in their own right.[2] The notes generated by refinements can themselves be primary chord tones (sometimes subject to further refinement); they can be repetitions of previous chord tones; they can be scale tones (chordal or nonchordal), which bind melodies by stepwise movement; or they can serve *ornamental* melodic functions as passing tones, neighboring tones, reaching tones, appoggiaturas, and so on.

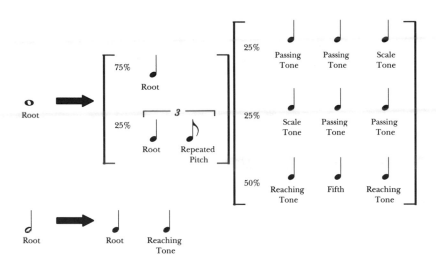

Figure 3. Rhythmic Refinements for Walking Bass Line

Figure 3 shows the rhythmic refinements employed to derive the walking bass line for the Cybernetic Composer's jazz genre. This is by far the simplest set of refinements used by the program. The arrow in each refinement should be interpreted as follows: "whenever in the current rhythm, a duration and melodic function matches the duration and melodic function on the left side of the arrow, replace the matched duration and function with one pattern described on the right side of the arrow." Rectangular brackets to the right of the arrow delimit alternative rhythmic streams, with percentages indicating the random weight associated with each stream.

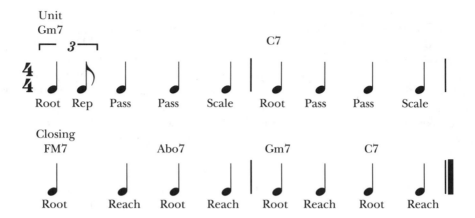

Figure 4. Sample Walking-Bass Rhythm.

Figure 4 illustrates one walking-bass rhythm, which might be obtained from the chordal rhythm in Figure 2.

Pitch

When the Cybernetic Composer creates a melody, it always describes the rhythm completely before it begins selecting any pitches. Selection of pitches is subject to several constraints: pitches must conform to instrumental capabilities; each note's pitch must be appropriate to the note's melodic function; chordal dissonances in the jazz and ragtime genres must be suitably resolved over the long term. Within these constraints, the program also biases pitch-selection with statistical feedback (Ames, 1990) so that melodies do not linger unintentionally upon particular scale

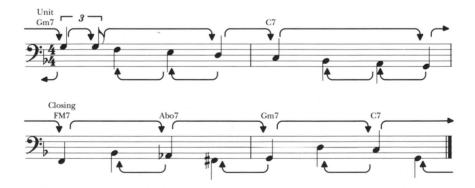

Figure 5. Order of Pitch Selection for Walking Bass Line.

degrees. Often these different objectives come into conflict with one another, so it becomes necessary to consider alternative solutions. This is where AI search (backtracking) comes into play

Figure 5 illustrates one sequence of pitches, which might have been selected for the rhythm shown in Figure 4. Arrows show the order of selection. The search selects pitches for primary notes (cadence tones, chordal tones, and scale tones) in the order in which these notes appear. When it comes to an ornamental note, the program skips forward in time to the next primary note, then works its way backward in time through the ornamental notes until all the ornamental pitches have been chosen. Sometimes the Cybernetic Composer finds itself at an impasse where no available pitch satisfies all the constraints; in such cases, the program backs up to an earlier-composed note, changes this earlier-composed note's pitch, and tries again.

Thematic Scheme

The thematic scheme of a model describes which sections of a composition employ original material and which sections imitate material from earlier sections. As with chordal schemes, thematic schemes can branch into alternative streams; such branching may or may not be coordinated with choices made in the chordal domain.

For originally-composed sections, the thematic scheme gives the Cybernetic Composer a style (where relevant), a point of pitch liaison, and a point of rhythmic liaison. A point of pitch liaison is only rarely needed. It allows the program to match the opening pitch of an original passage to an earlier pitch. This is useful in thematic schemes such as A B C B A; in this instance, specifying the opening of A as the point of pitch liaison for B directs the program to create an ending for B that will be compatible both with the opening of C and the opening of A. The point of rhythmic liaison enables the program to adapt the close of a newly-composed section so that the rhythm meshes properly into the section's successor (cf. Figures 6a-6b). If an originally-composed section is intended to be used as a repeated motive

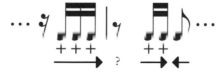

Figure 6a. False Rhythmic Mesh— Pickup Left Dangling.

Figure 6b. True Rhythmic Mesh— Pickup Resolved.

Measure	Chord	Section	Operation
1	C7	**A** (meas. 1)	Original; Verse style; Rhythmic liaison with **A**
2	F7	**B** (meas. 2)	Solo: Imitate **A** untransposed (diatonic) Bgnd: Imitate **A** untransposed (diatonic) Bass: Imitate **A** up a perfect fourth (real)
3	C7	**C** (meas. 3-4)	Imitate **A** untransposed (real)
4	C7		Imitate **A** untransposed (real)
5	F7		Imitate **B** untransposed (real)
6	F7		Imitate **B** untransposed (real)
7	C7		Imitate **C** untransposed (real)
8	C7		

Figure 7a. Thematic Scheme 1 for 16-Bar Blues Verse.

Measure	Chord	Section	Operation
1	C7	**A** (meas. 1-2)	Original; Verse style; Rhythmic liaison with **A**
2	F7		
3	C7	**B** (meas. 3-4)	Imitate **A** untransposed (real)
4	C7		
5	F7		50% Imitate **A** untransposed (diatonoic)
6	F7		50% Imitate **A** up a perfect fourth (diatonoic)
7	C7		Imitate **B** untransposed (real)
8	C7		

Figure 7b. Thematic Scheme 2 for 16-Bar Blues Verse.

Measure	Chord	Section	Operation
9	G7	**A** (meas. 9-10)	Original; Bridge style; Rhythmic liaison with **A**
10	F7		
11	G7		Imitate **A** untransposed (real)
12	F7		
13	G7		Imitate **A** untransposed (real)

Figure 7c. Thematic Scheme for 16-Bar Blues Bridge.

Measure	Chord	Section	Operation
15	G7	**A** (meas. 15, beats 1 & 2)	Original; Tag style; Rhythmic liaison with **A**
16 (1 & 2)	C7		Imitate **A** untransposed (real)
16 (3 & 4)	G7		Imitate **A** untransposed (real)
12	F7		Original; Tag style; Rhythmic liaison with verse

Figure 7d. Thematic Scheme for 16-Bar Blues Tag.

or as a riff, then the point of rhythmic liaison will be the section's own starting time. For imitative sections, the thematic scheme gives the Cybernetic Composer starting and ending times for a source section, a transposition, and a *strictness*. The strictest imitations are *real* imitations; these attempt to match pitches exactly. Next come *modal* imitations, which attempt to retain the same scale steps while allowing flexibility with accidentals. *Chromatic* and *diatonic* imitations permit deviations of one and two semitones from the original pitches, respectively. The least strict of Cybernetic Composer imitations retains the original rhythm and melodic functions but makes no attempt to match pitches. In some imitations the transposition and/or strictness will vary from layer to layer.

Figures 7a-7d detail the rock genre's thematic/chordal scheme for 16-bar blues. Figures 7a and 7b give alternative streams for the verse (measures 1-8); one or the other is chosen at random with equal probability of selection. The rock styles are detailed under the specific description of the rock genre; here it is sufficient to know that the Cybernetic Composer chooses from a variety of styles for each of three basic phrase types: verse, bridge, and tag.

Figure 8 illustrates how the program keeps track of thematic relationships. The arrows depict thematic links set up when the imitative rhythms were created (by copying notes from the source). The first three notes of measure 2 are a *modal* imi-

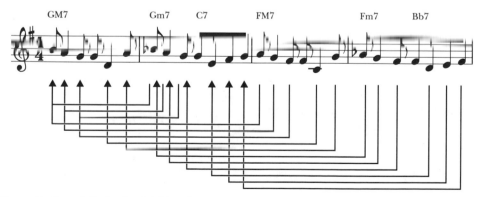

Figure 8. Sample Imitative Linking Structure.

tation of the first three notes of measure 1, while measures 3-4 are a *real* imitation of measures 1-2 transposed down a major second.

For an imitative passage, it is important to specify that the first few notes be *required* to match pitches with their counterparts in the source melody. This requirement prevents stylistic tendencies established immediately prior to an imitative passage (e.g., in Figure 8, measure 1, beats 3 & 4, just prior to measure 2's modal imitation of measure 1's opening notes) from overriding the imitative mandate. Whenever the opening pitches of an imitation fail to conform to these transitional tendencies, the program backtracks and changes transitional pitches until it discovers a suitable transition. Once the imitative character of a passage has been established, the program relaxes its matching requirement so that later imitative pitches can themselves be adjusted to transitional needs. The closest matches are attempted first, but if these do not work then the program seeks outward around the matching pitch until a stylistically appropriate pitch is found.

Such inflexibility at the opening of an imitation might lead to potential impasses without precautions. Consider what would happen if the imitation were at a transposition that shifted a source pitch outside the instrumental range: the Cybernetic Composer would have to backtrack all the way back to the source note before the impasse could be resolved. To prevent such impasses, the program checks all future incarnations of a note whenever it considers a source pitch. Thus when it selected the B at the opening of Figure 8, the program also checked that Bb would be suitable at the opening of measure 2, that A would be suitable at the opening of measure 3, and that Ab (derived from the opening B indirectly through the Bb in measure 2) would be suitable at the opening of measure 4.

The Genres

At this point the reader should understand generally how the Cybernetic Composer creates music. The remainder of this article details how the program emulates specific musical genres. In selecting which among the great variety of jazz, rock and ragtime practices should be incorporated into the program, we were guided primarily by our own background, tastes, and sense of what would be practical. Having played jazz and rock at one point, we had more than an academic awareness of how such pieces were made. All music composed by the Cybernetic Composer favors syncopated rhythms, in part because we enjoy syncopation and in part because we felt that livelier rhythms might provide some defense against the inevitable charge that computer-composed music must intrinsically be sterile. Our sense of the practical led us to avoid involvement with the many rock styles that depend upon nuances of pitch inflection (cf. Roth, 1984) and to avoid as well the nuances of rubato that are critical to slow music in any genre.

The Cybernetic Composer's "standard" jazz genre produces improvisations over chord changes—thematicism is employed only in the Latin jazz, rock and ragtime genres. The first chorus of each Latin jazz and rock piece is a fully composed tune; later choruses consist of improvisations following the tune's chordal scheme. Ragtime pieces are fully composed throughout.

"Standard" Jazz

The Cybernetic Composer's "standard" jazz improvisations reflect stylistic traits common to small jazz ensembles, which released recordings on the Blue Note label during the late 1950s and early 1960s. Among these traits are the "swing feel" and the dependence upon chordal designs derived from "standards" such as 12-bar blues, *I Got Rhythm,* or *How High the Moon.* The models are twelve–bar blues, AABA, ABAB, and ABCA. A general source of information on jazz idioms is Mehegan (1959-1965). The modal approach widely advocated by jazz theorists (and implemented in a composing program by Fry, 1980) does not give good results; Ames opted instead for a chordal framework with diatonic and chromatic ornaments.

The Solo Layer.   To compose a rhythm for the solo layer, the program applies two levels of refinement to a chordal rhythm such as the one illustrated in Figure 2. All notes generated by these refinements retain links to the chordal rhythm, so that the program can access this information rapidly when the time comes to assign pitches. The first level of refinement divides long chordal durations into successions of quarter notes, quarter rests, half notes, and half rests. The method of selection is weighted randomness, subject to the constraints that two rests may not occur consecutively and that cadential chords must always begin with notes. The placement of rests roughly determines the melodic phrasing, which is "fleshed out" by divisions at the second level of refinement:

Quarter notes (column 1 of Figure 9; appoggiaturas not shown) — the program selects a mode of division by weighted randomness:

a) no division (1 unit);

b) swing-eighth division (2 units);

c) triplet-note eighth division (3 units);

d) straight sixteenth-note division (4 units).

In modes (b) through (d), the program decides randomly whether the first unit in the division will function as an appoggiatura. If so, then the second unit becomes the primary chord tone; otherwise, the first unit of the division becomes the primary chord tone. Subsequent units (if any) are assigned any of three functions: secondary chord tone, passing tone, or reaching tone.

Quarter-note rests (column 2 of Figure 9)—the program selects one of divisions (a) through (d) above. In modes (b) through (d), the first unit of the division always becomes a rest; subsequent units become pickups to the next melodic phrase: scale tones, passing tones, or reaching tones

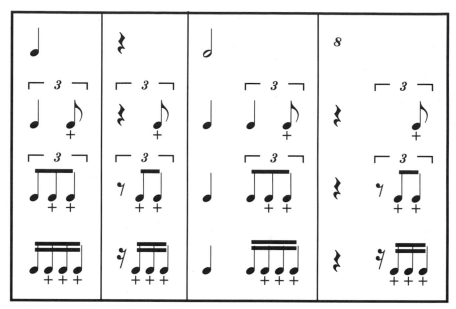

Figure 9. Standard Jazz Solo Embellishments for Quarter Note, Quarter Rest, Half Note, and Half Rest (without appoggiaturas). Each column represents an unrefined duration; each row represents a mode of division. Crosses show secondary chord tones, scale tones and/or ornamental melodic functions.

Half notes (column 3 of Figure 9; appoggiaturas not shown)—the program divides each half note into two tied quarter notes. For the first quarter note, it decides randomly whether to apply a swing-eighth appoggiatura. For the second quarter notes, the program selects one of divisions (a) through (d) listed above. The first unit of this retains the tie from the previous quarter; subsequent units become secondary chord tones, passing tones, or reaching tones.

Half-note rests—(column 4 of Figure 9) the program divides each half rest into two quarter rests. It leaves the first of these quarter rests alone. For the second quarter rest, the program selects one of divisions (a) through (d) above. The first unit of the division also becomes a rest; subsequent units become scale tones, passing tones, or reaching tones.

Pitches are chosen using a search similar to that described earlier for the walking bass line. Most constraints affecting standard jazz solo pitches can be inferred from the rhythmic functions, so the program delegates such constraints to a genre-independent pitch-testing routine. Augmenting these functional constraints are a test forbidding large compound leaps and a test requiring resolution of unstable consonances (e.g., chord thirds) and chordal dissonances (e.g., chord sevenths) within three primary notes. For consecutive primary notes, this test accepts as a resolution any chord tone lying within a major third of the unstable pitch; resolutions deferred for two or more primary notes must be stepwise. An exception is made if the unstable pitch (or an octave equivalent) reappears within the three-primary-note frame, in which case the instability transfers to the later note.

Ornaments are generated by a "standard ornament generator," which is also employed by the Latin jazz and ragtime genres. This ornament generator first determines a scale by consulting the goal pitch's link to the chordal rhythm. It next compiles a list of ornaments using the following one-note and two-note formulas:

For one-note ornaments, the standard ornament generator considers four candidates:

1) upper diatonic neighbor;
2) lower diatonic neighbor;
3) upper chromatic neighbor, but only if this pitch creates a descending chromatic line from the source pitch (taken from the primary note immediately preceding the ornament) to the goal pitch;
4) lower chromatic neighbor, but only if this pitch creates an ascending chromatic line from source to goal.

For two-note ornaments, the standard ornament generator considers six candidates:

1) the next-upper diatonic neighbor (the pitch two diatonic steps above the goal pitch) followed by the upper diatonic neighbor;
2) the upper diatonic neighbor followed by the upper chromatic neighbor, but only if the upper diatonic neighbor lies a whole step above the goal pitch; if this candidate is not applicable, then the following alternative is considered: the next-upper chromatic neighbor (the pitch two chromatic steps above the goal pitch) followed by the upper chromatic neighbor, but only if these pitches produce a descending chromatic line from source to goal;
3) the next-lower diatonic neighbor followed by the lower diatonic neighbor;
4) the lower diatonic neighbor followed by the lower chromatic neighbor, but only if the lower diatonic neighbor lies a whole step below the goal pitch; if this candidate is not applicable, then the following alternative is considered: the next-lower chromatic neighbor followed by the lower chromatic neighbor, but only if these pitches produce an ascending chromatic line from source to goal;
5) the upper diatonic neighbor followed by the lower diatonic neighbor;
6) lower diatonic neighbor followed by the upper diatonic neighbor.

Once the list of ornaments is derived, the program shuffles the list into random order (in genres employing imitation, the program sorts ornaments so that the closest imitative matches come first). The first ornament that conforms to the ornamental melodic functions (which may specify upper or lower neighbor, or which may forbid nonscale pitches) is the one used; if no ornament is suitable, then the ornament generator communicates its failure to the pitch-selection search, which discards the goal pitch and tries another candidate.

The Rhythm Section.   The rhythm section in a "standard" jazz ensemble lays out the points of reference—meter, phrasing, and harmony—from which the solo part takes its meaning. These points of reference are established through a partnership between the walking bass, background chords, and drums:

Walking Bass —The walking bass spells out chord roots and states the rhythmic pulse. It is composed using the procedures described in the first part of this article.

Background Chords —Background chords are usually limited to "punching" the chord changes. Punches tend to be balanced between on-the-beat punches and punches displaced by a swing-eighth note before or after the beat. The refinements used to generate jazz background rhythms differ significantly from the ones described so far: these refinements do not simply divide long notes into shorter notes and rests—they can also annex time from a preceding duration to create an anticipation.

Standard jazz background pitches are chosen in the following way: First, the program composes the topmost background part using the same procedures it uses to compose the solo part, but with the sparse, "punching" rhythms described above. This line is then thickened out in open-position block chords, using a table of chords with an entry for each chord type (e.g., tonic major, subdominant major, submediant minor, etc.) and for each chromatic pitch.

Drums —A jazz drummer combines the time-keeping role of the walking bass with the punches of the background chords; he also articulates the form by playing "turns' at the ends of phrases. Time-keeping is generally kept by playing beats 2 and 4 with the high-hat pedal and by playing common bebop ride-cymbal patterns. Snare and bass drums provide punches around beats 1 and 3 (cf. "Background Chords"). At phrase-endings, the time-keeping role is transferred from the ride cymbal to the bass drum; turns are played on the snare drums and tom-toms. Short (half-measure) turns announce 4-bar boundaries; long (full-measure) turns warn of impending new phrases and choruses.

Latin Jazz

Latin jazz is a hybrid of American Bebop and the Bossa Nova style popular in Brazil during the 1960s; its major champion was saxophonist Stan Getz. Some characteristics of the Latin jazz genre are a syncopated "straight eighth" feel, extended phrases, and chromatic chord-root movement. The models implemented by the Cybernetic Composer are: A only, AABA, and ABAC.

The Solo Layer.   The name of the game for Latin jazz solos is understatement. Latin jazz solos often proceed in sustained notes or in syncopated eighths and quarters. The greatest rhythmic activity usually happens in the pickups just before phrase boundaries; here one might encounter a run of several consecutive eighths, or even a bracketed tuplet. As likely as not, strong beats of the measure will be anticipated by an eighth note.

When it generates a Latin jazz solo, the Cybernetic Composer begins as always with the chordal rhythm. Long durations are usually divided up into whole and half notes; if a long note initiates a phrase, then the program sometimes contents itself with applying a pickup rhythm to the end of the note. Whole notes can also sustain with simply a pickup at the end; alternatively one of the appoggiaturas illustrated in Figure 10 can be applied—and possibly a pickup as well. Half notes can be left alone or refined by any of the refinements enumerated in Figure 11; these same refinements also generate pickup rhythms for longer notes. The pitch-selection procedures are identical with those used to compose the standard jazz solo part. Once a refinement has been applied, the program decides (with 50% weight of success, guided by statistical feedback) whether to apply an eighth-note anticipation to the note on the strong beat.

Figure 10. Some Characteristic Latin-Jazz Solo Appoggiaturas Applied to a Whole-Note A. Crosses show dissonances.

Figure 11. Local Rhythmic Refinements for Latin Jazz Solo Parts. The quintuplet may be used only as a pickup rhythm at phrase-endings

The Rhythm Section.   The Latin jazz soloist gets away with understatement because the Latin rhythm section is much more active than the standard jazz rhythm section. Two things that prevent this activity from intruding into the foreground are (1) the fact that the bass line and background chords have generally simple pitch usage and (2) the fact that although the drum riffs are complex in and of themselves, they quickly settle in with repetition.

Bass Line—The bass is strongly functional and limited almost exclusively to chord roots and fifths, with some reaching tones at chord changes. Downbeats and upbeats are obligatory only at chord changes; otherwise, the bass favors offbeat attacks.

Background Chords—Backgrounds avoid rhythmic intrusiveness by holding onto the same chord for several strokes at time. The pitch-selection procedures are identical with those used to compose the standard jazz background layer.

Drums—The drums play the quarter-note beat on the bass drum and accent the upbeats with the high-hat and left hand (snare and toms). The right hand plays on the ride cymbal or cowbell using syncopated eighth-note patterns. The Cybernetic Composer builds up a Latin jazz drum accompaniment by creating two-measure patterns for each phrase type(vamp, A phrase, B phrase, etc.). These patterns repeat constantly through the duration of a phrase; turns are not used.

Rock

Some consistent features of rock music are 4/4 and related meters and a syncopated straight-eighth feel. Chordal qualities tend to be homogeneous (e.g., all dominant seventh chords or all minor seventh chords)—at least throughout the span of a phrase. Chords roots favor scale degrees I, IV, V, bVI, bIII, bVII, II, and bII (in the key of C these roman numerals translate into C, F, G, Ab, Eb, Bb, D, and Db). Kaye (1969), Feldstein (1978), and Roth (1984) all influenced our formulation of rock idioms.

Phrase Types and Styles.   Choruses of the Cybernetic Composer's rock models are pieced together from three types of phrases: *verses*, *bridges*, and *tags*; how phrase types are assembled depends upon the model. The models are 16–bar blues; 8–bar verse with 4–bar bridge; repeated 4–bar verse with 8–bar bridge; and repeated 8–bar verse with repeated 4–bar bridge. Each verse, bridge, and tag can independently assume either a dominant-seventh quality or a minor-seventh quality. In addition, phrase types can independently assume any of four styles:

Eighth-note bass—background chords and drums punch beat 2 and/or eighth-note syncopations; bass mostly plays eighth notes;

Riff bass—background chords and drums as in eighth-note bass; bass plays riffs;

Fast funk—solo, background chords, bass, and drums all play highly active, sixteenth-note syncopations;

Double-time (bridges only)—sustained background chords; bass and drums in sixteenth-notes.

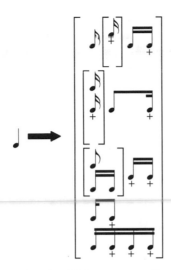

Figure 12. Some 'Regular' Refinements for the Quarter Note in the Rock Solo Layer. Rectangular brackets delimit alternative rhythmic streams; crosses show ornamental melodic functions.

Instrumental Roles.   Rock does not share with jazz and ragtime such rigid distinction between solo part and rhythm section. Although the solo part usually remains among the most active of layers, the background chords, bass line, and drums frequently contribute to the musical fabric on equal terms.

Solo—the rock genre employs two types of rhythm for the solo layer: "regular" and fast funk. Regular rhythms are used with the eighth-note bass, riff bass, and double-time styles; fast funk rhythms are used with the fast funk style. To generate regular rhythms, the program begins by dividing the chordal rhythm into quarter notes; each quarter note is then further elaborated by one of many rhythmic refinements. Five of these refinements are shown in Figure 12. Fast funk rhythms are based on the half note instead of the quarter; three fast-funk refinements are shown in Figure 13. The rock solo pitch-selection procedures are similar to those used in composing the standard jazz solo part, with two important qualifications:

1) Rock constraints are looser. Where chord thirds and sevenths are treated as unstable or dissonant in jazz and ragtime, in rock all chord tones are stable.

2) Instead of the standard ornament generator, the rock genre employs a specialized ornament generator, which lists specific, idiosyncratic ornaments (one to three notes) for each member of the basic dominant 7th and minor 7th sonorities. The rock genre also may substitute the fourth scale degree for a chord tone, provided that such notes are embellished by the flattened fifth—a classic rock blue note—and provided as well that such notes resolve downward by step.

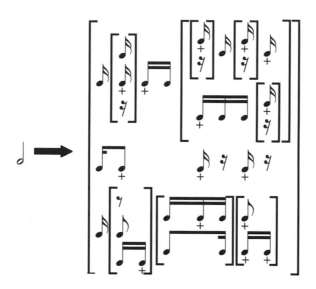

Figure 13. Some Fast Funk Refinements for Half Notes in the Solo Layer.

Bass—The eighth-note bass style is strongly functional, both rhythmically and chordally; the bass plays roots and reaching notes in eighths, dotted eighths, and sixteenths. The riff bass style alternates between strong metric stresses (especially of beats 1 and 2) and sixteenth-note anticipations. Fast funk bass lines feature staccato syncopations and emphatic offbeats. Double time bass parts employ a hard-driving, sixteenth-note ictus, but compensate for their heightened rhythmic drive by sticking mostly to chord roots. The pitch-selection procedures are very close to those used to compose the rock solo part.

Background—Against both the eighth-note bass and the riff bass, the background employs a common style alternating between upbeat stresses and eighth-note syncopations. Fast funk backgrounds emulate the organ playing on Tower of Power's *Urban Renewal* album. Against the double-time bass, the background rhythm consists mostly of sustained whole, half, and quarter notes, sometimes modified by sixteenth-note anticipations.

As with the jazz genres, rock background pitches are selected by first generating the topmost background part, and then thickening out this topmost part in blocked chords. However, nonchord rock ornaments are harmonized by parallel motion: the program skips forward to the next chordal tone, blocks out a chord there, and then works its way back using same chord in transposition for each ornament. The pitch-selection procedures for the topmost closely resemble the procedures used to compose the rock solo part.

Drums—For sample rock drum patterns, readers should refer to Feldstein (1979). Both the eighth-note bass and riff-bass styles employ variations of the less active riffs listed by Feldstein under "Hard Rock" and "Jazz-Rock." The fast funk styles employ variations of Feldstein's "Funky Rock" riffs, and the double-time style employs variations of Feldstein's more active "Jazz-Rock" riffs. The program builds up a rock drum accompaniment by creating one- or two-measure riffs and by repeating these riffs constantly, with turns prior to important phrase boundaries.

Ragtime

Ragtime is an early 20th century style epitomized by the piano compositions of Scott Joplin. Ragtime forms lend themselves to algorithmic generation. A chorus is invariably constructed of two phrases of eight 2/4 bars, each phrase is constructed in turn from two four-bar units. An individual unit may be through-composed, but more likely it will be built up of repeated half-measure, full-measure, or two-measure figures. Either the second or third unit can imitate the first unit; the fourth imitates either the second unit or the third. The form as a whole almost invariably follows the scheme AA BB A CC DD (The program also uses the abbreviated scheme ABACD), where the B phrase *sometimes* shifts into the dominant key, the C phrase *always* shifts into the subdominant key, and the D phrase either returns to the tonic or remains in the subdominant. Each Cybernetic Composer rag plays a monophonic solo part over an oom-pah accompaniment. Drums are not used.

Solo. Ragtime solo rhythm emphasizes eighths and sixteenths, with frequent sixteenth-note syncopations and anticipations. Figure 14 illustrates some half-note rhythmic patterns. Solo pitches for the ragtime layer are chosen using the exact constraints and ornament generator employed for the standard and Latin jazz genres.

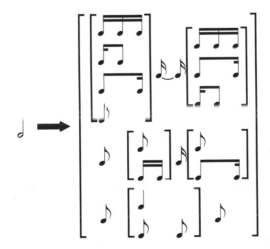

Figure 14. Some Solo Refinements to the Half Note in the Ragtime Genre.

Accompaniment. The ragtime accompaniment deviates strongly from the norm of Cybernetic Composer procedures in that the bass line and background chords are directly coordinated with one another. When it refines a primary note from the chordal rhythm, the ragtime-accompaniment procedure determines at the same moment how the bass and chords will complement one another.

Ragtime chordal progressions describe not only keys, roots, and qualities, but also the discretion available to the program in selecting chord tones for the bass. A common feature of Joplin's oom-pah bass lines is that even with nominal root-position chords, the root does not necessarily sound on the downbeat. Ragtime harmonies are also frequently characterized by passing inversions and by the classical device of a second-inversion tonic chord just before a cadence. All this is considered by the program as it composes its ragtime bass lines.

Once the bass pitches have been chosen, the program directs its attention to the background chords. Instead of filling in block chords under a background lead, ragtime backgrounds have true voice-leading with resolution of dissonances and leading tones, avoidance of parallel perfect consonances, and sensitivity to which chord tones are mandatory (e.g., thirds and sevenths) or optional (e.g., chord fifths). The process of background pitch-selection is aware of what the bass is playing, so the program can act to avoid parallel fifths or octaves with the bass. If the third appears in the bass, the background chords will exclude the third and include the root, and so on.

Acknowledgments

The Cybernetic Composer was instigated by Raymond Kurzweil and developed under a generous grant of funds and equipment from the Kurzweil Foundation. Dave Oppenheim of Opcode Systems supplied the MIDI interface driver; Paul DuBois wrote the Macintosh application skeleton. Our thanks also to Chet Graham, Christopher Yavelow, Wendy Dennis, and Alison Roberts for their advice and encouragement.

Notes

1. The incorporation of melodic functions into rhythmic descriptions was an important feature of Hiller and Ames's Mix and Match program. However, the Cybernetic Composer employs completely different techniques for rhythmic generation and thematic imitation.

2. This is only the latest of many applications of Chomsky's generative grammars to composing programs; see for example Holtzman, 1980 and Ames, 1987b. In Chomskian jargon, our "chordal rhythm" serves as the "axiom," while our "refinements" serve as "productions."

References

Ames, C. 1990. Statistics and Compositional Balance. *Perspectives of New Music* 28(1):80.

Ames, C. 1988a. *Concurrence*. *INTERFACE: Journal of New Music Research* 17(1): 3.

Ames, C. 1988b. How the Cybernetic Composer Works. Technical report, Kurzweil Foundation, 411 Waverley Oaks Drive, Waltham, Mass.

Ames, C. 1987a. Automated Composition in Retrospect: 1956-1986. *LEONARDO: Journal of the International Society for Science, Technology, and the Arts* 20(2): 169.

Ames, C. 1987b. Tutorial on Automated Composition. In *Proceedings* of the 1987 ICMC, 1.

Ames, C. 1986. Two Pieces for Amplified Guitar. *Interface* 15(1): 35.

Ames, C. 1985. Applications of Linked Data Structures to Automated Composition. In *Proceedings* of the 1985 International Computer Music Conference (ICMC), 251. San Francisco, Calif.: Computer Music Association.

Ames, C. 1982. *Protocol*: Motivation, design, and production of a composition for solo piano. *INTERFACE* 11(4): 213.

Ebcioglu, K. 1988. An Expert System for Harmonizing 4-part Chorales. *Computer Music Journal* 12(3): 43. Ebcioglu has published various descriptions of this program since it was first implemented in 1984.

Ebcioglu, K. 1980. Computer Counterpoint. In Proceedings of the 1987 ICMC, 534.

Feldstein, S. 1978. *Drum-Set Club Date Dictionary*. New York: Alfred Publishing Company.

Fry, C. 1980. Computer Improvisation. *Computer Music Journal* 4(3): 48.

Gill, S. 1963. A Technique for the Composition of Music in a Computer. *The Computer Journal* 6(2): 129.

Hiller, L. and Ames, C. 1985. Automated Composition: An Installation at the 1985 International Exposition in Tsukuba, Japan. *Perspectives of New Music* 23(2): 196.

Hiller, L. and Isaacson, L. 1959. *Experimental Music*. New York: McGraw-Hill.

Holtzman, S. 1980. A Generative Grammar Definitional Language for Music. *Interface* 9(1): 1.

Kaye, C. 1969. *How to Play the Electric Bass*. New York: Gwyn Publishing Company.

Mehegan, J. 1959-1965. *Jazz Improvisation*, in four volumes. New York: Watson-Guptill Publications.

Roth, A. 1984. *Arlen Roth's Complete Electric Guitar*. New York: Doubleday & Company.

Thomas, M.T. 1985. VIVACE, a Rule-Based AI System for Composition. In *Proceedings* of the 1985 ICMC, 267.

Abstract

In this chapter, we will examine the design and implementation of a system called WOLFGANG that composes tonal monodies. Our examination will focus on defining the evaluation criteria guiding WOLFGANG's compositional processing. The thesis of the work presented is derived from the hypothesis that a system's (innate) sense of musical sound strongly influences the development of its perception as well as composing habits. As the system develops its musical skills, it also develops a subjective use of a musical language biased by its sense of musical sound, and its adaptation to the cultural grammar of its environment.

Chapter 9

WOLFGANG—A System Using Emoting Potentials to Manage Musical Design

R. Douglas Riecken

AT&T Bell Laboratories/Rutgers Uniuversity

"That music gives pleasure is axiomatic. Because that is so, the pleasures of music as a subject for discussion may seem to some of you a rather elementary dish to place before so knowing an audience. But I think you will agree that the source of that pleasure, our musical instinct, is not at all elementary; it is, in fact, one of the prime puzzles of consciousness. Why is it that sound waves, when they strike the ear, cause 'volleys of nerve impulses to flow up into the brain,' resulting in a pleasurable sensation? More than that, why is it that we are able to make sense out of these 'volleys of nerve signals' so that we emerge from engulfment in the orderly presentation of sound stimuli as if we had lived through a simulacrum of life, the instinctive life of the emotions? And why, when safely seated and merely listening, should our hearts beat faster, our temperature rise, our toes start tapping, our minds start racing after the music hoping it will go one way and watching it go another, deceived and disgruntled when we are unconvinced, elated, and grateful when we acquiesce?"

Aaron Copland (Copland 1911)

By casual observation, one might consider the principle problem of investigation described within this chapter as a study in the composition of music by computer. While the body of work reported herein describes a computer software system for composing musical compositions, the composition process is actually a secondary problem of interest; mainly, *the composition process serves as a tool by which to examine the problem of how to define evaluation criteria able to guide a composition process.* An investigation of this problem entails the formal representation of a set of emotional properties which contribute to the formal structure and functioning of the system. These properties can be represented as (1) principles defining *epistemological adequacy*, or (2) *system components* which consistently and explicitly define aspects of system behavior, or (3) both.

Throughout this chapter, *epistemological adequacy* refers to the completeness of the corpus of knowledge encoded in system memory required to compose musical compositions. Due to this corpus, the system can follow, based on a first order logic embedded in the knowledge, a valid sequence of steps in composing a given musical work. *System components* are seen as influencing related components, especially system memory, by way of specific structures and functions. Specifically, system components manage and modify system memory (effect the access and use of knowledge encoded in memory), thus modifying the reasoning process.

What we hope to provide in this chapter is a plausible theory that demonstrates *how* a computer system might develop an ability to compose music in a personalized manner, and that determines what structures and functions possibly support the development of a personalized composition process. We attempt to provide a framework for such a theory based on the continuing study and design of the WOLF-GANG system. (This chapter reports on the second generation of the WOLFGANG system; WOLFGANG is presently being redesigned into a third generation model).

> "For at best, the very aim of syntax oriented theories is misdirected; they aspire to describe the things that minds produce—without attempting to describe how they're produced."
>
> *Marvin Minsky (Minsky 1981)*

Related Work

In reviewing the corpus of research focused on composition of music by computer, one observes that considerable grounding has resulted from the application of two distinct approaches of design and implementation. The first approach is based on such methods of probability as stochastic processes and Markov chains. This approach was quite active during the late fifties and the sixties (Hiller 1959, Hiller 1970, Hiller 1981; Pinkerton 1956). (Hiller 1970) reports on the development of other significant composing systems during this period by (1) Brooks, Hopkins, Neumann, and Wright, (2) Gill, and (3) Zaripov. The work of Brooks et al. is based on stochastic models for the analysis and synthesis of music. The work of Gill and Zaripov is based on the approach of design and implementation described below.

The second approach is based on production system models (see Note 1 in Glossary); such a model relies on the construction of propositions to define a system's knowledge. Such propositions are constructed by first-order logic using modus ponens (a typical approach for the construction of a first generation expert system). The system developed by Gill is based on heuristically-guided tree searching, while Zaripov's system appears to be a rule-based system.

During the 1970s and the 1980s, there appears to have been great interest in developing production systems which perform some set of musical tasks. This approach allowed researchers to construct models by which to simulate theories of cognitive processing, and to develop theories of composition. From the literature, one observes production system based models addressing such musical tasks as analysis of music (Rothgeb 1980; Smoliar 1980; Roads 1982), improvisation (Ulrich 1977; Levitt 1985, Levitt 1981), chorale harmonization (Ebcioglu 1984; Thomas 1985), development/machine learning (Schawanauer 1986; Riecken 1989), grammar-based composing (Ames 1982, Ames 1988, Ames 1985; Cope 1988, Cope 1987; Roads 1984), and music cognition by human or machine applied to composing and listening (Marsella 1988; Vincinanza 1989; Laske 1990, Laske 1988, Laske 1988, Laske 1977; Tenney 1980). Towards the end of the eighties, researchers have also begun to investigate a third design and implementation approach based on parallel processing and connectionism. While this work is fairly new, it has provided several useful results and several working systems (Vercoe 1988; Lischka 1987; Bharucha 1988).

The production systems described above have two salient features. First, their performance is based on a set of facts and rules (propositions); second, the knowledge embedded in these facts and rules is acquired from some theory of music. Examples of such theories of music include the generative theory of tonal music of Lerdahl and Jackendoff (Lerdahl 1983), and the theory of harmony authored by Piston (Piston 1941). Most of the research in composition undertaken by the described systems has entailed defining a representation of the adopted harmonic theory, often via a set of grammatical formalisms. From a review of production systems in the literature, it appears that many researchers have used grammatical formalisms to represent the musical facts and rules of their respective theories.

The design goals of WOLFGANG have evolved from the premise that a considerable percentage of cited work reporting the design and implementation of composing systems are based on establishing grammatical formalisms to construct propositions. Specifically, the knowledge contents of many of these systems result from knowledge-bases deriving from some *cultural grammar*. By *cultural grammar,* we refer to systems that guide composition processes by way of a musical theory reflecting the musical grammar of a given culture, such as, e.g., 19th century Western music.

Based on the assumption that a composer develops his or her skills based on some theories of music reflective of the composer's cultural development, I now put forth the following two propositions as guides to the research reported in this chapter. First, if WOLFGANG is to demonstrate an ability to compose music, then it must develop a musical skill that reflects its musical development within some environment. Thus, WOLFGANG would demonstrate cultural grammar based processing. Second, if WOLFGANG is to demonstrate cultural grammar based processing, then WOLFGANG must be designed with an (innate) ability to sense and attentively "perceive" musical sound, i.e., to utilize the musical characteristics it encounters in its environment.

> "A man, viewed as a behaving system , is quite simple. The apparent complexity of his behavior over time is largely a reflection of the complexity of the environment in which he finds himself."
>
> *Herbert A. Simon (Simon 1969)*

History of WOLFGANG Research Objectives

The WOLFGANG system began as a research project to study the development of compositional performance. This work focused on the application of Michalski's STAR methodology (Michalski 1983) for inductive machine learning in a knowledge-based system; it resulted in the first generation of WOLFGANG. In this first generation system, the evaluation criteria for guiding the composition process were derived from an implied grammar of Western music. This grammar was represented in terms of facts and rules in WOLFGANG's knowledge-base.

The second generation of WOLFGANG introduces emotional criteria; it allows a user to request a sixty-four measure monody composition that realizes an emotional characteristic chosen by the user. The set of emotional characteristics includes happiness, sadness, anger, and meditativeness. The second generation of the WOLFGANG addresses two different areas of research: (1) investigation of musical development, and (2) extension of the evaluation criteria guiding the composition process. Within this chapter we will focus on the second research area.

In developing the second generation WOLFGANG system, the following plausible hypothesis for how to guide the composition process was applied. The hypothesis states that *knowledge defining a system's (innate) sense of musical sound strongly influences the development of its musical perception and composing habits*. It is hypothesized further that as *such a system learns, it develops a personalized profile. This profile is forged from both the system's sense of musical sound and its adaptation to the cultural music grammar of its environment.*

To examine this hypothesis, WOLFGANG was designed to guide its composition process biased by a cultural grammar of music, as well as by a *disposition* for crafting musical phrases such that they express a specific emotional characteristic (see Note 2 in Glossary). Specifically, the evaluation criteria guiding WOLFGANG's composing process consists of: (1) a cultural grammar reflective of WOLFGANG's musical development, and (2) an ability to realize the emotive potential of musical elements represented in the respective cultural grammar.

An abstract description of WOLFGANG's composition process is as follows. Based on the grammatical context of a given compositional decision, WOLFGANG defines a set of valid solutions from its domain knowledge of music which satisfy the cultural grammar; then WOLFGANG selects from this set of valid solutions that solution which best satisfies WOLFGANG's current disposition, in order to endow the current musical phrase with a specific emotive potential.

Cultural Grammar and Disposition

Before examining the WOLFGANG system in depth, a brief discussion of the terms of *cultural grammar* and *disposition* should improve our understanding on their use throughout this chapter.

WOLFGANG's *cultural grammar* represents its complete body of domain knowledge for composing music. This knowledge is acquired and used by WOLFGANG over some period of its musical development. The knowledge consists of two classes of elements: (1) musical "methods" (e.g., methods of motivic development, methods of harmonization, etc.) and (2) musical "artifacts" (e.g., musical intervals, melodic ornamentation, etc.). A third category consists of musical elements that are examples of musical artifacts that have become part of WOLFGANG's musical lexicon during the development process. Also, specific elements from WOLFGANG's corpus of musical elements (both methods and artifacts), over time tend to demonstrate a higher frequency of use in specific contextual composing scenarios; this fact establishes patterns of composing habits. We might postulate that these patterns make up WOLFGANG's compositional signature.

WOLFGANG's *disposition* for crafting musical phrases such that they express specific emotive characteristics is supported by two design features. First, WOLFGANG is designed with a facility to express the emoting potential of musical materials. As WOLFGANG develops its musical skills, this facility not only permits emotional expressiveness; it also influences the construction of WOLFGANG's cultural grammar. Second, WOLFGANG's disposition is defined by its ability to realize specific emotions (viz., one of the four emotions supported by WOLFGANG). Changes in the dispositional state of WOLFGANG occur whenever the context dealt with during a composing session motivates change to a different emotion type. This design feature provides WOLFGANG with a range of possible behaviors during compositional processing.

System Architecture

Before addressing the actual functions of the WOLFGANG system, we should first examine the components that define the system architecture. These components provide the software structures by which WOLFGANG functions. WOLFGANG consists of the following five system components:

1) a corpus of K-nodes
2) a K-line network
3) a set of blackboard systems
4) a disposition feedback facility, and
5) logfiles.

Each of these components will now be discussed in detail; the discussion will focus on issues of architecture and function (purpose). Figure 1 shows the components that make up WOLFGANG's system architecture. Description of how the system components function (perform) will be presented in System Functioning.

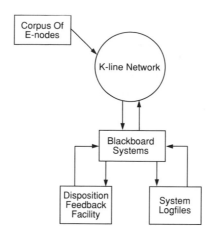

*Figure 1. Graphical Representation of System Components
Which Compose WOLFGANG's Architecture*

The Corpus of E-Nodes

The Notion of E-Node.   E-nodes (emotion-nodes) are the most fundamental system component. Informally, an E-node is a collection of information defining the emoting potential of a given *primitive musical artifact.* The term *primitive musical artifact* refers to higher-level music-structural elements such as musical modality, vertical harmonic structures (e.g., a tonic triad, a dominant seventh, etc.), horizontal harmonic structures (harmonic progressions consisting of paired vertical harmonic structures), amplitude, tempo, rhythm, and musical intervals between paired pitches. The use of the term *emotive* refers to a primitive musical artifact's potential to express emotion or sentiment in a demonstrative manner. The information provided by each E-node allows WOLFGANG to interpret the emoting potential of each primitive musical artifact. While the musical artifacts mentioned are actually quite complex structures (in terms of music theory), for the design of WOLFGANG they are viewed as simple (cognitive) elements, and in that sense, are taken for granted as elements of the musical imagination.

A critical issue concerning E-nodes must now be reviewed. E-nodes are not instances of musical knowledge as are primitive musical artifacts. An E-node is simply a qualification of the emotive potential of a given primitive musical artifact. In order for WOLFGANG to be knowledgeable of a given primitive musical artifact, a representation of the respective artifact must be encoded into system memory. Once this representation has been encoded, it inherits its emoting potential from the respective E-node. Thus E-nodes serve as (innate) system properties; they are not part of WOLFGANG's musical knowledge.

Now that we have an abstract sense of what an E-node is, let us review it in more detail. An E-node was defined as a collection of information; the actual composition of this information consists of a set of four numeric values. Each numeric value defines the emotive potential of a particular emotion, as realized by the primitive musical artifact represented by an E-node. The four distinct emotions represented by the four numeric values assigned to each E-node are Happiness, Sadness, Anger, and Meditativeness. The design of WOLFGANG provides each primitive musical artifact with its range of emoting potential over the defined set of emotions. (The number of individual emotions supported is currently restricted to four so as to minimize system complexity.)

The significance of E-nodes lies in their qualification of emoting potentials for the four emotions over the complete set of primitive musical artifacts. These emotive qualifiers perform a critical role during WOLFGANG's *development*; they serve as operands by which emoting values are computed and assigned to new primitive musical artifacts, or to a *compound musical artifact*. The term *development* refers to the acquisition of musical knowledge by WOLFGANG to improve its performance as a composer. The term *compound musical artifact* refers to a musical artifact composed directly or indirectly (or both) of two or more primitive musical artifacts. Thus, E-nodes provide emotive primitives (initial properties) used to derive the emoting potential for the combinatorial development of WOLFGANG's musical knowledge.

The decision to specify the emotive potential of all musical artifacts is motivated by our task of developing evaluation criteria for guiding the composition process. As we have learned thus far, one of the metrics which guides WOLFGANG's composition process consists of composing musical phrases that satisfy some current compositional *disposition*. This means that WOLFGANG will attempt to compose a musical phrase provoking a specific emotion that matches the current disposition of the system; at any moment, WOLFGANG's disposition is at some level of Happiness or Sadness, Anger or Meditativeness. Therefore, the selection of musical artifacts is biased towards those musical artifacts which provide the highest emotional potential matching WOLFGANG's current disposition; consequently, the system design of WOLFGANG requires a method to specify the emoting potential of all musical artifacts.

Motivation for Defining E-Nodes. As briefly discussed earlier, WOLFGANG is a research effort geared to understanding the composition process; it is, however, also geared to the effort of designing a system that develops the musical skill to compose music. My initial work with WOLFGANG was based on the hypothesis that musical development is biased by an organism's (innate) sense and perception of (musical) sound, and its adaptation to the musical sounds of its environment during cognitive development. Thus, my design goal in the use of E-nodes is to provide WOLFGANG with an (innate) sense of sound by which to bias its development of musical skills. Further, as WOLFGANG begins to acquire musical knowledge, its musical culture will also bias development. Metaphorically, E-nodes provide WOLFGANG with an (innate) "physiological" sense of musical sound.

If E-nodes provide the primitive basis due to which emoting potentials are computed for all musical artifacts (higher-level music-structural elements), then what criteria motivate the use of E-nodes as a system component? Psychological research in music perception addresses the extent to which the construction of a melody is influenced by factors *extrinsic to music* - in particular, by the natural pitches of the harmonic series and their effects on, and within, the human ear, and the human auditory system. For example, musical idioms of the world as a whole demonstrate a high salience for the octave, perfect fifth and perfect fourth due to the harmonic series (Jackendoff 1987; Balzano 1982; Clynes 1977, Clynes 1970; Jairazbhoy 1971; Dowling 1986). Thus, the idea is to define sets of E-nodes that attempt to represent plausible salient features found in many cultures of music.

As an example, repertoires for the kyoto, sitar, balalaika, lute, and guitar all demonstrate a high salience for octaves, perfect fifths, perfect fourths, cycles of fifths, and cadences built from perfect fifths. These musical components are strong, and support a sense of finality. They are useful in constructing resolution from tension or climax. Other primitive musical artifacts such as major/minor seconds, augmented fourths, minor sixths, and minor sevenths are less stable and are useful to generate tension or climax.

Time trajectories are another important property in music perception. For example, faster tempi support higher levels of energy while slower tempi perform the inverse (Minsky 1986; Clynes 1977). Another set of properties in music perception addresses the spatial and temporal proximity of pitches in a melodic sequence and their role in the effectiveness of memory recall of melodic phrases. Studies have shown that smaller size intervals, specific pitch groupings, and the tonal context of adjacent melodic phrases are processed and retained with greater accuracy (Deutsch 1982a, Deutsch 1982b, Deutsch 1975; Krumhansl 1979; Butler 1979; Sloboda 1985). Representation of these auditory properties by WOLFGANG provides useful metrics for the motivic development of musical phrases intended to provoke a given emotion.

The Implementation of E-Nodes.   E-nodes are implemented as frames composed of five slots (see Note 3 in Glossary). The first slot in each frame identifies the distinct primitive musical artifact represented by the E-node. For example, the symbol in the first slot could be major second to denote that the respective E-node represents the musical interval of a major second. The next four slots contain the four numeric values representing the four respective emotions. These numeric values are real numbers with a range from zero to one; these values remain constant over all of WOLFGANG's development. Figure 2 provides a graphical representation of an E-node frame. A second design decision regarding the corpus of E-nodes addresses their classification. The corpus of E-nodes is partitioned into classes based on their respective function. Examples of class functions include tempo, musical intervals, and modality. Each E-node class is represented as a list composed of the respective individual E-nodes. Partitioning the corpus of E-nodes into classes provides effective management and efficient access to all E-nodes by localization of functionality.

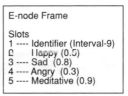

```
E-node Frame

Slots
1 ---- Identifier (Interval-9)
2        Happy (0.5)
3 ---- Sad  (0.8)
4 ---- Angry  (0.3)
5 ---- Meditative (0.9)
```

Figure 2. A Graphical Representation of an E-Node Frame

Memory Based on the K-Line Theory

The storage, access, and management of WOLFGANG's musical domain knowledge
is supported by a network of interconnected musical artifacts; these artifacts
reflect WOLFGANG's musical experiences and development. The principal
influence in the design of WOLFGANG's memory is Marvin Minsky's K-line theory
of memory (Minsky-86, Minsky-80).

> "When you 'get an idea,' or 'solve a problem,' or have a 'memorable experience,' you
> create what we shall call a K-line. This K-line gets connected to those 'mental agencies'
> that were actively involved in the memorable mental event. When that K-line is later
> 'activated,' it reactivates some of those mental agencies, creating a 'partial mental state'
> resembling the original."
>
> *Marvin Minsky (Minsky 1980)*

The K-line memory theory describes the behavior of a system by the dynamic relationships of linked agents called K-lines. The complexity of a K-line can range from
a representation defined by a single instance of information, a K-node, to extremely
complex representations of behavior defined by a K-line composed of a large set of
linked K-lines and K-nodes. Minsky's theory explains that sets of K-lines form societies of agents providing specific mental functions, and that these societies or
agents, or both, can dynamically form multiple connections (K-lines) with each
other to create new K-lines, thus increasing the body of knowledge. It is the activation of sets of K-lines (societies of agents) that bring about partial mental states. A
total mental state is composed of several partial mental states active at a single
moment in time. System development is supported by constructing new K-line connections within or between partial mental states.

Significance in Application of K-Line Memory Features

WOLFGANG's memory is another significant aspect of the system. In the second generation of WOLFGANG, great care was taken to design a system which demonstrated
improvement in its ability to develop. If WOLFGANG is to develop composing skills,
these skills should demonstrate some characteristic of personalized style. The

design of WOLFGANG's memory attempts to capture two powerful qualities found in
the K-line theory: *flexibility* and *recall of personalized habits*.

The term *flexibility* refers to WOLFGANG's ability to store and use diverse knowledge during its development as a composing system. The issue of flexibility provided critical motivation for the evolution from the first generation to the second generation of WOLFGANG. The first generation system consistently reached impassable
stages of development. This problem resulted due to the nature common to knowledge-based systems; these systems have historically demonstrated their ability to perform quite well over restricted sets of problems, except that the acquisition and representation of a large body of knowledge elements quickly promotes conflicting
assertions of facts and rules. The K-line model avoids conflicting assertions by allowing multiple patterns of diverse knowledge to represent different memorable experiences; musical experiences that provide good results during some composing session are therefore encoded as individual K-lines in WOLFGANG's memory. This
representation serves to minimize the number of rules governing methods and
facts, and thus to avoid the attending problems of complexity.

The concept *recall of personalized habits* refers to WOLFGANG's ability to develop
and apply its composing skills in a subjective manner reflecting its musical learning
experiences. This feature of system performance is a direct result of the explicit
method by which musical knowledge is encoded in WOLFGANG's memory (as individual instances (K-lines) of successful musical methods and facts). Thus, as WOLF-
GANG develops, it also develops a distinct style of composing; this results from the
frequent combinations of collaborating K-lines which, over time, are referenced as
one single compound K-line. By attempting to model features of Minsky's K-line
memory, WOLFGANG develops personal composing habits; these habits become the
system's compositional signature.

Design and Implementation of Memory

WOLFGANG's memory is implemented as a frame-based spreading-activation network; semantic relationships within the network form individual K-lines (see Note 4
in Glossary). Each K-line is represented by a discrete set of network links. Figure 3
presents a graphical representation of a K-line; in this figure, a K-line representing
a primary cycle harmonic progression (I, IV, V, I) is defined by an ordered set of
three supporting K-nodes. These links interconnect supporting K-lines or K-nodes,
or both, to represent some musical knowledge. All K-lines and K-nodes are implemented as frame structures known as K-line frames (KF). The slot values in each KF
identify the respective KF and its supporting structures and characteristics. The
overall K-line network is partitioned into two functional parts composed of: (1)
method facts (e.g., methods of motivic development, methods of harmonization, etc.)
and (2) *facts* (specific instances of intervals, harmonic structures, etc.). This design
decision will be discussed in the section on system functioning.

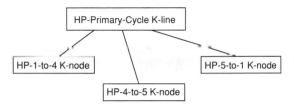

Figure 3. A Graphical Representation of a K-Line Composed of an Ordered Set of Supporting K-Nodes

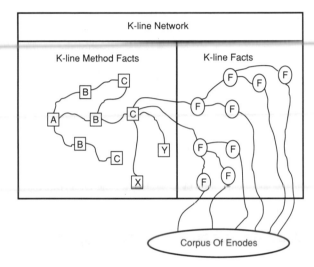

Figure 4. Diagram of Spreading Activation from Initial K-Line Method Fact Labeled A, to Supporting K-Line Method Facts. Supporting Method Facts Are in Turn Supported by K-Line Facts. The activation pathways which terminate as K-line facts define the actual method which satisfies a given goal during compositional processing

Figure 4 shows a minimal partitioned K-line network including interrelationships between K-line method facts and K-line facts; also, the figure shows K-line facts which have a direct correspondence with E-nodes. Within the network, K-lines are partitioned into different classes of musical artifacts, such as sets of intervals, rhythmic patterns, harmonic progressions, methods for motivic development, and so on. This is done to provide effective management and efficient access of system memory; the management and access of K-line classes is supported via blackboard technologies (see Note 5 in Glossary). Finally, each K-line class is implemented as a frame, called a musical-component-frame (MCF). Each MCF consisted of an arbitrary number of slots; each slot in the MCF references a distinct KF contained within the class. The MCFs are implemented as lists. Figure 5 provides a graphical presentation of a MCF representing harmonic substitutions.

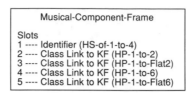

Figure 5. A Graphical Presentation of a MCF

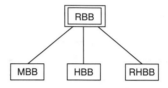

Figure 6. Relational Diagram of WOLFGANG's Blackboard Systems

Blackboards as Knowledge Negotiators

WOLFGANG's blackboard systems serve as knowledge negotiators. They manage the interactions of K-lines from different K-line classes as they collaborate to compose a musical work. The blackboard technologies are implemented in a distributed hierarchical model. The model consists of a primary blackboard system supported by (three) subordinate blackboard systems. The primary blackboard system, called the root blackboard (RBB), manages the overall composition process. The three subordinate blackboard systems include the melodic blackboard (MBB), the harmonic blackboard (HBB), and the rhythmic blackboard (RHBB). These three blackboard systems manage composing processes relating to melody, harmony, and rhythm respectively. Also, these three blackboard systems serve as blackboard knowledge sources (KS) to the RBB.

Each blackboard system is implemented as a shared memory allowing access to its respective K-line classes (e.g., K-line melody classes, K-line methods of motivic development classes, etc.). Activated K-lines within these classes serve as KSs which attempt to assert information provided by each active K-line onto the blackboard. This information is evaluated by a blackboard scheduler. Each blackboard system comprises a scheduler for managing blackboard functions. In WOLFGANG, the schedulers are implemented as inference engines composed of minimal sets of rules relating to the distinct tasks of each respective blackboard. (The schedulers are the only system components within the WOLFGANG architecture whose knowledge is defined by rules.) Figure 6 displays WOLFGANG's blackboard architecture. We will provide a more detailed description of the blackboard systems in the next section.

A Disposition Feedback Facility

The disposition feedback facility provides WOLFGANG with the ability to evaluate decisions made during a composing session. Evaluations are based on the emoting potential derived from each possible decision, and a ranking of each possible decision with regard to an ordered list of previous decisions that demonstrate high emoting potentials. This facility allows WOLFGANG to mark for future use during a given composing session specific musical artifacts that compute high emotional potentials, while satisfying the current disposition of the system.

Implementation of the disposition feedback facility consists of: (1) a feedback loop (2) a variable called the *dispositionValue* (3) an ordered list of decisions called the *listOfGoodElements*. Both variables, *dispositionValue* and *listOfGoodElements*, are asserted and maintained on the RBB. The variable *dispositionValue* maintains the current disposition of WOLFGANG as one of the four emotion types: happy, sad, angry, and meditative. The variable *listOfGoodElements* provides WOLFGANG with a list of musical elements which have been applied previously during the current composition session, and have provided high emoting potentials. This list is significant; it acts as a short term store of musical artifacts applicable in the motivic development of remaining musical phrases. Thus, during each composing session, WOLFGANG creates and appends to the variable *listOfGoodElements* musical features derived from decisions made during the session which provide high emoting potentials. The feedback loop is implemented as a background process that sends status messages to the RRB scheduler when an interesting event has occurred and has been posted on the RBB; the scheduler then appends the musical artifact associated with this event to the *listOfGoodElements*. Figure 7 shows the implemented design for supporting interactions between the disposition feedback facility and the RBB. Further discussion on the functioning of the disposition feedback facility appears later in this chapter.

System Logfile

The logfile insures that each composition is distinct; it provides information of previously composed works, so that WOLFGANG can avoid the excessive repetition of musical artifacts by reviewing its previous composing habits during a session. The logfile consists of trace data from the last twenty sessions stored off in a hard disk file.

System Functioning

Let us now examine the functionality of WOLFGANG. We begin by defining *what* WOLFGANG composes; we will then define *how*, in detail, WOLFGANG functions. Our examination of how WOLFGANG functions will be first at a general system level, and

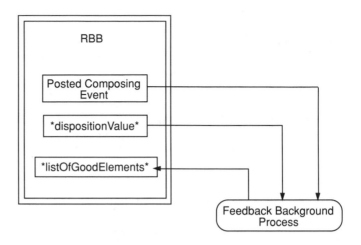

Figure 7. Graphical Representation of the Software Structures and Processes Which Support the Disposition Feedback Facility

then at a system component level. We will describe the general system level from both a user's perspective and a system perspective; the system component level will be presented only from a system perspective.

As previously described, WOLFGANG composes tonal monody compositions. In defining how WOLFGANG functions, our first concern is to define exactly *what* WOLFGANG composes. A completed musical composition is defined by a set of compositional constructs; examples of compositional constructs include the melody, meter, and form of a musical composition. So as to define a tractable composing process, the set of compositional constructs composed by WOLFGANG has been restricted. This set includes melody, modality, harmonic progression, rhythm, tempo, and method of motivic development. Other compositional constructs essential to the definition of a completed tonal composition are provided by WOLFGANG via a *skeletal planning* technique; they include meter, form, composition length, and cadential positioning.

WOLFGANG's *skeletal planning* technique consists of assigning a set of default values for the *meter, form, composition length,* and *positioning of cadences* of the composition to be realized; these values define the composition's skeletal structure. Of these four default values, only the positioning of cadences can be modified during the composition process; such modifications are allowed to support refinement or patching of system goals during the compositional process. The construction of a composition's skeletal structure serves to establish grammatical constraints over a composition process; it restricts the composition process to a tractable set of problems. We will examine the construction of a composition's skeletal structure in more detail shortly.

User and System Perspectives of the Composition Process

User Perspective. From a user perspective, a composing session with WOLFGANG is a two-phase process: (1) session priming, and (2) compositional processing. During session priming, a user provides specific information to initialize the composition process. The user performs three tasks by which initialization values are assigned to internal system structures; he provides WOLFGANG with three kinds of information: musical, emotional, and behavioral. First, the user enters a musical motif as a linear set of musical tones (pitches) with the respective temporal duration of each tone; the motif serves as the seed from which to compose the musical work; the size of the motif must be either two or four measures in length. Second, the user selects the emotional quality that the composition should represent (either happy, sad, angry, or meditative). The final task requires the user to define the behavior of WOLFGANG during the composition session as a type ranging from conservative to aggressive. This behavior metric directs the formulation of goals during the composition session. The idea is that with an aggressive behavior, WOLFGANG is not inhibited from trying new ideas or breaking rules to learn new facts or methods to extend its musical knowledge. Once session priming is complete, all subsequent actions performed by WOLFGANG are perceived by the user as WOLFGANG's composition process.

System Perspective. From a system perspective, a composing session consists of a three phase process: (1) assertion of user initialization values, (2) feature pattern analysis, and (3) compositional processing. From the user's perspective, the second and third phases (feature pattern analysis and compositional processing) are viewed together as the compositional processing phase.

During assertion of the user initialization values, WOLFGANG assigns the user supplied musical motif, the user requested emotion type, and the system behavior type to the respective structures on the RBB. During the feature pattern analysis phase, WOLFGANG performs two tasks: (1) define specific features of the user supplied musical motif which provide the best emoting potentials to match the user requested emotion type, and (2) develop a skeletal design for the composition to be composed.

WOLFGANG evaluates the user supplied motif to define a characterization of the motif that best matches the user requested emotion. This entails parsing the motif into simple elements called sub-motifs; each sub-motif consists of several notes. The selection of sub-motifs is based both on the system's melodic (cultural) grammar, and the emoting potentials derived for each sub-motif. WOLFGANG then maps sets of harmonic progressions onto the parsed motif; these progressions are valid within its cultural grammar and provide the highest desired emoting potentials. The results of this characterization are then stored on the RBB.

The characterization of a user supplied motif is represented on the RBB in the following structures. The pitches and rests from a user supplied motif are assigned as leaves in a *Time Span Tree (TST)* as described by Lerdahl and Jackendoff (Lerdahl et al. 1983). Important sub-motifs within the motif which establish the desired emotion type for the completed composition are then marked as useful elements. The location and composition of each marked sub-motif is added to a list of *good musical ideas for motivic development* called the Motivic Element List (MEL). The MEL is implemented as a list of links into the TST. The final structure, the List of Harmonic Links (LHL), is a list of nested lists. The top level list defines multiple harmonic progressions which support the entire motif and the user requested emotion type of the composition. Each expression in the list defines a specific harmony which is linked to a specific leaf in the TST. When multiple harmonies support the same leaf, then the respective expression for that leaf, when evaluated, returns a list of expressions; each expression contained in the returned list of expressions defines a valid harmony for the respective leaf. Figure 8 shows the internal representation of a user supplied motif on the RBB via the structures just discussed.

Skeletal Structure of the Composition. Once characterization of the user's musical motif is complete, WOLFGANG constructs a skeletal structure of the composition to be composed; this structure is represented on the RBB. WOLFGANG's skeletal structure defines the *length, meter, location of cadences,* and *form* for each composition. Each composition is exactly sixty-four measures in length with a meter of four-four time. The location of cadences is determined based on the length of the user's motif; if the motif is two measures in length then cadences occur every four mea-

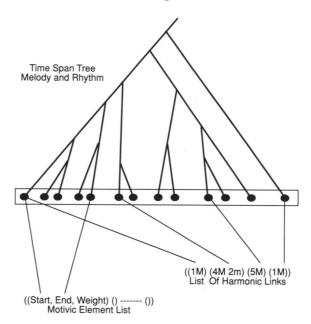

Figure 8. Diagram of the Internal Representation of a User Supplied Motif Represented on the RBB via a TST, a MEL, and a LHL. The dots in the box represent individual nodes; each node defines a specific musical pitch and rhythmic value; the nodes are ordered left to right representing the motif's melody.

sures, else if the motif is four measures in length then cadences occur every eight measures. Further, the musical form of each composition follows a *quasi sonata allegro* musical form. The sonata allegro form is partitioned into three sections: an *exposition section* of thirty-two measures which terminates with a modulation, a *development section* of sixteen measures in a new key or modality, or both, which ends with a modulation back to the original key and modality of the exposition section, and a *recapitulation section* comprised of the final sixteen measures in the original key.

A more detailed view of the skeletal defined form of a composition is as follows. The first sixteen measures of the exposition section first state the entire motif (theme) of the composition, and then motivically develop the motif or its submotifs with minimal variations. The second sixteen measures of the exposition section are dedicated to pure motivic development of the motif. The methods of development during this sixteen measure section are allowed great freedom. This section concludes with a modulation to another key or modality or both. The development section, the next sixteen measures, continues the motivic development of the motif in the new key or modality or both with the same degree of freedom allowed in the second half of the exposition section. The development section terminates with a modulation to the original key and modality of the exposition section. The recapitulation section begins by restating the entire original motif. The remainder of the recapitulation is then composed of several of the *most memorable* motivic artifacts developed in the exposition section. This is accomplished as follows: (as previously discussed) WOLFGANG's disposition feedback facility maintains an ordered list called the *listOfGoodElements*. This list contains specific musical elements (eg., submotivic developed phrases) which demonstrated a high emoting potential to satisfy a current dispositional state during the composing process. So, once the original motif has been restated in the opening measures of the recapitulation, WOLFGANG cuts and pastes specific musical phrases from the *listOfGoodElements* to complete the composition. The criteria for phrase selection consider only those musical phrases developed in the exposition section which have the highest emoting potentials matching the user requested emotion type.

The skeletal structure when represented on the RBB is actually represented as the musical score for the composition to be composed. This score is represented in the identical manner as the user supplied motif. The score consists of a TST to represent the sixty-four measures of melody. As the harmonic structures of the composition are composed, they are represented in a list. Each atom in the list is a specific vertical harmony. The temporal location of each atom is defined by its link to a specific leaf in the melody TST.

Summary of the First Two Phases. To summarize the system perspective of the first and second phases of the composition process, WOLFGANG has (1) asserted and characterized the user input information into internal structures, and (2) developed a skeletal structure of the composition. The internal representation of user input provides efficient access for a broad use of musical knowledge associated with the input; this information will influence motivic development during the composition process. The skeletal structure propagates specific constraints over the composition process; the structure defines the final composition with a fixed length, a fixed form, a fixed meter, and a tentative structure of musical phrases based on the location of cadences.

The Compositional Process Proper.   WOLFGANG final phase of the composition process is that of compositional processing proper. It is during this final phase that WOLFGANG composes musical phrases based on its musical knowledge encoded in the K-line network and its disposition for specific musical constructs. During the compositional processing phase, the K-line network and the blackboard systems together construct and represent the completed composition on the RBB. The activation of the network and blackboard systems is based on the context defined by the user input and the skeletal structure. We will examine how the system components perform this process shortly.

As each musical phrase is constructed during compositional processing, it is added to the skeletal structure on the RBB. As WOLFGANG constructs each musical phrase, the disposition feedback facility inserts any musical elements which provide a high emoting potential matching WOLFGANG's current dispositional state to the *listOfGoodElements*. At the conclusion of the composition processing phases, WOLFGANG saves the final composition and trace data in its logfile.

System Memory—System Component Level

Representation of Emotive Potential.   Let us now examine WOLFGANG at a system component level. We begin with a description of internal representation for the emoting potential of individual musical elements encoded in WOLFGANG's memory. We will subsequently discuss the partitioned functioning of the K-line network.

We have established that E-nodes provide fundamental values to represent the emoting potential of primitive musical artifacts. It remains to be described how these values influence the representation of compound musical artifacts, and how emoting potentials influence the actual composition process.

The propagation of E-node properties over a K-line network is accomplished through a set of algorithms which perform summing, averaging, and smoothing operations based on the compositional complexity of each respective K-line. When a K-line is instantiated, these operations are applied to all the emoting values associated with the individual components (other K-lines) that make up the newly created K-line. The results of these operations represent the emoting values for the newly instantiated K-line. This is to be understood in more detail as follows.

Each K-line is implemented as a frame structure called a K-line frame (KF). Each KF contains six slots. The first slot stores the K-line identification symbol. The second slot contains a list of links to supporting structures (eg., K-lines and K-nodes) whose knowledge defines the respective KF. For example, a given five note melody encoded in WOLFGANG's memory as a K-line could be represented by four supporting structures; each supporting structure being a K-line of an individual musical interval, a primitive musical artifact. If a KF represents a primitive musical artifact, then its second slot is set to a null value.

The remaining four slots represent the four emoting potentials (happy, sad, angry, and meditative) of the respective K-line. Each emoting potential is represented by a tuple (a pair of variables). The first variable is a quasi-static weight (QW) and the second variable is a dynamic weight (DW). These weights are used to control the firing of K-lines. Figure 9 displays a detailed representation of a K-line frame. When a K-line is first constructed, each emoting weight is computed and assigned to both variables in the respective tuples.

There are two cases to consider when computing emotional weights:

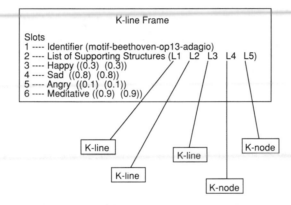

Figure 9. Detailed Diagram of a K-Line Frame. Slot two displays a linked set of supporting K-lines and K-nodes

1) If a KF represents a primitive musical artifact, then the respective KF weights are inherited from the respective E-node, and the K-line is considered a "very-low-level" instance of musical knowledge.

2) If a KF represents a compound musical artifact (a musical artifact composed directly or indirectly, or both directly and indirectly, by two or more primitive musical artifacts), then the respective KF weights are computed by a set of summing, averaging, and smoothing algorithms.

The summing and averaging algorithms compute a mean value for each emoting weight. The smoothing algorithm applies a ratio value to the final computation of the four emoting weights tuples; the ratio is dependent on the complexity of the newly created K-line which is defined by its composition of zero or more supporting K-lines and K-nodes.

Tuple Representation.   We have explained that a KF maintains a tuple for each of the four emoting types. It is important to understand the function of the tuple representation. Each time WOLFGANG initiates a composition session, the DW of each tuple is assigned the value of its respective tuple's QW. The DWs serve to determine which K-line offers the highest emoting potential to satisfy the system's current dispositional state while constructing a musical phrase.

During a composing session, the DWs change based upon events in the K-line network. For example: a current system goal is to fire (activate) the K-line with the highest sad DW which addresses the musical syntax of the current musical phrase being composed. Once this K-line has fired, its sad DW is decremented. This allows other K-lines a chance to fire. Eventually, the sad DW of this K-line is incremented back to the value of its QW; incrementing this DW occurs as related K-lines fire. There is also a special case for incrementing a DW: the system's disposition feedback facility can flag the use (firing) of a K-line as a very positive event and strongly recommend to the respective blackboard scheduler that this K-line be fired again in any similar cases. Under this condition the blackboard scheduler will then immediately assign the value of the QW to the DW.

We have observed that the QW serves as a control weight throughout a composition session, but over time (many sessions) the QW might change. WOLFGANG evaluates its composing habits via its logfile. If a given K-line shows an emoting pattern of high or low usage, the system will readjust the QW accordingly, thus adjusting its musical opinion and permitting WOLFGANG to develop. (Modification is not allowed for the QWs of K-lines representing primitive musical artifacts; this design insures that WOLFGANG maintains its sense of musical sound.)

Logical Pathways for Composition.   As discussed, the K-line network is partitioned into two functional parts. One portion of the network, the *methods-net,* serves as a composer's tool box. The methods-net contains different method-classes defining such compositional methods as cadential resolution, harmonization, transposition, and motivic development. It is important to note that the *methods-net is composed of facts and methods, not rules.* The other portion of the K-line net, the *facts-net,* defines explicitly such musical artifacts, as sets of intervals, rhythmic patterns and harmonic progressions.

Each method-class in the methods-net is constructed by interconnecting many smaller classes or individual K-lines, or both, defining specific types of methods. For example, the method-class defining motivic development is realized and accessed as a K-line composed of many smaller method societies defining types of motivic development, such as inversion, retrograde, and elongation. In turn, each type-of-motivic-development method (society) is represented by multiple K-lines representing facts in the facts-net; each fact being a representation of an actual instance for each respective type-of-motivic-development element encoded in memory. This architecture provides WOLFGANG with logical pathways along which to decompose both compound musical artifacts and composing-methods into multiple combinations of primitive musical artifacts; it is well suited for the application of a problem reduction approach during composition processing (see Problem Reduction of Compositional Processing Tasks). Further, each K-line is an instance of musical knowledge developed during WOLFGANG's life cycle; the topology of WOLFGANG's K-line network reflects a partially ordered sequence of supporting K-lines and K-nodes defining new K-lines. This ordering results from WOLFGANG's development.

There is one major difference between K-lines in the methods-net and the facts-net. K-lines in the facts-net are assigned emotional weights when created. The K-lines in the methods-net inherit emotional weight values temporarily during a composition session. When a given set of K-lines in the methods-net become active, the K-lines temporarily inherit the weights of the musical artifacts in the facts-net to which they correspond.

Blackboard and Schedulers Performance—System Component Level

Problem Reduction of Compositional Processing Tasks. How do the blackboard systems manage the composition process and the K-line network? We observed above how the architecture of WOLFGANG's memory provides logical pathways to decompose musical constructs representative of WOLFGANG's cultural grammar, and that this representation is suited for problem-solving (making decisions) via a problem reduction approach. This is important since the complex structure of a musical composition might require problem reduction techniques as noted in the work of Marsella and Schmidt (Marsella 1988; see also Marsella and Schmidt in this volume). We begin by demonstrating a compositional processing approach based on task reduction and the applicability of blackboard technologies.

Composing music can be viewed as a problem-reduction task; a composer decomposes the task of composing a musical work into several tasks collaborating with each other. Each task might be viewed as an active agent which formulates hypotheses and goals; it determines when its respective goals have been satisfied. For example, a composer crafts a musical phrase by constructing a melody with some harmonic accompaniment. This tasks reduces to such sub-tasks as define the notes, define the rhythm, define the harmony, and insure that all components integrate correctly. It is the role of WOLFGANG's blackboard systems to manage the many sub-tasks involved during a composition session.

In the design of WOLFGANG, the blackboard schedulers and knowledge sources (KS) serve as software agents to address these many sub-tasks that occur during a composition process. These sub-tasks are represented on the primary blackboard system (the root blackboard (RBB)), the three subordinate blackboard systems (the melodic blackboard (MBB), the harmonic blackboard (HBB), and the rhythmic blackboard (RHBB)), and in the K-line network.

The architecture of the K-line network is designed to provide many levels of reduction during a composing session. At the root level, problem reduction is applied to the initial goal: *compose a musical work*. This goal will be satisfied by a set of solutions to sub-problems which are further reduced. Each reduced level of problems is solved by the respective blackboard system's scheduler and KSs. Each level's solution is then applied as a possible contribution to develop a solution to its parent problem. This is recursively performed until the initial goal *compose a musical work* is satisfied.

For example, a given K-line class, called *melody-class*, is assigned the problem to compose a melody. This problem will reduce into the problems: (1) t*o select a set of intervals* and (2) t*o select a rhythm* from the classes of *intervals-class* and *rhythm-class*. The classes *intervals-class* and *rhythm-class* will determine their best solutions which meet both the context of the musical problem and WOLFGANG's current disposition. These two class solutions are computed on their respective blackboards and then applied by the KSs of the *melody-class* blackboard. When the partial solutions posted by the KSs on the *melody-class* blackboard collaborate within the bounds of WOLFGANG's cultural grammar and system dispositional state, the respective scheduler concludes that a melodic solution has been formulated.

From this approach of task reduction and task collaboration, we derive processing characteristics which are most appropriate for blackboard technologies. In the design of WOLFGANG, the blackboard systems provide the system facility for K-lines acting as KSs to collaborate and post possible contributions to solutions under the control of blackboard schedulers. The blackboard architecture provides an excellent computational structure for collaboration between many classes of KSs over many levels of reduced tasks and problems, as has been cited in the literature for distributed problem-solving and artificial intelligence (Durfee 1987; Engelmore 1988; Lesser 1988; Nii 1986, Nii 1988; Rice 1988).

Blackboard System Functions.   A distinction is to be made between the RBB and the three subordinate blackboard systems. The RBB manages the overall composition process. It is responsible for managing the construction of the composition-in-progress, and the dispositional feedback facility. The subordinate blackboard systems, the MBB, HBB, and RHBB, serve as KSs to the RBB and support task functions relating to melody, harmony, and rhythm respectively. Further, given K-lines also serve as KSs during compositional processing for the RBB.

Management functions performed by the RBB scheduler include: (1) formulation and evaluation of goals during the composition process (2) assignment of sub-tasks to the subordinate blackboard systems (3) activation and management of specific K-lines and K-line classes (4) maintenance of the system disposition variable (*dispositionValue*) (5) attenuation of QWs and DWs in the K-line network (6) creation and maintenance of K-lines and K-line classes, and (7) management of all information posted on the RBB.

The three subordinate blackboard systems support a restricted set of tasks for the RBB. They act as the RBB's KSs for sub-tasks relating to melody, harmony, and rhythm respectively. K-lines and K-line classes relating to musical domain knowledge of melody, harmony, and rhythm serve as KSs for the MBB, HBB, and RHBB. The respective schedulers for these three blackboard systems all perform the following functions: (1) formulation and evaluation of goals during the composition process, (2) activation and management of specific K-lines and K-line classes, (3) monitoring of the system disposition maintained on the RBB, and (4) management of all information posted on each scheduler's respective blackboard.

The collaborative behavior between given K-lines and the three subordinate blackboard systems all functioning as KSs for the RBB can best be described as that of dynamic heterarchical agents. As the RBB scheduler initiates different tasks during a composing session, given K-lines and the subordinate blackboard systems exchange leadership roles in constructing a given musical phrase. Figure 10 displays the relational architecture between all schedulers, blackboards, and KSs in the WOLFGANG system.

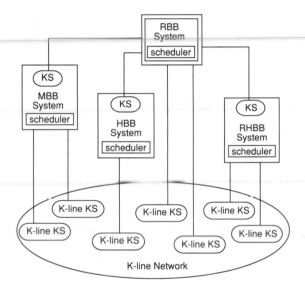

Figure 10. Detailed Diagram of the Relational Architecture between All Schedulers, Blackboards, and KSs in the WOLFGANG System. The diagram displays KSs as both subordinate blackboard systems and K-lines

Previously we mentioned that the blackboard schedulers are the only system component consisting of rules. These rules are formulated to define the functions performed by the different schedulers implemented in the WOLFGANG system; the rules act as laws throughout the complete system, some of them in a global, some in a local capacity. At the global level, RBB scheduler rules define: (1) how K-line classes develop, (2) what K-lines classes interact with each other, and (3) the protocols by which they interact. At a local level, the schedulers for the RBB, MBB, HBB, and RHBB define (1) how specific KSs (K-lines in a given class) formulate tasks and goals,

(2) how transformations are applied to knowledge posted on a given blackboard, (3) how generalizations and analogies are performed, and (4) how knowledge is represented and manipulated.

As different KSs for a given blackboard system attempt to post information to complete a given task or satisfy a given goal, the respective scheduler must establish an agenda to manage its KSs. Via some set of agenda algorithms, a scheduler can prioritize the ordering of KSs posting information on a blackboard. WOLFGANG's agenda algorithms qualify and rank a set musical characteristics for a given task or goal. Thus, a scheduler can determine which KS has the most useful information by computing priority values based on these agenda characteristics. These characteristics are defined by a hierarchy of musical parameters. When a composition process begins, WOLFGANG's agenda scheme places high importance on the harmonic structure of a composition, followed by the melodic structure, then the rhythmic structure. This ranking does change as needed during the initial stage of the composition process. As compositional processing continues, the ranking begins to place equal importance on both the harmonic structure and the melodic structure of the composition. This occurs since over time a general pattern of construction for the harmonic structure is established. (The design of WOLFGANG's agenda scheme evolved due in part to influences from work by Douglas Lenat (Lenat 1982) and Edmund Durfee (Durfee 1989)).

Functioning of the Disposition Feedback Facility—System Component Level

We have described the disposition feedback facility as a set of functions which maintains: (1) the *listOfGoodElements* composed of musical elements constructed during the current composition session that demonstrate a high emoting potential, and (2) WOLFGANG's current disposition state by assignment of a specific emoting value (happy, sad, angry, or meditative) to the variable *dispositionValue*. (Both of these variables are stored on the RBB.)

The posting of elements to the *listOfGoodElements* is provided by a background process functioning as a feedback loop. This process evaluates the construction of all musical elements during a composing session and posts those elements which compute high emoting potentials to the *listOfGoodElements*. This list is managed and accessed during a composing session by the RBB scheduler.

As discussed earlier, the RBB scheduler is designed and implemented to manage WOLFGANG's dispositional state. This entails (1) initializing the variable *dispositionValue* with the user requested emotion type to define WOLFGANG's initial disposition, and (2) changing the value stored in *dispositionValue* to a different emotion type as needed during a composing session.

As an example, assume WOLFGANG has been requested to compose a happy composition. For the first forty measures of the composition, WOLFGANG's disposition is to compose such as to convey a quality of happiness; as WOLFGANG begins to compose the next musical phrase starting at measure forty-one, a K-line in the method-net defining a need to change the emoting quality of the music is activated by a RBB scheduler. The information represented by this method K-line is then posted on the RBB as the goal: *change to a new emotionalstate for a short period of time, then return to the original user requested emotionalstate.* As this method K-line activates associated K-lines in the facts-net, WOLFGANG might satisfy this new goal as follows: *compose the next eight measures of the composition as "slightly" angry, then change the disposition back to happy for the remaining measures of the composition.* (All such changes in WOLFGANG's disposition result from processing events during a composition session; they are not user provoked.)

Future Direction and Conclusions

Currently, a new design for the next generation of WOLFGANG is being implemented. This design calls for the replacement of the emoting weights assigned to each K-line with links to different classes of K-lines representing different emoting potentials. These new classes are in constant resonance, the level of their activity being dependent on varying activation events over the entire K-line network, and within each respective emoting class of K-lines. These emoting classes function as "emotion centers/societies". The links between K-lines in the emoting classes and the different classes representing musical knowledge are bi-directional; thus K-lines representing emoting potentials and musical knowledge can activate each other.

In conclusion, WOLFGANG provides a working model of music composition in which "dispositions" are instrumental in deciding about steps in the elaboration of tonal monodies. The research and design of WOLFGANG has resulted from a subjective view of musical composing according to which the emoting potential of high-level musical constructs is more important to the musical logic of a monody than are their syntactic features. A musical composition is thought to be an artifact which stimulates the senses and cognitive awareness of both its creator and any intended listener. We therefore view composing as a process that creates an artifact to communicate some cognitive (emotional) effect. The composing process necessitates the development of a set of musical skills, and the application of these skills based on the disposition of the composer. We consider WOLFGANG's compositional processing as constrained by its cultural grammar, and guided by its disposition to musically communicate some emoting quality.

Glossary

The following notes are provided to define the use of given terms within this chapter. Further, these notes are intended to provide introductory information for those unfamiliar with given vocabulary applied in the field of artificial intelligence.

Note 1: Production System Model.   A model of processing based on a specific class of rule-based system composed of logical constructs called productions; where the left side of a production, the antecedent, states some condition to be satisfied, and the right side of a production, the consequence, states some action to be performed when the respective condition has been satisfied. In a production system, the productions are organized and represented in a collective body commonly referred to as a knowledge base. As the conditions of given productions become satisfied, the actions of these respective productions direct the performance of the system.

Note 2: Disposition.   In this chapter, the view of the term disposition is influenced by Marvin Minsky's use of this term in his 1980 paper on K-lines (Minsky 1980). In his paper Minsky's states as follows: "I use 'disposition' to mean 'a momentary range of possible behaviors'"; technically it is the shorter term component of the state. In a computer program, a disposition might depend upon which items are currently active in a data base, e.g., as in Doyle's flagging of items that are "in" and "out" in regard to making decisions (Doyle 1979). While the design of WOLFGANG makes use of the concept of dispositions, the current work in progress is an evolving attempt to integrate some of Minsky's ideas; considerable work is still required.

In this chapter, the term disposition refers to the range of valid states assigned to the variable *dispositionValue*; this variable maintains a temporary state defined by its current value of either happy, sad, angry, or meditative. During a composition process, the state changes based on the assignment of one of the four valid emotion types. The current assignment of a value to *dispositionValue* is determined by defining which of the four emotion types is most active at any given moment during a composition session. These four types are individual variables which store numeric values representing their respective levels of activity; the numeric values change based on the progress of the composition process.

Note 3: Frame.   A structure (schema) representing specific knowledge of some object or concept; the structure associates features which are descriptive of a given object or concept. These features are represented as attributes called slots. Slot values can be either some physical value (such as a symbol or numerical value), or some process to be invoked to perform some task. Frames were defined by Marvin Minsky as a framework for representing knowledge (Minsky 1975).

Note 4: Spreading-Activation Network.   In this chapter, a spreading-activation network means a network of interconnected nodes, where individual nodes represent given objects or concepts, and where these nodes are linked together based on specific relationships; this network serves as a knowledge representation. Within the network, attention to specific knowledge is provided by the activation of specific nodes which in turn propagate (spread) different levels of activation to related nodes. This spreading of activation to related nodes provides more (related) details to the nodes initially activated.

Note 5: Blackboard System.   H. Penny Nii (Nii 1989) provides the following description of a blackboard model which is consistent with the use of blackboard system technologies in the design of the WOLFGANG system. "Organizationally, the blackboard model consists of three components:

The knowledge sources. The knowledge needed to solve the problem is partitioned into knowledge sources, which are kept separate and independent.

The blackboard data structure. The problem-solving state data (objects from the solution space) are kept in a global data store, the blackboard. Knowledge sources produce changes to the blackboard which lead incrementally to a solution to the problem. Communication and interaction among the knowledge sources take place solely through the blackboard.

Control. What knowledge source to apply when and to what part of the blackboard are problems addressed in control.

In addition to the organizational requirements, a particular reasoning (computational) behavior is associated with blackboard systems: The solution to a problem is built one step at a time. At each control cycle any type of reasoning step (data driven, goal driven, forward chaining, backward chaining, etc.) can be used. The part of the emerging solution to be attended to next can also be selected at each control cycle. As a result, the selection and the application of knowledge sources are dynamic and opportunistic rather than fixed and preprogrammed."

Acknowledgments

The author is deeply indebted to Marvin Minsky and John Carson for their helpful interest and comments in this research project. I especially wish to thank Otto Laske and Stacy Marsella for their effort in reviewing, and providing valuable contributions to, the composition of this chapter. I gratefully acknowledge valuable discussions concerning both the WOLFGANG system and related research with Saul Amarel, Peter Clitherow, Harold Cohen, Jürgen Koenemann, Alex Kononov, Scott Robertson, Michael Rychener, Jack Mostow, and Chris Tong. I would like to thank Karl Kuffermann for creating the artwork included in this chapter.

References

Ames, C. and Domino, M. 1988. A Cybernetic Composer Overview. In Proceedings of the First Workshop on Artificial Intelligence and Music, Minneapolis/St. Paul, Minnesota: AAAI-88.

Ames, C. 1985. Applications of Linked Data Structures to Automated Composition. In Proceedings of the 1985 International Computer Music Conference, Burnaby, B.C., Canada: ICMC.

Ames, C. 1982. Crystals: Recursive Structures in Automated Composition. *Computer Music Journal*, Fall.

Balzano, G.J. 1982. The Pitch Set as a Level of Description for Studying Musical Pitch Perception. In *Music, Mind, and Brain: The Neuropsychology of Music*, ed. Clynes, M., New York, New York: Plenum Press.

Bharucha, J. 1988. Neural Net Modeling of Music. In Proceedings of the First Workshop on Artificial Intelligence and Music, Minneapolis/St. Paul, Minnesota: AAAI-88.

Butler, D. 1979. A Further Study of Melodic Channeling. *Perception and Psychophysics*, 25, pp. 264–268.

Clynes, M. 1977. *Sentics: The Touch of Emotions*. Garden City, New York: Anchor Press/Doubleday.

Clynes, M. and Milsum, J.H. 1970. *Biomedical Engineering Systems*. New York, New York: McGraw-Hill Book

Company.

Cope, D. 1988. Music: The Universal Language. In Proceedings of the First Workshop on Artificial Intelligence and Music,Minneapolis/St. Paul, Minnesota: AAAI-88.

Cope, D. 1987. An Expert System for Computer-Assisted Composition. *Computer Music Journal,* Winter.

Copland, A. 1944. *Copland On Music.* p. 24, New York, New York: W. W. Norton & Company.

Deutsch, D. 1982a. Grouping Mechanisms in Music. In *The Psychology of Music,* ed. Deutsch, D., New York, New York: Academic Press.

Deutsch, D. 1982b. The Processing of Pitch Combinations. In *The Psychology of Music,* ed. Deutsch, D., New York, New York: Academic Press.

Deutsch, D. 1975. Two-Channel Listening to Musical Scales. *Journal of the Acoustical Society of America,* 57, pp. 1156–1160.

Dowling, W. J. and Harwood, D. L. 1986. Music Cognition. New York, New York: Academic Press.

Doyle, J. 1979. A Truth Maintenance System. A.I. Memo No. 521, Artificial Intelligence Laboratory, Massachusetts Institute of Technology, Cambridge, Massachusetts. Cambridge, Massachusetts.

Durfee, E. H. 1989. *Coordination of Distributed Problem Solvers.* Boston, Massachusetts: Kluwer Academic Publishers.

Durfee, E. H., Lesser, V. R., and Corkill, D. D. 1987. Cooperation Through Communication in a Distributed Problem Solving

Network. In *Distributed Artificial Intelligence,* ed. Huhns, M. N., Los Altos, California: Morgan Kaufmann.

Ebcioglu, K. 1984. An Expert System for Schenkerian Analysis of Chorales in the Style of J. S. Bach. In Proceedings of the 1984 International Computer Music Conference, Paris, France: ICMC.

Engelmore, R. S., Morgan, A. J., and Nii, H. P. 1988. Hearsay-II. In *Blackboard Systems,* eds. Engelmore, R. S. and Morgan, A. J., New York, New York: Addison-Wesley.

Hiller, L. 1981. Composing with Computers: A Progress Report. *Computer Music Journal,* Winter.

Hiller, L. 1970. Music Composed with Computers: A Historical Survey. In *The Computer and Music,* ed. Lincoln, H.,

Ithaca, New York: Cornell University Press.

Hiller, L. 1959. Computer Music. Scientific American, December.

Jackendoff, R. S. 1987. *Consciousness and the Computational Mind.* Cambridge, Massachusetts: Bradford Book/MIT Press.

Jairazbhoy, N. A. 1971. *The rags of North Indian Music.* London, England: Faber and Faber (Weslayan University Press).

Krumhansl, C. L. 1979. The Psychological Representation of Musical Pitch in a Tonal Context. *Cognitive Psychology,* 11, pp. 346–374.

Laske, O. 1990. The Computer as the Artist's Alter Ego. *Leonardo,* Vol. 23, No. 1. Pergamon Press.

Laske, O. 1988. Introduction to Cognitive Musicology. Computer Music Journal, MIT Press, Spring.

Laske, O. 1980. Toward an Explicit Cognitive Theory of Music Listening. *Computer Music Journal,* MIT Press, Summer.

Laske, O. 1977. *Music, Memory, and Thought.* University Microfilms Intl., Ann Arbor, Michigan. (see also: Laske, O. 1981. *Music and Mind: An Artificial Intelligence Perspective.* Computer Music Association Reports, San Francisco.)

Lenat, D. B., and Davis, R. 1982. *Knowledge-Based Systems In Artificial Intelligence.* New York, New York: McGraw-Hill.

Lerdahl, F. and Jackendoff, R. 1983. *A Generative Theory of Tonal Music.* Cambridge, Massachusetts: MIT Press.

Lesser, V. R. and Erman, L. D. 1988. A Retrospective View of the Hearsay-II Architecture. In *Blackboard Systems,* eds. Engelmore, R. S. and Morgan, A. J., New York, New York: Addison-Wesley.

Levitt, D. A. 1985. A Representation for Musical Dialects. Doctoral Dissertation, Massachusetts Institute of Technology, Cambridge, Massachusetts.

Levitt, D. A. 1981. A Melody Description System for Jazz Improvisation. Masters Dissertation, Massachusetts Institute of Technology, Cambridge, Massachusetts.

Lischka, C. 1987. Connectionist Models of Musical Thinking. In Proceedings of the 1987 International Computer Music Conference, Urbana, Illinois: ICMC.

Marsella, S. and Schmidt, C. 1988. A Problem Reduction Approach to Automated Music Composition. Technical Report LCSR-TR-115, Rutgers University, New Brunswick, New Jersey.

Michalski, R. S. 1983. A Theory and Methodology of Inductive Learning. In *Machine Learning*, eds. Michalski, R.S., Carbonell, J. G. and Mitchell, T. M., Los Altos, California: Morgan Kaufmann.

Minsky, M. 1986. *The Society of Mind*. New York, New York: Simon and Schuster.

Minsky, M. 1981. Music, Mind, and Meaning. A.I. Memo No. 616, Artificial Intelligence Laboratory, February, Massachusetts Institute of Technology, Cambridge, Massachusetts.

Minsky, M. 1980. K-Lines: A Theory of Memory. *Cognitive Science Journal*, Volume 4, Number 2, April-June, Ablex Publishing. (see also: Minsky, M. 1979. K-Lines: A Theory of Memory. A.I. Memo No. 516, Artificial Intelligence Laboratory, June, Massachusetts Institute of Technology, Cambridge, Massachusetts.)

Minsky, M. 1975. A Framework for Representing Knowledge. In *The Psychology of Computer Vision*, ed. Winston, P. H., New York, New York: McGraw-Hill.

Nii, H. P. 1989. Introduction. In *Blackboard Architectures and Applications*, eds. Jagannathan, V., Dodhiawala, R., and Baum, L., New York, New York: Academic Press.

Nii, H. P., Aiello, N., and Rice, J. 1988. Frameworks for Concurrent Problem Solving: A Report on CAGE and POLIGON. In *Blackboard Systems*, eds. Engelmore, R. S. and Morgan, A. J., New York, New York: Addison-Wesley.

Nii, H. P. 1986. Blackboard Systems: The Blackboard Model of Problem Solving and the Evolution of Blackboard Architectures. *AI Magazine 7*, American Association for Artificial Intelligence, Menlo Park, California.

Pinkerton, R. 1956. Information Theory and Melody. Scientific American, February.

Piston, W. 1941. *Harmony*. W. W. Norton and Company, New York, New York.

Rice, J. 1988. The Elint Application on Poligon: The Architecture and Performance of a Concurrent Blackboard System. Knowledge Systems Laboratory Technical Report, Stanford University, Palo Alto, California.

Riecken, R. D. 1989. Goal Formulation With Emotional Constraints: Musical Composition by Emotional Computation. In Proceedings of AAAI - First Annual Conference on Innovative Applications of Artificial Intelligence. Stanford University, Palo Alto, California: IAAI.

Roads, C. 1984. An Overview of Music Representations. In Proceedings of the 1984 International Computer Music Conference. Modena, Italy: ICMC.

Roads, C. 1982. Interactive Orchestration Based on Score Analysis. In Proceedings of the 1982 International Computer Music Conference, Venice, Italy: ICMC.

Rothgeb, J. 1980. Simulating Musical Skills by Digital Computer. Computer Music Journal, Summer.

Schawanauer, S. 1986. Learning Machines and Tonal Composition. Doctoral Dissertation, Yale University, New Haven, Connecticut.

Simon, H. A. 1969. The Sciences of the Artificial. Cambridge, Massachusetts: MIT Press.

Sloboda, J. A. 1985. The Musical Mind: The Cognitive Psychology of Music. pp. 151-193, Oxford, England: Clarendon Press (Oxford Press).

Smoliar, S. 1980. A Computer Aid for Schenkerian Analysis. *Computer Music Journal*, Summer.

Thomas, M. T. 1985. VIVACE: A Rule-based AI System for Composition. In Proceedings of the 1985 International Computer Music Conference. Burnaby, B.C., Canada: ICMC.

Tenney, J. and Polansky, L. 1980. Temporal Gestalt Perception in Music. *Journal of Music Theory*.

Ulrich, W. 1977. The Analysis and Synthesis of Jazz by Computer. In Proceedings of IJCAI-77, Cambridge, Massachusetts: IJCAI.

Vercoe, B. 1988. Hearing Polyphonic Music with the Connection Machine. In *Proceedings of the First Workshop on Artificial Intelligence and Music*. Minneapolis/St. Paul, Minnesota: AAAI-88.

Vincinanza, S. and Prietula, M. 1989. A Computational Model of Musical Creativity. In *Proceedings of the Second Workshop on Artificial Intelligence and Music*. Detroit, Michigan: IJCAI-89.

Abstract

The expertise required to recognize musical structure or generate acceptable musical compositions has proven to be very difficult to capture within a computational model. This research addresses this issue from an unusual perspective. Our work in this area has grown out of an interest in understanding the control issues that arise in the use of the method of problem reduction. Musical composition was selected as one domain in which to experiment with problems of control because of the highly complex structure apparent in musical composition. This chapter discusses a problem reduction approach to automated music composition. The application of this approach to the task of writing melodies is then discussed and some examples are shown.

Chapter 10

On the Use of Problem Reduction Search for Automated Music Composition

Stacy C. Marsella and Charles F. Schmidt
*Laboratory for Computer Science Research and Department of Psychology,
Busch Campus, Rutgers University*

A musical composition is a highly structured artifact. An expert in the musical genre of the composition can decompose it into parts and recognize at least some of the various types of relationships between the parts. The expertise required to recognize musical structure or generate acceptable musical compositions has proven to be very difficult to capture within a computational model. Our own research addresses this issue from an unusual perspective. Our work in this area has grown out of our interest in understanding the control issues that arise in the use of the artificial intelligence (AI) search method known as *problem reduction* [Nilsson 1971, Bresina et al. 1987]. Musical composition appealed to us as one domain in which to experiment with problems of control because of the highly complex structure apparent in some musical composition (e.g., [Lerdahl and Jackendoff. 1983, Tenney 1986]).

One of the most apparent features of musical compositions is the presence of hierarchical structure. This has led some researchers to explore the adequacy of formal grammars as a basis for capturing some of the structural features of musical compositions (e.g., [Laske 1972, Lidov and Gab. 1973, Lerdahl and Jackendoff. 1983, Roads 1985a]). Grammars are particularly attractive formalisms by which to attempt to capture the structural properties of musical compositions because they allow for the generation of an infinite set of strings from a finite vocabulary, and because their use in generation or parsing assigns a hierarchical structure to the resulting terminal string. The non-terminal nodes of this hierarchical structure or tree provide a formal basis for representing the fact that the music is organized into larger and more abstract groupings such as phrases, contours, themes and the like. It is quite clear, however, that a context free grammar is not powerful enough to

capture all the apparent structure that can be discerned in most musical compositions. In particular, the use of repetition of note, motive, or theme, either unaltered
or under some transformation at discontinuous locations in the string, suggests a
structure of dependency across the "tree of derivation," as well as the hierarchical
dependency captured in the tree.

A dependency that holds between nodes of the tree of derivation that are not
dominated by a common parent node will be referred to as a horizontal dependency. A concern for such horizontal dependencies is evidenced in much of the musical grammar research. So, for instance, Holtzman employed a formal grammar
more powerful than context free, an unrestricted grammar [Holtzman 1980]. This
concern is also evidenced in researchers employing representations influenced by
AI, such as [Ebcioglu 1988].[1] As we shall see, such dependencies also pose interesting problems for the control of problem reduction search because the context is
non-local, in effect, it extends "arbitrarily" between nodes in the tree of derivation.

A simple musical example of such a horizontal dependency can be seen in
Beethoven's *Écossaise in G* shown in Figure 1. This piece can be analyzed as a two-
part or binary form. In this AB structure, the first eight measures constitute the A
section and the final 8 the B section. Note the similarity of the last two measures of
the A section and the last two measures of the B section. Horizontal dependencies
of this type cannot be naturally expressed within a context free grammatical formalism, and, indeed are difficult to generate efficiently within any AI search method,
including the computational framework provided by the standard problem reduction search method. Our interest in extending the problem reduction search
method to efficiently handle the generation of solutions that exhibit such horizontal dependencies motivated our use of music, more specifically melodic aspects of
music, as a domain in which to study the control problems posed by such horizontal
dependencies.

Figure 1. Excerpt from Beethoven's Écossaise in G

Problem Solving and Musical Structure

This computational approach led us to consider the way in which musical composition might be cast if it is viewed as the result of a problem solving process carried
out within the framework provided by the method of problem reduction. In this
view, the problem solver, or "composer," begins with two sets of specifications.
The first is a partial specification, usually quite abstract, of the musical material
that is to be used in forming a musical composition. Call this the *starting state* of
the composition problem. The second is again a partial specification, also usually
quite abstract, of the requirements that the musical composition should successfully satisfy. Call this the *goal state* of the composition problem. Using this pair, the
problem solver makes some pattern of choices that transforms the starting materi
al into a sequence of notes and their associated timing that satisfies the goal
requirement. A history of this pattern of choices and the associated context within
which these choices were made provides a structural representation of the com-
poser/problem solver's decisions.

From this viewpoint, it is important to note that whatever structure is discernable
in the sequence of notes is the result of, but may only partially reflect the structure
of, the decisions made by the problem solver. Thus, the structure of the composition itself is viewed as homomorphic to the structure that is reflected in the history
of the decisions made by the problem solver in forming the composition. It should
be recognized that this implies that the decisions made by the problem solver cannot necessarily be recognized unambiguously from any analysis applied to the
sequence of notes generated by the problem solving process. From this point of
view, the study of musical composition and its various forms can be understood as
the study of the control structure of the corresponding problem solving process
rather than the study of the structure of the resulting musical sequence of notes.
This point of view will not be defended. Rather it should be viewed as a general
hypothesis about a useful way in which to understand musical structure. The work
described in this chapter represents some preliminary research which begins to provide a basis for evaluating the plausibility and usefulness of this hypothesis.

With regard to this hypothesis, it should be noted that under a generic interpretation of "problem," there is considerable work that views composition as
either a problem solving process or a problem of making decisions (or choices). For example, see [Gill 1963, Hiller and Isaac. 1963]. In contrast, two points
should be stressed about the present work. First, the problem reduction model
provides an explicit, and technical, definition of what constitutes a problem
[Nilsson 1971]. Second, the intent, and consequences, of seeing composition as
a problem solving process are different. This research is concerned with the
control of problem reduction search. To this end, our concern is the *history* of
control decisions made in that search, as opposed to just the solution tendered,
or a hierarchical representation of that solution free of control issues. It is the
maintenance of this history, or pattern, of control decisions, not just the choic-

es, that is critical in the control of the problem reduction search.

The Method of Problem Reduction

The specific problem solving method we use to explore musical structure is problem reduction. This method involves recursively decomposing a complex problem into presumably simpler subproblems until only primitive subproblems remain whose solution is "obvious". The complex problem is solved if the solution to each of the primitive subproblems jointly imply a solution to the original complex problem. This condition trivially holds if each of the subproblems is independent of all other subproblems. Subproblem independence rarely holds. Consequently, the focus of the research on this problem reduction method has been on ways to recognize and solve problems where there exists some dependency between subproblems. Some of the areas that have been studied using this search method include the so-called robot planning problems [Fikes et al. 1971, Sacerdoti 1977], various puzzle domains [Amarel 1981], and the domain of logical proofs [Amarel 1967].

Because the method of problem reduction involves searching for a solution by recursively decomposing a problem, the history of the decompositions that yield a solution can be thought of as assigning a structure to that solution. However, the interest in AI research on problem reduction has typically emphasized the way in which this model can be used to *control* the decisions that must be made in searching for a solution to a given problem, rather than on the *structure* that such a model "assigns" to the solution created by this model. This focus on control naturally arises because problem reduction is studied as a general method for conducting a heuristic search for a solution to some problem. Further, there may typically be several ways in which to derive a particular solution as well as many possible solutions to a given problem. Consequently, there is no bias that dictates that a given solution should have a unique structure assigned to it. Additionally, in the problem reduction model, rather than viewing the starting state as some generic symbol as in a context-free grammar, there is the idea of satisfying or deriving a given goal from some specification of starting assumptions or resources. Consequently, a given goal coupled with differing starting assumptions or constraints will typically yield differing solutions.

The problem reduction method can be abstractly described as involving a cycle that includes a *decomposition* phase and a *composition* phase. The decomposition phase involves the recursive application of a process of problem decomposition. The structural representation of this process defines a hierarchically organized AND/OR tree of subproblems where the decomposition of a problem into subproblems is represented as an AND node and alternative decompositions as OR nodes. As in the case of the top-level problem, each subproblem also consists of two types of specifications. This pair of specifications will be referred to as the starting state and the final or goal state of the subproblem.[2] Together this state pair provides the context for the subsequent attempt to find a solution to the given subproblem. A decomposition rule, or in the parlance of problem reduction, a *non-terminal reduction rule*, rewrites the given problem state pair into a set of such problem state pairs. *Terminal reduction rules* serve to recognize primitive subproblems. A problem is solved when all terminal nodes of an AND tree in the AND/OR tree have been recognized as primitive, and the composition of each set of child subproblems implies the solution of their parent subproblem. Such an AND tree constitutes a *plan* to solve the problem.[3]

In order to explicate the control issues involved in problem reduction it will be useful to depict some of the ways in which control can be achieved in problem reduction search. To this end, a graphical depiction of a partially expanded AND tree is provided in Figure 2. Here the top or root node represents the start of the problem solving process. Associated with this node is the problem specification which is depicted as a black oval. The decomposition of the problem specification into two ANDed subproblems is represented by the nodes immediately dominated by the root node. The left-most subproblem is shown as further decomposed into two additional ANDed subproblems each of which is itself decomposed into two further subproblems. Each of these subproblems happens to be primitive and thus undergoes no further decomposition. The "wide" rectangles dominated by each of these terminal nodes represent a terminal partial solution. The composition of each of these pairs yields the partial SubSolution represented as "tall" rectangles associated with the parent node. These are then composed in turn to yield the SubSolution to their parent problem. Thus, at this point in the depiction of the search, the decomposition phase has been recursively applied to the leftmost portion of the tree followed by the recursive application of composition to yield the SubSolution to the left subproblem associated with the overall problem.

Note that the search has proceeded in one of the many possible orders in which the subproblems might be expanded. If all of the subproblems are independent then the order in which the frontier of this tree is expanded is irrelevant. However, subproblem independence is the exception rather than the rule. Consequently, the focus of AI research in problem reduction search has been on ways of detecting and efficiently handling subproblem dependence. Most of the approaches to handling subproblem dependencies have involved a control structure where subproblem independence is assumed to hold during the decomposition phase of this cycle, and then the validity of this assumption is tested during the composition phase [Fikes et al. 1971, Sacerdoti 1977]. The models of problem reduction search vary in the type of mechanism provided to deal with subproblem dependencies that are discovered during this composition phase. Our own approach to the development and implementation of a model of problem reduction search has involved extending the expressive power of the rules of decomposition to allow the nature of the dependency between subproblems to be specified. This information is then used to control the problem solving process. It is this ability to express the specific nature of subproblem dependencies and the usage of this knowledge in the control of the problem solver that we will exploit in our experiments in the domain of music composition.

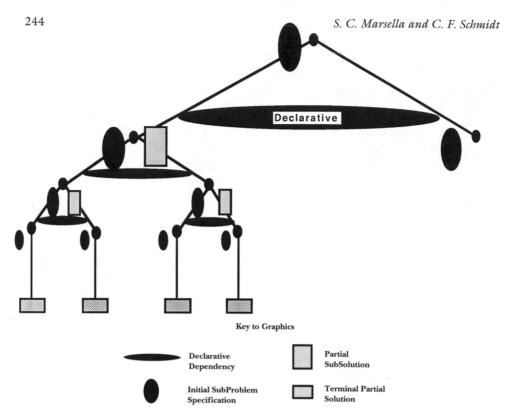

Figure 2. A Partially Expanded Problem Reduction AND Tree with Declarative Dependency

By specifying the contents of subproblem state pairs, a rule can indirectly affect the way each of its descendant subproblems will ultimately be solved. By indirectly affecting how the subproblems are solved, this specification can be employed to predictively handle dependencies between those subproblems. Furthermore, a subproblem high in the hierarchy of decompositions can leave a trace of its contributions to the surface structure of those terminal elements of the solution that it dominates.

The predictive specification of the contents of descendent subproblems is graphically depicted in Figure 2. Note the "wide" black ovals linking the sibling subproblems. This depicts the fact that the subproblem specification allows for the *implicit* expression of dependencies between the descendent subproblems. These are labelled a *declarative dependency* in the figure because their expression is based on how a given rule rewrites a parent problem into the subproblem state pairs (see [Marsella 1988] for further discussion). However, as we shall see, not all subproblem dependencies can be handled predictively within this hierarchical structure.

This explicates the relation between hierarchical structure present in the solution and the hierarchical history of problem decomposition. However, it does not explain how a terminal element of the tree, or more generally, a partial subtree, can affect parts that are not dominated by that subtree. This is the situation that holds in the description of the excerpt from Beethoven's *Écossaise in G* discussed

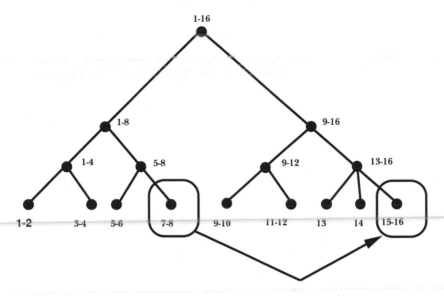

Figure 3. A Structural Representation of an Excerpt from Beethoven's Écossaise in G.

earlier and shown in Figure 1. A graphical representation of a simple structuring of this excerpt is shown in Figure 3. The numbers associated with each node refer to the measures dominated by that node. The node labelled 1–8 represents the A part, that labelled 9–16 the B part, of this binary form. Here the horizontal arrow points out the dependency between the node labelled 7–8 and that labelled 15–16. Note that node 7–8 is dominated by the node that represents the A part and node 15–16 by the node representing the B part. The only node that dominates both these nodes is the root node.

Dependencies of this type can be realized within a problem reduction method if an ordering is imposed on the expansion and solution of the subproblems in this tree. The imposition of an ordering on the solution to the subproblems allows aspects of the solved subproblems to be passed up the tree and across to disjoint branches of this tree. In this way the results of the solution to one subproblem can affect the way in which a quite distant subproblem is solved. In terms of the current example, this result can be achieved if it is known, at the time that the root node is expanded, that the terminal element of the solution to the "A" subproblem of the binary form is to be used as material for the terminal solution of the "B" subproblem. This can be achieved if the problem solver first completely solves the "A" subproblem, passes *aspects* of this solution to the "B" subproblem, and then essentially solves the "B" subproblem in a more or less "right to left" fashion so that the solution to node 15–16 can appropriately influence the solution to the remaining nodes in the "B" subproblem.

The important point is not the specific ordering suggested, but rather that a specific ordering is required. To arrive at the musical structure of this example

using a control strategy which does not in some sense "know" the ordering requirements at the time that the top node is expanded would be extremely difficult.

One limited approach, that extends the ability to control problem reduction
search, exploits the ability to order the solution of subproblems. This is graphically depicted in Figure 4. In this case, the subsolutions are passed back up the tree
during the composition phase. These partial subsolutions are depicted as "tall"
rectangles. These, then, in turn can provide additional specification of the
remaining subproblems. The "wide" gray rectangles represent the *solution derived
dependencies* that can be resolved once the subsolutions have been resolved. These
solution derived dependencies can be employed by virtue of the ordering that has
been imposed on subproblem expansion. In this figure, the ordering is from left
to right so that leftmost subproblems are expanded first. As denoted by the
curved gray lines, the entire solution for a subproblem composed during the composition phase is passed up the tree. This subsolution is used to specify the dependency between that subproblem and a subproblem in an adjoining branch of the
tree. This dependency is then employed to constrain the search for a solution to
that as yet unexpanded subproblem.

There is an inherent limitation in the use of solutions to specify dependencies
that is of particular relevance to musical composition. The solution must be *interpreted* in order to derive the dependency. For instance, reconsider the graphical representation of the excerpt from Beethoven's *Écossaise in G* shown in Figure 1. As
analyzed, the dependency is between the node labelled 7–8 and that labelled 15–16.
The dependency is not between the entire solution to the A part (the node labelled
1–8) and the B part (the node labelled 9–16). To express the actual dependency
between nodes 7–8 and 15–16 minimally requires details of the structure imposed
on the two parts (nodes 1–8 and 9–16) during their generation. This information is
not present in the solutions to those parts. It would have to be recovered, or
derived by analysis of the solutions.[4]

This limitation suggests an alternative approach that further extends our ability
to control problem reduction search. Consider Figure 5. Here again, an order is
imposed on expansion. However, instead of passing a solution constructed during
the composition phase, a structure termed a *design artifact* is built during the plan
generation or decomposition phase. The design artifact is passed between subproblems (now termed a Design SubArtifact Specification) to express a *plan derived
dependency*. In the figure, these are depicted as "wide" gray ovals that span sibling
subproblems. As we shall see in the section titled "Experiments," this design artifact
includes information about the decisions made in the generation of a subsolution
that can be readily employed to specify dependencies between that subsolution and
discontinuous subproblems.

The problem reduction method that we have developed, REAPPR (Reformulation
And Parallel Problem Reduction), is designed to allow the use of these various
mechanisms for specifying dependencies in controlling problem reduction search
[Bresina et al. 1987, Marsella 1988]. Rather than discuss REAPPR abstractly, we will
now turn to a discussion of its application in writing simple melodies.

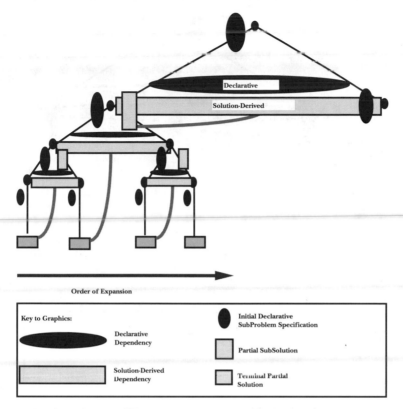

Figure 4. A Partially Expanded Problem Reduction AND Tree with Solution Derived Dependency Expressed through SubSolution Passing

Experiments

A series of simple experiments are being conducted as an initial illustration of our problem reduction approach to melody composition. The task for these experiments is to generate simple melodies using a fixed set of forms (e.g., rounded chanson, rondeau, etc.). In addition, stylistic constraints are placed on the rhythm, melodic motion, and tonal organization (e.g., tritone leaps were to be avoided, large leaps or chromatic intervals were to be used only rarely, major phrases should end on the tonic or dominant, etc.).

The problem solving process used in all the experiments proceeds by decomposing the composition task into a COMPOSE subproblem and a CRITIQUE subproblem. The major task for COMPOSE actually involves building and manipulating the *design artifact*. The design artifact represents those aspects of the composition structure that must be communicated in the plan (i.e., the AND tree) in order to handle horizontal dependencies. Thus, it represents a relation between parts of the composition

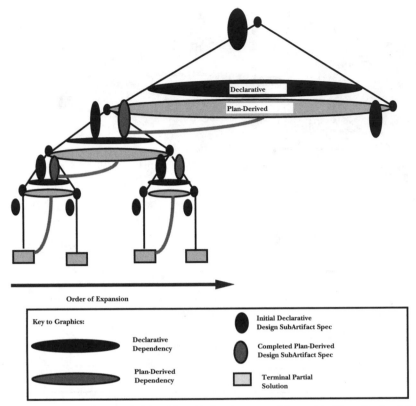

Figure 5. A Partially Expanded Problem Reduction AND Tree with Plan Derived Dependency Expressed through SubArtifact Passing

structure and the control decisions involved in creating it that permits a more predictive handling of the horizontal dependencies.

Originally these experiments used an interval based approach to melody writing. One of the first "melodies" (entitled here as "First Melody") composed by REAPPR under this approach is shown in Figure 6. Figure 7 shows some of the overlying structure that dominates parts of that melody. A left to right ordering of the frontier of the complete structure would recreate the melody shown in Figure 6. Note how the piece is broken into an **AABA'** structure at the highest level. In these experiments, structure forming rules that typically one would envision only being applicable at the highest level of the structure could also be recursively applied at lower levels. In keeping with this possibility, Figure 7 illustrates how the **A** is broken into **A1, A1, A2,** and **A1'** parts.

Building this structure also involves several subtasks. Tonal centers (as well as portions of the overall scale) are assigned to these phrases and subphrases. This assignment is based on the phrases' role in the overall melody, their depth in the hierarchy, and their relation to their "parent" phrase. So, for instance, the large intervallic leaps seen in the **B2** part are related to the fact that it is the middle of its parent section's **B1 B2 B3** structure which in turn is a middle section in the overall **AABA'** form.

The repetition and variation dependencies seen in this example are quite simple. Indeed, the lateral dependency suggested by the repetition of sibling parts was actually generated by REAPPR by virtue of its ability to specify the order (and repetition) of solution subsequences. It did not require non-hierarchical communication. Furthermore, the variations implied by the **A'** and **A1'** parts did not fully materialize in this piece due to rule selection decisions made lower in the hierarchy.

In more recent experiments, we have been moving to harmony based approaches to melody writing. These new experiments are better exemplars of the problem reduction control issues we are exploring, in part because the structure of the design artifact requires a more elaborate dependency structure in the plan that generates it.

A partial representation of a strongly dependent artifact is shown in Figure 8. In this partial design artifact, the overall melody is composed of three "sub"melodies (typically eight bar periods). The first of these submelodies is labelled Part A. In turn, Part A is composed of two submelodies (typically an antecedent and consequent, which has an implied musical dependency between them) labelled **a** and **b**. As opposed to such hierarchical structure, there is a lateral dependency between Part A and its sibling, Part Ar. Part Ar is a repetition of Part A. A more interesting lateral dependency is seen in the case of Part B, which is a "variation" built from one of Part A's submelodies, **b**. Thus Part B must be composed by modifying the sub-structure that describes **b**. This lateral dependency cuts across the hierarchy and between levels of that hierarchy. Thus, fragments of melodies (e.g., motives) can be employed at different points in the hierarchy as a source for variations and repetitions.

Besides fixing a pattern of repetition and variation, these lateral dependencies suggest the necessary control and flow of information for the problem reduction process. That is to say, the rules, and, in particular, a plan generated by those rules, must in some effective fashion deal with these dependencies. For instance, Part A must be planned prior to Part B and Part Ar. Moreover parts of the design artifact created for Part A must be provided to composition tasks which generate the artifact structure for Part B.

In order to understand the role this artifact would play in communicating dependency information in the plan tree, we will look at a rule that builds and employs the artifact. Figure 9 presents a stylized representation of part of such a non-terminal rule. At the top of the rule is the problem specification which describes the conditions under which the rule can be applied. This rule decomposes the problem of creating a melody based on an **ABA** pattern into three distinct subproblems. These subproblems require different kinds of knowledge in order to be solved and are in fact solved in different reduction spaces. In essence, this is a knowledge intensive approach that is modeling composition in terms of the design decisions that must be made. As denoted by the lateral arrows, *plan derived dependency* information

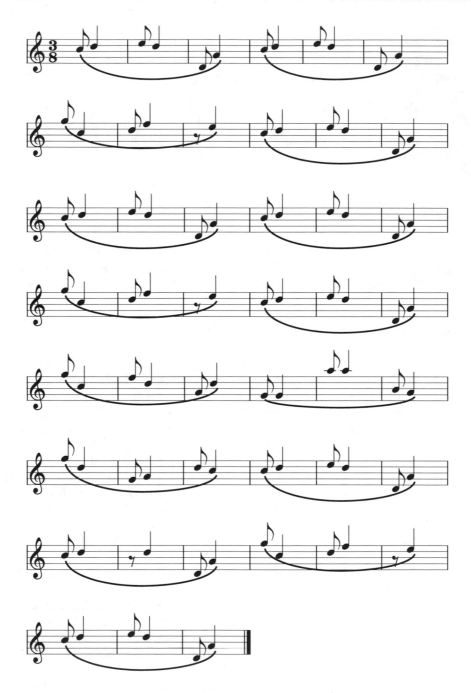

Figure 6. REAPPR's "First Melody"

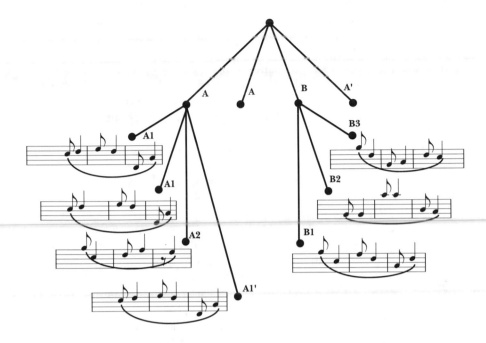

Figure 7. Partial Representation of REAPPR's "First Melody"

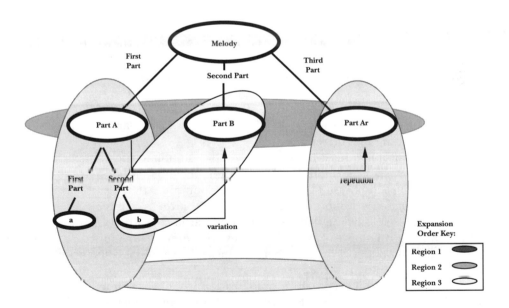

Figure 8. A Few Details of a Partial Design Artifact

acquired during the generation of a solution to one subproblem can be employed to further specify a subsequent subproblem. In other words, the order in which sub-problems are solved is part of the design decisions represented in the rule and determines how the various subproblems constrain each other. For instance, note the partial orders specified at the bottom of Figure 9 and the relation to the specifications of the subproblems. Subproblem1, which derives the chords and melodic contour, precedes the COMPOSE subproblems and as such constrains the solutions of those subproblems.

The structure of the decomposition and the segment of the plan it would create are related to, but distinct from, the artifact depicted earlier in Figure 8. Although not explicitly depicted in Figure 9, the design artifact of Figure 8 is specified incre-mentally, as the search for solutions to the subproblems proceeds. And, this evolv-ing design artifact in turn provides the local context required for the solution to the remaining open subproblems. The goal state of each subproblem determines what aspects of the design artifact it will reference as well as how it will modify/enhance the artifact. Relating the two figures, the DERIVE subproblems of Figure 9 modify the artifact by more fully specifying MELODY. In Figure 8, this is depicted as Region 1. Both COMPOSE subproblems build a hierarchical grouping structure. COMPOSE **A** takes the result of the DERIVE subproblem and builds additional structure that describes **A**. In the artifact, this additional structure corresponds to Region 2. COM-POSE **B** builds a variation by viewing just the **b** part built by the COMPOSE **A**, as depicted by Region 3 in Figure 8.

Note that this relation between **A** and **B** achieves several ends. The **B** subprob-lem's view of the artifact is restricted to just part of the overall state of the artifact. This localization is an important approach to generating subproblems whose solu-tions are simpler to find [Lansky 1986, Marsella 1988]. Furthermore, the depen-dency between the subproblems is predictively specified, or handled, at the time the rule is applied. In order to do this, **B** used knowledge of what **A**'s structure would be. This is not always available and it can be more difficult to specify predic-tively when these variations or associational structures[5] occur across widely disparate levels of the artifact. In such cases, either backtracking in the planning process or opportunistic planning may be required.

The DERIVE subproblem must be decomposed by additional rules which capture musical constraints, such as resolution to the tonic, melodic motion, etc. In addi-tion, at the level of each phrase (**A** and **B**), the selection of rhythmic patterns is per-formed. In part, these derivation decisions are based on the role a melodic phrase plays in the overall melody, the depth in the design artifact at which that phrase is positioned, and its relation to "parent" phrases. However, at this juncture of the experiment, the knowledge brought to bear on these derivations is quite primitive.

Additional rules would grow (i.e., recursively extend) the plan (and consequently the design artifact) until it eventually terminates at a frontier which tentatively rep-resents the notes of the melody. The Critique subproblem evaluates/modifies the artifact based on stylistic constraints (e.g., avoidance of tritones) and the goals implicit in the hierarchical view of the structure.

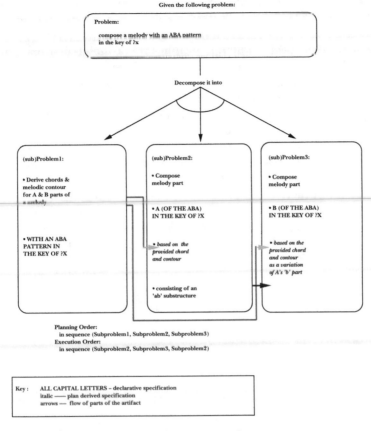

Figure 9. *Partial Representation of a Rule for an ABA Pattern*

Discussion of the Experiment

The preliminary computational experiment encourages our hypothesis that compositional expertise can be captured within this model of problem reduction. And, this model appears to provide a principled way in which to explore how various patterns of control create the surface structure of a musical composition.

Two structures, the problem reduction AND tree and the design artifact, lie at the heart of how this research explores the relation between patterns of control and surface structure. The full AND/OR search tree is created by recursive application of reduction rules that can express a variety of control patterns via the orders imposed on the search for subproblem solutions and the corresponding state specification mechanisms. This expressive power allows the decisions made in forming a musical composition to be modeled, and if need be, to be modeled at a fine grain. So, for instance, depending on how a rule is written, a melodic contour could be fixed for the entire melody or just a part of it. The contour can also be described abstractly and refined/modified later. And, different rules can potentially place different orders on when the contour decision is made relative to other decisions.

While the AND tree provides a hierarchical history of the recursive application of rules, it is the design artifact which must be introduced to allow for the efficient handling of horizontal dependencies. The design artifact provides the structure for selectively grouping information from various parts of the current state of the AND tree and then communicating this information to open subproblems in the tree. As depicted in Figures 8 and 9, this allows the composition process to be modeled effectively with problem reduction searches which take place in specialized search spaces. Each of these searches can access and build upon a different part or view of the artifact. The ideal is that the reduction search is provided with a local view of the relevant decisions that have been made. At the same time, information and constraints are communicated between the reduction searches by the effect each search has on the artifact. Finally, there is an overall strategy for controlling and ordering the subspace searches as well as for amalgamating and refining the partial results of those searches.

The design artifact thus provides more than a hierarchical description of the eventual surface structure. It also allows for encoding the parts of the design decision history which impose constraints on the solutions to the design subproblems. Different views of the design artifact selectively communicate these constraints across subproblems solved in different spaces. This allows the rich sets of constraints and interactions that a subproblem solution builds to be more readily incorporated by another subproblem's view.

The declarative specification of the design artifact provides a basis for comprehending what the system is doing. This comprehension is useful for both the system and its user. It allows the system to model decisions, and gives it the ability to modify and replan musical structures. For a human user, it opens the possibility of interacting with the system. In so far as the goals expressed in the design artifact are realized in the resulting melody, the artifact also provides a basis for evaluation.

Concluding Remarks

AI approaches to problem solving and design tasks typically involve some form of search through a space of alternative decisions or choices. Effective realization of such search paradigms typically depends on controlling the decisions which are taken, or considered (or re-considered in the case of systems that backtrack). So for instance, in exploring the use of AI search techniques in music production, researchers have explored the use of intelligent or dependency directed backtracking and search control heuristics (e.g. [Ebcioglu 1988, Ames 1987]).

The use of a problem reduction search paradigm in this research provides several benefits for the design task. By reducing a problem into a collection of design subproblems, the reduction approach allows a global view of the search for a completed design even though the search for solutions to those subproblems proceeds locally. Aspects of the overall design, and the role the subproblem solutions will play in that design, can be embedded in local searches, thus controlling them and reducing the need for backtracking. This ability is exploited when building the rich set of relations that provides for the assignment of tonal centers and scales, as well as the patterns of repetition and variation. This global view is in contrast to other search techniques such as state space search which tend to be constrained to a very local view of the ongoing search.

An interesting comparison can be made with the CHORAL expert system that harmonizes and performs a Schenkerian analysis of chorales in the style of J.S. Bach [Ebcioglu 1988]. The system employs a rich representational structure, views of which are tied to, and serve to structure, a rule based generate and test search. Based on these views, the search follows a repeated fixed control cycle of chord skeleton, fill-in, Schenker-bass, and Schenker-descant.

In contrast, our interest in studying control issues that arise in the use of problem reduction led us to explore the elevation of aspects of the search control to the level of the expertise encoded in the problem reduction rules. Thus control becomes an explicit, flexible part of the search decisions/compositional process. This interest in control issues is reflected in the fact that it is not so much musical knowledge that ends up being modeled, but rather knowledge about how to control the compositional process (cf. [Laske 1989]). A major concern for this research is whether problem solving expertise as captured in this problem reduction paradigm will elucidate structural issues in musical composition. At the present time, the approach looks promising, but final results must await further experimentation.

Acknowledgments

The authors gratefully acknowledge the help of John Bresina in the early phases of this research.

This work was supported in part by the National Science Foundation under Grant No. DCR83-18075.

Notes

1) See [Roads 1985b, Ames 1987] for surveys on the application of AI techniques to music.

2) When problem reduction is applied to the domain of planning sequences of physical actions [Nilsson 1971], the starting state and goal state each constitute a partial description of the state of the world. As we apply problem reduction to this music domain, the states typically refer to more abstract aspects of the musical design rather than the surface elements of the resulting composition.

3) The reader should be aware that some of the AI planning literature uses the term *plan* to denote just the solution. The distinction between the two uses of the term should become more salient as the discussion progresses.

4) This limitation is not peculiar to this domain or task. For instance, even in simple "Blocks World" robotic domains [Nilsson 1971, Sacerdoti 1977], planning often requires that the solution, a

sequence of robot actions, has to be re-interpreted as changes to the state of world.

5) Or, in the more general case, when any dependency occurs across widely disparate levels of the structure.

References

[Amarel 1981] Amarel, S. 1981. Problems of representation in heuristic problem solving: Related issues in development of expert systems.In *Methods of Heuristics*, eds. Groner, Groner and Bischof. Hillsdale, N.J.:Lawrence Erlbaum.

[Amarel 1967] Amarel, S. 1967. An approach to heuristic problem solving and theorem proving in the propositional calculus. In *Systems and Computer Science*, eds. J.F. Hart and S. Takasu. University of Toronto Press.

[Ames 1987] Ames, C. 1987. AI in Music. In *Encyclopedia of Artificial Intelligence*, ed. S. Shapiro, 638–642. John Wiley & Sons.

[Bresina et al. 1987] Bresina, J.L., Marsella, S.C. and Schmidt, C.F. 1987. Predicting subproblem interactions, Technical Report LCSR-TR-92, Laboratory for Computer Science Research, Rutgers University.

[Ebcioglu 1988] Ebcioglu, K. 1988. An Expert System for Harmonizing Four-Part Chorales. *Computer Music Journal*, 12(3):43–51.

[Fikes et al. 1971] Fikes, R.E., Hart, P.E. and Nilsson, N.J. 1971. STRIPS: A new approach to the application of theorem proving to problem solving. *Artificial Intelligence*, 2:189–208.

[Gill 1963] Gill, S. 1963. A technique for the composition of music in a computer. *The Computer Journal*, 6(2):129–133.

[Hiller and Isaac. 1963] Hiller, L. and Isaacson, L. 1963. Experimental Music. *The Modeling of Mind; Computers and Intelligence*, K. Sayre and F. Crosson, 43–71. Notre Dame, Indiana: University of Notre Dame Press.

[Holtzman 1980] Holtzman, S.R. 1980. A Generative Grammar Definition Language for Music. *Interface*, 9:1–47.

[Lansky 1986] Lansky, A.L. 1986. A representation of parallel activity based on events, structure, and causality. *Reasoning about Actions and Plans, Proceedings of the 1986 Workshop*, eds. M.P. Georgeff and A.L. Lansky. Los Altos: Morgan Kaufmann.

[Laske 1972] Laske, O. 1972. On Musical Strategies with a View to a Generative Theory of Music. *Interface*, 1:111–125.

[Laske 1989] Laske, O. 1989. Composition Theory: An Enrichment of Music Theory. *Interface*, 18:45–59.

[Lerdahl and Jackenfoff 1983] Lerdahl, F. and Jackendoff, R. 1983. *A Generative Theory of Tonal Music*. Cambridge, Mass.:MIT Press.

[Lidov and Gab. 1973] Lidov, D. and Gabura, J. 1973. A Melody Writing Algorithm Using a Formal Language Model. *Computer Studies in the Humanities and Verbal Behavior*, 4(3/4):138–148.

[Marsella 1988] Marsella, S.C. 1988. An Approach to Problem Reduction Learning, Technical Report LCSR-TR-110, Laboratory for Computer Science Research, Rutgers University.

[Nilsson 1971] Nilsson, N.J. 1971. *Problem Solving Methods in Artificial Intelligence*, 80–115. New York: McGraw-Hill.

[Roads 1985a] Roads, C. 1985. Grammars as Representations of Music. *Foundations of Computer Music*, eds. C. Roads and J. Strawn, 403–442. Cambridge, Mass.: MIT Press.

[Roads 1985b] Roads, C. 1985. Research in Music and Artificial Intelligence. *Computing Surveys*, 17(2):163–190.

[Sacerdoti 1977] Sacerdoti, E.D. 1977. *A Structure for Plans and Behavior*. New York: Elsevier.

[Tenney 1986] Tenney, J. 1986. *Meta-Hodos and META Meta-Hodos*. Oakland CA: Frog Peak Music.

Abstract

An overview of two knowledge acquisition systems built for the explicit purpose of eliciting, understanding, and modeling non-verbal music knowledge as utilized in composition tasks. The first system, OBSERVER (1971–77), deals with perception-based, real-time composition; the second system, PRECOMP (1987–1990), with symbolic, notation-based composition. In both cases, verbal knowledge is bypassed in order to focus directly on musical action, which is captured in so-called protocols. Protocols form the input material for the musicologist's knowledge modeling task.

Chapter 11

The OBSERVER Tradition of Knowledge Acquisition

Otto E. Laske

Music is one of the most ancient sciences of the artificial.

Herbert A. Simon (1969:81)

The Observer Tradition

The Acquisition of Non-Verbal Music Knowledge

In AI generally, and in AI and Music in particular, the acquisition of non-verbal knowledge is difficult, and no proven methodology exists. We report about two related approaches to computer-assisted knowledge acquisition in music, focusing attention on the epistemological problems in modeling knowledge data, not on technical details of the tools that generate or model the data. Both approaches bypass verbalization; they focus directly on underlying intuitions, dispositions, and explicit actions of a musical novice or expert in composition. Actions are monitored in the framework of a programmed task environment embodying a model of the task, which is either one of perception-based (OBSERVER), or of text-based (PRECOMP) composition. In both cases, the task model itself is based on knowledge data deriving from the work of expert composers, namely, P. Hindemith in the case of OBSERVER, and G.M. Koenig and O. Laske in the case of PRECOMP. The computer functions as a semi-active partner, viz., as a test case generator, analysis tool, interactive monitoring and knowledge acquisition device, as well as a tool for modeling elicited knowledge. One can speak of task-based knowledge acquisition. This use of the computer is in keeping with the goal of our research, to formulate a performance model of music composition.

Historical Background

In early writings on cognitive musicology (Laske 1971–1975), inspired by computer music and influenced by N. Chomsky, P. Schaeffer, and H. A. Simon, a distinction was made between models of musical knowledge (competence), on the one hand, and models of its use in real-time tasks (performance), on the other. In struggling with the complexities of competence models (which seemed to require one, among other things, to state musical universals), generative grammars—ten years later advocated by Lerdahl & Jackendoff—were judged as inappropriate to the task of modeling musical knowledge. Grammars were thought to be ethnocentric representations of the syntactic aspect of musical knowledge, conceived in isolation from semantic and sonological knowledge (i.e., grammatical knowledge about sound). This rejection of grammars as stand-alone competence models unrelated to semantic and sonological knowledge reflected the refusal, to restrict the notion of "grammar" to a model of the isolated syntactic component of musical knowledge (thus implying an emphatic use of the term "grammar" as a model of music-semantic and sonological knowledge as well; see also Blacking 1984); the refusal also implied the rejection of a grammar that is unrelated to concrete uses of competence in real time, within a particular musical culture, and at a certain point of its history (performance):

> For purposes of grammatical investigation as well as for an inquiry into performance, a sonological theory defined out of relation with syntax and semantics is useless; equally useless is a syntactical component whose definition fails to account for knowledge concerning the sound properties of musical structures
>
> *(Laske 1972: 69)*

This refusal is that of an epistemologist and anthropologist—rather than a musicologist—who, by profession, is aware of the variability of competence in different cultures, and within cultures over a period of time (Meyerson 1948, Vecchione 1990b), and who cannot accept the dichotomy between "structure" (syntax) and "sound" (sonology) that is basic to "music theory." From an epistemological point of view, what matters is not only the link of structure and sound, but also the distinction between merely psychoacoustic and sonological properties of sound, the latter being properties that pertain to sonic objects as designed artifacts (Simon 1969), or embodied objects (Laske 1973c), while the former pertain to sonic objects as merely perceptual entities.

It was decided that what primarily needed study were performance models of music (Laske 1972, 1973a, 1974b), preferably regarding tasks for which a controlled environment could be created with the aid of a computer. For such studies, a minimal model of competence, operationalized by the programmed task environment, was thought to be sufficient. As well, sonology, the study of sounds having a musical function, was considered as an artificial intelligence discipline (viz., a science of the artificial). These reminiscences describe the epistemological background of the work here reported, which extends over a period of nearly twenty years.

The OBSERVER Tradition

Knowledge acquisition in the OBSERVER tradition is a computer-assisted undertaking. The tradition has been established by two interactive systems, viz., OBSERVER and PRECOMP. In the context of Laske & Truax's OBSERVER programs (Laske 1973b, 1974a, 1975, 1977 [ch. 10], 1979), children of ages seven to twelve were monitored by a computer in their problem-solving in an elementary composition task employing electroacoustic sounds. Using a teletype interface, the children's decision-making during task performance was documented by "action protocols" keeping track of their activity as reflected in the use of operators. Following a production-system simulation of the resulting performance traces at Carnegie-Mellon University in 1975–77 (in PSG, forerunner of the OPS-languages), some of the OBSERVER protocols were analyzed manually (Laske 1979), in order to understand the development of the children's music-syntactic thinking. Fifteen years later, in a dissertation closely following the OBSERVER precedent, D. Cantor made use of G. M. Koenig's Project One program (Koenig 1969, 1979), and of O. Laske's personal knowledge as a composer using Project One (Laske 1990a-c, 1989b), to create parts of PRECOMP (Cantor 1989). PRECOMP is a professional tool for interpretive composition; in this type of composition, material in the form of an alphanumeric text is interpreted by a composer as material for a musical score.

In contrast to OBSERVER, which is entirely based on notions of music theory, thus public knowledge, the PRECOMP environment is based on formalizing personal knowledge about composition. OBSERVER has mainly been used with novices (children), whereas PRECOMP can be used only by experts in composition. In what follows, we discuss the OBSERVER tradition of knowledge acquisition and knowledge modeling, and its continuation in PRECOMP, in order to highlight issues in developing an empirical theory of compositional knowledge.

Methodological Considerations

In cases where human knowledge is mainly action knowledge, as in music, methods of verbalization, as used in different kinds of interview, are insufficient to capture an expert's knowledge (Laske 1986a). Intuitions and actions must be captured on-line. As first shown by Laske & Truax (Laske 1974a), this can be done by building a programmed environment embodying a model (a) of the expert's task, (b) of the expert's physical environment, and (c) of the cooperation between system and expert. The task environment must be congenial with the expert's way of working (i.e., it must be a professional tool); it must be capable of documenting the expert's actions in a form suitable for machine evaluation and computer modeling.

In both OBSERVER and PRECOMP, the focus is on action knowledge bypassing verbalization. Actions are conceived as designed, i.e., as based on the musician's theory-in-use (competence), to be elucidated inductively, by inference from empirical knowledge data. For practical purposes, a theory-in-use might be conceived of as a cognitive schema underlying action—in contrast to an expert's espoused theory which is composed of selective verbalizations of his knowledge (Argyris 1985).

The OBSERVER System

Interactive Knowledge Acquisition

OBSERVER is an interactive system for knowledge acquisition in monody composition. It was implemented on a PDP-15 computer by Barry Truax, Utrecht, during 1972–73, and, in a later version, by David J. Murray, Urbana, Illinois, on a PLATO workstation (1977–78). In this system, the competence assumed as required for pursuing monody composition is operationalized by a task model defining the user's working environment, basically an interface comprising compositional problem-solving operators. Figure 1 outlines the parts of the OBSERVER system. OBSERVER consists of two sets of programs, for: (1) knowledge acquisition by way of generating performance traces, or protocols (OBSERV, OBSVAR), and (2) the simulation of a monody composition task by computer (OBSYN). The two sets of programs are linked, because empirical insight into real-time composition processes is seen as a means for improving the simulation of the composition task undertaken in OBSYN. To allow for generic test cases (that one can submit to different users simultaneously, or to the same user at different times), OBSYN is used as a generator of test cases for OBSERV. An analysis program, PHRAN, is employed for carrying out a quantitative analysis of OBSYN output, as well as user-created monodies. (PHRAN embodies criteria, taken from (Hindemith 1935) and (Keller 1957), for defining the melic, rhythmic, and harmonic potential of a sound sequence, called its "type.")

Scope and Structure of an OBSERVER Task

In contrast to a PRECOMP task, which is based on an alphanumeric score text, an OBSERVER task is a real-time, perception-based task communicable in a form that musical novices can readily understand. We restrict attention to OBSERV, a program for creating monody (melodies) from an aleatoric repertory of electroacoustic sounds. (OBSVAR is a program dealing with the formation of variants of OBSERV output.) Composition in OBSERV starts with accepting a given sound sequence generated by OBSYN. Prior to its use, the sound sequence is classified by PHRAN as being of one of six types, viz., Mh, Mr, Rm, Rh, Hm, or Hr (W. Keller 1957), where the capital letter indicates the primary (most strongly weighted) parametrical dimension (M=melos, R=rhythm, H=harmony), and the small letter the second, subordinate dimension. This analytical classification, which remains unknown to the user, enables one to formulate elementary compositional goals, and to classify composi-

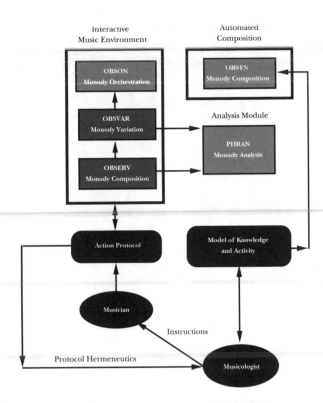

Figure 1. Knowledge Acquisition in OBSERVER (1971–1977).

tional outcomes. It is the user's task, (a) either to create a sound sequence of a certain type (properly circumscribed in the user's language), or (b) simply, as in the case of young children, to "compose a melody." PHRAN functions as a neutral arbiter posting the structural result of the user's problem-solving session. An example will help clarify these ideas.

An OBSERVER Protocol

Table 1 presents a protocol taken from OBSERV. The protocol is a performance trace documenting the relationship between modification operators (such as P, for changing the pitch of a sound), and tests verifying the perceptual result of their application. Each protocol entry represents a command to a sound synthesis system generating and transforming monophonic sound sequences in real time. The protocol is a snapshot of a composition process as reflected by the use of problem solving operators; it shows what a user has done at a particular point in time in the pro-

#	action	#	action
001	get 1,2 [first 2 sounds]	022	5, tel
002	tmel	023	5,P -3
003	tmel	024	5, tel
004	tmel	025	3,P +4
005	add 5 [sounds]	026	3, tel
006	tmel	027	tmel
007	end, write	;	
;		028	tmel
008	1,P 0	029	2,P -3
009	tmel	030	2, tel
010	tmel	031	2,P -4
011	tmel	032	2, tel
012	tmel	033	2,P -5
013	2,E +5	034	2, tel
014	2, tel	035	tmel
015	2, tel	036	2,P -1
016	tmel	037	2, tel
017	3,P +4	038	2,P +5
018	3, tel	039	2, tel
019	3, P-3	040	tmel
020	3, tel	041	tmel
021	5,P +5	042	end

input: Rmh [melic Rhythm; PHRAN weighting: R=2.0, M=3.5, H=3.5]
output: Mrh [rhythmic Melos, PHRAN weighting R=2.0, M=1.9, H=3.5]

Table 1. OBSERVER Protocol from Module OBSERV

cess of creating a melody of a particular type. At each step, not only are the user's commands carried out by the system; the user is also monitored both in what he does, and in the results of his decision-making (as analyzed by PHRAN). In this way, every step intermediate between the user's start and goal state is documented in both a procedural and declarative form.

The protocol in Table 1 is shown in two juxtaposed halves. To the right of the running entry number, mnemonic action identifiers are seen; some of these refer to perceptual tests (TMEL [test the melody], TEL [test a single sound]), others, to housekeeping actions (GET [sounds], ADD [add sounds], END [exit]). Modification operators serve the purpose of modifying the sound repertory initially accepted by the user; they have the form <n,P[T,E]+/-m>, where n is the integer name of a single sound, and P,T,E refer to the musical parameters of pitch (P), time delay (temporal distance between consecutive sounds, T), and the envelope (E) defining a sound. Compositional changes [+/-m] are quantified along a scale from -5.0 to

+5.0, where -5.0 is the highest negative, +5.0 the highest positive, degree of change. Accordingly, a command such as <5,P+5> means: "at this point, change the pitch of sound no. 5 by a maximal amount of +5.0." Since no tempered pitch system is used, the result of this command can only be assessed post facto, by hearing the melody generated by the change command. Melody composition is treated as a transformation task; a melody is "composed" by adjusting the parameters of a given repertory of sounds until a goal is thought to have been reached. The musicological task is to formulate a model of the musical knowledge documented by the performance trace, by taking into account the model of competence embodied by the task environment. (For a taxonomy of composition tasks, see Laske 1977, chapter 9).

Capturing Knowledge by Monitoring Musical Actions

Table 1 shows the protocol of an eleven year old (Tristram Koenig). Interpreting such a performance trace is a hermeneutic act; it leads to representing music activity as a kind of reasoning based on the recognition of sonological features (i.e., perceptual features having a music-grammatical function). Musical intuitions are rendered as inferences, in a more or less formal and explicit way. One might want to understand the protocol entries as the right side of rules of the form <if C[ondition], then A[ction]>, where the left side of the rule represents a conceptual, perceptual, or memory condition, and the right side, the resulting music action. The condition is then something to be inferred by the musicologist from protocolled actions, seen in the light of the competence model embodied by the task environment. (An operator such as "P" in the task model makes the claim that there exists an element of competence regarding pitch.) Such induction is not a simple matter; it is often rather an abduction, meaning a way of finding the most convincing interpretation. As is shown by the alternation of tests and transformations in the protocol, conception and perception are strongly interdependent in real-time composition; modification operators are never used randomly, but are treated as (procedural) working hypotheses in need of confirmation. Each protocol action is a consequence of a previous, perceptual and/or conceptual, insight, and is undertaken in view of goals refined during the ongoing performance (This makes the problem "ill-structured."). As the use of the operator TMEL indicates, the user's understanding does not primarily concern single sounds, but entire melodic sequences. For such sequences, only indirect, syntactic operators exist that must be used to satisfy semantic as well as sonological goals.

The following factors are of primary interest for understanding a performance trace:

1) the way in which perceptions are used to support (verify) the use of compositional operators;

2) the way in which global tests (TSEQ) reinterpret local ones (TEL);

3) the relative frequency of occurrence of particular modification operators P, T, E (i.e., their "interestingness ranking;" here P occurs 11 times out of 12);

4) the proportion of compositional changes [= 12] to tests [= 25, of which 13 are global] to housekeeping operators [= 5];

5) the temporal sequence of steps taken, and (6) the selection of tones focused on (here, #2, 3, 5, 3, 2).

The temporal resolution of the protocol is quite high: 42 steps in 11 minutes, or one action every 16 seconds on the average.

The Evidence of Expertise

Figure 2a is a notational representation of the input to the child's performance. This is a cludge, since no well-tempered or metric system is in use in OBSERVER; CMN notation is therefore approximate. We see a sound sequence of type Rmh (melic-harmonic Rhythm), viz., a melody of primarily rhythmic potential with an equal (PHRAN) weighting of the subsidiary dimensions M and H (R:2.0, M:3.5, H:3.5, where the lower score (i.e., 2.0) defines a higher potential). The target melody was defined as "a melody of same or very similar type" (understood in the sense of PHRAN). In a non-tempered system where operator P (pitch) simultaneously affects the melic (M) and the harmonic dimensions (H) of a melody, melic and harmonic competences have to be well established, to stay close to the melodic type of the initial repertory (input). Any use of P (which predominates the protocol considered) changes the harmonic dimension, thus threatening to turn the Rmh input into a different melodic type (for instance, an Hrm). In the present case, the solution melody, shown in Figure 2b, scored as a weakly defined rhythmic Melos—the scores for R and M are very close—with a weak harmonic dimension, Mrh (R:2.0, M:1.9, H:3.5). In this melody, the rhythmic and harmonic potential remained unchanged compared with the input, while the melic potential of the melody was significantly strengthened.

duration: 3.7"   4.2"   2.8"   2.3"   .5" 3.4"   2.9"

Figure 2a. CMN Rendition of Input Repertory to OBSERVER Protocol.

duration: 3.7"   4.2"   2.8"   2.3"   .5" 3.4"   2.9"

Figure 2b. CMN Rendition of Output Melody from OBSERVER Protocol.

Modeling the music knowledge implied by Table 1 means to produce a model of the use of competence in a real-time performance situation. Another purpose of modeling is to present a comparative analysis of several protocols relating to the same input and task, either performed by different children, or by the same child at different times. An important goal in OBSERVER was to employ the performance model resulting from the analysis of protocol data as a basis for enhancing the functioning of OBSYN, to develop OBSYN into a reasonably "intelligent" tool for automated melody composition. (This goal was never pursued to completion.) A comparative interpretation of Table 1 can be found in (Laske 1979).

The PRECOMP System

Knowledge Acquisition in a Composer's Assistant

PRECOMP is a composer's assistant implemented on a Macintosh computer with the aid of Hypercard; its purpose is to assist composers in producing a CMN score and, based on it, a musical form. One of the modules of PRECOMP is also a knowledge acquisition tool producing knowledge data that document a part of the composer's design process. PRECOMP comprises four modules, as shown in Figure 3. The first three were implemented by D. Cantor as part of a dissertation (D. Cantor 1989); the last one is in the process of being implemented.

A) a generator of score texts (called event lists), taken from Koenig's Project One program

B) a graphic score-text analyzer

C) a module giving a composer feedback on his design of a musical form, based on decisions about segmenting the score text, and yielding protocols documenting the composer's process in terms of "snapshots"

D) a module translating the score text output by module A (pseudo-score) into a note list (definitive score) as required by CSound, an orchestra language for programmed sound synthesis (Vercoe 1988).

Module A is based on G. M. Koenig's formalization and programming of his own compositional expertise; it exists in two forms: a 1969/1979, and a 1988, version. Modules (B) through (D) codify knowledge elements pertaining to compositional design, as well as analysis, verbally elicited from O. Laske. (Module D uses the later version of Project One since it gives composers a higher degree of freedom in their input specification.) Division of labor in PRECOMP is as follows. Module A generates the compositional material, module B assists in analyzing it, module C gives feedback on design decisions utilizing the material, and module D does the actual inter-

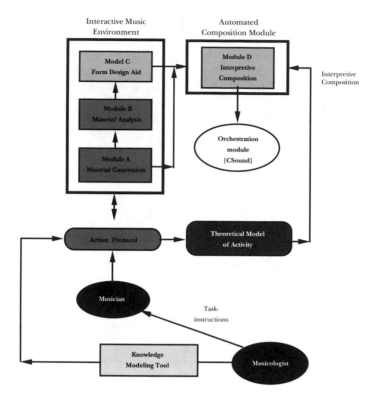

Figure 3. Knowledge Acquisition in PRECOMP (1987–1990).

pretive work, of deriving a musical score (note list) from event list material. The composer is free to skip modules B and C, and to proceed directly from module A to D, in order to produce a note list. (A note list is an interpreted event list, i.e., a definitive score).

PRECOMP is not an all-purpose compositional tool, nor is it, in and of itself, an intelligent tool. Rather, it is an assistant functioning as a composer's alter ego, which embodies, in objectified form, some part of the composer's musical working knowledge. PRECOMP is geared to interpretive composition, a task in which a computer-generated alphanumeric text (called an event list) is interpreted by the composer for the sake of creating a piece of music (see Laske 1990a/d, 1989a–c). Upon receiving a minimal input, the program produces sets of compositional material which, when interpreted competently, can be fashioned into a musical form. PRE-COMP's "intelligence" lies in challenging a composer to making interpretations of materials he would ordinarily not be able to produce by hand; it is a problem-posing, not a problem-solving, device.

In the following discussion of PRECOMP's knowledge acquisition module (C), emphasis will be given to the modeling of data relating to event list segmentation, a prerequisite task in designing a musical form. Segmenting is, above all, an analytical task. Segmenting an event list means determining ("finding") structural breakpoints capable of articulating parts of a musical form. While a human composer engaged in this task draws together information about all of the subscores of a composition, PRECOMP's segmentation module (C) takes a somewhat pedestrian approach, considering only a single score text at a time. Module C is not in any way intelligent; it is simply a good monitor. Its relevance for music research lies in its focussing of attention on the cognitive disposition that gives rise to a composer's decision-making, as will become apparent below, when commenting on a particular performance trace.

Scope and Structure of the PRECOMP Task

Composing with PRECOMP means engaging in a dialog with one's compositional alter ego. The process begins with planning the production of syntactic materials for an instrumental or tape composition. (For other dimensions of compositional knowledge, see Laske 1990a, and Riecken, in this volume.) In the framework of 20th century music composition, structural planning is frequently carried out by focusing on the so-called musical parameters, such as tone color, pitch, dynamics, octave register, and various temporal calibrations (duration, entry delay, tempo). In accordance with this approach, PRECOMP's module A requires the composer to specify a structure formula stipulating a crude measure of order/disorder (or of homogeneity /heterogeneity) of compositional materials, independent of their elaboration in time. The elaboration of these materials into a music-syntactic surface structure is left as a task to the composer. Module A provides a scale of seven degrees of order/disorder, ranging from 1 (highest degree; change from event to event) to 7 (highest degree of redundancy through repetition). An example of a structure formula is as follows:

P(itch)=6,R(egister)=6,T(imeDelay)=6,T(oneColor)=6,D(ynamics)=6 .

This formula specifies a high degree of redundancy for all parameters, with entirely different musical consequences for each. (T=6 will result in metric groupings, while P=6 will become manifest in repeating tone-, motive-, or row-centered events.)

Table 2 shows an event list produced by module A, based on the above specification. (There are 32767 possible outputs, depending on the random seed). In the event list, each row defines an abstract "event," and each column specifies the temporal changes, from event to event, of a particular parameter, such as, e.g., dynamics (second column from right). The composer's precompositional task is to understand the structure of the event list, and the implications of that structure for the design of a musical form interpreting the event list. The composer is helped in this task by module B, presenting him with graphic representations of analytic views

Match_I.2, version 2
Instr.= 6, E.D.= 6, Pitch Classes= 6, Registers= 6, Dynm. = 6

bar#	*previous disposition (breakpoints)*	*Ev*	*Instr.*	*E.D.*		*Pitch Classes*	*Order*	*Registers*	*Dynm.*	*present disposition (breakpoints)*
8		1 *	4 *	1/5	T=40.0 *	a# a f e	4 3 2 1	1 1 1 1	4	
		2	4	1/5		d# b	2 1	1 1	4	
		3	4	1/5		c# c g# g	3 4 1 2	1 1 1 1	4	
		4	4	1/5		f# d a#	2 1 3	1 1 1	4	
		5	4	1/5		a f	1 2	1 1	4	
9		6	4	1/5		e	1	1	4	
	[3]	7	4	1/5		d# b c# c	1 4 3 2	1 2 2 2	4	⑦
		8 *	1	1/5		g# g f# d	4 3 2 1	2 2 2 2	4	⑧
10	[1]	9	1 *	1/2	T= 43.0	a# a	1 2	2 2	8	⑥
	[10]	10	1	1/2		f e	1 2	2 2	8	
		11	1	1/2		d#	1	2	8	
		12 *	5	1/2		b	1	2	8	
		13	5	1/2		c# c	2 1	2 2	8	
	[4]	14	5	1/2		g# g	1 2	2 2	8	
		15	5	1/2		f# d	1 2	1 1	8	
		16	5	1/2		a# a	2 1	1 1	8	
11		17	5 *	3/2		f e	1 2	1 1	6	⑤
		18	5	3/2		d# b c#	3 1 2	1 1 1	6	
12		19	5	3/2		c	1	1	6	
		20 *	2	3/2		g# g	2 1	1 1	6	⑨
13	[7]	21	2	3/2		f#	1	1	6	
		22	2	3/2		d a# a f e	3 2 5 1 4	1 2 2 2 2	6	③
14	[5]	23	2 *	1/4	*	b	1	2	6	①
		24	2	1/4		c	1	2	6	
		25	2	1/4		d# b	2 1	2 2	3	
	[2]	26	2	1/4		c d#	1 2	2 2	3	
		27 *	3	1/4		b	1	2	3	
		28	3 *	1/8	T= 65.0	c	1	2	3	②
		29	3	1/8		d#	1	2	3	
		30	3	1/8		b	1	2	3	
		31 *	2	1/8		c	1	2	3	
		32	2	1/8		d#	1	2	2	
		33	2	1/8		b	1	2	2	
		34	2	1/8		c	1	2	2	
		35	2 *	1/2		d#	1	2	2	
15		36	2	1/2		b c d#	3 1 2	2 2 2	2	④
		37	2	1/2	*	f	1	2	2	
	[6]	38 *	1	1/2		e	1	2	2	
		39	1	1/2		c# d# d	3 2 1	2 2 2	2	
16		40	1 *	1/5		b	1	2	1	
		41	1	1/5		f# g a# g#	4 3 2 1	1 1 1 1	1	
		42	1	1/5		a	1	1	1	
	[9]	43	1	1/5		c f e c#	4 2 3 1	1 1 1 1	1	
17		44	1	1/5		d# d b f#	2 4 1 3	1 1 1 2	1	
18	[8]	45	1	1/5		g a# g# a	2 1 4 3	2 2 2 2	1	
		46 *	3	1/5		c	1	2	1	
		47	3	1/5		f e c#	3 2 1	2 2 2	1	
19		48	3 *	1/5		d# d b f#	3 1 2 4	2 2 2 2	5	⑩
		49	3	1/5		g a# g# a	3 1 2 4	2 2 2 2	5	
		50 *	4	1/5		c f	2 1	1 1	5	

Table 2. Annotated Event List Output from Module A of PRECOMP

of chosen material (Laske 1990a). After having produced and studied various graphic representations of the compositional materials for a section, the composer may wish to determine which events in the list could define subsections (serve as structural breakpoints). It is this determination which is monitored by module C.

A Protocol of Module C

Module C enables a musicologist (knowledge elicitor) to gauge the mental process underlying compositional design; it enables the composer to express his intuitions regarding event list segments, by using mouse clicks or keyboard actions. More precisely, the composer is given Hypercard buttons and fields for (1) stipulating values indicating his sensitivity to parametrical change in an event list (SEN), and (2) expressing the structural significance of chosen parameters (event list columns) for the musical form to be designed (REL). The composer's input to module C is based on his reading and understanding of the event list; it testifies to musical competence as well as imagination.

Reading an event list is a pattern recognition task that can be rendered by rules only to a limited extent. A pattern is a sequence of uninterpreted symbols as found in Table 2. Reading such a table is a knowledge-intensive task, in that it depends on insight (and/or imagination) as to how pattern changes in the list (rows or columns) might be reflected in musical sound and/or form. The dependency of pattern recognition on symbol manipulation in the reading task gives some justification to the approach followed in module C, of capturing knowledge in terms of rules whose variables are set by the composer (for technical details, see Cantor 1989). A protocol documenting the kind of intelligence-guided pattern recognition in question is shown in Table 3. One is dealing with the performance trace of a composer deliberating the relevance of the values of musical parameters spelled out in the columns of Table 2, and deciding about his own sensitivity to event-to-event changes of those values. One can say that Table 3 takes a snapshot of a composer's design process making use of data in Table 2.

In module C, compositional design proceeds by having a program compute structural breakpoints (score subsections). This is done initially, by giving quantitative answers to the program's questions regarding one's sensitivity to event list changes, and the relevance of certain form-defining musical parameters. The composer indicates his sensitivity to changes occurring in certain columns of Table 2 (SEN), as well as the relevance that certain parameters are meant to have in designing a form (REL). The composer's decision-making is documented under the column Value Changes (Table 3, column 5), to which an explanatory column, listing a calibration of stipulated changes has been added in column 6 of the table, entitled Disposition. The structural breakpoints resulting from the composer's Disposition, computed by module C, are posted by each session. In this way, module C provokes a debugging action that continues until the composer reaches an acceptable set of (ten) breakpoints.

Entry #	Time	Parameter Focused On [rule]	Aspect Chosen [slot]	Value Changes [from ⇒ to]	Disposition [Value difference]
001	9:12	Tempo [R1]	Intensity factor	2⇒0.5	SEN3 +1.5
002	9:13	Time-delay [R3]	Multiplier PL*	1⇒0.5	SEN3 +0.5
003	9:13	"	PL[seconds]	5⇒3	SEN1 +2.0
004	9:15	"	Minimum Δ	5⇒3	SEN2 +2.0
005	9:17	Chord-size [R4]	Multiplier PL	1⇒0.5	SEN3 +0.5
006	9:18	"	PL[seconds]	5⇒3	SEN1 +2.0
007	9:20	"	PL[events]	5⇒2	SEN1 +3.0
008	9:22	Pitch [R6]	Minimum Δ	4⇒1	SEN2 +3.0
009	9:23	Tone-color [R7]	Weight	5⇒3	REL -2.0
010	9:24	"	Multiplier PL	1⇒0.2	SEN3 +0.8
011	9:27	Register [R8]	PL[seconds]	5⇒3	SEN2 +2.0
012	9:28	"	PL[events]	5⇒3	SEN2 +2.0
013	9:30	Density [R10]**	Weight	5⇒2	REL -3.0
014	9:32	"	Minimum Δ	6⇒4	SEN2 +2.0
015	9:33	Register [R11]	Weight	5⇒1	REL -4.0
016	9:34	"	Minimum Δ	30⇒15	SEN2 +15.0
017	9:36	Pitch [R12]	Multiplier Δ	2⇒1	SEN3 +1.0
018	9:40	"	Minimum Δ	1⇒1.5	SEN2 -0.5

* PL = prelude length, i.e., the time period, in no. of events or seconds, that has to elapse for a parametrical change to be taken into account in breakpoint computation.

** Starting with rule 9 [R9], neighboring subsections are compared in terms of a specific musical parameter. Certain parameters are thus referred to both in analyzing single and neighboring subsections. For technical details, see D. Cantor 1989.

Table 3. PRECOMP Protocol from module C

In sequence from left to right, the columns in Table 3 document the following aspects of the composer's process:

1) column 1: the sequence of decisions made by the composer

2) column 2: the timing of the decisions, in seconds

3) columns 3-4: the musical parameter momentarily focused on, together with a specific aspect of that parameter singled out for attention (e.g., pitch changes in a single segment, or in two neighboring segments; for technical details on the rule/slot structure in module C, see Cantor 1989)

4) column 5: the change in value from a previous stipulation of the composer, indicated by the integer on the left, to a new stipulation shown by the integers on the right of the arrow "⇒"

5) column 6: a summary of the value changes in column 5 in terms of:
   (1) relevance of change (REL), and
   (2) sensitivity to change (SEN).

Figure 4. CMN Score of Match for Piano by Otto Laske (1989).

Sensitivity comes in three flavors: sensitivity to speed of change (SEN1), (2b) to amount of change (SEN2), and (2c) a reinforcement factor for changes occurring in a specific direction (SEN3; such as, e.g., changes from slow to fast tempo).

The performance trace in Table 3 is to be considered in the context of the composer's process of interpretation of Table 2. In the latter, each column represents a musical parameter, viz., column 1: event number; column 2: instrument (tone color); column 3: time delay between successive events, expressed in fractions of an interpretable unit measure (½) such as a half-note; column 4: pitch classes; column 5: pitch succession; column 6: octave (or other) register; column 7: dynamic levels (from 1 to 8, i.e., ppp to fff).

When the composer starts work on Table 2, the event list shows no sectional structure. This structure is introduced by the interpreting composer (somewhat analogous to a music analyst reading notation). Figure 4 shows the definitive CMN score resulting from the composer's interpretation of the event list. As can be seen, the composer has been inspired to conceive of Table 2 as defining 12 bars (Figure 4, bars 8 to 19) of a larger movement (see the bar nos. at the outer left of Table 2). To understand the composer's work, let us imagine that he is presently considering the inner structure of the event list. In his design deliberations, the composer deals with the function of parameter changes in Table 2 (Table 3, columns 3-4) as building stones of a musical form to be created. Module C enables the composer to make four kinds of decisions (Table 3, columns 5–6), viz., decisions regarding:

a) a parameter's overall design relevance (REL)

b) the time (in seconds or number of events) that must elapse between consecutive parameter changes, for them to be design-relevant (SEN1).

c) the degree of change required for a parameter change to count as design-relevant, defined in accordance with the parameter in question (SEN2, Minimum Δ)

d) a reinforcement factor (for REL overall) emphasizing a particular kind of change (SEN3).

Module C does more than just store the composer's proposed values, as listed under columns 3–4 of Table 3. It carries out computations to determine the segmentations resulting from the composer's stipulations. In order to give the composer feedback on his decisions, module C computes a ranking of the ten most important structural breakpoints in a score text, naming those events in Table 2 that could either start a new, or end a previous, score section. (For example, it might inform the composer that his SEN- and REL-stipulations result in defining a primary breakpoint at event no. 23 of Table 2. For further explanations as to breakpoints, see below). If the composer finds this result unconvincing, or in conflict with musical common sense, he will reflect on the stipulations made and revise them, as long as is required for him in order to find an acceptable set of structural breakpoints. Essentially, then, module C permits the composer to engage in dialog with himself, and to find out what are the structural equivalents of his intuitively adopted readings of the event list, as categorized by input to module C.

The composer is entirely free to make whatever decisions he wants to make. When inspecting the outer right column of Table 3, one sees that, in the present case, the composer has made three REL decisions, three SEN1 decisions, seven SEN2 decisions, and five SEN3 decisions (please note that a reduction in a SEN-related value (column 5) amounts to an increase of SEN (column 6), while the reduction of a REL-related value reduces REL). This configuration of decisions defines his Disposition. According to Table 3, the composer's present disposition is characterized by the fact that foremost on his mind is the degree of required minimal change of parameter values in the event list (SEN2=7), and the reinforcement of parameter change in a particular direction (SEN3=5), followed by speed of parametrical change (SEN1=3), and parameter relevance itself (REL).

As one notices under Value Changes (Table 3, column 5), values from the composer's previous disposition were consistently reduced (except in entry 018). As shown under Disposition (Table 3, column 6), this attitude amounts to a decisive increase in sensitivity to pattern change (SEN1-3), and a lessening of the overall relevance of specific parameters (REL) for defining breakpoints. In natural language terms, the composer is conveying that he is henceforth going to be more sensitive to changes in tempo, time delay, chord size, pitch, tone color, and register, as well as density, while simultaneously reducing the overall relevance of parameters tone color, density, and register. (From entry 013 on, the composer is comparing two neighboring segments of the event list, instead of dealing with single segments; for these technical details, see Cantor 1989). As a result, the sequence of break points computed initially (second column of Table 2) is replaced by the sequence of breakpoints listed in the outer right column of Table 2, entitled "present disposition."

Module C Protocols Document Mental Disposition

In (Minsky 1980), a disposition is defined as a "momentary range of possible behaviors," and it is thought that theories of memory ought to model dispositions as mental states that give rise to behavior. (It is thought, further, that new mental states derive from a mutual relationship between sensation and memory; see also Smoliar, in this volume). In the present context, Table 3 documents a range of possible compositional behaviors vis-à-vis the target material stated in Table 2. A sequence of "snapshots" such as Table 3 documents the composer's changes of mind regarding event list data, as he is molding this data into a musical form. (Regarding the non-computability of changes of mind, see Kugel, in this volume.) Here, each protocol entry is taken to refer to the intentional state (disposition documented by Table 3), with attention focused on particular musical parameters (i.e., columns of Table 2). In all cases, entries in Table 3 refer to a composer's previous mental state, that is, his memory, even if that state is only a default the composer happened to start out from. This previous mental state (now a memory) is under revision by the behaviors documented in Table 3. In a possible (still crude) interpretation of (Minsky 1980), a mental state as expressed in Table 3 can be said to "dispose" a musician to a certain range of behaviors in designing a musical form. These behaviors are spelled out by the individual protocol entries.

In a (possibly too) narrow and literal interpretation of Minsky's definition, Table 3 can be understood as an explication of a composer's disposition, in the context of which possible behaviors (regarding changes in musical parameters) are experimentally tried out. (There are actually two classes of behaviors, viz., the class of immediate behaviors of using module C as a segmentation assistant, and the class of virtual behaviors using module C output for designing a musical form.) Dispositions are high level strategies; they are indispensable when dealing with complex situations, or when managing possible (imagined) situations. (An event list has many different dimensions, and many relations obtain between them, thus many different actions can be taken regarding them.) Note that the relationships among the imagined musical objects implied by Table 2 are not logical, but, to speak with Piaget, "infralogical" ones (Laske 1974a).

Dispositions, then, are temporary "world views" that permit focused activity; they simplify an involved situation and focus the imagination. Module C enforces such simplification by requiring the composer to focus on a single parameter at a time. In entry 1 of Table 3, column 5, for instance, the composer conveys his decision to become more sensitive to tempo changes in Table 2 ($2 \Rightarrow 0.5$), especially where they occur in the direction from slow to fast [R1=Rule 1]. In entry 3, column 5, the composer expresses that a shorter time period than previously stipulated ($5 \Rightarrow 3$) will be required for changes in the temporal distance between events to be of relevance for determining structural breakpoints. As these examples show, the composer experimentally (and playfully) adopts a particular range of behaviors regarding a musical parameter; module C responds to his stipulations by informing the composer of the structural outcomes of his disposition in terms of structural breakpoints that will result, thereby elucidating for him the (declarative) results of changes in procedure (behavior). In the present case, module C ranked the events in Table 2 in the sequence: #23, 28, 22, 36, 17, 9, 7, 8, 20, and 48. This means that event #23 was assigned the highest potential for serving as the beginning of a score subsection, while event #48 has the lowest. The composer can use this feedback to improve the design (and his design behavior), changing his disposition as long as is required to reach his compositional goals. In this way, module C provides a history of the composer's "changes of mind" as determinants of musical form.

Clearly, a single phase of a musical design process, such as rendered by Table 3, is difficult to capture other than by computer. Were one to interpret the composer's decisions as actions that depend on conditions (as one would in a system of production rules), evidently the conditions could be extremely complex; they would have to include willful decisions which are, by nature, not computable (Kugel 1990; in this volume). Such a rule-based approach would certainly be very awkward.

Capturing Knowledge by Monitoring Actions

Knowledge acquisition in PRECOMP stresses that compositional activity concerns virtual (possible) musics (see also Farrett 1990). Correspondingly, it is emphasized that the subject matter of knowledge elicitation regards possible compositional behaviors and their structural outcomes (as computed by module C) —not some kind of preordained knowledge one can ossify in a "knowledge base." Also, the "expert interviewed" by module C does not speak, but act, exercising the elements of the craft the knowledge elicitor is in search of. In this regard, PRECOMP implicitly criticizes the epistemological assumptions of a majority of knowledge acquisition enterprises, for which knowledge is conceived as something "out there" (in the task environment) or "in here" (viz., in the mind), but not as something virtual, spontaneous, constantly changeable.

An expert may not be able to verbalize what he knows, but he can surely show an observer (such as a musicologist) how he proceeds on account of his knowledge—if only one can capture his actions by way of a suitably monitored task environment. This regards, in particular, processes based on complex cognitive schemata that cannot easily be factored into their constitutive elements.

In module C, competence regarding the use of parameters in musical design is cast into the form of rules. Each parameter, such as tempo, is represented by one or more rules comprising slots which represent the REL- and SEN-aspects of a parameter. A rule in module C is a composition-theoretical, thus musicological, device for capturing knowledge about possible musics. Considered in abstract terms, a rule says to the user: "if your adopted disposition regarding event list parameter z (column of Table 2) is X, then set the slot Y of rule Z to N" (where N is the new value to the right of "$\Rightarrow$" under column #5 of Table 3). Rules are thus utilized as a medium in which to codify mental states, and the behaviors they give rise to; rules provoke reasoning about a possible state of affairs (Farrett 1990). The task of interpreting such reasoning is a knowledge modeling task. Formulating a knowledge model for module C protocols consists of representing disposition X on the basis of empirical findings regarding the slot(s) Y[N] of rule (parameter) Z. (For technical details regarding the machinery for generating protocols in PRECOMP, see Cantor 1989. As many other writings in the knowledge acquisition literature, Cantor's thesis suffers from the methodological misconception that building the tool, not evaluating and modeling the knowledge data it generates, is the main knowledge acquisition task.)

The Evidence of Expertise

In PRECOMP, as in OBSERVER, the emphasis is on understanding the structure of expert knowledge, and its utilization in real-time performances. In PRECOMP, the emphasis is on virtual music and associated possible behaviors, rather than on actual behavior, as in OBSERVER. This difference might be rendered as that between creativity (possible behaviors) and competence (actual behaviors). Regardless of this distinction, in interpreting knowledge acquisition findings, the crucial referent ist the outcome of a performance. A PRECOMP performance results in a musical score as shown in Figure 4 (bars 8 to 19 of Match for Piano by O. Laske [1989]). To help in understanding the relationships between the source material and the resulting score, Table 2 has been annotated by way of integers (in circles or square brackets) indicating two different rankings of events, one that is due to a previous, and another that is due to the current, disposition. (The plain integers at the outer left of Table 2 refer to bar numbers in Figure 4.)

In Table 2, the circled integers on the outer right side, (namely, ① to ⑩), specify the event ranking resulting from the actions documented in Table 3 (column 5, integers to the right of '⇒'), while the integers on the left side, in square brackets, refer to a previous disposition (Table 3, column 5, integers to the left of "⇒"). The sequence of compted breakpoints changes from (event #9, 26, 7, 4, 23, 38, 21, 45, 43, 10) to (event #23, 28, 22, 36, 17, 9, 7, 8, 20, 48). On account of the change in disposition documented by Table 3, the highest-ranking breakpoint of the previous disposition (namely, event #9) has been replaced by event #23.

In what follows, we briefly discuss the compositional treatment of the three most important breakpoints computed by module C on the basis of Table 3. To do so, we need to relate the two tables to Figure 4. (In Figure 4, all annotations refer to Table 2; integers in circles indicate breakpoints, and integers preceded by "#," indicate events.) In the score, the three most important structural breakpoints are located in bars 13 and 14. As shown, the composer opted for considering:

a) event 23 (breakpoint 1, tone B [lower voice, bar 14])

b) event 28 (breakpoint 2, tone C, [upper voice, last tone, bar 14])

c) event 22 (breakpoint 3, chord D, A# F [lower voice, bar 13])

(compare Table 2 with Figure 4) as important design determinants. In the score, this is conveyed by rests separating events 22 and 23 [bars 13–14], on the one hand, and events 28 and 29 [bars 14 and 15], on the other.

To accommodate the first (#23) and third (#22) breakpoints, the composer separated parts of the lower voice of bars 13 and 14 by silences; he chose to state events 24–25 (tone C [with an insertion of A from event 22]; chord D#, B [upper voice, bar 14]) temporally prior to event 23 (B [lower voice, bar 14]), and skipped the repetitions (of events 24–25) occurring in events 26-27, merging the tone C in event 26 with the C in event 28 [upper voice, bar 14]. To do justice to the second most important breakpoint at event 28, the composer delimited tone C from its successor (29-30, tones D#, B [upper voice, bar 15]) by a further rest [end of bar 14, start of bar 15] and, following events 29–30, jumped directly to events 37–38 (tones F, E [upper voice, bar 15]), thereby omitting events 31 to 36 (as well as breakpoint no. 4). The score is a result of a series of the composer's changes of mind regarding Table 2. It would be interesting to discuss at length all of the minute and global interpretations the composer adopted to arrive at the score in Figure 4. However, this is impossible in the context of this chapter.

Musicological Knowledge Modeling

From Knowledge Acquisition to Knowledge Modeling

All of the humanities can, with good reason, be viewed as knowledge modeling enterprises. Cognitive Musicology is no exception. In knowledge modeling, acquiring empirical knowledge data in and by itself is only the beginning of the enterprise. The crucial task is that of formulating a model of the acquired knowledge, in a more or less formal and explicit way. The resulting knowledge model can have a number of different uses: (1) formulating an empirical theory of composition, (2) building simulations of a musical process, (3) assisting novices, or simply (4) improving existing interfaces, are examples. Here, the main concern is musicological knowledge modeling for the sake of theory, in particular, an empirical theory of compositional thought. This is a topic in knowledge representation; it poses the interesting problem, to develop computer-assisted tools for representing complex mental processes, such as compositional changes of mind. Since composition has to do, above all, with possible (not with existing) musics (Laske 1989a, 1990c), tools for modeling virtual behaviors, like modal logics and hypermedia, are of special relevance (Farrett 1990).

For present purposes, a classical production system model of the dispositions in Table 3 would be cumbersome, due to the complexity of the conditions entering into design decisions. Even less suitable would be a grammar, since the knowledge data gathered are those of a performance model, not a competence model, for music. When formulated in an object-oriented form (that is, permitting references to complex objects on both its LHS and RHS), a rule-based model might be satisfactory, since it leaves behind the data/programm distinction. Such a model could be developed by using a special language suiting the purpose of the modeling (Klahr et al. 1987; Farrett 1990 [who speaks of "knowledge programming"]). However, rule systems, whether production systems, grammars or other, are post facto selective codifications of knowledge that lack predictive power; they are not useful for anticipating possible performances, nor do they have sufficient expressive power for representing experiential knowledge, or imagined behaviors. An interesting alternative for knowledge codification is the class of hypermedia tools (Goldfarb et al. 1990). Such tools, when geared to the musicological enterprise, can accept not just alphanumeric text, but also music notation and, via videodisk, musical sound. One could speak of musicological workstations (Figure 6, see below).

Four Layers of Musical Knowledge

In terms of the "Knowledge Acquisition and Documentation Structuring" (KADS) methodology developed by (G. Schreiber et al.1988; Wielinga 1989a/b), a conceptual model of expertise—task environment aside—comprises four layers:

1) Domain Layer (domain knowledge)
2) Inference Layer (inferential knowledge)
3) Task Layer (structure of the task)
4) Strategy Layer (alternative subtask sequences for achieving a goal).

Adopting this paradigm for present purposes, one can say that while layers (1) and (3) are embodied in the PRECOMP system itself (thereby defining a task envi-

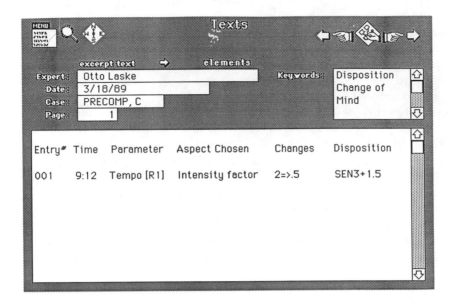

Figure 5. Card from PRECOMP Text Stack in CAMEO.

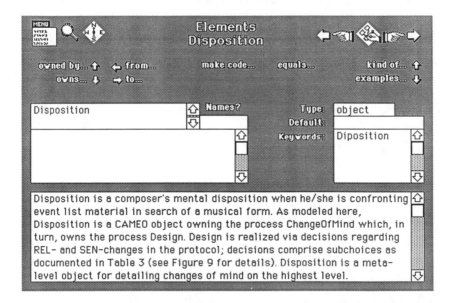

Figure 6. Card from PRECOMP Element Stack in CAMEO.

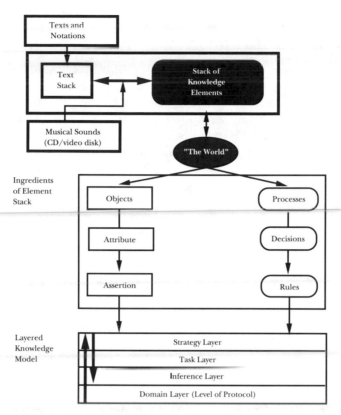

Figure 7. A Hypermedia Model of Musical Knowledge.

ronment), protocols generated by module C provide empirical evidence suitable for elucidating layers (2) and (4). The musicologist's task is to formulate a model of layers (2) and (4) on the basis of layers (1) and (3). Modeling the musician's Inference Layer means to show how the musician reasons regarding Table 2; modeling the musician's Strategy Layer amounts to showing what are alternative strategies utilized by musicians regarding the same design material.

A hypermedia tool for modeling knowledge needs to fulfill two main requirements: it must enable the knowledge modeler (musicologist) to (a) model all four layers of knowledge, as indicated above, and (b) elucidate their relationship. These requirements are fulfilled by CAMEO (Jones 1990a/b), developed for structuring and modeling human task knowledge, and implemented in HyperCard. CAMEO helps a knowledge elicitor/observer in documenting and structuring his understanding of knowledge data deriving from some kind of text (protocol or interview). CAMEO comprises two types of stacks (of cards), a Text Stack, into which raw knowledge data is read (Figure 5), and an Element Stack, for modeling the knowledge contents of the hypertized text (Figure 6). As shown in Figure 7, middle, ingredients of the Element Stack adhere to certain types, some of which are predefined, while others can be added by the knowledge modeler. Predefined element types in CAMEO are objects owning attributes about which assertions can be made, and processes (and-goals) comprising decisions (or-goals) owning rules (which are conjoinments of assertions). On the basis of an "ownership" hierarchy linking these key categories, one can define a componential model of performance knowledge comprising, first, a data model, and second, a process model. The data model specifies the data needs of the mental processes a task performance consists of; a process model details the strategy and decisions deployed by an expert using the modeled data. On the basis of the data model, CAMEO computes a network of rules showing the inference structure of a particular task, in terms of conjoinments of assertions about the state of the world dealt with. CAMEO also displays local and global graphs of all knowledge elements to facilitate a bird-eye's view of the modeled universe of knowledge.

The Cognitive Musicologist at Work

Figure 8 documents the assumption that, at the highest level of modeling, a musician's "World" consists of the object Disposition owning the process ChangeOfMind and its subprocess Design. On the basis of this assumption, Figure 9 renders the Task Layer of the composer's design process. Design is based on Decisions regarding REL- and SEN-changes (Table 3, columns 5–6), changes which, in turn, relate to the musical parameters stated as columns in Table 2. Figure 9 shows the details of the Task Layer of the compositional process, namely, what is involved in making a musical design based on REL- and SEN-specific information in the event list.

The Domain Layer of the musician's knowledge is embodied by the structure of module C itself (see Figure 7, bottom). Once the Task Layer has been explicated, the musicologist can begin to formulate a data model of the composer's decision-making (here not shown). The purpose in doing so is to model the Inference and Strategy Layers of the composer's performance in reference to the data serving as mental objects of his performance. In terms of Figure 7 (bottom), the task of the musicologist in using CAMEO is to ascend from the Domain Layer to the Strategy Layer of the composer's task knowledge. To do so, the musicologist, after defining a process and data model of the composer's performance knowledge, formulates assertions reflecting the changing state of the materials the composer is using. The musicologist then conjoins these assertions—about parameters (objects) and REL/SEN-aspects (attributes)—to arrive at a body of CAMEO rules reflecting the task's overall inference structure. At a metalevel, the musicologist may define metarules whose assertions deal with task-level rules, in order to explicate alternative compositional strategies.

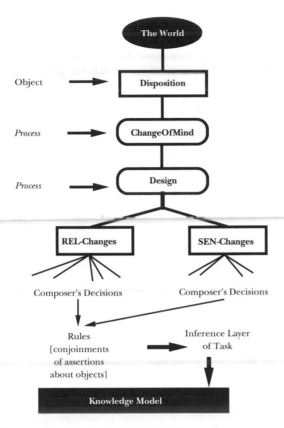

Figure 8. Levels of Hypermedia Model of a PRECOMP Protocol.

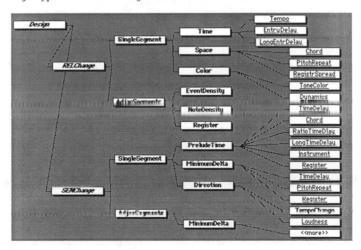

Figure 9. CAMEO Graph of Task Layer of Compositional Knowledge in PRECOMP Protocols.

Cognitive Musicology versus Traditional Musicology

The purpose of modeling data contained in module-C protocols is to develop an empirical musicological theory of compositional thought. Since module C itself embodies the Domain and Task Layers of design expertise in its very structure, attention is focused on elucidating the Inference and Strategy Layers of that expertise. ("Expertise" is taken to be a performance, not a competence, notion.) Actions are modeled on the knowledge level; they are conceived as processes conjoining four layers, each of which comprises its own specific objects and processes. In this way, an object-oriented representation (in the sense of Hypercard) of compositional expertise is elaborated which, when modelings of different protocols are compared, may lead to a theory of compositional design in a specific cultural task environment.

In contrast to traditional musicological research, the effort in PRECOMP is to go beyond assertions regarding the Domain Layer that merely restate a musicologist's notational findings—findings that, as processes, ordinarily never get modeled. What is scrutinized here is not only the end state of the musical process (namely, the frozen results of the compositional process codified in Figure 4), but the material on which the score is based (Table 2), as well as the process that led to it, as captured by the performance trace (Table 3). Initial-, intermediate-, and end-state analyses of music are thus combined (Laske 1977). Given an expanded repertory of musicological knowledge data, and a hypermedia tool such as CAMEO, it becomes possible to formulate a theory of the Inference and Strategy Layers of a musical process, and of the relationship of these layers to the Domain and Task Layers.

In the OBSERVER tradition, the claim is that only if one models all four layers of musical knowledge, is it possible to claim to be on the level of the activity being modeled. Consequently, traditional musicological research must be said to operate below the epistemological level defining its subject matter, thus failing to do justice to it. Both traditional musicology and "music theory" (Lerdahl et al. 1983) isolate the Domain Layer of task knowledge from the other three layers; in consequence thereof, they mistake scores—which are instructions for an interpreter/performer, and thus templates meant to provoke possible behaviors—for knowledge representations of an idealized listener (who often has to carry the burden of playing the role of composer, performer, and musicologist simultaneously). Due to their fixation on notated music as a valid representation of musical experiences, both of these disciplines fail to present a task analysis of compositional activity. For such an analysis, they substitute that of an idealized listening process far removed from the compositional one (see also Smoliar, in this volume). In fact, these disciplines reduce composition to listening, thereby committing the philosophical error of *katabasis eis allo genos,* in that from composition, they jump to a different generic class of tasks (Laske 1991a, 1990b). The only benefit of such a procedure lies in the competence model (for listening) that is produced. However, in this "knowledge modeling in reverse," the competence model arrived at is rarely if ever substantiated empirically, nor is it acknowledged that composition is not just a variety of listening, but an autonomous task that fundamentally differs from listening. (For compo-

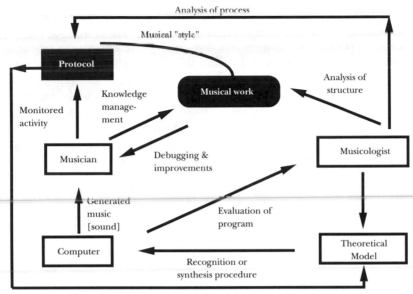

Figure 10. The Musicological Hexagon.

sition as a form of design, see Simon 1969).

Historical Placement of the Methodology

The methodology outlined in this paper dates back to Laske and Truax's OBSERVER program of the early seventies (Laske 1973b, 1974a/b, 1975); it is based on epistemological insights documented in (Laske 1973c). The methodology is geared to producing empirical knowledge data for four related purposes:

1) understanding processes of musical (and musicological) thinking empirically
2) formulating criteria for the critical evaluation of compositional tools
3) formulating guidelines for musical pedagogy using computer-assisted media
4) explicating the relationship between the mental processes (as documented by a performance trace), and the structure of the musical work resulting from that process (whether scored or not).

The latter purpose is considered to be one of the crucial tasks of Cognitive Musicology (see also Marsella, in this volume).

According to this methodology, musicological research takes place within the framework defined by Figure 10 (an adaptation of Figure 1 of Kippen & Bel 1989). Here, the musicologist works much like an anthropologist, by collaborating with practicing musicians of a particular culture. Due to this collaboration the traditional triangle "musicologist—musical work—theoretical model" is expanded into a hexagon comprising computer—musician—protocol. What in Figure 10 is called "musical work," could equally be a musicological study, musicology and music theory being treated as musical activities like any other. The expansion resulting from this concept of musicological research fundamentally changes the nature of the theoretical model aimed for. The musicologist chooses a musical task (such as composition), and formulates a theoretical model of the task that can be embodied in a computer program. Subsequently, the musicologist cooperates with one or more musicians who, by using the task model operationalized by the program, record both their mental processes, and the music generated by them. As exercised in (Bel 1990a), this approach leads to a situation where the programmed task environment acts not only as a monitor, but as an active partner.

The fact that the musical task is carried out in a programmed environment can count as an advantage, in that the environment pre-structures the task and, in many ways, makes it well-defined (in the sense of a musical exercise). Insights into this constrained environment might be extended to tasks characterized by a greater degree of freedom (for which not only musical competence, but artistic creativity is required). As a consequence, there is some possiblity that the crucial anthropological question, of how the control structure of mental processes determines, and is reflected in, the structure of the resulting work (Meyerson 1948) might be answered in an empirical way. For an anthropologically oriented musicology, answers to this question provide essential criteria for judging the discipline's legitimacy and success.

Acknowledgments

This chapter is for Barry Truax.

References

Argyris, C. et al. 1985. *Action Science.* San Francisco, California: Jossey-Bass Publishers.

Balaban, M. 1988. The Cross Fertilization Relationship between Music and Artificial Intelligence. Proceedings, First International Workshop on A. I. and Music, AAAI-88.

Bel, B. 1990a. Acquisition et représentation de connaissances en musique. Thèse du doctorat. Faculté des Sciences et Techniques, Université d'Aix-Marseille III, Marseille, France.

Bel, B. and B. Vecchione eds. 1990b. *Actes Colloque Musique et assistance Informatique.* Marseille, France: Laboratoire Musique et Informatique Marseille.

Blacking, J. 1984. What Languages Do Musical Grammars Describe? In *Musical Grammars and Computer Analysis,* eds. M. Baroni and L. Callegari. Florence, Italy: Leo S. Olschki.

Blevis, E. 1990. Foundations of a Music Logic: The CALM System. Ph. D. dissertation. Department Computer and Information Sciences, Queens University, Kingston, Ontario, Canada.

Boose, J. H. et al. eds.1988. Proceedings, European Knowledge Acquisition Workshop. Bonn-Birlinghoven, F.R.G.: GMD. GMD-Studien Nr. 143.

Cantor, D. 1989. A Knowledge Acquisition System for Segmentation in Music. Ph.D. dissertation., Department of Computer Science, Boston University, Boston, Massachusetts.

Clancey, W. J. 1983. The Epistemology of a Rule-Based Expert System: A Framework for Explanation. *Artificial Intelligence* 20(3).

Cope, D. 1987. Experiments in Musical Intelligence. Proceedings of the 1987 ICMC, San Francisco, California: Computer Music Association.

Dreyfus, H. L. et al. eds. 1982. Husserl, *Intentionality and Cognitive Science.* Cambridge, MA: The MIT Press.

Ebcioglu, K. 1987. An Efficient Logic Programming Language and its Application to Music. Logic Programming: Proceedings of the Fourth International Conference. Cambridge, MA: The MIT Press.

Goldfarb, C. F. and Newcomb, S. R. 1990. X3V1.8M Working Draft, ANSI Project X3.749-D. Hypermedia/Time-based Structuring Language (HyTime). IBM Almaden Research Laboratory.

Farrett, P. 1990. Intensional Composer: A Knowledge Acquisition System for Creative Design Applications. Ph. D. dissertation., Department of Information and Computer Sciences, Queens University, Kingston, Ontario, Canada.

Fodor, J. A. 1983. *The Modularity of Mind.* Cambridge, MA: The MIT Press.

Fodor, J. A. 1981. *Representations.* Cambridge, MA: The M.I.T. Press.

Jones, W. P. 1990a. CAMEO: Computer-Aided Modeling of Expertise in Organizations. Technical Report. Cambridge, MA: Arthur D. Little, Inc.

Jones, W. P. 1990b. Bringing Corporate Knowledge into Focus with CAMEO. *Knowledge Acquisition,* 2:207–239.

Johnson-Laird, P. N. 1983. *Mental Models.* Cambridge, MA: Harvard University Press.

Hindemith, P. 1942. *The Craft of Musical Composition.* New Haven, CT: Yale University Press.

Keller, W. 1957. *Handbuch der Tonsatzlehre I: Tonsatzanalytik.* G. Bosse Verlag, Regensburg, F.R.G.

Kippen, J., and Bel, B. 1989. Can the Computer Help Resolve the Problem of Ethnographic Description? *Anthropological Quarterly,* 62.3. Washington, D.C.: The Catholic University of America Press.

Klahr D. et al, 1987. *Production System Models of Learning and Development.* Cambridge, MA.: The MIT Press.

Koenig, G. M. 1988. *Project One.* (Newest program version). Den Haag, The Netherlands: Koninglijk Conservatorium.

Koenig, G. M. 1979. *Protocol.* Utrecht, The Netherlands: Institute of Sonology.

Koenig, G. M. 1969. *Project One.* Utrecht, The Netherlands: Institute of Sonology.

Kugel, P. 1990. Myhill's Thesis: There's More Than Computing in Musical Thinking. Computer Music Journal, 14(3):12-25. Cambridge, MA: The M.I.T. Press.

Kunst, J. 1976. Making Sense in Music I: The use of mathematical logic. *Interface,* 5:3-68.

Laske O., 1992. An Epistemic Approach to Systematic Musicology. In *Music Processing,* ed. G. Haus. New York: J.A.I. Press Inc. Publications.

Laske O. 1991a. Toward an Epistemology of Composition. *Interface,* 20(3-4). 235-269, ed. O. Laske. Amsterdam, Holland: Swets & Zeitlinger.

Laske, O. 1991b. Sciences humaines comme science de l'artificiel. *Interface,* 21(1-2), ed. B. Bel and B. Vecchione. Amsterdam, Holland: Swets & Zeitlinger.

Laske, O. 1990a. The Computer as the Artist's Alter Ego. *Leonardo,* 23(3): 53–66. New York: Pergamon Journals.

Laske, O. 1990b. Two Paradigms of Music Research: Composition and Listening. In Proceedings, Colloque Musique et Assistance Informatique, eds. B. Bel et al. Marseille, France: Laboratoire Musique et Informatique Marseille.

Laske, O. 1990c. Composition et Assistance Informatique: un exemple de composition interprétative." In Proceedings, Colloque Créativité en art, eds. B. Bel et al. Aix-en-Provence, France: Centre de Recherche en Sciences de la Musique, Université Aix-en-Provence.

Laske, O. 1989a. Composition Theory: An Enrichment of Music Theory. *Interface,* 18(1-2): 45-59. Lisse,

The Netherlands: Swets & Zeitlinger.

Laske, O. 1989b. Composition Theory in Koenig's Project One and Project Two. In *The Music Machine.*, ed. C. Roads. Cambridge, MA. : The MIT Press. (Reprinted from Computer Music Journal, vol. 5(4):54–65. Cambridge, MA..: The M.T Press, 1981.)

Laske, O. 1989c. Music Composition as Hypothesis Formation: A Blackboard Concept of Musical Creativity. In *Knowledge-Based Systems,* ed. V. Marik, 3(1): 36–41. Guildford, Surrey, U.K.: Butterworth Scientific.

Laske, O. 1989d. Ungelöste Probleme bei der Wissensakquisition für Expertensysteme. In K. I. zwischen Hoffnung und Realität. Wiesbaden, F.R.G.: Betriebswirtschaftlicher Verlag Dr. Th. Gabler.

Laske, O. 1989e. DECOMPILE: Automatic Knowledge Acquisition from Concurrent Expert Reports Using Production System Architectures. *Communication and Cognition,* vol. 6(2-3):111–136. Ghent, Belgium: Babbage Institute for Knowledge and Information Technology.

Laske, O. 1988. A Three-Phase Approach to Building Knowledge-Based Systems. *Communication and Cognition,* 5(2):19–30. Ghent, Belgium: Babbage Institute for Knowledge and Information Technology.

Laske, O. 1987. A Decompilation Approach to Knowledge Acquisition. In Proceedings, First European Workshop on Knowledge Acquisition., ed. T.R. Addis. Whiteknights, West Sussex, United Kingdom: University of Reading.

Laske, O. 1986a. A Course in Applied Epistemology. Technical Report, Arthur D. Little, Inc., Cambridge, MA.: Applied Artificial Intelligence Center.

Laske, O. 1986b. On Competence and Performance Notions in Expert System Design. In Actes, Sixièmes journées internationales sur les systèmes experts & leurs applications, ed. J.-J. Rault, 257–297. Paris La Défense: Agence de l'Informatique.

Laske, O. 1979. Goal Synthesis and Goal Pursuit in a Musical Transformation Task for Children Between Seven and Twelve Years of Age. *Interface,* 8: 207–235. Lisse, The Netherlands: Swets & Zeitlinger.

Laske, O. 1977. *Music, Memory, and Thought: Explorations in Cognitive Musicology.* Ann Arbor, Michigan: University Research Press.

Laske, O. 1975. "Toward a Theory of Musical Cognition." *Interface,* 4(2): 147–208. Lisse, The Netherlands: Swets & Zeitlinger.

Laske, O. 1974a. The Information Processing Approach to Musical Cognition. *Interface,* 3(2):109–136. Lisse, The Netherlands: Swets & Zeitlinger.

Laske, O. 1974b. In Search of a Generative Grammar for Music. *Perspectives of New Music,* Spring/Summer, 351-378. Annondale-on-Hudson, N.Y. (also in *Machine Models of Music,* eds. S. Schwanauer et al. Cambridge, MA: The MIT Press., 1990.)

Laske, O. 1973a. *Introduction to a Generative Grammar of Music.* Utrecht, The Netherlands: Institute of Sonology.

Laske, O. 1973b. Toward a Musical Intelligence System: Observer. *Numus West,* 4:11–16. Mercer Island, Washington.

Laske, O. 1973c. On the Understanding and Design of Aesthetic Artefacts. In *Musik und Verstehen,* eds. Peter Faltin et al. Cologne, F.R.G.: Arno Volk Verlag.

Laske, O. 1972. *On Problems of a Performance Model for Music.* Utrecht, The Netherlands: Institute of Sonology.

Laske, O. 1971. An Acoulogical Performance Model for Music. *Electronic Music Reports* 4: 33–64. Utrecht, The Netherlands: Institute of Sonology.

Lischka, C. 1986. "A Constraint-based Approach to Musical Knowledge Representation." Proceedings of the 1986 ICMC. San Francisco, California: Computer Music Association.

Meyerson, I. 1948. *Les fonctions psychologiques et les oeuvres.* Paris, Vrin.

Minsky, M. 1980. "K-Lines: A Theory of Memory." *Cognitive Science,* vol. 4, 117–133.

Minsky, M. 1986. *The Society of Mind.* New York: Simon and Schuster.

Roads, C. 1981. IT: An Intelligent Composer's Assistant." Unpublished manuscript. M. I. T. Experimental Music Studio.

Rumelhart, D., and McClelland, J. 1987/1988. *Parallel Distributed Processing.* Cambridge, MA.: The MIT Press.

Schreiber, G. et al.1988. Modelling in KBS Development Boose, in Proceedings, European Knowledge Acquisition Workshop, eds. J. H. Boose et al. Bonn-Birlinghoven, F.R.G.: GMD. GMD-Studien Nr. 143.

Seeger, C. 1977. *Studies in Musicology: 1935–1975.* Berkeley, California: University of California.

Simon, H. A. 1969 [1981]. *The Science of the Artificial.* Cambridge, MA: The MIT Press.

Vecchione, B. 1990a. Méthodologie de la composition: le raisonnement créateur. *Actes, Colloque Musique et assistance informatique,* eds. B. Bel and B. Vecchione. Marseille, France: Laboratoire Musique et Informatique Marseille.

Vecchione, B. 1990b. La révolution musicologique des années 1970–1980. *Actes, Colloque Musique et assistance informatique,* Marseille, France: Laboratoire Musique et Informatique Marseille.

Vercoe, B. 1988. *CSound Manual.* Media Laboratory, MIT, Cambridge, MA.

Wielinga, B. et al. 1989a. A Knowledge Acquisition Perspective on Knowledge-Level Models. *Proceedings,* Banff Knowledge Acquisition Workshop KAW 1989.

Wielinga, B. et al. 1989b. Synthesis Report, KADS. *Deliverable Y3, Esprit Project P1098.* Department of Social Science Informatics: University of Amsterdam.

Winner, E. 1982. *Invented Worlds: The Psychology of the Arts.* Cambridge, MA.: Harvard University Press.

Section Four

Analysis

Musical analysis is a difficult mental task, and modeling the behavior of music analysts with computer programs is one of the interesting challenges facing the AI and music field. Computers have already been proved to be useful to the music analyst in several ways not directly related to AI; early examples that come to mind are projects for making a thematic index of works by Josquin, or for using statistical analysis to determine authorship of a given piece of music (Lincoln 70). Attempts have also been made to construct computer models of the tasks performed by a music analyst. Some examples are programs for performing the harmonic analysis of Bach Chorales (Winograd 68), or for verifying a Schenkerian analysis of the middleground of pieces, according to different proposed formalisms for Schenker's approach (Smoliar 80, Kassler 75, Snell 79). We will not try to give an exhaustive bibliography; for a bibliography on earlier work, including AI-related approaches, the reader is referred to, e.g., (Battier and Arveiller 75, Lincoln 70).

Analysis by Discovery

Human music analysts often concentrate on discovering features of given pieces of a composer that are likely to be considered unusual, elegant or profound, according to the contemporary trends in analysis (e.g., a golden section in the motets of Dufay (Sandresky 81)). This discovery is done probably by utilizing a vast degree of musical and general knowledge, and by investing significant research effort. The task of automating this discovery process in musical analysis has not yet, to our knowledge, attracted attention (with the exception of a system proposal for making analytical discoveries about Debussy's *Syrinx* (Laske 84)). By contrast, the similarly difficult problem of automating mathematical discovery, has been attempted by A.I. researchers (Lenat 1976).

Analysis by Synthesis

An alternative, and perhaps ambitious, approach to style analysis by computer has been to write programs that attempt to generate pieces in the same style as a given set of musical pieces. By writing an algorithm for generating new pieces similar to a given set, researchers hope to gain a more detailed understanding of music in that style, and to eliminate the vague and incomplete verbal statements that are hard to avoid in the traditional approaches to music analysis. Attempts have been made to algorithmically generate music in different styles, such as Lutheran chorale melodies (Baroni and Jacoboni 76), and folk melodies (Zaripov 69). The chapters by Ebcioglu and Cope in this analysis section of this book belong to this latter analysis-by-synthesis category, while the chapter by Maxwell concentrates on the task of harmonic analysis by discovery.

Although the analysis-by-synthesis technology is still far from the stage of providing substantially complex new pieces "that the original composer could have written," the chapters in this section include some computer-generated scores, which raise our hopes for further research in the area.

In current rule-based analysis-by-synthesis approaches, the rules are usually encoded manually by a musician, and the addressed style is rather specific (See, e.g. (Ebcioglu 80, Schottstaedt 84) for species counterpoint, (Ames 83) for contemporary music composition with similar techniques). A longer term research agenda for the analysis-by-synthesis field, therefore, includes the automatic acquisition of the knowledge base for a style simulation task, which could simplify the design of such systems, and the modeling of the evolution of musical styles. The task of automatic acquisition of a rule-base for a style from musical pieces has already been attacked by some chapters in this volume (e.g. Widmer), however we feel that it would be prudent to stress the long term nature of this challenging research agenda.

Overviews of the Chapters in this Section

The chapter "An Expert System for Harmonizing Chorales in the Style of J. S. Bach" by K. Ebcioglu, is an attempt to create an algorithmic model of a four-part chorale harmonization task. Ebcioglu's expert system, named CHORAL, automatically produces the bass, tenor and alto parts when the soprano part (the chorale melody) is given. The resulting four-part score is printed in conventional music notation. The author describes a new logic programming language, BSL, that he has designed to accomplish this task. The program's knowledge base contains 350 rules written as logic formulas; these are subdivided into groups that represent knowledge about the chorale from multiple viewpoints, such as harmony and melody. The harmonization is generated stage by stage, using algorithms called intelligent backtracking and heuristic search, derived from A.I. research (Nilsson 71, Pearl 83). The author stresses the inadequacy of treatise-like rules alone for describing a style; the CHORAL program incorporates many weighted *heuristic* rules to choose between the correct continuations of a partial harmonization, in addition to *absolute* rules that aim to define the correctness of a partial harmonization. Issues and design tradeoffs in modeling the complexities of the Bach chorale style are discussed, such as bold clashes of simultaneous inessential notes. Harmonization results automatically produced by the program are presented, along with Bach's harmonizations of some of the same melodies, for comparison.

The next chapter by H. John Maxwell, "An Expert System for Harmonic Analysis of Tonal Music," describes a rule-based expert system for performing the harmonic analysis of certain movements of J. S. Bach's Six French Suites. The author's program assigns chord symbols to each beat (or subbeat, depending on the harmonic rhythm) in a given score. While the present trends in harmonic analysis (by humans) have concentrated mostly on the Schenkerian approach (Schenker 69, Beach 88), the chord symbol assignment problem already constitutes a challenge for a computational model, and solving this problem is perhaps a prerequisite for a more ambitious automated analysis of harmony. Some of J. S. Bach's French Suite movements contain complex note encounters that tend to make an algorithmic solution difficult; the author has chosen a rule based, artificial intelligence approach to tackle this problem. The chapter discusses the 55 rules of the author's expert system in detail, and also reports the program's results on three French Suite movements. Maxwell's program does demonstrate the usefulness of a rule based approach for solving musical analysis problems, and also sheds light on the possible ways of attacking the problem of more general harmonic analyses.

The chapter "On Algorithmic Representation of Musical Style," by David Cope, gives a summary of the author's ongoing research on his EMI system, that aims to generate new pieces of music using Augmented Transition Networks (ATNs). ATNs were originally developed for parsing natural language sentences (Woods 70). Musical examples written by a given composer are fed to the system, which are then processed, and incorporated into EMI's Augmented Transition Network. This ATN is subsequently used for generating pieces in the same style; however, the algorithmic details of this process are not sufficiently elaborated in this summary chapter. The author describes analogies between the parsing of natural language and the parsing of music. A two-part invention-like keyboard piece is given as an output example from the EMI system. In general, EMI seems to offer a promising environment for testing new algorithms for the analysis and resynthesis of various musical styles.

References

Ames, C. 1983. "Stylistic Automata in Gradient," *Computer Music Journal*, 7(4).

Baroni, M. and Jacoboni, C. 1976. "Verso una Grammatica della Melodia"," Università Studi di Bologna.

Battier M. and Arveiller, J. 1975. "Musique et Informatique: Une Bibliographie Indexée," Universite de Paris VIII.

Beach D. 1988. "The Fundamental Line from Scale Degree 8: Criteria for Evaluation," *Journal of Music Theory*, 32(2): 271-294.

Ebcioglu, K. 1980. "Computer Counterpoint," *Proceedings of the 1980 International Computer Music Conference*, Computer Music Association, San Francisco.

Lincoln, H. B. (ed) *The Computer and Music*, Cornell University Press, 1970.

Kassler, M. "Proving Musical Theorems I: The Middleground of Heinrich Schenker's Theory of Tonality," Basser Department of Computer Science, University of Sydney, August 1975.

Laske, O. 1984. "KEITH: A Rule-System for Making Music-Analytical Discoveries." In *Musical Grammars and Computer Analysis*, Baroni et al. (eds), 165-199. Florence, Italy: Leo S. Olschki.

Lenat, D.B. "A.M.: An Artificial Intelligence Approach to Discovery in Mathematics and Heuristic Search" STAN-CS-76-570, Ph.D. thesis, Department of Computer Science, Stanford University, July 1976.

Nilsson, N. "Problem Solving Methods in Artificial Intelligence," McGraw Hill, 1971.

Sandresky, M.V. 1981. "The Golden Section in Three Byzantine Motets of Dufay," *Journal of Music Theory*, 25.2.

Schenker, H. "Five Graphic Analyses," Felix Salzer, ed., Dover, 1969.

Schottstaedt, B. 1984. "Automatic Species Counterpoint," CCRMA, Report no. STAN-M-19, Department of Music, Stanford University.

Smoliar, S.W. "A Computer Aid for Schenkerian Analysis," *Computer Music Journal*, 4, Summer 1980.

Snell, J. L. "Design for a Formal System for Deriving Tonal Music," M.A. thesis, State University of New York at Binghamton, 1979.

Winograd, T. 1968. "Linguistics and Computer Analysis of Tonal Harmony," *Journal of Music Theory*, 12:2-49.

Woods, W. A. 1970 "Transition Network Grammars for Natural Language Analysis," *Communications of the Association for Computing Machinery*, 13, 10, pp. 591-606.

Zaripov, R. K. "Kibernetika i Muzyka," English translation by J.G.K. Russel, in Perspectives of New Music, 7, 2, Spring/Summer 1969.

Abstract

This chapter describes an expert system called CHORAL, for harmonization of four-part chorales in the style of Johann Sebastian Bach. The system contains about 350 rules, written in a form of first-order predicate calculus. The rules represent musical knowledge from multiple viewpoints of the chorale, such as the chord skeleton, the melodic lines of the individual parts, and Schenkerian voice leading within the descant and bass. The program harmonizes chorale melodies using a generate-and-test method with intelligent backtracking. A substantial number of heuristics are used for biasing the search toward musical solutions. The CHORAL knowledge base provides for style-specific modulations, cadence patterns, and complex encounters of simultaneous inessential notes; it imposed difficult constraints for maintaining melodic interest in inner voices. Encouraging results have been obtained, and output examples are given. BSL, a new and efficient logic-programming language fundamentally different from PROLOG, was designed to implement the CHORAL system.

In this chapter, we will describe CHORAL, a knowledge based expert system for harmonization and hierarchical voice leading analysis of chorales in the style of J.S. Bach. We will first briefly outline a logic programming language called BSL that was designed to implement the project, and then describe the CHORAL system itself.

Chapter 12

An Expert System for Harmonizing Chorales in the Style of J. S. Bach[1]

Kemal Ebcioğlu

BSL: An Efficient Logic Programming Language

At the outset of our CHORAL project, we considered a number of alternative knowledge representation techniques, and we finally decided to use first-order logic for representing musical knowledge. First order logic was felt to be well-suited to the application, because it allowed us to make precise, concrete assertions about properties of a piece of music, and because it was more formal and tractable than some other AI paradigms, such as unrestricted production systems [Forgy and McDermott 77]. We started with over a hundred assertions in first-order predicate calculus, which later formed the seed of the knowledge base. These assertions were not in clausal form, and made free use, e.g., of existential and universal quantifiers, as in the assertions one would use to extend English in a formal treatment such as [Rogers 67]. However, the PROLOG interpreter then available to us on the VAX 11 architecture did not have a natural way of coding quantifiers; moreover, it did not offer the most efficient way for utilizing the native resources of a traditional CPU. On the other hand, our music application was well-suited to the native data types and operations of a traditional architecture, and was also known to be extremely computation intensive (we did have a fair idea about the potential problems of the application, because we had previously written a smaller-scale 16th-century strict counterpoint program using a similar heuristic search method [Ebcioglu 79, 81]). We were thus led to look for a different logic programming language for implementing our project. Our requirements were: (1) the language had to have a natural way of coding universal and existential quantifiers directly; (2) the language had to utilize the native resources of a traditional architecture efficiently, in a manner competitive with deterministic Algol-class languages, so that we could use it to produce very high quality music in a reasonable time; (3) the language had to have a natural way of specifying preferred solutions as well as just correct ones (the musical importance of this will be explained in the sequel); (4) the language had to have a streamlined design in order to increase its chances of being theoretically tractable; moreover, we felt that striving to use a streamlined design was a better way to approach a large project. While we were going back and forth between the logical assertions and ways of "executing" them, a logic programming language called BSL (Backtracking Specification Language) was designed, which appears to satisfy each of the above-mentioned requirements.

The design of the BSL language constitutes an unusual approach to the use of logic in computer programming, but is extremely traditional in the sense of the execution paradigm. Unlike languages such as PROLOG, BSL is not a descendant of resolution theorem-proving research [Robinson 65]: BSL is merely a nondeterministic language with Pascal-style data types, where more than one explicit assignment to a variable is forbidden. BSL has a Lisp-like syntax and is compiled into C via a Lisp program. We have provided BSL with formal semantics, in a style inspired from [de Bakker 79] and [Harel 79]. The semantics of a BSL program F is defined via a ternary relation Ψ, such that $\Psi(F, \sigma, \sigma')$ means program F leads to final state σ' when started in initial state σ, where a *state* is a mapping from variable names to elements of a "computer" universe, consisting of integers, arrays, records, and other ancillary objects. Given an initial state, a BSL program may lead to more than one final state, since it is nondeterministic, or it may lead to none at all, in case it never terminates. What makes BSL different from ordinary nondeterministic languages [Floyd 67, Smith and Enea 73, Cohen 79] and relates it to logic is that there is a simple mapping that translates a BSL program to a formula of a first-order language, such that if a BSL program terminates in some state σ, then the corresponding first-order formula is true in σ [where the truth of a formula in a given state σ is evaluated in a fixed "computer" interpretation after replacing any free variables x in the formula by $\sigma(x)$.] A BSL program is very similar in appearance to the corresponding first-order formula, and for this reason, we call BSL programs formulas.

In this chapter, we will only give an informal overview of the BSL language. A formal description of BSL, and a proof of its soundness can be found in [Ebcioğlu 87a]. We will start with an example of a simple BSL program to solve a little puzzle, followed by its first-order translation: Place 8 queens on a chess board, so that no queen attacks another (i.e. no two queens are on the same row, column or diagonal). Assume that the rows and columns are numbered from 0 to 7, and that the array elements p[0],... p[7] represent the column number of the queen in row 0,...,7, respectively:

```
(include stdmac)                          ;include standard macro definitions
(options registers (k j n))               ;allocate k,j,n in registers
(E ((p (array (8) integer)))
    (A n 0 (< n 8) (1 + n)
        (E j 0 (< j 8) (1 + j)
            (and (A k 0 (< k n) (1 + k)
                (and  (!= j (p k))
                      (!= (- j (p k)) (- n k))
                      (!= (- j (p k)) (- k n))))
                (:= (p n) j)))))))
```

First-order translation:

$$(\exists p \mid type(p) = \text{``(array (8) integer)''})$$
$$(\forall n \mid 0 \leq n < 8)$$
$$(\exists j \mid 0 \leq j < 8)$$
$$[(\forall k \mid 0 \leq k < n)\ [j \neq p[k]\ \&\ j - p[k] \neq n - k\ \&\ j - p[k] \neq k - n]$$
$$\&\ p[n] = j\ ]$$

Because of the similarity between a BSL formula and its logical counterpart, a BSL formula is like a specification for its own self: it describes what it computes. As the reader can readily see, the BSL formula shown above specifies what a solution to the eight-queens problem should satisfy, assuming we read an assignment symbol as equality, and we translate the quantifiers to a conventional notation. This BSL formula compiles into an efficient backtracking program in C that finds and prints instantiations for the array p that would make the ($\exists$p)-quantified part of the corresponding first-order formula true in the fixed interpretation. The register declarations shown in the option list are passed to C, and cause the C compiler to place the quantifier indices k,j,n in registers if possible, for faster execution. The original BSL compiler was written in Franz Lisp, and generated code acceptable by the Berkeley UNIX C compiler, on a VAX 11 computer. We have now ported the BSL compiler to Lisp/VM and IBM 3081-3090 computers: it now generates code acceptable by the C version of the PL.8 compiler [Warren et al. 86], and also the AT&T C compiler.

We can observe some examples of BSL language features in this eight-queens program: The basic building blocks of BSL are constants that consist of integers (such as -2, 0, 3); record tags (which are identifiers such as ssn, salary); and variables, which are identifiers such as x, p, n, or emp (for convenience, we assume that variables are distinct from record tags). Each variable and constant is a BSL term, and if t_1 and t_2 are BSL terms, and *binop* is one of the binary operators +,-,*,/, sub, and dot, then (*binop* t_1 t_2) is also a BSL term. Examples of BSL terms are 0, (+ x 2), and (* 2 (dot emp salary)). The constructs (1+ x), (1- x) may be used as abbreviations for (+ x 1) and (- x 1), respectively. A BSL lvalue is either a variable or a term of the form $(f_1 \ldots (f_{n-1}(f_n\ x\ \ldots)\ldots)\ldots)$ where each of $f_1, \ldots f_n$ is either sub or dot, and where x is a variable. Lvalues are terms that can appear as the left-hand operand of an assignment, and are exemplified by x (dot emp salary) or (sub p n). Lvalues can also be abbreviated as long as their normal notation can be inferred from context, for example the latter two lvalues can be written as (salary emp) and (p n) in the proper contexts. A BSL atomic formula is either an assignment of the form (:= l t_1) or a test of the form (*relop* t_1 t_2), where l is an lvalue, t_1, t_2 are terms, and *relop* is one of == (equal), != (not equal), <, >=, <=, or >. A BSL atomic formula is a BSL formula. On the assumption that F_1 and F_2 are BSL formulas, then so are the following: (and F_1 F_2), (or F_1 F_2),[2] (A x *init cond incr* F_1), (E x *init cond incr* F_1), and (E ((x *typ*)) F_1), where x is a variable, *init, incr* are terms where *init* does not contain x, and *cond* is a BSL formula not containing any occurrences of A, E, or :=, and *typ* is type. The BSL types are similar to the type declarations of an Algol-class language, and allow integer, array and record declarations. Examples of BSL types are integer, (array (3) integer), and (record (ssn integer) (salary integer)). In general, "integer" is a BSL type, and if *typ*, typ_1,..., typ_k are BSL types, $k \geq 1$ and y_1,..., y_k are distinct record tags, and n is a positive integer, then (array (n) typ) and (record (y_1 typ_1)...(y_k typ_k)) are BSL types.

We give here an informal description of the nondeterministic program semantics of BSL: The variables of BSL can range over objects, each of which has a corresponding type. Objects of type integer are constants such as -2, 0, 3, and U (called the unassigned constant). An object can also be an *array*, which is a list of objects of the same type, or a *record*, which is a list of alternating record tags and objects, not necessarily of the same type. Arrays and records are exemplified by (1 2 U), which is an object of type (array (3) integer), and (ssn 999123456 salary 25000), which is an object of type (record (ssn integer) (salary integer)). The value of a BSL term, in a particular state during execution, is computed by using the usual meanings of the binary operators +,-,*,/,sub, and dot. Here sub is defined to be the subscript operator which takes an array object and an integer i and returns the i'th element of the array object (the array elements are numbered starting from 0); and dot is defined to be an operator that extracts a subobject of a given record object as determined by a given record tag (it performs a function similar to the dot within the expression "employee.salary" in PL/I). BSL atomic formulas, i.e. assignments and tests, are executed in the conventional manner: the tests are executed by performing the indicated comparison operation after computing the current values of the two terms to be compared; and the assignments are executed by computing the current value of the right hand side term, and then destructively changing the value of the left hand side term to reflect the current value of the right hand side term. If the comparison operation indicated in a test comes out to be true, the effect of the test is a no-op. However, if a test does not come out to be true, or if an assignment is attempted when the current value of the left hand side is not U, or when the current value of the right hand side is not an integer, or if an attempt is made to perform an illegal computation (such as using a variable whose value is U in an arithmetic operation or comparison, or dividing by zero), execution does not terminate. The formula (and F_1 F_2) is executed by first executing F_1, then F_2. The formula (or F_1 F_2) is executed by executing one of F_1 or F_2. The formula (A x *init cond incr* F_1) is similar to the C "for" loop: it is executed by saving the old value of x, setting x to *init*, while *cond* is true repetitively executing F_1 and setting x to *incr*, and restoring the old value of x if and when *cond* is finally false. (E x *init cond incr* F_1) is executed by saving the old value of x, setting x to *init*, setting x to *incr* an arbitrary number of times (possibly zero times), and finally deciding not to set x to *incr* any more, executing F_1, and then restoring the old value of x. Here *cond* must be true after x is set to *init* and after each time x is set to *incr*, or else execution does not terminate. (E ((x *typ*)) F_1) is similar to a "begin-end" block with a local variable: it is executed by saving the old value of x, setting x to an object of type *typ* all of whose scalar (i.e. integer) subobjects have the value U, executing F_1, and then restoring the old value of x.

The translation of a BSL program to the first-order assertion that is true at its termination states, is for the most part obvious, as exemplified by the eight-queens program above; however, both the assignment symbol (:=) and the equality test (==) of BSL get translated to the equality symbol in the logical counterpart, that is, the program contains procedural information not present in its logical counterpart. First, assume that F' denotes the first-order translation of a BSL term, formula or operator F. The translation of BSL terms to first-order logic is straightforward: for example (+ x 2), (dot (sub emp i) salary), translate into +(x,2), dot(sub(emp,i),salary) (which can also be abbreviated as x+2, emp[i].salary). The first-order translations of the comparison operators <, >=, <=, >, ==, != are the predicate symbols $<, \geq, \leq, >, =, \neq$, respectively. Tests such as (*relop* t_1 t_2), and assignments such as (:= l t_1) translate into the first-order atomic formulas t'_1 *relop'* t'_2 and $l' = t'_1$, respectively. (and F_1 F_2) translates into [F'_1 & F'_2], (or F_1 F_2) translates into [$F'_1 \vee F'_2$], and (E ((x typ)) F_1) translates into $(\exists x \mid \text{type}(x)="typ")[F'_1]$. For a simple subset of BSL, where the only allowable looping constructs are of the form (A x t_1 (< x t_2) (1+ x) F), (E x t_1 (< x t_2) (1 + x) F), and variants thereof, the translation of these to bounded quantifiers of first-order logic, namely $(\forall x \mid t_1 \leq x < t'_2)[F]$, $(\exists x \mid t'_1 \leq x < t'_2)[F']$,..., works; where t'_1, t'_2 are the first-order translations of BSL terms t_1 and t_2, respectively, and where x does not occur in either t_1 or t_2. However, for the general case involving arbitrary *cond* and *incr* expressions, which we will not elaborate here, the rigorous translation of BSL formulas involves associating a different function symbol of the first-order language with every quantified formula of BSL, and is less natural.[3]

The following translation examples should demonstrate the intuition behind the relationship of a BSL program to its first-order translation: When either (:= x 0) is successfully executed (i.e. x is initially U) or (-- x 0) is successfully executed (i.e. x is initially 0), the assertion x=0 is true at the termination state. When (or (== x 0) (== x 1)) is successfully executed (i.e. x is initially 0 or 1, and the proper subformula of the "or" is chosen for execution), the assertion [x=0 $\vee$ x=1] is true at the termination state. When

(A i 0 (< i 10) (1 + i) (E ((j integer)) (and (or (:= j 0) (:= j 1)) (:= (sub a i) j))))

is successfully executed (i.e., "a" is initially an array object whose first ten elements are U),

$(\forall i \mid 0 \leq i < 10)(\exists j \mid \text{type}(j)="integer")[[j = 0 \vee j = 1] \ \& \ a[i] = j]$

is true in the termination state. This assertion says that the first 10 elements of "a" are an arbitrary sequence of 0's and 1's. To see why this assertion is true at the termination state of the program, observe that during the execution of the program, for each i = 0,…,9, the assertion (∃j | type(j) = "integer") [[j = 0 ∨ j = 1] & a[i]= j] was made true by creating (for each i) an integer j equal to 0 or 1, and then making a[i] = j true by assigning j to a[i]. The first-order translation of (and (:= x 0) (:= x (1+ x))) is [x = 0 & x = x + 1], but such a BSL formula can never reach a termination state, no matter what the initial value of x is, because it violates the single assignment rule enforced by the program semantics of BSL (the single assignment rule is the one that verifies that the left hand side is U, and the right hand side is an integer, before each explicit assignment). The intuitive purpose of the single assignment rule is to ensure that the continuation of execution does not destroy the truth of the assertions that were previously made true. Top-level formulas (i.e. complete programs) of the BSL subset we are describing, such as the eight-queens program given above, do not contain free variables, so the truth of the assertions corresponding to such formulas is not affected by the value of any variable in the termination state. Successfully executing such a top-level BSL formula is equivalent to constructively proving that the corresponding first-order sentence is true in a fixed interpretation that involves integers, arrays, records, and operations on such objects (or in all models of a suitably axiomatized "theory of integers, arrays, and records").

A BSL program of the form (E ((x typ)) F) is implemented on a real, deterministic computer via a modified backtracking method, which in principle attempts to simulate all possible executions of the BSL program, and prints out the value of x just before the end of every execution that turns out to be successful. Whenever a choice has to be made between executing F_1 and executing F_2 in the context (or F_1 F_2), the current state is pushed down to enable restarting by executing F_2, and F_1 is executed. Whenever a choice has to be made between executing F and setting n to *incr* in the context (E n *init cond incr F*), the current state is pushed down to enable restarting by setting n to *incr*, and F is executed. Whenever a test (*relop t_1 t_2*) is found to be false, or if *cond* is found to be false in the context (E n *init cond incr F*), or if the top level (E ((x typ))…) is successfully executed and x is printed, the state that existed at the most recent choice point is popped from the stack, and execution restarts at that choice point. Attempting to make more than one explicit assignment to a scalar variable or to a scalar subpart of an aggregate variable, and illegal computations (such as attempting to add a number to a variable whose value is U) are considered errors and should never occur during the backtracking execution of a correct BSL program (however, the run time checks for detecting such errors can be omitted for efficiency reasons). Execution begins with an empty choice-point stack and ends when an attempt is made to pop something from an empty stack.

A modification is made to this basic backtracking technique for the case of assignment-free formulas F_1 in the context (or F_1 F_2), or (E n … F_1). After a formula F_1 in such a context is successfully executed, the most recent choice point on the stack is discarded (which would be the choice point for restarting at F_2, or F_1 with a different value of n, assuming the modification is uniformly applied). This convention, similar to the "cut" operation of PROLOG, serves to prevent duplicate solutions for x from being printed out (or redundant failures from occurring) when F_1 and F_2 do not express mutually exclusive conditions, or when F_1 is true for more than one n in its quantifier range. Here is an example that demonstrates the motivation behind this modification to backtracking: suppose that many elements of an array "a" are equal to 0 in a particular state during backtracking execution; if in this state, an assignment free subformula (E i 0 (< i N) (1+ i) (== (a i) 0)) is executed and succeeds after finding that for a particular i, a[i] = 0, and immediately thereafter a failure occurs (or some solution is printed), there is no point in backtracking to the point in the subformula where i is set to i + 1, and then succeeding again after finding another element of "a" that is equal to 0, because the program will then fail in exactly the same way as before (or will print the same solution that it printed before). So the choice point for backtracking to i = i + 1 is discarded when (E i ...) succeeds.

Since backtracking is a notoriously inefficient search technique, we had to be careful about its implementation in BSL, in the hope of making the language usable for substantial applications. From the compiler implementation viewpoint, the backtracking semantics described above that entails saving the entire program state for later restarting at the next alternative, would appear to be an inefficient mechanism; since the program state would seemingly include the current values of all the variables that are active at the point of nondeterministic choice [the active variables are the the variables that are declared within the quantifiers enclosing the choice point; nested quantifiers that use the same variable x, such as (E x ... (A x ...)...), are eliminated by renaming the inner x throughout its scope]. But in case run-time checks of single assignment are omitted, as they are in the present implementation, the single assignment nature of BSL allows a significant reduction in the amount of information that needs to be saved at a choice point. In the present implementation, where variables are allocated in static storage or in registers (for the BSL subset we are describing), the following observation applies to a typical scalar variable or scalar subpart of a variable, when the state is being pushed down at a choice point: if the variable already has an integer value, then it does not need to be saved, since it will not have been assigned again and its storage space will have remained intact when backtracking later occurs to this choice point; and if the variable is currently unassigned, then it still does not need to be saved, since its current value will not be used after a backtracking return is made to this choice point. In fact, the only variables that are pushed down at a choice point (called the *destructible variables*) are precisely the variables that are both active at the choice point, and that are also declared within the scope of a universal quantifier (A n ...) enclosing the choice point.[4] These variables typically consist of quantifier indices. It is this smallness of state that enables a BSL program to rapidly push down the entire program state at a nondeterministic choice point, and to return to the most recent choice point directly when a failure later occurs, without having to execute statements in the backward direction as in older nondeterministic languages [Floyd 67, Cohen 79], and without having to restore variables on a "trail" stack to their previous value, as in many PROLOG implementations [e.g. Fagin and Dobry 85, Turk 86]. The BSL compiler also uses a technique for eliminating or reducing the need for pushing down choice points: If a subformula F_1 in the context (or F_1 F_2) and (E n *init cond incr* F_1) is assignment free, the BSL compiler does not generate code for pushing down the state before the execution of F_1, and emits compare and branch statements for F_1 that directly jump to next alternative when F_1 fails (the next alternative is F_2, or the setting of n to *incr*), and that directly jump to the continuation of (or F_1 F_2) or (E n ... F_1) when F_1 succeeds, using a standard compilation technique for Boolean expressions [Aho and Ullman 77] extended with bounded quantifiers. This standard compilation technique is equivalent to, but much more efficient than the original "cut"-like semantics given above that involves first pushing down, and then discarding a choice point.[5] Moreover, even when there are assignments in a subformula F_1 in the context (or $F_1 F_2$) or (E n *init cond incr* F_1), the compiler delays the pushdown operations that would normally precede the code for F_1, and emits compare and branches for as large an initial segment of F_1 as possible, as long as assignments are not yet encountered in F_1; the code for this initial segment jumps directly to the next alternative when F_1 fails (the possibility exploited here is that F_1 may fail before the state needs to be pushed down.)[6]

It should also be noted that BSL operates on the native data types of a traditional computer such as integers and arrays of integers, rather than machine words which contain both data and tags, as is the case in a typical PROLOG implementation; moreover, bounded quantifiers in BSL are native to the language and often compile into simple loops, which enable traditional compiler optimizations such as code motion, strength reduction or induction variable elimination.

Some performance comparisons between BSL and PROLOG and Lisp on exhaustive search algorithms, which may help to quantify the advantage of using BSL, were given in [Ebcioğlu 87b]. BSL's method of combining extended Boolean tests and backtracking is perhaps a natural way to "execute" a logical specification on a computer; however, the possible logical specifications are limited to those that correspond to valid BSL programs, and it is required that the programmer indicate which equalities in the specification are to be executed as assignments, and which are to be executed as tests.[7] The language subset described up to here is called L^*, and constitutes the "pure" subset of BSL. The full BSL language also allows user-defined predicates in addition to <, >, ..., user-defined functions in addition to +, sub, ..., global variable declarations, macro and constant definitions, "if" and "case" statements, enumeration types, real types, and a richer set of primitive operations. The user-defined predicates of BSL are nondeterministic recursive procedures analogous to PROLOG procedures, but whether a parameter of a BSL predicate is used (i.e., is an input) or is assigned to (i.e., is an output) during the predicate call is fixed by the programmer. Facilities include a "(with...)" construct that allows convenient abbreviations for certain lvalues that would otherwise have to be written out with long chains of sub and dot operators. A "not" connective is allowed as long as we can move the "not" in front of the atomic formulas at compile time with de Morgan-like transformations, and then change (not (== ...)) to (!= ...), etc., and still get a valid BSL formula. BSL is also extended with heuristics, which are BSL formulas themselves, which can guide the choices made during the backtracking execution of a BSL program. As a preparation to the next section that depicts the use of BSL for implementing expert systems, we will describe the heuristics feature of BSL below.

Normally, the order of enumeration of the possible successful executions, or termination states of a BSL formula F during a backtracking simulation is determined in a somewhat trivial way via factors such as which subformula occurs first in an (or ... ...). This order is fine for applications where all solutions have to be found, but in applications such as music generation, the list of all solutions is of impractical length and is quite boring. It is thus necessary to alter the order of enumeration of termination states, so that a better solution will tend to come out first. A more sophisticated order of enumeration of the termination states of a BSL formula F can be obtained by enclosing F in the construct (H F (l_1... l_n) F_k ... F_0), where l_1, ..., l_n are (not necessarily scalar) lvalues that are assigned during F, and F_k, ..., F_0 are side-effect-free BSL formulas, called heuristics.

(H F ...) is simulated as follows: First all executions of F are simulated, and whenever an execution of F terminates successfully, the termination state of the current execution, as represented by the assignments to l_1, ..., l_n, is assigned a numerical worth by executing each heuristic F_k, ..., F_0 in the current termination state. The heuristics are weighted by decreasing powers of two, and the worth of a termination state is computed to be the sum of the weights of the heuristics that it makes true. Thus, if a heuristic F_i is true in the current termination state, $k \geq i \geq 0$, it increases the worth of the current termination state by 2^i; otherwise, it does not affect the worth of the current termination state. Then the assignments to l_1, ..., l_n in the current termination state are saved in a list along with their worth, and a failure return is forced in order to obtain more termination states of F. If and when all termination states of F are exhausted (as defined by the modified back-tracking simulation), the resulting list is sorted according to the worth of each termination state (i.e. assignment to l_1, ..., l_n). Ties are resolved with explicit randomness by shuffling the list randomly before sorting, in order to defeat any extra unwanted "heuristics" that may result from the regularity in the generation of the list. Then (H F ...) succeeds first with the highest valued termination state of F, then if backtracking occurs, with the next highest valued termination state, etc., and finally backtracks to a previous choice point when there are no more assignments left in the list. This feature of BSL forms the basis for the BSL generate-and-test paradigm, which is described next.

The Generate-and-Test Paradigm in BSL

Despite its Spartan data types, BSL can be used for designing large and complex expert systems in a structured manner. The formal analog of a knowledge based system based on the generate-and-test method [Stefik 78] can be implemented in BSL via a very long formula of the following form:

```
(E ((s (array (N) typ1 )))
    (E ((inp typ2))
       (and "initialize inp"
            (A n 0 (< n N) (1+ n)
               (H  (and
                       (or (and conditions₁ actions ₁)   ;
                              ...                          ; generate section
                           (and conditionsₖ actionsₖ))    ;
                           constraint₁ ;
                              ...              ; test section
                           constraintₘ);
                       ((s n))
                       heuristic₁          ;
                          ...              ; recommendations section
                       heuristicⱼ)))))     ;
```

In the generate-and-test paradigm of BSL, the computation proceeds by "generate-and-test steps," where each step consists of selecting and assigning an acceptable value to the n'th element of the solution array "s" depending on the elements 0,..., $n - 1$ (and also on the input data structure "inp"). The condition-action pairs given here are the formal analogs of production rules [Davis and King 76], as they are used in a generate-and-test application. The conditions are subformulas that typically perform certain tests about elements 0,..., $n - 1$ of the solution array, and the actions are subformulas that typically involve assignments to element n of the solution array. Thus a condition-action pair has the informal meaning "IF conditions are true about the partial solution, THEN a new element as described by the actions can be added to the partial solution."[8] The constraints are subformulas that assert absolute rules about the elements 0,..., n of the solution array. They have the procedural effect of rejecting certain assignments to element n (this effect is also called *early pruning* in AI literature [Hayes-Roth, Waterman, Lenat 83]). The heuristics are subformulas that assert what is desirable about elements 0,..., n of the partial solution: they have the procedural effect of having certain assignments to element n tried before others are. The condition-action pairs are called the *generate section*, the constraints are called the *test section*, and the heuristics are called the *recommendations section* of the knowledge base. Each step of the program is executed as follows [we are repeating the explanation given above for the (H ...) construct]: All possible assignments to the n'th element of the partial solution are sequentially generated via the production rules. If a candidate assignment does not comply with the constraints, it is thrown away; otherwise its worth is computed by summing the weights of the heuristics that it makes true, and it is saved in a list, along with its worth. When there are no more assignments to be generated for solution element n, the resulting list is sorted according to the worth of each candidate. The program then attempts to continue with the best assignment to element n, and then, if a dead-end is later encountered and a backtracking return is made to this point, with the next best assignment, etc., as defined by the sorted list. The reason we chose the particular powers-of-two weighting scheme described above for the heuristics was because of its clarity, freedom from unconstrained numerical weights, and efficient implementation.

Heuristic search is an important topic that has attracted considerable research interest, and many alternative approaches have been studied [e.g., Nilsson 71, 80, Pearl 83, Newell and Simon 63]. Although BSL's heuristic search paradigm is itself simple, the heuristic criteria that one can specify with ease in BSL can be quite sophisticated, because heuristics have the generality of logic formulas. Heuristics have no effect on the nondeterministic semantics of a BSL formula, or on its first-order translation: the first-order translation of (H F ...) is taken to be the same as the first-order translation of F; moreover, in the nondeterministic execution semantics of BSL, (H F ...) is executed by executing merely F.

Within the production rules, constraints, and heuristics, the existential and universal quantifiers of BSL can provide capabilities equivalent to the pattern matching capabilities of a true production system [Forgy and McDermott 77]. For example, assume that we are dealing with a molecular genetics application similar to the one described in [Stefik 78]. In this problem, the solution object can be represented as a sequence of elements, each having two attributes, a "site" and a "segment."[9] The problem is to find some or all of the solutions, that are consistent with the rules of the domain and the results of laboratory experiments given as input. In the context of this application, in order to specify a production rule that says "IF certain conditions are true, THEN the segment whose length is the smallest among a given array of segments can be added to the partial solution," one could write[10]

```
(and "certain conditions"
    (E i 0 (< i maxsegs) (1+ i)
        (and (A j 0 (< j maxsegs) (1+ j)
                (imp (!= i j)
                    (< (seg_list i) (seg_list j))))
            (:= (segment (s n)) (seg_list i)))))
```

Based on appropriate type declarations for seg_list and s, the logical translation of this subformula is:

["certain conditions" &
$(\exists i | 0 \le i < maxsegs)$
$[(\forall j | 0 \le j < maxsegs) [i \ne j \rightarrow seg\_list[i] < seg\_list[j]]$
& s[n].segment = seg_list[i]]].

Similarly, a constraint asserting "IF certain conditions are true, THEN the 'site' that has just been added to the solution cannot have more than one previous occurrence in the solution" can be written as:

```
(imp "certain conditions"
    (not (E i (1- n) (> i 0) (1- i)
            (E j (1- i) (>= j 0) (1- j)
                (and  (== (site (s i)) (site (s n)))
                    (== (site (s j)) (site (s i)))))))))
```

whose logical translation is:

["certain conditions" ⇒
   not[($\exists i \mid n - 1 \geq i > 0$) ($\exists j \mid i - 1 \geq j \geq 0$) [s[i].site = s[n].site & s[j].site =s[i].site]]].

Operations that may normally require more than one recognize-act cycle in an ordinary production system can also be performed in a single generate-and-test step in the present paradigm; e.g. more than one attribute of the next item to be added to the solution, where each attribute involves several nearly independent choices, can be decided in a single step. For example, assuming each solution element has two attributes, "site" and "segment," the generate section of the knowledge base can be constructed as follows:

```
(and
      (or "condition-action pairs to choose the n'th site")
      (or "condition-action pairs to choose the n'th segment"))
```

where the n'th segment may depend on the n'th site. (Note that in a production system language, one normal way of achieving the same effect could take two recognize-act cycles, involving choosing the site during the first recognize-act cycle, and then changing the "current task" to be that of choosing the segment, and choosing the segment during the second recognize-act cycle.)

In fact, the generate section of the fill-in knowledge base of the CHORAL system decides the attributes of the three voices bass, tenor, alto, as well as other relevant attributes, in a single step, and has the form:

```
(and ...
     (A v bass (< v soprano) (1+ v)
       (or
          "condition-action pairs to choose attributes of voice v at the n'th step"))
          ...)
```

Our experience while writing large knowledge bases in BSL has suggested that such knowledge bases can attain a very high degree of complexity, and some discipline is required for managing them (PROLOG and general purpose expert system shells are also not immune to this problem): The production rules, constraints and heuristics of a knowledge base need not be enumerated in an unstructured manner as shown here; to enhance legibility, they can be hierarchically grouped according to subject, similar to chapters and paragraphs of a musical treatise (in a larger project, perhaps different teams can design the different chapters, based on an agreement on the shared data structures and a written outline of the knowledge base). Similarly, distinguishable concepts (e.g. parallel motion of two voices, doubling the fifth of a chord) can be implemented through hierarchies of predicate, function, or macro definitions, so constraints and heuristics are short and are as close as possible to an English paraphrasing of them. Other points we learned through experience are that nested AND-OR-AND-OR structures must be avoided (multiplied out, normalized), and that long lists of similar constraints or production rules should be replaced by a compact table that is interpreted by a single production rule or constraint, and constraints or heuristics longer than a screenful of lines should be broken down. But if a proper design methodology is followed, the BSL paradigm indeed allows the benefits of a true production system in an important class of generate-and-test applications.

Representing Knowledge with Multiple Viewpoints

The paradigm shown above is suitable only for simple generate-and-test problems, such as Stefik's GA1 system [Stefik 78]. It uses a single model of the solution object, as represented by the primitives allowed by the solution array's type declaration. Representing knowledge about multiple viewpoints, or multiple models of a solution object is a need that often arises in the design of complex expert systems: the Hearsay-II speech understanding system [Erman et al. 80] was such an example, where there was a need to observe the interpretation of speech simultaneously as mutually consistent streams of syllables, words, and word sequences. In logic, a good way to describe an object from different viewpoints is to use different primitive functions and predicates for each view; since without the appropriate primitives, logic formulas for describing a concept can be unnecessarily long. But since BSL allows efficient manipulation of the native data types of a traditional computer, such as arrays and records, it is preferable to implement multiple viewpoints in BSL with pseudo functions and predicates, through data structures. In BSL, each viewpoint is represented by a different data structure, typically an array of records, that serves as a rich set of primitive pseudo functions and predicates for that view. For example, assuming that we wish to have a viewpoint that observes the chord skeleton of a musical piece with two primitive functions $p(n,v)$ and $a(n,v)$, representing the pitch and accidental of voice v of chord n, BSL lvalues of the form $c[n].p[v]$ and $c[n].a[v]$, where c is the array of records of the view, can be used as a pseudo notation to abbreviate $p(n,v)$ and $a(n,v)$.

BSL's multiple view paradigm has the following procedural aspect, which amounts to interleaved execution of generate and test: It is convenient to visualize a separate process for each viewpoint, which constructs that particular view of the solution, in close interaction with other processes constructing their respective views. A process typically executes in units of "generate-and-test steps." The purpose of each step, as before, is to assign acceptable values to the n'th element of an array of records, depending on the values of the array elements $0,\ldots, n-1$, and external input, e.g. elements of external arrays of records, whose values have been assigned by other processes. The processes, implemented as BSL predicate definitions, are arranged in a round-robin scheduling chain. With the exception of the specially designated process called the clock process, each process first attempts to execute zero or more steps until all of its input are exhausted, and then schedules (calls) the next process in the chain with parameters that indicate how far each process has progressed in assigning values to its output arrays. The specially designated *clock process* attempts to execute exactly one step when it is scheduled; all other processes adjust their timing to this process.

In certain cases a view may be completely dependent on another; i.e. it may not introduce new choices on its own. In the case of such redundant views, it is possible to maintain several views in a single process, and share heuristics and constraints, provided that one master view is chosen to execute the process step and comply with the paradigm. One way to do this is as follows: at the n'th step of such a process, the generate section is executed to produce a candidate assignment to the attributes of the n'th element of the master view; the subordinate views are then updated according to the chosen master view attributes, and then a mixture of constraints and heuristics from both the master and subordinate views are used to decide if the candidate assignment to the n'th element of the master view is acceptable and desirable. It is evident that the framework described here is in contrast with the more common techniques for constructing expert systems, where some emphasis is placed on sophisticated control structures. We should therefore explain why we have chosen such a streamlined architecture for designing an expert system, rather than a more complex paradigm such as the multiple demon queues of [Stallman and Sussman 77], or the opportunistic scheduling of [Erman et al. 80]. We strongly believe that striving to use simpler control structures is a better approach to the design of large systems. Our design approach is in fact a deliberate choice, and is analogous to a recent approach to computer architecture [Patterson et al. 81, Hennessy et al. 82, Radin 82]: It is a preliminary attempt at reducing the semantic gap between the top and bottom levels of the hardware-software complex that implements an expert system, by designing a streamlined set of system primitives that directly correspond to the target problem[11] [cf. Myers 82]. The paradigm described here has served to simultaneously represent knowledge about and construct multiple models of the solution object for the chorale program. We suspect that it can also be used for any generate-and-test application where (1) execution efficiency is mandatory during all stages of the development phase, and (2) the solution can be conveniently represented as one or more Pascal-style data structures. Note that programming such a demanding application in BSL would be much easier than programming it in C or Pascal, since BSL is indeed a high-level declarative language that gives access to the expressive richness of concepts of first-order predicate calculus, despite the fact that there is little trade-off of efficiency in choosing BSL over conventional low-level languages. However, like some of the other knowledge engineering paradigms, such as diagnosis-oriented skeletal systems [Buchanan and Shortcliffe 84], BSL has a limited scope of applicability; in particular, the BSL paradigm would be unsuitable for applications that cannot do without list processing: in music, we could get away with mere arrays and records, because music can be represented as a uniform sequence of events.

A Compilation Technique for Intelligent Backtracking

Ordinary, or chronological, backtracking may sometimes be inefficient when no choices can be found for successfully executing the current generate-and-test step, and the immediately preceding step is irrelevant to the failure of the current step. In this case, a substantial amount of computation that will look useless to a human observer will be done until the most recent step that caused the failure is reached: For example, assuming the current step is the n'th step and the choice responsible for the failure of the current step was made at step $n - k$, $k > 2$, then there will be a seemingly useless sequence of backtrackings to step $n - 1$ until all of the choices at step $n - 1$ are exhausted, and then there will be a backtracking to the step $n - 2$, and then there will again be many backtrackings to step $n - 1$, and so on. The BSL compiler attempts to alleviate the overhead associated with backtracking by a special compilation technique triggered by a compiler option. We have expressly tried to find an intelligent backtracking heuristic with very low overhead, since we have observed that overly ambitious intelligent backtracking schemes can introduce so much overhead that they can actually slow down the typical applications. In our technique, it is assumed that the computation proceeds as a sequence of generate-and-test steps. Otherwise the technique is domain-independent, and will produce the same solutions as ordinary backtracking would. Each scalar variable or each scalar member of an aggregate variable has a tag associated with it. At run time, things are arranged so that the tag always contains the stack level to backtrack to in order to get a different choice for the value of the corresponding variable. During the execution of a step, a running maximum is maintained of the tags of all variables that occur in the failing tests. When a step cannot be executed and backtracking is necessary, the program returns to this computed most recent responsible step for the failure, which is not necessarily the chronologically preceding step.[12] There have been a number of research projects in A.I. and logic programming that also have addressed the intelligent backtracking problem, using alternative approaches [e.g. Stallman and Sussman 77, Doyle 79, Bruynooghe and Pereira 81, Pereira and Porto 80, de Kleer and Williams 86].

The main use of this heuristic is for eliminating the need for Conniver-style [Sussman and McDermott 72] programmed return to an earlier-than-normal step, or the PROLOG-style "cuts" to labels specified by the programmer. This sort of inelegant intrusion into the backtracking mechanism would have otherwise been mandatory in the chorale program, since when a step of the chord skeleton view fails, it must at least backtrack to the previous step of the chord skeleton view, which is not necessarily the immediately preceding step (the immediately preceding step can be totally irrelevant to the failure). Because of this property of the scheduling order of the viewpoints, the intelligent backtracking technique causes the chorale program to run much faster than it would without it. However, we have encountered cases in the chorale program where this conservative and domain-independent intelligent backtracking mechanism is not intelligent enough. In particular, it appears to be desirable to detect not only the responsible step, but also the precise change that is required at that step (as it was done in [Schmidt et al. 78]), but we do not presently know of an easy way to compile such an intelligent backtracking algorithm; similarly we do not know whether the additional overhead would be justified. To remedy the problem, we have added an incomplete search feature to the compiler that gives a fixed number of chances to the intelligent backtracking technique when there are repetitive failures at a given step, and then forces the program to backtrack to a step earlier than the step recommended by the intelligent backtracking technique. The earliness of the step to backtrack to is increased, while the failures continue to occur in the same step as they did before. This feature cannot be used in more mundane applications where all solutions must be found, but it did give satisfactory results in the present application.[13]

The Knowledge Models of the CHORAL System

We are now in a position to discuss the CHORAL system itself. We will be able to give here only a brief overview of the knowledge base of CHORAL, which is in reality very long and complex. The CHORAL system uses the back-trackable process scheduling technique described above to implement the following viewpoints of the chorale: The *chord skeleton view*, which corresponds to the clock process, observes the chorale as a sequence of rhythmless chords and fermatas, with some unconventional chord symbols underneath them, indicating key and degree within key. The primitives of this view allow referencing attributes such as the pitch and accidental of a voice v of any chord n in the sequence of skeletal chords. This is the view where we have placed, e.g., the production rules that enumerate the possible ways of modulating to a new key, the constraints about the preparation and resolution of a seventh in a seventh chord, and the heuristics that prefer "Bachian" cadences. The *fill-in view* observes the chorale as four interacting automata that change states in lockstep, generating the actual notes of the chorale in the form of suspensions, passing tones and similar ornamentations, depending on the underlying chord skeleton. This view reads the chord skeleton output. For each voice v at fill-in step n, the primitives allow referencing attributes of voice v at a weak eighth beat and an immediately following strong eighth beat, and the new state that voice v enters at fill-in step n (the states are suspension, descending passing tone, and normal). At each one of its steps, the fill-in view generates the cross product of all possible inessential notes (suspensions, passing tones, neighbor notes, miscellaneous embellishments specific to the chorale style, etc.) in all the voices, and then filters out the unacceptable combinations and selects the desirable combinations, using a rather complex list of constraints and heuristics. In this view we have placed, e.g., the production rules for enumerating the long list of possible inessential note patterns that enable the desirable bold clashes of simultaneous passing tones and suspensions, a constraint about not sounding the resolution of a suspension above the suspension, and a heuristic on following a suspension by another in the same voice (a "Bachian" cliché).[14]

The *melodic-string view* observes the sequence of individual notes of the different voices from a purely melodic point of view. The primitives of this view allow referencing the pitch and accidental of any note i of a voice v. This is the view where we have placed, e.g., a constraint about sevenths or ninths spanned in three notes and a heuristic about continuing a linear progression.

The *merged melodic-string view* is similar to the melodic-string view except that it observes the repeated pitches merged together. This view was used for recognizing and advising against certain bad melodic patterns that we feel are not alleviated even if there are repeating notes in the pattern.

The *time-slice view* observes the chorale as a sequence of vertical time-slices each of which has a duration of a small time unit (an eighth note) and imposes harmonic constraints. The primitives of this view allow referencing the pitch and accidental of a voice v at any time-slice i, and whether a new note of voice v is struck at that time-slice. We have placed, e.g., a constraint about consecutive octaves and fifths in this view.

The *Schenkerian analysis view* is based on our formal theory of hierarchical voice leading, inspired from [Schenker 69, 79] and also from [Lerdahl and Jackendoff 77, 83]. The core of this theory consists of a set of rewriting rules, which, when repeatedly applied to a starting pattern, can generate the bass and descant lines of a chorale. The Schenkerian analysis view uses our rewriting rules to find separate parse trees for the bass and descant lines of the chorale, employing a bottom-up parsing method, and using many heuristics for choosing (among the alternative possible actions at each parser step) the action that would hopefully lead to the musically most plausible parsing. Unlike Lerdahl and Jackendoff's theory, which is based on a hierarchy of individual musical events (e.g. chords, noteheads), our theory is based on a hierarchy of slurs, and is more in line with Schenker's theory. The discussion of our voice-leading theory is beyond the scope of this chapter, and the details can be found in [Ebcioğlu 87a]. The Schenkerian analysis view observes the chorale as the sequence of steps of two nondeterministic bottom-up parsers for the descant and bass. This view reads the fill-in output. The primitives of this view allow referencing the output symbols of a parser step n, the new state that is entered after executing step n, and the action on the stack at parser step n. The rules and heuristics of this view belong to a new paradigm of automated hierarchical music analysis, and do not correspond to any rules that would be found in a traditional treatise: In this view we have placed, e.g., the production rules that enumerate the possible parser actions that can be done in a given state, a constraint about the agreement between the fundamental line accidentals and the key of the chorale, and a heuristic for proper recognition of shallow occurrences of the Schenkerian D-C-B-C ending pattern. The fill-in, time-slice and melodic string views are embedded in the same process, with fill-in as the master view among them.

The order or scheduling of processes is cyclically chord skeleton, fill-in, Schenker-bass, Schenker descant. Each time chord skeleton is scheduled, it adds a new chord to the chorale; each time fill-in is scheduled, it fills-in the available chords, and produces quarterbeats of the actual music until no more chords are available. Each time a Schenker process is scheduled, it executes parser steps until the parser input pointer is less than a lookahead window away from the end of the currently available notes for the descant or bass.[15] When a process does not have any available input to enable it to execute any steps when it is scheduled, it simply schedules the next process in the chain without doing anything. The chorale melody is given as input to the program.

There are currently a total number of approximately 350 production rules, constraints and heuristics in the chorale program. The rules and heuristics were found mainly from empirical observation of the chorales and personal intuitions, although we used a number of traditional treatises (such as [Louis and Thuille 06] or [Koechlin 28]) as an anachronistic, but nevertheless useful point of departure. The current version of the chorale program aims only to harmonize an existing chorale melody, and assign an analysis to it. All parts of the chorale program are written in BSL, except for the graphics routines and the routine to read in and pre-process the chorale melody, which are written in C. In the VAX 11/780 version of the program, it used to take typically 15–60 minutes of CPU time to harmonize a chorale. In the present version, which has a larger knowledge base and some extremely difficult rules intended to increase the output quality, it typically takes about 3–30 minutes of IBM 3081 CPU time to harmonize a chorale, although there have been a few chorales that have required several hours.

The program has presently been tested on about 70 chorales (by consuming inordinate amounts of CPU time) and has reached an acceptable level of competence in its harmonization capability; we can say that its competence approaches that of a talented student of music who has studied the Bach chorales. The program has also produced good hierarchical voice leading analyses of descant lines, but the Schenkerian analysis knowledge base still reflects a difficult basic research project in music analysis, and is not as powerful as the harmonization knowledge base. We were also not able to get any good parsings involving the basses so far.

The CHORAL system takes an alphanumeric encoding of the chorale melody as input, and outputs the chorale score in conventional music notation and the descant parse trees in Schenkerian slur-and-notehead notation. The output can be directed to a graphics screen, or can be saved in a file for later printing on a laser printer. The BSL compiler inserts a simple interactive interface in "(H F ...)" constructs that can explain the choices made at any step of a viewpoint, and other kinds of debugging tools are built into the program itself, such as a graphic display of the progress of the composition.

In the section Examples of Harmonizations, we present five examples of harmonizations produced by the program at the end of the paper (all the chorale numbers in this paper are from [Terry 64]). The reader will notice that some notes are too high or too low for the range of some of the voices in these examples: this is because the program does not generate the chorale with the voices in their proper ranges, but it ensures that there exists a transposition interval that will bring all the voices to their proper ranges. Also note that the parallel fifths between the soprano and tenor that accompany the anticipation pattern at the ending of the second phrase of chorale no. 75 (Figure 10) and at the ending of the last phrase of chorale no. 68 (Figure 9) are allowable in the Bach chorale style; see, for example, no. 383 in [Terry 64]. Bach's harmonizations of two of the same melodies, no. 128 and no. 48, are also given for comparison. Occasionally, the program's harmonizations can be quite similar to Bach's, as in no. 128 (Figures 6 and 7), but in other cases, the program has its own different, less austere style, as in no. 48 (Figures 11 and 12). Many more output examples and the complete list of rules of the system in English (about 77 single-spaced book pages) can be found in [Ebcioğlu 87a].

As a concrete example as to what type of knowledge is embodied in the program, and how such musical knowledge is expressed in BSL's logic-like notation, we take a constraint from the chord skeleton view. The following subformula asserts a familiar constraint about false relations (this is the most recent revision of this constraint; an earlier version of this constraint was given in our previous publications):

> When two notes which have the same pitch name but different accidentals occur in two consecutive chords, but not in the same voice, and no single voice sounds these notes via chromatic motion, then the second chord must be a diminished seventh, or the first inversion of (a dominant seventh or a major triad), and the bass of the second chord must sound the sharpened fifth of the first chord and must be approached by an interval less than or equal to a fourth, or the soprano of the second chord must sound the flattened third of the first chord. In case the bass sounds the sharpened note of the false relation and moves by ascending major third (matching the pattern e-g# in a C-major–E-major chord sequence), then some other voice must move in parallel thirds or tenths with the bass (matching the pattern g-b).[16] False relations are also allowed unconditionally between phrase boundaries, when there is a major-minor chord change on the same root.

(The exception where the bass sounds the sharpened fifth of the first chord is commonplace, the less usual case where the soprano sounds the flattened third, can be seen in the chorale *Herzlich thut mich verlangen*, no. 165. The case where there is a major-minor chord change on phrase boundaries can be seen in chorale no. 46 or no. 77. These exceptions are still not a complete list, but we did not attempt to be exhaustive). The complexity of this rule is representative of the complexity of many of the production rules, constraints and heuristics in the CHORAL system. We see the BSL code for this rule below.

```
(A u bass (<= u soprano) (1 + u)
    (A v bass (<= v soprano) (1 + v)
        (imp(and(> n 0)
                (!= u v)
                (== (mod(p1 u) 7) (mod(p0 v) 7))
                (!= (a1 u) (a0 v))
                (not(E w bass (<= w soprano) (1 + w)
                        (and  (== (mod(p1 w) 7) (mod(p1 u) 7))
                              (== (p0 w) (p1 w)))))))))
```

```
(or  (and (member chordtype0
                (dimseventh domseventh1 major1))
          (or(and (== (a0 v)  (1 + (a1 u)))
                  (== v bass)
                  (== (mod(- (p0 v) root1) 7) fifth)
                  (<= (abs(- (p1 v) (p0 v))) fourth)
                  (imp (thirdskipup (p1 v) (p0 v))
                       (E w tenor (<= w soprano) (1 + w)
                           (and(== (mod(- (p1 w) (p1 v)) 7) third)
                               (thirdskipup (p1 w) (p0 w))))))
              (and (== (a0 v) (1- (a1 u)))
                   (== v soprano)
                   (== (mod(- (p0 v) root1) 7) third))))
      (and (> fermata1 0)
           (== root0 root1)
           (== chordtype1 major0)
           (member chordtype0 minortriads)))))))
```

Here, n is the sequence number of the current chord, (pi v), $i = 0,1,\ldots$, is the pitch of voice v of chord n $-$ i, encoded as 7*(octave number)+(pitch name), (ai v), $i = 0,1,\ldots$, is the accidental of voice v in chord n $-$ i, and chordtype$i$ and root$i$, $i = 0,1,\ldots$, are the pitch configuration and root of chord n $-$ i, respectively. fermata i, $i = 0,1,\ldots$, indicates the presence of a fermata over chord n $-$ i when it is greater than 0. The notation p0, p1, etc. is an abbreviation system obtained by an enclosing BSL "with" statement that allows convenient and fast access to the most recent elements of the array of records representing the chord skeleton view. (thirdskipup p_1 p_2) is a macro which signifies that p_2 is a third above p_1. We repeat the constraint below in a more standard notation for clarity, using the conceptual primitive functions of the chord skeleton view instead of the BSL data structures that implement them:

$(\forall u \mid \text{bass} \leq u \leq \text{soprano})$ $(\forall v \mid \text{bass} \leq v \leq \text{soprano})$

$[[n > 0 \ \& \ u \neq v \ \& \ \text{mod}(p(n-1,u),7) = \text{mod}(p(n,v),7) \ \& \ a(n-1,u) \neq a(n,v) \ \&$
$\quad \text{not}(\exists w \mid \text{bass} \leq w \leq \text{soprano})$
$\quad\quad [\text{mod}(p(n-1,w),7) = \text{mod}(p(n-1,u),7) \ \& \ p(n-1,w) = p(n,w)]]$

$\Rightarrow$

$[[\text{chordtype}(n) \in \{\text{dimseventh,domseventh1,major1}\} \ \&$
$\quad [[a(n,v) = a(n-1,u) + 1 \ \& \ v = \text{bass} \ \& \ \text{mod}(p(n,v) - \text{root}(n-1),7) = \text{fifth} \ \&$
$\quad\quad \text{abs}(p(n-1,v) - p(n,v)) \leq \text{fourth} \ \&$
$\quad\quad [\text{thirdskipup}(p(n-1,v),p(n,v)) \Rightarrow$
$\quad\quad\quad (\exists w \mid \text{tenor} \leq w \leq \text{soprano}$
$\quad\quad\quad\quad [\text{mod}(p(n-1,w) - p(n-1,v),7) = \text{third} \ \&$
$\quad\quad\quad\quad \text{thirdskipup}(p(n-1,w),p(n,w))]]]$

$\quad\quad \vee$

$\quad\quad [a(n,v) = a(n-1,u) - 1 \ \& \ v = \text{soprano} \ \& \ \text{mod}(p(n,v) - \text{root}(n-1),7) = \text{third}]]]$

$\quad \vee$

$[\text{fermata}(n-1) > 0 \ \& \ \text{root}(n) = \text{root}(n-1) \ \& \ \text{chordtype}(n-1) = \text{major0} \ \&$
$\quad \text{chordtype}(n) \in \text{minortriads}]]]$

Before showing an example of a heuristic, it is appropriate to touch upon the significance of heuristics for music generation. It is a known fact that absolute constraints are not by themselves sufficient for musical results: Composers normally use much additional knowledge to guide their choices among the possible solutions. Our limited powers of introspection prevent us from exactly replicating the thought process of such choices in an algorithm; but there exist algorithmic approximations, based on large amounts of precise domain-specific heuristics, or preferences, that tend to give good results in practice (cf. [Lenat 76]). The chorale program uses an extensive body of heuristics, which are used for selecting the preferred choice among the list of possibilities at each step of the program, as previously described in the section on the BSL generate-and-test paradigm. Examples of heuristics would be to continue a linear progression or to follow a suspension by another one in the same voice.

To exemplify the BSL code corresponding to a heuristic, we again take the chord skeleton view. The following heuristic asserts that it is undesirable to have all voices move in the same direction unless the target chord is a diminished seventh. Here the construct (Em Q $(q_1\ q_2\ ...)$ $(F\ Q)$) is a macro which expands into (or $(F\ q_1)$ $(F\ q_2)...$), thus allowing us to use the second order concept of quantification over a set of predicates.

```
(imp  (and  (> n 0)
            (Em Q (< >)
                (A v bass (<= v soprano) (1 + v)
                    (Q (p1 v) (p0 v)))))
      (== chordtype0 dimseventh))
```

We again provide the heuristic in a more standard notation for clarification:

$$[n > 0\ \&\ (\exists Q \in \{<, >\})(\forall v \mid bass \le v \le soprano[Q(p(n-1,v),p(n,v))] \Rightarrow$$
$$chordtype(n) = dimseventh].$$

On the Use of Constraints and Heuristics for Music Generation

It is worthwhile to discuss certain practical issues related to the use of constraints and heuristics for music generation. We will first explain the motivation behind the use of constraints and heuristics for algorithmic production of music.

The Motivation behind Constraints and Heuristics

A composition is written incrementally, typically from left to right in a direct fashion for short pieces, or perhaps as a sequence of successively refined plans for large-scale works. At each stage of the composition, the composer either decides to add an item (e.g. a chord, a phrase, or a plan for a movement, assuming a traditional idiom) to the partial composition, so that the added item will hopefully lead to the best completion of the composition, or decides that the partial composition needs revising, and makes a sequence of erasures and changes in the previously written parts of the composition in order to make the composition ready for extension again. Given a partial composition x and an item y, the question whether "x is acceptable, and one of the best ways to extend x is to add y to it" holds for (x,y) can be answered by a composer with a limited degree of accuracy and consistency; similarly, for a given acceptable partial composition x, the composer can find items y such that this question can be answered positively for (x,y). However, the set of pairs (x,y) for which the answer is yes, which can be called the *extension set*, is difficult to define with mathematical rigor. Moreover, the extension set does not remain constant between styles and historical periods, and evolves even during the course of the composition of a single piece. The general approach of this research was to select a relatively fixed style, the Bach chorale, attempt to approximate the extension set with a precise definition, and then use the precise definition in a computer algorithm for generating music in that style.[17] Inspired by our own experience with a strict counterpoint program [Ebcioğlu 79, 81] and the recent artificial intelligence research in expert systems, we have designed the present knowledge-based method for describing the extension set, which appears to work, and succeeds in generating non-trivial music that is of some competence by educated musician standards. In the following paragraphs we will discuss the general problems associated with the constraints and heuristics used in this knowledge-based method, and also describe the possible sources for constraints and heuristics.

The Difficulty of Using Absolute Rules to Describe Real Music

A major part of the knowledge of the chorale program is based on constraints, or absolute rules in other words. Absolute rules, such as those expressed by treatises on harmony, counterpoint, or *fugue d'école*, assert, in a very inflexible manner, which pieces are acceptable, and which others are not. For artificial styles such as harmony, counterpoint and fugue exercises, absolute rules are part of the usual musical knowledge and practice. However, some problems are encountered when we try to describe a real style of music with absolute rules, rather than an artificial style. The rules in the book do not work, and many treatises mention to what extent great composers break the rules [Morris 46, Koechlin 33]. Schenker [Schenker 79] provides some modifications of traditional rules on fifths and octaves, so that the liberties taken by the masters are considered acceptable when the liberty no longer exists in a middleground reduction; unfortunately Schenker's rules do not meet the level of precision typically found in a traditional treatise. A number of treatises on composition attempt to describe the free compositional style [D'Indy 12, Durand n.d. (1898), Czerny 79] ([Messiaen 44, Schillinger 46] could also be considered in this category), but such treatises do not characterize the existing style of any master; they often reflect a particular normative view of music. In general, prescribing rules for the music of a master is recognized to be undoable. Nevertheless, this fact alone does not imply that good approximations of a real style cannot be obtained with the aid of a judiciously chosen set of such rules: for example, [Jeppesen 39], which describes real 16th-century counterpoint, as opposed to school exercises, is a treatise in this direction. Moreover, absolute rules are a powerful software tool in an expert system; although they appear to impose stringent demands on the knowledge base designer, in reality they are (in our opinion), conceptually clearer and easier to handle than assertions with numerical truth values [Zadeh 79, Shortcliffe 76, Buchanan and Shortcliffe 84] in an application as complex and as subjective as the present one. We therefore decided to take a constructive approach toward the use of absolute rules for describing a real style of music, namely the Bach chorales.

How Absolute Rules Can Be Found

We will now discuss the sources from which absolute rules are obtained.

A good source for finding absolute rules is the traditional harmony treatise. In the chorale program, we used a number of treatises, such as [Louis and Thuille 06, Lovelock n.d. (1956), Durand n.d. (1890), Dubois 21, Koechlin 28, Bitsch 57], as useful points of departure, despite their anachronism. However, since treatises are usually tailored for school exercises rather than for real Bach chorales, rules from such books had to be amended to fit the actual chorales themselves. For example the familiar rule about parallel fifths had to be amended to allow a diminished fifth followed by a perfect fifth when the parts are moving by ascending step, because of the consistent occurrence of these fifths in the chorale style.[18] We see an example of such an occurrence in chorale no. 73 shown in Figure 1 (at the phrase ending, between alto and soprano).[19]

Unfortunately, if we try to make our rules comprehensive, such amendments

Figure 1. Chorale No. 73 (Bach).

tend to never reach an end. We would have liked to have absolute rules that would accept every chorale. However, attempting to do so results in the unwieldy proliferation of allowable, conditional violations of some rules. Moreover, there are cases where the extenuating condition for the violation is hard to find. Consider the fifths by contrary motion in chorale no. 18 in Figure 2 (between tenor and soprano). We found it difficult to explain this liberty (except perhaps by the remote extenuating effect of the first inversion of the dissonant dominant seventh chord).[20] In certain cases, we therefore used our own judgement in deciding where to cut the list of conditional violations.

Figure 2. Chorale No. 18 (Bach).

Another source for rules is empirical observation and inductive reasoning on the chorales themselves. For example, most chorale phrases end on a chord with the root doubled, which suggests an implicit absolute rule. Such rules are also not without exception, and it is again impractical to codify the precise reasons for all the exceptions. To distinguish which exceptions are truly representative of the style, it is necessary to use musical judgement in order to make an educated guess as to where Bach did what he wanted to do and where he did what he had to do. For example in chorale no. 100 given in Figure 3, this rule is violated by doubling the third in the phrase ending; the reason is obvious: doubling the root would have resulted in a parallel octave between the alto and bass or some other unacceptable error. Moreover it is desirable to keep the cadence as it is because of the nice linear progression in the tenor. However, this exception is not a good candidate for inclusion in the program, since it would be marginal in loyalty to the style and would require complex extenuating conditions to be specified to prevent the backtracking algorithm from using this license in inappropriate contexts. So we overruled Bach in this case and declared that a phrase should end with the root doubled as an absolute rule, with exceptions allowing the fifth to be doubled in a IV^7–V ending in the minor mode (see chorale no. 51 for an example), and the third to be doubled in a V–VI ending (commonplace).

Figure 3. Chorale No. 100 (Bach).

The arbitrariness of this constraint definition mechanism needs some elucidation. It would probably be easy to reduce the corpus of chorales to a tractable size and write constraints that accept all members of the corpus, thus making the method more scientific (It would probably be more difficult to do the same without reducing the corpus). However, we know by experience that the property of exact agreement of the constraints with the corpus per se would be of little help in improving the quality of the music produced by the knowledge base (Baroni and Jacoboni [Baroni and Jacoboni 76] make a similar observation). Moreover, we feel that regarding music knowledge base design as more of an art and giving full liberty to the knowledge base designer's goodwill and musical intuitions in both the heuristics and constraints would produce more competent programs, without having to restrain the corpus of music that the knowledge base designer would draw upon. We are not saying that it is undesirable to have a rule set that would exactly characterize a large musical corpus, similar to a theory that explains the outcomes of chemical experiments; however musical pieces apparently do not enjoy the simplicity of other natural phenomena, and for the time being we may have to stay with inexact rule sets rather than have none at all.

The Significance of Heuristics

The second kind of difficulties faced by the music knowledge base designer is related to finding adequate heuristics. The purpose of heuristics is to estimate, at each step, which among the possible ways of extending the partial chorale will lead to its best completion. Heuristics are very important, since programs without heuristics that are based solely on absolute rules and random selection tend to quickly get trapped in a very unmusical path, and generate gibberish instead of music.[21] In the chorale program, we are using a natural extension of a heuristic technique we had used in an early strict counterpoint program [Ebcioğlu 79, 81] which was very successful for its purpose. Note that in theory it would be possible to characterize any finite set of "best" solutions with solely absolute rules. In fact, a research effort for generation of Bach chorale melodies [Baroni and Jacoboni 76] has used the absolute-rule approach. However, heuristics have a different and more human-composer-like flavor of describing what constitutes a good solution, because heuristics, in contrast to constraints, are rules that are to be followed whenever it is possible to follow them.[22] The main advantage of heuristics vs. pure absolute rules and random search is the following: heuristics lead the solution path away from a large number of unmusical patterns; if there were no heuristics, unmusical patterns would probably be generated by the bundle, would have to be painstakingly diagnosed, and then carefully ruled out with potentially complex constraints. Thus, a system based on heuristics can get away with less constraints and/or less complex constraints than a similar system based on random search. However, in case the research goal itself is to make a fair measurement of the musical power of a set of absolute rules, then heuristics cannot be used, since heuristics strongly bias the solution path toward a particular style, whereas random search can produce a relatively unbiased selection among all the possible solutions that are accepted by the rule set.

An Algorithmic Problem with Heuristic Ordering

As described in the previous section on the operational details, heuristics are strictly prioritized in the chorale program, and tied to a backtracking scheme. This strict priority scheme is easy to understand and debug, and avoids dealing with problems associated with arbitrary numerical weighting schemes. It is also quite rich and expressive, because the prioritized heuristics have the generality of BSL formulas. However, there is an algorithmic problem associated with the stack-based backtracking scheme and the heuristic ordering. At a given step, the heuristics may make an erroneous estimate: i.e. the item that the heuristics choose among the possibilities for adding to the chorale may not be on the path that leads to the best completion of the partial chorale. The reason such an error is possible is because heuristics typically depend only on a simple local property of the partial solution and on the item to be added to it. If the erroneous choice leads to a blind alley, the choice will eventually be undone by the backtracking mechanism. However, a locally good choice dictated by the heuristics may also later force a mediocre passage, which could have been avoided by a different, perhaps locally bad choice, or a locally good choice may force the program to miss a cliché or other "desirable" progression, which would not have been missed by a different, perhaps locally bad choice. Although such problems could be remedied by maintaining a priority queue of partial chorales, sorted by a numerical evaluation function [Nilsson 71, 80, Lenat 76], and/or by using heuristics with several levels of lookahead, we preferred to keep the conceptual simplicity of BSL's stack based mechanism, and we used additional constraints in an attempt to provide remedies for these problems. In the cases where we understood the precise pattern that made a passage mediocre, we made mediocre passages either unconditionally forbidden or conditionally forbidden via constraints of the form "pattern x is not allowed" or "if pattern x could have been avoided, then it should have been avoided," respectively. For the case where a locally good choice misses a future cliché opportunity, whereas a locally bad choice does not, we used a conditional backtracking scheme to provide a selective degree of heuristic lookahead: Whenever there is an opportunity for a cliché progression, the chorale program first prefers to generate that cliché and enters a cliché state; while in that state, the cliché must be at least partially fulfilled. If this is not possible, the program will backtrack to the originating step where it will not enter the same cliché state and perhaps choose what is best according to the local heuristic criteria.

How Heuristics Can Be Found

Now we come to the problem of finding heuristics.

One major source of heuristics are the preferences of general good counterpoint practice, such as moving by step rather than by skip, avoiding following a scalar motion by a skip in the same direction, etc., which a counterpoint treatise will tell us in some probably unalgorithmic recipe [e.g. Koechlin 26]. The knowledge base designer must possess the minimal ability of making such preferences precise and algorithmic in a reasonable way, using his or her musical judgement. Another source of heuristics is the chorales themselves. Heuristics from this source are style-awareness heuristics, and roughly correspond to the informal knowledge acquired by a composer when he or she sets out to understand a style. These heuristics are developed by observing a very broad range of chorales. Examples are to follow a suspension by another in the same part, and to prefer certain recurring patterns—we can call them Bach chorale clichés. We see in chorale no. 22 (Figure 4) an example of the repeating suspension pattern in the alto in the first measure, and in the fourth measure we see a cliché chord progression, a cadence cliché in this case. The chorale program currently knows 11 such cliché progressions. However, getting such recurring patterns to be used is a different and less predictable matter within the extremely intense computation of chorale generation, since whenever the use of a pattern is seemingly appropriate, it may result unexpectedly in e.g., a forbidden melodic motion in an inner voice. (Being more vulnerable to accusations of unmusicality, our program is more concerned with melodic motion in the inner parts than Bach is).

Figure 4. Chorale No. 22 (Bach).

A third and valuable source is hand simulation of an algorithm in an attempt to generate specific chorales exactly as written by Bach. This exposes all details, causes one to find the plausible reasons underlying each choice, and allows postulating priorities for heuristics. For example, the heuristics behind the first two measures of chorale no. 210, *Jesu meine Freude* (Figure 5), can be explained as a concern to move by step and continue a linear progression in the bass and in the other parts and to prefer a cadence cliché. The layout of the chords is affected by a preference to use triads rather than seventh chords and to double the root in triads. The inserted diminished seventh on the weak eighth beat of the third chord is explained as a desire at the fill-in view to change the plagal progression IV–I in the skeleton to one of the more desirable VII–I or V–I progressions. The reasons for the suspension in the first measure of the bass are a concern to hide the second inversion of a chord, and a concern to continue eighth-note movement.

Figure 5. Chorale N. 210. Jesu Meine Freude (Bach).

We have made these concerns heuristics in the chorale program. We can see many interesting applications of these particular heuristics in very different contexts in the examples of [Ebcioğlu 87a]. Unfortunately, there are cases where we cannot find any plausible reason for choosing certain possibilities rather than others, or sometimes a choice that appears to be locally bad is made by Bach. Such situations tend to agree with the backtracking search model. However, because of the labor intensive nature of such very detailed hand simulation, conclusive results for validating the backtracking search model of composition can only be reached by drastically restricting the corpus. We were not primarily interested in validating a cognitive model for a composer, so we did not push far enough in this direction. However, we feel that explicating the decisions made during such an algorithmic resynthesis of a piece could be an instructive future research direction to pursue in the field of music analysis that is likely to yield results of profound nature.

Emotional Content of Computer-Composed Music

In this section, a final remark must be made about some common misconceptions about the "emotional content" of music generated by computers. Often it is taken for granted that mechanical music cannot have emotional content. Unfortunately, existing computer generated compositions in traditional styles sometimes confirm this opinion. However, the factor responsible for the apparent lack of feeling is more often than not an inadequate program which lacks the knowledge base to characterize a sufficiently sophisticated style. In all cases of practical interest, the set of pieces in the desired style with the desired feelings is finite, thus there is no inherent theoretical problem against an algorithmic description of music with emotional content.[23] A study by [Meyer 56] ties emotion to concrete musical events, such as the delaying of expectations of chordal and melodic progressions. The whole burden is therefore on the expert system designer, who must algorithmically encode the emotional content in rules and/or heuristics, where we are assuming that the set of desired solutions largely overlaps the set of solutions with emotional content. This is no small burden, however. In fact, actual composition of music in any decent style is invariably easier than characterizing precisely what that style is in terms of concréte attributes, and such characterization attempts appear to be limited to styles that are well understood. What is well understood is of course strictly dependent on the competence of the knowledge base designer. However, each knowledge base designer may also have a limit that applies to him or her: sometimes compositional ideas discovered after lengthy unconscious search are not well understood, these ideas, similar to sufficiently hard proofs, unfortunately tend to be the most valuable ones. Thus, it is unknown to what extent human compositional ability can be algorithmically replicated. However, there is no obstacle against establishing higher and higher standards in algorithmic composition, in fact, substantially higher than the existing norms. Moreover, large knowledge bases in an efficient computing environment have an encouraging synergistic effect that sometimes transcends the naiveness of the individual rules and heuristics [Lenat 70, 82].

Examples of Harmonizations

This last section presents actual examples of harmonizations. The CHORAL harmonization of chorale no. 128 is shown in Figure 7, and Bach's is shown in Figure 6 for comparison. The CHORAL harmonization of chorale no. 286 is shown in Figure 8, and those of chorales no. 68 and no. 75 are shown in Figures 9 and 10, respectively. The CHORAL harmonization of chorale no. 48 is shown in Figure 12, and Bach's is shown in Figure 11 for comparison.

Conclusions

In this chapter, we have described a knowledge-based heuristic search technique for

Figure 6. Chorale No. 128 (Bach).

Figure 7 (above). Chorale No. 128 (CHORAL).

Figure 8 (right). Chorale No. 286 (CHORAL).

Figure 9. Chorale No. 68 (CHORAL).   Figure 10. Chorale No. 75 (CHORAL).

Figure 11. Chorale No. 48 (Bach).

Figure 12. Chorale No. 48 (CHORAL).

generating tonal music, which seems to work and which produces musical results. While it is imprudent to make claims about the accuracy of this algorithmic model for the human composition process, our work indicates that heuristic search, coupled with large, complex knowledge bases, can be effective for the purpose of music generation. Although a heuristic evaluation function was used in a very early program for generating simple serial music [Gill 63], research in algorithmic composition has since then concentrated mainly on non-heuristic search techniques, such as random selection of attributes of notes according to statistical distributions [Xenakis 71, Hiller 70] or generation of music through terse formal grammars [Jones 81] or other mathematical artifacts [Kendall 81] (these are mostly avant-garde approaches; computer generated tonal music has somehow failed to be popular among computer musicians, perhaps because of its reactionary overtones). However, the knowledge-based heuristic search technique that we described here, which is based on [Ebcioğlu 79, 81], is not at all restricted to tonal music: with the proper set of rules, it can certainly be used for the purpose of more general algorithmic composition as well. We thus hope that our techniques can be of help to computer music researchers who may be looking for alternative approaches to algorithmic composition.

In this chapter, we have also described a multiple-viewpoint knowledge representation technique, which is analogous to the multiple levels of knowledge in the Hearsay-II expert system [Erman et al. 80], but which is based on first-order predicate calculus and which uses different primitive functions and predicates for representing each viewpoint. Another AI issue concerning the present research is the efficient, compiled representation of musical knowledge in the CHORAL knowledge base, which can be seen as a step toward the goal of knowledge compilation [Hayes-Roth,Waterman, and Lenat 83], a goal which has been predicted to be an important one for the ambitious expert systems of the future. Finally, we have adopted a streamlined approach to the design of a complex expert system, and we have advocated the reduction of the semantic gap. Although a streamlined approach is not easy to defend with a "logical" argument, computer science experience with large software/hardware systems, as well as considerations on mathematical tractability, seems to suggest that it is a desirable approach. In this chapter, we have also described a new logic programming language BSL, which was designed to implement the CHORAL system. Logic programming is a clearly desirable means to implement large AI applications. It provides a fuller understanding of the declarative meaning of the knowledge in the program and the relationship of this declarative meaning to the actual execution of the program (this is not at all true for the OPS family and many other inference engines [Hayes-Roth, Waterman and Lenat 83], where no adequate formalism exists for understanding the declarative meaning of the rules). Also, the knowledge representation techniques in an expert system written in a logic programming language can be more easily made to follow a formal discipline, since the properties of the desired outputs of the expert system are specified with precise logic formulas. But we feel that logic programming research should not confine itself to a narrow PROLOG-and-variants paradigm, since PROLOG is not the only medium to achieve such benefits of logic programming. In the context of the present research, we have designed and implemented BSL, a logic programming language radically different from PROLOG. BSL has a sound formal basis; it allows the programmer to use the concepts of first-order logic including universal and existential quantifiers, and is not limited to the clausal form of logic; moreover, it allows the benefits of an efficient Algol-class language for coping with substantial applications. We hope that our work with BSL will be of use to researchers who would like to use the concepts of logic in computation-intensive applications.

Acknowledgments

I am indebted to my thesis advisor, the late Professor John Myhill, for encouraging me to study computer music and getting me interested in the mechanization of Schenkerian analysis. I would also like to thank Professor Pat Eberlein for her encouragement, which led to the receipt of a two-year NSF grant for this project. The research environment and the computing resources at IBM Yorktown Heights were invaluable during the later stages of this research. I am in particular thankful to John Darringer and Abe Peled for their support, to Jean-Louis Lassez for helpful discussions on logic programming, and to Josh Knight and Phil Perry for their unselfish help with the software problems I had in porting BSL and CHORAL to the IBM environment. I am also grateful to the referees for their useful comments on this chapter.

Notes

1) This chapter is based on the author's Ph.D. dissertation "An Expert System for Harmonization of Chorales in the Style of J.S. Bach," Technical report 86-09, March 1986, Dept. of Computer Science, S.U.N.Y. at Buffalo, and on about a year of additional work done at IBM Research. This research was supported by NSF grant no. DCR-8316665, and the major portion of it was done at S.U.N.Y at Buffalo, under the direction of the author's advisor John Myhill. This chapter originally appeared in *Journal of Logic Programming,* 1990:8:145–185. Reprinted by permission of Elsevier Science Publishing Co., Inc.

2) In the eight-queens program above, the construct (and F_1 F_2 F_3) abbreviates (and F_1(and F_2 F_3)). In general, "and" and "or" associate to the right, and thus (and...) and (or...) can contain more than two subformulas.

3) See [Ebcioğlu 87a] for details. In practice, the general case is rarely needed, because BSL programs are often first conceived as first-order assertions rather than, say, "while" loops.

4) This is because n may be re-incremented, and the other variables declared within (A n...) may be destroyed through re-use of their storage space during the continuation of execution, due to the static nature of the storage. For example, in the eight-queens program above, j and n (but not p) need to be pushed down within (E j...) for the purpose of later backtracking to the setting of j to j + 1.

5) [Gergely and Szots 84] have proposed a logic programming language called Logic of Cuttable Formulas, whose formulas are compiled into efficient programs that have essentially the same semantics as the assigment-free subset of BSL.

6) For example, in the eight-queens example above, no pushdown operations are executed within (E j...(and...)) until just before the assignment (:= (p n) j). If (and...) fails before reaching the assignment, it jumps directly to the setting of j to j+1. A detailed compilation algorithm is given in [Ebcioğlu 87a].

7) In contrast to BSL, the unification algorithm [Robinson 65] and certain nonlogical systems such as "Constraints" [Sussman and Steele 80], defer the choice between making equality and checking for it to run time. But the unification algorithm has the elegant consequence of being able to answer different questions about a relation without reprogramming, such as using the same code for finding the parents of a given x, or finding the children of a given y, or checking if a given y is a par-

ent of a given x, or finding pairs (x,y) such that y is a parent of x. BSL is suitable for generate-and-test applications where such versatility, which is useful but usually costly, is not of prime importance, and where the question is fixed (e.g. given the result of laboratory experiments, find the solutions to a molecular genetics problem, not the other way around, as exemplified by [Stefik 78]).

8) Note that this condition-action paradigm captures only the generate-and-test application of production rules, which is the intended application of BSL. In general, production systems can allow very arbitrary control, such as self-modification [Waterman 75] or blackboards [B. Hayes-Roth 85].

9) The sites are enzyme names labeling points on a circular DNA molecule where that enzyme has made a cut, and the segments are integers indicating the length of the DNA molecule segment from one site (cut point) to the next. Stefik [Stefik 78] describes the problem in detail.

10) Here, (imp F_1 F_2) is a macro that expands into (or (not F_1) F_2).

11) An alternative successful approach is to reduce the semantic gap between existing A.I. software paradigms and hardware, by designing specialized hardware for Lisp and PROLOG. The BSL paradigm, on the other hand, is destined for well-understood RISC or supercomputer architectures. As for the parallel execution of BSL, we expect that significant speedup of BSL programs will be achievable in the future, via the emerging "Very Long Instruction Word" (VLIW) architectures and compilation techniques [Ellis 86, Nicolau 85, Ebcioğlu 87c], which are intended for parallel execution of general, ordinary sequential programs.

12) Here is some more detail: In normal code, when an assignment is made to a scalar variable or a scalar subpart of an aggregate variable, the stack level to backtrack to for undoing this assignment is placed in the tag of the variable (the additional assignment is compiled inline). Tests are executed as usual in normal code. During the execution of a generate-and-test step (a subformula specially designated by the programmer, where we are interested in finding the most recent responsible stack level to backtrack to, in case this subformula fails), whenever a variable is assigned a value, its tag is set to the maximum of the tags of the variables on the right hand side of the assignment. Whenever a test within the generate-and-test step succeeds, execution proceeds as usual, but when the test fails, a "current estimate" (a running maximum) for the most recent responsible stack level is updated, if it is less than any of the tags of the variables that were part of the failing test, via additional code compiled inline after the test. If the current generate-and-test step fails, this estimate is used for selecting the stack level to backtrack to; otherwise, the tags of the variables assigned during the current step are changed to point to the next alternative for the current step, and execution continues, typically with the next generate-and-test step. Various optimizations are performed on top of these basic principles. See [Ebcioğlu 87a] for further details.

13) The incomplete search technique was later disabled on the IBM 3081-3090 version of the program, because we felt we could afford more search on the faster hardware.

14) We felt that enabling the bold clashes of multiple simultaneous inessential notes was indispensable for obtaining a "Bachian" melodic-harmonic flow. Not allowing multiple simultaneous inessential notes or style-specific modulations in the harmonization, would have greatly simplified the problem domain, but then, we would probably not obtain music.

15) The lookahead window gradually grew bigger as our ideas evolved, and in the recent versions, for the sake of reducing module sizes, we have found it expedient to place the Schenker processes in a separate post-processing program that reads its input from a file produced by the other views. Note that the technique of using a separate program for a particular process is not necessarily outside the nondeterministic parallel processes paradigm; it is rather an optimization of a degenerate case of the same paradigm.

16) Both of these thirds are filled in with a passing note at the fill-in view.

17) Mechanizing the evolution of the extension set over time is a potentially more difficult problem that has not been attacked in the scope of the present research.

18) It is interesting to note that [C.P.E. Bach 49] allows such fifths in the non-extremal parts, declaring them to be better than descending fifths where the first is diminished. He also allows quite a few other combinations of the diminished and perfect fifth, not often seen in the chorales [McHose 47]

is another treatise which correctly points out that the ascending diminished fifth—perfect fifth sequence is legal in the Bach chorale style.

19) All the Bach chorale examples in this article have been reprinted by permission from C.S. Terry (ed.), *The Four-part Chorals of J.S. Bach,* copyright 1929 and 1964, Oxford University Press.

20) However, it appears that these fifths are not an oversight after all: they also occur in chorale no. 352 in the same context. They could be license of the style when a descending fifth in the soprano is harmonized in this specific manner.

21) It should be noted that there are contexts where music generated by extremely naive random number generation methods [Xenakis 71], let alone absolute rules, is not necessarily gibberish; it may offer a refreshing sense of liberation from the traditional or modern constraints and clichés, and a sense of beauty from a sophisticated aesthetic viewpoint, in fact, a natural evolution of Western art music through the centuries. In this particular research we are obviously looking at the problem of computer music from a stubbornly traditional aesthetic point of view; in real life, we do not necessarily have such an approach. However we feel that our present approach is useful, because answering the unanswered questions in computer generation of traditional music could also help to answer the many (nowadays unasked and) unanswered fundamental questions in the field of algorithmic composition.

22) In fact, it would not be desirable to always satisfy a heuristic such as continuing a linear progression, because a piece consisting merely of scales could ensue from such a practice. Heuristics are therefore only meaningful in conjunction with constraints that prevent them from being satisfied all the time.

23) [Hofstadter 79, 82], perhaps overly impressed by an older topic in recursive function theory, believes that works of art must be a productive set; i.e. given any algorithm, a work of art that is not generated by this algorithm can be found, or the algorithm can be shown to generate a non-work-of-art. For the case of music, we feel that the set of all "pieces" that can be encoded via digital recordings of some fixed sampling rate and that take less than a reasonable time limit is a satisfactory superset of the set of interesting music. The finiteness of this otherwise huge set does not of course make the discovery of a practical algorithmic description of music less difficult; it merely points out that productiveness is an incorrect model of the true difficulty. Also, even if we momentarily accept that we are dealing with an infinite set, Hofstadter's choice of a productive set (rather than, say, an immune set) actually works against the point he wants to make: a productive set has an infinite recursively enumerable subset [Rogers 67], which by Hofstadter's hypothesis would mean that there exists an algorithm which will produce infinitely many different works of art, but never a non-work-of-art. Note, however, that the conjecture that art objects, like the true sentences of a sufficiently complex formal system, could be a productive set was indeed elegant in its own right when the repercussions of Goedel's incompleteness theorem were strong [Myhill 52]; thus, this particular stance of Hofstadter is marred primarily by its bad timing.

References

Aho, A.V. and Ullman, J.V. 1977. *Principles of Compiler Design,* Addison-Wesley. Bach, C.P.E. 1949. 1949. *Essay on the True Art of Playing Keyboard Instruments,* Tr. W.J. Mitchell, W.W. Norton and Company Inc..

Baroni, M. and Jacoboni, C. 1976. *Verso una Grammatica della Melodia,* Universita Studi di Bologna.

Bitsch, M. 1957. *Précis d'Harmonie Tonale,* Alphonse Leduc et Cie, Paris.

Bruynooghe, M. and Pereira, L.M. 1981. "Revision of Top-down Logical Reasoning through Intelligent Backtracking," Centro di Informática da Universidade Nova de Lisboa, report no. 8/81.

Buchanan, B.G. and Shortcliffe, E.H. (eds.) 1984. *Rule Based Expert Systems: The MYCIN Experiments of the Stanford Heuristic Programming Project,* Addison-Wesley.

Cohen, J. 1979. "Non-deterministic algorithms," *Computing Surveys* Vol. 11, No. 2.

Czerny, C. 1979. *School of Practical Composition*, Tr. John Bishop, Da Capo Press, New York..

Davis, R. and King, J. 1976. "An Overview of Production Systems," Elcock and Michie (eds.), *Machine Intelligence 8*, Wiley.

de Bakker, J. 1979. *Mathematical Theory of Program Correctness*, North Holland.

de Kleer, J. and Williams, B. 1986. "Back to Backtracking: Controlling the ATMS," *Proceedings of the Fifth National Conference on Artificial Intelligence*.

D'Indy, V. 1912. *Cours de Composition Musicale*, Durand et Cie, Paris.

Doyle, J. 1979. "A truth maintenance system," *Artificial Intelligence* 12, 231–272.

Dubois, Th. 1921. *Traité d'Harmonie Théorique et Pratique*, Heugel, Paris.

Durand, E. (n.d., ca. 1890?). *Traité de l'Accompagnement au Piano*, Alphonce Leduc et Cie, Paris.

Durand, E. (n.d., ca. 1898?). *Traité de Composition Musicale*, Alphonse Leduc et Cie, Paris.

Ebcioğlu, K. 1979. "Strict Counterpoint: A Case Study in Musical Composition by Computers," M.S. Thesis (in English), Department of Computer Engineering, Middle East Technical University, Ankara.

Ebcioğlu, K. 1981. "Computer Counterpoint," *Proceedings of the 1980 International Computer Music Conference*, held in Queens College, New York, Computer Music Association, San Francisco, California.

Ebcioğlu, K. 1987a. "Report on the CHORAL project: An Expert System for Harmonizing Four-part Chorales," research report RC12628, IBM Thomas J. Watson Research Center, Yorktown Heights. (This is a revised version of the author's Ph.D. dissertation, "An Expert System for Harmonization of Chorales in the Style of J.S. Bach," technical report TR 86-09, Dept. of Computer Science, S.U.N.Y. at Buffalo, March 1986.)

Ebcioğlu, K. 1987b. "An Efficient Logic Programming Language and its Application to Music," *Proc. 4th ICLP*.

Ebcioğlu, K. 1987c. "A Compilation Technique for Software Pipelining of Loops with Conditional Jumps," *Proc. 20th Annual Workshop on Microprogramming (MICRO 20)*, ACM Press.

Ellis, J.R. 1986. *Bulldog: A Compiler for VLIW Architectures*, MIT Press.

Erman, L.D. et al. 1980. "The Hearsay-II Speech Understanding System: Integrating Knowledge to Resolve Uncertainty," *Computing Surveys*, Vol 12, No 2.

Fagin, B. and Dobry, T. 1985. "The Berkeley PLM Instruction Set: An Instruction Set for PROLOG," Report no. UCB/CSD 86/257, Computer Science Division (EECS), University of California at Berkeley.

Feigenbaum E.A. 1979. "Themes and Case Studies in Knowledge Engineering," in *Expert Systems in the Micro-Electronic Age*, Donald Michie (ed.). Edinburgh University Press.

Floyd, R. 1967. "Nondeterministic Algorithms," *Journal of the Association for Computing Machinery*, Vol. 14, no. 4.

Forgy, C. and McDermott, J. 1977. "OPS: A Domain Independent Production System Language," *Proceedings of the fifth International Joint Conference in Artificial Intelligence*.

Gergely, T. and Szots, M. 1984. "Cuttable Formulas for Logic Programming," *1984 International Symposium on Logic Programming*.

Gill, S. 1963. "A Technique for the Composition of Music in a Computer," *Computer Journal* 6-2.

Harel, D. 1979. "First Order Dynamic Logic," Lecture Notes in Computer Science, Goos and Hartmanis (eds.), Springer-Verlag.

Hayes-Roth, B. 1985. "A Blackboard Architecture for Control," *Artificial Intelligence* 26, pp. 251–321.

Hayes-Roth, F., Waterman, D. and Lenat, D.B. (eds.) 1983. *Building Expert Systems*, Addison-Wesley.

Hennessy et al. 1982. "The MIPS Machine," *Digest of Papers—Compcon Spring 82*.

Hiller, L. 1970. "Music Composed with Computers: A Historical Survey," in *The computer and music*, H.B. Lincoln (ed.), Cornell University Press.

Hofstadter, D.R. 1979. *Goedel, Escher, Bach: An Eternal Golden Braid*, Basic Books.

Hofstadter, D.R. 1982. "Metafont, Metamathematics, and Metaphysics," Technical Report No. 136, Indiana University Computer Science Department.

Jeppesen, K. 1939. *Counterpoint: The Polyphonic Vocal Style of the Sixteenth Century*, Tr. Glen Hayden, Prentice-Hall.

Jones, K. 1981. "Compositional Application of Stochastic Processes," *Computer Music Journal*, Vol 5, No. 2.

Kendall, G.S. 1981. "Composing from a Geometric Model: Five-leaf Rose," *Computer Music Journal*, Vol. 5, No. 4.

Koechlin, Ch. 1926. *Précis des régles de Contrepoint*, Paris, Heugel.

Koechlin, Ch. 1928–1930. *Traité de l'Harmonie*, Volumes I, II, III, Éditions Max Eschig, Paris.

Koechlin, Ch. 1933. *Étude sur l'Écriture de la Fugue d'École*, Éditions Max Eschig, Paris.

Lenat, D.B. 1976. "A.M. : An Artificial Intelligence Approach to Discovery in Mathematics and Heuristic Search," Report no. STAN-CS-76-570, Department of Computer Science, Stanford University.

Lenat, D.B. 1982. "The Nature of Heuristics," *Artificial Intelligence* 19.

Lerdahl, F. and Jackendoff, R. 1977. "Toward a Formal Theory of Tonal Music," *Journal of Music Theory* 21.

Lerdahl. F. and Jackendoff, R. 1983. *A Generative Theory of Tonal Music*, MIT press.

Louis, R. and Thuille, L. 1906. *Harmonielehre*, C. Grüninger, Stuttgart.

Lovelock, W. *First Year Harmony, Third Year Harmony*, Hammond and Co., London, not dated and 1956, respectively.

McHose, A.I. 1947. *The Contrapuntal Harmonic Technique of the 18th Century*, Prentice-Hall.

Messiaen, O. 1944. *Technique de mon Langage Musical*, Alphonse Leduc et Cie, Paris.

Meyer, L.B. 1956. *Emotion and Meaning in Music*, University of Chicago Press.

Morris, R.O. 1946. *The Oxford Harmony*, Oxford University Press.

Myers, G.J. 1982. *Advances in Computer Architecture*, Wiley Interscience.

Myhill, J. 1952. "Some Philosophical Implications of Mathematical Logic: Three Classes of Ideas," *Review of Metaphysics*, Vol. VI, no. 2.

Newell, A. and Simon, H. 1963. "GPS: A Program that Simulates Human Thought," in *Computers and Thought*, Feigenbaum and Feldman, eds., McGraw Hill.

Nicolau, A. 1985. "Percolation Scheduling: A Parallel Compilation Technique," TR 85-678, Dept. of Computer Science, Cornell University.

Nilsson, N. 1971. *Problem Solving Methods in Artificial Intelligence*, McGraw-Hill.

Nilsson, N. 1980. *Principles of Artificial Intelligence*, Tioga.

Patterson, D.A. et al. 1981. "RISC-I: A Reduced Instruction Set VLSI computer," Eighth Annual Symposium on Computer Architecture.

Pearl, J. (ed.) 1983. Special Issue on Search and Heuristics, *Artificial Intelligence* 21.

Pereira, L.M. and Porto, A. 1980. "Selective Backtracking for Logic Programs," Report no. 1/80, Centro di Informática da Universidade Nova de Lisboa.

Radin, G. 1982. "The 801 Minicomputer," *Proc. ACM Symposium on Architectural Support for Programming Languages and Operating Systems*.

Robinson, J.A. 1965. "A Machine Oriented Logic Based on the Resolution Principle," *Journal of the Association for Computing Machinery* 12.

Rogers, H. 1967. *Theory of Recursive Functions and Effective Computability*, McGraw-Hill.

Schenker, H. 1969. *Five Graphic Analyses*, Felix Salzer, ed., Dover.

Schenker, H. 1979. *Free Composition* (Der freie Satz), Translated and edited by Ernst Oster. Longman.

Schillinger, J. 1946. *The Schillinger System of Musical Composition*, C. Fischer, New York.

Schmidt, C.F. et al. 1978. "The Plan Recognition Problem: An Intersection of Psychology and Artificial

Intelligence," *Artificial Intelligence,* Volume 11, nos. 1, 2.

Shortcliffe, E.H. 1976. *Computer Based Medical Consultations: MYCIN,* Elsevier, New York.

Smith, D.C. and Enea, H.J. 1973. "Backtracking in Mlisp2," *Proceedings of the third International Joint Conference in Artificial Intelligence.*

Stallman, R.M. and Sussman, G.J. 1977. "Forward Reasoning and Dependency-Directed Backtracking in a System for Computer-Aided Circuit Analysis," *Artificial Intelligence* 9.

Stefik, M. 1978. "Inferring DNA Structures from Segmentation Data," *Artificial Intelligence* 11.

Sussman, G.J. and McDermott, D.V. 1972. "From PLANNER to CONNIVER—A Genetic Approach," *Proc. AFIPS 1972 FJCC.* AFIPS Press, pp. 1171–1179.

Sussman, G.J. and Steele, G.L. 1980. "Constraints—A Language For Expressing Almost-Hierarchical Descriptions," *Artificial Intelligence* 14, 1–39.

Terry, C.S. (ed.) 1964. *The Four-voice Chorals of J.S. Bach,* Oxford University Press.

Turk, A.W. 1986. "Compiler Optimizations for the WAM," Proc.

Warren, S.H., Auslander, M.A., Chaitin, G.J., Chibib, A.C., Hopkins, M.E., and MacKay, A.L. 1986. "Final Code Generation in the PL.8 Compiler," report no. RC 11974, IBM T.J. Watson Research Center.

Waterman, D.A. 1975. "Adaptive Production Systems," *Proceedings of the fourth International Joint Conference in Artificial Intelligence.*

Xenakis, I. 1971. *Musique—Architecture,* Casterman.

Zadeh, L.A. 1979. "A theory for approximate reasoning," in J.E. Hayes, D. Michie and L.I. Mikulich, eds., *Machine Intelligence 9,* Wiley.

Chapter 13

An Expert System for Harmonizing Analysis of Tonal Music

H. John Maxwell

Implementing computer programs to perform music analysis is beneficial to the music theorist because it necessitates an explication of the musical methods and knowledge required to accomplish the analysis. When a computer program is used to carry out music analysis, it can only perform as well as the robustness of the algorithms it uses and the musical knowledge it possesses.

Although several music analysis programs have been built over the last twenty-five years, most of them have had limited success. The majority of them have attempted what is best termed *computer-assisted analysis*, in which the program generates data about surface-level features in the music, and the theorist studies that data to draw some sort of analytical conclusions. Good examples of computer-assisted analysis include recognition of melodic patterns in Bach's *Orgelbüchlein* (Brinkman 80) and a set of programs (Gross 1975), which were envisioned as part of a comprehensive music system (Byrd 1977) at Indiana University. Programs that attempt to fully implement music analysis are naturally more complex than those that only generate and tabulate data about surface features. For example, Gross attempted harmonic chord labelling in one of her programs, but ran into considerable difficulty when she "realized that the definitions found in textbooks were entirely insufficient for even the analysis of a Haydn minuet." (Gross 1975, p. 3)

A few studies have tackled problems related to harmonic analysis of tonal music. These can be divided into two groups: (1) programs that *generate* music from some initial structure using theoretical principles, such as Rothgeb's harmonizations of figured bass lines (Rothgeb 1968) or Smoliar's Schenkerian transformations (Smoliar 1980), and (2) truly analytical programs that start with the actual music and look for the underlying functions, such as the analysis of jazz harmonies in (Ulrich

1977) and of Bach chorales in (Winograd 1968) and (Winold and Bein 1983). The project described here is analytical, not generative, and owes much to the ideas developed in the Bach chorale studies.

One of the greatest challenges in creating either analytical or generative programs is that the musical theories and rules used by human analysts often prove to be inadequate or impractical in a computational treatment. This problem was noted, for example, by Rothgeb, who found that rules from treatises by Heinichen and Saint-Lambert for harmonizing figured bases did not constitute a sufficient computational methodology (Rothgeb 1968). An analogous problem exists in the field of linguistics, where some attractive linguistic theories do not lend themselves well to computation, and numerous alternatives have been proposed that can be better computed. Consequently, the current project did not tie itself to any one theory of tonal harmony, but invented its rules and heuristics in an empirical fashion. A serious attempt was made to model intuitive judgements about how people perform similar analysis, while iteratively revising methods that did not yield adequate results.

We have developed a rule-based expert system that performs harmonic chord function analysis for tonal music. Analyses by the expert system of three movements of J. S. Bach's *Six French Suites* are discussed below. The three pieces were chosen because they present varying levels of complexity for the expert system: the Sarabande from Suite No. 1 in D Minor is in four-part harmony with numerous non-harmonic tones; the Menuet from Suite No. 2 in C Minor is entirely in two voices with continuous contrapuntal movement; and the Gavotte from Suite No. 5 in G Major has a varying contrapuntal texture. All of these pieces are more complex texturally than the Bach chorales analyzed in earlier research, and thus they better approximate the task a music theorist faces in analyzing harmonies of literature from the common practice period.

As was pointed out in (Winold and Bein 1983), two strongly-interacting problems must be faced in constructing rules for harmonic analysis: (1) determining which vertical sonorities are chords worthy of a function label, and (2) determining the tonal regions in which chords are to be analyzed. These two problems cannot be solved independently. It is the tonality that makes a sonority a chord with a function, but at the same time it is the chords with their sequence and relationships to each other that create the tonality. A chord-analysis system must search for an optimal analysis for a piece from among the combinatorially large number of possible analyses. However, we would like to accomplish this search in a manner that is more intuitive than the branch-and-bound, right-to-left method used in (Winograd 1968, p. 27).

Problem One: Which Vertical Sonorities Are Chords?

If the music we had to analyze were a series of block chords from a music theory textbook, this problem would not exist. In music such as the Bach keyboard pieces to be analyzed here, there are many dissonant and non-harmonic sonorities. A good analysis will not consider every vertical sonority that occurs in a piece as a chord. Furthermore, it is not reasonable to analyze every triad or seventh chord that appears in a piece as an independent chord function; some must be regarded as linear chords because of rhythmic, metrical, or voice-leading considerations.

We use the terms "sonority," "vertical," and "vertical sonority" to denote individual simultaneities in music that are delineated by each note attack and release that occurs. The term "chord" denotes verticals that can or should be given a function label. Analyses may differ on the number of chords that should be labeled in a given musical passage, depending on their particular view of the harmonic rhythm in the passage, or on differing levels of harmonic abstraction of the entire analysis.

The first step towards choosing which sonorities in a piece are to be promoted to the status of "chordship" is to recognize consonance and dissonance, which are defined as follows:

Rule 1 & Rule 2.　IF a sonority consists of only one note, OR it consists of two notes that form a consonant interval other than a perfect fourth, OR it consists of three or more notes forming only consonant intervals, THEN it is a *consonant vertical*, OTHERWISE it is a *dissonant vertical*.

Rule 3 & Rule 4.　IF an interval forms a unison, minor third, major third, perfect fourth, perfect fifth, minor sixth, major sixth, or octave, THEN it is a *consonant interval*, OTHERWISE it is a *dissonant interval*.

Obviously, by this definition many diatonic chords (especially the seventh chords) are dissonant. This does not mean that these sonorities cannot be analyzed as chords, but does indicate that they should be examined for the presence of nonharmonic tones. Another property of verticals can be established:

Rule 5.　IF the pitches of a vertical can be arranged so that each note is separated from its neighbor(s) by a third or fifth, and the pitches all lie within a single octave, THEN it is *tertian*.

Still another necessary concept is whether or not an event in a piece is rhythmically accented. Assuming a moderate tempo, accents fall upon the regular "beats" of the meter.

Rule 6.　IF a musical event falls on the "primary beat unit" of the meter (as defined by a table relating meters to beat units) THEN it is *accented*.

With some grasp on whether an event is accented, it is possible to define the concept of "contextual dissonance" for vertical sonorities (the "tertian dissonance levels" are established by Table 1):

Rule 7.　IF a sonority is not tertian OR it is accented AND dissonant AND the next sonority is tertian AND the next sonority has a lower tertian-dissonance level OR it is unaccented AND dissonant AND the last sonority is tertian AND the last sonority has a lower tertian-dissonance level, THEN the sonority is *dissonant in context*.

Dissonance Level	*Chord Quality*
1	consonant intervals
	major triads
	minor triads
2	tritone
	diminished triad
	minor-minor seventh
	major-minor seventh
3	augmented fifth
	augmented triad
4	half-diminished seventh
	fully-diminished sevenths
	augmented-sixth sonorities
5	verticals with major sevenths
	anything else

Table 1. Levels of Tertian Dissonance.

If a sonority is dissonant, it probably contains some notes that can be classified according to various types of non-harmonic tones. There are two rules to determine whether a given note is indeed a dissonant note.

Rule 8.   IF a note is in a vertical that is both "dissonant" and "dissonant in context," AND the note forms a dissonant interval with another note in the vertical, AND the vertical is accented, AND the note is not continued or repeated in the next vertical, THEN the note is a *dissonant note.*

Rule 9.   IF a note is in a vertical that is both "dissonant" and "dissonant in context," AND the note forms a dissonant interval with another note in the vertical, AND the vertical is unaccented, AND the note is not continued or repeated from the previous vertical, THEN the note is a *dissonant note.*

The various types of non-harmonic tones are identified by Rules 10 through 19, but for the sake of brevity, the rules are not listed. They identify passing tones, neighboring tones, appoggiaturas, escape tones, suspensions, retardations, and anticipations. These are familiar patterns that are described in most first year theory texts. Except for the suspensions, however, the recognition of these patterns does not play a crucial role in separating chords from non-chords. The characteristic of being "dissonant in context" is far more important in determining the status of a sonority, and it guides the process of grouping non-chord verticals with an appropriate chord.

Meter	Beat	Strength
⁴⁄₄ (quarter note beat)	1	0
	2	3
	3	1
	4	3
³⁄₄ (quarter note beat)	1	0
	2	3
	3	2
²⁄₂ (half note beat)	1	0
	2	1

Table 2. Beat Strength for Various Meters (lower strength number indicates stronger beat).

Having located dissonance in the music, it is necessary to decide how often chords ought to appear. This could be influenced by a number of factors: meter, tempo, musical genre, the density of chord changes—all of the factors that constitute the rather nebulous realm of harmonic rhythm. For our present purposes, however, it will suffice to build a single chord on each primary beat of the meter wherever this is possible, occasionally allowing more than one chord per beat. We then combine or reduce chords so that there is only one per strong beat of the meter. The strength of beats is defined in Table 2.

Beats that have a strength rating of one or zero are considered strong beats. For some meters (such as ³⁄₄), this means that the second level of reduction will aim to produce only one chord per measure wherever it is reasonable or logical, and for other meters there may be more than one chord per measure.

Relative consonance and metrical placement are the first criteria used to separate chords from non-chords, as embodied in the following rules.

Rule 20. IF a vertical is tertian AND its duration is at least as long as the primary beat of the meter, THEN it is a chord.

Rule 21. IF a vertical is tertian AND it is accented AND it is not "dissonant in context," THEN it is a chord.

Rule 22. IF a vertical is unaccented AND it is tertian AND the previous vertical is tertian AND they both have the same root, THEN the vertical is subordinate to the previous vertical.

Rule 23.   IF a vertical is accented AND it is dissonant in context AND the next vertical is tertian, THEN it is subordinate to the next vertical, and is not an independent chord.

Rule 24.   IF a vertical is unaccented AND it is not dissonant in context AND the last vertical is dissonant in context, THEN the vertical is a chord.

Rule 25.   IF a vertical is tertian AND it is unaccented AND the previous vertical is tertian AND the previous vertical is not dissonant in context AND the two verticals do not have the same root, THEN the vertical is a chord, but is marked *passing.*

Rule 26.   IF a vertical is not tertian AND it is accented, THEN it is subordinate to whatever chord follows.

Rule 27.   IF a vertical is not tertian AND it is unaccented, THEN it is subordinate to whatever chord precedes it.

Rule 28.   IF a vertical contains a suspension AND the resolution note of the suspension can be substituted for the suspension note to form an implied tertian vertical AND the implied tertian vertical is more consonant than the original vertical, THEN the implied vertical should be substituted for the suspension vertical, and is made a chord.

The rules we have given will suffice to select chords from non-chords in a three- or four-voice texture, but for music in only two voices, two more rules are necessary:

Rule 29.   IF a vertical is unaccented AND it is not dissonant in context AND it is a two-voice sonority AND the previous vertical is a two-voice sonority AND the notes of the vertical can be combined with the notes of the previous vertical producing an implied tertian sonority with the same root as the previous vertical, THEN the unaccented vertical should be subordinate to the previous vertical, and its notes can be included with those of the previous vertical.

Rule 30.   IF a vertical consists of a single note from a single voice, THEN the vertical is subordinate to the previous chord.

Assuming for the moment that a key is established and that chords have been analyzed, several rules can be laid down for combining chords so that those with strong harmonic functions subsume those with weaker functions (The relative strengths of the harmonic functions are defined in Table 3):

Rule 31.   IF a chord is in the same key as the previous chord AND the chord has the same harmonic function as the previous chord AND they have the same inversion, THEN the chord can be subordinated to the previous chord.

Level	Harmonic Functions
0	I V vii
1	ii IV (iv) vi (VI)
2	iii (III)
	secondary V,vii
3	borrowed chords (diatonic in parallel major/minor)
4	altered chords (Neapolitan, augmented sixths, etc.)
5	anything else

Table 3. Harmonic Function Strength (a lower number indicates greater strength).

Rule 32.   IF a chord is accented AND it is followed by a chord with a weaker harmonic strength, which is followed by a chord with the same function as the first chord, THEN the second two chords can be subordinated to the first chord.

Rule 33.   IF a chord is accented AND it is followed by a chord that is unaccented AND the second chord has a weaker harmonic function than the first, THEN the second chord is subordinate to the first.

Rule 34.   IF a chord contains a suspension AND the resolution of the suspension note can be substituted for the suspension note to produce a chord with a greater function strength than the original chord, THEN the new function should be substituted for the old function. (This rule does not combine chords, but can cause other rules to do so.)

There are two final rules for combining chords, which do not depend directly on the levels of functional strength:

Rule 35.   IF a chord is accented AND it is on a strong beat AND it is a six-four chord AND the next chord has the same bass note AND the next chord is in root position, THEN the first chord is subordinate to the second.

Rule 36.   IF a chord is a two-voice chord AND the previous chord is accented AND the two chords are in the same measure AND the notes of the chord can be combined with those of the previous chord without changing the root of the previous chord, THEN the chord is subordinate to the previous chord.

In summary, the location of chords is a two-stage process that first combines verticals together to form chords (mostly by considering relative consonance and accent) and then combines subordinate chords with (metrically and harmonically) stronger chords.

Problem Two: What Is the Key?

In the past, several approaches have been used to decide the key in which to analyze chords. Ulrich set up "tonal segments" throughout the piece based on the possible functions of chords, and then attempted to merge the segments into larger tonal regions (Ulrich 1977). This island-growing approach has an appealing, organic quality; "islands of tonal clarity" can be imagined that spread their influence and "grow" into areas of tonal ambiguity. Winograd made an initial pass over the music to locate evidence of key establishment, and then performed a retrograde parse of the piece, examining possible functions of every chord according to each of the keys found in the first pass (Winograd 1968). Winold and Bein used a method custom-fitted to the Bach chorales for determining the main key, and relied on the tonal implications of the clearly-marked cadences to determine keys during a front-to-back parse of the chorale (Winold and Bein 1983).

The approach taken here will be to let the analysis proceed from the beginning of a piece to the end, analyzing as long as possible in the currently-established key, and only attempting to modulate when a certain threshold of functional weakness is exceeded. Before the analysis can take place, it is assumed that the vertical sonorities have been properly grouped by the rules we have listed in the preceding section. It is also useful to have a notion of what the overall tonality of the piece is. In the Baroque dance movements we will analyze (and in most common practice music) it is unnecessary to perform some complicated routine to determine this. A human analyst glances at the key signature and the final cadence (if necessary) and makes a quick judgement. Our method will be the same. If the final cadence or chord contradicts the key signature, the algorithm should look at the opening measures for evidence of a key establishment. In general we can assume that the final key is the main key, and also that the main key is established in the opening measures. Thus the main key is assumed to be the "current key" when analysis starts at the beginning of the piece.

The chord analysis algorithm begins with the first chord and makes a single pass through the piece from beginning to end, looking ahead in the piece when necessary for information. The following rules apply to the analysis of each chord:

Rule 37.   IF the previous chord has not been analyzed, THEN defer analysis of this chord until the previous chord is done.

Rule 38.   IF the chord can be assigned a function in the key in which the previous chord was analyzed, THEN assign the strongest possible function in that key.

Rule 39.   IF the chord is a secondary dominant or leading-tone chord, AND the next chord is not its natural resolution, THEN mark the chord's analysis as doubtful.

Rule 40.   IF [the chord cannot be analyzed in the key of the previous chord OR the analysis is "doing badly"] AND [not enough is known about future keys to look for a better key], THEN defer analysis of this chord until more is known about keys established later in the piece.

Rule 41.   IF [the chord cannot be analyzed in the key of the previous chord OR the analysis is "doing badly"] AND [enough *is* known about future keys to look for a better key], THEN determine which key will provide the strongest analysis of the next few chords or measures, modulate to that key, analyze the present chord in the new key, and assign pivot functions to some previous chords.

Because of the general language of the rules, a few rather imprecise concepts must be explicated in order to turn our approach into a computer program. First of all, what does it mean for the analysis to be "doing badly?" This occurs when the functional strength of the last few chords that have been analyzed drops beyond a certain threshold. Another vague phrase that requires definition is "enough evidence of future key establishment to determine a better key." Cadences are the most obvious evidence of key establishment, but are not always easy to find. Instead of searching for only true cadences, we seek all harmonic patterns that indicate the potential establishment of tonalities, the strongest of which will be the true cadences. We call such patterns *p-cadences* (for *potential-* or *pseudo-* cadences). P-cadences are sought by applying the following rules to chords:

Rule 42.   IF a chord is accented AND is a triad or major-minor seventh AND the previous chord is tertian AND the root motion between the two chords is a descending or ascending perfect fifth, major second, or minor second, THEN the chord is the *goal chord* of a p-cadence.

Rule 43.   IF the root motion from pre-cadence chord to goal chord of a p-cadence is a descending perfect fifth AND the pre-cadence chord contains a major third above the root, THEN the p-cadence is *authentic,* and its strength should be increased by 20.

Rule 44.   IF the pre-cadence chord of a p-cadence is a major-minor seventh, THEN increase the strength of the p-cadence by 10.

Rule 45.   IF the root motion between the pre-cadence and goal chords of a p-cadence is an ascending minor second AND the pre-cadence chord contains a tritone, THEN the p-cadence is a *leading-tone* p-cadence, and its strength is increased by 15.

Rule 46.   IF the goal chord of a p-cadence falls on a strong beat of the meter, THEN increase its strength by 20.

Rule 47. IF the goal chord falls on a strong beat, AND the goal chord is either a major triad or a major-minor seventh, AND the root motion from pre-cadence chord to goal chord is an ascending or descending perfect fifth or major second or a descending minor second; AND when the root motion is a descending fifth, the precadence chord is not a potential dominant; AND when the root motion is an ascending fifth the pre-cadence chord is triadic (no seventh); THEN the p-cadence is a *half cadence,* and its strength increases by 10.

Rule 48. IF the goal chord of a p-cadence is in root position, THEN increase its strength by 10.

Rule 49. IF the pre-cadence chord of a p-cadence is in root position, THEN increase its strength by 10.

Rule 50. IF the p-cadence falls on a measure number that is evenly divisible by four, THEN increase its strength by 10.

Rule 51. IF a p-cadence occurs an even number of measures after the previous p-cadence, THEN increase its strength by 10.

Rule 52. IF a prospective p-cadence cannot be labelled authentic, leading-tone, or half OR if its strength is no greater than 10, THEN it is *not* a p-cadence.

Rule 53. IF a p-cadence is authentic or leading-tone, THEN it implies the establishment of a key where the goal chord is the tonic.

Rule 54. IF a p-cadence is a half p-cadence, THEN it implies the establishment of a key where the goal chord is the dominant.

The p-cadences can be used to find key establishment when the following rule applies:

Rule 55. IF [at least two p-cadences have been found ahead of the chord] OR [at least one p-cadence has been found ahead of the chord and there are at least eight intervening chords] OR [one p-cadence has been found ahead of the chord and the p-cadence is at the end of piece], THEN there is enough evidence of key establishment ahead of a chord to guide the search for a better key in which to analyze it.

When one of these conditions is met, the keys implied by the p-cadences that have been found ahead of the chord are collected together with the previous key and they are tested to see which one will provide the strongest functional analysis of the next few chords (or measures). All the chords from the "problem chord" through the first or second p-cadence after the chord are analyzed in each implied key, and the analysis modulates to the key with the strongest functional analysis.

The problem chord is then analyzed in the new key. If the new key is different from the previous key, an attempt is made to extend the analysis backwards a few chords, changing their functions and key as long as the new analysis has greater functional strength. If an analysis in the new key will not improve the strength of the previous chords, but they can be analyzed in the new key, they are given secondary pivot functions in the new key. In this way the algorithm can find a smooth transition between keys using a pivot chord (or chords), and can catch exceptional cases where the modulation occurred so smoothly that it was not detected until somewhat beyond the pivot point.

Implementation Issues

The notes, durations and other information in the score are encoded for each piece in a LISP-oriented notation that falls into the same tradition as DARMS or MUSTRAN [1] encoding. A preprocessor reads this notation and forms an internal representation of the music consisting of interconnected, frame-like nodes for notes and other events. During the course of the analysis, new frames representing non-harmonic tones, chords, and cadences are linked into the network by the actions of the rules.

The antecedent-consequent structure of the analysis rules stated above clearly hints at a rule-based, production system implementation. They were stated in this manner so that their logic would be as transparent and modular as possible, with the goal in mind that alternative analytical biases could be interchanged.

The implementation of the rules was carried out in LISP, each rule having a fairly regular syntax for the conditions, but with more arbitrary LISP for the actions. The granularity of the rules varies considerably; the non-harmonic pattern recognition rules (numbers 10–19) are generally quite simple, whereas Rule 41 for finding pivot points for modulations requires much more extensive processing.

The rules are interpreted by a forward-chaining inference engine that uses a prioritized agenda to control conflict resolution. The rulebase is partitioned into various phases of analysis such as non-harmonic tone identification, chord recognition, determination of cadence and modulation, and functional analysis of chords. This partitioning, along with priorities that are assigned to individual rules, helps to focus the activity of the system. In addition, the mechanism that matches rules against the musical network uses a list of currently active nodes called a "focus of attention" to restrict the size of the conflict set. Several control-oriented rules were added which manipulate the agenda and the focus of attention.

The analysis is complete when the system runs out of instantiations to fire. When the system stops, the network representation of the music has been altered to contain new structures representing the analysis. Utility routines are used to generate formatted reports of the analysis by reading it from the network.

Resulting Analyses

Having described the musical considerations that determined the rules of the system and pertinent aspects of the implementation, we now examine the resulting analyses. The chord function notation used is typical of that found in most undergraduate music theory textbooks. Since the non-harmonic tone analysis is not our primary concern here, and would clutter the examples considerably, it has been omitted. More detail about the output produced by the system (such as non-harmonic tone and p-cadence reports and traces of rule firings) can be found in (Maxwell 1984).

Analysis of D-Minor Sarabande

The system's harmonic analysis of the D-Minor Sarabande is shown in Figure 1. This piece is a logical starting point for testing the system for several reasons: it is short (only 24 measures), its texture generally consists of four voices that produce full-bodied chords, and it contains an abundance of non-harmonic activity without complex embellishments or passage-work. Its texture is considerably more complex than that of a chorale, especially with regard to harmonic rhythm—in some measures of the Sarabande there is only one chord per measure, while elsewhere chords change on every eighth note. This presents a significant challenge to the logic that governs the pseudo-reduction process of combining verticals and chords together (done by Rules 20 through 36).

Figure 1. Harmonic Analysis of D-Minor Sarabande.

Figure 1 (continued). Harmonic Analysis of D-Minor Sarabande.

The analysis in Figure 1 demonstrates that the program has performed quite well in meeting one of the primary challenges of the Sarabande: finding the right chords to analyze in the jumble of non-harmonic tones and passing sonorities. Where possible, single functions have been assigned to entire measures. The slow harmonic rhythm of the opening eight bars is especially clear. Furthermore, the modulations chosen by the system are sensible and are made in appropriate places. The p-cadences identified by rules 42–55 provided sufficient evidence of key establishment to guide the analyses. Some might object to the short modulation to F major, preferring to see the program return immediately to D minor and treating mm. 17–18 within the main key of the piece. The choice of the program in this case is certainly justifiable, however, considering the ambiguous succession of secondary dominants in mm. 17–20. In any case, the pivot functions in D minor that the program assigned the chords in these measures illustrates the alternate modulatory scheme.

Although most of the analysis is unremarkable (because it is essentially correct), a few items in it deserve special comment. In some cases the rules out-smart themselves, producing analyses that are rather odd. On the downbeat of m. 12, for example, the suspension in the soprano caused Rule 28 to infer the presence of a dominant six-five chord. Because the rest of m. 12 is a leading-tone seventh, the suspension sonority probably should not have been discarded. Measure 11 elicited an analysis from the rules that illustrates their general preference for consonant sonorities. Even though there is an accented leading-tone seventh on the third beat that might seem preferable (because of the similar sonority on the first beat) to the subdominant six-four chord, it is considered "dissonant in context" relative to the inverted triad. The last two beats of m. 11 are a bit ambiguous in any case, being a point of modulation, and a human analyst might view it in several ways.

Analysis of C-Minor Menuet

In the analysis of the Sarabande the program was fortunate to have an abundance of complete four-voice chords on which to base its judgements. In the C Minor Menuet this is obviously not the case, as the entire movement is in two voices, both of which are fairly melodic, though the bass moves generally in slower rhythmic values. A two-voice texture can be much more ambiguous with regard to chord functions unless the analyst is able to view the music with a sufficiently broad perspective; if every harmonic interval is inspected for possible tonal functions, a two voice piece can produce a bewildering number and variety of incomplete triads and their functions. Much of the C Minor menuet exhibits harmonic rhythm that changes chord function every measure, while in some measures the functions change on every quarter note. The ability of the rules to perform a reduction of vertical sonorities to legitimate chords is even more crucial here than in the Sarabande.

The modulation scheme chosen for the Menuet by the system is quite reasonable (see Figure 2), although it demonstrates a stronger willingness to modulate than might have been expected, given the general preference of the rules for remaining in the same key as long as possible. The program is also a bit short-sighted in choosing keys; the modulation back to C minor might have occurred as soon as m. 17, with m. 18 analyzed as a secondary dominant. The distance ahead of a "problem" area that the program will search for a new key varies according to the density of p-cadences (see Rules 41 and 45). Looking forward from the end of m. 17, the program sees several p-cadences in succeeding measures: an authentic p-cadence implying E-flat major (m. 19), an authentic p-cadence implying A-flat major (m. 20), and a half p-cadence implying C minor (m. 22). The search procedure usually only rates chords as far ahead as the second p-cadence, which means that from m. 17 it continues only to m. 20. This is not far enough to see the strength of C minor in the following measures. Although the short modulation to E-flat major in mm. 17-20 is acceptable, it seems that the search for key establishment needs more flexibility in determining how far it should proceed in order to make the best decision about where (or whether) to modulate.

The chord analysis in Figure 2 shows that the rules proved quite successful in spacing chords in accordance with what we would perceive as the harmonic rhythm of the Menuet. One of the most productive rules in this respect is Rule 32, which allows two chords of similar function to "swallow" an intervening chord that has a weaker functional strength. It is this rule that ultimately reduces mm. 1, 2, 4, 12, 14 and 16 to single chords. Interestingly enough, it failed to reduce m. 9 in spite of the obvious similarity to m. 1 (obvious to us at least, mainly because of the identical voice-leading patterns). Unfortunately, Rule 32 cannot absorb two intervening chords; the third beat of m. 9 implies a consonant mediant, which is never subordinated to the tonic that follows. In m. 1 the third beat is obviously dissonant in context relative to the tonic on the last eighth note, and the program never considers the possibility of a mediant chord. The inability of the program to recognize the obvious similarity of these measures demonstrates the ignorance of the rules toward voice-leading or melodic patterns.

Figure 2. Harmonic Analysis of C-Minor Menuet.

Figure 2 (continued). Harmonic Analysis of C-Minor Menuet.

Figure 3. G-Major Gavotte, mm. 17–20.

One might wonder why the harmonies in mm. 18, 20, and 22 are not analyzed as seventh chords rather than simple triads. The sevenths (which appear on the fourth eighth note of each of these measures) are unfortunately discarded very early in the reduction process by Rule 27, which subordinates unaccented verticals that are "dissonant in context." The significance of these sevenths is their role in forming a 7-10-7-10-7-10 contrapuntal pattern at the measure level, but the system is completely unaware of this level of abstraction.

Analysis of G-Major Gavotte

Much of the analysis done of this piece demonstrates nothing new and has been omitted. However, several passages in the Gavotte present an additional level of complexity and melodic embellishment beyond what the system faced in the Sarabande and Menuet. The failure of the rules to deal with these passages adequately is interesting because it points out certain types of knowledge that are not embodied in the rules.

One of these passages is mm. 17–20, the analysis of which is shown in Figure 3. There are two problems here: (1) lengthy successions of consonant eighth note motion that are interpreted too literally as strings of passing chords, and (2) the lack of knowledge in the rules concerning linear patterns that carry harmonic information.

A music theorist considering m. 17 of the Gavotte would quickly recognize the entire measure as a dominant to G major with a resolution to a G major chord on the first beat of m. 18. The C major chord is disguised by an ornamented appoggiatura. The major difficulty for the system in the second beats of mm. 17 and 18 is that the counterpoint is entirely consonant during four successive verticals in each beat. The rules have no other recourse but to generate passing chords for each vertical—in the absence of dissonance, no other chord-combining rules can be applied. These scalewise passages do not carry significant harmonic information, but they are "taken literally" by the system.

Although the program successfully identifies the tonic chord inherent in the counterpoint of the second half of m. 19, it errs dramatically in the first half of m. 19 and throughout m. 20 because of its dogged preference for consonance and its ignorance of common melodic patterns, such as arpeggiation, that have obvious harmonic meaning. The first half note of m. 19 would be best analyzed as a dominant seventh chord. In fact, the diverging scalar motion of the second half of m. 18 and the first half of m. 19 would be better combined into a single dominant seventh function. The program does not recognize the outlines of the dominant seventh chord in the notes emphasized by their placement on strong beats in mm. 18 and 19. In m. 18 it identifies four implied chords during the second half note, and in m. 19 it considers the initial seventh "dissonant in context" relative to the succeeding sixth. Consequently, the first beat of m. 19 is ultimately given a supertonic function.

A similar inappropriate preference for consonance causes the program to identify a supertonic function on the second beat of m. 20. This entire measure is obviously based on dominant seventh harmony. Unfortunately, by the time the rules for determining chord function and for combining chords have a chance to act, Rule 23 has long since discarded the accented sonority on the second beat of m. 20 in favor of the relative consonance of the succeeding vertical. In many cases, such an action would have been completely correct, but here the overwhelming functional strength of the dominant seventh and the obvious arpeggiation of the dominant seventh in both the bass and treble voices should establish it as predominant, overriding any other considerations. Here consonance is subordinate to tonal function and the dictates of linear patterns, but the rules are designed to perform an initial reduction of verticals to chords that is based on relative consonance and accent. This could be improved by making better use of melodic patterns as harmonic indicators. For example, there is nothing currently in the rulebase that allows the program to recognize an obvious arpeggiation in the bass voice during the first half of this measure. Yet this provides the human analyst with a singularly powerful indication of harmonic function. In florid passages, where the notes come much faster than changes in harmony, a melodic reduction might be performed that chooses out rhythmically emphasized notes and arpeggiations. The resulting melodic skeleton would lend itself better to harmonic analysis. The rule-based structure of the system should enable such enhancements to be tried with minimal difficulty.

Conclusions

At its inception, it was hoped that this project would accomplish two goals: that it would demonstrate some analytical success on the test pieces and that its failures would illuminate and clarify some of the issues and problems inherent in building a knowledge base for music analysis. The project has accomplished these goals.

The rule-based format for capturing musical knowledge and procedures has proved to be an extraordinary boon to the development process of what turned out to be an intricate program. Expressing the knowledge as rules made the knowledge base modular and extensible, although the production system architecture sometimes made it difficult to exert control over the order in which various phases of analysis were performed.

Although there is room for improvement in the analyses done by the program for the Sarabande and Menuet, the analyses are generally correct and occasionally insightful, especially with regard to the reductive process that finds chords in the midst of abundant linear activity. The analysis of the Gavotte demonstrated some important weaknesses in the musical knowledge possessed by the program, but these weaknesses point toward possible enhancements to the program's knowledge base and future avenues for research.

References

Brinkman, A. R. 1980. Johann Sebastian Bach's *Orgelbüchlein*. *Music Theory Spectrum* 2:46–73.

Byrd, D. 1977. An Integrated Computer Music Software System. *Computer Music Journal* 1:55–60.

Gross, D. S. 1975. A Set of Computer Programs to Aid in Music Analysis. Ph.D. dissertation, Indiana University.

Maxwell, H. J. 1984. An Artificial Intelligence Approach to Computer-Implemented Analysis of Harmony in Tonal Music. Ph.D. dissertation, Indiana University.

Rothgeb, J. 1968. Harmonizing the Unfigured Bass: A Computational Study. Ph.D. dissertation, Yale University.

Smoliar, S. W. 1980. A Computer Aid for Schenkerian Analysis. *Computer Music Journal* 4:41–59.

Ulrich, J. W. 1977. The Analysis and Synthesis of Jazz by Computer. In Proceedings of the Fifth International Joint Conference on Artificial Intelligence, 865-72. Menlo Park, Calif.: International Joint Conferences on Artificial Intelligence.

Winograd, T. 1968. Linguistics and Computer Analysis of Tonal Harmony. *Journal of Music Theory* 12:2–9.

Winold, A., and Bein, J. 1983. BANALYZE: An Artificial Intelligence System for Harmonic Analysis of Bach Chorales. Unpublished manuscript, School of Music, Indiana University.

Abstract

The author herein asserts that the metaphor of "music as a universal language" should be taken seriously. Fundamental pitch, rhythm and timbre parallels with language may hold profound implications for music analysis, theory and composition. The author first describes a hierarchical (Forte, 1967) language/music parsing technique, which has both context-driven and context-free representations and which exposes the hidden structure of diverse musical surface representations. This is followed by a description of an augmented transition network (ATN) which generates new works in diverse styles.

Chapter 14

On Algorithmic Representation of Musical Style

David Cope

Professor of Music, University of California Santa Cruz

Background

While creating an algorithmic compositional tool and finding machines lacking in inspiration, the author decided to treat seriously the comparisons of music to language. From this concept, a computational model for generating music linguistically was constructed. Perceiving musical gestures as grammars seemed natural and more logical then those based in mathematics.

EMI (Experiments in Music Intelligence) was founded (1981) on linguistic principles. Emphasis was and continues to be placed on cognition of musical style. Replication of recognizable examples of various composers' styles represents one form of corroboration of successful perception and is the essence of work at EMI (Cope, 1991).

Commonalties Between Language and Music

That music and language share pitch, rhythm and meter associations seems relatively clear (Chomsky, 1965). Pitch and timbre have literal rather than metaphoric equivalence as do rhythm and meter. Even subtler manifestations such as accent, tempo, etc., have musical/language parallels. These relationships are frequently discussed in relevant literature even if vagueness suggests that the relationships are more implied than explicit (Winograd, 1968; Lerdahl and Jackendoff, 1983; Pelinski, 1986).

It is not at all clear, however, what exists beyond these simple comparisons. Questions continue about how, at a deeper level, musical phrases relate to sentences and the nature of equivalents in music to word representations (musical nouns and verbs). The consequences of making the parallels more explicit and hence powerful are even less clear. Further questions include: 1) Do (should) one perceive music as a language? 2) What would such perception mean for current analytical and compositional models? 3) Would such parallels produce important revelations that non-language based analytical systems miss?

In an attempt to respond to these questions, the author has emphasized hierarchy and abstraction of function. The metaphor to language is particularly useful here. Italian, French and English all have verbs, for example, and protocols for their use have significant similarities. Dictionaries in any two of these languages would, however, be strikingly different to any but those with extensive knowledge of common (i.e. Latin) word roots.

Language Parsing

Figure 1 shows a simple sentence which provides a basis for presenting the traditional concepts of parsing. While prosaic, this kind of statement reveals how language may invite comparisons to music. First, language conforms to a powerful hierarchical model. Some words here are critical to the meaning of the statement while others can be removed without sacrificing intent. While creating poor grammar and loss of nuance (information), the fundamental meaning is not detrimentally influenced. Dropping the word "to," for example, produces "I am driving the country," which, while poor English, conveys almost exactly the same message as does the whole sentence. Leaving out "country," in contrast, removes an essential element. Changing it to "funeral," for example, produces an entirely different meaning. On the other hand, dropping all words except "I country," provokes a general reference to the first statement. "Am the," on the other hand, is virtually meaningless.

"I am driving to the country."

Figure 1

Hierarchical Parsing

A second important concept of language parsing is that of abstracting function from surface detail. Figures 2a and 2b demonstrate the parsing procedures as used in EMI. Here, hierarchy descends (most to least important) with all logical processions of delineated words. Arrows demonstrate logical modifier processions (such as

"I country" and "I driving country."). Subjects followed by verbs and prepositions preceding articles adhere to the basic protocols of English. The sentence flows in word order (left to right). In Figure 2b, however, abstraction replaces words with the various "parts of speech" (functions).

Musical Parallels

Figure 3 presents a simple musical line. Its C-major quality possesses as much information as did the equally simple "I am driving to the country." From Schenkerian layer analysis (Lidov and Gabura, 1973; Schenker, 1933) one can easily obtain the background prolongation of tonic from the first to the last C.

Figure 4 parses Figure 3. Hierarchically, this reduction (only one of the many possible correct extrapolations) has the final C as most important note of the phrase with the incipient C as second in priority. The inclusion of the G at the next stage demonstrates basic consequent motion in tonal music. Subtler observations show how the scale-tones of the first full measure relates to the cadence. This representation is context-driven, with pitch still a constituent part of the analytical process.

EMI Symbology

The symbols used by EMI are called "identifiers." These are OSAC (ornamental, statement, antecedent and consequent in priority order) in three different levels of importance (1–3, least to most significant). In the current incarnation of the program, these numbers represent foreground, middleground and background respectively.

Figure 5 abstracts the pitch content of Figure 4 using identifiers to provide representations of projected musical functions. Here S1 logically precedes A3 and O2 follows S2. The arrows have been retained from the previous example since they still apply. All possible parsings are correct as was the case with the English example. As in language, observing the motion and hierarchy of phrases in a context-free environment corroborates the existence of inherent structure. With little coercion, it seems possible to convert a language model to a musical one.

Augmented Transition Networks (ATN)

Augmented transition networks (ATN) in grammar allow for an increased level of finer detail between context-free and context-driven environments. Using ATN, one can make plural or singular nouns and verbs agree. Tense becomes essential as does location of pronouns and first, second or third person point-of-view. Figure 6 provides a simple parsing (with an ATN extension) of the sentence of Figure 1. By refining speech functions, more local information surfaces. The "noun" subject becomes a first person singular pronoun (and by a process of elimination: "I").

a)

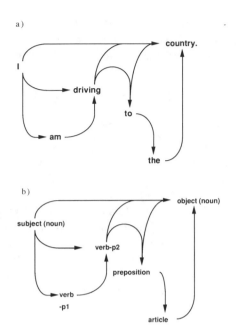

b)

Figure 2. The Parsing Procedures Used in EMI.

Figure 3. A Simple Musical Line.

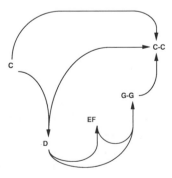

Figure 4. A Parse of Figure 3.

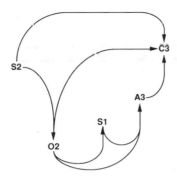

Figure 5. Abstracing the Pitch Content of Figure 4.

Generating New Music

In EMI, a similar form of ATN enhances the refinement of details in a given musical generation as shown in Figure 7. At this point it is important to notice that style depends not on just the immediate circumstance but on consequences of actions quite temporally distant from their formal antecedents. The manner in which a supertonic first-inversion-seventh-chord here forces the use of dominant seventh rather than just dominant is mirrored at more sophisticated levels such as relating cadences of various sections of a work (bottom of Figure 7). Much of what the example generates results from inheritance (top of Figure 7). Conversely, surface detail is framed in a local voice-leading (counterpoint) rules-base. The tonic "I" in the first instance, rather than tonic-six or tonic-six-four, is as inevitable as the "I" in the ATN of Figure 6.

Style Replication

EMI relies on a parser/generator which follows specific protocol routines in the ordering of context-free symbols. At this level, no musical detail exists, only precedence and succession rules. A strictly classical tonal model can be expressed in a straightforward set of conditionals. The actual generation of music follows hierarchical processes whereby each phrase begins as a single symbol (the most important) and incrementally grows by a fleshing out (top-down) of the phrase and motive structure. This process, a separate but related issue and hence not discussed here in depth, is called non-linear composition (Cope, 1980).

EMI then employs dictionaries of local gestures derived from the original works of the composer under study. Explicit meanings are given to each of the symbols previously limited only by order (syntax). This creates an expression or interpretation of the correctly generated symbols and ultimately rough surface detail (seman

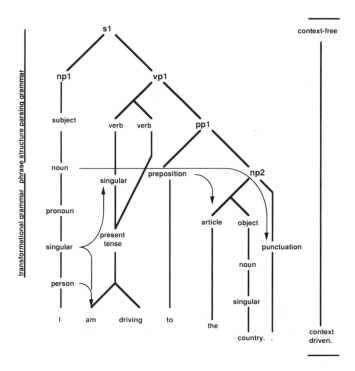

Figure 6. A Simple Parse with an ATN *Exception of the Sentence in Figure 1.*

tics; see Laske, 1973). In the case of a Bach replicator, Baroque qualities of motor-rhythm, part-writing, etc., are factored into the process in order to translate the formal constraints into new musical examples.

Musical Examples

One of the most difficult aspects of computer composition is creating a program capable of composing large-scale forms. A correctly parsed/generated style can plod endlessly onward, sounding right for the moment, but never coming to a proper closure. In EMI, form results from an work-tree with both vertical and horizontal elements equivalent to the context-free abstractions found in the phrase parsings. In fact, the latter represent deductions derived from a single identifier which is then split, as previously discussed. At each level, the rules nested in the protocol of the system, prescribe exactly which identifier can precede and follow another. Each level inherits its logic from the one created before it, embellishes it in a correct manner, and then acts as a base for the next level. Works produced in this manner follow logical routes to end points so that the music does not simply stop—it ends.

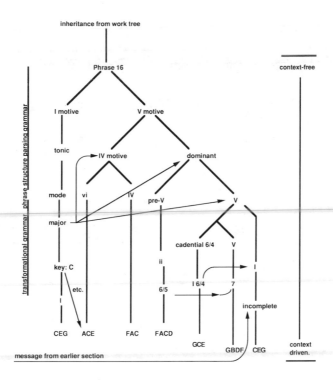

Figure 7. ATN *Enhances the Refinement of Details ina Given Musical Generation.*

It is often necessary to coerce certain aspects of the identifier detail into more focus to ensure that the ultimate surface detail will be stylistically correct (the ATN component). This is accomplished by coercing connections between various identifiers already in place. For example, cadences can be altered with respect to their position in a work. Motives which stylistically represent situations in which a composer might more logically choose another variation or repeat exactly can be ensured. This kind of mid-level communication between elements of the work guarantees that corrections will not have to be made after a surface note has been created (i.e. no backtracking).

The short work in Figure 8 (a Bach-like keyboard invention) exemplifies EMI's approach to machine-composed imitations. As with most of the work at EMI it is for a keyboard instrument performed live rather than using a synthesizer or sampling systems. It is completely machine-composed (no editing) and was the first composition generated after honing the texture and tessitura components. While brief (space limitations) this imitative two-voice piece of counterpoint demonstrates the results of generating larger segments with the refinement of ATN into recognizable sequences, imitations, convincing cadences, hints at the dominant key and occasional variants

Figure 8. Emi's Approach to Machine-Composed Imitation.

Conclusions

At present, the musical language metaphor has produced vague semblances of classical styles at EMI. It has also provided the author and others with a composing partner capable of enhancing the speed of their creative work. On the whole, however, the interface between surface detail and background abstraction remains too remote to say that actual personal styles have been reproduced. Future plans include the refining of the ATN engine to personalize the replication of the creative process and allow, hopefully, more accurate representations of style integrity.

At this point, EMI has taken the metaphor of music as a language seriously and launched a new approach to both analysis and composition. If the assumptions made here and in the cited articles are correct, they may hold valuable import for others in analytical, theoretical, performance and compositional music fields. Music may or may not be the "universal language," but the evidence that it is a language seems substantial.

References

Chomsky, Noam. *Aspects of the Theory of Syntax.* Cambridge, MA: MIT Press, 1965

Cope, David. "Experiments in Musical Intelligence (EMI): Non-Linear Linguistic-Based Composition." *Interface* 18, 1–2 (1989)

Cope, David. *Computers and Musical Style.* Madison, WI: A-R Publications, 1991

Forte, A. "Computer-implemented Analysis of Musical Structure." *Computer Applications in Music,* 1967

Laske, O. "Musical Semantics: A Procedural Point of View." Proceedings of the International Conference on the Semiotics of Music. Belgrade, 1973

Lerdahl, Fred, and Ray Jackendoff. *A Generative Theory of Formal Music.* Cambridge, MA: The MIT Press, 1983

Lidov, D., and J. Gabura. "A Melody Writing Algorithm Using a Formal Language Model." *Computer Studies in the Humanities.* 4(¾): 138–148, 1973

Pelinski, Ramón. "A Generative Grammar of Personal Eskimo Songs." In *Musical Grammars and Computer Analysis.* Edited by M. Baroni e L. Callegari. Firenze (Italy): Societa Italiana de Musicologia, 1986

Schenker, Heinrich. *Five Analyses in Sketchform.* New York: David Mannes School of Music, 1933.

Winograd, T. "Linguistics and the Computer Analysis of Tonal Harmony." *Journal of Music Theory.* 12 (Spring): 2–49, 1968

Section Five

Performance

The competence vs. performance discussion has been the subject of a long-standing debate in linguistics. In musicology, the new, emerging trend of cognitive musicology presents a shift in emphasis, from studies of what can be called competence theories in composition and analysis, to performance theories, both in the traditional areas of composition and analysis, and in newer areas such as improvisation.

This section presents work on two very different topics in this new research direction: A study of improvisational techniques in Indian drum music, and a study of the visual recognition and performance of simple sheet music by a musical robot. The latter study breaks away from traditional musicology and also from most software-based AI and music projects, in the sense that it is a preliminary attempt to literally build a human-like performer and listener.

In B. Bel and J. Kippen's chapter, "Bol Processor Grammars," the authors develop a theory of generative grammars meant to capture the transformations and operations characterizing musical improvisation. This work emerged from a study of Indian drum music. The authors concentrate on the form of "theme and variations" which is fundamental to this music. However, unlike traditional approaches, they are not interested in an abstract theory of the musical form, but in an operational theory of music performance in real time, i.e., in an ethnomusicological theory making explicit the techniques and transformations used by Indian musicians. The authors show that traditional, Chomskian grammars are, indeed, sufficiently expressive to account for the musical form in question (as the languages are all regular), but that they fail to single out the important operations characterizing the generative process by which this music is produced, (i.e., their descriptive power is poor). This insight leads to the development of a theory of generative grammars deriving from the theory of pattern languages, called BP grammars, and to extending that theory by operational notions such as templates, negative contexts, rule weights, and remote contexts, to list just a few. The authors envision that BP grammars can account for musical activities beyond the one they were originally designed for.

The chapter "A New Approach to Music Through Vision," by S. Ohteru and S. Hashimoto, gives us a glimpse of Japanese research on modeling human activities related to music and dance. In this case, the authors have given their computer model a more anthropomorphic appearance. Their chapter describes a musical robot called "Wabot-I" that was built at Waseda University. Equipped with a CCD camera and a speech synthesizer, this robot can read nursery rhyme scores and play them on an electronic keyboard with ten fingers, can recognize and pronounce the names of different types of dance by observing human dancers, and follow the baton of a human conductor directing an ensemble. Moreover, the robot can also automatically transcribe simple sheet music to Braille music notation.

From the vantage point of a general theory of music processing systems, Ohteru and Hashimoto's work can be viewed as the *grounding module* in such systems. So far, it is, indeed, unclear how systems targeted at modeling different stages of music processing can be combined, but this situation in AI and music is no different from the general state of affairs in other domains of AI.

Abstract

Bol Processor grammars are an extension of unrestricted generative grammars allowing a simple representation of string "patterns," here taken to mean repetitions and homomorphic transformations. These have been successfully applied to the simulation of improvisatory techniques in traditional drum music, using a production-rule system called "Bol Processor BP1." The basic concepts and parsing techniques of BP1 are presented.

A new version of Bol Processor, namely "BP2," has been designed to serve as an aid to rule-based composition in contemporary music. Extensions of the syntactic model, such as metavariables, remote contexts, substitutions and programmed grammars, are briefly introduced.

Chapter 15

Bol Processor Grammars

Bernard Bell and Jim Kippen

Although in the field of computer-aided composition considerable time has been devoted to new sound generation techniques, many studies of structural models have been restricted to the analysis of Western staff-notated music. Beyond this domain (particularly in ethnomusicology) there have been early attempts to borrow concepts from linguistics on the basis of assumed parallels between language and traditional musical systems. Some provocative papers, however, resulted in the virtual rejection of purely abstract speculations that Feld had termed "the hollow shell of formalism":

> Only Blacking [...] and Lindblom and Sundberg [...] have dealt explicitly with basic theoretical issues... The rest of the literature ignores issues like the empirical comparison of models, a metatheory of music, evaluation procedures, and the relation of the models to the phenomena they supposedly explain.
>
> *[Feld 1974:210]*

The project which initiated the work presented in this chapter has been an in-depth study of the music of a group of drummers in North India [Kippen 1988]. The oral tradition encountered differed markedly from the few descriptions of improvisational formulae in the limited and often unreliable literature. This meant a shift in focus from purely analytical models (embodying a hypothetical descrip-tion of musicians' competence versus performance) to models of musical perfor-mance. Analytical models attempt to describe structural regularity in a particular musical piece (e.g. [Jackendoff & Lerdahl 1982]) or in a set of related variations. In the first case, the structure that is discovered by the analyst (possibly with the help of a computer) claims to reflect an underlying musical (or perceptive) system which may be called the *competence* of an "ideal listener." In the analysis of variations, a model of the competence of an "ideal musician" is sought. However, both approaches rely on epistemological considerations (borrowed from linguistics) that do not take into account individual "deviations," i.e. models of performance: the originality of a particular musical work or, simply, the creativity of a musician. In this respect, music is more comparable to literature (or poetry) than to language.[1]

Our experimental work[2] on traditional tabla drumming was mainly focussed on computer simulations of improvisation schemata called *qa'ida*.[3] A computer program called Bol Processor (BP1) was implemented on the Apple™ IIc, i.e. the only computer (at the time, 1982–85) portable enough to be taken to locations where the interaction with expert musicians could take place "in context." A detailed description of the BP1's modus operandi may be found in [Kippen & Bel 1989a]. Results and problems arising from the BP methodology have been discussed in [Kippen 1987]. The transfer of knowledge from human informants to machines using automatic rule generation is presented in [Kippen & Bel 1989b-d] and [Bel 1990a].

This chapter is an introduction to the Bol Processor grammatical model. We first demonstrate the scope and limitations of conventional generative grammars on the basis of a simple musical example borrowed from the qa'ida repertoire. In response to these limitations we introduce a rule format for the representation of "string patterns" (repetitions and homomorphic transformations). Then the method for parsing unrestricted BP grammars is outlined, and additional features allowing a control of derivations are shown. In the end we describe the main features of a new version of Bol Processor, namely BP2, meant to be used as a compositional tool dealing with a wider variety of musical systems.

Generative Grammars in Bol Processor BP1

It is assumed that, in some musical systems, elementary musical objects ("atoms") may be transcribed with the aid of a non-empty finite set of symbols Vt, namely the alphabet of terminal symbols. The set of all finite strings over an alphabet A is notated A*. A music sequence may therefore be represented as string belonging to Vt*.[4] Any properly defined subset of Vt* is a *formal language*.

For example, many pieces of tabla music are transliterated with onomatopoeic syllables representing sounds and strokes on the drums, called *bols*.[5] (Using onomatopoeic languages for the transmission and occasionally the performance of traditional drum music is a common practice both in Asia and in Africa.) A terminal alphabet used in many tabla compositional types is for instance

Vt = {tr, kt, dhee, tee, dha, ta, ti, ge, ke, na, ra, -}

in which the hyphen indicates a silence (or the prolongation of a resonant stroke).[6] Symbols "tr" and "kt" are shorthand for "tira" and "kita." In general, any finite set of labels for sound-objects (e.g. notes) may be used as a terminal alphabet for music.

The Scope of Work with the Bol Processor

A number of ethnomusicologists have attempted to use generative grammars to represent sets of "acceptable" variations of a musical theme. The relevance of a concept like "acceptability" should of course be understood in relation to the musical system under study. Players of the tabla themselves claim that there is a precise system underlying "correct" variations although its rules are generally not explicit. The main motivations of our project, therefore, have been (1) to make rules explicit for some compositional types, and (2) to check the consistency of musicians' assessments of correctness both in music teaching and performance situations.

The compositional type most fundamental to an understanding of composition and improvisation in tabla playing is the qa'ida, the "theme and variations" form par excellence. Not only do beginners learn qa'idas, usually with sets of "fixed variations" composed by their teachers (thus providing models of the crucial art of music improvisation), but advanced players use them too, particularly in solo performances, to demonstrate their technical mastery and mental skills. Furthermore, musicians postulate that unless one can improvise on qa'ida themes, one is not adequately equipped to improvise on any of the other theme and variations forms.

The Hierarchy of Generative Grammars and Formal Languages

Throughout this chapter we will refer to Chomsky's hierarchy of generative grammars. A generative grammar is an ordered fourtuple (Vt, Vn, S, F) in which Vt is an alphabet of terminal symbols, Vn an alphabet of variables (with Vt $\cap$ Vn = $\varnothing$), S a distinguished symbol of Vn, and F a finite set of rewriting rules P $\rightarrow$ Q such that P and Q are strings over the alphabet (Vt $\cup$ Vn) and P contains at least one symbol from Vn. We call P and Q the *left* and *right argument* of the rule respectively.

We use the notation $|X|$ to designate the length of a string X. The empty string is notated λ. One of many (equivalent) ways of defining the hierarchy of generative grammars is:

Type 0 (phrase-structure): unrestricted phrase-structure (type-0) grammar

Type 1 (length-increasing or context-sensitive):
$|P| \leq |Q|$ except possibly for the rule S $\rightarrow \lambda$

Type 2 (context-free): $|P| = 1$ and $|P| \leq |Q|$ except possibly for the rule S $\rightarrow \lambda$

Type 3 (regular or finite-state): every rule has form either X $\rightarrow$ a Y or Z $\rightarrow$ b, where X, Y, and Z are variables and a and b terminal symbols.

Every type n grammar generates a formal language of type n', for some n' $\geq$ n. This yields a proper hierarchy of language classes [Révész 1985:7]. For instance, it can be proved that every finite language is regular, hence context-free, etc., so that it may be generated by a grammar of any type.

Throughout this chapter small letters are used for terminal symbols, and variables start with a capital letter.

Context-Free Grammars for Qa'idas

As a result of some basic observations about the structure of qa'idas—the regular alternation of fixed and variable sections, and the predominance of permutation

dha ti dha ge	na dha tr kt	dha ti dha ge	dhee na ge na
dha tr kt dha	ti dha ge na	dha ti dha ge	tee na ke na
ta ti ta ke	na ta tr kt	ta ti ta ke	tee na ke na
dha tr kt dha	ti dha ge na	dha ti dha ge	dhee na ge na

Figure 1. The Theme of a Qa'ida.

and substitution as improvisatory devices—it was thought that formal language models would be suited to the construction of grammatical models.

Figure 1 is an example of variation on a well-known qa'ida theme. A theme may itself be viewed as one particular variation—here in Figure 1 the kernel of the theme is represented in the first line with a variation of it in the second. It should be read from left to right as plain text. The durations of all syllables (including "tr" or "kt" as composites) are identical. Syllables are grouped into beats, therefore we may say that this piece has a *stroke density* of four strokes per beat. Since each line contains four beats, the total metric duration of the piece is sixteen beats (anything from eight to twelve seconds in performance depending on interpretation).

Some strokes on the tabla have a voiced (resonating) and an unvoiced (dampened) version. Here, the cadential string "dha ti dha ge dhee na ge na" is repeated at the end of each line in its voiced as well as partly-voiced ("dha ti dha ge tee na ke na") and fully-unvoiced ("ta ti ta ke tee na ke na") transformations. The complete mapping of voiced to unvoiced strokes in this qa'ida will be shown in Figure 7.

The piece in Figure 1 belongs to a set of acceptable variations that may be very large although it is certainly finite since all pieces are bound by the metric cycles, i.e. a duration of sixteen or thirty-two beats. A complex variation is given in the section Parsing a Variation. However, let us for a while consider only the first lines of a subset of ten simple variations.

dha tr kt dha	tr kt dha ge	dha ti dha ge	dhee na ge na
dha tr kt dha	tr kt dha dha	dha ti dha ge	dhee na ge na
dha ti dha tr	kt dha tr kt	dha ti dha ge	dhee na ge na
dha tr kt dha	ti - dha ti	dha ti dha ge	dhee na ge na
dha tr kt dha	ti dha tr kt	dha ti dha ge	dhee na ge na
ti - dha ti	dha dha tr kt	dha ti dha ge	dhee na ge na
ti dha tr kt	dha dha tr kt	dha ti dha ge	dhee na ge na
tr kt dha ti	dha dha tr kt	dha ti dha ge	dhee na ge na
tr kt tr kt	dha dha tr kt	dha ti dha ge	dhee na ge na
tr kt dha tr	kt dha ge na	dha ti dha ge	dhee na ge na

Figure 2. The First Lines of 10 Variations of the Qa'ida.

Figure 3. Basic Transitions in a Finite Acceptor.

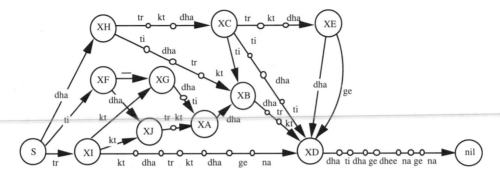

Figure 4. A Finite Acceptor for the Language Shown in Figure 2.

This set can easily be described using a regular/finite-state (type-3) grammar. A regular grammar can be represented as a *finite acceptor*, i.e. a directed graph in which X, Y, and Z are state labels, and a and b transition labels (see Figure 3). Using a rule X → a Y to rewrite "X" as "a Y" is equivalent to jumping from state X to state Y following the transition labelled a. The second type of rule, Z → b, is represented as a transition from state Z to an accepting state nil (see Figure 3).[7]

The state from which all paths originate is labelled S, the initial symbol in the grammar. To analyze a string, each of its component symbols (from left to right) is used as a "road sign." The string is grammatically correct if it is possible to move from S to an accepting state following all the road signs. For example, a finite-state acceptor recognizing exactly the ten examples given in Figure 2 could be the one shown in Figure 4.

The purpose of this representation is twofold: (1) it serves as a "classifier" telling whether or not a given string belongs to the set of original examples in Figure 2, and (2) it can be used to generate any string belonging to the set. However, it is not unique and its musical relevance will even be questioned in the section Generalizing Grammars. To simplify the representation, only those states which are (diverging or converging) nodes of the graph have been labelled. Other states appear as small circles. This suggests an alternate equivalent representation using a "two-layer acceptor" as in Figure 5. This new acceptor is equivalent to the generative grammar of Figure 6. The mapping of transitions to grammar rules is self-explanatory.

Some variable labels have numbers indicating the metrical values of terminal strings which are derived therefrom. Thus, "TA7" denotes a string of seven strokes. Although this information is not used by the Bol Processor, it facilitates checks of the grammar when variations are of fixed length, here for instance the sum of met-

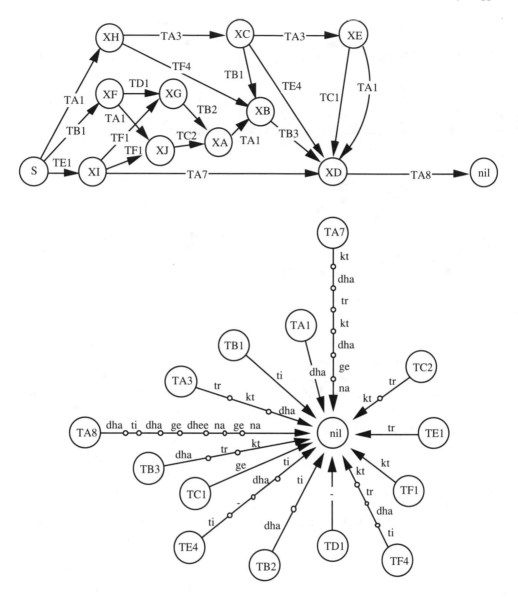

Figure 5. An Equivalent "Two-Layer Finite Acceptor."

rical values along each path of the upper acceptor is 16 (meaning four beats in stroke density 4).

This grammar is context-free (type-2) grammar although it generates a finite (type-3) language. Rules shown on the right side of Figure 6 are called *lexical rules*. Their right arguments are chunks of strokes that have been repeated several times in the examples of Figure 2, presumably "words" of the language

S	→	TE1 XI	TA7→kt dha tr kt dha ge na		
XI	→	TA7 XD	TC2	→	tr kt
XD	→	TA8	TE1	→	tr
XI	→	TF1 XJ	TF1	→	kt
XJ	→	TC2 XA	TF4	→	ti dha tr kt
XA	→	TA1 XB	TD1	→	-
XB	→	TB3 XD	TB2	→	dha ti
XI	→	TF1 XG	TE4	→	ti - dha ti
XG	→	TB2 XA	TC1	→	ge
S	→	TA1 XH	TB3	→	dha tr kt
XH	→	TF4 XB	TA8	→	dha ti dha ge dhee na ge na
XH	→	TA3 XC	TA3	→	tr kt dha
XC	→	TE4 XD	TB1	→	ti
XC	→	TA3 XE	TA1	→	dha
XE	→	TA1 XD			
XE	→	TC1 XD			
XC	→	TB1 XB			
S	→	TB1 XF			
XF	→	TA1 XJ			
XF	→	TD1 XG			

Figure 6. A Grammar Equivalent to the Two-Layer Acceptor.

although they do not bear any semantic value.

The music segmentation of musical pieces into "significant chunks" has been discussed in great detail by musicologists, e.g. Ruwet [1972] and Nattiez [1976]. In brief, lexical rules define the vocabulary of the piece as presumably perceived by musicians, a task that requires some presupposed knowledge about what is "meaningful" and what is not [Kippen & Bel 1989b:203]. In fact, the vocabulary displayed by the grammar in Figure 6 was not assessed as correct, therefore another grammar was constructed on the basis of musicians' comments that eventually yielded a correct segmentation of the variations. (See [Kippen & Bel 1989b:210]).

A context-free grammar in the format of Figure 6 may be viewed as a combination of two "transformational subgrammars" corresponding to the two automata shown in Figure 5. The term "transformational" is borrowed from formal language theory [Kain 1981:24], not linguistics. To generate a variation, the first subgrammar (rules on the left side) is used until no further derivation is possible, for instance:

S
TE1 XI
TE1 TA7 XD
TE1 TA7 TA8

Then rules of the second subgrammar (right side of Figure 6) are applied in an arbitrary order:

TE1 TA7 TA8
TE1 kt dha tr kt dha ge na TA8
tr kt dha tr kt dha ge na TA8
tr kt dha tr kt dha ge na dha ti dha ge dhee na ge na

The module that takes care of (enumeratively or randomly) selecting rules in order to generate variations is part of the inference engine of the Bol Processor. The other part of the inference engine is the parsing module that will be described in the section Parsing Variations with BP Grammars.

Generalizing Grammars

Despite some musicians' claims that they follow systematic procedures in constructing sets of variations, it is difficult to discover what that system may be as they rarely create more than six to eight variations in any given situation. Furthermore, few players are able or willing to describe in words what procedures they follow, and even then we have observed that there is a considerable discrepancy between what is said and what is actually done.

Therefore, the main problem in formalizing improvisation schemata as found in qa'ida is the inference of a grammar recognizing large sets of correct variations on the basis of a small set of typical examples. This problem belongs to *structural pattern*[8] *recognition* (see for instance [Fu 1982], [Miclet 1984]), where a pattern classifier is inferred from a relatively small set of training examples. The classifier is expected to assign correct class numbers to a (possibly infinite) number of new patterns. Finite acceptors (equivalently, regular grammars) are sorts of string classifiers working with only two classes: "acceptable" and "unacceptable."[9] In addition, they can also generate any string belonging to the "acceptable" class.

Given a sample set of correct and incorrect variations, i.e. positive and negative instances of the language, a learner (human or mechanical) should be able to construct a grammar that eventually accepts/generates all possible correct variations and rejects the incorrect ones. We can imagine that this learning process is strictly incremental: each time a new (positive or negative) instance is supplied, the learner is expected to adjust the currently guessed grammar accordingly. This inference process belongs to inductive generalization because the new grammar may become smart enough to recognize/generate variations that have not yet been supplied as examples.[10]

Take for instance the finite acceptor of Figure 4 and suppose that the eleventh example supplied by the musician were:

ti dha dha ti   dha dha tr kt   dha ti dha ge   dhee na ge na

A new acceptor recognizing this example could be obtained by merging states XJ and XG. This would yield an acceptor recognizing/generating one more variation that has not yet been assessed by the musician:

ti - tr kt   dha dha tr kt   dha ti dha ge   dhee na ge na

If this variation is incorrect, then other inferences may be tried, for example constructing a path of two transitions labelled "dha" and "ti" connecting XJ to XA.

Any inference, therefore, requires an assessment of newly generated variations. When training a pattern classifier, negative instances are supplied so that incorrect inferences may eventually be detected. In music teaching or performance situations this is generally not the case. Therefore the validity of generalizations is assessed by instructing the Bol Processor to generate variations that are submitted to informants: any variation which they reject is then considered as a negative instance.

Implications of the Generalization Technique on the Grammatical Model

Regular grammars (equivalently, finite acceptors) have been used extensively in syntactic pattern recognition. (See for instance [Fu 1982].) A major reason is that there exist relatively efficient inductive inference methods for the identification of regular (type-3) languages. *Identification in the limit* means that, once a finite number of positive and negative instances of an unknown language have been supplied to the learner, the currently guessed grammar no longer requires modification, and this grammar recognizes exactly the target language.[11] Gold's theorem [1967] says that (1) any enumerable class of decidable languages (see Parsing Variations with BP Grammars) can be identified in the limit using positive and negative instances of the language, and (2) no class of formal languages containing all finite languages and at least one infinite language may be identified in the limit using exclusively positive instances.

An implication of Gold's theorem is that there is little scope for identifying languages in the absence of negative instances. Angluin {1980a] has given useful characteristic properties of languages that can be identified from exclusively positive sample sets.

An algorithm for inferring context-free grammars (in the format shown in Context-Free Grammars for Qa'idas) has been designed [Bel 1990a] and successfully tried in support to the analytical work with the Bol Processor. (See the QAVAID[12] system in [Kippen & Bel 1989b]) This approach provides interesting results insofar as variations may be considered sequences of words taken from an unknown vocabulary: the algorithm yields the vocabulary and a grammar determining the segmentation and deep structure of any variation.

There are human limits as to the number of examples that can be supplied to the machine, let alone problems of time/space complexity in the grammatical inferencer. Therefore, even though the identification of finite languages like qa'ida could be performed mechanically, part of the generalization process is still left to human experts for the sake of heuristic efficiency. In the absence of a music theory able to account formally for the scores of several hundreds of qa'idas performed by a group of musicians, the major part of the work is being accomplished by a human analyst.

This has obvious implications for the grammatical model used for representing music. It is difficult, for instance, to reconcile one's musical intuitions with a context-free grammar in the restrictive format shown in Context-Free Grammars for Qa'idas, all the more so if the number of rules is bound to exceed a few hundred. This reflects an obvious discrepancy between machine- and human-oriented representations.

For this reason, we developed a grammatical model that is general and inclusive of representations aimed at limiting the number of rules needed to account for significant musical ideas. Only now that many qa'idas have been identified could we envisage looking for a unified restrictive grammar format encompassing this whole musical system. Meanwhile, Bol Processor BP1 supports generative grammars in unrestricted (type-0) format. It is the task of the analyst to stick to rule formats enabling the machine to generate and recognize the same language. As indicated in Parsing Variations with BP Grammars, parsing variations is generally not possible with arbitrary grammar formats.

Pattern Rules in BP Grammars

So far we have dealt only with permutations of "words." In order to find an appropriate representation of periodic structures (systematic repetitions, etc.) we developed the idea of pattern rules.

We call a *string pattern* any element of $(V_n \cup V_t)^*$, i.e. a string containing variables and terminal symbols. Every variable in a string pattern may in turn be replaced with another arbitrary string pattern. Replacing all occurrences of a variable with the same non-empty string is called a *substitution*.

Consider for example the alphabets

Vt = {a, b, c, d, ..., z} Vn = {A, B, C, ..., Z}

and a string pattern "A a b A B c B." Substitutions of this pattern may be:

A a b A B c B	Original string pattern
C e C a b C e C c d c c d	Substitute "A" with "C e C" and "B" with "c d."
f g h e f g h a b f g h e f g h c d c c d	Substitute "C" with "f g h."
etc...	

If p is a string pattern and s a substitution, then s(p) is a *derivation* of p. A string pattern containing no variable is called a *terminal derivation*. The set of all terminal derivations of p is called the *pattern language* generated by p [Angluin 1980b].

We felt it would be interesting to combine the representational power of pattern languages (in terms of periodicity) with the versatility of generative grammars. Generative grammars are rather counterintuitive for the representation of string-patterns.[13] Consider for instance the following grammar (proposed by [Salomaa 1973:12]) generating the language derived from string pattern "X X" over terminal alphabet Vt = {a,b}.

```
S        → A B C
A B      → a A D
A B      → b A E
D a      → a D
D b      → b D
E a      → a E
E b      → b E
D C      → B a C
E C      → B b C
a B      → B a
b B      → B b
A B      → λ
C        → λ
```

This grammar is non-restricted (type-0). In addition, most derivations of the starting symbol "S" halt on a string that still contains variables; therefore it is difficult to control the generative process so that only terminal strings are produced.

To overcome these limitations we developed an extension of the rule format that we call *pattern rules* [Bel 1990c:41-43]. Informally, a pattern rule generating the "X X" pattern language (on any terminal alphabet) would be the following:

S → (= X) (: X)

in which brackets indicate that all derivations of the occurrences of "X" must be identical. The leftmost expression "(= X)" is the reference and "(: X)" its copy. We call brackets containing "=" or ":" pattern delimiters. There may be several copies of the same reference, e.g.:

S → (= A) (= B) (: A) (: B) (: A)

Repetitions may not always be strict. In many musical systems a number of transformations affecting terminal symbols have been proposed. In Context-Free Grammars for Qa'idas, for instance, we suggested that strokes on the tabla may be either voiced or unvoiced. Figure 7 shows the mapping of the corresponding voiced/unvoiced transformation, which stands for all qa'idas using these strokes.

This mapping may be extended to any string over the terminal alphabet Vt (yielding a λ-free homomorphism, see [Révész 1985:10]). For instance, the unvoiced image of "dha ge na" is "ta ke na." To indicate a homomorphic transformation we insert a special symbol (a *homomorphic marker*) before the pattern delimiter, indicating the part of the string in which the transformation must be performed. The marker used for the voiced/unvoiced transformation is an asterisk. For instance, the grammar

S → (= D) * (: D)
D → dha ge dhee na ge na

yields the terminal derivation

(= dha ge dhee na ge na) * (: ta ke tee na ke na)

which is internally represented with the help of a master-slave assignment pointer (See Figure 8).

This internal representation is economical in terms of memory space. The algo-

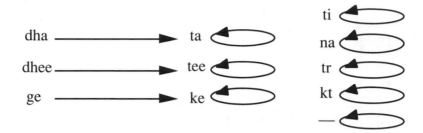

Figure 7. A "Voiced/Unvoiced" Mapping in Tabla Music.

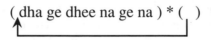

Figure 8. Master-Slave Assignment Pointer.

rithm for rewriting assignment pointers in string patterns is presented in [Bel 1990c:43–45]. It applies to multilayered representations as well.

The variation given in Figure 1 may be represented as:

(= dha ti dha ge	na dha tr kt	dha ti dha ge	dhee na ge na)
(= dha tr kt dha	ti dha ge na)	(= dha ti dha ge	tee na ke na)
* (: ta ti ta ke	na ta tr kt	ta ti ta ke	tee na ke na)
(: dha tr kt dha	ti dha ge na)	(= dha ti dha ge	dhee na ge na)

This variation is produced by the grammar shown in Figure 9, using rules 1, 4, 7, 8, etc.

Rules defining V8, V16 and V24 may be context-free as shown in Context-Free Grammars for Qa'idas. An elaborated version of the grammar of this qa'ida is given in the section A BP1 Grammar for a Qa'ida.

We call a Bol Processor grammar any type-0 grammar containing pattern rules.

Parsing Variations with BP Grammars

When designing Bol Processor BP1 we wanted a machine that could not only gener-ate variations which would be submitted to musicians, but also one that could evalu-ate musical pieces proposed by musicians as correct examples. In this process (called a *membership test*), the inference engine verifies that a given variation is well-formed according to the rules of the grammar. The membership test is performed by the *parsing module* of the inference engine. Only when a grammar agrees with the expert after both generating and parsing variations can one then suggest that it reflects the musician's knowledge of the "language."

[1] S	→	(=A16) (=V8) A'8 *(:A16) (:V8) A8
[2] S	→	(=V16) A'16 *(:V16) A16
[3] S	→	(−V24) A'8 *(:V24) A8
[4] A16	→	dha ti dha ge na dha tr kt dha ti dha ge dhee na ge na
[5] A'16	→	dha ti dha ge na dha tr kt dha ti dha ge tee na ke na
[6] A8	→	dha ti dha ge dhee na ge na
[7] A'8	→	dha ti dha ge tee na ke na
[8] V8	→	... define permutations of eight strokes
[9] V16	→	... define permutations of sixteen strokes
etc...		

Figure 9. A Grammar with Three Pattern Rules.

One of the major reasons why the BP could be used successfully for modelling part of the musical behavior of traditional musicians was its ability to display compositional and analytical processes in two different ways. Information on how correct variations can be composed is generally supplied higgledy-piggledy. This fits well with a grammatical representation in which the order of rules is arbitrary. On the other hand, if a musician/musicologist is prompted to describe how a variation is analyzed, he/she is likely to come up with an ordered set of instructions such as:

> In the analytical process, the first significant chunks to be recognized are those appearing in fixed positions (e.g. the cadential part "dha ti dha ge dhee na ge na," see Context-Free Grammars for Qa'idas). Then variable parts are analyzed. Large chunks or "words" are recognized first.

This type of description indicates a human preference for a data-driven (i.e. bottom-up) procedure that starts from the string under analysis and rewrites it until a "success/failure" flag is obtained (see Parsing a Variation).

The main problem with the membership test arises when there is disagreement between a human expert and the machine regarding the acceptability of a varia tion. Usually the variation is a correct one, and yet the machine rejects it thereby pointing to a defect in the grammar. In order to understand why the variation has been rejected, the analyst should be able to repeat the procedure step by step. This may lead to a clue provided that the trace reflects an intuitive analytical process. (See, for example, Parsing a Variation.) For instance, tracing a parsing procedure is difficult if the procedure is non-deterministic, i.e. if it backtracks on failures. Therefore we opted for a deterministic parsing procedure.

Another problem is purely theoretical. The class of languages for which there exist membership tests (i.e. decidable languages) contains the class of context-sensitive (type-1) languages, but there are also unrestricted (type-0) languages that are undecidable. In addition, membership tests for classes of languages properly containing the class of context-free (type-2) languages often lead to inefficient parsing procedures. (See [Loeckx 1970], [Révész 1970].) The design of an efficient procedure, therefore, implies restrictions on the grammar format.[14]

BP1 Parsing Procedure

The procedure which we implemented in Bol Processor BP1 is data-driven, deterministic, and quite efficient in terms of time/space complexity.[15] Informally, the algorithm is the following:

1) If G is a transformational grammar, its dual is obtained by swapping the left and right argument in every rule.

2) Given G_1, ..., G_n, the subgrammars of the language, and their respective duals G'_1, ..., G'_n, the membership test is the result of the context-sensitive canonic rightmost derivation of the string under analysis by G'_n, ..., G'_1 in this order.

3) If the membership test has yielded S, the starting symbol, the input string is "accepted." It is rejected in any other case.

Informally, the grammar is turned "upside down" and rules in each subgrammar are applied in reverse. If for instance a string "dha tr kt dha ti dha ge na" is generated using the subgrammar

(1) V3	→ dha ge na
(2) V2	→ tr kt
(3) V1	→ dha

then during its analysis by BP1 the dual subgrammar

(1') dha ge na	→ V3
(2') tr kt	→ V2
(3') dha	→ V1

should be used. This introduces ambiguity because, if rule (3') is used first, then the string is rewritten "V1 tr kt V1 ti V1 ge na" so that no further rule is applicable. Indeed this goes against the intuitive reasoning that suggests "large chunks should be recognized first." Therefore the parsing procedure is expected to impose a (partial) ordering of rules and set preferences for the position of derivations. This is accomplished by the canonic rightmost derivation.

Canonic Rightmost Derivation

The concept of context-sensitive canonic (leftmost) derivation was defined by Hart [1980:82] for strictly *context-sensitive* (type-1) *grammars*, i.e. grammars in which all the left arguments of rules contain no more than one variable. We first extended

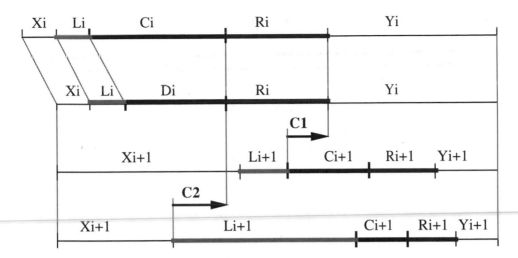

Figure 10. Context-Sensitive Rightmost Derivation.
Suppose that neither conditions C1 nor C2 are satisfied. Since C2 is not true, rule f_{i+1} could have been applied before f_i as $L_{i+1}C_{i+1}R_{i+1}$ would be a substring of R_iY_i. Besides, since C1 is not true, applying rule f_{i+1} would only modify Y_i without changing the context R_i. In such a case the order of application of f_i and f_{i+1} might have been inverted. This change in the order would have been justified since all symbols rewritten by f_{i+1} are to the right of those rewritten by f_i.

---

[1] (=...............) (=.........).........*(:...............) (:.........).........
[2] (=...............).................*(:...............).................
[3] (=.......................).........*(:............................).........

Figure 11. Templates.

this definition to all length-increasing (type-1) grammars. Then we adapted it to the dual grammars in which rules are always length-decreasing, i.e. their right arguments are shorter than their left ones.

Let W_i be the string under derivation after the i-th derivation step. (Each step corresponds to the application of a rule of the grammar.) The context-sensitive rule used for the i-th derivation may be written

$$L_iC_iR_i \rightarrow L_iD_iR_i$$

in which L_i and R_i are the left and right contexts respectively. C_i is the part of the string W_i that will be rewritten as D_i. Since the rule is length-decreasing, $|D_i| \leq |C_i|$.

Context-Sensitive Rightmost Derivation. Let G be a length-decreasing grammar. The derivation in G:

$$W_0 \Rightarrow W_1 \Rightarrow \dots \Rightarrow W_n$$

is context-sensitive rightmost iff:

$\forall i \in [0, n\text{-}1], W_i = X_i L_i C_i R_i Y_i$,
$W_{i+1} = X_i L_i D_i R_i Y_i$ after having applied rule $f_i: L_i C_i R_i \rightarrow L_i D_i R_i$,
the next rule to be applied will be $f_{i+1}: L_{i+1} C_{i+1} R_{i+1} \rightarrow L_{i+1} D_{i+1} R_{i+1}$
        such that $W_{i+1} = X_{i+1} L_{i+1} D_{i+1} R_{i+1} Y_{i+1}$,

and at least one of the two following conditions is satisfied:

(C1) $|C_{i+1} R_{i+1} Y_{i+1}| > |Y_i|$
(C2) $|L_{i+1} C_{i+1} R_{i+1} Y_{i+1}| > |R_i Y_i|$

The diagram and commentary of Figure 10 illustrate conditions C1 and C2. This derivation is *canonic* because if C1 or C2 is satisfied for all derivations then the possible choice of every f_i was unique.

An indication of how the context-sensitive rightmost derivation is used to handle ambiguity in the parsing procedure is given below. Let W_i be the string under derivation. Candidate rules are those whose left arguments[16] are substrings of W_i. Consider two candidate rules:

f_i $L_i C_i R_1 \rightarrow L_i D_i R_i$
f'_i $L'_i C'_i R'_i \rightarrow L'_i D'_i R'_i$
        given $X_i L_i C_i R_i Y_i = X'_i L'_i C'_i R'_i Y'_i = W_i$

The selection criterion is: f_i will have priority over f'_i if one of the following conditions (in this order) is satisfied:

(D1) $|X_i L_i C_i| > |X'_i L'_i C'_i|$
(D2) $|X_i L_i C_i R_i| > |X'_i L'_i C'_i R'_i|$
(D3) $|L_i C_i R_i| > |L'_i C'_i R'_i|$
(D4) $i > i'$

It can be proved that, if D1 is not satisfied (i.e. $|X_i L_i C_i| = |X'_i L'_i C'_i|$), D2 is no longer relevant and the ambiguity between f_i and f'_i may therefore be handled by D3 and D4 [Bel 1987a:8]. D3 makes a decision on the basis of the length of the left arguments of the two rules, and D4 is a final arbitrary decision that takes into account the order in which the rules appear in the grammar. In the BP membership test, rules are tried from the bottom to the top of the grammar.

To save computation time, D3 is not evaluated by the inference engine, so that the following partial ordering of rules is imposed on the grammar:

"Chunk" Rule. In a BP subgrammar, the right argument of rule f_i may not be a substring of the right argument of f_j such that $j < i$. This conforms to the intuitive statement that "large chunks should be recognized first." Rules in the subgrammar shown in Context-Free Grammars for Qa'idas should therefore be arranged in either way:

(1) V1 $\rightarrow$ dha   (1) V1 $\rightarrow$ dha   (1) V2 $\rightarrow$ tr kt
(2) V3 $\rightarrow$ dha ge na   (2) V2 $\rightarrow$ tr kt   (2) V1 $\rightarrow$ dha

(3) V2 → tr kt   (3) V3 → dha ge na   (3) V3 → dha ge na

In a practical implementation, this partial ordering of rules may be computed by the machine when exiting the rule editor.

Templates

Variations can only be parsed when represented along with their pattern delimiters, homomorphic markers, etc. However, the Bol Processor is meant to perform membership tests on large amounts of data comprising examples to which it is not always easy to assign a structure, as for instance the variation analyzed in Parsing a Variation. Understandably, one could expect the machine to complete the missing information on the basis of structural knowledge contained in pattern rules of the grammar. To this effect, the inference engine of the Bol Processor has been given the ability to generate *templates* from a grammar, i.e. a list of possible structures in which dots are used to represent the locations of imaginary unitary terminal symbols. For instance, the templates generated by the first three rules of the grammar in Figure 9 are shown in Figure 11. It may be noticed that each template contains exactly sixty-four dots since all variations have a metric duration of sixteen beats in stroke density 4.

Templates are stored along with the grammar file. When analyzing a variation the Bol Processor attempts to superimpose it on each template in turn. The membership test is tried whenever the variation matches a template (See Parsing a Variation). Several templates may lead to successful membership tests, thereby pointing at structural ambiguity.

Controlling the Generation Process

We present a few additional features of Bol Processor grammars that were introduced to help the musicologist formalize certain musical ideas in a straightforward and intuitive manner. These are meant to control the selection of candidate rules in generation, although this selection is also taken into consideration by the parsing module. Other features allowing a control of the position of derivation have been discussed at length in [Kippen & Bel 1989a].

Negative Context

Negative context is a practical way of writing a rule when all but one variable/terminal symbol are allowed as context. See for instance rule [28] in subgrammar 5 in A BP1 Grammar for a Qa'ida:

[28] #tt V V V V → #tt tt dha tr kt

This rule means that "V V V V" may be rewritten as "ti dha tr kt" only if it is not preceded by "ti." This reflects the idea that it is not acceptable to duplicate "ti" in a sequence (both for technical and aesthetic reasons). Procedures for matching and rewriting expressions with (possibly several) negative context(s) are described in detail in [Bel 1990c:55–60].

Wild Cards

Wild cards are metavariables notated "?" in BP syntax. These are used by the inference engine when it looks for candidate rules in the generation or parsing process. A wild card may be matched with any variable or terminal symbol. In subgrammar 6 in A BP1 Grammar for a Qa'ida, wild cards are used to define the locations of "fixed chunks."

Special Structural Symbols

Special symbols like "+" and ";" are used as position markers in variations. For instance, in the grammar in A BP1 Grammar for a Qa'ida, ";" indicates the end of a variation while "+" is the end of a line of four beats. These symbols are used as contexts for controlling the selection of candidate rules, see for instance subgrammar 3. Special symbols also appear in templates. It may be noticed that templates [16] and [20] are identical except that [16] contains a "+" marker after forty-eight dots, i.e. at the end of the third line of the variation. (Each line represents four beats of the metric cycle, see Context-Free Grammars for Qa'idas.) When parsing a variation, therefore, template [16] assumes that the thirteenth beat should fall on the beginning of a word, which is not the case with template [20].

Stochastic Production

Since the actual sets of correct variations of a qa'ida are very large, the only realistic way of checking the generative precision of a grammar is to instruct the Bol Processor to produce randomly chosen variations. If the variation is assessed as correct by the expert, the procedure is invoked again and another variation (sometimes the same one) is generated. The grammar is considered "correct" if it has been in full agreement with the expert over a sufficient number of work sessions.

Since the correctness of a grammar can never be fully assessed in this way—indeed, like musicians themselves, machines may be allowed casual mistakes—it is important to enable the stochastic production process to generate variations from a wide and representative subset of the language. This can be achieved by weighting the decisions of the inference engine. Weights (and their associated probabilities) are used to direct the Bol Processor's production along paths more likely to be followed by musicians. The use of weighted rules resulted in a marked improvement in the quality of the generated music. This went a long way towards solving the problem of musical credibility encountered in earlier experiments with BP1, a problem that arose from the complete randomness of the generative process.

The stochastic model in Bol Processor is inspired from probabilistic grammars/automata [Booth & Thompson 1973], the difference being that a weight rather than a probability is attached to every rule. The probability of a rule is computed each time it is a candidate in a generation process. (Candidate rules are those whose left argument matches a substring of the string under derivation.) Before any derivation, the inference engine calculates the sum W of weights of all candidate rules. If the weight of a candidate rule is 0 then its probability remains 0; in any other case its probability is the ratio of its weight to the sum W. Consider for example the set of rules

[1]	<100>	V3	→	dhagena
[2]	<100>	V3	→	dhatrkt
[3]	<50>	V3	→	dha—
[4]	<5>	V3	→	dhati-

in which the sum of weights is W = 100+100+50+5 = 255. The probability of choosing candidate rule [4] in the derivation of a string containing "V3" is therefore $\frac{5}{255}$ =0.0196

In some context-free grammars—those that fulfill a "consistency" condition defined by Booth & Thompson [1973:442–447]—weights may also be used for computing the probability of occurrence of each variation generated by the grammar. Grammars in the format shown in Figure 6 are consistent for any weight assignment. This probability is displayed by Bol Processor BP1 for each variation which has been generated or parsed, thereby yielding a graduation of its acceptability. Another remarkable feature of consistent grammars is that rule probabilities can be inferred from a subset of the language [Maryanski & Booth 1977:525]. This leads to an interesting method for weighting the rules—even in inconsistent grammars as demonstrated in [Kippen & Bel 1989a] with the qa'ida such as in A BP1 Grammar for a Qa'ida. The method is the following: a grammar is given along with a sample set of the language that it recognizes (for instance variations taken from a performance of an expert musician). Let all rule weights be set to 0; then analyze every variation of the sample set, incrementing by one unit the weights of all rules used in the parse.[17] Rules that have not been used in the parse of the sample set may then be scrutinized to check whether they are incorrect or whether they point to unexplored parts of the language. To this effect, their weights are set to a high value so that the Bol Processor is likely to select them and generate variations that may then be assessed.

Bol Processor BP2

We now introduce the syntactic model of the new version of Bol Processor (BP2).[18] Other important features, such as polymetric structures and the representation of sound objects, are presented in another chapter of this volume

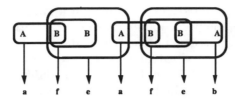

Figure 12. A Context-Sensitive Substitution.

Since BP2 is meant to be part of a computer environment for rule-based composition, the grammar format has been (and is still being) extended on the basis of requests formulated by composers. These may be based on well-defined compositional ideas, or simply exploratory.

Under such conditions, the correctness of a grammar is assessed exclusively on the basis of the music it generates. The composer may instruct the machine to generate many variations and then select those he/she wants to keep. Selected items may even be edited further using a music sequencer. Only in improvisational situations is a grammar expected to generate only "good" variations. For this reason we did not feel it necessary to implement a parsing module in BP2. This allows the user complete freedom as to the grammar format that will best reflect his/her intuitions, even if the grammar is undecidable.

Metavariables

Metavariables are a set of ordered tokens notated "?1," "?2," etc. Each may match a variable or a terminal symbol. If a rule like

   ?1 ?1 ?2 ?3   → ?1 ?3 ?2 ?1

is applied, BP2 scans the string under derivation looking for a sequence of four variables or terminal symbols in which the first two occurrences are identical, e.g. "A A B C"; it then rewrites it swapping the second and fourth occurrences, i.e. "A C B A." Metavariables are local to the rule in which they appear. A typical application is proposed in the section A BP2 Grammar.

Remote Context

Formal (e.g. Chomsky-type) grammars make it difficult (although theoretically possible) to control productions on the basis of a "remote context," i.e. the occurrence of a string located anywhere to the left or right side of the derivation position. Therefore a special syntax of remote contexts is available in BP2.

Remote contexts are represented between ordinary brackets in the left argument of a rule.[19] For instance, a rule like (a b c) X Y (c d) → X e f

means that "X Y" may be rewritten as "X e f" only if "a b c" is found somewhere before "X Y" in the string under derivation, and "c d" somewhere after "X Y." Note that "X" itself is a left context in the sense of conventional generative grammars.

A remote context may contain any string in BP syntax, including string patterns and metavariables. (See, for instance, A BP2 Grammar). It may also be negative. For instance,

#(a b c) X → c d e

means that "X" may be rewritten as "c d e" only if not preceded by "a b c" in the string under derivation.

Context-Sensitive Substitutions

Substitutions may be viewed as a "parallel rewriting" of the string under derivation: in a single step, each symbol of the string is replaced with another string of symbols (defined by a rule). All occurrences of the same symbol are replaced likewise. *Constant-length substitutions*, in which all replacement strings have identical lengths, yield (infinite) sequences whose structure is intermediary between periodicity and chaos [Allouche 1987]. This property is useful for the design of rhythmic structures, as shown by Allouche & Mouret [1988]. A less restrictive formalism that we call "context-sensitive substitution" has been implemented in BP2. Substitution rules can also be weighted, use remote contexts, etc.

For instance, the substitution grammar

Substitution		
S	→	A B B A B B A
A B	→	a B
B A	→	B b
A A	→	c c
A B A	→	A d A
B B A	→	B e A
B B	→	f B

produces "a f e a f e b" in two derivation steps. The first derivation yields "A B B A B B A," which is then derived as illustrated in Figure 2

In A BP2 Grammar, subgrammar 4 uses a context-sensitive substitution to realize the sonological interpretation[20] of strings of "A," "B," "C," "D."

Programmed Grammars

When a generative grammar is used to derive a string, rule order is intrinsically predetermined by the availability of variables in the string under derivation. This process is generally non-deterministic because there may be several candidate rules. The idea of a programmed grammar, as suggested by Laske [1973a:303], is to impose an extrinsic

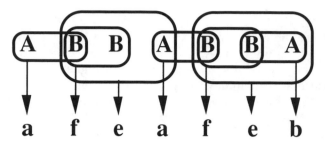

Figure 12. A Context-Sensitive Substitution.

ordering of rules reflecting a certain manner in which the generation process is envisaged by the composer. Programmed grammars in BP2 use flags taking positive integer values. Suppose we need to generate random variations of length 12 containing "a" and "b," yet with approximately two times more "a" than "b." We may write:

[1]	S	→	X X X X X X X X X X X X /flag1/ /flag1/ /flag2/
[2]	/flag1/ X	→	a	/	fl	a	g	2	/
[3]	/flag2/ X	→	b	/flag1/ /flag1/

The first rule generates "X X X X X X X X X X X X" and three flags. More precisely, "flag1," being generated twice, is set to integer value 2, while "flag2" is set to 1. These are used as conditions for the application of rules [2] and [3]: a rule may be applied only if the value of its condition flag is strictly positive. Each time the rule is applied the value of its condition flag is decremented. For example, rule [2] generates "a" while it decrements "flag1" and increments "flag2" with the effect of validating [3] as a candidate rule. Rule [3] decrements "flag2," generates "b" and increments "flag1" by 2 units, which will make it possible to apply rule [2] twice.

A BP1 Grammar for a Qa'ida

Below is the grammar of a qa'ida; taught by the late Afaq Husain Khan of Lucknow. It was elaborated in many work sessions and later revised on the basis of the musician's actual performance. An interesting feature of this improvisation schemata is the possible change of tempo within a single variation. Tempi are notated by way of integer numbers following slashes. For instance, "/4" indicates a stroke density of 4 strokes per beat.[21] A variation with a change of tempo may be found in Parsing a Variation. Rules [18] to [20] in subgrammar 2 indicate a change to density 6 followed with a change back to density 4.

Subgrammar 1

[1] S → /4 (= + S64 ;) Default stroke density is 4
[2] S → ... Other possible structures

Subgrammar 2

[1] S64 → L16 + S48
[2] S64 → L14 S50
[3] S64 → L12 S52
[4] S64 → L24 S40
[5] S48 → M16 + S32
[6] S48 → M14 S34
[7] S48 → M40 O8
[8] S50 → M18 + S32
[9] S50 → M34 + S16
[10] S50 → M18 + * (= + N14) O18
[11] S16 → O16
[12] S50 → V10 A'8T * (= N18 +) + O16
[13] S50 → M20 * (= N14 +) + O16
[14] S52 → V28 A8T O18
[15] S52 → M20 + S32
[16] S40 → M8 + S32
[17] S32 → * (= + N16 +) + S16
[18] S32 → * (= /6 + V12 /4 A8 +) + O16
[19] S32 → * (= /6 + A16 V8 + /4) + O16
[20] S32 → * (= /6 + V24 + /4) + O16
[21] S32 → * (= /8 + N'16 + A16 + /4) + O16
[22] S32 → * (= + N14) O18
[23] S34 → O34
[24] S34 → * (= N18 +) + S16
[25] S16 → /8 + A16 O16 ; /4

Subgrammar 3

[1] M16 → V16
[2] N18 → V18
[3] (= + L16 → (= + A16
[4] (= + L16 → (= + V10
[5] (= + L14 → (= + V10 A'6T
[6] M14 → A'16T
[7] (= + L14 → (= + A16T
[8] (= + L14 → (= + A'16T
[9] (= + L12 → (= + A16TT
[10] (= + L24 → (= + V24
[11] + M16 + * → + V10 A'6 + *
[12] + M16 → + A'16
[13] M8 + * → A'8 + *
[14] M16 + * → V8 A'8 + *
[15] M11 → V0 A'8T

[16] M18 + * → V10 A'8 + *
[17] M18 + * → V18 + *
[18] M34 + * → V28 A'6 + *
[19] M34 + * → V26 A'8 + *
[20] M20 + * → V12 A'8 + *
[21] M20 → V20
[22] M40 → V8 A'8T V26
[23] * (= /8 + N'16 → * (= /8 + V16
[24] * (= /8 + N'16 → * (= /8 + N16
[25] N16 + → V12 A4 +
[26] N16 + → V8 A8 +
[27] N16 + → V10 A6 +
[28] * (= + N16 → * (= + A16
[29] M14 → V8 A8T
[30] * (= + N14 → * (= + V8 A8T
[31] * (= + N14 → * (= + A16T
[32] N14 + → V6 A8 +
[33] O8 ; → A8 ;
[34] O34 ; → V26 A8 ;
[35] O18 ; → V10 A8 ;
[36] O16 ; → V8 A8 ;
[37] + O16 ; → + A16 ;

Subgrammar 4

[1] V30 → V V V28
[2] V28 → V V V26
[3] V26 → V V V24
[4] V24 → V V V V V20
[5] V20 → V V V18
[6] V18 → V V V16
[7] V16 → V V V V V12
[8] V12 → V V V10
[9] V10 → V V V8
[10] V8 → V V V6
[11] V6 → V V V V V V

Subgrammar 5

[1] ? V → ? -
[2] V → dha
[3] V V → trkt
[4] V V → dheena
[5] V V → teena
[6] V V → dhati

[7] V V → gena
[8] V V → dhage
[9] + V V → +tidha
[10] - V V → -tidha
[11] kt V V → kttidha
[12] na V V → natidha
[13] ge V V → getidha
[14] - V V → -ti-
[15] kt V V → ktti-
[16] ge V V → geti-
[17] na V V → nati-
[18] V V V → dhagena
[19] V V V → teenake
[20] V V V → dheenage
[21] V V V → dhatrkt
[22] V V V → trktdha
[25] V V V V → tidhagena
[26] V V V V → dhagedheena
[27] V V V V → teena-ta
[28] #ti V V V V → #ti tidhatrkt
[29] V V V V → dheenagena
[30] V V V V → teenakena
[31] V V V V V → dhagenadheena
[32] V V V V V → dhagenateena
[33] V V V V V → dhagenadhati
[34] V V V V V → dhatrktdhati
[35] V V V V V → dhatidhatrkt
[36] V V V V V → dhatidhagena
[37] V V V V V V → dheenagedhatrkt
[38] V V V V V V → genagedhatrkt
[39] V V V V V V → dhagedheenagena
[40] V V V V V V → dhageteenakena
[41] #ti V V V V V V → #ti tidhagedheenage
[42] V V V V V V → teenakegenage
[43] V V V V V V V V → dhagenagenanagena
[44] V V V V V V V V → dhatidhagedheenagena
[45] V V V V V V V V → dhatidhageteenakena
[46] V V V V V V V V A8 → dhatrktdhatidhatrkt A8
[47] V V V V V V V V A'8 → dhatrktdhatidhatrkt A'8

Subgrammar 6

[1] + ? ? ? ? ? ? ? ? ? ? A'6T → + ? ? ? ? ? ? ? ? ? ? dhageteena
[2] + ? ? ? ? ? ? ? ? ? ? A6T → + ? ? ? ? ? ? ? ? ? ? dhagedheena
[3] + ? ? ? ? ? ? ? ? ? ? A'6T → + ? ? ? ? ? ? ? ? ? ? dhageteena
[4] + ? ? ? ? ? ? ? A8T → + ? ? ? ? ? ? ? dhatidhagedheena
[5] A8T ? ? ? ? ? ? ? ? ? ? ? ? ? ? ? ? ? ? ; → dhatidhagedheena ? ? ? ? ? ? ? ? ? ? ? ? ? ? ? ? ? ? ;

[6] + ? ? ? ? ? ? ? ? A'8T → + ? ? ? ? ? ? ? ? dhatidhageteena

[7] + ? A'8T → + ?
dhatidhageteena

[8] A'6 + → dhageteenakena +

[9] A'8 + → dhatidhageteenakena +

[10] A4 + → dheenagena +

[11] A6 + → dhagedheenagena +

[12] A8 + → dhatidhagedheenagena +

[13] A8 ; → dhatidhagedheenagena ;

[16] + A16TT → + dhatidhagenadhatrktdhatidhage

[17] + A16T #ge → + dhatidhagenadhatrktdhatidhagedheena #ge

[18] + A'16T #ke → + dhatidhagenadhatrktdhatidhageteena #ke

[19] + A16 → + dhatidhagenadhatrktdhatidhagedheenagena

[20] + A'16 → + dhatidhagenadhatrktdhatidhageteenakena

Templates Generated by This Grammar

[1] /4 (= +...............+...............+ * (= +...............+) +...............;)

[2] /4 (= +...............+...............+ * (= +...............+) + /8 +...............; /4 ;)

[3] /4 (= +...............+...............+ * (= /6 +........... /4........+) +...............;)

[4] /4 (= +...............+...............+ * (= /6 +...................+ /4) +...............;)

[5] /4 (= +...............+...............+ * (= /8 +...............+...............+ /4) +...............;)

[6] /4 (= +...............+...............+ * (= +...............) ....;)

[7] /4 (= +...............+...............................;)

[8] /4 (= +...............+............... * (=...............+) +...............;)

[9] /4 (= +...............+............... * (=...............+) + /8 +...............; /4 ;)

[10] /4 (= +...............+...............+ * (= +...............+) +...............;)

[11] /4 (= +...............+...............+ * (= +...............+) + /8 +...............; /4 ;)

[12] /4 (= +...............+...............+ * (= /6 +........... /4........+) +...............;)

[13] /4 (= +...............+...............+ * (= /6 +...................+ /4) +...............;)

[14] /4 (= +...............+...............+ * (= /8 +...............+...............+ /4) +...............;)

[15] /4 (= +...............+...............+ * (= +...............) ....;)

[16] /4 (= +...+...............;)

[17] /4 (= +...+ /8 +...............; /4 ;)

[18] /4 (= +............... * (=...............+) +...............;)

[19] /4 (= +............... * (=...............+) +...............;)

[20] /4 (= +...;)

Parsing a Variation

The following is part of the trace showing the parsing of a variation by the grammar above. This demonstrates template matching (see Templates) and the canonic rightmost derivation (see BP1 Parsing Procedure). The complete process took less than 2 minutes on an Apple IIc. The variation is:

/4 dhatidhage	nadhatrkt	dhatidhage	dheenatrkt
dhadhatrkt	dhatidha-	dhatidhage	teena-ta
teena-ta	titakena	tatitake	teenakena
/8 dhatidhagenadhatrkt	dhatidhagedheenagena	gena-dhatidhagena	dhatidhagedheenagena

Trying templates:

[1] /4 (=+dhatidhagenadhatrktdhatidhagedheenatrkt+dhadhatrktdhatidha-dhatid-
hageteena-ta+*(=+teena-tati takenatatitaketeenakena+)+dhatidhagenadhatrktd-
hatidhagedheenagena;)
Incomplete template: failed...

[2] /4 (=+dhatidhagenadhatrktdhatidhagedheenatrkt+dhadhatrktdhatidha-dhatid-
hageteena-ta+*(=+teena-tatitakenatatitaketeenakena+)+ /8 +dhatidhagenadhatrktd-
hatidhagedheenagenagena-dhatidhagenadhatidhagedheenagena ; /4 ;)   Acceptable template

Trying a membership test on this template:

/4 (=+dhatidhagenadhatrktdhatidhagedheenatrkt+dhadhatrktdhatidha-dhatidhage-
teena-ta+*(=+teena-tatitakenatatitaketeenakena+)+ /8 +A16 gena-dhatidhagenadhatidhagedheenagena; /4 ;)

/4 (=+ A16T trkt+dhadhatrktdhatidha-dhatidhageteena-ta+*(=+teena-tatitakenatatitake-
teenakena+)+ /8 + A16 gena-dhatidhagenadhatidhagedheenagena; /4 ;)

/4 (=+ A16T trkt+dhadhatrktdhatidha-dhatidhageteena-ta+*(=+teena-tatitakenatatitake-
teenakena+)+ /8 + A16 gena-dhatidhagena A8 ; /4 ;)

/4 (= + A16T trkt+dhadhatrktdhatidha-dhatidhageteena-ta+*(=+teena-tatitakena A8+)+
/8 +A16 gena-dhatidhagena A8 ; /4 ;)

/4 (= + A16T trkt+dhadhatrktdhatidha- A'8T -ta+*(=+teena-tatitakena A8+)+ /8 +A16
gena-dhatidhagena A8 ; /4 ;)

/4 (= +A16T trkt+dhadhatrktdhatidha- A'8T -ta+*(=+teena-tatitakena A8+)+ /8 +A16
gena- VVVVV A8 ; /4 ;)

/4 (= +A16T trkt+dhadhatrktdhatidha- A'8T -ta+*(=+teena-tatitakena A8+)+ /8 +A16
gena VVVVVV A8 ; /4 ;)

/4 (= +A16T trkt+dhadhatrktdhatidha- A'8T -ta+*(=+teena-tatitakena A8+)+ /8 +A16
VVVVVVVV A8 ; /4 ;)

/4 (= +A16T trkt+dhadhatrktdhatidha- A'8T -ta+*(=+teena- VVVVV A8+)+ /8 +A16
VVVVVVVV A8 ; /4 ;)

/4 (= +A16T trkt+dhadhatrktdhatidha- A'8T -ta+*(=+teena VVVVVV A8+)+ /8 +A16
VVVVVVVV A8 ; /4 ;)

/4 (= +A16T trkt+dhadhatrktdhatidha- A'8T -ta+*(=+VVVVVVVV A8+)+ /8 +A16
VVVVVVVV A8 ; /4 ;)

/4 (= +A16T trkt+dhadhatrktdhatidha- A'8T V ta+*(=+VVVVVVVV A8+)+ /8 +A16
VVVVVVVV A8 ; /4 ;)

/4 (= +A16T trkt+dhadhatrktdhatidha V A'8T V ta+*(=+VVVVVVVV A8+)+ /8 +A16
VVVVVVVV A8 ; /4 ;)

/4 (= +A16T trkt+dhadhatrktdhati VV A'8T V ta+*(=+VVVVVVVV A8+)+ /8 +A16

VVVVVVV A8 ; /4 ;)

/4 (= +A16T trkt+dha VVVVVV A'8T V ta+*(=+VVVVVVV A8+)+ /8 +A16 VVVVVVV A8 ; /4 ;)

/4 (= +A16T trkt+VVVVVVV A'8T V ta+*(=+VVVVVVV A8+)+ /8 +A16 VVVVVVV A8 ; /4 ;)

/4 (= +A16T VV+VVVVVVV A'8T V ta+*(=+VVVVVVV A8+)+ /8 +A16 VVVVVVV A8 ; /4 ;)

/4 (= +A16T VV+VVVVVVV A'8T V ta+*(=+VVVVVVV A8+)+ /8 +A16 VVV6 A8 ; /4 ;)

/4 (= +A16T VV+VVVVVVV A'8T V ta+*(=+VVVVVVV A8+)+ /8 +A16 V8 A8 ; /4 ;)

/4 (= +A16T VV+VVVVVVV A'8T V ta+*(=+VV V6 A8+)+ /8 +A16 V8 A8 ; /4 ;)

/4 (= +A16T VV+VVVVVVV A'8T V ta+*(=+V8 A8+)+ /8 +A16 V8 A8 ; /4 ;)

/4 (= +A16T VV+VVV6 A'8T V ta+*(=+V8 A8+)+ /8 +A16 V8 A8 ; /4 ;)

/4 (= +A16T VV+V8 A'8T V ta+*(=+V8 A8+)+ /8 +A16 V8 A8 ; /4 ;)

/4 (= +A16T VV+V8 A'8T V ta+*(=+V8 A8+)+ /8 +A16 O16 ; /4 ;)

/4 (= +A16T VV+V8 A'8T V ta+*(=+N16+)+ /8 +A16 O16 ; /4 ;)

/4 (= +A16T VV+M14 V ta+*(=+N16+)+ /8 +A16 O16 ; /4 ;)

/4 (= +L14 VV+M14 V ta+*(=+N16+)+ /8 +A16 O16 ; /4 ;)

/4 (= +L14 VV+M14 V ta+*(=+N16+)+S16 ;)

/4 (= +L14 VV+M14 V ta+S32 ;)   Membership test failed...

Trying more templates:

...

[5] (=+dhatidhagenadhatrktdhatidhagedheenatrkt+dhadhatrktdhatidha-dhatidhage-
teena-ta+*(= /8 +teenatatitakenatatitaketeenakena+dhatidhagenadhatrktdhatid-
hagedheenagena+ /4)+gena-dhatidhagenadhatidhagedheenagena;)   Acceptable template...

Trying membership test on this template: failed...
Trying more templates:

...

[11] (=+dhatidhagenadhatrktdhatidhagedheenatrktdhadhatrktdhatidha-dhatidhage-
teena-ta+*(=+teena-tatitakenatatitaketeenakena+)+ /8 +dhatidhagenadhatrkt
dhatidhagedheenagena gena-dhatidhagena dhatidhagedheenagena ; /4 ;) Acceptable template...

Trying membership test on this template:

/4 (= +dhatidhagenadhatrktdhatidhagedheenatrktdhadhatrktdhatidha-dhatidhage-
teena-ta+*(=+teena-tatitakenatatitaketeenakena+)+ /8 +A16 gena-dhatidhagenadhatidhagedheenagena; /4 ;)

/4 (= +A16T trktdhadhatrktdhatidha-dhatidhageteena-ta+*(=+teena-tatitakenatatitake-
teenakena+)+ /8 +A16 gena-dhatidhagenadhatidhagedheenagena; /4 ;)

/4 (= +A16T trktdhadhatrktdhatidha-dhatidhageteena-ta+*(=+teena-tatitakenatatitake-
teenakena+)+ /8 +A16 gena-dhatidhagena A8 ; /4 ;)

/4 (= +A16T trktdhadhatrktdhatidha-dhatidhageteena-ta+*(=+teena-tatitakena A8+)+

/8 +A16 gena-dhatidhagena A8 ; /4 ;)

/4 (= +A16T trktdhadhatrktdhatidha-dhatidhageteena-ta+*(=+teena-tatitakena A8+)+
/8 ⊦A16 gena VVVVV A8 ; /4 ,)

/4 (= +A16T trktdhadhatrktdhatidha-dhatidhageteena-ta+*(=+teena-tatitakena A8+)+
/8 +A16 gena VVVVVV A8 ; /4 ;)

/4 (= +A16T trktdhadhatrktdhatidha-dhatidhageteena-ta+*(=+teena-tatitakena A8+)+
/8 +A16 VVVVVVV A8 ; /4 ;)

/4 (= +A16T trktdhadhatrktdhatidha-dhatidhageteena-ta+*(=+teena- VVVVV A8+)+ /8
+A16 VVVVVVV A8 ; /4 ;)

/4 (= +A16T trktdhadhatrktdhatidha-dhatidhageteena-ta+*(=+teena VVVVV A8+)+ /8
+A16 VVVVVVV A8 ; /4 ;)

/4 (= +A16T trktdhadhatrktdhatidha-dhatidhageteena-ta+*(=+VVVVVVV A8+)+ /8
+A16 VVVVVVV A8 ; /4 ;)

/4 (= +A16T trktdhadhatrktdhatidha-dhatidhage VVVV+*(=+VVVVVVV A8+)+ /8
+A16 VVVVVVV A8 ; /4 ;)

/4 (= +A16T trktdhadhatrktdhatidha-dhati VVVVVV+*(=+VVVVVVV A8+)+ /8 +A16
VVVVVVV A8 ; /4 ;)

/4 (= +A16T trktdhadhatrktdhatidha- VVVVVVVV+*(=+VVVVVVV A8+)+ /8 +A16
VVVVVVV A8 ; /4 ;)

/4 (= +A16T trktdhadhatrktdhatidha VVVVVVVVV+*(=+VVVVVVV A8+)+ /8 +A16
VVVVVVV A8 ; /4 ;)

/4 (= ⊦A16T trktdhadhatrktdhati VVVVVVVVVV+*(–+VVVVVVV A8+)+ /8 +A16
VVVVVVV A8 ; /4 ;)

/4 (= +A16T trktdha VVVVVVVVVVVVVV+*(=+VVVVVVV A8+)+ /8 +A16
VVVVVVV A8 ; /4 ;)

/4 (= +A16T VVVVVVVVVVVVVVVVVV+*(=+VVVVVVV A8+)+ /8 +A16 VVVVVVV
A8 ; /4 ;)

/4 (= +A16T VVVVVVVVVVVVVVVVVV+*(–+VVVVVVV A8⊦)⊦ /8 ⊦A16 VVV6 A8 ; /4
;)

/4 (= +A16T VVVVVVVVVVVVVVVVVV+*(=+VVVVVVV A8+)+ /8 +A16 V8 A8 ; /4 ;)

/4 (= +A16T VVVVVVVVVVVVVVVVVV+*(=+VV V6 A8+)+ /8 +A16 V8 A8 ; /4 ;)

/4 (= +A16T VVVVVVVVVVVVVVVVVV+*(=+V8 A8+)+ /8 +A16 V8 A8 ; /4 ;)

/4 (= +A16T VVVVVVVVVVVV V6+*(=+V8 A8+)+ /8 +A16 V8 A8 ; /4 ;)

/4 (= +A16T VVVVVVVVVV V8+*(=+V8 A8+)+ /8 +A16 V8 A8 ; /4 ;)

/4 (= +A16T VVVVVVVV V10+*(=+V8 A8+)+ /8 +A16 V8 A8 ; /4 ;)

/4 (= +A16T VVVVVV V12+*(=+V8 A8+)+ /8 +A16 V8 A8 ; /4 ;)

/4 (= +A16T VV V16+*(=+V8 A8+)+ /8 +A16 V8 A8 ; /4 ;)

/4 (= +A16T V18+*(=+V8 A8+)+ /8 +A16 V8 A8 ; /4 ;)

/4 (= +A16T V18+*(=+V8 A8+)+ /8 +A16 O16 ; /4 ;)

/4 (= +A16T V18+*(=+N16+)+ /8 +A16 O16 ; /4 ;)

/4 (= +A16T M18+*(=+N16+)+ /8 +A16 O16 ; /4 ;)

/4 (= +L14 M18+*(=+N16+)+ /8 +A16 O16 ; /4 ;)

/4 (= +L14 M18+*(=+N16+)+S16 ;)

/4 (= +L14 M18+S32 ;)

/4 (= +L14 S50 ;)

/4 (= +S64 ;)

        S   Membership test successful…

Trying more templates, etc…

A BP2 Grammar

This grammar is inspired by *tintinnabulation*, the art of ordering peals of church bells in England [Jaulin 1980]. The grammar is expected to build a sequence chaining distinct permutations of four sounds: "A," "B," "C" and "D." All acceptable changes from one permutation to the next are listed in subgrammar 2: these rules restrict changes of positions of a given sound yielding a structure in which an average periodicity of 4 is suggested but never clearly shown. Negative remote contexts make sure that the permutation newly generated is occurring for the first time. Variable "Cut" is used to separate permutations. When no further rule in subgrammar 2 is applicable, the inference engine jumps to subgrammar 3 in which all remaining variables (except of course "A," "B," "C," "D") are erased. Subgrammar 4 uses a context-sensitive substitution to replace variables with notes. Following standard solfège, "re4" stands for "D octave 4." Notes proposed here are arbitrary pitches unrelated to the traditional tuning of bells. A detailed presentation of this grammar and its variants is available in [Bel 1990b].

Subgrammar 1

    S → A B C D Cut B A C D X12
    S → A B C D Cut A C B D X23
    S → A B C D Cut A B D C X34
    S → A B C D Cut B A D C X1234

Subgrammar 2

  #(?1 ?2 ?4 ?3) ?1 ?2 ?3 ?4 X12 → ?1 ?2 ?3 ?4 Cut ?1 ?2 ?4 ?3   X34
  #(?2 ?1 ?4 ?3) ?1 ?2 ?3 ?4 X12 → ?1 ?2 ?3 ?4 Cut ?2 ?1 ?4 ?3   X1234
  #(?2 ?1 ?4 ?3) ?1 ?2 ?3 ?4 X34 → ?1 ?2 ?3 ?4 Cut ?2 ?1 ?4 ?3   X1234
  #(?2 ?1 ?3 ?4) ?1 ?2 ?3 ?4 X34 → ?1 ?2 ?3 ?4 Cut ?2 ?1 ?3 ?4   X12
  #(?2 ?1 ?4 ?3) ?1 ?2 ?3 ?4 X23 → ?1 ?2 ?3 ?4 Cut ?2 ?1 ?4 ?3   X1234
  #(?2 ?1 ?3 ?4) ?1 ?2 ?3 ?4 X1234 → ?1 ?2 ?3 ?4 Cut ?2 ?1 ?3 ?4 X12

#(?1 ?3 ?2 ?4) ?1 ?2 ?3 ?4 X1234 → ?1 ?2 ?3 ?4 Cut ?1 ?3 ?2 ?4 X23
#(?1 ?2 ?4 ?3) ?1 ?2 ?3 ?4 X1234 → ?1 ?2 ?3 ?4 Cut ?1 ?2 ?4 ?3 X34

Subgrammar 3

Cut   → λ
X12   → λ
X23   → λ
X34   → λ
X1234 → λ

Subgrammar 1: Sonological Interpretation

(Context-sensitive substitutions)

A B → do3 B
A #B → do4 #B
B → sol4
C → re5
D A → mi4 A
D #A → mi5 #A

A sequence generated by this grammar is:

| do3 sol4 re5 mi5 | sol4 do4 mi5 re5 | sol4 mi4 do4 re5 | mi5 sol4 re5 do4 |
| mi5 re5 sol4 do4 | re5 mi4 do4 sol4 | re5 do4 mi5 sol4 | do4 re5 sol4 mi5 |

The pseudo-periodicity of all occurrences of "do," "sol," "re" and "mi" is clearly visible in this sequence. Tabulations delimit permutations.

Conclusion

Work with the Bol Processor has been beneficial in finding a workable compromise between general formal language models whose mathematical properties are well established (although they often bear little musical relevance) and ad hoc representations fulfilling the requirements of only particular musical tasks. Our problem is not so much finding a universal abstract representation of music but identifying certain forms of musical "thinking" that may be rendered operative in the design of tools for computer-aided music creation, performance, and analysis.

Bol Processor grammars lend themselves to descriptions of music that may be normative when dealing with highly constrained systems (e.g. improvisation in traditional music) or empirical when applied to the modelling of compositional processes.

We are currently engaged in two projects that originated from this field of investigation. The first is a study of the inference of formal languages under the control of

human experts (see [Kippen & Bel 1989b], [Bel 1990a]). The second one is the design
of software tools for rule-based music composition/improvisation (see [Bel 1990d]).

Notes

1) Regarding aesthetic communication, see for instance [Laske 1973b]. Theories of individual compositions viewed as products of rule-governed artistic creativity are named *counter-grammars* by Laske
[1973a:359].

2) Initial work was part of a research scheme by the *International Society for Traditional Arts Research*
(ISTAR, New Delhi) generously funded by the *Ford Foundation* and the *National Centre for the Performing Arts* (NCPA, Bombay). Kippen's work was also supported by the *Leverhulme Trust* and the *Economic
and Social Research Council* in the UK.

3) *Qa'ida* may be thought of as "theme and variations" in which the variations are variously referred to
as *palta, vistar, bal, penc*, etc.

4) A string representation of non-sequential structures is proposed in the second part of "*Symbolic and
sonic representations of sound-object structures*" in this volume.

5) From the verb *bolna*, "to speak," in North Indian languages; for this reason the machine was named
"Bol Processor."

6) A system for transliterating tabla strokes to non-ambiguous symbolic representations has been proposed by Kippen [1988:xvi–xxiii].

7) We call "finite acceptor" a kind of finite automaton with a univocal mapping of the set of states to
the set {"acceptable," "unacceptable"}. This suggests that other mappings can be envisaged, see for
instance [Allouche 1987].

8) The word "pattern" is used here in a less restrictive sense than in Pattern Rules in BP Grammars.

9) These can also be adapted to deal with more than two classes. Probabilistic grammars, for instance,
may be viewed as pattern classifiers on an arbitrary number of classes. See [Booth & Thompson 1973].

10) See [Case & Lynes 1982] for a formal introduction.

11) More flexible learning criteria have been defined, among others, by Case & Lynes [1982].

12) "Question-Answer-Validated Analytical Inference Device." This acronym is also a word meaning
"grammar" in Arabic/Urdu—*Qava'id* is the plural of *qa'ida*.

13) The class of pattern languages is properly included in the class of unrestricted (type 0) languages,
but it is not comparable with any other class.

14) Restrictions on BP grammars are not described here. See [Bel 1987a–b].

15) The number of derivation steps needed for parsing a string is smaller than its length; space complexity is linear.

16) Since we are considering the dual grammar, these are the right arguments of original rules.

17) Unlike the algorithm by Maryanski and Booth [1977], this method works on arbitrary sample sets
even if some rules are not used in the parse.

18) A prototype version of BP2 for Macintosh computers is available as shareware from authors.

19) These brackets are distinct from pattern delimiters that contain either "=" or ":".

20) See the first section of "Symbolic and sonic representations of sound-object structures" in this volume.

21) This notation is elaborated in §6.1 of "Symbolic and Sonic Representations of Sound-Object Structures," in this volume.

References

Allouche, J.P. 1987. Automates finis en théorie des nombres, *Expositiones Mathematicae* 5:239–66

Allouche, J.P. and Mouret, A. 1988. Libertés non anarchiques, automates finis et champs matriciels. *Colloque International "Structures Musicales et Assistance Informatique,"* Marseille:45–50.

Angluin, D. 1980a. Inductive inference of formal languages from positive data. *Information & Control*, 45, 2:117–35.

Angluin, D. 1980b. Finding patterns common to a set of strings. *Journal of Computer and System Sciences* 21:46–62.

Bel, B. 1990a. Inférence de langages réguliers. In *Proceedings of "Journées Françaises de l'Apprentissage" (JFA)*, 5–27. Lannion: CNET.

Bel, B. 1990b. *Grammaires BP pour des airs de sonneurs de cloches.* Technical Report, Laboratoire Musique et Informatique de Marseille.

Bel, B. 1990c. *Acquisition et Représentation de Connaissances en Musique.* Thèse de Doctorat en Sciences, Faculté des Sciences de St-Jérôme, Université Aix-Marseille III, Marseille.

Bel, B. 1990d. Bol Processor BP2: reference manual. ISTAR France, Marseille.

Bel, B. 1987a. *Les grammaires et le moteur d'inférences du Bol Processor,* Internal Report n°237, GRTC, Centre National de la Recherche Scientifique, Marseille.

Bel, B. 1987b. Grammaires de génération et de reconnaissance de phrases rythmiques. In *Proceedings of "6ème Congrès AFCET: Reconnaissance des Formes et Intelligence Artificielle,"* 353–366. Paris: Dunod Informatique.

Booth, T.L. and Thompson, R.A. 1973. Applying Probability Measures to Abstract Languages. *IEEE Transactions on Computers*, C-22, 5:442–450.

Case, J. and Lynes, C. 1982. Machine Inductive Inference and Language Identification. In *Proceedings of the International Colloquium on Algorithms, Languages and Programming (ICALP).* Springer Verlag:107–115.

Feld, S. 1974. Linguistic Models in Ethnomusicology. *Ethnomusicology*, 18,2:197–217.

Fu, K.S. 1982. *Syntactic Pattern Recognition and Applications.* Englewood Cliffs: Prentice Hall.

Gold, E.M. 1967. Language Identification in the Limit. *Information and Control*, 10:447–74.

Hart, J.M. 1980. Derivation Structures for Strictly Context-Sensitive Grammars. *Information and Control*, 45:68–89.

Jackendoff, R. and Lerdahl, F. 1982. A Grammatical Parallel between Music and Language. In *Music, Mind and Brain: the Neuropsychology of Music,* ed. M. Clynes, 83–117. New York: Plenum Press.

Jaulin, B. 1980. L'art de sonner les cloches. In *Sons et Musique.* Paris: Belin:100–111.

Kain, R.Y. 1981. *Automata Theory: Machines and Languages.* Malabar: Krieger.

Kippen, J. 1988. *The Tabla of Lucknow: a Cultural Analysis of a Musical Tradition.* Cambridge: Cambridge University Press.

Kippen, J. 1987. An ethnomusicological approach to the analysis of musical cognition. *Music Perception*, 5:173–95.

Kippen, J. and Bel, B. 1989a. Modelling music with grammars: formal language representation in the Bol Processor. In *Computer Representations and Models in Music,* eds. A. Marsden and A. Pople. London: Academic Press. Forthcoming.

Kippen, J. and Bel, B. 1989b. The identification and modelling of a percussion "language", and the emergence of musical concepts in a machine-learning experimental set-up. *Computers and Humanities* 23, 3:199–214

Kippen, J. and Bel, B. 1989c. Can a computer help resolve the problem of ethnographic description? *Anthropological Quarterly*, 62, 3:131–144.

Kippen, J. and Bel, B. 1989d. From word-processing to automatic knowledge acquisition: a pragmatic application for computers in experimental ethnomusicology. *ALLC/ICCH Conference,* Toronto, 6–10 June. Forthcoming

Laske, O. 1973a. In Search of a Generative Grammar for Music. *Perspectives of New Music,* Fall-Winter 1973, Spring-Summer 1974:351–378.

Laske, O. 1973b. On the Understanding and Design of Aesthetic Artifacts. In *Musik und Verstehen,* eds. P. Faltin and H.P. Reinecke, 189–216. Köln: Arno Volk.

Loeckx, J. 1970. The Parsing for General Phrase-Structure Grammars. *Information and Control,* 16:443–464.

Maryanski, F.J. and Booth, T.L. 1977. Inference of Finite-State Probabilistic Grammars. *IEEE Transactions on Computers,* C-26, 6:521–536. [Some anomalies of this paper are corrected in B.R. Gaine's paper "Maryanski's Grammatical Inferencer," *IEEE Transactions on Computers,* C-27, 1, 1979:62–64]

Miclet, L. 1984. *Méthodes structurelles pour la reconnaissance des formes.* Paris: Eyrolles.

Nattiez, J.J. 1976. *Fondements d'une sémiologie de la musique.* Paris: Union Générale d'Editions 10–18.

Révész, G. 1985. *Introduction to Formal Languages.* New York: McGraw-Hill.

Révész, G. 1971. Unilateral Context Sensitive Grammars and Left-to-right Parsing. *Journal of Computer and System Sciences,* 5:337–352.

Ruwet, N. 1972. *Langage, musique, poésie.* Paris: Seuil.

Salomaa, A. 1973. *Formal Languages.* New York: Academic Press.

Abstract

It is needless to say that music is the art of sound. Therefore, in engineering, studying music has been done mainly in the field of "music and acoustics". It is, however, evident that vision is also important in music. Since ancient times, music has been written in pictorial patterns known as a score, so that musicians can recognize and reproduce music through vision. Moreover, a singer's facial expression and the actions of a performer have a visual impact on the audience. Music video is now growing more popular than plain audio tapes.

Although many studies have been reported recently on music and AI, as far as we know there have been no attempts to create a general approach to music through vision technology. Computer vision may not be good enough yet to play an important role in music, though there are several areas of computer music where computer vision at its present level can be effectively applied.

In the following sections, we introduce some recent topics which our laboratory of "music and vision" has developed during the last ten years.

Chapter 16

A New Approach to Music Through Vision

Sadamu Ohteru and Shuji Hashimoto

Waseda University and Toho University

Automated Recognition System for Musical Score

One of the most important problems, at the current initial stage of the application of AI methods to music, is entering musical scores into the computer. There are various manual or half-automated methods and types of equipment to input musical data, but all of them require a lot of time and effort.

We have developed an automatic score recognition system using a computer vision technique (Matsushima et al. 1985a). Figure 1 shows an example of its recognition results. The reading time for a commercially available nursery song music score that has three parts is approximately 10 seconds. Once the data acquisition has been performed, wider applications are possible in the fields of computer music and musical information processing. Our musician robot WABOT-2 reads a musical score in real time and plays an electronic organ with its own fingers (Matsushima et al. 1985b).

Two-Way Translation System Between Printed Music and Braille Music

It is not always easy for blind people to obtain braille music scores, because braille music production requires a knowledge of music, braille, and braille musical notation. This makes "mastering braille music as difficult as mastering a foreign language". We have developed an Automatic Printed-Music-to-Braille Translation System, which has the capability of translating almost all the symbols used in piano musical scores

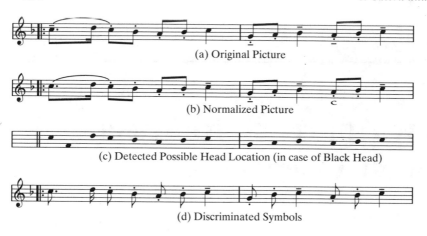

(a) Original Picture

(b) Normalized Picture

(c) Detected Possible Head Location (in case of Black Head)

(d) Discriminated Symbols

(e) Output Score Data (after Analysis)

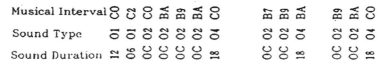

(e) Output Score Data (after Analysis)

Figure 1. An Example of Recognition

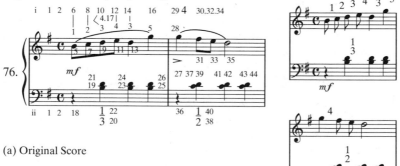

(a) Original Score

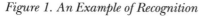

(b) Produced Braille Music

(c) Inverse Transformation Result from (b)

Figure 2. An Example of Automatic Printed-Music-to-Braille Transformation and Its Inverse Transformation

within seconds, and embossing them out to the braille-writer automatically (Matsushima et al. 1988a). Figure 2 shows an example. The system is now under practical testing in several places in Tokyo; including schools for the blind and rehabilitation centers.

Through our experience in constructing this braille translation system, we have been able to implement AI capabilities for an inverse translation system, that analyzes sequential braille code, and produces the corresponding printed-music automatically. Both printed-music and braille music are "universal languages" that are now used commonly in the world; thus two-way translation between them may be one of the most interesting problems even in the fields of AI.

A Computer Music System That Can Follow a Human Conductor

One of the biggest defects of automated musical performance systems is the lack of improvisation (Mathews 1989). In order to improve this situation, we have developed a computer music system which can follow a human conductor, as illustrated in Figure 3 (Morita et al. 1989). The vision system consists of a CCD camera, feature extraction hardware, and a movement analyzer that interprets the conductor's intentions by analyzing the movement of his baton with the aid of a knowledge base for conducting. Tempo is expressed by the vertical movement of the baton, and strength is expressed by the trajectory length of the baton. A typical movement of the feature point is shown in Figure 4. A linear prediction method is used to evaluate the changes in tempo and to compensate for them. The effects of misdirection and involuntary movements of the baton are also eliminated.

The recognition results are sent to MIDI control units to improvise the performance in real time. The behavior of the system is similar to that of human players, so the system can play in concert with human performers, and even be a member of a symphony orchestra. The human players in the orchestra need not synchronize themselves with the machine performance, because both the humans and the machine are following the same human conductor. The authors believe that this system suggests a new style of automated music performance, in which AI can play an important role.

Computerized Dance-Step Recognition and Musical Accompaniment

Music and dance or human body movement have been closely related since ancient times. Music has created new dances and dances have produced new music. However, in the field of modern computer music, the link between music and human body movement is not yet very strong (Rokeby 1988). We propose a new dance accompaniment system named 'MAI' (the name of an old Japanese style of dance) which can

Figure 3. The Baton Now Becomes the Perfect Human Interface

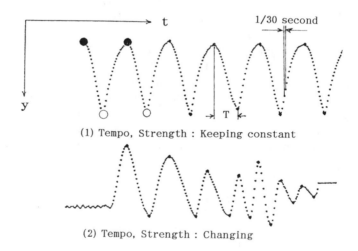

Figure 4. Trajectory of the Baton

recognize a dance pattern in real time and can generate appropriate dance music by selecting a score from a previously stored data base (Namekawa et al. 1989).

A pair of dancers on the stage start dancing, for example, a waltz without music. As shown in Figure 5, a high resolution CCD video camera attached to the ceiling follows the white silk hat of the male dancer. After approximately 15 seconds from the start of the dance, the computer answers by a speech synthesizer; if the dance is a waltz, the synthesizer announces "This is Waltz." At the same time, MIDI instruments controlled by the computer play music to accompany the dance, and the corresponding segments of the musical score are shown on the CRT display one by one in order. Dance-steps used in the present experiment have been limited to the six ballroom dances: Waltz, Tango, Slow Fox-trot, Quick Step, Viennese Waltz, and Blues. The standard pattern of the each dance-step can be updated by a learning method.

The evolution of the dancing movement is not governed by physical time, but by the musical rhythm expressed in the score. Indeed, almost all dance notations are expressed using the musical score as the time base (Hutchinson 1985, Calvert 1986). In real time, our system can display the musical score and the corresponding movement vectors (velocity and acceleration) as the output of the dance pattern recognition process, as shown in Figure 6. This output may be called *dynamic* orchesography or choreography.

The present system not only is promising for harmonizing dance with computer music, but can also be applied to other performances in which movement and music are combined, such as musical accompaniment for animation, or for synchronized swimming.

In this connection, we are trying to read Laban notation automatically using vision technology, and display or print out its meaning and its corresponding body movement by animation. This latter attempt can be called a dance construction system, as opposed to a dance recognition system.

An Integrated Music Information Processing System

Although each of the above systems is fundamentally an independent single purpose system, by combining them we are now developing an integrated music system PSB-er (Performance, Score and Braille music system in WASEDA University for education and research) in which musical information can be exchanged among the systems as shown in Figure 7, by computers and communication lines (public telephone lines) (Matsushima et al. 1988b).

The representation of musical information is different for performance (playing, conducting and dancing), printed score, and braille score. Performance is time dependent and demands analog, acoustic, or visual information. A printed score is a two-dimensional graphic image presenting analog and digitized characters. A braille music score is a digitized one-dimensional sequence of braille characters. The information contained in each of these three forms of musical data is quite different. Consequently, we contrived a new way of representing musical data named SMX (standard music expression), which is based on score information. Although our integrated system has not been completed, it can accept and produce any of the music representations mentioned above, using an SMX format data link. Moreover, it can play MIDI instruments under the control of a human conductor, and can visually recognize dance movements and provide accompaniment.

Figure 5. Computerized Dance-Step Recognition and Musical Accompaniment "MAI"

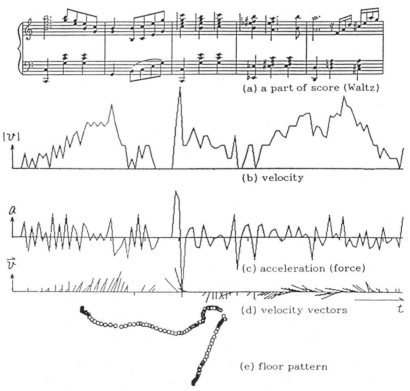

(a) a part of score (Waltz)

(b) velocity

(c) acceleration (force)

(d) velocity vectors

(e) floor pattern

Figure 6. Dynamic Choreography

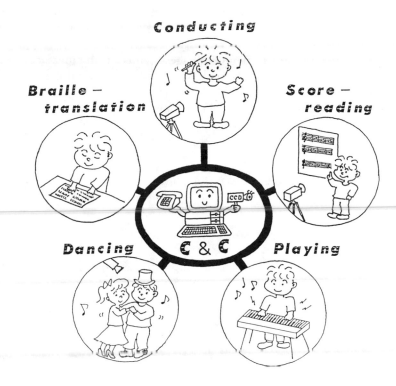

Figure 7. An Integrated Music Information Processing System

As a proper computer network system for music, SMX will stimulate new applications of music information processing. The results of the above experiments suggest some new applications. For example, since only a few copies of most musical scores are sold, a store selling musical scores must stock a few copies each of a large variety of musical scores. For a music information center, one way to alleviate this problem is to keep numerous kinds of scores in a data base that users can receive via public communication lines, and print at will at their own location. This technique will obviously be very useful for braille music, where the demand is smaller and more storage space is required for a copy of a score in the embossed braille form.

Conclusions

We are now searching for a new field of "music and vision" to stand alongside "music and acoustics." The present chapter shows that even performance and rhythmical body movement can take part in a computer music system with the help of the recently developed computer vision technology. We believe that this attempt will not only expand AI applications for music but also raise the standards of computer music, including computer performance, by using interesting and amusing human interfaces.

Among the artistic activities human beings engage in, music is the most logical and mathematically well-founded, which has made it suitable for the application of AI techniques. On the other hand, music has an illogical aspect like the other arts, which could lead AI to the new frontier of emotional information processing.

Acknowledgments

The authors are obliged to the members of the Ohteru laboratory: Messrs. H. Ueda, T. Harada, I. Sonomoto, T. Matsushima, K. Kanamori, D. Shin, N. Namekawa, K. Naoi and H. Morita.

References

Calvert, T. W. 1986. Toward a Language for Human Movement. *Computers & Humanities* 20: 35–43.

Hutchinson, A. 1984. *Dance Notation.* New York: Dance Horizons.

Mathews, M. V. 1989. The Conductor Program and Mechanical Baton. Int. Symposium on Music and Information Science.

Matsushima, T., Sonomoto, I., Harada ,T., Kanamori, K. and Ohteru, S. 1985a. Automated High Speed Recognition of Printed Music. Proc. of Int. Conference on Advance Robotics, 477–482.

Matsushima, T., Harada, T., Sonomoto, I., Kanamori, K., Uesugi, A., Nimura, Y., Hashimoto,S. and Ohteru, S. 1985b. Automated Recognition System for Musical Score -The Vision System of WABOT-2 -. Special Issue on WABOT-2, Bulletin of Science and Engineering Research Laboratory (112): 25–52 Waseda Univ.

Matsushima, T. 1988a. Automated Printed-Music-to-Braille Translation System. *Journal of Information Processing* 11(4): 249–257.

Matsushima, T., Ohteru, S. and Hashimoto, S. 1988b. An Integrated Music Information Processing System: PSB-er. Proc. of 14th ICMC

Morita, H., Ohteru, S. and Hashimoto,S. 1989. Computer Music System which Follows A Human Conductor. Proc. of 15th ICMC.

Namekawa, N., Furukawa, T., Ohteru, S. and Hashimoto, S. 1989. Computerized Dance-step Recognition and Musical Accompaniment. Convention Record of Acoustical Society of Japan (in Japanese).

Rokeby, D. 1988. Body Language. ACM Siggraph Art Show, Aug.1–5, Atlanta.

Section Six

Perception

Modeling music perception as an activity has in the past been undertaken by psychoacoustics, the psychology of music and in studies on music education. By contrast, music theorists and musicologists have focused on the study of the end products of perceptual activities. Between these two kinds of studies very few, if any, links have been forged. The study of musical perception within the framework of the cognitive sciences and AI is a new trend that will hopefully remedy this deficiency.

When speaking of musical perception, one should keep in mind the epistemological status of perception in listening. Listening is a broad concept in which not only perception, but also cognition, problem solving, analogical and metaphorical reasoning, and emotional mapping have their place. Today, only vague hypotheses as to the relationships of these elements in listening are available. It is, however, beyond doubt, that what is perceived is interpreted on many different levels, and it is the accumulation and, perhaps, synthesis, of different viewpoints of one and the same perceptual event which is called listening.

The following section presents three chapters on the subject, two on the perception of meter, and one on time quantization. For the reader's convenience, we have also added a list of references.

The chapter "On Analyzing and Representing Musical Rhythm," by Christiane Linster, describes a neural network approach to the task of performing a hierarchical grouping of a given rhythmic sequence. The input to the system is a sequence of notes with durations, but without pitches. The output of the system is an encoding of a parse tree that shows the division of the given input sequence into hierarchical subunits, such as measures, beats, and subbeats, where the terminal nodes of the parse tree are the individual notes of the input sequence. Linster's network is trained using a backpropagation algorithm, which is given as input a number of rhythmic sequences along with their correct analysis (parse trees). After training, the system is able to find the hierarchical analyses of new inputs in the same style, with good accuracy.

B. O. Miller, D. L. Scarborough and J. A. Jones, in their chapter "On the Perception of Meter," study and compare two contrasting psychological approaches to modeling the development of hierarchical representation of metric structures by listeners: A rule-based approach versus a parallel constraint satisfaction network approach. Underlying their work is the assumption that listeners indeed possess a hierarchical conception of meter, of the sort described by Lerdahl and Jackendoff. The question is: "How does a listener develop such a hierarchical conception?". Lerdahl and Jackendoff's theory does not provide an answer for such questions, nor does it provide a complete algorithm for associating only musically valid hierarchies with a given rhythmic pattern. The authors try to shed some light on this hard problem, by comparing the performance of two programs that simulate the process of listening, according to the cognitive models of perception mentioned above.

The rule-based model uses knowledge about metrical hierarchies, based on the theory of Lerdahl and Jackendoff, and on ideas taken from Longuet-Higgins and Lee. In a single pass through a given string of note durations, stripped from all other musical information, the program suggests a metrical hierarchy. In the network-based model, observed time intervals coupled with phases in the input are modeled by objects that make up the network. Objects can be excited by signals from note-onset intervals and from other objects. The internal reactions between the network's objects were designed by the researchers, so that they indirectly reflect the principles of metrical hierarchy. The final status of these objects, once the input is scanned, is the proposed hierarchy.

So far, no clear-cut answers as to the nature of meter perception in humans can be given. Considering the difficulty of the task, and the fact that meter perception, probably, cannot be separated from the perception of other musical parameters, this is not surprising.

The chapters of Linster and of Miller et al., although concentrated around the same musical task, differ in goals, approach and means. Linster's work is more like an engineering experiment: An off-the-shelf algorithm is applied to rhythmic examples; results are observed, and the appropriateness of the tool for performing the desired task is discussed and evaluated. Miller et al.'s work is motivated by psychological inquiry into the nature of meter perception in humans. Hence they use two cognitive models that they believe to be psychologically plausible, and compile into them knowledge about meter perception, such as rules of rhythmic hierarchy. Of particular interest is the compilation of such knowledge into weak and strong interactions between network objects (representing note-onset intervals). Their experiments do not produce a tool for rhythmic analysis, but rather build another step into the possible future understanding of meter perception.

The chapter "The Quantization Problem: Traditional and Connectionist Approaches," by P. Desain and H. Honing, describes and compares approaches to the problem of time quantization in music, i.e., the problem of how musical continuity is segmented into bounded and discrete units by the listener. The authors first define the problem and explain its importance for both cognitive modeling and for the automatic transcription of performed music, and studies of expressive timing in "no score" music. Then, the authors survey several numerical and structure based methods, and point to typical problems with each. Finally, the authors describe a network model that is similar to Miller et al.'s network, with objects standing for inter-onset intervals, their summations, and interactions. They claim that the performance of a quantizer built around this approach is context sensitive and maintains consistency at higher levels, even in complex situations, where quantizers usually break down. However, evidence demonstrating this latter claim are not provided.

References

Dowling, W. J. and Harwood, D. L. 1986. *Music Cognition,* Orlando, FL: Academic Press.

Erman, L. D. Hayes-Roth, F. Lesser, V. R.; and Reddy, D. R. 1980. "The Hearsay-II Speech Understanding System: Integrating Knowledge to Resolve Uncertainty," *Computing Surveys* 12:213-253.

Fraisse, P. 1947-48. "Mouvements Rythmiques et Arythmiques," *L'Anne Psychologique* 4748 - 21.

Fraisse, P. 1982. "Rhythm and Tempo," In *The Psychology of Music,* ed. D. Deutsch, 149-180. New York: Academic Press.

Hopfield, J. J. and Tank, D. W. 1985. "Neural Computation of Decisions in Optimization Problems," *Biological Cybemetics,* 52:141-152.

Jones, J. A. Miller, B. O. and Scarborough, D. L. 1988. "A Rule-based Expert System for Music Perception," *Behavior Research Methods, Instruments & Computers* 20:255-262.

Lerdahl, F. and Jackendoff, R. 1983. *A Generative Theory of Tonal Music,* Cambridge, MA: MIT Press.

Longuet-Higgins, H. C. and Lee, C. S. 1982. "The Perception of Musical Rhythms", *Perception* 1 1:1 15-128.

Marr, D. 1982. *Vision.* San Francisco: W.H. Freeman.

McClelland, J. L.and Rumelhart, D. E. 1981. "An Interactive Model of Context Effects in Letter Perception: Part I. An Account of Basic Findings," *Psychological Review* 88: 375-407.

McClelland, J. L.and Rumelhart, D. E. 1988. *Explorations in Parallel Distributed Processing,* Cambridge, MA: MIT Press.

Miller, B. O. 1991. "Simulation and Evaluation of a Model of Meter Perception," Unpublished doctoral dissertation, City University of New York.

Miller, B. O. Scarborough, D. L. and Jones, J. A. 1988. "A Model of Meter Perception in Music," In *Proceedings of the Tenth Annual Conference of the Cognitive Science Society,* 717723. Hillsdale, NJ.: Lawrence Erlbaum Associates.

Miller, B. O. Scarborough, D. L. and Jones, J. A. 1989. "Rule-Based versus Constraint Satisfaction Approaches to the Perception of Meter in Music," In *Proceedings of the Second Intemational Workshop on Artificial Intelligence and Music, Intemational Joint Conference on Artificial Intelligence* (IJCAI-89). 26-35. Menlo Park, CA: American Association for Artificial Intelligence.

Newell, A. and Simon, H. A. 1972. *Human Problem Solving,* Englewood Cliffs, NJ: Prentice-Hall.

Povcl, D.-J. and Essens, P. 1985. "Perception of Temporal Pattems," *Music Perception,* 2:411440.

Rumelhart, D. E., Smolensky, P. McClelland, J. L; and Hinton, G. E. 1986. "Schemata and Sequential Thought Processes in PDP Models," In *Parallel Distributed Processing: Explorations in the Microstructures of Cognition. Vol 2: Psychological and Biological Models,* Ch 14, 7-57. Cambridge, MA: MIT Press.

Tumer, F. and Poppel, E. 1983. "The Neural Lyre: Poetic Meter, the Brain, and Time," *Poetry,* 142:277-310.

Abstract

In this chapter we show that it is possible to represent musical structures with neural networks. For reasons of simplicity we put our initial focus on rhythm. Hierarchical structures as a representation scheme for rhythmic grouping are discussed as well as the mapping of this representation onto the processing elements of a neural network. We show the scope of applicability of our representation scheme on three different applications: rhythm analysis, rhythm classification and rhythm driven performance.

Chapter 17

On Analyzing and Representing Musical Rhythm

Christiane Linster

"Grouping is arguably the most important level of musical understanding. Modelling how listeners understand melodies may be restricted to the problem of how they assign grouping structures to tonal melodies by processing discrete serial input pitches, in combination with their knowledge of other pieces"

[Baker 1989]

The musical structures and patterns that are represented in a listener's mind are composed of three musical dimensions: melody, harmony and rhythm. To simplify the first steps of the approach, we focus on the analysis of one musical dimension: rhythm. The search for a useful representation of musical knowledge with neural networks is the main motivation of our work. Perception of rhythm and a representation scheme for rhythmic events which can be applied to several aspects of the handling of musical rhythm information are discussed. Then the mapping of this representation onto the processing elements of a neural network is realized.

Based on the assumption that the ability to recognize patterns and structures in music depends on cultural background and musical training, and that familiar patterns are better recognized than unfamiliar ones, it seems plausible to use a network structure which may learn by experience. In this approach, a three layer, feedforward neural network trained by error-backpropagation is used.

In three applications we discuss the quality of the chosen representation and network architecture: rhythm analysis, rhythm classification and rhythm driven performance.

Perception and Representation of Rhythm

The fact that sounds stand in relation to each other is the principal characteristic of music. The listener must start to notice relationships and identify significant groupings. At the lowest level they will be relatively simple features of the sound patterns

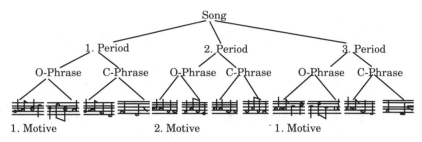

Figure 1. Form Structure of "Alle Voegel Sind Schon Da."

characterizing small groups of notes [Sloboda 1985]. At a very high musical level, such groupings will be very complex, corresponding to formal structures within a work.

Based on the assumption that classic western music compositions are very clearly structured and symmetrically built, their formal structure can be represented as a hierarchical tree. A formal analysis of a simple song leads to the representation in Figure 1.

Deutsch has provided experiments to support the theory that hierarchical structures seem to be implied in the way we represent complex information in music. She asked musicians to recall melodies by dictation. Some of the melodies could be described as hierarchical structures, others could not. Recall for the former type was 94 percent, for the latter 52 percent. If the structured melodies were temporally segmented into groups corresponding to the major hierarchical subdivisions, performance rose to 99 percent [Deutsch 1980].

The formal structure of a composition may be viewed as *"high level rhythm"*. If one concentrates on single rhythm events (i.e. notes) of a work, a different level of the music is represented. The tree structures that can be built from this reduced (no melody) information (Figure 2) are very similar to those in Figure 1. Rhythm events are analyzed in respect to neighboring events, instead of looking at higher level formal groupings. This representation is called *"low level rhythm"* in opposition to the higher level structural rhythm defined above.

The simplest type of rhythm has a regular pulse, so that regular multiples of the pulse are stressed. A perceived pulse marks off equal intervals in time. Pulses tend to be grouped. Within the groups, strong and weak pulses alternate in ways that reflect hierarchical organization.

In performance, the hierarchy of rhythm events is expressed by physical cues. In music notation sounds of different durations are grouped together to give information about accentuations and stresses.

Several authors have described computer models for analysis of simple rhythms using hierarchical representations of metrical structure. [Rosenthal 1988], [Miller & Scarborough & Jones 1988]. These approaches use recursive parsing and are rule based. We are concerned with learning by examples, and do therefore apply a different approach: the time window representation. This approach allows us to simultaneously represent a limited sequence of rhythmic events. This representation is

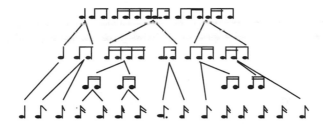

Figure 2. Hierarchical Tree of Rhythmical Events.

also suggested by Todd in a model of algorithmic composition [Todd 1990] and is
similar to the time window approach common in speech applications. Large chunks
of time are presented simultaneously, in parallel, with different locations in time
captured by different positions of processing units.

Encoding

A fundamental concern in the construction of neural networks for musical applications is the representation of input to the system and output from the system, e.g. the
mapping of a chosen representation of events onto the processing elements of the
network. The way in which input is presented is determined by several factors: the
theoretical view point of the designer, the use of the network and available computational resources, like preprocessors and interfaces [Laden & Keefe 1990]. Both low
level and high level representation are needed here. The input to the network represents only low level rhythmic information. Feature extraction is done by the system,
and higher level information about grouping structures is represented by the output.

It is assumed that in rhythm analysis, only the placement of event onsets relative
to one another is important, and the duration of each event is unimportant. Therefore, the set of input units for the network represents a span of time, with individual
units representing ordered, equally spaced points in that span. The interval
between two points corresponds to the smallest quantization interval used by a nor-
malizing algorithm for preprocessing of the rhythm events, and corresponds to the
smallest interval between notes which can be represented.

Figure 3 illustrates the input representation of a particular note sequence. In this
illustration, active units corresponding to note onsets are darkened.

In this binary activation scheme a unit is either on or off because we do not
represent pitch in the input vector. The level of activation of each unit corresponding to a note onset could be used however to represent other information,
such as the pitch or amplitude of each note. Other encoding schemes, such as
coding the duration of notes in a group of binary units have been explored, and

Figure 3. Encoding of Rhythmic Events.

the differences in network performances for a number of encoding schemes have been explained in detail [Linster 1989]. In this chapter, only the time span approach will be discussed.

It is important to remember that the rhythmic inputs were normalized with respect to time [Hipfinger & Linster 1990]. That is, an event representing a particular note duration was always represented by the same interval in the input vector, whereas in actual performance, notes of nominally equivalent duration will differ.

The encoding of output information depends on the applications; it will be explained in more detail in the corresponding paragraphs.

Network Structure

Based on the assumption that the function we want to approximate is complex, we chose to train a multi-layer perceptron. Connectivity between layers is complete, but no connections exist within layers. The musical input is presented as an n-dimensional vector to the input layer units and is recoded in the hidden layer (internal representation). The output vector is computed from the internal representation vector and not from the input vector.

Error-backpropagation [Rumelhart, Hinton & Williams 1986] is a method of gradient descent, using the generalized delta rule. The learning procedure requires a set of pairs of input and desired output patterns (target patterns). In a first step, the input vector is propagated through the layers, and an activation vector for the output layer is computed. The output units take continuous values between −1 and +1 due to their non-linear activation function. The sum of the quadratic errors between the computed unit activations and the corresponding target values (−1, +1) is used to perform weight changes to decrease error. Several parameters for the training phase have to be adjusted: the learning-rate (step size for gradient descent), the momentum term (influence of the weight changes calculated at the preceding steps) and the number of units in the hidden layer.

Training the Network

Training sets and test sets are formed by rhythm sequences copied from the works of several classic, modern or jazz composers. For one experiment, the quantization interval is fixed for all the training and test patterns. This interval defines the smallest note value which can be represented. The set of available examples is divided into a training and a test set. The number of input units and output units depends on the maximal length of the sequences and on the quantization interval. Training on the same set of examples, we varied the number of hidden units in order to find the optimal network structure.

Weights are initialized to small random values (between −0.1 and +0.1) before training. We kept the learning-rate small (0.01) and we did not use a momentum term or other acceleration methods. During training, patterns are presented to the network in random order. We applied the stochastic gradient algorithm, meaning that weight changes are computed after the presentation of each example. The training procedure is stopped when the average error between the potential of the output units and the desired values over all output units and over all examples is smaller than 0.01.

For testing, the sigmoidal units of the output layer are replaced by binary units. An output vector is considered "wrong" if one or more output units is of the wrong sign.

Applications

Rhythm Analysis

The time-window representation allows us to simultaneously input a limited sequence of rhythm events. From this information, the network computes a hierarchical structure which should best fit the sequence. The input represents a sequence of rhythmic events in time, without information on meter and measure or pitch. The output represents the same sequence of events, to which the structural information has been added. Figure 4 shows input to the network and output from the network as well as the corresponding unit vectors for a simple rhythm structure.

The units of the output layer represent the hierarchical grouping of the rhythmic events. The hierarchy consists of groups of notes, the higher groups (e.g.) using the lower ones (e.g.)) as building blocks. This grouping represents the composer's rhythmic guideline for the performer. For each moment on the time axis, groups of output units represent the beginning and the ending of the grouping of the rhythmic events . In the example of Figure 4 the time scale represents $\frac{1}{16}$th notes. There are three levels of groupings represented in the output vector. For each moment of the time scale, a group of units represents possible beginnings and endings of groupings for each level of the hierarchy.

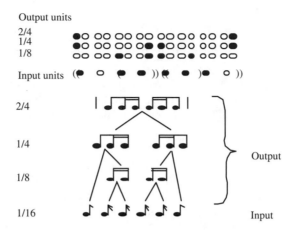

Figure 4. *Example of Input and Output Encoding.*

Figure 5. *The Four Possible Groupings for the First Experiment.*

For the first experiment, a small training set of simple ²⁄₄ₜₕ measures was invented. All the patterns were of the same length (4 measures). The quantization interval corresponded to ¹⁄₃₂ₙd note value. The training set comprised 15 sequences which were randomly chosen combinations of the four building blocks shown in Figure 5.

After the training phase, the network was tested with sequences of different combinations of the four blocks and we computed the desired output for all of them. Two completely different rhythm sequences were chosen for further testing (Figure 6).

The result of the first example of Figure 6 is very similar to the desired output. The grouping structure is incomplete, but not musically wrong (Figure 7).

The result for the second example shows that the network could not compute the desired grouping structure for the syncopation (Figure 8). This is not surprising, because in all the training patterns, grouping always began on the strong beats. Later experiments show that it is hard to train one and the same network on even and uneven rhythms. A network cannot learn the difference between ¾ syncopations and ⁶⁄₈ rhythms because the same input sequences would require different output representations.

Another network was trained on a pattern set comprising 200 rhythm sequences from Mozart piano sonatas. These patterns varied in length, tempo and bar, including examples from ²⁄₄ₜₕ, ³⁄₄ₜₕ and ⁴⁄₄ₜₕ measures. After the training phase the network was tested on a set of 100 different sequences from the same sonatas, as well as on 50 sequences from the third part of the clarinet sonata by Hindemith (Figure 9).

Figure 6. Two Unknown Examples.

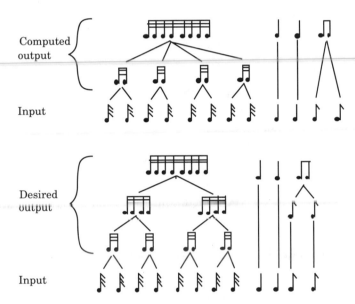

Figure 7. Interpretation of the Output Obtained for the First Example from Figure 6 and the Desired Output.

The desired output for each rhythm sequence is the original grouping written by the composer. According to this criteria, 82 patterns from the test set were associated with their desired output. For nine of the remaining patterns, the grouping computed by the network was different from the original grouping, but was not "musically wrong". ¾th rhythms were grouped as incomplete ¼th, ¼th with upbeat as ¾th and so on. The remaining patterns presented rhythm sequences including syncopations of 4th and 8th beats. Only 12 of the training examples included syncopated rhythms, these rhythms have not been "learned" by the network. This shows that our training set was not representative.

The performance on the second test set was very low: 10%. This is due to the variety of rhythms in the pattern set (triplets, syncopes with triplets).

The 50 examples from this set were used to train another network, which showed

Figure 8. Result for the Second Unknown Example of Figure 6.

Figure 9. Rhythm Sequence from the Clarinet Sonata.

over 90% success on the test set from Mozart sonatas. Other similar experiments have been presented before [Linster 1988]. In conclusion we might say that a trained network can handle any sequences built of familiar rhythm structures. These do not have to be presented in the same order or in the same combinations as in the training set.

In order to find the relevant features in the input signals that the network uses to compute the desired output, a simple algorithm is proposed. After the training phase, the weights of the network are fixed for a given set of training patterns. The network is tested for good generalization with similar input patterns, which do not belong to the training set. The following procedure helps to identify the important features in the input pattern:

1) clamp a pattern onto the input units
2) choose an active input unit
3) change the value of the input unit to inactive
4) compute the values of the output units for the new input pattern
5) if the output pattern changed (not the wanted output anymore), reset the input unit into active state
6) if the output pattern did not change (beyond a fixed limit), leave the input unit in inactive state.

In order to keep the input perturbation independent of the order in which input units are selected for perturbation, these are selected in a random order. The perturbation procedure is repeated several times for the same input vector, and the results are compared. The number of active units is reduced considerably. Only those input units which are necessary to compute the desired output remain in an active state. Analyzing a certain number of sequences can give a cue as to what information is important for the correct behavior of the system. In a classification system the number of input features can often be reduced considerably after such analysis. The same algorithm has been proposed by the author to reduce a set of

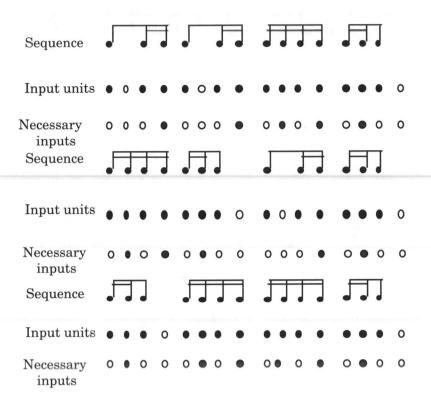

Figure 10. Analysis Result.

200 input features for medical coma diagnosis to a set of fifty relevant inputs [Rom & Grims & Linster 1990].

The system has been trained and tested with the same simple rhythm combinations as described above, but with a quantization interval corresponding to ¹⁄₁₆th note. Figure 10 shows the pattern in notational form, the initial activation pattern of the input units, and the remaining pattern after analysis.

Several input units are active for all patterns because the rhythm patterns are very regular. In these examples, on every quarter beat both ¹⁄₈th notes are present. The input sequences only differ by the presence of the ¹⁄₁₆th notes on the offbeat of the ¹⁄₈th beats. After the analysis algorithm only those input units remain that stand for these offbeats. The network has eliminated all the information which is common to all the input patterns. For more complex input patterns, the analysis result is less regular. If syncopations are included, the on-beat information becomes equally important to the network. A network which learned to distinguish ³⁄₄th from ⁹⁄₈th patterns will

Figure 11. Ambiguous Sequence.

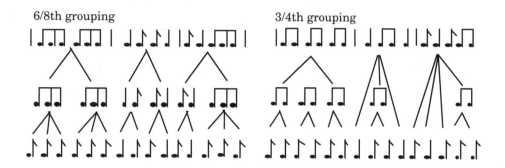

Figure 12. Two Possible Groupings for the Rhythm from Figure 12.

look for information on the third, fourth and fifth beat, the first beat is eliminated due to the equal length of the two measures.

Rhythm Classification

In the course of this work, we encountered some ambiguous situations. For some rhythm sequences no grouping preference can be defined a priori (Figure 11).

Two or more solutions are possible, depending on the types of measures (⁶⁄₈, ¾...) which have been included in the training patterns (Figure 12).

A neural network will find the solution which is closest to the average of patterns presented during the training phase. It might not always settle to one stable solution but find a solution in between, if more solutions are equally probable.

This experience led to the idea of designing a rhythm classifier. The model designed for the distinction of rhythmic sequences built of classical ⁶⁄₈th and ¾th measures has two output units, each representing one class (grand-mother units). The network was trained on 60 sequences which are clearly identifiable. Examples from both classes include the same number of beats and a same sequence of note values can occur in both cases. Using a time resolution of ¹⁄₆₄th note values and presenting four measures of rhythmic events, we need 192 input units. Two hidden units were sufficient for good generalization in this example. The rhythm sequences are encoded into the input layer in the same form as in the previous examples. The test sequences were taken from the same music pieces (Marcel Bitch: Etudes rhythmiques pour clarinette) as the training sequences. It is useful to introduce a third activation state for the output units: the "don't know" state defined by an activation level near 0. If one of the sequences from Figure 12 is presented to the input layer, both output units take values around 0. This means that no decision can be made, because the input sequence represents both classes equally well (the two classes overlap in the representation space).

More experiments have been made involving rhythm classification, including different music styles, baroque dances, rag-time, reggae, tangos, to name only a few. The number of different classes varied from two up to four. All results were equally satisfactory and unsurprising and need not be discussed in further detail.

Rhythm Driven Performance

Music styles, like baroque dances, classic waltzes or jazz styles have different formal, harmonic and rhythm structures. As we consider only simple, monophonic music, the important aspect is the rhythm structure. In performance, it is expressed by accentuations, loudness and rhythmic stresses. We consider music styles which are primarily defined by their rhythm and accentuation. A bolero for instance will be recognized as such, if composed in baroque or modern style because of its strong rhythmic peculiarities. If a neural network is trained to find the grouping preferences for one specific style, then it will impose that style's particular rhythm structure to any melody that it analyzes, and can be used for rhythm driven performance. The network structure, as well as the encoding of the input pattern, is the same as in the above described applications.

The neural network is trained to output musical information to a MIDI instrument. For performance the grouping information encoded in the output units has to be translated into accentuations of single events. The hierarchical tree contains more information than is needed. Instead of encoding all the structural information into the output vector it is simpler to directly represent accentuations. The output units represent the same time axis as the input units, but they take discrete activation values corresponding to the level of accentuation.

The number of output units has been reduced considerably by this encoding. Using a time resolution of $\frac{1}{32}$nd notes and presenting three $\frac{3}{4}$ measures, 96 input units and 96 output units are necessary.

There are two possible network architectures: one network per music style or encoding of several music styles within one network. For the first architecture, two or more networks are trained with training sets from different music styles. After the training phase, all the networks are accessible from the same interface. A melody is entered using a MIDI instrument and the user must choose which network

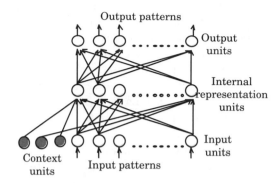

Figure 13. Network Structure with Context Units.

to activate. Another, more compact architecture requires additional input units, called context units. Only one network structure is trained with all the training patterns (including several music styles). The corresponding music style is encoded into the context units (Figure 13).

The network has to differentiate similar input sequences only by the context units. The results are very interesting to listen to. We did not make the usual generalization tests with this architecture, due to the good results in previous experiments. We only judged by listening.

Conclusion

We have shown the possibility of representing knowledge about musical rhythm in a neural network. Different aspects of human rhythm handling have been successfully solved by our representation scheme: rhythm analysis, rhythm classification and rhythm driven performance. We are aware of the simplifications we have made in this first approach, especially the lack of temporal information. The next steps in research will have to be taken into this direction, including dynamic neural networks.

Acknowledgments

Special thanks to Christoph Lischka, who enabled the collaboration at the expert system group, Gesellschaft fuer Mathematik und Datenverarbeitung, St. Augustin, FRG in 1988, and who had the initial idea for this project. Thanks to Marc Linster and Stefan Knerr for spending much time on carefully reviewing initial drafts. Last but not least thanks to an anonymous reviewer for helpful and justified criticism.

References

[Baker 1989] Baker, M. 1989. An artificial intelligence approach to musical grouping analysis" *Contempo-rary Music Review* Spring 1989, special issue on Music and the Sciences.

[Deutsch 1980] Deutsch, D. 1980. The processing of structured and unstructured tonal sequences. *Perception and Psychophys.* 28, 381–389.

[Hipfinger & Linster 1990] Hipfinger, G. and Linster, C. 1990. Preprocessing of musical information and applications for neural networks. In proceedings of the Tenth European Meeting on Cybernetics and Systems Research, Vienna.

[Laden & Keefe 1990] Laden, B. and Keefe, D. H. 1990. The Representation of Pitch in a Neural Network Model of Chord Classification. *Computer Music Journal.* Vol 13, Number 4.

[Laske 1980] Laske, O. E. 1980. Toward an Explicit Cognitive Theory of Musical Listening. *Computer Music Journal.* Vol 4, No2, Summer 1980 pp: 73–83.

[Lerdahl & Jackendoff 1983] Lerdahl, F. and Jackendoff, R. 1983. *A generative Theory of tonal music.* Cambridge: MIT Press.

[Linster 1990] Linster, C. 1990. A neural network which learns to play in different musical styles. In proceedings of the International Computer Music Conference, Glasgow.

[Linster 1989] Linster, C. 1989. Get Rhythm, a Musical Application for Neural Networks. Arbeitspapiere der GMD 365.

[Linster 1988] Linster, C. 1988. Rhythm Analysis with backpropagation. In proceedings of Connectionism in Perspective, SGAICO, Zürich.

[Miller, Scarborough, & Jones 1988] Miller, B. O., Scarborough, D. L.and Jones, J. A. 1988. A Model of Meter Perception in Music. In proceedings of the AAAI workshop on AI and Music.

[Rom, Grim & Linster 1989] Rom, G., Grim, R. and Linster, C. 1990. Medical decision support based on databases, expert systems and neural networks. In proceedings of the IFAC world congress, Tallinn USSR.

[Rumelhart, Hinton & Williams 1986] Rumelhart, D. E., Hinton, G. E. and Williams, R.J.1986. Learning internal representations by error-propagation. In *Parallel Distributed Processing*, ed D. E. Rumelhart and J. L. McClelland.Cambridge: The MIT Press.

[Sloboda 1985] Sloboda, J.A. 1985. *The Musical Mind, The cognitive psychology of music.* Oxford psychology series No. 5, Clarendon Press Oxford.

[Todd 1990] Todd, P. M. 1990. A Connectionist Approach to Algorithmic Composition. *Computer Music Journal.* Vol 13, Number 4.

Abstract

A basic problem in music perception is how a listener develops a hierarchical representation of the metric structure of the sort proposed by Lerdahl and Jackendoff (1983). This paper describes work on two contrasting approaches to developing psychologically plausible solutions to this problem. One approach uses a set of rules that specify the ways in which musical events are used in constructing a metric structure, and express the formal requirements that a metric structure should fulfill. The second approach uses parallel constraint-satisfaction in which many independent agents respond to events in the music, with a representation of the metric structure emerging as a result of distributed local interactions between the agents (Marr, 1982).

Chapter 18

On the Perception of Meter

Benjamin O. Miller, Don L. Scarborough, and
Jacqueline A. Jones

How do people perceive meter? How do we know when to clap in order to clap along with the music? Which aspects of music (e.g. duration, pitch, accent) are relevant to this perceptual task? How do we use such information to discover an appropriate temporal framework to organize the sequence of events in the music? These are the questions that have motivated the simulation models described in this chapter.

Meter is a perceived pulse that marks off equal temporal intervals in music. These pulses tend to be grouped perceptually, with the first of each group heard as accented; within groups, pulses appear to alternate between weak and strong in a regular way that reflects a hierarchical organization, as illustrated below. In this notation, introduced by Lerdahl and Jackendoff (1983) in *A Generative Theory of Tonal Music* (henceforth, *GTTM*), the numbers along the top represent successive equally spaced points in time, and the dots below them are pulses. The first row of dots shows a pulse at each successive point in time and might represent time intervals corresponding to, say, eighth notes. The second row of pulses, corresponding to every other pulse of the first row, groups pulses in the first row by twos and therefore represents a quarter note pulse. The third row represents half notes. Moments with dots at more than one level (e.g., time points 1, 3, 5 and 9) are perceived as stressed relative to others, and in this example they hierarchically organize pulses into pairs, pairs of pairs, and so on. Of these levels (e.g. eighth, quarter, half), the most perceptually salient is what we intuitively call the *beat* or what Lerdahl and Jackendoff call the *tactus*, a level in the hierarchy that corresponds to a moderate foot-tapping tempo. It is important to note that a structure of alternating strong and weak beats is generally heard even when listening to a sequence of equally spaced, equally intense tones, indicating that the hierarchical organization is a property of perception (Fraisse, 1982).

Time										
1	*2*	*3*	*4*	*5*	*6*	*7*	*8*	*9*	*10 etc.*	
Metric Level 1 •	•	•	•	•	•	•	•	•	•	
2 •		•		•		•		•		
3 •				•				•		

In *GTTM*, a hierarchy's structure is constrained by *metric well-formedness rules*, which require that every note onset must be represented by a beat[1] at the lowest metric level (level 1 in the above example) and, conversely, that every beat at a given level must also be a beat at all lower levels. At each level, beats must be evenly spaced in time and must group beats at the next lower level by twos (as in the above example) or by threes. *Metric preference rules* specify how to decide among several possible well-formed hierarchies. The most basic of these rules gives preference to a metric hierarchy in which stressed notes (strong beats in the music) correspond to the highest levels of the metric hierarchy. Metric analysis is a matter of constructing a metric hierarchy that is legal (i.e. obeys the metric well-formedness rules) and most closely fits the music (according to the metric preference rules).

Metric structures provide frameworks for the emergence of rhythm. For example, syncopated rhythms occur when perceived musical accents are heard at relatively unstressed times in the metric structure. Thus, musical events are heard within the context of the metric structure, but a listener must use those same musical events to discover the metric structure in the first place.

We have developed two psychological simulation models of this meter extraction process. The *BEATS* program (Miller, Scarborough and Jones, 1988) is a rule-based approach that is part of a larger simulation of the meter and grouping stages of *GTTM* (Jones, Miller & Scarborough, 1988). BEATS is a rule-based production system (Newell & Simon, 1972), using a Hearsay II "blackboard" type of architecture (Erman, Hayes-Roth, Lesser & Reddy, 1980). The blackboard model has been popular in psychological modeling (e.g. McClelland & Rumelhart, 1981) because it was designed to deal with temporally unfolding input with multiple levels of interpretation. *BeatNet*, a network approach to meter extraction that currently stands alone (Miller, Scarborough & Jones, 1989), is a one-layer cooperative-competitive network (McClelland & Rumelhart, 1988).

Input to both BEATS and BeatNet is limited to a symbolic representation of note durations taken from music scores, without pitch, key, time signature, or placement of bar lines. This limitation is not meant to suggest that duration is the only cue to meter, or even that it is a sufficient cue. On the contrary, we assume that accents and melodic structure contain important metric cues, and that listeners have flexible perceptual strategies for using whatever cues are available. Our goal in limiting these models to duration information is to understand the possibilities and the limitations of duration as a cue to meter.

The metric rules of *GTTM* specify what a metric hierarchy ought to look like when an analysis is finished, but do not specify how such a hierarchy should be produced. Well-formedness rules are explicit constraints in BEATS, but not in BeatNet, where any well-formedness in the output reflects the structure and operation of the network. Both models make a single left-to-right pass through a score. This constraint is intended to respect the linear experience that we have of music, and does not deny the importance of short-term memory in listening. It does, however, rule out processes which require random access to the entire score. As the models move through a piece of music, they identify candidate metric levels, which can be thought of as metronomes. A metronome is characterized by its rate and phase, as shown below:

	Time										
	1	*2*	*3*	*4*	*5*	*6*	*7*	*8*	*9*	*10*	*etc.*
Metronome 1	• •	• •	• •	• •	• •	• •	• •	• •	• •	• •	
2	•	•	•	•	•	•	•	•	•	•	
3	•	•	•	•	•	•	•	•	• •		

Metronomes 1 and 2 differ in rate (1 ticks twice as often as 2), while metronomes 2 and 3 have the same rate but differ in phase.

A Rule-Based Approach to Meter Perception

BEATS operates in a single pass, and uses an input window to simulate short-term memory. An example of an input window is an index card with a rectangular cutout in its center a few inches wide and as high as a line of text. Reading text through the cutout as the card is passed along each line on the page demonstrates the effect of the input window. The narrower the cutout, the more difficult reading will be, as input covered by the card is no longer available to the visual perceptual processes responsible for reading. When the input is auditory, the width of the window is measured not in inches but in seconds; the briefer the temporal width of the window, the more difficult it will be to make sense of the input. That which is beyond the window is gone, but input inside the window can be examined repeatedly. In BEATS the width of the input window is five seconds (Dowling & Harwood, 1986; Turner & Poppel, 1983).

BEATS incorporates both bottom-up and top-down components. The bottom-up components simply construct metronomes (i.e., metric units) based on time intervals between successive note onsets as they occur. Top-down components include: a) processes that use these intervals and combinations thereof to predict future events, with different intervals leading to different predictions; and b) processes that evaluate hypothesized metric units for consistency with a well-structured hierarchy as specified by *GTTM*, eliminating inconsistent units when necessary.

BEATS is based on metric hypothesis testing: the occurrence of an interval (note onset to note onset) generates a hypothesis that this interval is a level in the metric hierarchy, which will be either confirmed or disconfirmed by future events. Confirmed hypotheses produce levels in the growing metric hierarchy. BEATS also contains rules, adapted from those of Longuet-Higgins and Lee (1982), that create new metric levels from existing ones (thus producing metric levels larger than any note duration). We have added to these rules by providing three things: a way to generate the entire hierarchy; criteria for excluding levels generated by the rules but not acceptable in the context of *GTTM*; and a means of generating those levels not generated by Longuet-Higgins and Lee's rules but required by *GTTM*. BEATS' rules are given here, followed by a detailed example of their operation.

Setup.

> IF 1—the onset of the second note has been reached
> and 2—the time frame has not been created
> THEN create the time frame.

Induce.

> IF 1—a new onset interval is found
> and 2—the interval stands in an integral ratio to the nearest existing metronome
> THEN add a new metronome corresponding to the new onset interval.

Double.

> IF 1—the time frame predicts a future note onset
> and 2—the hypothesis is confirmed
> and 3—the time frame is smaller than some limit (e.g. a whole note)
> THEN double the time frame and add a new metronome to the hierarchy.

Upbeat.

> IF a new onset interval is longer than any previous interval and longer
> than the time frame
> THEN the first onset of the new interval becomes the downbeat.

Longnote.

> IF 1— the Upbeat rule has just applied
> and 2—the time frame predicts an onset earlier than one actually occurs
> THEN enlarge the time frame so that it predicts the next onset, and add
> a new metronome to the hierarchy.

Interpolate.

> IF a new metronome is created that divides the nearest existing
> metronome by 3 or $\frac{1}{3}$
> THEN interpolate a third metronome that stands in a 1:2 or 1:3 ratio to
> the first two metronomes.

Stretch.

> IF 1—an onset occurs before the next predicted onset
> and 2—the interval beginning there is longer than the previous interval
> THEN enlarge the time frame and create a new metronome.

Slide.

    IF 1—the onset predicted by the time frame is reached
  and 2—the Double rule does not apply because the size limit has been
           reached (see Double, condition 3)
  THEN slide the time frame by moving T1 to T2, T2 to T3,
           and T3 to T2 + (T2 − T1).

Remove/1.

    IF 1—the ratio between two adjacent metronomes is nonintegral
  and 2—the Interpolate rule has no solution
  and 3—one of the problem metronomes is not consistent with the largest
           metronome in the hierarchy
  THEN remove the inconsistent metronome.

Remove/2.

    IF 1) the ratio between two adjacent metronomes is nonintegral
  and 2) the Interpolate rule has no solution
  and 3) each of the metronomes is consistent with the largest
           metronome in the hierarchy
  THEN 1) estimate the meter by finding the larger of 2x or 3x the smallest
           metronome that integrally divides the largest metronome
  and 2) determine which of the problem metronomes is inconsistent with
           the estimated meter
  and 3) remove the inconsistent metronome.

The order of priority of these rules is 1–Setup, 2–Induce, 3–Longnote, 4–Upbeat 5–Stretch, 6–Double, 7–Remove, 8–Interpolate, 9–Slide.

Figure 1 shows BEATS' analysis of the beginning of Mozart's symphony no. 40 (first violin part). None of the metric levels begins on the first note of the symphony, because neither BEATS nor a listener can construct a metric hierarchy before hearing a few notes. Once BEATS has identified metric levels, it generates expectations at each level, like a listener who has "got the beat," producing a metric structure that conforms to the well-formedness rules of *GTTM*. That is, a dot marks every note onset, and the temporal intervals (represented by distance between dots at any level) are uniform. Also, if there is a dot at level L (e.g., quarter note) there is a dot at L-1 (e.g., eighth note), and dots at level L group dots at L-1 either by twos or by threes. Note also that strong beats (those with dots at higher levels) coincide with onsets of longer notes and coincide with Mozart's bar lines.

BEATS works by processing a piece note by note and trying to discover a time interval that will provide a basis for a hierarchical metric structure. Initial hypotheses about an appropriate time interval are based on the time intervals between successive note onsets. An observed time interval is then used to predict the time of future events in the piece. The mechanism for this is the *time-frame*, a set of three equally-spaced times: T1, T2 and T3. When analysis begins, T1 anchors the beginning of the metric structure at the onset of the first note. T2 corresponds to the beginning of the second note. BEATS now hypothesizes that the interval defined by the two onsets (the *frame interval*) represents a metric unit in the music, and predicts that another onset will occur at time T3, one frame interval further on. This hypothesis is instantiated in a *metronome*, a process that represents a level in the metric hierarchy. At this point, the frame interval is an eighth note, so a metronome with a period of an eighth-note is created. The "ticks" of this metronome at successive time intervals are represented by dots in the metric hierarchy.

Figure 1. Mozart Symphony No. 40, First Movement (first violin).

Once BEATS has created a metronome, its processing is influenced both by events in the music and by the occurrence of metronome ticks. The next processing step always occurs at the closer of two events: the next note onset or the next tick of the lowest level (smallest time interval) metronome. In this example, the time to the sole metronome's next tick is the same as the distance to note 3, so BEATS moves to this location.

The third note coincides with a tick of the eighth-note metronome, supporting the hypothesis that the eighth-note is a metric unit. On the strength of this, BEATS hypothesizes a higher-level temporal grouping at double the metric unit just confirmed. The reason for doubling rather than tripling a metric unit to generate the next higher level is that two is the most common grouping in the subjective organization of identical, isochronous tones (Fraisse, 1982), and in spontaneous tapping (Fraisse, 1947–1948). Thus, BEATS uses a *Double* rule to establish a new time frame with a frame interval of a quarter-note. The resulting quarter-note metronome now becomes the highest level of the metric structure anchored at the first note. Based on this new time frame, BEATS now moves T3 to note 4, thus predicting that the next significant metric event will occur at the next tick of the quarter-note metronome. There are now two metronomes, with different periods.

The interval to the next note onset is a quarter-note, while the unit of the lowest metronome is an eighth-note, so the next location is halfway between the onset of the third and fourth notes. BEATS examines each metronome. The eighth-note metronome is set to tick here, but there is no onset here. This is acceptable because metric pulses frequently occur during sustained notes or during rests.

The next tick of the quarter-note metronome occurs at the onset of the fourth note, so we might expect BEATS again to double the frame interval and create a new half-note metronome. However, something more important has happened. At the onset of the fourth note, BEATS reaches the end of the third note and it recognizes that this quarter-note is longer than any note it has heard before. Because longer notes usually initiate higher-level metric groupings (Povel and Essens, 1985), and since it is still early in the piece, BEATS reinterprets the first two notes as upbeats to the third note. Accordingly, an *Upbeat* rule specifies that the time frame and the anchor point (i.e. T1) for the metric structure should be shifted forward from the first note so as to coincide with the onset of the third note. The frame interval is not changed, so T2 is now set to the onset of the fourth note. Because of this change, the Doubling that seemed warranted at this location is no longer possible because T3 has been projected to a point (the onset of note six) we have not yet reached: thus, no new metronome is created.

At the onset of the sixth note, BEATS has reached T3 and accordingly Doubles the quarter-note frame interval to a half note, and makes a half-note metronome. Note that because of the previous Upbeat operation, which shifted the anchor point T1, every second tick of the half-note metronome coincides with a bar line in the score. At the ninth note, BEATS again reaches T3, and the Double rule enlarges the frame interval to a whole note and creates a new metronome corresponding to a whole-note interval beginning at the anchor point, which is still set to coincide with the third note.

We do not allow enlargement of the frame interval beyond a temporal limit which in practice is about the duration of a typical measure. As a result, our analysis does not produce *GTTM*'s two-measure, four-measure and higher metric levels. The point of this limitation is that higher levels are: a) less perceptually salient (they are far above the tactus); and b) better understood as defining phrasal boundaries than metric units (Longuet-Higgins and Lee, 1982).

Based on the four metronomes (the eighth-, quarter-, half-, and whole-note levels), BEATS generates the full metric hierarchy. As it proceeds, it evaluates the adequacy of each of the metronomes by noting how well they match events in the music. If a change in the meter of the music were to occur, this would be reflected in a poor match between the existing metronomes and events in the music. This mismatch can then trigger a re-evaluation of the metronomes and the metric structure at that point.

BEATS' analysis of Mozart's Piano Sonata K331, shown in Figure 2, illustrates another important operation. When BEATS gets to the second note, it creates a dotted eighth-note metronome, and the interval from the second to the third note leads to the creation of a sixteenth-note metronome. Upon reaching the fourth note and the next tick of the dotted-eighth note metronome, Beats creates an eighth-note metronome corresponding to the third note. BEATS also realizes that the third note, while not the longest so far, is longer than the previous note. The previous note, a sixteenth-note, falls at the beginning of a metric unit at the highest metric level (i.e., dotted eighth note). On the assumption that longer notes should initiate higher level metric units, a *Stretch* rule specifies the creation of a new larger time interval by stretching the dotted-eighth note interval to span the interval from the first note to the third note, corresponding to a quarter-note metronome. T1, the anchor point, remains at the first (longest) note. However, the Stretch rule also specifies that the metronome corresponding to the interval that was stretched (the dotted eighth note) should be eliminated. Intuitively, the purpose of the Stretch rule is to handle dotted notes. A dotted note is usually followed by a complementary note which, added to the dotted note, yields a duration that fits the metric hierarchy at a higher level than either of the notes alone.

Figure 2. Mozart Piano Sonata K331, First Movement.

BEATS now has sixteenth-, eighth- and quarter-note metronomes. However, the new quarter-note metronome now incorrectly predicts a note onset in the middle of the fourth note. Because the quarter-note metronome is the largest metric unit, and because its prediction of a note onset is disconfirmed, this suggests that the quarter-note interval is incorrect, and therefore should be enlarged. The most conservative enlargement is made by Stretching the interval to a dotted quarter-note and creating a new dotted quarter-note metronome. Again, the application of the Stretch rule leads to the elimination of the quarter-note metronome, meaning that the quarter-note level is no longer a part of the listener's metric representation. Both applications of the Stretch procedure illustrate a common principle: whenever an interval is enlarged by some means other than doubling, it is assumed that the old interval is incorrect.

In general, BEATS will create a metronome that corresponds to the onset interval between any two successive notes, provided that such a metronome is consistent with the current frame interval. By consistent, we mean that the interval in question is an integral multiple or divisor of the frame interval. For example, consider the beginning of the last movement of Mozart's symphony no. 41 ("Jupiter") in Figure 3. At the outset, BEATS establishes only a whole-note metronome. Later it hears the first of the quarter-notes. Since the first quarter-note is consistent with the whole-note metronome, BEATS creates a quarter-note metronome. However, although its period is consistent with the current frame interval, the metric hierarchy now violates another *GTTM* rule that limits the ratio between the time intervals at adjacent metric levels to values of two or three. The solution is to interpolate a half-note metronome between the quarter- and whole-note levels. Thus, in this case, BEATS creates a metric level that does not correspond to any onset-onset interval in the piece up to that point. A few notes later we hear a dotted half-note; this, too, is smaller than the whole-note interval, but since it is not consistent, no metronome is made. After the dotted half, we hear a sixteenth note, and it is again necessary to create a new metronome, as well as an interpolated eighth-note level.

Figure 3. Mozart Symphony No. 41 (Jupiter), First Movement.

Based on note-by-note processing, BEATS yields musically plausible metric analyses that conform to *GTTM*'s rules for a wide variety of scores. However, there are many scores that it does not analyze correctly. This is not surprising, because music provides many cues to metric structure (e.g., accent, harmony) other than the time intervals between successive notes. The extent to which BEATS succeeds reflects the redundancy between rhythmic, melodic and harmonic dimensions in most music. The important question is whether those scores that BEATS cannot analyze are also difficult for human listeners when only time interval information is presented. Recent work in our laboratory (Miller, 1991) suggests that the answer is a qualified yes. Overall, BEATS is able to predict listeners' metric perceptions in over 40% of all trials. The table below shows the correspondence between BEATS' analyses and listeners' perceptions.

		BEATS' Analysis		
		Correct	*Wrong Meter*	*Wrong Phase*
Subject's Perception	Correct	55*	26	29
	Wrong Meter	24	38*	33
	Wrong Phase	14	18	36*

(percentages are by column)

The table shows, for example, that scores that were correctly analyzed by BEATS were correctly perceived by subjects in 55% of the trials, were perceived by subjects with the wrong meter in 24%, and were perceived by subjects with the right meter but the wrong phase 14% of the time. Starred cells represent agreement between subjects and BEATS; as predicted, each of these is the largest in its column. This significant association between BEATS' analyses and subjects' perceptions suggests that BEATS does capture some aspect(s) of meter perception. On the other hand, the association that is found when data are considered over many subjects and many trials conceals a puzzling inconsistency. Subjects tended not to hear a given score the same way on repeated listenings. This is puzzling in that models like BEATS predict that a listener will hear a given score the same way every time. A possible interpretation of this result is to suppose that there are nondeterministic aspects of meter perception that are not modeled by BEATS, whose analysis may reflect an average of listeners' perceptions.

A Parallel Constraint-Satisfaction Approach to Meter Perception

BEATS is an example of a rule-based symbolic system in which decisions about metric levels are generated and selected on the basis of rules that embody expectations about meter. In contrast to BEATS, our second model, BeatNet, is a simple one-layer parallel distributed processing network that performs more or less the same task, not by a sequence of decisions, but by satisfying a set of weak constraints in a cooperative-competitive network (Rumelhart, Smolensky, McClelland & Hinton, 1986).

The BeatNet model starts from the assumption that every level in a metric hierarchy will correspond to the duration and phase of a single note or small group of adjacent notes somewhere in the piece. This assumption suggests a strategy for discovering the metric hierarchy. If we first measure the durations of notes and note groups, the observed time intervals will define a set of candidate metric levels that will include the correct metric levels. Although many durations in a piece will not correspond to appropriate metric levels, if a subset within the candidate set can be found that jointly produces a well-formed hierarchy, then these intervals represent a plausible metric interpretation. Therefore BeatNet's task is first to identify the time intervals that occur in the score. Each observed interval then defines a metric level and a class of metric levels that are related to it by ratios of 2 and 3 or integer multiples of these ratios. The metric level defined by this observed interval is potentially compatible with each of the metric levels in this class in a complete hierarchy. Similarly, each observed interval also defines a second disjoint class of incompatible metric levels. Thus each interval found in the score is evidence for or against the inclusion, in a particular well-formed metric hierarchy, of metric levels corresponding to other observed intervals.

The BeatNet model consists of a one-dimensional array of very low frequency (i.e. less than 10 Hz) oscillators. The idea is that something similar to such oscillator time keepers underlies the ability of people to perceive metric levels and the relations between them. We assume that these oscillators respond to external events, in particular to the onset-to-onset time intervals that occur in a score. Each oscillator is driven by events in the score. That is, an oscillator is like a pendulum with a specific periodicity. Just as a pendulum begins swinging when set into motion by a push, an oscillator begins oscillating when "pushed" by the occurrence of an interval between two note onsets in the piece that matches the period of the oscillator. In addition, just as the period remains the same but the amplitude of the arc of a pendulum increases if the pendulum is pushed again at the end of each swing, so a BeatNet oscillator oscillates with greater amplitude if subsequent note onsets in the score occur at the right time to give the oscillator additional pushes. An additional assumption is that there can be oscillators with the same frequency but with different phases. By analogy, two pendula could swing at the same frequency, but one might tick when the other tocks.

The oscillators in BeatNet are ordered by frequency and are represented by a one-dimensional array of nodes. Each oscillator node has an activation level that is initially 0. In response to external and internal events, an oscillator's activation level can vary between a maximum level of 1.0 and a minimum level of -0.2. Events can be either excitatory or inhibitory, and an activation level greater than 0 represents an excited oscillator, while an activation below 0 represents an inhibited oscillator. An oscillator is excited to the extent that notes matching the period and phase of an oscillator occur in the score. Thus, a sequence of eighth notes at a particular tempo will strongly activate the corresponding eighth-note oscillator node. In addition, if the eighth-note intervals stop, the activation of the oscillator node decays with time, just as a pendulum eventually comes to rest when no longer pushed. Once an oscillator has been excited, the rate of decay determines how long that oscillator will remain above some minimum level of activation and will affect other oscillators, as described below. Thus, the decay rate defines a time window that determines how long earlier events continue to play a role. In our simulations, the decay rate was chosen such that an oscillator loses about half its excitation within one measure.

A score is presented to BeatNet as a sequence of note onsets. As BeatNet moves through the score, the time between one note onset and another leads to the excitation of an oscillator with that period. Each oscillator has a phase, which is defined by where it starts, and a period that spans some onset-onset interval in the piece. As a piece is heard, a subset of the oscillators is excited by the time intervals that occur. The activation of an oscillator, then, depends on the detection of a specific time interval or period in the stimulus with a particular phase. If a period is detected with more than one phase, each period/phase combination activates a corresponding oscillator with the corresponding period and phase. Oscillators that do not correspond to onset-onset intervals are initially inactive.

Simply activating oscillators that correspond to onset-onset intervals does not lead to a coherent metrical structure. For example, a series of eighth notes will activate an oscillator corresponding to an eighth note, as well as oscillators corresponding to a quarter note, a dotted-quarter note, a half note, and so on. Furthermore, these additional oscillators will be activated in several phases. For example, there will be a quarter-note oscillator in phase with the first eight-note, and a second quarter-note oscillator in phase with the second eight-note but out of phase with the other quarter-note oscillator. However a metric analysis that conforms to the Lerdahl and Jackendoff rules will allow only the subset of these oscillators that make a well-formed hierarchy. This suggests that oscillators that appear to be inconsistent with the metric structure should be suppressed or inhibited, while oscillators that are consistent should be further strengthened. To do this, we let the oscillator nodes interact as described below in ways that represent constraints on the network that are likely to lead to a coherent metric structure.

The activation level of an oscillator is affected by several factors. Once an oscillator is activated, its activation increases if it predicts future note onsets, i.e., it ticks concurrently with a note onset, but, in the absence of continued excitatory input, the activation level will decrease to 0 because of decay. In addition, internal events affect the activation level. For example, an oscillator's activation is increased by excitatory inputs from compatible oscillators. On the other hand, an oscillator's activation level is decreased from time to time by inhibitory effects from incompatible oscillators. These interactions are described more fully below when two versions of the BeatNet model are presented. Finally, activation is indirectly affected by two other features of BeatNet. First, each oscillator node has a threshold. An oscillator's activation level must be above this threshold for it to have any effect, either excitatory or inhibitory, on other oscillators, though it may continue to tick and can still receive excitation and inhibition. Second, in time perception, as with pitch perception, people are most responsive or sensitive to events of a particular frequency, and this peak sensitivity is the basis for the tactus, the metric level that is perceived as most salient, and which is generally around 2 Hz (Fraisse, 1947–48). Therefore, oscillators closest to the tactus are most sensitive to events, and sensitivity decreases with distance from the tactus.

We created two versions of this general BeatNet oscillator model. In the first version, called the Broadcast model, we built a minimum of interactive constraints into the network structure. Interactions between network nodes are based on a few simple principles that only indirectly embody the requirements for a well-formed hierarchy. The question was whether such a simple architecture could nonetheless produce metric analyses that were well-formed in the Lerdahl and Jackendoff sense. The second model, called the Resonance model, makes stronger assumptions about the nature of the interactions between oscillators.

The Broadcast Model

In the Broadcast model, oscillator nodes respond only to signals that are "broadcast" to all the nodes. That is, there are no specific connections between nodes, but rather an event affects all nodes. These broadcast signals originate from both external and internal events. An externally generated signal is broadcast to all nodes whenever a note onset occurs. The effect of this signal is that all oscillators that would tick at that instant are further activated. The second source of broadcast signals comes from the internal ticking of the oscillators themselves. A tick of an oscillator is, functionally, much like a note onset, in that it excites other (compatible) oscillators that also tick at that moment. In addition, we assume that when an oscillator ticks, it inhibits all oscillators with smaller periods that do not tick. Thus, the effect of an event on a node is determined by the state of the node (ticking or not ticking) at the time of the event. The strength of these excitatory and inhibitory signals depends on how many oscillators tick at the same time. However, we assume that a ticking oscillator has the greatest effect on nearby oscillators (those with similar periods) and weaker effects on more distant oscillators (which are more remote in period). That is, the influence of one oscillator on another in the oscillator array is a decreasing function of the distance between them. Distance, for purposes of calculating the effect of one oscillator on another, is defined in terms of the ratio of the periods of the two oscillators. Close neighbors show strong excitatory or inhibitory interactions, while more distant oscillators are hardly affected. Finally, as described above, oscillators closest to the tactus are most sensitive to events, and sensitivity decreases with distance from the tactus. The activation level of each oscillator is updated at intervals corresponding to a 128th note. The change in an oscillator's activation level at each update depends on the net input to the oscillator from all external and internal events. The change in activation level also depends on the current level of activation as described by McClelland & Rumelhart (1988, p 13).

The idea that oscillators that tick at the same time strengthen each other is a weak way to implement the constraint that, in a well-formed hierarchy, an oscillator with a period T should be in phase (tick at the same time) with other oscillators whose periods are related to T by small integer ratios, e.g., 2T or 3T, and ½T or ⅓T. Oscillators that are in phase with each other will tick together more often than out-of-phase oscillators. In addition, the tick of an oscillator inhibits all oscillators with shorter periods that do not tick at that time. This implements the constraint that a pulse at one metric level must coincide with pulses at all the lower metric levels. The asymmetry between excitation and inhibition can be seen in the nature of a well-formed metric hierarchy: a beat at a given level need not be a beat at higher levels, but it must be a beat at all lower levels (Lerdahl and Jackendoff, 1983). The Broadcast model's patterns of inhibition and excitation are such that oscillators that together constitute a well-formed hierarchy will tend to strengthen one another and inhibit outsiders.

Figure 4 shows in graphic form BeatNet's analysis of Mozart's 40th symphony. Results from the Broadcast model are shown in Figure 4a. The figure illustrates oscillator activation levels and interactions. The Y axis represents the activation level of an oscillator. The X axis, representing time, intersects the Y axis at an activation level of 0. The horizontal dashed line above the X axis represents the threshold that an oscillator must reach before it can affect other oscillators. The short vertical dash lines mark the note onsets in this piece. The very first note onset occurs at the Y axis. Each curve represents the activation level of a single oscillator over time. The most active oscillator is an eighth note, the second most active is a quarter note, and the third most active is a half note. A whole-note oscillator is also weakly activated. These four oscillators are indicated by the note symbols on the right side of the panel. Although it is not easy to see in this representation, these oscillators are in phase with each other, indicating that BeatNet has produced a well-formed metric hierarchy.

Unlike the analysis by the BEATS rule-based model shown in Figure 1, the overall BeatNet interpretation in Figure 4a is out of phase with Mozart's bar lines in that the whole-note metric level begins on the second beat of the measure. This shift in

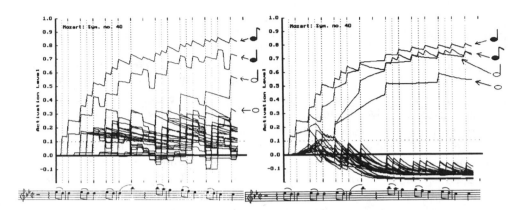

Figure 4. Mozart Symphony No. 40: a. Broadcast Model; b. Resonance Model.

the metric structure can be seen by noting the location of the increase in the activation levels of the half- and whole-note oscillators; this increase occurs on the second quarter note rather than on the first quarter note of the last measure shown. It is not clear that this is a failing of the model, for the initial rhythmic structure is in fact ambiguous. On the other hand, in the BEATS and BeatNet models we are assuming that initial analysis of the metric structure is based on duration-only data. A further stage of analysis would be needed to incorporate and integrate other information, such as pitch, tonal progression and grouping, and this additional analysis would disambiguate many metric structures. Thus, we propose that listeners, presented with duration-only information, might produce the same sorts of analyses produced by BeatNet.

Figure 5a shows the Broadcast model's interpretation of Mozart's Piano Sonata K331. At the end of this segment, the sixteenth- and eighth-note oscillators are most active. However, both a quarter- and a dotted-quarter note oscillator are also activated. Either of these oscillators would produce a well-formed metric hierarchy in conjunction with the sixteenth- and eight-note oscillators. However, as it stands, this is an illegal hierarchy. With additional measures, which are not shown, the dotted-eight oscillator wins out, in agreement with Mozart's score, and the quarter-note oscillator is weakened. In addition, a dotted-half note oscillator emerges, although it is out of phase with Mozart's bar lines by half a measure. Again, this last outcome is reasonable because, based only on duration information, the first three notes of the piece can easily be heard as an upbeat to the first quarter note.

All in all, the Broadcast model seems to do a fairly good job of inducing appropriate metric structures on the basis of some simple assumptions about how the oscillators might interact. Further, within wide limits, the model's output does not depend critically on the values of the parameters that determine the interactions of

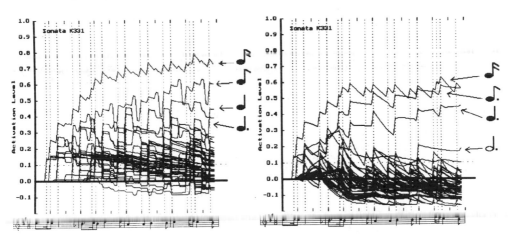

Figure 5. Mozart Piano Sonata K331: a. Broadcast Model; b. Resonance Model.

oscillators. The important point is that the principles for oscillator interaction do not explicitly embody the concept of a metric hierarchy. Instead, the metric hierarchy evolves from the effects of many local distributed interactions.

The Resonance Model

In the Resonance model, as in the Broadcast model, we assume: 1) that we have an array of oscillators; 2) that each oscillator is excited by the occurrence of note-onset intervals that match its period and phase; and 3) that the activation level of each oscillator decays over time. However, the architecture of the Resonance model makes more specific assumptions about the pattern of interactions. In particular, this model assumes that excitatory and inhibitory interactions continue to occur in the interval between ticks and note onsets. For this to happen, we must assume that all oscillators are connected. Any two oscillators are connected by an excitatory or an inhibitory connection depending on whether or not those two oscillators are in phase, and on whether their periods form a simple integer ratio. This assumption leads to a pattern of interactions that produces much quicker sorting out of "bad" oscillators. In addition, depending on the strength of the interactions, the Resonance model does resonate, in that a particular subset of the oscillators can form a pattern of interactions in which the strength of the internal signals alone is sufficient to hold the oscillators in a stable pattern of activation. This may not be an unreasonable characteristic of the model because it means that the same structure that recognizes a metric structure can continue to maintain that metric structure, just as a listener, after hearing a few bars of a piece, can anticipate the rhythmic pattern thereafter.

Figure 4b shows the analysis of the Resonance model for Mozart's symphony no. 40. A well-formed metric structure is created, but it is incorrectly aligned with respect to Mozart's bar lines. However, in contrast to the results for the Broadcast model shown in the left panel, a different whole-note metric level emerges that begins with the upbeat. In general, the selected metric levels stand out much more clearly from the other metric levels in the Resonance model than in the Broadcast model.

Figure 5b shows the Resonance model's analysis of Mozart's piano sonata, K331. Unlike the Broadcast model results (Figure 5a), the Resonance model correctly identifies the dotted-quarter and dotted-half note metric levels within the first four measures. Though this is a well-formed metric structure, the dotted-half note oscillator is again out of phase with Mozart's bar lines by half a measure.

There are two problems in evaluating BeatNet. First, BeatNet does not necessarily produce a well-formed hierarchy, and, as a result, the model's analysis is often neither completely correct (i.e. containing all and only the correct oscillators) nor completely incorrect (i.e. containing no correct oscillators). Second, BeatNet's output does not explicitly identify a specific set of oscillators as constituting an appropriate metric hierarchy for the score under analysis. In the case of the Resonance model, there is often a small set of oscillators with much higher activation levels than the rest of the oscillators; in such cases it seems reasonable to treat that small set as BeatNet's candidate metric hierarchy. However, the Broadcast model tends to produce a more continuous range of activation levels, and in any event it is hard to say what criterion should be used to distinguish between those oscillators that belong in the metric hierarchy and those that do not. These aspects of the model prevent evaluating it by asking whether the metric hierarchy produced by the model does or does not correspond to the correct hierarchy for a given piece. Instead, we have made a different comparison. The correct analysis of a score is one that corresponds to the score's time signature and bar lines. If a correct analysis of the score has four metric levels up to, say, a whole-note level, then the corresponding four oscillators should be the strongest in BeatNet's analysis. By the same token, the proportion of the strongest n oscillators in BeatNet's analysis that match metric levels in the correct analysis gives a rough indication of the model's performance.

We compared BeatNet's analyses of 19 folk-song scores to the correct analyses of the same scores. In all of BeatNet's analyses, the set of most strongly activated oscillators included at least one correct oscillator, and in some (3 Broadcast analyses, 6 Resonance analyses), this set included all oscillators found in the correct analysis. On average, both models included two thirds of the correct oscillators. Despite equal mean performance, there is a clear difference between the Broadcast and Resonance models in that the latter is more likely to be completely correct or quite wrong. Another notable result is that BeatNet performs best with duple-meter scores. For such scores, the Broadcast model's mean proportion of correct oscillators was 0.77 and the Resonance model's was 0.79; for triple-meter scores, the Broadcast model's mean proportion was 0.57 and the Resonance model's was 0.54. The lower performance for triple-meter scores arises because BeatNet has a propensity to produce duple metric hierarchies. A possible explanation of BeatNet's duple-meter bias is that the oscillators in a duple hierarchy tick together more often than oscillators in a triple hierarchy. The resulting difference in activation would, other things being equal, favor those oscillators that constitute a duple hierarchy.

We also compared BeatNet's and BEATS' analyses of the same scores. The proportion of oscillators in BeatNet's analyses that were also in BEATS' was 0.59 for the Broadcast model and 0.60 for the Resonance model. In a larger sample, which included the folk songs used in this comparison, BEATS correctly analyzed 38% of the scores. For the present comparison, scores were selected to represent all of BEATS' characteristic errors as well as correct analyses. Of the 19 scores selected, 15 are incorrectly analyzed by BEATS; for 10 of these, BeatNet's analysis corresponded more closely to the correct analysis than to BEATS' (incorrect) analysis. On the other five scores, BeatNet's analysis matched BEATS' as well as or better than it matched the correct analysis.

Conclusion

BEATS has a single agent, or inference engine, that makes decisions about metric structure using a set of rules, and knowing about the current score events and the current state of the metric analysis. In contrast, in a distributed network approach such as BeatNet, many weak constraints are represented in parallel by the interactions between nodes, and there is no single agent, no centralized knowledge, and no database of rules. Instead, each node and its interactions with other nodes embody constraints that an analysis of the meter should satisfy. Each node acts as one of many agents in influencing other nodes, with each agent embodying only a small piece of knowledge. Through interactions, the nodes affect each other in a way that is simple at the level of each node but complex for the network taken as a whole (Hopfield and Tank, 1985).

Another obvious difference between BEATS and BeatNet has to do with the kind of information the score provides in each case. BEATS considers only the period from one onset to the very next; it uses a set of rules to generate metric levels that do not correspond to note-to-note onset intervals, and it uses additional rules to correct phase errors. BeatNet, on the other hand, finds all evidence for oscillators in the score, and it uses a network of weak constraints rather than rules to weed out inappropriate oscillators. In BEATS, period and phase are tied together by the fact that, for a given period, only one phase is considered at a time. In BeatNet, period and phase are entirely independent in that there can be several oscillators with the same period but with different phases. Both phase conflicts and period conflicts are resolved in the same way, namely by the interplay of excitation and inhibition. Another important difference between the models has to do with tempo. Whereas BEATS ignores tempo altogether, BeatNet uses tempo information to weigh oscillators near the tactus more heavily.

The BeatNet models succeed in producing reasonable metric analyses for many pieces. In other cases, the output does not match our intuitions regarding the score. However, it is possible that a human listener would produce a similar wrong interpretation if deprived of all information other than time intervals. While Beat-Net solves or promises to solve some of the shortcomings of rule-based models, it is not without problems. A difficulty with BeatNet that is inherent in network models is the virtual impossibility of predicting the model's output and the difficulty in understanding the relation of this output to the many parameters. However, in general we have tried to constrain the system parameters based on a priori judgments about what is reasonable. While a rule-based system such as BEATS has few parameters and is very predictable—on the whole it can produce only one analysis of a given score—BeatNet produces different output as the values of its initial state and parameters are changed. Exploring the various configurations of values over a number of parameters is a daunting task, but we are encouraged by the fact that a configuration that works well with one score tends to work well with other scores.

Acknowledgments

This work was supported by an NSF Pre-Doctoral Fellowship to Miller and by PSC-CUNY Faculty Research Awards to Jones and to Scarborough.

Notes

1) *Beats* are durationless, equally spaced units of counting. *Meter* is the grouping of beats at the next higher level in a hierarchy of temporal relations. *Metric grouping* can be thought of as an accent structure (Dowling & Harwood, 1986) imposed on equally spaced beats. *Rhythm* emerges from the interaction of a metric structure and a sequence of note durations.

References

Dowling, W. J.; and Harwood, D. L. 1986. *Music Cognition.* Orlando, FL: Academic Press.

Erman, L. D.; Hayes-Roth, F.; Lesser, V. R.; and Reddy, D. R. 1980. The Hearsay-II Speech Understanding System: Integrating Knowledge to Resolve Uncertainty. *Computing Surveys* 12:213–253.

Fraisse, P. 1947–48. Mouvements Rythmiques et Arythmiques. *L'Annee Psychologique* 47–48:11–21.

Fraisse, P. 1982. Rhythm and Tempo. In *The Psychology of Music,* ed. D. Deutsch, 149–180. New York: Academic Press.

Hopfield, J. J; and Tank, D. W. 1985. "Neural" Computation of Decisions in Optimization Problems. *Biological Cybernetics,* 52:141–152.

Jones, J. A.; Miller, B. O.; and Scarborough, D. L. 1988. A Rule-based Expert System for Music Perception. *Behavior Research Methods, Instruments & Computers* 20:255–262.

Lerdahl, F.; and Jackendoff, R. 1983. *A Generative Theory of Tonal Music.* Cambridge, MA: MIT Press.

Longuet-Higgins, H. C.; and Lee, C. S. 1982. The Perception of Musical Rhythms. *Perception* 11:115–128.

Marr, D. 1982. *Vision.* San Francisco: W.H. Freeman.

McClelland, J. L.; and Rumelhart, D. E. 1981. An Interactive Model of Context Effects in Letter Perception: Part I. An Account of Basic Findings. *Psychological Review* 88: 375–407.

McClelland, J. L.; and Rumelhart, D. E. 1988. *Explorations in Parallel Distributed Processing.* Cambridge, MA: MIT Press.

Miller, B. O. 1991. *Simulation and Evaluation of a Model of Meter Perception.* Unpublished doctoral dissertation, City University of New York.

Miller, B. O.; Scarborough, D. L.; and Jones, J. A. 1988. A Model of Meter Perception in Music. In *Proceedings of the Tenth Annual Conference of the Cognitive Science Society,* 717–723. Hillsdale, NJ.: Lawrence Erlbaum Associates.

Miller, B. O.; Scarborough, D. L.; and Jones, J. A. 1989. Rule-Based versus Constraint Satisfaction Approaches to the Perception of Meter in Music. In *Proceedings of the Second International Workshop on Artificial Intelligence and Music, International Joint Conference on Artificial Intelligence (IJCAI-89).* 26–35. Menlo Park, CA: American Association for Artificial Intelligence.

Newell, A.; and Simon, H. A. 1972. *Human Problem Solving.* Englewood Cliffs, NJ: Prentice-Hall.

Povel, D.-J.; and Essens, P. 1985. Perception of Temporal Patterns. *Music Perception,* 2.111–140.

Rumelhart, D. E.; Smolensky, P.; McClelland, J. L; and Hinton, G. E. 1986. Schemata and Sequential Thought Processes in PDP Models. In *Parallel Distributed Processing: Explorations in the Microstructures of Cognition. Vol 2: Psychological and Biological Models,* Ch 14, 7–57. Cambridge, MA: MIT Press.

Turner, F.; and Poppel, E. 1983. The Neural Lyre: Poetic Meter, the Brain, and Time. *Poetry,* 142:277–310.

Abstract

Quantization separates continuous time fluctuations from the discrete metrical time in performance of music. Traditional and AI methods for quantization are explained and compared. A connectionist network of interacting cells is proposed, which directs the data of rhythmic performance towards an equilibrium state representing a metrical score. This model seems to lack some of the drawbacks of the older methods. The algorithms of the described methods are included as small Common Lisp programs.

Chapter 19

The Quantization Problem: Traditional and Connectionist Approaches

Peter Desain and Henkjan Honing

The Quantization Problem

Musical time can be considered as the product of two time scales: the discrete time intervals of a metrical structure, and the continuous time scales of tempo changes and expressive timing (Clarke 1987). In the notation of music both kinds are present, though the notation of continuous time is less developed than that of metric time (often just a word like rubato or accelerando is notated in the score). In the experimental literature, different ways in which a musician can add continuous timing changes to the metrical score have been identified. There are systematic changes in certain rhythmic forms, e.g., shortening triplets (Vos & Handel 1987) and consistent time asynchronies between voices in ensemble playing (Rasch 1979). Deliberate departures from metricality such as rubato seem to be used to emphasize musical structure, as exemplified in the phrase-final lengthening principal formalized by Todd (1985). Alongside these effects, which are collectively called expressive timing, are non-voluntary effects, such as random timing errors caused by the limits in the accuracy of the motor system (Shaffer 1981), and errors in mental time-keeping processes (Vorberg & Hambuch 1978). These non-intended effects are generally rather small, in the order of 10 milliseconds.

To make sense of most musics, it is necessary to separate the discrete and continuous components of musical time. We will call this process quantization, although the term is generally used to reflect only the extraction of a metrical score from a performance. This quantization process transforms incoming time intervals between subsequent note onsets, i.e., *inter-onset intervals*, into discrete note durations (as can be found in the score) and a tempo factor that reflects the deviation from this exact duration. It is solely based on inter-onset intervals: any other information like note offsets, dynamics and pitch is ignored. The output of the quantization process can serve as input for processes extracting higher level structural descriptions like meter.

Apart from its importance for cognitive modelling, a good theory of quantization has technical applications. It is one of the bottle-necks in the automatic transcription of performed music, and is also important for compositions with a real-time interactive component where the computer improvises or interacts with a live performer. It is indispensable in the study of expressive timing of music for which no score exists.

Traditional Methods

The quantization problem has been approached from different directions, the resulting solutions ranging from naive and inept to elegant and plausible. We will describe here first the methods that construct the solution in a straightforward numerical way.

Inter-Onset Quantization

This simple method rounds the inter-onset intervals of the notes to the nearest note duration on a scale containing all multiples of a smallest duration (time-grid unit or *quantum*). In Figure 1 an architecture for this method with standard signal processing modules is shown. Note that this method runs in *event-time:* one cycle of processing is done for each new incoming inter-onset interval, resulting in a quantized interval. The module divides the input by the smallest allowed value and rounds it to the nearest integer. It also yields a relative error in proportion to the quantum (between -0.5 and 0.5). When given a list of intervals and a value for the quantum the method will produce a list of quantized intervals with respect to this quantum. Given the inter-onset intervals of the rhythm of Figure 2, and a quantum of 100 ms (32th triplet at tempo 50), it will result in the list of multiples of this quantum (12 6 3 3 4 3 4 6 6 3 3 3 3 12) which does not represent the right quantization: (12 6 3 3 4 4 4 6 6 3 3 3 3 12). This method, when it makes a round-off error, will shift the absolute onset of all subsequent notes. When used in polyphonic music, an error in one stream of notes will permanently de-synchronize it with respect to the other streams.

Onset Quantization

At first sight, quantizing the absolute onsets of the notes themselves, instead of the inter-onset intervals, will be a solution to the de-synchronization problem. This method simply maps each onset-time to the nearest point in a fixed grid with a resolution equal to the quantum. Small but consistent deviations in the inter-onset intervals,

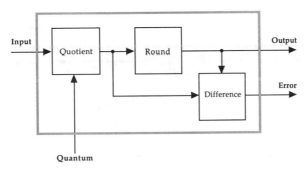

Quantum

Figure 1. Inter-Onset Quantizer.

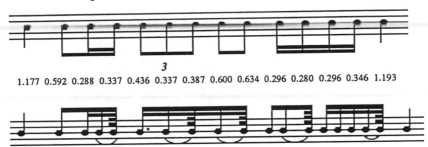

1.177 0.592 0.288 0.337 0.436 0.337 0.387 0.600 0.634 0.296 0.280 0.296 0.346 1.193

Figure 2. Played Score (performance inter-onset intervals in seconds) and its organization by a commercial package (using a solution of 1/64 note).

as occur in slight tempo fluctuations, will add-up and produce an onset-time deviation that is the sum of all previous interval deviations. So this method is more sensitive to small tempo fluctuations than inter-onset quantization. Occasionally an onset-time will topple over the boundary between two grid points and the note will not be quantized correctly, but the quantized data will not be permanently de-synchronized.

Commercially available sequencer and transcription software packages use this simple onset quantization method. They cannot notate a non-trivial piece of music without errors (see Figure 2). This is not surprising, considering the large deviations of up to 50% and the ambiguity that has to be dealt with, especially in the case where both binary and ternary divisions are present. Most of these packages force the interpreter to play along with a metronome to give an acceptable result, or require a precise tuning of parameters (e.g. are triplets allowed) for different sections of the piece.

Tempo Tracking

The methods mentioned above can be enhanced by repeatedly adapting the duration of the quantum to the performance. When the performer accelerates, the

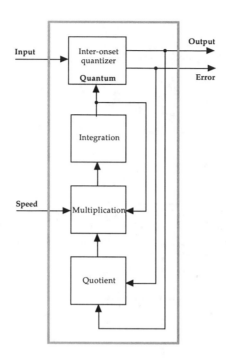

Figure 3. Tempo Tracker.

onset times will all tend to fall before the grid points. Adapting the quantum (decreasing it) will enable the system to follow the tempo change of the performer and to keep quantizing correctly. This set-up is shown in Figure 3. A required adjustment is calculated that, when the quantum is increased with this value, would have accounted for the interval perfectly. The fastest response possible for the tempo tracker would be to increase its quantum (one interval later) with that proportion. But such a progressive approach may allow the tempo to stray on the first note that is played imprecise. It is rather difficult to design a good control module that adjusts tempo fast enough to follow a performance, but not so fast that it reacts on every 'wrong' note. A common solution is to build in some conservatism in the tempo tracker by using only a fraction of the proposed adjustment. If this fraction, called the adjustment speed, is set to 0.5 the new tempo will be the mean of the old tempo and the proposed ideal.

Tempo Tracking with Confidence Based Adjustments

A more sophisticated tempo tracker adapts its tempo only when there is enough confidence to do so. An onset that occurs almost precisely between two grid points

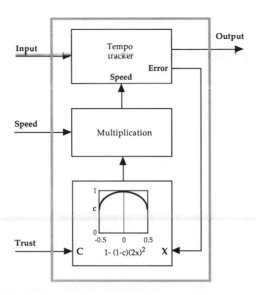

Figure 4. Tempo Tracker with Confidence Based Adjustment.

will give no evidence for adjusting the tempo (because it is not sure in what direction it would have to be changed). In Figure 4 the details are shown. The quantization error (the difference between the incoming interval and the quantized output of the system) is expressed as a fraction of the quantum. A simple function will calculate a confidence level, on the basis of this error and has a maximum near zero errors. The confidence level also depends on the parameter *trust,* that expresses its sensitivity for errors. If we now use this confidence level as a scale factor for the adjustment, speed of the tempo tracker will enhance its performance.

Of course, even this method is vulnerable to errors. Dannenberg and Mont-Reynaud report a 30% error rate for their 'real time foot tapper' which uses a variant of this method (Dannenberg and Mont-Reynaud 1987). This poor performance, considering their careful tuning of parameters and their preprocessing of the musical material (taking only 'healthy' notes into account), is disappointing.

The Algorithm

Since the methods mentioned above can be considered as extensions of each other, the last method can emulate the less sophisticated ones by supplying zero- or one-valued parameters. In Figure 5 a micro version of a this general traditional quantizer is given. Experimenting with it, changing parameter values and feeding it with different musical material quickly shows the limitations of these kinds of systems and their lack of robustness.

```
;;; MICRO TRADITIONAL QUANTIZER
;;; (C)1990, Desain & Honing
;;; in Common Lisp (uses loop macro)

;;; utilities

(defun square (x)(* x x))

(defun quantize (intervals &key (speed 0.0) (trust 1.0)
                                (quantum (first intervals)))
  "Quantize time intervals in multiples of quantum"
  ;; speed = 0, trust = 1 :inter-onset quantizer
  ;; 0<speed<1, trust = 1 :tempo tracker
  ;; 0<speed<1, 0<trust<1 :tempo tracker with confidence
  (loop for in in intervals
        as out = (quantize-ioi in quantum)
        as error = (quantization-error in out quantum)
        do (incf quantum
                 (* (delta-quantum error out quantum)
                    (confidence error trust)
                    speed))
        collect out))

(defun quantize-ioi (time quantum)
  "Return approximation of time in multiples of quantum"
  (round (/ time quantum)))

(defun quantization-error (in out quantum)
  "Return error of quantization"
  (- (/ in quantum) out))

(defun delta-quantum (error out quantum)
  "Return the quantum change that would have given a zero error"
  (* quantum (/ error out)))

(defun confidence (error trust)
  "Return amount of confidence in a possible tempo adjustment"
  (- 1 (* (- 1 trust) (square (* 2 error)))))


;;; example: real performance data: no luck
(quantize '(1.177 0.592 0.288 0.337 0.436 0.337 0.387 0.600
            0.634 0.296 0.280 0.296 0.346 1.193)
          :quantum 0.1 :speed 0.5)
-> (12 6 3 3 4 3 4 6 6 3 3 3 4 13)
```

Figure 5. The Traditional Algorithm.

```
;;; LONGUET-HIGGINS QUANTIZER
;;; (C)1990, Desain
;;; Stripped version: no articulation analysis, metrical structure
;;; or tempo tracking
;;; in Common Lisp (uses loop macro)

;;; utilities

(defun make-onsets (intervals)
  "Translate inter-onset intervals to onset times"
  (loop for interval in intervals
        sum interval into onset
        collect onset into onsets
        finally (return (cons 0.0 onsets))))

(defun make-intervals (onsets)
   "Translate onset times to inter-onset intervals"
  (loop for onset1 in onsets
        for onset2 in (rest onsets)
        collect (- onset2 onset1)))

(defun alternative (metre &rest states)
  "Return alternative metre plus unaltered states"
  (cons (case (first metre) (2 '(3)) (3 '(2)))
        states))

(defun extend (metre)
  "Return alternative metre plus unaltered states"
  (or metre '(2)))

;;; main parsing routines

(defun quantize (intervals &key (metre '(2)) (tol 0.10)
                 (beat (first intervals)))
  "Quantize intervals using initial metre and beat estimate"
  (loop with start = 0.0
        with onsets = (make-onsets intervals)
        for time from 0
        while onsets
        do (multiple-value-setq (start figure metre onsets)
             (rhythm start beat metre onsets time 1 tol))
        append figure into figures
        finally (return (make-intervals figures))))
```

Figure 6. The Longuet-Higgins Algorithm.

```
(defun rhythm (start period metre onsets time factor tol)
  "Handle singlet and subdivide as continuation"
  (singlet
    start (+ start period) metre onsets time tol
    #'(lambda (figure onsets)
        (tempo figure start period metre onsets time factor tol))))

(defun singlet (start stop metre onsets time tol cont)
  "Handle singlet note or rest"
  (if (and onsets (< (first onsets) (+ start tol)))
    (singlet-figure stop metre (list time) (rest onsets) tol cont)
    (singlet-figure stop metre nil onsets tol cont)))

(defun singlet-figure (stop metre figure onsets tol cont)
  "Create singlet figure and subdivide in case of more notes"
  (let* ((onset (first onsets))
         (syncope (or (null onset) (>= onset (+ stop tol))))
         (more? (and onset (< onset (+ stop (- tol))))))
      (if more?
        (apply #'values (funcall cont figure onsets))
        (values (if syncope stop (first onsets))
                figure metre onsets syncope))))

(defun tempo (figure start period metre onsets time factor tol)
  "One or two trials of subdivision using alternative metres"
  (rest (generate-and-test #'trial
                      #'(lambda (syncope stop &rest ignore)
                          (and (not syncope)
                               (< (- stop tol)
                                  (+ start period)
                                  (+ stop tol))))
                      #'alternative
                      metre figure start period onsets time factor
tol)))

(defun generate-and-test (generate test alternative &rest states)
  "Control structure for metre change"
    (let ((result1 (apply generate states)))
      (if (apply test result1)
        result1
        (let ((result2 (apply generate (apply alternative states))))
          (if (apply test result2)
            result2
            result1)))))
```

Figure 6. The Longuet-Higgins Algorithm (continued).

```
(defun trial (metre figure start period onsets time factor tol)
   "Try a subdivision of period"
  (loop with pulse = (pop metre)
        with sub-period = (/ period (float pulse))
        with sub-factor = (/ factor pulse)
        repeat pulse
        for sub-time from time by sub-factor
        do (multiple-value-setq
              (start sub-figure metre onsets syncope)
              (rhythm start sub-period (extend metre) onsets
                   sub-time sub-factor tol))
        append sub-figure into sub-figures
        finally
         (return
           (list syncope start (append figure sub-figures)
                        (cons pulse metre) onsets)))))

;;; example
(quantize '(1.177 0.592 0.288 0.337 0.436 0.337 0.387 0.600 0.634
            0.296 0.280 0.296 0.346 1.193) :tol 0.15)
->(1 1/2 1/4 1/4 1/3 1/3 1/3 1/2 1/2 1/4 1/4 1/4 1/4 1)
```

Figure 6. The Longuet-Higgins Algorithm (continued).

Use of Structural Information

Because of the poor performance of the methods described above, techniques that make use of knowledge of the hierarchical structure of rhythms were proposed for quantization. Longuet-Higgins (1987) describes a hybrid method based on tempo tracking plus the use of knowledge about meter. In this method the tempo tracking is done with respect to a beat (that can span one or more notes). This beat is recursively subdivided in 2 or 3 parts looking for onset times near the start of each part. The best subdivision is returned, but the program is reluctant to change the kind of subdivision at each level. The start and length of the beat or subdivision thereof is adjusted on the basis of the onsets found, just as in the simple tempo tracking method. Next to the quantized results, this program delivers a hierarchical metrical structure. A more detailed study of the behavior of this elegant method can be found in (Desain, 1990).

The Algorithm

Because Longuet-Higgins published the rather complicated program in POP-2, it seems appropriate to restrict ourselves here to a stripped version (see Figure 6), concentrating only on the essential aspects (see Desain, 1990). It incorporates the basic ideas about stability of meter, the tolerance with respect to which all decisions on onsets are made, and the beat length that has to be supplied as an initial state of the system. But the analysis of articulation, delivery of metrical structure and the sophisticated tempo tracking are removed. When given the inter-onset intervals of the rhythm in Figure 2, it will result in the correct quantization: (1 1/2 1/4 1/4 1/3 1/3 1/3 1/2 1/2 1/4 1/4 1/4 1/4 1).

Knowledge Based Methods

The automatic transcription project at CCRMA (Chowning et al. 1984) is a particularly elaborate example of a knowledge based system. It prefers simple ratios and uses context dependent information to quantize correctly. This knowledge based approach uses information about melodic and rhythmic accents, local context, and other musical clues to guide the search for an optimal quantized description of the data. Using even more knowledge could possibly contribute to the quantization problem. e.g. harmonic clues could be used to signal phrase endings where the tempo may be expected to decrease at the boundary (phrase final lengthening) and repetition in the music could be used to give more confidence in a certain quantization result. However these knowledge based approaches seem to share the same problems of all traditional AI programs: the better they become, the more domain dependent knowledge (depending on a specific musical style) must be used for further advance, and such programs will break down rapidly when applied to data outside their domain.

Multiple Alternatives

All methods above can be enhanced by using them repeatedly on the same data, but with different parameters, searching for the best solution. These analyses could even go on in parallel. Dannenberg and Mont-Reynaud (1987) propose multiple 'foot tappers' all running at the same time. For Chung (1989) the parallel exploration of multiple alternatives is essential. Using Marvin Minsky's paradigm (Minsky 1986) he describes his system as consisting of multiple intelligent agents. These proposals are distributed models with a 'coarse' grain: each part-taking processor consists of a complete traditional symbolic AI program. However, it is possible to use a very fine grained parallelism to tackle the quantization problem, where each processor is very simple, but the interaction between them is crucial.

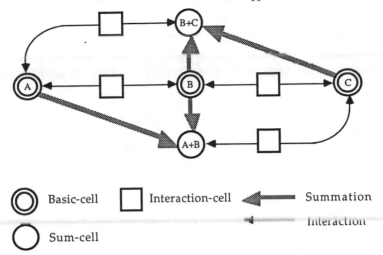

Figure 7. Topology of a Connectionist Network of a Rhythm of Three Inter-Onset Intervals.

Connectionist Methods

Connectionism provides the possibility for new models which have characteristics that traditional AI models lack, in particular their robustness and flexibility (see Rumelhart & McLeland 1986). Connectionist models consist of a large number of simple cells, each of which has its own activation level. These cells are interconnected in a complex network, the connections serving to excite or inhibit other elements. The general behavior of such a network is that from a given initial state, it converges towards an equilibrium state. An example of the application of such a network to music perception is given by Bharucha (Bharucha 1987) in the context of tonal harmony, but the connectionist approach has not yet been used for quantization.

The quantization model that will be presented now is a network designed to reach equilibrium when metrical time intervals have been achieved, and which converges towards this end point from non-metrical performance data. It is implemented as a collection of relatively abstract cells, each of which performs a complex function compared to standard connectionist models. We will now give a condensed overview of the model.

A Connectionist Quantizer

The proposed network consists of three kinds of cells: the *basic-cell* with an initial state equal to an inter-onset interval, the *sum-cell* to represent the longer time interval generated by a sequence of notes, and the *interaction-cell* that is connected in a bidirectional manner to two neighboring basic- or sum-cells. Figure 7 shows the

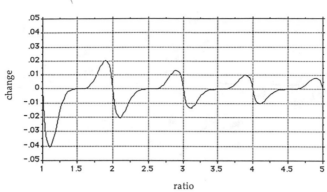

ratio

Figure 8. Interaction Function.

topology of a network for quantizing a rhythm of four beats, having its three inter-onset intervals set as initial states of the three basic-cells, labeled A, B, and C, and the two summed time intervals A+B and B+C represented by the corresponding sum-cells. There are four interaction-cells connecting cell A to cell B, B to C, A+B to C, and A to B+C respectively. Each interaction-cell steers the two cells, to which it is connected, toward integer multiples of one another, but only if they are already close to such a multiple.

The two connected cells receive a small change calculated from the application of an interaction function (see Figure 8) to the quotient of their states. One can see that if the ratio is slightly above an integer it will be adjusted downward, and vice versa. The interaction function has two parameters: *peak*, describing how stringent the function requires an almost integer ratio to calculate a correction and *decay*, expressing the decreasing influence of larger ratios. Each cell accumulates the incoming change signals from the connected interaction-cells. The interaction of a sum-cell with its basic-cells is bidirectional: if the value of the sum-cell changes, the basic-cells connected to it will all change proportionally, as well as the other way around. This process is repeated, updating the values of the cells a little bit in each iteration, moving the network towards equilibrium. The system produces promising results. It is *context sensitive*, with precedence of local context. For this reason the example in Figure 2 is quantized correctly (for more details see Desain & Honing, 1989). The system also exhibits *graceful degradation*. When the quantizer breaks down in a complex situation it is often able to maintain musical integrity and consistency at higher levels. The resulting error will only generate a local deformation of the score.

The Algorithm

A micro version of the program is given in Figure 9. In this program the sum-cells are not represented explicitly, their value is recalculated from the basic-cells. Also the interaction-cells are not represented explicitly. Their two inputs from the con-

```
;;; MICRO CONNECTIONIST QUANTIZER
;;; (C)1990, Desain & Honing
;;; in Common Lisp (uses loop macro)

;;; utilities

(define-modify-macro multf (factor) *)
(define-modify-macro divf (factor) /)
(define-modify-macro zerof () (lambda(x) 0))

(defmacro with-adjacent-intervals
    (vector (a-begin a-end a-sum b-begin b-end b-sum) &body body)
  "Setup environment for each interaction of (sum-)intervals"
  `(loop with length = (length ,vector)
        for ,a-begin below (1- length)
        do (loop for ,a-end from ,a-begin below (1- length)
                sum (aref ,vector ,a-end) into ,a-sum
                do (loop with ,b-begin = (1+ ,a-end)
                        for ,b-end from ,b-begin below length
                        sum (aref ,vector ,b-end) into ,b-sum
                        do ,@body))))

;;; interaction function

(defun delta (a b minimum peak decay)
  "Return change for two time intervals"
  (let* ((inverted? (<= a b))
         (ratio (if inverted? (/ b a)(/ a b)))
         (delta-ratio (interaction ratio peak decay))
         (proportion (/ delta-ratio (+ 1 ratio delta-ratio))))
    (* minimum (if inverted? (- proportion) proportion))))

(defun interaction (ratio peak decay)
  "Return change of time interval ratio"
  (* (- (round ratio) ratio)
     (expt (abs (* 2 (- ratio (floor ratio) 0.5))) peak)
     (expt (round ratio) decay)))


;;; quantization procedures

(defun quantize
    (intervals &key (iterations 20) (peak 5) (decay -1))
  "Quantize data of inter-onset intervals"
  (let* ((length (length intervals))
         (changes (make-array length :initial-element 0.0))
         (minimum (loop for index below length
```

Figure 9. The Connectionist Algorithm.

```
                    minimize (aref intervals index))))
        (loop for count to iterations
              do (update intervals minimum changes peak decay)
              finally (return (coerce intervals 'list)))))

(defun update (intervals minimum changes peak decay)
  "Update all intervals synchronously"
  (with-adjacent-intervals intervals
    (a-begin a-end a-sum b-begin b-end b-sum)
    (let ((delta (delta a-sum b-sum minimum peak decay)))
      (propagate changes a-begin a-end (/ delta a-sum))
      (propagate changes b-begin b-end (- (/ delta b-sum))))))
  (enforce changes intervals))

(defun propagate (changes begin end change)
  "Derive changes of basic-intervals from sum-interval change"
  (loop for index from begin to end
        do (incf (aref changes index) change)))

(defun enforce (changes intervals)
  "Effectuate changes to intervals"
  (loop for index below (length intervals)
        do (multf (aref intervals index)
                  (1+ (aref changes index)))
           (zerof (aref changes index))))


;;; example (the result is rounded)
(quantize (vector 1.177 0.592 0.288 0.337 0.436 0.337 0.387 0.600
                  0.634 0.296 0.280 0.296 0.346 1.193))
->(1.2 .6 .3 .3 .4 .4 .4 .6 .6 .3 .3 .3 .3 1.2)
```

Figure 9. The Connectionist Algorithm (continued).

necting sum-cells are calculated in the main loop, as is their final effect on basic-cells. All updates to the basic-cells are collected first, only to be effectuated once per iteration round (i.e., synchronous update).

Recent Research

Since this chapter was written we elaborated on several aspects of the model. It has been extended to a process model (Desain, Honing, & de Rijk, 1989), a rigorous mathematical description is given in Desain & Honing (1991), and a detailed comparison with the Longuet-Higgins model and its interpretation as a cognitive model is described in Desain (1991).

Acknowledgments

We would like to thank Eric Clarke, Jim Grant, and Dirk-Jan Povel, for their help in this research, and their comments on the first version of this chapter. This research was partly supported by an ESRC grant under number A413254004.

Notes

1) This chapter was presented at the first AI and Music Workshop, St. Augustin, Germany in September 1988. It has been updated with references to new work and some material from (Desain & Honing 1991). Micro versions of the main algorithms were added as well.

References

Bharucha, J.J. 1987. Music Cognition and Perceptual Facilitation, A Connectionist Framework. *Music Perception* 5.

Chowning, J., L. Rush, B. Mont-Reynaud, C. Chafe, W. Andrew Schloss, & J. Smith, 1984. Intelligent systems for the Analysis of Digitized Acoustical Signals. CCRMA Report No. STAN-M-15.

Chung, J.T. 1989. An Agency for the Perception of Musical Beats or If I Only Had a Foot. Masters Thesis, Department of Computer Science, MIT, Boston.

Clarke, E., 1987. Levels of Structure in the Organization of Musical Time. *Contemporary Music Review* 2:212–238.

Dannenberg, R. B. & B. Mont-Reynaud, 1987. An on-line Algorithm for Real Time Accompaniment. In Proceedings of the 1987International Computer Music Conference. San Francisco: Computer Music Association.

Desain, P. & H. Honing,1989. Quantization of Musical Time: A Connectionist Approach. *Computer Music Journal* 13(3), also in Todd & Loy (1991).

Desain, P., H. Honing, & K. de Rijk. 1989 A Connectionist Quantizer. In Proceedings of the 1989 International Computer Music Conference. San Francisco: Computer Music Association.

Desain, P. 1991. A Connectionist and a Traditional AI Quantizer, Symbolic versus Sub-symbolic Models of Rhythm Perception. In Proceedings of the 1990 Music and the Cognitive Sciences Conference, edited by I. Cross. *Contemporary Music Review*. London: Harwood Press. (forthcoming).

Desain, P. 1990 Parsing the Parser, a Case Study in Programming Style. *Computer Music Research*, vol 2.

Longuet-Higgins, H.C., 1987. *Mental Processes*. Cambridge, Mass.: MIT Press.

Minsky, M. 1986. *Society of Mind*. New York: Simon and Schuster.

Rasch, R. A. 1979. Synchronization in Performed Ensemble Music *Acustica* 43(2):121–131.

Todd, P. & Gareth Loy. D. eds. 1991. *Music and Connectionism*, Cambridge, Mass.: MIT Press. Forthcoming.

Rumelhart, D.E. & McClelland. J.E. eds. 1986. *Parallel Distributed Processing*. Cambridge, Mass.: MIT Press.

Shaffer, L.H. 1981. Performances of Chopin, Bach, Bartok: Studies in Motor Programming. *Cognitive Psychology* 13:326–376.

Todd, N. P. 1985. A Model of Expressive Timing in Tonal Music. *Music Perception* 0(1):00 00.

Vorberg, D. J. & R. Hambuch, 1987. On the Temporal Control of Rhythmic Performance. In: J. Requin (Ed.) *Attention and Performance* VII.

Vos. P. & Handel, S. 1987. Playing Triplets: Facts and Preferences. In: A Gabrielsson (Ed.) *Action and Perception in Rhythm and Music*. Royal Swedish Academy of Music. No. 55:35–47.

Section Seven

Learning and Tutoring

Musical learning has been a topic of studies in music education. These studies have mainly been based on psychological insight, and on empirical studies in the behavior of music students. Despite considerable research in music education, very little is known even today about how musical competence is acquired by children, and broadened by adolescents, and about the relationship between musical skill (performance) and knowledge (competence). For this reason, the attempt to approach these problems from the vantage point of AI is most welcome.

The chapters in this section demonstrate two modes of using the theory of machine learning: In Intelligent Tutoring Systems (ITS)—for student modeling, and in expert systems—for discovery of rules.

The chapter "An Architecture for an Intelligent Tutoring System," by M. J. Baker suggests an architecture for a system that guides novice students in the study of various musical tasks. The idea is that neither traditional methods based on matching the student's performance with an expert one, nor domain independent approaches, are appropriate: The first are too weak due to their severe requirements, the latter are too weak due to their extreme generality. Instead, the author suggests that in non-analytical domains, where existing theories only partially account for the given phenomena, the system can provide intelligent tutorial guiding on the subject. The author applies these ideas to the subjects of analyzing musical structures, and teaching musical interpretation. The system operates by first generating, possibly multiple, expert accounts of the problem in question, associated with their justifications, and then leading the student through a negotiation dialog, based on the expert accounts. The author claims that representation of related knowledge is domain dependent. Hence, the representation selected for the two musical tasks in question, depends on their specific characteristics; no generality is claimed. Other modes of input/output for the tutoring system, such as gestural performance are also discussed.

The chapter entitled "The Importance of Basic Musical Knowledge for Effective Learning" by Gerhard Widmer, is an application of the explanation based learning technique used in AI (Mitchell et al 86), to the field of species counterpoint. Here, the goal is not only to create a rule based expert system for writing two part species counterpoint, but also to infer the rules of this expert system automatically, by generalizing on the basis of music fragments labeled good, bad or unacceptable by the user. Domain knowledge for inferring rules from musical examples is incorporated in the knowledge base of Widmer's system. Such domain knowledge allows the system to minimize the number of questions it has to ask the user, until the desired general rule is inferred. Thus, for example, when provided with the user feedback that a fragment of a counterpoint exercise it just generated is unacceptable (e.g. parallel fifths), Widmer's system can efficiently produce a new generalized rule about this music fragment using its algorithms for creating rules, thus making this music fragment and similar ones forbidden in the future (but each new rule is subject to interactive approval by the user). Avoiding the direct coding of music expert systems by using automated learning of rules is an important issue; the task of making this learning process efficient is the interesting research area that this chapter addresses.

Abstract

Adult and novice musicians who lack technical and theoretical knowledge have little educational access to the important skill of musical interpretation. We describe how recent research in the cognitive psychology of music, computer-music technology and intelligent tutoring systems (ITS) can be combined in the design of an ITS architecture which addresses this problem. Our approach is based on generating intelligent guidance on the use of computer-music tools for graphically editing and gesturally performing melodies, which free the student from the cognitive load of producing the notes. The architecture includes a parser for musical structures, an advisor on the application of interpretive variations and a differential modelling component for comparing simplified gestural performances with the previously edited version. These components are united by a general model for negotiative tutorial dialogues, used for discussing concepts underlying knowledge of musical structure and interpretation. Work has concentrated on implementing prototypes of the tutorial dialogue model and the musical parser, since domain restrictions of the parser limit the educational scope of the system.

Chapter 20

Design of an Intelligent Tutoring System for Musical Structure and Interpretation

Michael J. Baker

Centre National de la Recherche Scientifique

"Once we accept that composition, audition and performance are activities central to music, we are then obliged to notice that a lot of what takes place under the heading of 'music teaching' seems to be concerned with something else."

(Swanwick 1979, p. 44–45)

Applying Cognitive Science to Teaching Musical Performance Skills

Few would dispute that the primary focus of music teaching should be on the central concrete musical activities of composition, audition and performance. In a sense, however, this threefold distinction is misleading, since audition is clearly an important factor in both composition and performance, knowledge of compositional techniques may have important effects on a performer's understanding of how to perform a piece, and knowledge of the performance potentialities of instruments is an important part of the composer's art [Slo 1985]. In this chapter, our aim is to describe ways in which recent research in the fields of Artificial Intelligence and Music and in Intelligent Tutoring Systems could facilitate the teaching of musical performance skills.

Before an Intelligent Tutoring System (ITS) is designed and built it should be clear that it fulfills a real educational need. Two simple criteria are that the computer should not perform an educational activity any worse than a human teacher, and that the computer should not merely re-implement knowledge which already resides in some other educational medium. A large number of different skills are required of musical performers, including (at least) the ability to understand musical notation and transfer it to aural imagination, to play what one hears mentally, to improvise, to transform notation into an interpretation, and to perform the required motor skills. In designing an ITS for musical performance skills, we must therefore carefully select which of these component skills are in some sense "essential" to the primary skill itself, and then try to decide whether the computer can make a genuine educational contribution to their acquisition by learners. Rather than using the computer to re-implement existing educational practice, the design of an ITS for a musical activity therefore provides us with an opportunity to consider afresh a number of problems in music teaching, and possibly to exploit the powerful educational leverage to be gained from AI models of music cognition. It is a common experience in teaching musical performance skills that beginners become so preoccupied with technical aspects such as finger positions and musical notation that the cognitive and physical load imposed is too great to allow them to attend to the finer points of *musical interpretation*. We argue therefore that a computer-music system which gave adult novice musicians some degree of access to learning musical interpretation from the beginning of their studies, without requiring advanced technical and notational ability, would constitute an effective ITS according to our previously stated criteria. In the remainder of this chapter we review some existing approaches to using computers to teach musical performance skills and describe how existing research in Music and the Cognitive Sciences, in computer music technology, and in Intelligent Tutoring Systems could be combined to design an ITS architecture which addresses this problem in music education.

Existing Computer-Based Approaches to Teaching Musical Performance Skills

To date there have been few attempts to apply AI and Cognitive Science research to the teaching of musical performance skills, in marked contrast to musical composition ([Taf 1985],[Des 1986],[Hol 1989]). Most existing computer-music applications have concentrated on teaching activities which may be viewed as *supportive* to the primary musical activity of performance. By *supportive* activities we understand skills such as reading musical notation and performing traditional "aural tests," which are traditionally claimed to support the primary activity of musical performance. For example, there are a number of tutors available for traditional aural skills and simple music theory [Hof 1981], the educational purpose of which is to administer standard tests effectively, thus lightening the human teacher's workload and allowing students to learn at their own pace. From the point of view of music education, the relevance of such tests to performance ability is now viewed as questionable [Swa 1979]. There are, however, a number of other aural abilities which are clearly relevant to musical performance, and independent of knowledge of musical notation. These include the ability to play what one hears, and to use aural feedback to correct one's own performance.

The ability to "play by ear" may be viewed as a form of aural ability which is much more important in musical performance, given the link between the kinaesthetic sense and musical memory. The "Tunemaster" program [Klr 1986] aimed to teach playing by ear using the motivating power of engaging the student in a computer-based game. The objective was to "beat the machine" by playing back a melody generated by the system within a given period of time, using a touch-tablet. An advantage of the system was that it did not require knowledge of conventional musical notation, and so in a sense addressed directly a central aspect of musical performance skills. The work of Lamb and Buckley [Lam 1985] addressed the problem that students often experience difficulty in attending to their own performances in order to make fine adjustments. Their approach was essentially to provide additional *visual feedback* in the form of a "piano roll" graphical interface, on the durations and attack points of notes played on a synthesiser keyboard. Whilst this approach may be of some help in playing trills evenly, for example, its use requires guidance from a human teacher, and may even have the effect that students aim to play *everything* evenly, to the detriment of musical interpretation. Yoshinori and Nagaoka [Yos 1985] have produced a similar interface which also included a graphical display of "expert" performances for the student to imitate. Although such an approach could have the short term benefits that students may produce acceptable performances of a number of specific pieces, it seems unlikely that such knowledge would assist in developing more general interpretive abilities, and may even prevent students from learning general principles of musical interpretation which would enable them to develop an original style of their own. A similar approach was adopted in the Piano Tutor project [San 1987], which aimed to give tutorial feedback on the accuracy of novice keyboard performances. The system combined a matcher for comparing the student's performance on a synthesiser keyboard with prestored expert performances, a curriculum of pieces to be played, and interactive videodisks of a human teacher. In practice mode the system gave feedback on wrong notes and other differences between the student and expert performances, and in a tutorial mode adopted a directive instructional style with respect to prestored lesson plans. The major problem with such an approach lies in its reliance on comparing the student's performance with prestored expert ones. There is a very large range of different interpretations for a given piece of music which are musically acceptable, in the sense of not contradicting fundamental musical structures. Without a more explicit model for the generation of interpretive variations in the context of the structure of the piece in question, it is difficult to see how a non-arbitrary distinction can be made between those differences between student and expert which are within the space of musically acceptable interpretations and those which are not.

In summarizing this brief review we can see that existing approaches to computer-based teaching of musical performance skills have either implemented questionable existing educational practices (such as traditional aural tests), or else have concentrated on giving feedback on the accuracy of keyboard performances. Paradoxically, such approaches may be argued to encourage unreflective copying and the elimination of interpretive variations to produce a mechanical playing style. No existing approaches have attempted to use the computer to teach one of the most fundamental skills in musical performance—that of *musical interpretation.* Our central claim in this chapter is therefore that it is possible to design an Intelligent Tutoring System which makes a genuine contribution to music education in virtue of giving adult novice musicians access to learning an important skill—musical interpretation—which is otherwise difficult to acquire without extensive technical ability and theoretical knowledge. Such a system should be based on a deeper model of the cognitive psychology of musical performance. In the next section we describe the general cognitive model for musical interpretation on which or design of an ITS architecture is based.

Cognitive Models for Musical Performance

The process of transforming a literal rendition of a musical score into an interpretation which expresses the character of the music is an extremely complex and subtle one. It includes such factors as communicating structural boundaries in the music to the listener, expressing emotional content or tension and relaxation in the music, and the observance of historical constraints on musical styles. The basic framework within which psychologists of music have worked is that in skilled performances, expressive variations bear a systematic relationship to musical structure. Clarke [Cla 1985] states the common working hypothesis as follows :

> "With accurate measurement, discrepancies are always found between the temporal properties of the performance and those indicated by the score. It is a fundamental hypothesis of this research that those discrepancies are related to structural properties of the music and to the ways which performers organise those properties."

([Cla 1985] p. 210)

The implications of this basic hypothesis can be summarised as the following two points, each of which are supported by psychological evidence:

1) performers possess an abstract cognitive representation of the music which they play ;
2) systematic variations in musical parameters are applied in performance, which relate to this abstract representation.

The first hypothesis is supported by evidence from studies of how melodies are reproduced ([Att 1971],[Slo 1985]), where singers were found to systematically produce variations upon a general structural representation of the music. In addition, the hypothesis of a generalised structural representation in human memory has been used successfully to explain data from studies of the rhythmic structure of piano performances ([Sha 1981],[Cla 1985],[Tod 1985],[Tod 1989]). With respect to the second point, the fact that interpretive variations are largely consistent for a given performer has led a number of researchers to hypothesise that such knowledge is stored as a set of (production) rules. Thus Sloboda states that:

"One simple test of how principled a performer's expressive playing is, is to ask him to provide two consecutive performances of a relatively unfamiliar piece. If he is able to provide very similar expressive changes on the two occasions, in the absence of explicit score instructions, then we can infer the existence of some rule-based system for assigning variation to his performance."

([Slo 1985], p.82)

Extensive research on specifying such rules has been carried out by Sundberg and co-workers ([Sun 1983],[Fri 1986]), and the work of Todd ([Tod 1985],[Tod 1989]) has recently permitted precise mathematical modelling of the degree to which performance parameters are applied in the case of rubato. A cognitive model for interpretation of music could therefore be specified within something like a standard production-system cognitive architecture [And 1983]. In such a model, declarative knowledge would consist principally of musical structures, providing working memory traces to match with conditions of production rules whose consequents specify the interpretive variations to be applied. In the case of interpretation of music, however, it is implausible to neglect the specific motor programs which control actions required to achieve cognitive goals. This is because many expressive devices are intimately related to the physical capacities of the human body and to physical constraints imposed by specific instruments. For example, the conventions that higher notes in a melody are considered as more expressive and that ascending passages are accompanied by crescendo are related to the fact that singing higher notes requires more effort. Even our notions of musical structure are related to physical capabilities, since, as Schoenberg [Sch 1967] states "The term *phrase* means, structurally, a unit approximating to what one could sing in a single breath." (p. 3). We therefore argue that a cognitive model for musical interpretation which could serve as the basis for intelligent tutoring must take account of the psychomotor aspects of musical performance. In the next section we describe how this general cognitive model may be applied to the design of an ITS architecture.

From Cognitive Model to ITS Architecture

Our basic approach depends on providing a form of intelligent tutorial guidance on the use of computer-music tools, which is specifically adapted to the *cognitive characteristics* of our chosen musical domain. We begin with a discussion of approaches to giving guidance in computer-based education.

Research in AI and Education has been dominated by two main tendencies, which may be described as the tutoring approach and the environment approach. The former is well represented by the relatively early collection of articles in Sleeman and Brown [Sle 1982]. It depends on the view that AI techniques may be developed for diagnosing student's knowledge and learning styles, based on a structured representation of the teaching domain, and that this knowledge may be used to determine appropriate teaching strategies for knowledge communication and correction [Wen 1987]. The environment approach basically claims that we should provide students with a rich computer-based environment and the tools required to achieve their learning goals—an approach initially associated with Papert [Pap 1980] and LOGO. This dichotomy has recently begun to break down, with the idea of providing a flexible degree of guidance for a student's discovery in an environment [Els 1990], and various approaches to viewing the computer as a *collaborator* rather than instructor [Gre 1988]. We claim that the choice of a specific tutoring approach depends crucially on properties of the domain in question. For example, teaching arithmetic, where knowledge can be readily formalised, must be quite different from teaching a subject such as moral philosophy.

With reference to the general cognitive model described in the previous section, the domain properties which must be taken into account include *ambiguous* and *uncertain knowledge* on the part of AI programs for analysis of musical structures, and the existence of *multiple possible solutions* to the choice of interpretive factors which may be applied to communicate structure. As Lerdahl and Jackendoff [Ler 1983] have shown, tonal melodies are often intrinsically ambiguous in structure—i.e. there is more than one set of structural boundaries which may be perceived in musically acceptable interpretations. With respect to AI music analysis programs, recent research has shown ([Bak 1989a],[Bak 1989b], Miller, Scarborough and Jones, this volume) that relatively few pieces provide sufficient structural cues to enable unambiguous parsing. These two facts mean that it is both musically inappropriate and technically unrealistic to expect an intelligent tutoring system to possess *certain knowledge* concerning musical structures in automatically analysed pieces. This does not, however, mean that no educational guidance can be given, or that prestored structural analyses should be used instead (see our criticisms of existing work in the previous section), but rather that appropriate tutorial dialogue strategies should be developed which can provide guidance on the basis of *uncertain justified beliefs*. We therefore need to find an alternative to either a directive tutorial style based on comparing the student's performance with that of an expert, or an open-ended environment approach, in which no guidance is given at all. We suggest that the most appropriate tutorial style is one in which the system and student *negotiate* a range of possible solutions to structural analysis and preferred interpretation in a *critical argument*. We describe such a model for tutorial dialogue in a later section of this chapter.

In the introduction to this chapter, we stated that novice instrumentalists are often so concerned with physically "playing the notes" that they cannot simultaneously attend to finer points such as musical interpretation. One possibility of using computers to overcome this educational problem would therefore be to assign the task of actually producing the notes to a computer music system, and allow the student to specify precisely how the piece should be interpreted by controlling performance variations such as timbre, articulation and dynamics. Two principal kinds of tools that can give this possibility to learners are graphic music editors [Bux 1980], and gestural control devices [Mat 1980]. There are also numerous commercially available gestural control devices (such as the Roland Octapad™, which allows MIDI events to be triggered by striking a drumpad) and computer-based graphical music editing tools. Since these tools do not give novice musicians *educational guidance* on their use, we propose that a system could be designed which combines computer controlled tools with the intelligent tutoring approach outlined above. In terms of our general cognitive model for musical performance, such a system would need to teach:

1) knowledge of musical structures in a given piece of music ;

2) knowledge of the way in which various performance parameters (dynamics, articulation, timbre, ...) may be manipulated to communicate musical structures in interpretation ;

3) psychomotor skills required for controlling performance parameters in real-time.

The following is a summary of our proposed general tutorial strategy:

1) *Choosing a Melody to Edit.*   The student inputs a tonal melody by selecting dialogue boxes for pitches using the mouse, or using a synthesiser keyboard. A period of checking that the system has stored what the student wants (quantisation) follows. Alternatively, the student selects a prestored melody (input by the student or stored in the system). The initial portion of the melody is displayed on a graphical interface in either conventional or pianoroll musical notation.

2) *Analysing Musical Structures in the Melody.*   A parsing program analyzes musical structures in the melody, storing its results in frames and a propositional network of beliefs and justifications. This is fully explained in the next section of the chapter.

3) *Tutorial Dialogue about Musical Structures.*   A negotiated tutorial dialogue is conducted between system and student concerning musical structures in the input melody, centred on the graphic editing tool display. Both user and system can indicate possible phrase boundaries, and the system can play sections of the melody for demonstration, via an interfaced touch-sensitive synthesiser. Typed dialogue is generated in a separate window. For example, the student indicates a phrase boundary at position p1 on the interface, the system responds that it agrees that this is a phrase boundary, but that it does not agree with the justifications for believing this to be the case input by the student.

4) *Performance Editing Phase.*   A set of menus for performance variations are available to the student, which can be applied to the graphically represented melody. The resulting edited version can be played via the synthesiser at any point by menu selection. A variety of tutorial strategies are used here to acquaint the student with the relationship between these variations and musical structure. The result of this phase is an ideal performance edit (more than one version could be saved) which results from a cooperative dialogue between the student and system.

5) *Gestural Performance Phase.*   The student performs the "ideal performance edit" by triggering successive pitches of the melody using a gestural input device (a Roland Octapad™), where dynamics are controlled using the sen

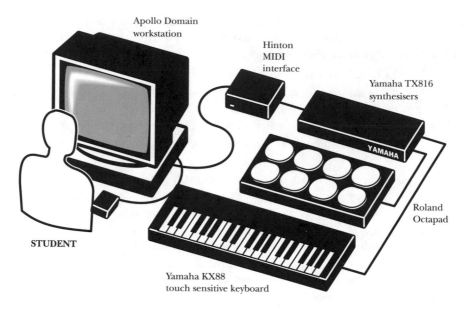

Figure 1. Hardware Configuration for INTERPRET.

sitivity of the pad. The system gives educational feedback on the degree of match between the gestural performance and the original ideal performance edit, suggesting sections to practice and perhaps a revision of the original interpretation edit.

As we discuss in conclusion, these phases do not necessarily have to be followed in this order. The general hardware setup which we assume is shown in Figure 1. In the remainder of the chapter we describe how elements of this tutorial strategy could be implemented as components of an ITS architecture.

Components of an ITS Architecture for Musical Structure and Interpretation

The system which we propose for generating the previously described general tutorial scenario consists of the following components: (1) a musical parser for tonal melodies ; (2) a model for sustaining tutorial dialogues ; (3) an advisor on plans for musical interpretation ; (4) a differential modelling program, for comparing gestural performances with melodies edited using a graphic editing tool.

For ease of reference, we shall refer to the integrated system as INTERPRET.

Tutoring Knowledge of Musical Structures

One approach to representing knowledge of musical structures in an ITS would be for a human analyst to prestore this information for a finite set of pieces. Ideally, however, we want to be able to deal with melodies input and chosen by the student (within certain limits), without having to rely on prestored analyses. We therefore need to derive structural analyses automatically, which would also enable us to use knowledge of the musical factors which influenced the program's decisions as a basis for tutorial explanations. As we discuss in conclusion, this design decision has the effect of severe restriction on the musical competence of the system.

Automated Analysis of Musical Structures. A number of approaches have been applied to analysing musical structures, including grammars [Ste 1984], blackboard architectures ([Ash 1989] ; Miller, Scarborough and Jones, this volume), and connectionist models ([Lis 1987],[Bha 1989]). The choice of such a model as a basis for intelligent tutoring depends to a large extent on the "transparency" of its reasoning methods and the resulting degree of communicability of the knowledge derived [Wen 1987]. For example, it is unlikely that a connectionist network for analysing musical structures could (*alone*) provide a sufficiently symbolic and high-level knowledge representation for explaining the presence of musical structures in a given piece to a student. The method which we chose relies on a combination of "top-down" recognition of musical phrase-structure schemata, parsing using musical chord functions, and "bottom-up" recognition of features on the "musical surface" [Ler 1983]. We shall not describe the model in detail (this has been done elsewhere in [Bak 1989a],[Bak 1989b]), and restrict ourselves to sufficient detail to enable its use in intelligent tutoring to be understood. In the subsequent discussion the model is referred to as GRAF (GRouping Analysis with Frames).

The position of phrase boundaries in tonal melodies relates to a number of interacting musical factors. The most obvious determinants of musical phrases are the standard chord progressions known as *cadences,* which usually end on chord V or chord I. Other factors include "surface features" such as relatively large interval leaps, changes in dynamics, and micropauses (described by the Lerdahl and Jackendoff, 1983, "grouping preference rules"), and repeated musical patterns [Sim 1988] In terms of harmony, rhythm and melodic contour. GRAF was based on the idea that a system for analysing musical structures must incorporate a model for how a number of these diverse processes interrelate, and that it must combine top-down and bottom-up processes (in analogy with speech understanding systems—[Erm 1980]. For example, we would argue that an attempt to base grouping analysis solely on the surface features incorporated in Lerdahl and Jackendoff's (1983) grouping preference rules [Ash 1989] is essentially inappropriate since other processes are not taken into account, and in any case, precise numerical weightings of rules should be specified at the acoustical level. In GRAF the top-down element consists of a set of frames [Min 1977] for knowledge of grouping structure schemata, which have been used to explain experimental data in musical perception [Sto 1985]. The frames used relate to both the "normal form" for reductional analysis of Lerdahl and Jackendoff and the top-level chord grammar rules used by Steedman [Ste 1984] as input to other rules. They incorporate "templates" for chord progressions in musical phrases, such as "<I x I>" and "<I V>," the elements of which may be expanded by chord grammar rules to regenerate a chord progression which harmonises the melody analysed. For example, a melody harmonized by the chord sequence "I IV V I ii V I" (upper case symbols such as "V" are major chords, lower case, such as "ii," minor chords) could match with the templates "<I V>' and "<I x I>," since it can be rewritten to them using the following chord grammar rules: V → ii V, I → I IV, x → V. Note that the simple occurrence of a chord V in a harmonization does not necessarily indicate a phrase boundary, since the preceding melodic unit must in fact *function harmonically* as a phrase. The matching process thus depends on isolating a section of the melody which is a *candidate phrase,* assigning sets of possible chord functions to it (itself a difficult problem), and attempting to rewrite chord functions to match with the template stored in the frame. Candidate phrase units are identified in two ways: firstly, by calculating default values for phrase boundaries, on the assumptions of even phrasing (one of Lerdahl and Jackendoff's well-formedness rules), and by identifying strongly reinforced possible phrase boundaries according to the surface features described in Lerdahl and Jackendoff's grouping preference rules. The system makes a simple left-to-right pass through the melody, and returns frame hypotheses with positions for phrase boundaries as output. An important feature is the fact that the type of surface feature or default which led to the phrase boundary's recognition are recorded. An example output is:

    Frame-1:
       phrase_1: <I x I>
          position : (0 8)
          factors : (interval_leap (progression I ii V I))
       phrase_2 : <I x I>
          position : (9 15)
          factors : (end (progression I vi ii V I))
    Frame-2:
       phrase_1 : <I x I>
          position : (0 6)
          factors : (micropause (progression I IV V I))
       phrase_2 : <I V>
          position :(7 12)
          factors : (default (progression I V))
       phrase_3 : <I x I>
          position : (13 15)
          factors : (end (progression I IV ii V I))

This is interpreted as follows. There are two hypothesized sets of phrase boundaries, the first of which identifies a phrase boundary from the first to the eighth note of the melody, and from the ninth to the fifteenth. The musical factors that led to the identification of these boundaries are the relatively large interval leap, and the end of the melody (trivially, a boundary), as well as the parsed harmonic progressions. In the second set, phrase boundaries are identified between the sixth and seventh and twelfth and thirteenth notes. These relate to micropauses, a default assumption of metrical symmetry, and the end of the melody. The model thus provides some limited account of how the musical factors of top-down recognition of schematic structures, unconscious inference of harmony, and perception of features on the musical surface interrelate in perception of phrase boundaries. It is presently restricted to recognising simple English nursery rhyme melodies [Moo 1912].

From the point of view of an ITS, it is important to note that the musical recognition system produces a number of *plausible* and justified hypotheses concerning musical structures. Such a representation is not, however, sufficient for tutorial purposes, since a novice musician may not understand the musical terms involved. For example, an explanation for the presence of a phrase boundary of the type "... it is a phrase because there is a plagal cadence IV—I, and there is a leap of a minor sixth surrounded by seconds.." would not be suitable for a complete novice. The results of the parser are therefore integrated into a *propositional network* [And 1983], which contains representations for related musical concepts. For example, with respect to the frames described earlier, propositions are represented for explaining all terms mentioned as factors which influenced the recognition process ("interval," "chord," "chord V," "chord progression," etc.). Since our model for tutorial dialogue does not include natural language recognition or generation capabilities, these nodes have attached explanatory text.

A Model for Generating Human-Computer Dialogue. Our concern here is with possible contributions of artificial intelligence to teaching music. We shall not therefore describe our model for tutorial dialogue which operates upon this domain representation in detail, but rather give a brief annotated example of dialogues generated by the system, which is described fully in ([Bak 1989c],[Bak 1989d],[Bak 1991]). The dialogue model is *specific to teaching music* in the sense of being appropriate for the characteristics of its musical knowledge domain, and *general* in the sense of being appropriate to other domains which share those characteristics. For example, dialogues about politics [Far 1988] may also be concerned with justified belief.

The KANT (Kritical Argument Negotiated Tutoring) system [Bak 1989c] is a computational model for generation of high-level tutorial dialogue [Kis 1986]. It consists of the specification of a set of representations for cognitive states of interlocutors, and a set of processes which generate dialogue exchanges, at the level of propositions rather than individual sentences. The set of fundamental data representations used in the model are termed the *dialogue state* [Pow 1979]. They include the beliefs of each participant about the domain (a propositional network); beliefs of each participant concerning the beliefs of the other; a set of dialogue goals; and a restricted memory of the recent utterances of each speaker in the dialogue.

Belief representations and mechanisms for their encoding in dialogue exchanges are based on Anderson's [And 1983] theory of semantic memory, where the phenomenon of *spreading activation* is used to control dialogue focus [Gro 1981]. Dialogue goals, similar to *speech act operators* ([Sea 1969],[Coh 1990]), are incorporated in the system for generating a critical argument [Tou 1979], in terms of communicating beliefs, justifying them, and critiquing the beliefs communicated by the other speaker. A set of processes operate on these representations in order to decide which goal to negotiate, and to decide whether to cooperate with a goal negotiated by the other speaker, as well as updating the conversants' belief representations. The dialogue generation mechanism is briefly as follows. The system searches a hierarchical tree of dialogue goals top-down, in order to find a sequence of goals to pursue. Goals are marked as *relevant* if their preconditions are satisfied with respect to the *dialogue state*. For example, a speaker cannot challenge a claim unless some claim has been made, the concept to be negotiated is sufficiently in focus, the speaker has the knowledge required with which to challenge, and so on. Revelant goals are *negotiated:* if negotiation succeeds, any associated dialogue actions are performed (for example, informing the student of the system's beliefs), otherwise, the conversational turn [Sch 1973] shifts to the student. A number of other important features include the use of educational preferences to discriminate between multiple relevant goals, the use of spreading activation to control dialogue focus, and the algorithms used for deciding which concept to discuss at any point in the dialogue.

When it is the student's turn to speak, the same mechanisms are used, except that the dialogue goals are presented to the student for choice. Preconditions of dialogue goals also play a role in the system's procedure for deciding whether or not to cooperate with goals proposed by the student: if the preconditions of the negotiated goal are satisfied as *relevant* from the point of view of the system, then it cooperates, otherwise not. We can best illustrate some of these features with a short extract from a trace generated by the system. We must emphasise that this is not intended to be a dialogue which is presently practically usable with students, but is rather an interactive trace of program execution. Lines have been subsequently numbered for reference, and student input is in italics.

INTERACTION TRACE OF THE KANT SYSTEM
   1/My turn over ... your move
   2/Are you sure you want to continue the discussion? (y or n)
   3/*y*
   4/Please type who you want the SPEAKER to be ...(student or system)
   5/*student*
   6/Please type in the concept you want to talk about (if you want a full list of possibilities, type "show")
   7/*phrase_boundary*
   8/Please type in the instance position you want to talk about
   9/*p10*
   10/I will tell you if I agree to cooperate ... Ok, I will cooperate
   11/Please choose one but not both of the goals to pursue:
   12/ CHALLENGE = make a challenge to a previous claim
   13/ CLAIM = make a claim concerning a concept
   14/*claim*

15/I will tell you if I agree to cooperate ... Ok, I will cooperate

16/Please choose one but not both of the goals to pursue:

17/ CONCRETE_CLAIM = make a specific claim about a concept instance

18/ ABSTRACT_CLAIM = make a general explanatory claim about a concept

19/*concrete_claim*

20/I will tell you if I agree to cooperate ... Ok, I will cooperate

21/Please choose a goal to pursue:

22/MAKE_INSTANCE_CLAIM = state a claim about an instance

23/SUPPORT_INSTANCE_CLAIM = state justifications for an instance claim

24/*make_instance_claim*

25/I will tell you if I agree to cooperate ... Ok, I will cooperate

26/You are pursuing the dialogue goal MAKE_INSTANCE_CLAIM, with

27/PHRASE_BOUNDARY as a concept, and P10 as its instance. Please confirm or dis
  confirm your intentions (y/n)

28/*y*

29/Ok, I'll remember that.

30/Please choose a goal to pursue:

31/SUPPORT_INSTANCE_CLAIM = state justifications for an instance claim

32/*support_instance_claim*

33/Please type in the justification(s) for the instance P10

34/(CONTRAST PARALLELISM)

35/I will tell you if I agree to cooperate ... Ok, I will cooperate

36/You are pursuing the dialogue goal SUPPORT_INSTANCE_CLAIM, with

37/PHRASE_BOUNDARY as a concept, P10 as its instance, and (CONTRAST PAR
  ALLELISM)

38/as the justifications. Please confirm or disconfirm your intentions (y/n)

39/*y*

40/Are you sure you want to continue the discussion? (y or n)

41/*y*

42/My move ...

43/Do you accept that we pursue the dialogue goal CHALLENGE (== make a challenge to a previous claim) (y/n?)

44/*y*

<<continues ...>>

The extract has been taken from the middle of an interaction, and shows an extended negotiation phase (lines 1-35), followed by a dialogue action (lines 36-39). At the start, it is the student's negotiated turn, and the system presents the available dialogue goals to the student, together with choice of parameters for the concept and instance to discuss. After each choice, the system substitutes the chosen parameters (for example, concept parameter = "phrase_boundary") into the preconditions for the chosen goal, and evaluates them in order to decide whether to cooperate or not (lines 10, 15, 20, 25, ...). The final claim of the student is that there is a phrase boundary at position P10 in a given melody, justified by the existence of musical parallelism (recurring patterns) and a musical contrast of some kind. Since the student has performed a dialogue action, the system updates its memory representations, the concept "phrase boundary" becoming a source of activation in its propositional network representation. At line 40 it is now the system's turn to converse, and at 43 it decides to challenge the student's claims. We do not have space here to continue this commentary, but in the subsequent dialogue, the system agrees with the student's claim, agrees with the justification "parallelism," disagrees with the justification "contrast," and proposes a third kind of justification, which it asks the student to attempt to specify.

The principal contribution of the model to ITS research consists in the definition of a model for negotiation in intelligent tutoring dialogues. It is not, however, presently suitable for use with real students. Further work on this component includes developing such a usable interface, evaluating coherence of the model with real students, and extending the capability of the model to deal with conflict. Much of the verbosity of this trace could be eliminated by conjoining negotiation of goals into something like "Do you accept that I make a claim about phrase boundaries?" However, in the case of non-acceptance, we do need to retain the more fine-grained negotiation mechanism, in order to identify and negotiate the source of disagreement (does the student disagree that the system should speak, that phrase boundaries should be the topic, etc.?). At present the model only deals with dialogues concerning musical structures. In the following sections we describe how it could be extended to discuss other kinds of knowledge related to musical interpretation.

Tutoring Interpretation of Music

We propose that adult novices musicians, who lack technical instrumental skills, may be able to gain access to learning musical interpretation by interacting with a graphic music editing tool under guidance from an appropriately designed Intelligent Tutoring System. A design for such a graphical music editor is shown in Figure 2. The design of an ITS approach to teaching musical interpretation presents similar problems of representing knowledge in an effectively communicable form to those which we described for knowledge of musical structures. Results in the psychology of musical performance ([Sun 1983],[Cla 1983]) have been formalized as a set of rules of the form:

IF <musical structure s1 present> THEN <apply interpretive variations v1, v2, v2 ...>

However, it is now almost a byword of ITS research that a knowledge representation in the form of such rules is not sufficient alone as a basis for communicating that knowledge to a student (witness Clancey's recent work, [Cla 1988]). The classic example is of course the early version of GUIDON [Cla 1987], built on top of the MYCIN expert system for medical diagnosis. Later versions of GUIDON addressed this problem by relating rules into groups and adding further explanatory layers—a method which has become a general tendency in Second Generation Expert sytems research [Ste 1987]. We therefore propose an alternative representation of the concepts embodied in musical performance rules, which pulls them apart to generate a much more abstract representation called a *goal abstraction hierarchy*. For example,

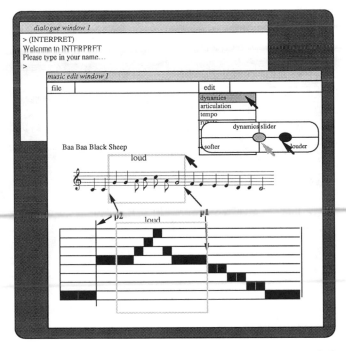

Figure 3. INTERPRET Dialogue and Music Edit Windows.

suppose we have two (simplified) rules, and that one overall goal of interpretation is to communicate musical structure:

R1—IF <phrase boundary present> THEN <apply dynamics contrast>
R2—IF <phrase boundary present> THEN <insert micropause>

We can view these rules as statements of how to perform *actions* with the graphic editing tool (the right hand sides of the rules) to achieve the *goal* (the rule left hand sides) "communicate phrase boundary," with the precondition that a phrase boundary is present.

The two rules shown above may thus be represented as goal operators (Fikes and Nilsson 1971):

```
GOAL : communicate_structure(s1)
    preconditions : (musical_structure s1)
    subgoals : (G1 G2)
    action : nil
    effects : nil

GOAL : G1
    preconditions : (phrase_boundary s1)
    subgoals : nil
    action : (dynamics ("piano" before s1) ("forte" after s1))
    effects : ((dynamics (phrase 0 s1) "piano") (dynamics (phrase s1 s2) "forte")
```

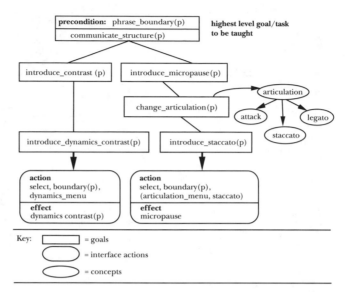

Figure 3. An Abstract Plan Hierarchy for Tutoring Application of Performance Variations Using a Graphic Music Editing Tool.

GOAL : G2
    preconditions : (phrase_boundary s1)
    subgoals : nil
    action : insert_micropause(phrase_boundary)
    effects : ((silence 0.2 seconds) (position s1))

The general tutorial objective of defining this knowledge representation is to provide a means of imposing an abstract structure on the domain, so that students can be taught to *generalize* from one type of action to achieve a goal, to other similar kinds of action. For example, the action in goal G1 (above) of applying a dynamics contrast to the edited melody is obviously similar to the action of applying a contrast in timbre. What we therefore want the student to understand is the more general fact that the goal of communicating musical structure can be achieved by applying *any form of musical contrast*. This requires representing further levels of abstract goals, between the highest level goal and lower level goals which have corresponding actions in the editing environment, examples of which are shown in Figure 3.

In order to understand the ways in which musical goals may be generally achieved, novices will also need to understand a number of musical *concepts*. For example, in order to understand the way in which changes in articulation may provide musical contrast, the novice may need to understand the concepts of *staccato*, *legato*, and so on. Appropriate semantic networks [Qui 1968] may therefore be linked to abstract goals in order to provide a knowledge representation which facilitates this. An example of the knowledge representation which we propose is shown in Figure 3. It shows a set of subgoals to the goal of communicating musical structure in an interpretation, some concepts linked to the goals, and actions in the music editing tool attached to terminal subgoals.

Given such a knowledge representation, a large body of the existing ITS literature can be fruitfully exploited to specify a set of strategies for recognising students' plans for interaction with the editing tool ([Mil 1982],[Woo 1988]), and for tutoring their acquisition. We restrict our comments to tutorial strategies for plan aquisition. Essentially, these consist of algorithms for traversing the domain representation in a way which is intended to faciliate learning. For example, the top-down "successive refinement" strategy of the BRIDGE system [Bon 1988], or the bottom-up "cognitive apprenticeship" strategy [Col 1989]. The DOMINIE system [Spe 1988] combines a variety of teaching strategies, together with algorithms for choosing between them at any given point in the interaction. This system also addressed the problem of teaching the *concepts* underlying the procedures to be learned (for using a computer interface) in the way in which we described previously, but simply presented text templates in order to do this, without giving any control over the interaction to the student. The *KANT dialogue model*, described in the previous section, could therefore be used for teaching the concepts underlying abstract performance plans, thus producing an ITS design which contains closely integrated components.

In summary, the following approaches to using plans in ITS are included in our design of the performance editing component of INTERPRET:

1) Knowledge of interpretive variations can be tutored using a combination of approaches to traversing an abstract plan hierarchy. The general objective is to extend the range of actions known to the student with which to achieve a given goal. The approach is based on teaching the use of a graphic music editing tool, which applies interpretive variations to a given input melody.

2) The concepts required to understand abstract goals, and to generalise to similar ways of achieving them, can be taught using the dialogue mechanisms of KANT, rather than using text templates.

3) The activity of students using the music editing tool could be monitored using plan recognition algorithms, in combination with student modelling techniques for determining which of the subconcepts of abstract goals are known to the student.

Given the connection between the abstract performance plans and the use of KANT in teaching related musical concepts, there need not be a rigid distinction between phases concerned with teaching musical structure and interpretation, although some discussion of structure will often be a necessary precursor. It is even possible that students may wish to revise their views on structure as a result of exploring the effect of various interpretive variations on the way in which the melody is perceived.

A number of research problems remain, the most important of which concerns giving tutorial guidance on how editing operations may be *combined*. For example, human performers may mark a phrase boundary using micropauses, diminuendo, and a slight decelerando. Furthermore, the kind of variations used will generally be applied throughout the piece of music with some degree of consistency in a coherent interpretation. In our present design, we assume that this is left to the student's musical intuitions, but some indications as to how such knowledge could be formalised can be derived from the work of Sundberg [Sun 1983] and co-workers. A further limitation is that we have only specified abstraction hierarchies for performance rules which have the goal of communicating structure. Similar approaches could be adopted for rules for vocal modelling and musical expression. Finally, our present design does not include guidance on the precise *degree* to which any particular performance variation should be applied. In future work it would be possible to design an expert component for demonstrating and correcting the appropriate degree of an interpretive musical factor, based on the work of Todd [Tod 1989] and Friberg and Sundberg [Fri 1986].

Tutoring Psychomotor Skills in Musical Interpretation

So far we have described an ITS architecture that tutors structural analysis and interpretation via a static graphic representation of the music. However, musical interpretation and perception is intimately connected with movement in time. As is well documented, [Slo 1985] much of what we understand by expression in music is related to bodily gestures. For example, the micropause inserted between interval leaps relates to necessary shifts in hand positions on many string instruments. For novice performers, however, the *complexity* of the physical gestures required to play many instruments effectively excludes them from active involvement in interpretation. In order to give novices some degree of involvement, we propose to *simplify* the instrumental techniques required using a computer-music gestural input device. An example of such a device is the Roland Octapad™, where the performance gestures required are simplified to the striking of one of eight "pads" with hands or drumstick, each of which can be assigned to trigger MIDI events stored in the computer, with precise articulation, rhythm, tempo and dynamics. The tutorial principle here is analogous to the "factoring out" of the activities involved in a complex motor skill, such as flying an aeroplane, commonly used in flight simulators. For example, the strength with which the student hits the pad can be assigned to control the volume (velocity) and start-time of each note of a melody stored in the computer. Due to technological limitations, only one factor can be considered at a time, subsequent playings being required for controlling other factors.

The user's gestural performance can be captured via MIDI and stored in a file for comparison with their original edited version. For example, if the student controls dynamics in the gestural "performance," and the edited version includes a dynamics contrast at a particular phrase boundary, we can determine whether the student has succeeded in reproducing this in their interpretation. By analysis of the musically significant differences between the two musical representations, educational feedback could be given. Use of this module of the architecture could be freely mixed with the other two phases, since students may wish to revise their original conception of an interpretation to be more in accordance with their present gestural performance abilites. Since research in the psychology of music [Tuc 1977] has established that visual feedback can be sufficient for correction in real-time performances, gestural performances would therefore benefit from a simultaneous animated graphical display, similar to that described by Lamb and Buckley [Lam 1986]. The display would need to be combined with a graphical notation of the performance editing operations applied to the melody—the "score" which the student "plays"—in order to reduce the memory load of remembering the ideal edited version.

Given that significant differences can be analysed between gestural and edited interpretations (itself a considerable research problem), we need to define ways in which they may be used in an effective intelligent tutoring approach. This tutorial paradigm is similar to "differential modelling" approaches in "coaching environments' such as the WEST system [Bur 1982]. WEST was based on the idea of identifying "issues" to tutor by observing the student's activity with a computer-based game and comparing it with optimal or expert game strategies. A number of effective tutorial rules were incorporated in the system—such as "do not interrupt too often, "let the student discover things for himself"—which could be applied to tutoring gestural performance. For example, if on two successive performances most differences are identified in terms of precise placing of the onset of notes, then "rubato" may be identified as an issue to tutor. "Issues" can be viewed as possible foci upon which our general dialogue model described earlier could operate, thus integrating this component with the two others.

The approach which we propose is, therefore, essentially different from those discussed in our earlier review of related work. Existing approaches ([Yos 1985],[Ste 1989]) compare a performance with a conventional keyboard with a presitored expert *performance,* or attempt to assist the student in correcting variations from a strict interpretation of musical notation ([Lam 1986],[San 1987]). In our case, a *simplified gestural performance* is compared with an *ideal edited version* which was initially specified during a *cooperative dialogue* between an ITS and a student. We argue that this would enable students to have a deeper understanding of the rationale behind their own interpretations, which would thus transfer more easily to other pieces and styles.

Finally, we need to consider how the component for tutoring psychomotor skills in performance could be integrated with other components of the architecture. A lesson on musical performance between a human teacher and learner may include elements of musical analysis, discussion of interpretation in front of the musical score, practical demonstration with musical examples, and critique of the performance in terms of the features discussed. The latter may lead to a return to discussing interpretive and analytical factors in the music. No simple pattern can therefore be identified such as: "structural analysis → interpretation analysis → performance and critique." We have already described how discussion of musical concepts may be relevant when applying performance variations, but the problem of making pedagogical choices between tutoring cognitive and psychomotor components of an activity has not been previously explored by ITS research. We speculate that this problem may be addressed to some extent by the fact that our dialogue model could integrate all three components of the knowledge and skills required for musical performance, and that these diverse learning goals are *negotiated* between system and student.

Conclusion

Our aim in this chapter has been to establish links between research in artificial intelligence, the cognitive psychology of music and intelligent tutoring systems, in order to address a specific problem in music education. In conclusion, we assess possible contributions to music education and ITS research which full implementation of this architecture could make. In terms of music education, INTERPRET constitutes an effective use of an ITS and of computer-music technology, since it could give novice musicians access to higher level skills which they cannot easily gain by conventional musical means. Learning the skills of musical analysis and interpretation by traditional implicit and intuitive methods usually involves extensive musical training. It is therefore possible that discussing these skills in an explicit manner with an ITS could serve to accelerate learning in the early stages of a novice musician's education. Clearly, there are many more dimensions to interpretive performance than the system can deal with, such as emotional involvement and the subtleties of rapport in ensemble playing. We would therefore argue that a system like INTERPRET should not be a student's sole means of access to such knowledge.

Intelligent Tutoring Systems research is now sufficiently advanced so that it can concentrate on specific problems such as applying machine learning techniques to student modelling, decision algorithms for choice amongst alternative teaching strategies and models of expert reasoning (see [Wen 1987],[Sel 1988],[Els 1990]). Nevertheless, we claim that due to their interconnectedness, specific subcomponents of an ITS must be developed within the framework of a more general architectural design, which addresses a real educational problem. For this reason, we have concentrated initial research on the design and implementation of the GRAF model for perception of musical structures, and the KANT dialogue model, both of which have been implemented in Common Lisp running on an Apollo Domain AI workstation and on the Macintosh-II. Elements of the components for teaching musical performance variations and gestural performance have been designed, but have not been implemented. Our principal contribution to ITS research is to have designed and implemented a model for tutorial dialogue which includes negotiation phases between system and student, and which is adapted to teaching in domains where we can not assume complete and unambiguous knowledge on the part of the system. Future work will concentrate on modelling conflict resolution mechanisms in dialogue and on extending the severe domain restrictions of the musical parser, which greatly limit the range of educational guidance provided by the system.

Acknowledgements

This research was supported by award number 86313101 from the Science and Engineering Research Council of Great Britain. Many thanks to Mark Elsom-Cook for guidance.

References

[And 1983] Anderson, J.R. (1983). *The Architecture of Cognition*. Harvard University Press.

[Ash 1989] Ashley, R.D. (1989). Modeling music listening: General considerations. Contemporary Music Review (4), 295–310.

[Att 1971] Attneave, F. and Ohlson, R.K. (1971). Pitch as a medium: a new approach to psychophysical scaling. *American Journal of Psychology* 84, 147–166.

[Bak 1989a] Baker, M.J. (1989a). An artificial intelligence approach to musical grouping analysis. *Contemporary Music Review* Vol. 3, pp. 43–68, Harwood Academic Publishers, London.

[Bak 1989b] Baker, M.J. (1989b). A computational approach to modeling musical grouping structure. *Contemporary Music Review* Vol. 4, pp. 311–325, Harwood Academic Publishers, London.

[Bak 1989c] Baker, M.J. (1989c). A Model for Tutorial Dialogues based on Critical Argument. In *Artificial Intelligence and Education,* (eds.) Bierman, D., Breuker, J. and Sandberg, J. IOS Publishing, Amsterdam.

[Bak 1989d] Baker, M.J. (1989d). *Negotiated Tutoring: An Approach to Interaction in Intelligent Tutoring Systems*. PhD thesis, Centre for Information Technology in Education, The Open University (GB).

[Bak 1991] Baker, M.J. (1991, in press). Negotiating Goals in Intelligent Tutoring Dialogues. In Costa, E. (ed.) *New Directions in Intelligent Tutoring Systems*. Springer Verlag, NATO ASI series.

[Bha 1989] Bharuca, J.J. and Olney, K.L. (1989). Tonal cognition, artificial intelligence and neural nets. *Contemporary Music Review* (4), 341–356.

[Bon 1988] Bonar, J.G. and Cunningham, R. (1988). BRIDGE: an intelligent tutor for thinking about programming. In Self, J. (ed.) *Artificial Intelligence and Human Learning*, Chapman Hall, London.

[Bur 1982] Burton, R.R. and Brown, J.S. (1982). An investigation of computer coaching for informal learning activities. In *Intelligent Tutoring Systems,* (eds.) Sleeman, D. and Brown, J.S., Academic Press.

[Bux 1980] Buxton, W., Reeves, W., Fedorkow, G., Smith, K.C. and Baecker, R. (1980). A microcomputer-based conducting system. *Computer Music Journal* 4,1, 8–21.

[Cla 1987] Clancey, W. (1987). *GUIDON: Knowledge based tutoring*. MIT Press.

[Cla 1988] Clancey, W. (1988). The role of qualitative models in instruction. In Self, J. (ed.) *Artificial Intelligence and Human Learning*, Chapman and Hall, London.

[Cla 1985] Clarke, E. (1985). Structure and Expression in Rhythmic Performance. In *Musical Structure and Cognition,* (eds.) Howell, P., Cross, I. and West, R., Academic Press, London.

[Coh 1990] Cohen, P.R., Morgan, J. and Pollack, M.E. (1990). *Intentions in Communication*. MIT Press, Cambridge (Mass.).

[Col 1989] Collins, A. and Brown, J.S. (1989). Cognitive Apprenticeship: teaching students the craft of reading, writing and mathematics. In Resnick, L.B. (ed.) *Cognition and Instruction: Issues and Agendas*. Lawrence Erlbaum Associates, Hillsdale New Jersey.

[Des 1986] Desain, P. and Honing, H. (1986). LOCO: Composition Microworlds in LOGO. *Proceedings of the International Computer-Music Conference*, The Hague.

[Els 1990] Elsom-Cook, M. (1990). (ed.) *Guided-Discovery Tutoring*. Paul Chapman, London.

[Erm 1980] Erman, L.D., Hayes-Roth, F., Lesser, V.R. and Reddy, D.R. (1980). The Hearsay-II speech understanding system: Integrating knowledge to resolve uncertainty. *ACM Surveys* 2 (2).

[Far 1988] Farrell, R. (1988). Facilitating Self Education by Questioning Assumptive Reasoning. *Proceedings of the Seventh National Conference on Artificial Intelligence* (AAAI-88), 2-6.

[Fik 1971] Fikes, R.E. and Nilsson, N.J. (1971). STRIPS: A new approach to the application of theorem proving to problem solving. *Proceedings of the Second International Joint Conference on Artificial Intelligence,* Imperial College, London.

[Fri 1986] Friberg, A. and Sundberg, J. (1986). A Lisp environment for creating and applying rules for musical performance. *Proceedings of the International Computer Music Conference,* pp.1–3, The Hague, Netherlands.

[Gre 1988] Greif, E. (1988). *Computer-supported cooperative work: a book of readings.* Morgan Kaufmann.

[Gro 1981] Grosz, B.J. (1981). Focusing and description in natural language dialogues. In Joshi, A.K., Webber, B.L. and Sag, I.A. (eds.) *Elements of Discourse Understanding.* Cambridge University Press.

[Hof 1981] Hofstetter, F. (1981). Computer-based aural training: The GUIDO system. *Journal of Computer-Based Instruction,* 7 (3), 84–92.

[Hol 1989] Holland, S. (1989). *Artificial Intelligence, Education and Music: The use of artificial intelligence to encourage and facilitate music composition by novices.* PhD dissertation, Centre for Information Technology in Education, The Open University (GB).

[Kir 1986] Kirshbaum, T. (1986). Using a touch-tablet as an effective, low-cost input device in a melodic dictation game. *Journal of Computer-Based Instruction.* Vol.13, (1), 14–16.

[Kis 1986] Kiss, G. (1986). *High-level dialogue in Man-machine Interaction.* A Survey Commissioned by the Alvey Directorate, Human Cognition Research Laboratory, The Open University (GB).

[Lam 1985] Lamb, M. and Buckley, V. (1985). A user-interface for teaching piano keyboard techniques. In Shackel, B. (ed.) *Interact* 1985.

[Ler 1983] Lerdahl, F. and Jackendoff, R. (1983). *A Generative Theory of Tonal Music.* MIT Press.

[Lis 1987] Lischka, C. (1987). Connectionist Models of Musical Thinking. *Proceedings of the International Computer- Music Conference,* University of Illinois at Urbana-Champaign (USA), 190–196.

[Mil 1982] Miller, M.L. (1982). A structured planning and debugging environment for elementary programming. In Sleeman, D. and Brown, J.S. (eds.) *Intelligent Tutoring Systems,* Academic Press.

[Mat 1980] Matthews, M.V. and Abbott, C. (1980). The Sequential Drum. *Computer Music Journal,* Winter 1980 Vol. 4 (4).

[Min 1977] Minsky, M. (1977). Frame-system theory. In Johnson-Laird, P.N. and Wason, P.C. (eds.) *Thinking: Readings in Cognitive Science.* Cambridge University Press.

[Moo 1912] Moorat, J. (1912). *Thirty Old-Time Nursery Songs.* Thames and Hudson, London.

[Pap 1980] Papert, S. (1980). *Mindstorms.* The Harvester Press, Brighton, Great Britain.

[Pow 1979] Power, R. (1979). The Organisation of Purposeful Dialogues. *Linguistics* 17, (1979) , 107–152.

[Qui 1968] Quillian, M.R. (1968). Semantic Memory. In Minsky, M. (ed.) *Semantic Information Processing,* 227- 270, MIT Press, Cambridge Mass.

[San 1987] Sanchez, M., Joseph, A., Dannenberg, R. Miller, P.L., Capell, P. and Joseph, R. (1987). *Piano Tutor: An Intelligent Keyboard Instruction System.* Unpublished Report of the Center for Art and Technology, Carnegie-Mellon University, USA.

[Sch 1973] Schegloff, E.A. and Sacks, H. (1973). Opening Up Closings. *Semiotica* 8 (4); 289–327.

[Sch 1967] Schoenberg, A. (1967). *Fundamentals of Musical Composition.* Faber, London.

[Sea 1969] Searle, J. (1969). *Speech Acts: An Essay in the Philosophy of Language.* Cambridge University Press.

[Sel 1988] Self, J. (1988). (ed.) *Artificial Intelligence and Human Learning.* Chapman Hall, London.

[Sha 1981] Shaffer, H. (1981). Performance of Chopin, Bach and Bartok: studies in motor programming. *Cognitive Psychology* 13, 326–76.

[Sim 1968] Simon, H.A. and Sumner, R. (1968). Pattern in Music. In *Formal Representation of Human Judgement* (ed.) Kleinmuntz, B. Wiley and Sons, London.

[Sle 1982] Sleeman, D. and Brown, J.S. (1982). *Intelligent Tutoring Systems.* Academic Press, London.

[Slo 1985] Sloboda, J. (1985). *The musical mind: the cognitive psychology of music.* Oxford University Press, Oxford.

[Spe 1988] Spensley, F. and Elsom-Cook, M. (1988). *Dominie: Teaching and assessment strategies.* Open University CAL Research Group Technical Report No. 74, Milton Keynes, Great Britain.

[Ste 1984] Steedman, M. (1984). A generative grammar for jazz chord sequences. *Music Perception* vol.2, no.1.

[Ste 1982] Steele, D. and Wills, B. (1982). Micro-computer assisted instruction for musical performance skills. *Technological Horizons in Education,* 9 (1), 58–60.

[Ste 1987] Steels, L. (1987). The Deepening of Expert Systems. *Artificial Intelligence Communications* Vol. 0 (1)

[Sto 1985] Stoffer, T.H. (1985). Representation of Phrase Structure in the Perception of Music. *Music Perception* Vol. 3 (2), 19–220.

[Sun 1983] Sundberg, J. (1983). (ed.) *Studies of Musical Performance.* Royal Swedish Academy of Music Publications.

[Swa 1979] Swanwick, K. (1979). *A Basis for Music Education.* NFER Publishing, London.

[Taf 1985] Taft-Thomas, M. (1985). VIVACE: A Rule-based AI system for composition. *Proceedings of the International Computer-Music Conference,* Vancouver, pp. 267–274.

[Tod 1985] Todd, N. (1985). A Model of Expressive Timing in Music. *Music Perception,* Fall 1985 vol.3 (1), pp.33–58.

[Tod 1989] Todd, N. (1989). Towards a cognitive theory of expression: The performance and perception of Rubato. *Contemporary Music Review* (4), 405–416.

[Tou 1979] Toulmin, S., Rieke,R. and Janik, A. (1979). *An Introduction to Reasoning.* Macmillan Publishing Co., New York.

[Tuc 1977] Tucker, W.H., Bates, R.T.H., Frykberg, S.D., Howarth, R.J., Kennedey, W.K., Lamb, M. and Vaughan, R.G. (1977). An interactive aid for musicians. *International Journal of Man-Machine Studies* 9, 635–651.

[Wen 1987] Wenger, E. (1987). *Artificial intelligence and tutoring systems: computational and cognitive approaches to the communication of knowledge.* Morgan Kaufmann Inc., Los Altos, California,

[Woo 1988] Woodroffe, M.R. (1988). Plan recognition and intelligent tutoring systems. In Self, J. (ed.) *Artificial Intelligence and Human Learning,* Chapman and Hall, London.

[Yos 1985] Yoshinori, Y. and Nagaoka, K. (1985). Computerised methods for evaluating musical performances and for providing instruction techniques for keyboard instruments. *Computing and Education,* Vol.9 (2),

Abstract

The chapter describes the first results of an ongoing project that is being pursued at the Austrian Research Institute for Artificial Intelligence. The long-term goal of the project is the development of a new generation of flexible and adaptive musical systems. The central concern is therefore with techniques of machine learning, and with research into the role that general musical knowledge plays in a system that is to learn new musical concepts. The first test domain for our system was two-voice counterpoint composition. The starting point for the project was the realization that "intelligent" learning requires a considerable amount of domain-specific knowledge. We will describe our approach to defining some basic knowledge about tonal music which can serve as the basis for learning processes. We will also briefly describe the integrated learning strategy which can take advantage of such knowledge during learning. Finally, the paper also suggests that intelligent, knowledge-based learning systems could be useful tools for testing general theories about music.

Chapter 21

The Importance of
Basic Musical Knowledge for
Effective Learning

Gerhard Widmer

Introduction

This chapter describes a project whose long-term goal is the development of a new generation of flexible and adaptive musical systems. Flexibility requires the ability to learn. Thus, for the moment we concentrate on the development of learning methods that are suited to the task of learning musical concepts and rules. The first test domain for our system is two-voice counterpoint composition.

Two main ideas will be expounded in this paper: the first is that "intelligent" learning requires a considerable amount of domain-specific, but possibly abstract, knowledge, that is, knowledge about the *structure* of the domain whose concepts are to be learned. This leads us to the problem of identifying and formalizing what we consider basic musical knowledge. It will be argued in this chapter that there is indeed something like common musical "knowledge" shared by most Western music listeners; and a model that captures some of this knowledge (with respect to two-voice counterpoint) will be presented. The second problem then consists in devising learning algorithms that can take advantage of that knowledge to learn both more "intelligently" and more effectively. We will present a new learning algorithm that has this desired property. Some examples of the algorithm at work will also be presented.

The second underlying idea is not new, but may not yet have been considered in connection with machine learning: we see intelligent learning systems as extremely useful tools for testing general theories in many domains. For a theory of perception of tonal music, this means that the theory can be tested by experimenting with a learning system and analyzing how certain assumptions and *a priori* knowledge affect the "learnability" of musical constructs and rules. This could lead to new insights concerning the connection between assumptions about perception, and specific systems of musical rules or styles.

This chapter tries to address two groups of researchers with possibly very different areas of interest and equally different backgrounds, namely, specialists in artificial intelligence (and machine learning, in particular), and musicologists. It seems therefore necessary to give a short introduction to those concepts in the field of machine learning that are relevant to our project, in particular the concept of "knowledge-based" learning. As our first application—two-voice counterpoint—is a very restricted and comparatively simple (some might say artificial) musical problem, we assume that the reader is familiar with the basic rules and concepts of that domain.

Machine Learning: Some Important Concepts

Machine learning (ML) is the discipline that tries to develop theories and models of learning processes, and to build working computer systems that can learn and adapt to new situations. "Learning" is a very broad term; in principle, it covers adaptation to new environments and situations, building new concepts and relations from experience and observation, acquiring knowledge from teachers and textbooks, acquiring specialized skills through practice, learning to avoid mistakes, and many more such scenarios. In the field of machine learning, the idea of learning *general rules or concepts* from specific *examples* has received by far the most interest. If we define the notion of a "rule" or "concept" broadly enough, this research direction covers many of the learning scenarios listed above. The system to be presented here will learn general *problem solving rules* from specific instances of correct and incorrect counterpoint compositions.

Empirical Versus Analytical Learning

The field of machine learning has seen a major shift of interest in recent years. During the early stages of ML, most work went into the development of *inductive, empirical* learning algorithms, where a system is expected to learn some concept solely from positive and negative examples (see, for instance, Dietterich & Michalski 1981; Michalski 1983; Mitchell 1982; Winston 1975). The past few years have brought a tendency towards *knowledge-based*, i.e, essentially *deductive, analytical* learning.

The main motivation for this shift lies in the problems that are inherent to *logical induction*. Inductive generalization from examples is problematic for at least two reasons. First, it is not logically justifiable: we have no guarantee that an empirical generalization drawn from the observation of a finite number of examples of a concept will be correct. Coincidental similarities between the limited number of known examples may lead a learning system to consider lots of incorrect or nonsensical generalizations that have nothing to do with the concept to be learned. Given just the examples and no other information, a learner has no way of judging the plausibility or correctness of a generalization. A related problem is that of the search space: the number of possible generalizations is huge for any non-trivial concept description language (Rendell 1987), and "blind" search of the space of generalizations is prohibitively expensive.

The solution to these problems lies in the use of *knowledge* to guide the learning process. There seem to be very few situations where people learn "blindly," without trying to *explain* the observed phenomena with the help of some prior knowledge (or by way of analogy). Such explanations, if possible, both reduce the number of plausible generalizations and act as justifications of generalizations.

The main result that came out of the new interest in knowledge-based learning was a methodology known as *Explanation-Based Learning* or *EBL* (Mitchell *et al.* 1986; DeJong & Mooney 1986). Learning in EBL consists of *explaining* why and how an example belongs to the concept to be learned, and *generalizing* this explanation. This process yields a description of a whole class of objects or situations which satisfy the same explanation structure and hence also belong to the goal concept. These explanations are in the form of *deductive proofs*. They are derived from the system"s *a priori* knowledge about the problem domain; the sum total of this knowledge is called the system's *domain theory*.

The EBL method is the exact opposite of knowledge-free inductive learning in that it requires *complete knowledge* about the thing to be learned, in order for learning to be possible. Learning is essentially reduced to re-expressing existing knowledge in a form that is more efficient and more directly applicable (or *operational*, in EBL terminology). While such an approach may be fruitful in some domains, it is clear that there are many more fields which do not permit the formulation of a complete *a priori* theory, and hence are not amenable to such purely deductive techniques. Music is but one of them. But even though EBL is not applicable in such domains, we do not want to resort to "blind" inductive learning. What we are looking for are learning methods that use all the knowledge available, without requiring completeness and consistency of that knowledge.

In the field of music theory, some attempts at automatic learning of musical rules have already been made, but most of these projects were along the lines of purely inductive learning (e.g., induction of musical grammars from examples). We are pursuing an alternative methodology: we provide the system with basic musical knowledge (the kind of knowledge that is intuitively clear to us), and devise algorithms that can take advantage of that knowledge during the process of learning.

Learning Apprentice Systems

In order to give the reader an idea of the scenario in which our system learns, we briefly introduce the concept of *Learning Apprentice Systems*. Mitchell *et al.* (1985) define a Learning Apprentice as:

...an interactive knowledge-based consultant that directly assimilates new problem-solving knowledge by observing and analyzing the problem solving steps contributed by its users through their normal use of the system.

Two things to note here are that a human expert (teacher) is assumed to be present and that learning should occur, as far as possible, during *normal* use of the system, which means that the system should learn primarily by observing the problem solving steps of the expert. But if the learning system does not have a complete *a priori* theory, and if we want it to learn reliably, it will sometimes have to ask questions of the expert. By using domain-specific background knowledge in the process of interpreting the user's actions, the number of questions that have to be asked can be kept to a minimum, and the system can make many plausible generalizations without any help from the teacher.

The system we have constructed, then, is a Learning Apprentice for two-voice counterpoint composition, and the *a priori* knowledge we have endowed it with are the kinds of "intuitive" perceptions that every ordinary person has acquired from years of (conscious or unconscious) exposure to tonal music.

The Domain: Two-Voice Counterpoint Composition

The problem for which the system is to learn rules is defined as follows:

Given: Key, time signature, and melody (the *cantus firmus*) of a counterpoint piece.

Problem: Complete the piece by writing a second line (the *counterpoint*) in such a way that the constraints of counterpoint style are satisfied.

Figure 1 shows a simple counterpoint piece of first species (whole notes against whole notes).

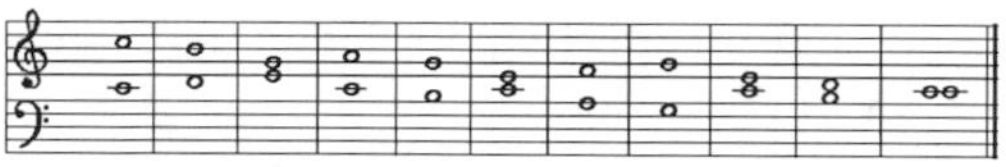

Figure 1. A Simple Counterpoint Piece.

The system learns three classes of rules:

good (P,N) if <conditions>
    note N is a good solution in a particular context in piece P if <conditions> (a conjunctive expression) is satisfied. <conditions> specifies the structure of the context and the attributes that note and context must satisfy for N to be a good solution.

bad (P,N) if <conditions>
    note N is bad in a particular context in piece P if <conditions> hold.

unacceptable (P,N) if <conditions>
　　note N is illegal in a certain context in piece P if <conditions> hold.

Figure 2 shows a simple rule and a musical situation to which it applies (succession of perfect consonances). Learned rules are ordinary PROLOG clauses; variables are capitalized; mnemonic variable names were substituted by the author.

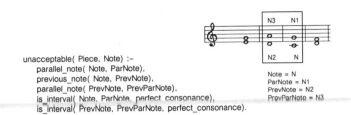

```
unacceptable( Piece, Note) :–
    parallel_note( Note, ParNote),
    previous_note( Note, PrevNote),
    parallel_note( PrevNote, PrevParNote),
    is_interval( Note, ParNote, perfect_consonance),
    is_interval( PrevNote, PrevParNote, perfect_consonance).
```

Note = N
ParNote = N1
PrevNote = N2
PrevParNote = N3

Figure 2. A Simple Counterpoint Rule.

General Musical Knowledge as a Basis for Learning about Music

In our system, the "technical" basis for reasoning about music is a hierarchical knowledge base defining the basic musical concepts (notes, intervals, scales, keys, etc.) along with their intrinsic properties (pitch, duration, degree of consonance, etc.). The knowledge base is implemented as a hierarchical frame system.

Given this information and some examples of acceptable and unacceptable counterpoint pieces, the system could learn counterpoint rules *inductively*, i.e., by comparing the different examples and hypothesizing general rules on the basis of commonalities and differences. A large number of (carefully selected) examples would be necessary, and the system would come up with many nonsensical hypotheses.

But we can do better than that; surely nobody learns counterpoint without prior musical knowledge. In fact, every ordinary person "knows" a lot about music (sometimes without knowing it) just from having been exposed to music (or Muzak, as the case may be) for years. This kind of tacit knowledge is usually called "habits of perception" or "musical intuition," or sometimes simply the "musical ear." It is this general knowledge that we want to model and give to the program as a basis for the learning process. We want to provide the computer with an "ear," as it were, so that it has the same possibilities for learning as humans.

A Hierarchical Model of Perception: Events and Effects

We have devised a simple (and rather naive) model of the perception of two-voice counterpoint to serve as a basis for the formulation of simple musical knowledge (see Figure 3). The model rests on the notions of *events* and *effects*.

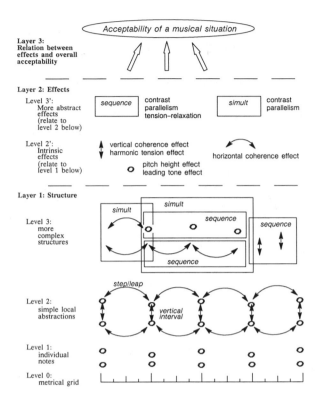

Figure 3. A Simple Model of the Perception of Two-Voice Counterpoint.

Events: The Structure of Musical Situations. At the moment we are experimenting with the simplest species of counterpoint, i.e., whole notes against whole notes, so we can use a rather simple model of the structure of a piece. The lower half of Figure 3 depicts successively more abstract views of a musical situation: level 1, the level of the individual notes, is not adequate as a reasonable basis for the description of situations; it is too unstructured. It seems safe to postulate that people make at least very simple *local abstractions* when listening to music: a note can be perceived as a single entity in its own right; two simultaneous notes are often heard as a unit, a *vertical interval*, and two consecutive notes can be perceived as forming a unit of melodic motion, a *step* or *leap*. How we perceive notes depends on the musical context and on the phenomena we are concentrating on. Accordingly, our representation system rests on three types of *events* (level 2):

1) *Single note* (a single note is viewed as such)

2) *Vertical interval* (two simultaneous notes are represented as a unit)

3) *Step/leap* (two consecutive notes are viewed as a unit)

Any situation in a piece can then be represented as a composition (sequence or simultaneity) of events and any combination of these compositions (level 3). Because of the multiple role of single notes (atomic event as well as part of some composite events), more than one parsing (or *view*) of a situation is usually possible. Our representation language is a context-free grammar, very similar to Stephen Smoliar's tree representation for Schenkerian analyses (Smoliar 1980). When applied to a collection of specific notes, it returns a typed parse tree for each possible structural view of this musical situation.

Instead of listing the entire grammar, let us demonstrate the principle by way of an example: Figure 4 shows a simple situation in a piece. The four notes b, d, g, and e can be interpreted as a sequence of vertical intervals, a pair of two simultaneous horizontal steps/leaps, or any combination of these with single notes. This is expressed in the parse trees of Figure 4. The labels composite_situation, sequence, vertical_interval, etc. correspond to non-terminal symbols in the grammar and specify the *type* of a subexpression. Strongly typed expressions permit clean formulation of rules and background knowledge: for every rule or other piece of knowledge, an attached type label identifies the kinds of objects or situations to which the rule is applicable.

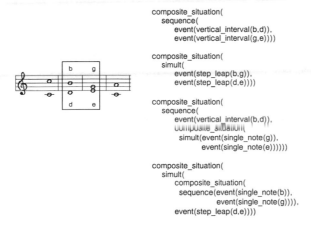

Figure 4. A Musical Situation and Four Parse Trees.

Effects: The Sound of Musical Situations.   Given this structural view of musical situations, we can now attempt to describe how certain situations *sound*. The central notion around which our approach revolves is that of an *effect*; effects correspond to simple kinds of more or less direct *sensations* in the listener. Every event has some *intrinsic effects* (level 2' in layer 2 of Figure 3), depending on its type, and more complicated (and more abstract) effects emerge when events are juxtaposed (in sequences or simults)—this is level 3' in Figure 3.

For instance, all events of type vertical interval have intrinsic effects *harmonic tension* and *vertical coherence*. The former depends primarily on the degree of consonance of the interval, whereas the latter is defined through the interval's width. Events are lined up along *scales of intensity* for each effect; this is part of the system's *a priori* knowledge. It knows, for example, that perfect consonances have an extremely low degree of harmonic tension (that is, they sound "empty," "smooth"), whereas most dissonances (especially narrow, altered intervals) have a very high harmonic tension effect (they sound extremely "tense").

Effects that arise from the juxtaposition of events correspond to more abstract sensations in a listener. Some of these "second order" effects are *contrast, coherence, parallelism, tension,* and *relaxation,* where contrast, for instance, is defined as arising from a combination of intrinsic effect differences between the events involved in the situation.

The Representation of Musical Knowledge

The kind of knowledge about effects listed above is mainly definitional. It is not sufficient to improve learning. Knowledge about *dependencies* between effects and the acceptability of a musical situation is needed. We believe that people have this knowledge, if only in a very general form. Even people with no explicit musical knowledge can usually say what it is that bothers them in an "awkward" musical situation.

In our system, this kind of knowledge comes in three forms: *deductive rules, determinations,* and *plausibility heuristics.* The following sections will describe each of these in turn and demonstrate how they contribute to an effective learning process.

Deductive Rules. Parts of the musical "knowledge" referred to above can be formulated as a set of hierarchically dependent rules (an *incomplete domain theory* (Mitchell *et al.* 1986)). These rules relate certain lower- and higher-order effects to the general acceptability of a musical situation.

Figure 5 gives a simplified sketch of some of these rules and shows how they allow the system to learn a simple rule from just one training example (the note c in the training example was labelled as bad by the teacher). The rule that is learned says that perfect vertical consonances are bad and should be avoided (rationale: they sound "dull" because of a lack of harmonic tension). The learning method is straightforward Explanation-Based Learning (EBL)—the system finds an explanation for why the c may sound bad, and then generalizes the explanation by turning constants into variables. Finally, a general rule is extracted from the explanation by collecting the leaves of the generalized explanation tree.

Many of these deductive rules describe factors that influence the way that music listeners intuitively rate the quality of a simple piece (for instance, that harmonic tension, contrast, and parallelism are related to the "interestingness" of a musical situation). If this knowledge were complete in the sense that it could explain all the rules of counterpoint, our apprentice could learn all the rules perfectly by EBL. Not much to the surprise of anyone who knows anything about music, this is not the case. But after some introspection, it is easy to formulate some weaker forms of general musical knowledge.

```
bad(Piece,Note) :- in_context(Note,C), incoherent(C).
bad(Piece,Note) :- in_context(Note,C), dull(C).
...
dull(C) :- intrinsic_effect(C,E,S), dull_effect(E,S).
...
```
⎫ Knowledge relating
⎬ abstract effects to
⎭ the acceptability of
    a solution

```
intrinsic_effect(vertical_interval(N1,N2),harmonic_tension,low) :-
    is_interval(N1,N2,perfect_consonance).
...
dull_effect(harmonic_tension,low).
...
```
⎫ Knowledge about
⎬ perceivable effects
⎭ of simple music

```
in_context(N,vertical_interval(N,N1)) :-
    parallel_note(N,N1).
...
```
⎫ Grammar capable of
⎬ describing the structure
⎭ of simple pieces

Figure 5a. Set of Given Deductive Rules (simplified).

Piece p:

Figure 5b. A Training Instance.

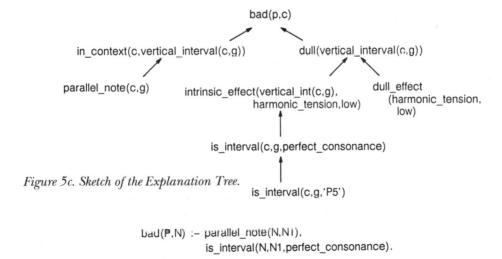

Figure 5c. Sketch of the Explanation Tree.

```
bad(P,N) :- parallel_note(N,N1),
            is_interval(N,N1,perfect_consonance).
```

Figure 5d. Rule Extracted from Generalized Explanation.

Determinations.   Determinations (Russell 1986) are a formalism for the expression of weaker knowledge. They are statements of *general dependencies* between attributes of a situation. They do not contain information that is specific enough for problem solving or for explaining new situations, but they can serve as a basis for the search for plausible explanations.

Figure 6a shows a rather general and powerful determination from our system, and the rest of Figure 6 sketches how it is used in the process of learning the "parallel fifths" rule (actually, a generalization thereof). The learning method used here is a combination of EBL and determinations. The determination's role is essentially to point to possible explanations for a phenomenon; these can then be verified by the user or by reference to other, known situations which satisfy the same determination in the same way (Davies & Russell 1987).

Determinations are a natural and attractive form for the formulation of general, abstract knowledge. The one depicted in Figure 6 is a very simple, intuitively clear musical heuristic; when writing it down, one need not know in advance for which cases and combinations of events and effects it will hold. This will be learned by the system.

Plausibility Heuristics.   The weakest form of knowledge in our system comes in the form of *heuristics for inductive generalization*. These are meant to describe very weak and overly general intuitions about music.

Here is an example of a plausibility heuristic:

> When trying to explain why a solution is bad or unacceptable, prefer hypotheses that contain some extreme or unusual event/effect.

This allows for a *heuristic search* for the best explanation and hence for the best inductive generalization (see below). The main effect is that more "plausible" hypotheses are tried first. Not only does this speed up the learning process, but it also saves the user the trouble of having to reject a lot of—in his/her eyes—"nonsensical" and unexpected hypotheses presented by the system for verification.

The Integrated Learning Strategy

The Learning Algorithm

The three types of explicit background knowledge—deductive rules, determinations, heuristics—require three different learning methods, namely, EBL, determination-based learning, and inductive generalization. Our apprentice combines and integrates these rather different methods in a framework of *explaining and generalizing*: given a training example (a musical situation) classified as good, bad, or unacceptable by the user, the system tries to explain why this might be so. An explanation is a tree reducing the goal (say, bad(P,N)) to simpler, easily testable ("operational") conditions. These are then generalized to yield the conditions for a generally applicable rule.

determines(bad_effect(Event1, Effect1, Degree1) &
        bad_effect(Event2, Effect2, Degree2),
        unacceptable_situation(sequence(Event1, Event2))).

A sequence *of two events* Event1, Event2 *which are both* bad *may be* unacceptable; *whether or not this is the case depends on exactly what the effects are that make the two events bad* (Effect1, Effect2), *and how strong they are* (Degree1, Degree2).

Figure 6a. A Determination.

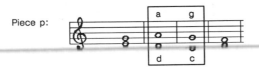

Piece p:

Figure 6b. A Training Instance.

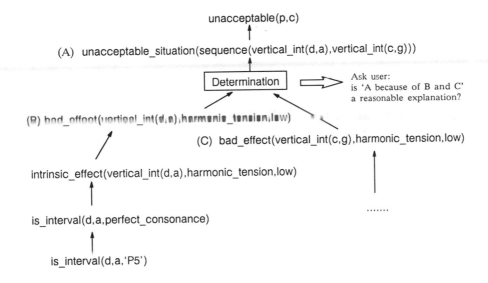

Figure 6c. Explanation Process (combination of determination and EBL).

unacceptable(P,N) :- parallel_note(N,N1),
                  previous_note(N,N2),
                  parallel_note(N2,N3),
                  is_interval(N,N1,perfect_consonance),
                  is_interval(N2,N3,perfect_consonance).

Figure 6d. Rule Extracted from Generalized Explanation.

determines(((bad(Piece, Note) :– Reason1,
          (bad(Piece, Note) :– Reason2,
          notequal(Reason1, Reason2))),
      unacceptable(Piece, Note)).

A note that is bad for two different reasons may be totally unacceptable; whether or not this is the case is determined by the particular reasons for which the note is bad.

Figure 7a. A Given Determination.

RULE 15: bad(N) :– previous_note(N,N1) & scale_degree(N, second) &
                  scale_degree(N1,root) & is_interval(N1,N,min7).

Figure 7b. A Specific Rule Already Learned.

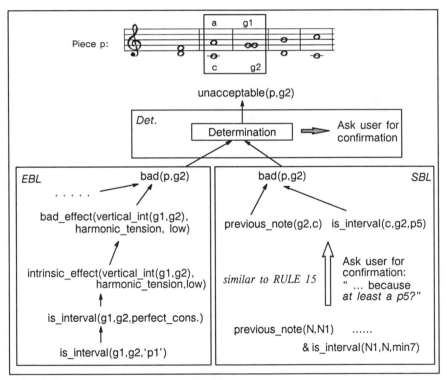

Figure 7c. A Training Instance and Its Explanation.

unacceptable(P,N) :– parallel_note(N,N1) & is_interval(N,N1,perfect_consonance) &
                   previous_note(N,N2) & at_least_interval(N2,N,p5)

Figure 7d. New Rule Extracted from Generalized Explanation.

In every step of the explanation process, the system tries to apply the strongest forms of knowledge available:

a) if a deductive rule is applicable to the current explanation subgoal, an EBL step is performed (see Deductive Rules).

b) if the current subgoal matches the latter part of a determination, the determination's preconditions are evaluated recursively (using methods (a), (b), or (c)), and the user is asked to verify the resulting explanation (see Determinations).

c) if neither (a) nor (b) is possible, the system tries to "explain" the current subgoal on the basis of its *similarity* to other known situations or to rules that have already been learned. Since there are usually several alternatives, all the available heuristics are used to determine which of these is the most plausible one (see Plausibility Heuristics). Again, the user is asked to verify such explanation steps. This type of "explanation" step leads to effects of inductive generalization.

Explanations based on "weak" knowledge (steps (b) and (c) above) are presented to the user for confirmation or rejection. In this way, the learned rules will be strongly justified, even if the underlying knowledge was unreliable. However, using all its knowledge, the system tends to come up with plausible explanations very quickly, so that this is not too much of a burden on the human teacher. The reader interested in machine learning is referred to (Widmer 1989) for details of the learning algorithm.

An Example

The following example demonstrates how the various learning modes are integrated in a more complex learning situation. Suppose that the apprentice has already learned the very specific rule depicted in Figure 7b, which says that a note is bad if it forms an interval (jump) of a minor seventh (min7) with its predecessor. Suppose also that at some point during problem solving, the system creates the solution depicted in Figure 7c, at which point the teacher interrupts it to say that note g2 is unacceptable. Figure 7c shows the explanation tree built by the system. The tree is constructed as follows:

- Trying to find an explanation for unacceptable(g2), the system finds the determination of Figure 7a and tries to establish its preconditions, that is, it attempts to show that g2 is bad for two different reasons.

   —First, it succeeds in proving bad(g2) using the deductive rules in Figure 5a. This results in the left subtree in Figure 7c and establishes an EBL-type sub-explanation ("g2 is bad because it forms a perfect consonance—specifically, a perfect unison (p1)—with g1, and perfect consonances have low harmonic tension, which sounds dull").

—Trying to show that bad(g2) holds for a second reason, the system comes across the specific rule already learned and listed in Figure 7b and, using some heuristics, finds that the rule is rather similar to one aspect of the current situation (namely, the jump c-g2, which is an interval of a perfect fifth (p5)). The two situations are similar in that in both cases, there is a melodic jump which is *at least as big as a p5*. This similarity is presented to the teacher as a hypothesis for bad(g2) ("Is the jump from c to g2 bad because it is at least a p5?"), and the teacher agrees, which establishes precondition 2 of the determination and introduces an inductive generalization into the explanation.

- Finally, the need to establish the relevance of the determination prompts another question to the teacher ("unacceptable(g2) because <sub-explanation1> and <sub-explanation2>?"). The teacher agrees again, and this completes the explanation.

The generalized rule extracted from the explanation is shown in Figure 7d. The rule basically says that it is prohibited to "jump into" a perfect consonance (perfect consonances should be introduced by stepwise motion). Note that this rather general rule was learned on the basis of one training instance, using three different kinds of background knowledge plus a previously learned rule and two very specific questions to the teacher.

Examples of the kinds of rules the system can learn appear in the next section, where a particular experiment with the system is presented.

An Experiment

The experiment described below demonstrates how the availability of general musical knowledge greatly improves the efficiency of the learning process. The setup was as follows: we settled on a set of eight rules which the system should learn. They are sketched below.

Rule 1. A first species conterpoint piece must not begin with an imperfect consonance (unacceptable).

Rule 2. Perfect consonaces should rarely be used (bad).

Rule 3. Sequences of perfect consonances are illegal (unacceptable).

Rule 4.   Paralel motion tends to be bad (bad).

Rule 5. Introducing perfect consonances by paralel motion is not allowed (unacceptable).

Rule 6. Melodic jumps bigger than a perfect fourth tend to be bad (bad).

Rule 7. Motion in opposite directions is good (good).

Rule 8   Melodic jumps bigger than an octave are not allowed (unacceptable).

The system was then run in two modes: once with the full domain theory (perception model), the second time without it (only the musical heuristics—see Plausibility Heuristics—were left in the system). That is, in the second case (without domain theory), all the rules would have to be learned in a purely *inductive* way. We then measured the number of training examples the apprentice would require, and the number of questions it would have to pose to the teacher, in order to learn just this set of rules. The results show the positive effect of *a priori* knowledge very clearly: the eight rules were completely learned in both cases. However, in case 1 (with domain theory), the apprentice needed *10 examples* and asked a total of *18 questions*, whereas in case 2 (almost no musical knowledge), *24 examples* and *42 questions* were needed for the system to learn the same set of rules. It must be stressed that no changes were made to the system—we just varied the amount of available musical knowledge.

Conclusion

We believe that our learning apprentice project represents a case of a fruitful marriage of artificial intelligence and music. On the one hand, it leads to the development of more flexible and reliable learning algorithms, which is beneficial to the entire field of machine learning. On the other hand, attempts to model some basic features of musical perception and experiments with a system that uses this model as a basis for learning may lead to interesting insights into the structure of tonal music. Such attempts may provide us with indications concerning the logical connection between musical perception theories and specific musical conventions by answering questions like the following:

- How do different sets of *a priori* knowledge affect the "learnability" of the rules of a given musical style?

- Is there a certain *regularity* to the connection between the underlying theory and the operational "surface" rules?

- Which part of the rule system of a particular musical style follows "naturally" from which set of underlying assumptions about perception?

We believe that the kinds of knowledge structures described in General Musical Knowledge as a Basis for Learning about Music represent a legitimate first step to providing a computer with the equivalent of a simple "ear." We are still far from having a satisfactory theory of musical events and effects. In particular, first species counterpoint is too simple a musical problem to allow for musicologically interesting experiments. In the meantime (1990–1991), the project has advanced beyond this rather simple type of music; a new, more ambitious system has been implemented that can learn to harmonize given melodies. That system is based on a more complex and also more general theory of musical perception (see Widmer 1990a, b, c).

First experimental results are very encouraging. The ultimate goal is to construct a general (qualitative) model of human musical perception, based on common-sense observations and intuitions. That kind of musical model could then be used in experiments to yield meaningful answers to the kinds of questions hinted at above.

Acknowledgments

I would like to thank Bernhard Pfahringer, Peter Kerstan, Paolo Petta, and John Matiasek for interesting discussions. Thanks are also due to Prof. Robert Trappl for his support of the project. Support for the Austrian Research Institute for Artificial Intelligence is provided by the Austrian Federal Ministry for Science and Research. Parts of this research were sponsored by the Austrian *Fonds zur Foerderung der wissenschaftlichen Forschung.*

The Learning Apprentice has been implemented in Quintus Prolog and runs on an Apollo DN3000 workstation. It communicates with the user via a graphical, mouse-sensitive music editor (written in C).

References

Davies, T. and Russell, S. (1987). A Logical Approach to Reasoning by Analogy. In *Proceedings of IJCAI-87, Milan.* Morgan Kaufmann Publishers.

DeJong, G. and Mooney, R. (1986). Explanation-Based Learning: An Alternative View. *Machine Learning* 1(1).

Dietterich, T. and Michalski, R. (1981). Inductive Learning of Structural Descriptions: Evaluation Criteria and Comparative Review of Selected Methods. *Artificial Intelligence* 16(3).

Michalski, R. (1983). A Theory and Methodology of Inductive Learning. In R. Michalski, J. Carbonell, T. Mitchell, eds., *Machine Learning: An Artificial Intelligence Approach*, Palo Alto, CA: Tioga.

Mitchell, T. (1982). Generalization as Search. *Artificial Intelligence* 18(2).

Mitchell, T., Mahadevan, S. and Steinberg, L. (1985). LEAP: A Learning Apprentice for VLSI Design. In *Proceedings IJCAI-85, Los Angeles.* Morgan Kaufmann Publishers.

Mitchell, T., Keller, R. and Kedar-Cabelli, S. (1986). Explanation-Based Generalization: A Unifying View. *Machine Learning* 1(1).

Rendell, L. (1987). Similarity-Based Learning and Its Extensions. *Computational Intelligence* 3.

Russell, S. (1986). *Analogical and Inductive Reasoning.* Ph.D. Thesis, Report STAN-CS-87-1150, Stanford University, Stanford, CA.

Smoliar, S. (1980). A Computer Aid for Schenkerian Analysis. *Computer Music Journal* 4(2).

Widmer, G. (1989). A Tight Integration of Deductive and Inductive Learning. In *Proceedings of the Sixth International Workshop on Machine Learning. Ithaca, N.Y.. Morgan Kaufmann. Extended version available* as Technical Report TR-89-3, Austrian Research Institute for Artificial Intelligence, Vienna.

Widmer, G. (1990a). The Usefulness of Qualitative Theories of Musical Perception. In *Proceedings of the International Computer Music Conference (ICMC-90),* Glasgow, U.K.

Widmer, G. (1990b). *A Qualitative Model of the Perception of Melodies and Harmonizations.* Report TR-90-12, Austrian Research Institute for Artificial Intelligence, Vienna.

Widmer, G. (1990c). *Using a Qualitative Perception Model to Learn Harmonization Rules for Melodies.* Report TR-90-13, Austrian Research Institute for Artificial Intelligence, Vienna.

Winston, P. (1975). Learning Structural Descriptions from Examples. In P. Winston, ed., *The Psychology of Computer Vision.* New York: McGraw Hill.

Index